LESSON
21

LESSON
22

LESSON
23

LESSON
24

Review
LESSON
25

Grade 2 • Theme 5

At a Glance

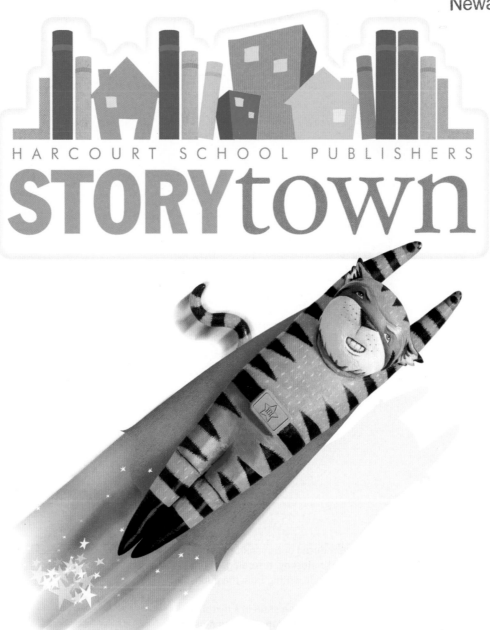

HARCOURT SCHOOL PUBLISHERS

STORYtown

Blast Off!

TEACHER EDITION

Senior Authors

Isabel L. Beck • Roger C. Farr • Dorothy S. Strickland

Authors

Alma Flor Ada • Roxanne F. Hudson • Margaret G. McKeown
Robin C. Scarcella • Julie A. Washington

Consultants

F. Isabel Campoy • Tyrone C. Howard • David A. Monti

T 57984

SCHOOL PUBLISHERS

www.harcourtschool.com

Program Authors

SENIOR AUTHORS

Isabel L. Beck
Professor of Education and Senior Scientist at the Learning Research and Development Center, *University of Pittsburgh*

RESEARCH CONTRIBUTIONS:
Reading Comprehension, Vocabulary, Beginning Reading, Phonics

Roger C. Farr
Chancellor's Professor Emeritus of Education and Former Director for the Center for Innovation in Assessment, *Indiana University, Bloomington*

RESEARCH CONTRIBUTIONS:
Instructional Assessment, Reading Strategies, Reading in the Content Areas

Dorothy S. Strickland
Samuel DeWitt Proctor Professor of Education and The State of New Jersey Professor of Reading, *Rutgers University, The State University of New Jersey*

RESEARCH CONTRIBUTIONS:
Early Literacy, Elementary Reading/ Language Arts, Writing, Intervention

AUTHORS

Alma Flor Ada
Professor Emerita, *University of San Francisco*

RESEARCH CONTRIBUTIONS:
Literacy, Biliteracy, Multicultural Children's Literature, Home-School Interaction, First and Second Language Acquisition

Roxanne F. Hudson
Assistant Professor, Area of Special Education *University of Washington*

RESEARCH CONTRIBUTIONS:
Reading Fluency, Learning Disabilities, Interventions

Margaret G. McKeown
Senior Scientist at the Learning Research and Development Center, *University of Pittsburgh*

RESEARCH CONTRIBUTIONS:
Vocabulary, Reading Comprehension

Robin C. Scarcella
Professor, Director of Academic English and ESL, *University of California, Irvine*

RESEARCH CONTRIBUTIONS:
English as a Second Language

Julie A. Washington
Professor, College of Letters and Sciences, *University of Wisconsin*

RESEARCH CONTRIBUTIONS:
Understanding of Cultural Dialect with an emphasis on Language Assessment, Specific Language Impairment and Academic Performance; Early Childhood Language and Early Literacy of African American Children

CONSULTANTS

F. Isabel Campoy
President, Transformative Educational Services

RESEARCH CONTRIBUTIONS:
English as a Second Language, Applied Linguistics, Writing in the Curriculum, Family Involvement

Tyrone C. Howard
Associate Professor Urban Schooling, *University of California, Los Angeles*

RESEARCH CONTRIBUTIONS:
Multicultural Education, The Social and Political Context of Schools, Urban Education

David A. Monti
Professor Emeritus Department of Reading and Language Arts, *Central Connecticut State University*

RESEARCH CONTRIBUTIONS:
Reading Comprehension, Alternative Assessments, Flexible Grouping

Theme 5: Better Together

Theme Resources **T2**
Leveled Resources **T4**
Digital Classroom **T6**
Monitor Progress **T7**
Theme at a Glance. **T8**
Planning for Reading Success **T10**
Theme Project **T12**
Build Theme Connections. **T14**

Lesson 21   T16

Plot. T34
Vocabulary T44

A Chair for My Mother T46
by Vera B. Williams • REALISTIC FICTION

Saving Money T72
by Mary Firestone • NONFICTION

Connections T74

Paired Selections

Theme Writing — **Reading-Writing Connection** T106

Student Writing Model: Description

Lesson 22   T118

Plot. T136
Vocabulary T146

Serious Farm T148
by Tim Egan • FANTASY

Beyond Old MacDonald. T174
by Charley Hoce • *illustrated by Eugenie Fernandes* • POETRY

Connections T176

Paired Selections

SOCIAL STUDIES

SOCIAL STUDIES

LANGUAGE ARTS

Lesson 23 — T206

🔄 **Use Graphic Aids** T224
Vocabulary T234

The Bee T236
by Sabrina Crewe • NONFICTION

California Bee Business T262
by Dimarie Santiago • NONFICTION

Paired Selections

Connections T264

Lesson 24 — T298

🔄 **Use Graphic Aids** T318
Vocabulary T326

Watching in the Wild T328
by Charnan Simon • from *Click* • NONFICTION

Chimp Computer Whiz T346
from *Ask* • MAGAZINE ARTICLE

Paired Selections

Connections T348

Lesson 25 Theme Review — T380

SOCIAL STUDIES

READERS' THEATER
Town Hall T400
INTERVIEW

LANGUAGE ARTS

COMPREHENSION STRATEGIES
A Time for Patience T435
from *Fables from Aesop* • retold by Tom Lynch • FABLE

Theme Wrap-Up and Review T454
Theme Project Presentations T455
Monitor Progress T456

Reference Materials

Small-Group Instruction

● **Lesson 21**
Phonics / S2
Fluency / S4
Plot / S6
Compare and Contrast / S8
Vocabulary / S10
Grammar and Writing / S12

● **Lesson 22**
Phonics / S14
Fluency / S16
Plot / S18
Compare and Contrast / S20
Vocabulary / S22
Grammar and Writing / S24

● **Lesson 23**
Phonics / S26
Fluency / S28
Use Graphic Aids / S30
Synonyms / S32
Vocabulary / S34
Grammar and Writing / S36

● **Lesson 24**
Phonics / S38
Fluency / S40
Use Graphic Aids / S42
Synonyms / S44
Vocabulary / S46
Grammar and Writing / S48

Assessment

● **Overview**

● **Prescriptions**
• Lesson 21 / A2
• Lesson 22 / A3
• Lesson 23 / A4
• Lessons 24 and 25 / A5
• Theme 5 Test / A6

Additional Resources

- **Rubrics**
  - Using Rubrics / R2
  - Retell and Summarize Fiction / R3
  - Summarize Nonfiction / R4
  - Presentations / R5
  - Writing Rubric: Short and Extended Responses / R6
  - 6-Point Rubric for Writing / R7
  - 4-Point Rubric for Writing / R8

- **Additional Reading** / R9

- **Lesson Vocabulary** / R10

- **Cumulative Vocabulary and High-Frequency Words** / R11

- **Handwriting Instruction and Models** / R12

- **Student Edition Glossary and Index of Titles and Authors** / R18

- **Professional Bibliography** / R22

- **Program Reviewers & Advisors** / R24

- **Scope and Sequence** / R26

- **Index** / R34

- **Acknowledgments** / R86

Data-Driven Instruction

1 ASSESS

Use assessments to track student progress.

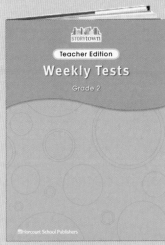

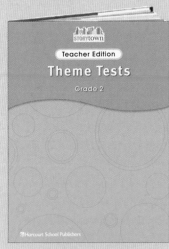

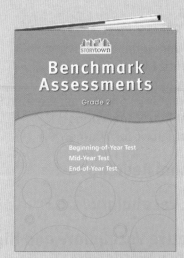

▲ Weekly Lesson Tests (grades 1–6)

▲ Theme Tests

▲ Benchmark Assessments
- Beginning-of-Year
- Mid-Year
- End-of-Year

Online Assessment, *StoryTown*

2 TEACH

Provide instruction in key areas of reading.

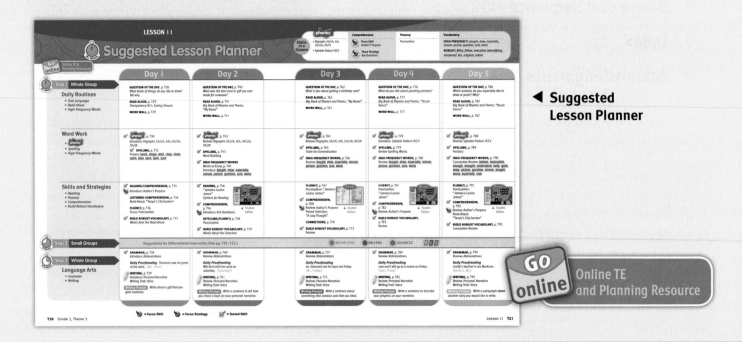

◀ Suggested Lesson Planner

3 DIFFERENTIATE INSTRUCTION

Use daily Monitor Progress notes to inform instruction.

MONITOR PROGRESS

Partner Reading

IF students need more support in fluency-building and in using appropriate pace,	THEN have them echo-read with you, paying close attention to punctuation marks to direct their pace.

Small-Group Instruction, p. S105:
- BELOW-LEVEL: Reteach
- ON-LEVEL: Reinforce
- ADVANCED: Extend

▲ Suggested Small-Group Planner

4 ASSESS, REMEDIATE, AND EXTEND

Use assessment results to remediate instruction.

INTENSIVE INTERVENTION PROGRAM

▲ Strategic Intervention Resource Kit

▲ Challenge Resource Kit

▲ Intervention Station, Primary
- Phonemic Awareness
- Phonics
- Comprehension
- Vocabulary
- Fluency

Overview of a Theme

FIRST FOUR LESSONS

- **Explicit Systematic Instruction**

- **Spiraled Review of Key Skills**

- **Abundant Practice and Application**

- **Point-of-Use Progress-Monitoring**

- **Support for *Leveled Readers***

- **Digital Support for Teachers and Students**

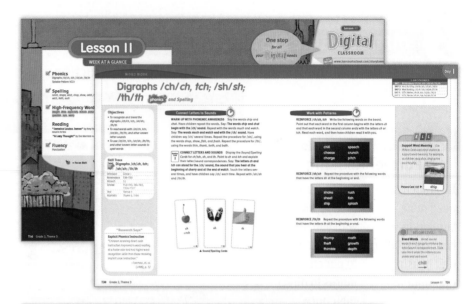

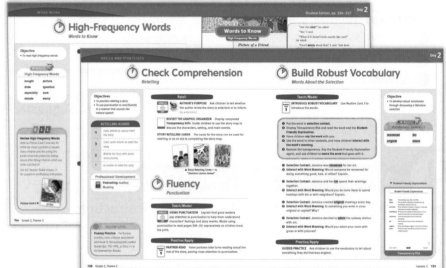

FIFTH LESSON THEME REVIEW

- **Review Skills and Strategies**

- **Build and Review Vocabulary**

- **Celebrate with Readers' Theater**

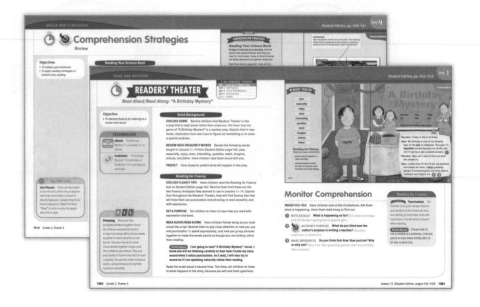

READING-WRITING CONNECTION

- **Reading-Writing Connection in *Student Edition***

- **Instruction in *Teacher Edition***

- **Focus on the Six Traits of Good Writing:**
  - Organization
  - Ideas
  - Sentence Fluency
  - Word Choice
  - Voice
  - Conventions

- **Develop a Variety of Writing Strategies**

- **Develop <u>One</u> Major Form Through the Writing Process:**
  - Personal Narrative
  - Respond to a Story
  - Friendly Letter
  - Story
  - Description
  - Research Report

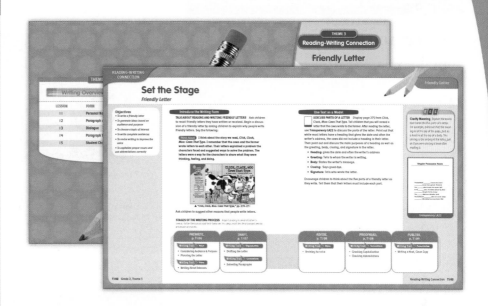

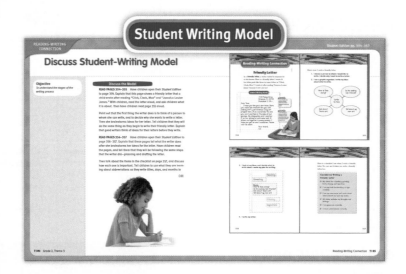

Student Writing Model

Overview of a Lesson

- **Lesson Resources**

- **Suggested Lesson Planner**
- **Suggested Small-Group Planner**

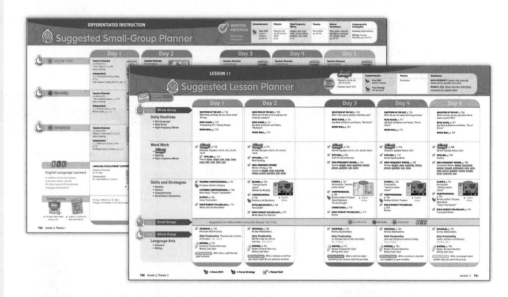

- *Leveled Readers* and **Leveled Practice**

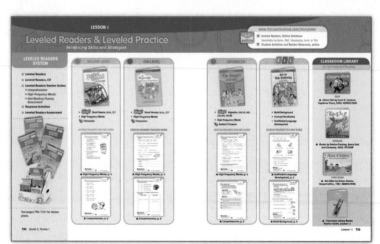

ROUTINES

- **Oral Language**
- **Read Aloud**
- **Word Wall**

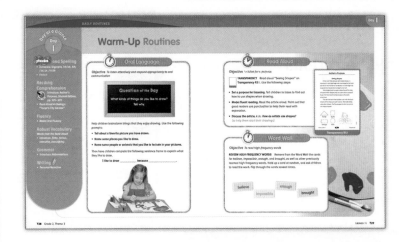

PHONICS/SPELLING

- **Connect Letter and Sound**
- **Word Building**
- **Work with Patterns**
- **Spelling Pretest and Posttest**
- **Introduce and Review Structural Elements**

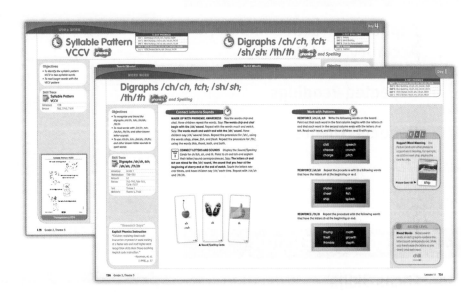

Overview of a Lesson (continued)

READING

- **Main Selections**
- **Paired Selections**

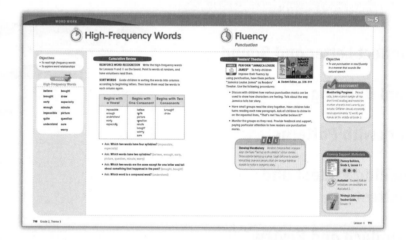

FLUENCY

- **Explicit Instruction in Rate, Accuracy, and Prosody**
- **Repeated Readings**
- **Readers' Theater**

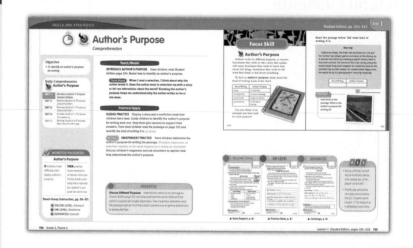

COMPREHENSION

- **Focus Skills**
- **Focus Strategies**
- **Listening Comprehension**

ROBUST VOCABULARY

- **Robust Vocabulary**
  - Tier Two Words

- **Instructional Routines**

- **Student-Friendly Explanations**

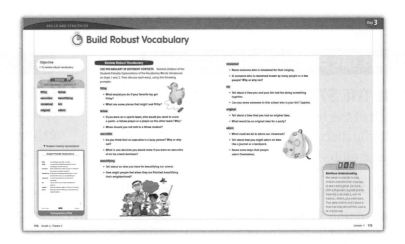

LANGUAGE ARTS

- **Grammar**

- **Writing**

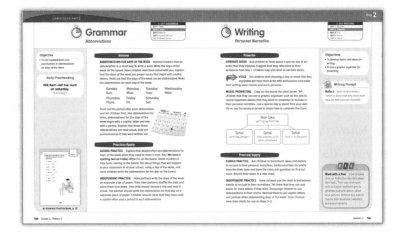

LEVELED READERS

- **Reinforce Skills and Strategies**

- **Review Vocabulary**

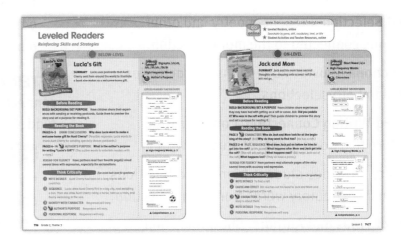

Introducing the Book

EXAMINE THE *STUDENT EDITION* Have children turn to each of the following features in the *Student Edition*. Briefly discuss how each part helps readers use the book and understand the stories.

- **Contents** Shows titles, authors, and page numbers.

- **Comprehension Strategies** Describes tools readers can use to read well.

- **Theme Overview** Lists literature, skills, and strategies in that theme.

- **Lesson Overview** Lists literature, focus skill, and focus strategy in that lesson.

- **Focus/Phonics Skill** Provides instruction in skills related to the literature.

- **Words to Know/Vocabulary** Introduces new high-frequency words or robust vocabulary words from the selection.

- **Genre Study** Describes the characteristic of the selection's genre.

- **Focus Strategy** Tells how to use strategies during reading.

- **Paired Selection** Presents poetry and other selections connected to the main selection.

- **Connections** Provides questions and activities related to both selections.

- **Reading-Writing Connection** Connects the literature to a good model of student writing.

- **Glossary** Provides student-friendly explanations for robust vocabulary words from each selection.

- **Index of Titles and Authors** Show titles and authors in alphabetical order.

Introduce Strategies

USING *STUDENT EDITION* PAGES 10–13 Have children open their *Student Editions* to page 10, and explain to them that these pages will help them think about ways to better understand what they read. Tell them that these ways are called "strategies," and that they can use strategies before they read, while they read, and after they read.

BEFORE YOU READ Tell children that before they read, they can think about what they already know about a topic to help them understand. They can also set a purpose for reading.

> **Think Aloud** If I was going to read a book about dogs, I could think about what I already know about dogs. I could also think about why I'm reading. These would help me understand the book better.

WHILE YOU READ Model strategies children can use while they read as follows:

> **Think Aloud** Asking questions about what I'm reading helps me know if I'm understanding it. If I'm not understanding, I can go back and reread parts of the book. When I answer questions about a book, I can be sure that I understood it.

AFTER YOU READ Explain how retelling and making connections can help children understand what they read. Say:

> **Think Aloud** After I read something, I tell myself what I just read. This helps me remember and understand. I also think about other things I have read, heard, or learned. Sometimes I can make connections between two different books.

Comprehension Strategies

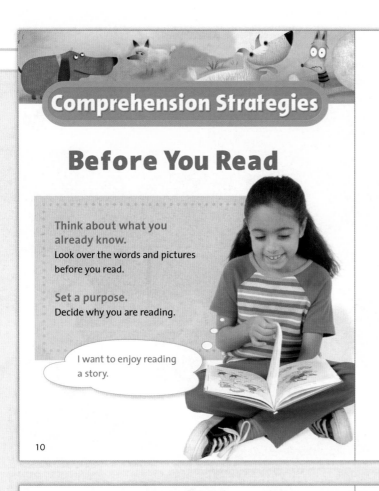

Before You Read

Think about what you already know.
Look over the words and pictures before you read.

Set a purpose.
Decide why you are reading.

I want to enjoy reading a story.

While You Read

Use story structure.
Think about a story's characters, setting, and plot.

Use graphic organizers.
Use a story map, web, or chart to help you read.

Monitor your reading.
Use fix-up strategies such as reading ahead or rereading.

Ask questions.
Ask yourself and others questions about what you read.

Answer questions.
Answer your teacher's questions to help you understand what you read.

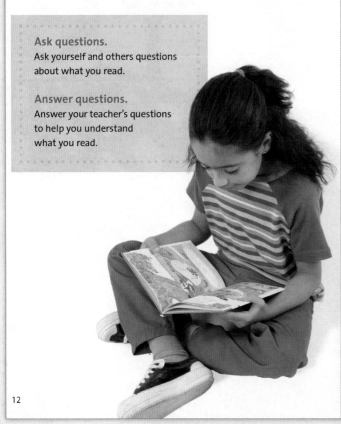

After You Read

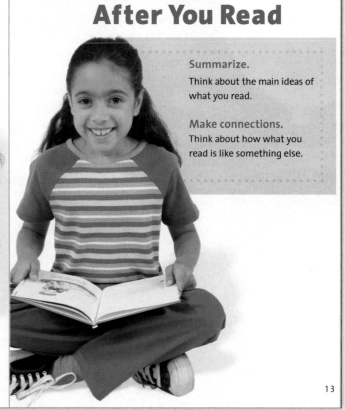

Summarize.
Think about the main ideas of what you read.

Make connections.
Think about how what you read is like something else.

Better Together

Theme Resources

 eBook STUDENT EDITION

STUDENT EDITION LITERATURE

Lesson 21

PAIRED SELECTIONS

"A Chair For My Mother," pp. 166–191
REALISTIC FICTION

"Saving Money," pp. 192–195
NONFICTION

Lesson 24

PAIRED SELECTIONS

"Watching in the Wild," pp. 284–297
NONFICTION

"Chimp Computer Whiz," pp. 298–299
MAGAZINE ARTICLE

Lesson 22

PAIRED SELECTIONS

"Serious Farm," pp. 208–233
FANTASY

"Beyond Old MacDonald," pp. 234–235
POETRY

Lesson 25 Theme Review

READERS' THEATER

"Town Hall," pp. 304–315
INTERVIEW

COMPREHENSION STRATEGIES

"A Time For Patience," pp. 316–319
FABLE

Lesson 23

PAIRED SELECTIONS

"The Bee," pp. 244–273
NONFICTION

"California Bee Business," pp. 274–275
NONFICTION

 Literature selections are available on Audiotext Grade 2, CD5.

THEME 5 CLASSROOM LIBRARY

For Self-Selected Reading

▲ **Treasure Map,** *by Stuart J. Murphy*
An old map leads the Elm Street Kids' Club to a buried time capsule.

▲ **A Log's Life,** *by Wendy Pfeffer*
Introduction to the life cycle of a tree.

▲ **Classroom Library Books Teacher Guide**

ADDITIONAL RESOURCES

▲ **Writer's Companion**

▲ **Grammar Practice Book**

▲ **Spelling Practice Book**

▲ **Literacy Center Kit**

▲ **Reading Transparencies**

▲ **Language Arts Transparencies**

▲ **Fluency Builders**

▲ **Picture Card Collection**

- **Professional Development Book**
- 📱 **Videos for Podcasting**

Leveled Resources

 BELOW-LEVEL

- phonics
- Vocabulary
-  Focus Skills

 ON-LEVEL

- phonics
- Vocabulary
- Focus Skills

Leveled Readers System

- **Leveled Readers**

- **Leveled Readers CD**

- **Leveled Readers Teacher Guides**
  - Vocabulary
  - Comprehension
  - Oral Reading Fluency Assessment

- **Response Activities**

- **Leveled Readers Assessment**

 ADVANCED

E L L

- phonics
- Vocabulary
- Focus Skills

- **Build Background**
- **Concept Vocabulary**
- **Scaffolded Language Development**

TECHNOLOGY

 www.harcourtschool.com/storytown

✔ **Leveled Readers Online Database** *Searchable by Genre, Skill, Vocabulary, Level, or Title*

✔ **Student Activities and Teacher Resources,** *online*

Teaching suggestions for the Leveled Readers can be found on pp. T102–T105, T202–T205, T294–T297, T376–T379, T450–T453

Strategic Intervention Resource Kit,
Lessons 21–25

Strategic Intervention Interactive Reader: *Balancing Act*
- "Pam's Big Plan"
- "Fun Farm"
- "Ants"
- "Tell Me"
- "Way to Grow!"

Also available:

- Strategic Intervention Teacher Guide
- Strategic Intervention Practice Book
- Audiotext CD
- Skill Cards
- Teacher Resource Book
- Strategic Intervention Assessment Book

 Strategic Intervention Interactive Reader eBook

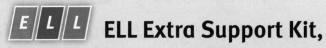 ELL Extra Support Kit,
Lessons 21–25

- ELL Student Handbook
- ELL Teacher Guide
- ELL Copying Masters

Challenge Resource Kit,
Theme 5

- Challenge Book Packs
- Challenge Teacher Guide
- Challenge Student Activities

Leveled Practice

 BELOW-LEVEL
Extra Support Copying Masters

 ON-LEVEL
Practice Book

 ADVANCED
Challenge Copying Masters

INTENSIVE INTERVENTION PROGRAM

Intervention Station, Primary

GRADES K–3 Sets of intervention material providing targeted instruction in

- Phonemic Awareness
- Phonics
- Comprehension
- Vocabulary
- Fluency

Digital Classroom
to go along with your Print Program

 GO online www.harcourtschool.com/storytown

FOR THE TEACHER

Prepare

GO online Professional Development

in the Online TE

📱 Videos for Podcasting

PROFESSIONAL DEVELOPMENT

Plan & Organize

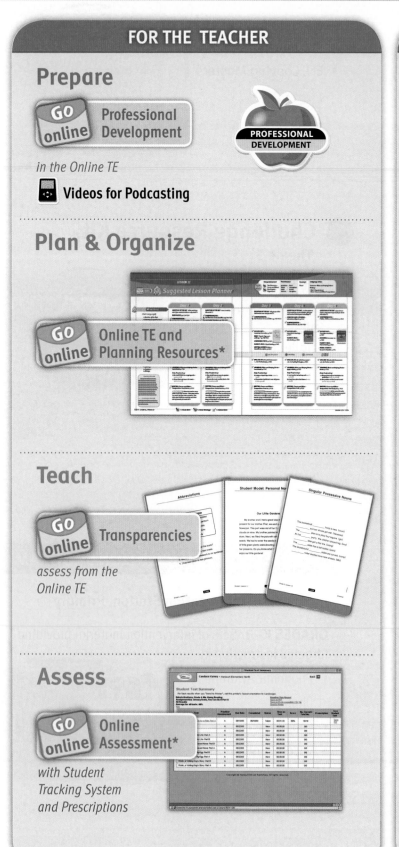

GO online Online TE and Planning Resources*

Teach

GO online Transparencies

assess from the Online TE

Assess

GO online Online Assessment*

with Student Tracking System and Prescriptions

FOR THE STUDENT

Read

GO online Student eBook*

GO online Strategic Intervention Interactive Reader

Balancing Act

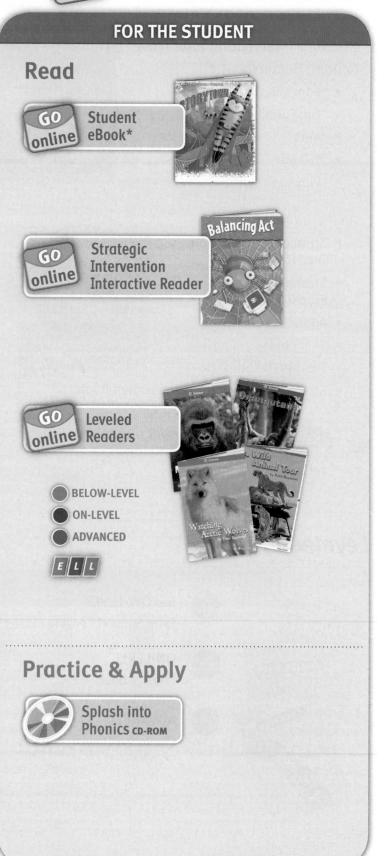

GO online Leveled Readers

🔴 BELOW-LEVEL
🔴 ON-LEVEL
🔴 ADVANCED

ELL

Practice & Apply

💿 Splash into Phonics CD-ROM

---

 *Also available on CD-ROM

Monitor Progress

 Plan Ahead

to inform instruction for Theme 5

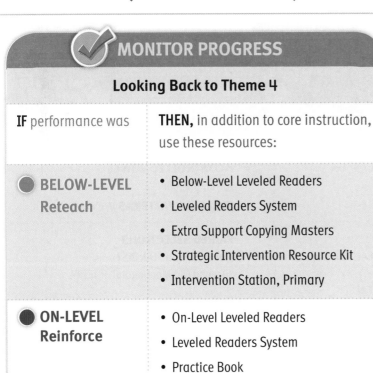 MONITOR PROGRESS

Looking Back to Theme 4

IF performance was	THEN, in addition to core instruction, use these resources:
BELOW-LEVEL **Reteach**	• Below-Level Leveled Readers • Leveled Readers System • Extra Support Copying Masters • Strategic Intervention Resource Kit • Intervention Station, Primary
ON-LEVEL **Reinforce**	• On-Level Leveled Readers • Leveled Readers System • Practice Book
ADVANCED **Extend**	• Advanced Leveled Readers • Leveled Readers System • Challenge Copying Masters • Challenge Resource Kit

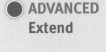 ONLINE ASSESSMENT

✓ Prescriptions for Reteaching
✓ Weekly Lesson Tests
✓ Theme Test
✓ Student Profile System to track student growth

 www.harcourtschool.com/storytown

Tested

THEME 5 TESTED SKILLS

Domain	Skills
PHONICS/SPELLING	• Vowel Diphthong /ou/*ou, ow* • *r*-Controlled Vowel /ôr/*or, ore, our* • Vowel Variant /o͞o/*oo, ew, ue, ui, ou* • *r*-Controlled Vowel /âr/*air, are*
COMPREHENSION	• Comprehension of Grade-level Text 🎯 Plot 🎯 Use Graphic Aids
VOCABULARY	• Robust Vocabulary
FLUENCY	• Oral Reading Fluency 📱 Podcasting: Assessing Fluency
GRAMMAR	• Present-Tense Action Verbs • Subject-Verb Agreement • Past-Tense Verbs • Forms of *be*
WRITING	• Description
WRITING TRAITS	• Sentence Fluency • Word Choice

Theme at a Glance

	LESSON 21 pp. T16–T105 	LESSON 22 pp. T118–T205 
• **Phonics/Spelling**	**VOWEL DIPHTHONG** /ou/*ou, ow* **ABBREVIATIONS**	*r*-**CONTROLLED VOWEL** /ôr/*or, ore, our* **SYLLABLE PATTERNS** V/CV and VC/V
• **Reading**	**PAIRED SELECTIONS** "A Chair For My Mother" REALISTIC FICTION "Saving Money" NONFICTION	**PAIRED SELECTIONS** "Serious Farm" FANTASY "Beyond Old MacDonald" POETRY
• **Comprehension**	Plot Use Story Structure	Plot Use Story Structure
• **Robust Vocabulary**	**ROBUST VOCABULARY** *allowance, rosy, bargain, spoiled, comfortable, boost, exchanged, delivered, thrifty, industrious*	**ROBUST VOCABULARY** *acquired, assumed, serious, extremely, admit, barely, hilarious, witty, absurd, attempt*
• **Fluency**	**FLUENCY:** Expression	**FLUENCY:** Expression

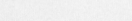 **Theme Writing** ▸ **Reading-Writing Connection** ▸ Description, pp. T106–T117

• **Grammar**	**GRAMMAR:** Present-Tense Action Verbs	**GRAMMAR:** Subject-Verb Agreement
• **Writing**	**WRITING FORM:** Personal Narrative	**WRITING FORM:** Fantasy
	WRITING TRAIT: Sentence Fluency	**WRITING TRAIT:** Sentence Fluency

THEME 5
Theme Project:
School Community
Mural

 = **Focus Skill**    = **Focus Strategy**    = **Tested Skill**

LESSON 23
pp. T206–T297

- **VOWEL VARIANT** /oo/oo, ew, ue, ui, ou
- **PREFIXES** mis-, re-, un-

PAIRED SELECTIONS
"The Bee" NONFICTION
"California Bee Business" NONFICTION

  Use Graphics Aids
 Summarize

ROBUST VOCABULARY
thickens, plentiful, crowd (v.), sealed, carefully, attack, pattern, disappear, role, diligent

FLUENCY: Reading Rate

LESSON 24
pp. T298–T379

- **r-CONTROLLED VOWEL** /âr/air, are
- **CONTRACTIONS**

PAIRED SELECTIONS
"Watching in the Wild" NONFICTION
"Chimp Computer Whiz" MAGAZINE ARTICLE

  Use Graphic Aids
 Summarize

ROBUST VOCABULARY
extinct, pledge, blended, cradled, raggedy, distance, personalities, crumpled, patience, tedious

FLUENCY: Reading Rate

Theme Review
LESSON 25
pp. T380–T453

READERS' THEATER

"Town Hall"

- **Build Fluency**
- **Review and Build Vocabulary**

COMPREHENSION STRATEGIES

"A Time for Patience"

REVIEW FOCUS STRATEGIES

 Use Story Structure

 Summarize

Writing Traits Sentence Fluency, Word Choice

GRAMMAR: Past-Tense Verbs

WRITING FORM: Paragraph of Information

WRITING TRAIT: Word Choice

GRAMMAR: Forms of *be*

WRITING FORM: Paragraph that Compares (or Contrasts)

WRITING TRAIT: Word Choice

ADDITIONAL REVIEW

 Focus Skills

- Plot
- Use Graphic Aids

 **and Spelling**

Grammar

 Writing: Revise and Publish

Planning for Reading Success

Tested Skill	Teach/Model	Monitor Progress	Additional Support
PHONICS/SPELLING • Vowel Diphthong /ou/*ou, ow* • *r*-Controlled Vowel /ôr/*or, ore, our* • Vowel Variant /o͞o/*oo, ew, ue, ui, ou* • *r*-Controlled Vowel /âr/*air, are*	Lesson 21, pp. T30–T33 Lesson 22, pp. T132–T135 Lesson 23, pp. T220–T223 Lesson 24, pp. T312–T315	Lesson 21, p. T42 Lesson 22, p. T144 Lesson 23, p. T232 Lesson 24, p. T324	Small-Group Instruction, pp. S2–S3 Small-Group Instruction, pp. S14–S15 Small-Group Instruction, pp. S26–S27 Small-Group Instruction, pp. S38–S39
ROBUST VOCABULARY	Lessons 21–25, pp. T37, T44, T61, T139, T146, T163, T227, T234, T253, T319, T326, T337, T398, T407, T417	Lessons 21–24, pp. T98, T198, T290, T372	Small-Group Instruction, pp. S10–S11, S22–S23, S34–S35, S46–S47
COMPREHENSION 🌀 Plot	Lesson 21, pp. T34–T35	Lesson 21, p. T34	Small-Group Instruction, pp. S6–S7, S18–S19
🌀 Use Graphic Aids	Lesson 23, pp. T224–T225	Lesson 23, p. T224	Small-Group Instruction, pp. S30–S31, S42–S43
COMPARE AND CONTRAST	Lesson 21, pp. T70–T71	Lesson 21, p. T70	Small-Group Instruction, pp. S8–S9, S20–S21
SYNONYMS	Lesson 23, pp. T268–T269	Lesson 23, p. T268	Small-Group Instruction, pp. S32–S33, S44–S45
DIBELS FLUENCY • Expression • Reading Rate	Lesson 21, p. T60 Lesson 23, p. T252	Lesson 21, p. T84 Lesson 23, p. T276	Small-Group Instruction, pp. S4–S5, S16–S17 Small-Group Instruction pp. S28–S29, S40–S41
WRITING CONVENTIONS Grammar	Lessons 21–24, pp. T38, T62, T78, T140, T164, T180, T228, T254, T270, T320, T338, T354	Lessons 21–24, pp. T100, T200, T292, T374	Small-Group Instruction, pp. S12–S13, S24–S25, S36–S37, S48–S49
WRITING	Lesson 21, p. T39 Reading-Writing Connection, pp. T106–T117 Lesson 22, p. T141 Lesson 23, p. T229 Lesson 24, p. T321	Scoring Rubric, p. T101 Scoring Rubric, p. T115 Scoring Rubric, p. T201 Scoring Rubric, p. T293 Scoring Rubric, p. T375	Small-Group Instruction, pp. S12–S13, S24–S25, S36–S37, S48–S49

🌀 = Focus Skill

Review	Assess
Lesson 21, pp. T42–T43, T66–T67 Lesson 22, pp. T144–T145, T168–T169 Lesson 23, pp. T232–T233, T258–T259 Lesson 24, pp. T324–T325, T342–T343	Weekly Lesson Tests 21, 22, 23, 24 Theme 5 Test
Lessons 21–24, Cumulative Review, pp. T101, T201, T293, T375	Weekly Lesson Tests 21–25 Theme 5 Test
Lesson 21, pp. T69, T85, T97 Lesson 22, pp, T136–T137, T171, T187, T197	Weekly Lesson Tests 21, 22 Theme 5 Test
Lesson 23, pp. T261, T277, T289 Lesson 24, pp. T316–T317, T345, T361, T371	Weekly Lesson Tests 23, 24 Theme 5 Test
Lesson 22, pp. T172–T173	Weekly Lesson Tests 21–22
Lesson 24, pp. T352–T353	Weekly Lesson Tests 23, 24
Lesson 22, p. T162 Lesson 24, p. T336	Oral Reading Fluency Tests
Lesson 25, pp. T408, T418, T428, T440, T448	Weekly Lesson Tests 21–24 Theme 5 Test
Lesson 25, pp. T409, T419, T429, T441, T449	Theme 5 Test

☑ INTEGRATED TEST PREP

In the *Teacher Edition*

- 4-point Rubric, p. R8
- Daily Writing Prompts, pp. T20–T21, T122–T123, T210–T211, T302–T303, T384–T385
- Writing on Demand, pp. T116–T117
- Short Response, pp. T59, T161, T251
- Extended Response, p. T335

TEST PREP SYSTEM

- Practice Workbook: Reading and Writing

☑ TEST PREP MINUTES

For early finishers, beginning of class, or anytime:

- **PAST-TENSE VERBS Write a few sentences that use past-tense verbs.** (Possible answer: I ran in a race yesterday at P.E.)

- **WRITING/SUMMARIZE Write a paragraph that summarizes what you did in school yesterday.** (Answers will vary but should include a summary of the day's events.)

- **ROBUST VOCABULARY Think of some things that you find absurd. Write a sentence about it. Draw a picture if you have time.** (Possible answer: I think a dog talking would be absurd.)

- **WRITING Think about a time when a group of people have worked together to solve a problem or make something better. Write a sentence about it. Draw a picture if you have time.** (Responses will vary.)

Theme Project
School Community Mural

Objectives
- *To gather information by taking notes*
- *To organize and present information in a mural*

Materials
- butcher or mural paper
- pencils, markers, crayons
- yardstick
- notebook paper

See **Project Ideas from The Bag Ladies,** pp. 10–11

Getting Started

Tell children to listen to this list and think about what all the things have in common: *neighborhood, class, town, team*. Children should recognize that the four words are names for kinds of communities—groups of people who share a place and often work together. Write the word *community* on the board, and tell children that they will learn about everyone who works in a special community—their own school. They will then make a mural together to show what they have learned.

Along the Way

1. **Brainstorm** Ask children to name all the school workers they can think of, including not only the teachers and administrators, but also the bus drivers, kitchen staff, custodial staff, and others. Talk about how all the jobs might be shown in a mural.

2. **Research** Lead children on a field trip through the school to see the staff at work at a variety of jobs. Have children carry paper and pencil with them to jot down notes that answer *Who* and *What* questions. Pairs of children may later take additional notes by interviewing staff members to learn more about what they do.

3. **Plan** Have the whole class help you make a chalkboard sketch of the mural that shows who will be shown in the different sections and how they will be shown. Discuss the captions that will explain who and what. Then assign sections to groups.

4. **Complete the Display** Have each group use pencils to sketch before drawing and coloring their mural section. Remind them that their captions must be neatly written and easy to read.

LISTENING AND SPEAKING

Children can develop listening and speaking skills as they conduct their interviews and as they work in small groups to complete a project. Emphasize the rules of effective listening and speaking:

- **Show interest while listening to a speaker.**
- **Ask follow-up questions to help you understand the speaker's points.**
- **Wait for a speaker to finish before making comments.**
- **Contribute to group discussions with comments that are on topic.**
- **Speak loudly and clearly enough for your listeners to hear and understand.**

SUGGESTIONS FOR INQUIRY

The theme project can be a springboard for inquiry into a variety of topics and ideas. Help children formulate questions about school communities, such as:

- **What are schools like in other parts of the world?**
- **What is "school pride" and how can we show it?**

Guide children in locating answers to some of their questions. Invite them to present their findings to the class.

Mrs. Musco, School Nurse
    makes sure kids have
    medicine, checks for
    fever, checks cuts and
    scrapes
Mr. James, Technology Specialist
    teaches kids how to use
    computers

Translate Names Guide children to complete this sentence frame for each school worker: Our *‹worker›'s job is to _____*. Work with children to use appropriate terms to describe each job.

BELOW-LEVEL

Support Concepts Guide children in making a web to show the connections among the different school workers. Encourage them to write a sentence that gives a main idea about "Our School Community."

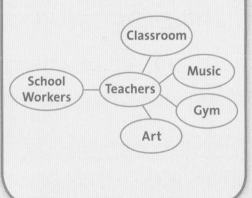

 School-Home **Connection**

Children may share their plans for their section of the mural with family members. Suggest that children ask for suggestions about showing the information in an interesting way.

Build Theme Connections
Better Together

Discuss Community Activities   Have children tell about their own experiences participating in events or activities with their whole school or neighborhood. Talk about why people come together for these activities. Children may observe that community activities such as fairs, parades, or block parties help people meet one another, while fundraisers and cleanups help make the community better. Then read the following poem aloud.

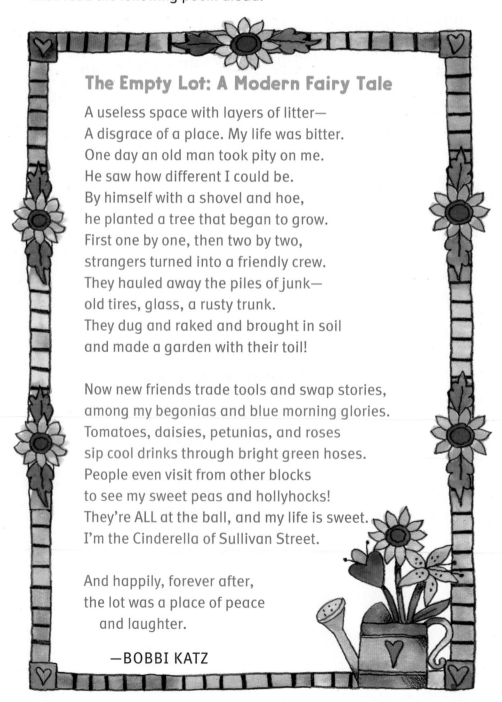

The Empty Lot: A Modern Fairy Tale

A useless space with layers of litter—
A disgrace of a place. My life was bitter.
One day an old man took pity on me.
He saw how different I could be.
By himself with a shovel and hoe,
he planted a tree that began to grow.
First one by one, then two by two,
strangers turned into a friendly crew.
They hauled away the piles of junk—
old tires, glass, a rusty trunk.
They dug and raked and brought in soil
and made a garden with their toil!

Now new friends trade tools and swap stories,
among my begonias and blue morning glories.
Tomatoes, daisies, petunias, and roses
sip cool drinks through bright green hoses.
People even visit from other blocks
to see my sweet peas and hollyhocks!
They're ALL at the ball, and my life is sweet.
I'm the Cinderella of Sullivan Street.

And happily, forever after,
the lot was a place of peace
    and laughter.

—BOBBI KATZ

Theme 5 **Better Together**
Balloons for a Dime, Jonathan Green

	Lesson 21 ▶	Lesson 22 ▶	Lesson 23 ▶	Lesson 24 ▶	Lesson 25 Review
Selection Titles	**A Chair For My Mother** Saving Money	**Serious Farm** Beyond Old MacDonald	**The Bee** California Bee Business	**Watching in the Wild** Chimp Computer Whiz	**Town Hall** A Time For Patience
Comprehension Strategies	Use Story Structure	Use Story Structure	Summarize	Summarize	Review Skills and Strategies
Focus Skills	Plot	Plot	Words with *oo, ew, ue, ui, ou*	Use Graphic Aids	

READING-WRITING CONNECTION

158   159

Talk About the Theme

DISCUSS THE THEME TITLE   Have children read the
theme title, "Better Together," and offer several ideas
about its possible meanings. Talk about the group
activity shown in the painting. Ask children what the
painting might have to do with the theme of activities
being "better" when done "together."

PREVIEW THE THEME   Have children page through the
selections in this theme. Tell them to read the story and
article titles and look at the illustrations. Ask for ideas
about the kinds of group activities that might be shown
in this theme—among fictional characters and among
real-life people and animals.

Talk About Fine Art

DISCUSS THE PAINTING   Have children look closely at
Balloons for a Dime by Jonathan Green. Tell children that
the artist often paints his memories of growing up in
an African-American community in South Carolina. Ask:
**How does the artist show the mood of joy? What do you
notice about the balloons? What round shapes do you
see? What other shapes do you see?** Encourage children
to give more than one answer and to ask their own
questions about the painting.

Lesson 21

WEEK AT A GLANCE

 Phonics
Vowel Diphthong /ou/*ou, ow*
Abbreviations

 Spelling
out, town, count, crowd, ground, now, found, crown, sound, down

Reading
"A Chair for My Mother" by Vera B. Williams
REALISTIC FICTION

"Saving Money" by Mary Firestone NONFICTION

 Fluency
Expression

 Comprehension
 Plot
Compare and Contrast
 Use Story Structure

 Robust Vocabulary
allowance, rosy, bargain, spoiled, comfortable, boost, exchanged, delivered, thrifty, industrious

 Grammar
Present-Tense Action Verbs

Writing
Form: Personal Narrative
Trait: Sentence Fluency

Weekly Lesson Test

 = Focus Skill   = Focus Strategy   = Tested Skill

One stop *for all* your **Digital** *needs*

Lesson 21

Digital
CLASSROOM

 www.harcourtschool.com/storytown
To go along with your print program

FOR THE TEACHER

Prepare Professional Development

 Videos for Podcasting

Plan & Organize Online TE & Planning Resources*

Teach Transparencies

access from Online TE

Assess Online Assessment*

with Student Tracking System and Prescriptions

FOR THE STUDENT

Read  Student eBook*

 Strategic Intervention Interactive Reader

 Leveled Readers

Practice & Apply Splash into Phonics CD-ROM

 Also available on CD-ROM

Literature Resources

STUDENT EDITION

 **GO online** eBook STUDENT EDITION

Vera B. Williams

A CHAIR FOR MY MOTHER

CALDECOTT HONOR BOOK

Genre: Realistic Fiction

Saving Money

by Mary Firestone

Genre: Nonfiction

 ◄ **Audiotext** *Student Edition selections are available on Audiotext Grade 2, CD 5.*

Accelerated Reader® ◄ *Practice Quizzes for the Selection*

THEME CONNECTION: BETTER TOGETHER

Comparing Realistic Fiction and Nonfiction

Paired Selections

 SOCIAL STUDIES **A Chair for My Mother, pp. 166–191**

SUMMARY After a fire destroys their home, a girl's family saves coins in a jar to buy a big, comfortable chair for them all to enjoy.

SOCIAL STUDIES **Saving Money, pp. 192–195**

SUMMARY This informational book gives an introduction to the basic concepts of saving.

Support for Differentiated Instruction

 LEVELED READERS

 **BELOW-LEVEL**

 **ON-LEVEL**

 **ADVANCED**

E L L

LEVELED PRACTICE

◄ **Strategic Intervention Resource Kit,** Lesson 21

◄ **Strategic Intervention Interactive Reader, Lesson 21**

Strategic Intervention Interactive Reader Online

◄ **ELL Extra Support Kit, Lesson 21**

◄ **Challenge Resource Kit, Lesson 21**

BELOW-LEVEL

Extra Support Copying Masters, pp. 162, 164–168

ON-LEVEL

Practice Book, pp. 162–169

ADVANCED

Challenge Copying Masters, pp. 162, 164–168

ADDITIONAL RESOURCES

- Decodable Book 17
- Spelling Practice Book, pp. 67–69
- Grammar Practice Book, pp. 73–76
- Reading Transparencies R106–R112
- Language Arts Transparencies LA41–LA42
- Test Prep System
- ◄ **Literacy Center Kit, Cards 101–105**
- Sound/Spelling Cards
- ◄ **Fluency Builders**
- ◄ **Picture Card Collection**
- Read-Aloud Anthology, pp. 76–79

ASSESSMENT

✓ **Monitor Progress**

✓ **Weekly Lesson Tests, Lesson 21**
- Comprehension
- Phonics and Spelling
- Focus Skill
- Robust Vocabulary
- Grammar
- Compare and Contrast

 www.harcourtschool.com/ storytown
Online Assessment
Also available on CD-ROM—Exam View®

Suggested Lesson Planner

 Go online Online TE & Planning Resources

	Day 1	**Day 2**
Step 1 Whole Group **Daily Routines** • Oral Language • Read Aloud • High-Frequency Words	**QUESTION OF THE DAY,** p. T28 *What is something special that you would save money for?* **READ ALOUD,** p. T29 *Transparency R106: Peng's Plan* **WORD WALL,** p. T29	**QUESTION OF THE DAY,** p. T40 *What are some things that make people feel good?* **READ ALOUD,** p. T41 *Big Book of Rhymes and Poems, "Grown-Ups"* **WORD WALL,** p. T41
Word Work • phonics • Spelling	**phonics**, p. T30 Introduce: Vowel Diphthong /ou/*ou, ow* **SPELLING,** p. T33 Pretest: *out, town, count, crowd, ground, now, found, crown, sound, down*	**phonics**, p. T42 Review: Vowel Diphthong /ou/*ou, ow* **SPELLING,** p. T43 Word Building
Skills and Strategies • Reading • Fluency • Comprehension • Build Robust Vocabulary	**READING/COMPREHENSION,** p. T34 Introduce: Plot **LISTENING COMPREHENSION,** p. T36 Read-Aloud: "The Just-Right Gift" **FLUENCY,** p. T36 Focus: Expression **BUILD ROBUST VOCABULARY,** p. T37 *Words from the Read-Aloud*	**BUILD ROBUST VOCABULARY,** p. T44 *Words from the Selection* Word Detective, p. T44 **READING,** p. T46 "A Chair for My Mother" *Options for Reading*  Read! **COMPREHENSION,** p. T46 Introduce: Use Story Structure ▲ Student Edition **RETELLING/FLUENCY,** p. T60 Expression **BUILD ROBUST VOCABULARY,** p. T61 *Words About the Selection*
Step 2 Small Groups	**Suggestions for Differentiated Instruction (See pp. T22–T23.)**	
Step 3 Whole Group **Language Arts** • Grammar Quick Write • Writing	**GRAMMAR,** p. T38 Introduce: Present-Tense Action Verbs ***Daily Proofreading*** Mike is shortest than mr. Small. (shorter, Mr.) **WRITING,** p. T39 Introduce: Personal Narrative Writing Trait: Sentence Fluency **Writing Prompt** *Write about an important experience you have had at school.*	**GRAMMAR,** p. T62 Review: Present-Tense Action Verbs ***Daily Proofreading*** Dad asked Jane, "Will you help I bake cookies." (me, cookies?) **WRITING,** p. T63 Review: Personal Narrative Writing Trait: Sentence Fluency **Writing Prompt** *Record what makes a personal narrative different than a story.*

  = Focus Skill    = Focus Strategy    = Tested Skill

Skills at a Glance

phonics	Comprehension	Fluency	Vocabulary
• Vowel Diphthong /ou/*ou, ow* • Abbreviations	Focus Skill Plot Focus Strategy Use Story Structure	Expression	**ROBUST:** *allowance, rosy, bargain, spoiled, comfortable, boost, exchanged, delivered, thrifty, industrious*

Day 3

QUESTION OF THE DAY, p. T64
What are some ways people show their feelings?

READ ALOUD, p. T65
Big Book of Rhymes and Poems, "Grown-Ups"

WORD WALL, p. T65

, p. T66
Review: Vowel Diphthong /ou/*ou, ow*

 SPELLING, p. T67
State the Generalization

FLUENCY, p. T68
Expression: "A Chair for My Mother"

COMPREHENSION, p. T69
Review: Plot
Introduce:
Compare and Contrast
Paired Selection: "Saving Money"

 ▲ Student Edition

CONNECTIONS, p. T74

 BUILD ROBUST VOCABULARY, p. T76
Review

Day 4

QUESTION OF THE DAY, p. T80
What words would you use to describe how you would like things to be at home?

READ ALOUD, p. T81
Big Book of Rhymes and Poems, "Home"

WORD WALL, p. T81

, p. T82
Introduce: Abbreviations

SPELLING, p. T83
Review Spelling Words

FLUENCY, p. T84
Expression: "A Chair for My Mother"

COMPREHENSION, p. T85
Review: Plot
Maintain: Make Predictions
Maintain: Setting

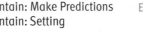 ▲ Student Edition

BUILD ROBUST VOCABULARY, p. T88
Review

Day 5

QUESTION OF THE DAY, p. T92
What makes a home quiet, peaceful, and lasting?

READ ALOUD, p. T93
Big Book of Rhymes and Poems, "Home"

WORD WALL, p. T93

, p. T94
Review: Abbreviations

SPELLING, p. T95
Posttest

FLUENCY, p. T96
Expression: "A Chair for My Mother"

COMPREHENSION, p. T97
Review: Plot
Read-Aloud:
"The Just-Right Gift"

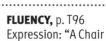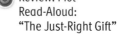 ▲ Student Edition

BUILD ROBUST VOCABULARY, p. T98
Cumulative Review

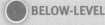 BELOW-LEVEL ON-LEVEL ADVANCED ELL

GRAMMAR, p. T78
Review: Present-Tense Action Verbs

Daily Proofreading
Molly gave Mrs brown some flowers.
(Mrs. Brown)

WRITING, p. T79
Review: Personal Narrative
Writing Trait: Sentence Fluency

Writing Prompt *Write about another way that "A Chair for My Mother" might have ended. Explain what might have caused the story to end differently.*

GRAMMAR, p. T90
Review: Present-Tense Action Verbs

Daily Proofreading
The shorter month of all is february.
(shortest, February)

WRITING, p. T91
Review: Personal Narrative
Writing Trait: Sentence Fluency

Writing Prompt *Compare something that you wrote earlier in the year to something you wrote recently. How has your writing changed?*

GRAMMAR, p. T100
Review: Present-Tense Action Verbs

Daily Proofreading
Does Sheenas grandmother live in richmond? (Sheena's, Richmond)

WRITING, p. T101
Review: Personal Narrative
Writing Trait: Sentence Fluency

Writing Prompt *Write a list of ideas for a new topic of your choice for writing.*

Suggested Small-Group Planner

45-60+ Minutes

	Day 1	Day 2

BELOW-LEVEL
15-20+ Minutes

Day 1

Teacher-Directed
Leveled Reader:
"The Book Sale," p. T102
Before Reading

Independent
⭐ Listening/Speaking Center, p. T26
Extra Support Copying Masters, pp. 162, 164

▲ Leveled Reader

Day 2

Teacher-Directed
Student Edition:
"A Chair for My Mother," p. T46

Independent
⭐ Reading Center, p. T26
Extra Support Copying Masters, pp. 165–166

▲ Student Edition

ON-LEVEL
15-20+ Minutes

Day 1

Teacher-Directed
Leveled Reader:
"Jackson's Tree," p. T103
Before Reading

Independent
⭐ Reading Center, p. T26
Practice Book, pp. 162, 164

▲ Leveled Reader

Day 2

Teacher-Directed
Student Edition:
"A Chair for My Mother," p. T46

Independent
⭐ Letters and Sounds Center, p. T27
Practice Book, pp. 165–166

▲ Student Edition

ADVANCED
15-20+ Minutes

Day 1

Teacher-Directed
Leveled Reader:
"Happy Again," p. T104
Before Reading

Independent
⭐ Letters and Sounds Center, p. T27
Challenge Copying Masters, pp. 162, 164

▲ Leveled Reader

Day 2

Teacher-Directed
Leveled Reader: "Happy Again," p. T104
Read the Book

Independent
⭐ Word Work Center, p. T27
Challenge Copying Masters, pp. 165–166

▲ Leveled Reader

ELL

English-Language Learners

In addition to the small-group instruction above, use the ELL Extra Support Kit to promote language development.

LANGUAGE DEVELOPMENT SUPPORT
Teacher-Directed
ELL TG, Day 1
Independent
ELL Copying Masters, Lesson 21

▲ ELL Student Handbook

LANGUAGE DEVELOPMENT SUPPORT
Teacher-Directed
ELL TG, Day 2
Independent
ELL Copying Masters, Lesson 21

▲ ELL Student Handbook

Intervention

▲ Strategic Intervention Resource Kit   ▲ Strategic Intervention Interactive Reader

Strategic Intervention TG, Day 1
Strategic Intervention Practice Book, Lesson 21

Strategic Intervention TG, Day 2
Strategic Intervention Interactive Reader, Lesson 21

▲ Strategic Intervention Interactive Reader

MONITOR PROGRESS

Small-Group Instruction

Comprehension	Phonics	Comprehension	Fluency	Robust Vocabulary	Language Arts Checkpoint
Focus Skill Plot pp. S6–S7	Vowel Diphthong /ou/*ou, ow* pp. S2–S3	Compare and Contrast pp. S8–S9	Expression pp. S4–S5	*allowance, rosy, bargain, spoiled, comfortable, boost, exchanged, delivered, thrifty, industrious* pp. S10–S11	**Grammar:** Present-Tense Action Verbs **Writing:** Personal Narrative pp. S12–S13

Day 3

Teacher-Directed
Leveled Reader: "The Book Sale," p. T102
Read the Book

Independent
⭐ Word Work Center, p. T27
Extra Support Copying Masters, p. 167

 ▲ Leveled Reader

Teacher-Directed
Leveled Reader: "Jackson's Tree," p. T103
Read the Book

Independent
⭐ Writing Center, p. T27
Practice Book, p. 167

 ▲ Leveled Reader

Teacher-Directed
Leveled Reader: "Happy Again," p. T104
Think Critically

Independent
⭐ Listening/Speaking Center, p. T26
Challenge Copying Masters, p. 167

 ▲ Leveled Reader

LANGUAGE DEVELOPMENT SUPPORT

Teacher-Directed
Leveled Reader: "In Our Neighborhood," p. T105
Before Reading; Read the Book
ELL TG, Day 3

Independent
ELL Copying Masters, Lesson 21

 ▲ Leveled Reader

Strategic Intervention TG, Day 3
Strategic Intervention Interactive Reader, Lesson 21
Strategic Intervention Practice Book, Lesson 21

 ▲ Strategic Intervention Interactive Reader

Day 4

Teacher-Directed
Leveled Reader: "The Book Sale," p. T102
Reread for Fluency

Independent
⭐ Letters and Sounds Center, p. T27

 ▲ Leveled Reader

Teacher-Directed
Leveled Reader: "Jackson's Tree," p. T103
Reread for Fluency

Independent
⭐ Word Work Center, p. T27

 ▲ Leveled Reader

Teacher-Directed
Leveled Reader: "Happy Again," p. T104
Reread for Fluency

Independent
⭐ Self-Selected Reading: Classroom Library Collection
Writing Center, p. T27

 ▲ Leveled Reader

LANGUAGE DEVELOPMENT SUPPORT

Teacher-Directed
Leveled Reader: "In Our Neighborhood," p. T105
Reread for Fluency
ELL TG, Day 4

Independent
ELL Copying Masters, Lesson 21

 ▲ Leveled Reader

Strategic Intervention TG, Day 4
Strategic Intervention Interactive Reader, Lesson 21

 ▲ Strategic Intervention Interactive Reader

Day 5

Teacher-Directed
Leveled Reader: "The Book Sale," p. T102
Think Critically

Independent
⭐ Writing Center, p. T27
Leveled Reader: Reread for Fluency
Extra Support Copying Masters, p. 168

 ▲ Leveled Reader

Teacher-Directed
Leveled Reader: "Jackson's Tree," p. T103
Think Critically

Independent
⭐ Listening/Speaking Center, p. T26
Leveled Reader: Reread for Fluency
Practice Book, p. 168

 ▲ Leveled Reader

Teacher-Directed
Leveled Reader: "Happy Again," p. T104
Reread for Fluency

Independent
⭐ Reading Center, p. T26
Leveled Reader: Reread for Fluency
Self-Selected Reading: Classroom Library Collection
Challenge Copying Masters, p. 168

 ▲ Leveled Reader

LANGUAGE DEVELOPMENT SUPPORT

Teacher-Directed
Leveled Reader: "In Our Neighborhood," p. T105
Think Critically
ELL TG, Day 5

Independent
Leveled Reader: Reread for Fluency
ELL Copying Masters, Lesson 21

 ▲ Leveled Reader

Strategic Intervention TG, Day 5
Strategic Intervention Interactive Reader, Lesson 21

 ▲ Strategic Intervention Interactive Reader

Leveled Readers & Leveled Practice
Reinforcing Skills and Strategies

LEVELED READER SYSTEM

- **Leveled Readers**
- **Leveled Readers, CD**
- **Leveled Readers Teacher Guides**
  - *Comprehension*
  - *Vocabulary*
  - *Oral Reading Fluency Assessment*
- **Response Activities**
- **Leveled Readers Assessment**

See pages T102–T105 for lesson plans.

BELOW-LEVEL

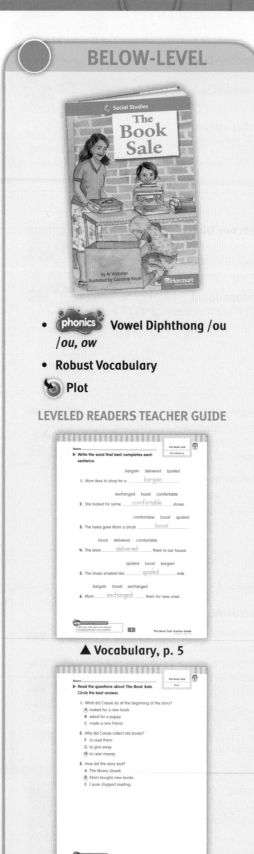

- **phonics** Vowel Diphthong /ou/ /ou, ow
- **Robust Vocabulary**
- **Plot**

LEVELED READERS TEACHER GUIDE

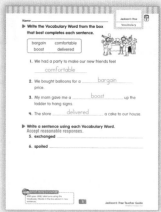

▲ Vocabulary, p. 5

▲ Comprehension, p. 6

ON-LEVEL

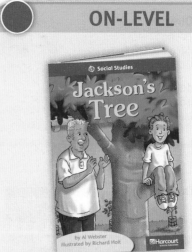

- **phonics** Vowel Diphthong /ou/ ou, ow
- **Robust Vocabulary**
- **Plot**

LEVELED READERS TEACHER GUIDE

▲ Vocabulary, p. 5

▲ Comprehension, p. 6

www.harcourtschool.com/storytown

GO online

★ Leveled Readers, Online Database
Searchable by Genre, Skill, Vocabulary, Level, or Title
★ Student Activities and Teacher Resources, online

ADVANCED

Social Studies

Happy Again

by Al Webster
illustrated by Debbie Mourtzios

Harcourt

- **phonics** Vowel Diphthong /ou/
  ou, ow
- **Robust Vocabulary**
- **Plot**

LEVELED READERS TEACHER GUIDE

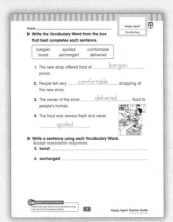

▲ **Vocabulary, p. 5**

▲ **Comprehension, p. 6**

E L L

Social Studies

In Our Neighborhood

by Al Webster,
illustrated by Anna Godwin

Harcourt

- **Build Background**
- **Concept Vocabulary**
- **Scaffolded Language Development**

LEVELED READERS TEACHER GUIDE

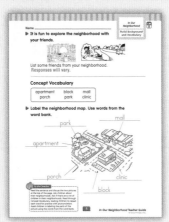

▲ **Build Background, p. 5**

▲ **Scaffolded Language Development, p. 6**

CLASSROOM LIBRARY

for Self-Selected Reading

EASY

▲ *Treasure Map* by Stuart J. Murphy.
FICTION

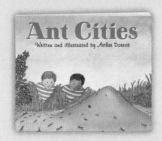

AVERAGE

▲ *Ant Cities* by Arthur Dorros.
NONFICTION

CHALLENGE

▲ *A Log's Life* by Wendy Pfeffer.
NONFICTION

▲ **Classroom Library Books
Teacher Guide, Lesson 21**

Literacy Centers
15 Min. each

Management Support

While you provide direct instruction to individuals or small groups, other children can work on literacy center activities.

▲ **Literacy Center Pocket Chart**

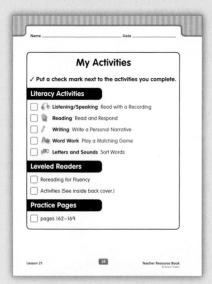

▲ **Teacher Resource Book, p. 54**

 ## Homework for the Week

TEACHER RESOURCE BOOK, PAGE 24

The *Homework Copying Master* provides activities to complete for each day of the week.

GO online www.harcourtschool.com/ storytown

 ### LISTENING/SPEAKING

Read with a Recording

Objective
To develop fluency by listening to familiar stories and reading them aloud

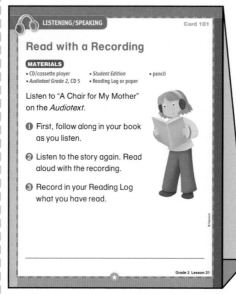

⭐ **Literacy Center Kit • Card 101**

 ### READING

Read and Respond

Objective
To develop comprehension by rereading familiar stories and responding to them

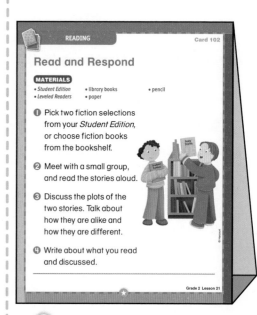

⭐ **Literacy Center Kit • Card 102**

---

www.harcourtschool.com/storytown

Go online

★ Additional Literacy Center Activities
★ Resources for Parents and Teachers

Differentiated
for Your Needs

✏️ WRITING

Write a Personal Narrative

Objective
To practice writing a personal narrative

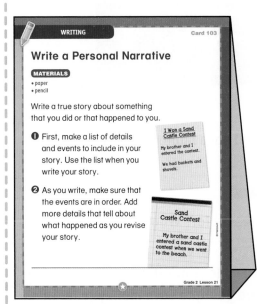

⭐ **Literacy Center Kit** • Card 103

🍎 WORD WORK

Play a Matching Game

Objective
To use vocabulary words

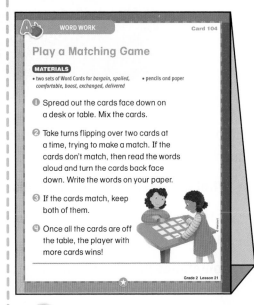

⭐ **Literacy Center Kit** • Card 104

🔤 LETTERS AND SOUNDS

Sort Words

Objective
To read and write words using known letter/sound correspondences

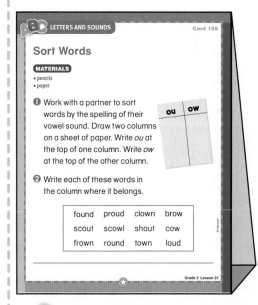

⭐ **Literacy Center Kit** • Card 105

Day at a Glance

Day 1

 phonics and Spelling

- Introduce: Vowel Diphthong /ou/*ou, ow*
- Pretest

Reading/ Comprehension

 Introduce: Plot, *Student Edition*, pp. 162–163

- *Read-Aloud Anthology:* "The Just-Right Gift"

Fluency

- Model Oral Fluency

Robust Vocabulary

Words from the Read-Aloud
- Introduce: *allowance, rosy*

Grammar *Quick Write*

- Introduce: Present-Tense Action Verbs

Writing ✎

- Personal Narrative

Warm-Up Routines

 ### Oral Language

Objective *To listen attentively and respond appropriately to oral communication*

> ### Question of the Day
>
> What is something special that you would save money for?

Help children brainstorm things they would save money for. Use prompts such as the following:

- **What is something you would like to buy?**

- **Is there someone you want to buy a present for? What would you buy for the person?**

- **Sometimes people save money to go to college or other schools to learn special information or skills. If you were going to save money to learn something, what would you like to learn?**

Then have children complete the following sentence frame to tell what they would save money for.

I would save money for _____

because _____.

Read Aloud

Objective *To listen for a purpose*

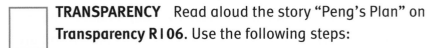

TRANSPARENCY Read aloud the story "Peng's Plan" on **Transparency R106**. Use the following steps:

- **Set a purpose for listening.** Tell children to listen to find out what Peng's plan is.

- **Model reading with expression.** Read the story aloud. Point out that when good readers read the characters' words, they read with expression to show how the characters feel. Explain that reading with expression makes a story more enjoyable to read and to listen to.

- **Discuss the story.** Ask: **What is Peng's plan?** (She wants to raise money to plant flowers in the schoolyard to make the school look cheerful.)

Plot

Peng's Plan

Winter was almost over. At the Carver School, Miss Cline and her class were thinking of ways to make their old school look cheerful. Everyone agreed that the school looked kind of gloomy.

"We could plant flowers in the schoolyard!" said Peng. "We could earn money for the supplies by having a bake sale and doing a talent show."

"We like Peng's plan!" said everyone in the class.

"Well, then, let's get to work," said Miss Cline.

In the next two months, the class held two bake sales. In late March, the students held a big talent show with the rest of the school. Many people paid two dollars for a ticket.

By early April, the class had earned a lot of money. Miss Cline took them to a garden supply store to get supplies.

Two weeks later, the school looked beautiful. The class had worked hard to plant flowers all around the building.

"Thank you," Principal Sanchez said to the class. "The school looks cheerful!"

Grade 2, Lesson 21   **R106**   Comprehension

Transparency R106

Word Wall

Objective *To read high-frequency words*

REVIEW HIGH-FREQUENCY WORDS Review the following words from the Word Wall: *already, woods, curve, accept, coming,* and *worry*. Randomly point to a word card and ask children to read the word. Repeat several times.

already	woods	curve
accept	coming	worry

Vowel Diphthong /ou/ ou, ow

 phonics *and Spelling*

Objectives

- *To recognize and blend the vowel diphthong sound /ou/ of* ou *and* ow
- *To read words with /ou/ou, ow, and other known letter-sounds*
- *To use /ou/ou, ow, and other known letter-sounds to spell words*

Skill Trace

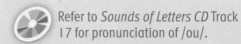

Tested **Vowel Diphthong /ou/ou, ow**

Introduce	Grade 1
Reintroduce	**T30–T33**
Reteach	S2–S3
Review	T42–T43, T66–T67, T394–T395
Test	Theme 5

Refer to *Sounds of Letters CD* Track 17 for pronunciation of /ou/.

Connect Letters to Sounds

WARM UP WITH PHONEMIC AWARENESS Say the words *out* and *owl*. Have children say the words. Repeat with the words *about* and *brown*. Say: **The words *out* and *owl* begin with the /ou/ sound, and the words *about* and *brown* have the /ou/ sound in the middle.** Have children say /ou/ several times. Then tell children you are going to say some words and ask them to raise their hand if they hear the /ou/ sound in the word. Use these words: *on, ounce, dawn, down, pond, pound, around, scoot, scout, scowl, clown, gone, gown,* and *golf.*

Routine Card 1 **CONNECT LETTERS AND SOUNDS** Display the *Sound/Spelling Card* for vowel diphthong /ou/ou, ow. Point to the letters *ou* and review their letter/sound correspondence. Say: **The two letters *ou* together can stand for the /ou/ sound, the sound you hear in the middle of *found*.** Touch the letters *ou* several times, and have children say /ou/ each time. Repeat the process for the letters *ow,* using the word *town.*

▲ **Sound/Spelling Card**

Day 1

5-DAY PHONICS
DAY 1 Reintroduce /ou/*ou, ow*
DAY 2 Word Building with: /ou/*ou, ow*
DAY 3 Word Building with: /ou/*ou, ow*
DAY 4 Abbreviations; Review /ou/*ou, ow*
DAY 5 Abbreviations; Review /ou/*ou, ow*

Work with Patterns

REINFORCE /ou/*ou* Write the following words on the board. Point out that each word in the first column begins with the letters *ou* and that each word in the second column has the letters *ou* in the middle. Read each word, and then have children read it with you.

outside	loud
ouch	scout
ounce	couch
outline	hound

REINFORCE /ou/*ow* Repeat the procedure with the following words that have the letters *ow* in the middle and at the end.

howl	allow
shower	vow
flower	now
gown	wow

Vowel Diphthong /ou/*ou*, *ow*
phonics *and Spelling*

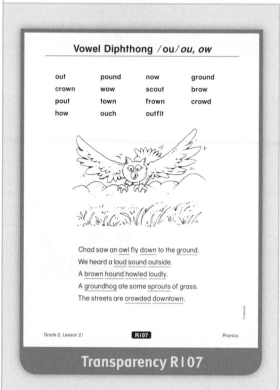

Vowel Diphthong /ou/*ou, ow*

out	pound	now	ground
crown	wow	scout	brow
pout	town	frown	crowd
how	ouch	outfit	

Chad saw an owl fly down to the ground.
We heard a loud sound outside.
A brown hound howled loudly.
A groundhog ate some sprouts of grass.
The streets are crowded downtown.

Grade 2, Lesson 21 **R107** Phonics

Transparency R107

Reading Words

GUIDED PRACTICE Display **Transparency R107** or write the words and sentences on the board. Point to the word *out*. Read the word, and then have children read it with you.

INDEPENDENT PRACTICE Point to the remaining words in the top portion, and have children read them. Then have children read aloud the sentences and identify words with /ou/*ou* or *ow*.

Decodable Books

Additional Decoding Practice

- **Phonics**
  Vowel diphthong /ou/*ou, ow*
- **Decodable Words**
- **High-Frequency Words**
  See the lists in *Decodable Book 17*.

  See also *Decodable Books*, online (Take-Home Version).

▲ **Decodable Book 17**
"Meg and the Groundhog"

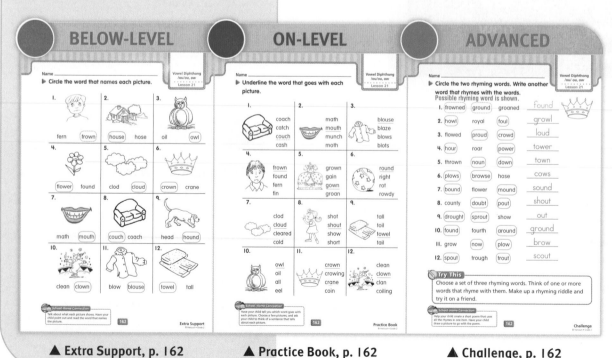

▲ **Extra Support, p. 162**   ▲ **Practice Book, p. 162**   ▲ **Challenge, p. 162**

ELL

- Group children according to academic levels, and assign one of the pages on the left.

- Clarify any unfamiliar concepts as necessary. See *ELL Teacher Guide* Lesson 21 for support in scaffolding instruction.

5-DAY SPELLING

DAY 1 Pretest
DAY 2 Word Building
DAY 3 State the Generalization
DAY 4 Review
DAY 5 Posttest

Introduce Spelling Words

PRETEST   Say the first word and read the dictation sentence. Repeat the word as children write it. Write the word on the board and have children check their spelling. Tell them to circle the word if they spelled it correctly or write it correctly if they did not. Repeat for words 2–10.

Words with Vowel Diphthong /ou/*ou* or *ow*

1.	out	Bree goes **out** to play after school.
2.	town	Tamara was born in a **town** in Russia.
3.	count	Belin can **count** to a thousand.
4.	crowd	Carlos joined the **crowd** in front of the pet shop.
5.	ground	Ashley's mitten fell to the **ground.**
6.	now	You are writing spelling words **now.**
7.	found	Tran **found** a quarter.
8.	crown	The princess wore a sparkling **crown** on her head.
9.	sound	The **sound** of soft music is relaxing.
10.	down	David watched the water swirl **down** the drain.

ADVANCED

Challenge Words   Use the challenge words in these dictation sentences.

11.	surround	Fences **surround** the zoo.
12.	without	Myra wanted a cake **without** frosting.
13.	cowboy	The **cowboy** rounded up the cattle.
14.	powerful	A **powerful** ox can haul heavy loads.
15.	cloudless	A sky without clouds is **cloudless.**

Spelling Words

1.	**out***	6.	**now***
2.	**town**	7.	**found***
3.	**count***	8.	**crown**
4.	**crowd**	9.	**sound**
5.	**ground**	10.	**down***

Challenge Words

11.	**surround**	14.	**powerful**
12.	**without**	15.	**cloudless**
13.	**cowboy**		

* Words from "A Chair for My Mother"
and "Saving Money"

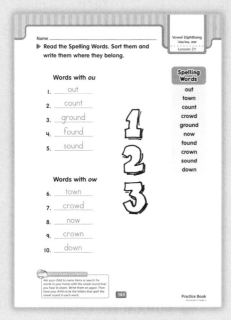

▲ Practice Book, p. 163

Lesson 21   **T33**

Plot
Comprehension

Objectives

- *To identify the plot of a story*
- *To identify the problem and solution in a story*

Daily Comprehension

Plot

DAY 1:	Introduce Plot *Student Edition*
DAY 2:	Review Plot *Student Edition*
DAY 3:	Review Plot *Student Edition*
DAY 4:	Review Plot *Transparency*
DAY 5:	Review Plot *Read-Aloud Anthology*

✓ MONITOR PROGRESS

Plot

IF children have difficulty identifying the story's plot, including its problem and solution,	**THEN** help them by asking what the main character has to do. Then ask what steps he or she takes to find a solution, and how everything turns out.

Small-Group Instruction, pp. S6–S7:

- ● **BELOW-LEVEL:** Reteach
- ● **ON-LEVEL:** Reinforce
- ● **ADVANCED:** Extend

Teach/Model

INTRODUCE PLOT   Have children read *Student Edition* page 162. Model how to use the story map to identify the problem and solution.

> **Think Aloud**   The *plot* tells what happens during a story. By looking at the story map and reading the boxes on page 162, I can tell what Ashley's problem is, important events in the story that tell how Ashley tries to solve her problem, and the solution to the story.

Practice/Apply

GUIDED PRACTICE   Display **Transparency GO7** or draw a story map like the one on *Student Edition* page 163. Then have children read "A Present for Mom." Guide them to identify the problem and important events that might help solve the problem. Ask: **What problem does Jill have?** (She doesn't have enough money to buy her mom flowers.) Add the information to the chart.

Try This   **INDEPENDENT PRACTICE**   As children tell about important events that lead to a solution, add their responses to the chart. (Events: Jill sets up a lemonade stand. She makes ten dollars in one day. Solution: Jill has enough money to buy her mom flowers for her birthday.) Have children use the completed story map to tell how Jill solves her problem.

Clarify Vocabulary   Use photographs to clarify unknown vocabulary in "A Present for Mom." For example, if children do not know the meaning of flowers, show *Picture Card 55* and point to the flower as you say, **This is a flower.**

Picture Card 55 ▶

flower

Focus Skill

Plot

Every story has characters, a setting, and a plot. The **plot** is what happens during the beginning, middle, and end of a story.

- The beginning introduces the characters and tells about a problem they have.

- The middle tells how they deal with the problem.

- The end tells how they solve it.

Read this story map. What problem does Ashley have? How does she solve it?

Problem
Ashley wants a new bicycle. She doesn't have enough money to buy one.

↓

Important Events
Ashley helps her brother do yard work. He pays her. She saves her money.

↓

Solution
Ashley saves enough money to buy a bicycle.

162

Read this story. What problem does the character have?

A Present for Mom

Mom's birthday was coming. Jill wanted to buy her flowers, but she had saved only $1.89. That wasn't enough for the flowers.

Then Jill had an idea. She would make some lemonade and set up a lemonade stand. After one day, Jill had made ten dollars. Now she could buy her mom flowers for her birthday.

Problem

↓

Important Events

↓

Solution

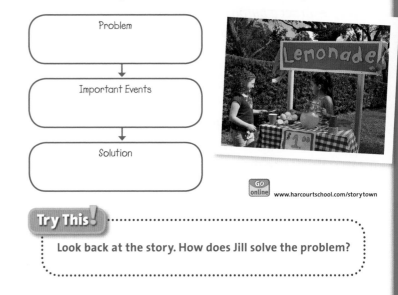

Go online www.harcourtschool.com/storytown

Try This!

Look back at the story. How does Jill solve the problem?

163

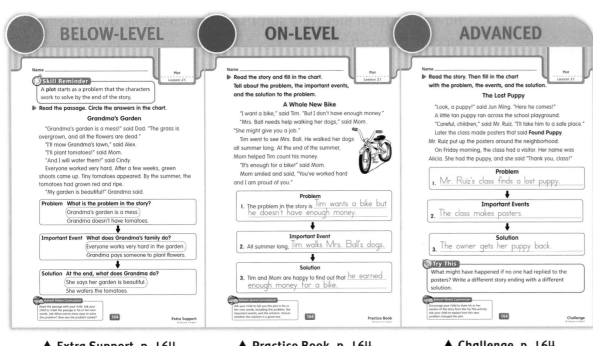

BELOW-LEVEL

Name _____

Skill Reminder
A **plot** starts as a problem that the characters work to solve by the end of the story.

▶ Read the passage. Circle the answers in the chart.

Grandma's Garden

"Grandma's garden is a mess!" said Dad. "The grass is overgrown, and all the flowers are dead."
"I'll mow Grandma's lawn," said Alex.
"I'll plant tomatoes!" said Mom.
"And I will water them!" said Cindy.
Everyone worked very hard. After a few weeks, green shoots came up. Tiny tomatoes appeared. By the summer, the tomatoes had grown red and ripe.
"My garden is beautiful!" Grandma said.

Problem What is the problem in the story?
 Grandma's garden is a mess.
 Grandma doesn't have tomatoes.

Important Event What does Grandma's family do?
 Everyone works very hard in the garden.
 Grandma pays someone to plant flowers.

Solution At the end, what does Grandma do?
 She says her garden is beautiful.
 She waters the tomatoes.

School-Home Connection
Read the passage with your child. Ask your child to retell the passage in his or her own words. Ask What events cause a way to solve the problem? How was the problem solved?

164 Extra Support

ON-LEVEL

Name _____

▶ Read the story and fill in the chart.
Tell about the problem, the important events, and the solution to the problem.

A Whole New Bike

"I want a bike," said Tim. "But I don't have enough money."
"Mrs. Ball needs help walking her dogs," said Mom. "She might give you a job."
Tim went to see Mrs. Ball. He walked her dogs all summer long. At the end of the summer, Mom helped Tim count his money.
"It's enough for a bike!" said Tim.
Mom smiled and said, "You've worked hard and I am proud of you."

Problem
1. The problem in the story is Tim wants a bike but he doesn't have enough money.

↓

Important Event
2. All summer long, Tim walks Mrs. Ball's dogs.

↓

Solution
3. Tim and Mom are happy to find out that he earned enough money for a bike.

School-Home Connection
Ask your child to tell you the plot in his or her own words, including the problem, the important events, and the solution. Discuss whether the solution is a good one.

164 Practice Book

ADVANCED

Name _____

▶ Read the story. Then fill in the chart with the problem, the events, and the solution.

The Lost Puppy

"Look, a puppy!" said Jun Ming. "Here he comes!"
A little tan puppy ran across the school playground.
"Careful, children," said Mr. Ruiz. "I'll take him to a safe place."
Later the class made posters that said **Found Puppy**.
Mr. Ruiz put up the posters around the neighborhood.
On Friday morning, the class had a visitor. Her name was Alicia. She had the puppy, and she said "Thank you, class!"

Problem
1. Mr. Ruiz's class finds a lost puppy.

↓

Important Events
2. The class makes posters.

↓

Solution
3. The owner gets her puppy back.

Try This
What might have happened if no one had replied to the posters? Write a different story ending with a different solution.

School-Home Connection
Encourage your child to share his or her version of the story from the Try This activity. Ask your child to explain how this new problem changed the plot.

164 Challenge

ELL

- Group children according to academic levels, and assign one of the pages on the left.

- Clarify any unfamiliar concepts as necessary. See *ELL Teacher Guide* Lesson 21 for support in scaffolding instruction.

▲ **Extra Support, p. 164**   ▲ **Practice Book, p. 164**   ▲ **Challenge, p. 164**

Listening Comprehension
Read Aloud

Objectives
- *To set a purpose for listening*
- *To identify the plot of a story*

Build Fluency

Focus: Expression   Tell children that good readers read a character's words and thoughts with expression. They use their voice in a way that shows how each character feels. If the character is happy and excited, the reader should sound happy and excited when reading that character's words. If the character is sad, the reader should make that character sound sad.

Clarify Meaning   Help children understand that *just right* means "perfect." Have children pantomime giving gifts to you. One child can offer a sheet of paper. Another child can offer a notebook. For the first gift, respond by saying, "Thank you, but this gift is not quite right. I need more than one sheet of paper for my work." For the notebook, say "Thank you. This is just right. I need many sheets of paper for my work!"

Before Reading

CONNECT TO PRIOR KNOWLEDGE   Tell children that they will listen to a story called "The Just-Right Gift." Explain that the story is about a girl named Gina who wants to buy a gift that is just right for her mother's birthday. Ask children to share any experiences they have had with choosing gifts.

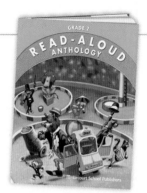

▲ Read-Aloud Anthology, "The Just-Right Gift," p. 76

Routine Card 2   **GENRE STUDY: REALISTIC FICTION**   Tell children that "The Just-Right Gift" is fiction. Remind them that realistic fiction stories are make-believe but may have parts that are like real life. The characters may have the same kinds of problems that real people have. Read aloud the first paragraph of "The Just-Right Gift."

Think Aloud   **I see that Gina's problem is that she wants to buy a birthday gift that is just right for her mother. Gina's big brother Donny agrees to take Gina to the store to shop for a gift.**

After Reading

RESPOND   Discuss the ending of "The Just-Right Gift" with children. Have them tell if they were surprised by Gina saying Donny helped pick out the scarf.

REVIEW PLOT   Remind children that every fiction story has a plot with a problem, important events, and a solution. Have children tell the important events in the story. (Possible response: Gina finds several things that she thinks are just right, but Donny points out that there's something wrong with all of them. Then Gina decides to buy a colorful scarf.) **Then ask children to tell the solution.** (Possible response: Mom drapes the scarf around her shoulders and says that it is special.)

Build Robust Vocabulary

Words from the Read-Aloud

Teach/Model

Routine Card 3

INTRODUCE ROBUST VOCABULARY   Use *Routine Card 3* to introduce the words.

❶ Put the word in **selection context**.
❷ Display Transparency R111 and read the word and the **Student-Friendly Explanation**.
❸ Have children **say the word** with you.
❹ Use the word in other contexts, and have children **interact with the word's meaning**.
❺ Remove the transparency. Say the Student-Friendly Explanation again, and ask children to **name the word** that goes with it.

❶ **Selection Context:** Gina had been saving her **allowance** for months so she could buy her mother a birthday gift.
❹ **Interact with Word Meaning:** When I was little, I got an allowance each week for helping to set the table. Would someone get an allowance for doing the dishes or for breaking them?

❶ **Selection Context:** Mom looked **rosy** and bright like the morning sun.
❹ **Interact with Word Meaning:** A rosy sunset fills the sky with red and pink colors. Which of these might you describe as rosy—a sunburn or dark brown hair?

Practice/Apply

GUIDED PRACTICE   Ask children to do the following:
- Give an example of something you might do to earn an *allowance*.
- Show or draw an example of something that is *rosy*.

Objective

- *To develop robust vocabulary through discussing a literature selection*

Tested

INTRODUCE ✓

Vocabulary: Lesson 21

allowance   **rosy**

▼ **Student-Friendly Explanations**

Student-Friendly Explanations

allowance	If you get money for doing chores or helping at home, you get an allowance.
rosy	If something looks rosy, it looks pink.
thrifty	If you are thrifty, you are careful about spending money.
industrious	If you are industrious, you are hard-working.

Grade 2, Lesson 21   R111   Vocabulary

Transparency R111

 Grammar **Quick Write**
Present-Tense Action Verbs

5-DAY PHONICS	
DAY 1	Introduce Present-Tense Action Verbs
DAY 2	Present-Tense Endings: -s, -es
DAY 3	Combining Sentences with the Same Verb
DAY 4	Apply to Writing
DAY 5	Weekly Review

Objectives

• *To identify and read present-tense action verbs*

• *To use present-tense action verbs correctly*

Daily Proofreading

Mike is shortest than mr. Small.

(shorter, Mr.)

Writing Trait

Strengthening Conventions

Grammar Use this short lesson with children's own writing to build a foundation for revising/editing longer connected text on Day 5.

Present-Tense Action Verbs

1. Donny and Gina go to a store.
2. Gina shops for a birthday gift for Mom.
3. They see many goods for sale.
4. Gina waves a timer in the air.
5. She and her brother smell perfume.
6. At last, Gina sees a silky scarf.
7. She wraps it with pretty paper.
8. Mom puts the scarf around her neck.

Grade 2, Lesson 21   **LA41**   Grammar

Transparency LA41

Teach/Model

INTRODUCE PRESENT-TENSE ACTION VERBS Explain that an **action verb** is a word that tells what someone or something does. A verb that tells about an action that is happening now is called a present-tense action verb.

Write this sentence on the board about "The Just-Right Gift" (*Read-Aloud Anthology,* p. 76):

> **Gina finds a just-right gift.**

Read aloud the sentence. Explain that the present-tense action verb in the sentence is *finds*. The verb *finds* tells what someone—*Gina*—does now.

Guided Practice

IDENTIFY PRESENT-TENSE ACTION VERBS Display **Transparency LA41**. Explain that each sentence has a present-tense action verb. Read the first sentence aloud, and identify the present-tense action verb (*go*). Explain that the verb *go* tells about an action that Donny and Gina are doing now. Guide children to identify the present-tense action verb in the remaining sentences and to tell what action is being done now.

Practice/Apply

INDEPENDENT PRACTICE Have children write sentences with a present-tense action verb. Have pairs of children read aloud their sentences to each other and tell what action in each sentence is being done now.

Writing
Personal Narrative

5-DAY WRITING	
DAY 1	Introduce
DAY 2	Prewrite
DAY 3	Draft
DAY 4	Revise
DAY 5	Revise

Teach/Model

INTRODUCE PERSONAL NARRATIVE Display **Transparency LA42,** and explain that this story tells about something the writer did. Read aloud the story, and discuss what the writer does. Develop a list of characteristics for a personal narrative.

Personal Narrative

- A personal narrative tells about an important experience the writer really had.
- The beginning tells what the personal narrative is about.
- The writer uses the words *I* and *me*.
- Details and words describe the setting, characters, objects, events, and feelings.
- The ending tells how things work out.

 SENTENCE FLUENCY: AVOIDING *I* Discuss the writer's use of the word *I*. Point out that the writer avoids starting each sentence with *I*. Explain that using a variety of sentence beginnings helps a story flow smoothly and makes it interesting.

Guided Practice

SHARE AN EXPERIENCE SENTENCE Model writing a sentence about an experience you had that was important to you. Have children share sentences about an important experience of their own.

Practice/Apply

SHARE SENTENCES ABOUT YOURSELF Have children orally share experiences they've had. Then have children write a sentence about one of their experiences. Children should save their sentences for use on Days 2–5.

Objectives

- *To read and respond to a personal narrative*
- *To share oral sentences about experiences*
- *To write sentences about experiences*

Writing Prompt

Write About School Have children write about an important experience they have had at school.

Student Model: Personal Narrative

A Birthday Present for My Mom

It was almost my mom's birthday, and I still had not bought her a gift. I was shopping with Mom when we stopped at a shop that sold music boxes. Mom smiled when she looked at the boxes. That was when I got my idea.

When I got home, I whispered my idea to Dad. The next day, Dad and I went back to the shop. I spotted the perfect music box for Mom. It had little figures of a boy and a girl on it. They held flowers and a present. The girl even looked like me!

When Mom opened her birthday gift she smiled and hugged me. Then she wound up the music box. "Happy Birthday" tinkled through the air.

Now Mom winds up her music box when anyone in our family has a birthday. Each time it makes me think of when Dad and I went shopping for it.

Grade 2, Lesson 21   **LA42**   Writing

Transparency LA42

Day at a Glance

Day 2

 **and Spelling**
- Review: Diphthong /ou/ou, ow
- Build Words

Robust Vocabulary
Words from the Selection
- Introduce: *bargain, spoiled, comfortable, boost, exchanged, delivered*

Comprehension
 Use Story Structure

 Plot

Reading
- "A Chair for My Mother," *Student Edition*, pp. 166–191  **Read!**

Fluency
- Expression

Robust Vocabulary
Words About the Selection
- Introduce: *thrifty, industrious*

Grammar
- Review: Present-Tense Verbs

Writing
- Personal Narrative

Warm-Up Routines

 Oral Language

Objective *To listen attentively and respond appropriately to oral communication*

Question of the Day
What are some things that make people feel good?

Help children brainstorm activities and events that make them feel good, and record their responses in a word web. Use prompts such as the following:

- **What are some outdoor activities that make you feel good? Indoor activities?**
- **What are some fun places to go?**
- **What are some special celebrations that you enjoy?**
- **How does a person feel when someone gives him or her a present?**

Read Aloud

Objective *To listen for a purpose*

BIG BOOK OF RHYMES AND POEMS Display the poem "Grown-Ups" on page 37 and read aloud the title. Ask children to listen for the grown-ups who are mentioned in the poem. Then read the poem aloud. Invite children to name the grown-ups mentioned in the poem. (mothers, fathers) Ask children to name the words that tell what the child wants her mother and father to be. (happy and glad)

▲ **Big Book of Rhymes and Poems, p. 37**

Word Wall

Objective *To read high-frequency words*

REVIEW HIGH-FREQUENCY WORDS Review the following words: *eight, straight, ago, sure, board,* and *popular*. For each word, have children read it, count the syllables, and finally read it again.

eight	straight	ago
sure	board	popular

Vowel Diphthong /ou/*ou, ow*

 phonics *and Spelling*

Objectives

- *To blend sounds into words*
- *To spell words with vowel diphthong /ou/ou, ow*

Skill Trace

✓ Tested **Vowel Diphthong /ou/*ou, ow***

Introduce	Grade 1
Reintroduce	T30–T33
Reteach	S2–S3
Review	T42–T43, T66–T67, T394–T395
Test	Theme 5
Maintain	Theme 6, T360

Spelling Words

1. **out***	6. **now***
2. **town**	7. **found***
3. **count***	8. **crown**
4. **crowd**	9. **sound**
5. **ground**	10. **down***

Challenge Words

11. **surround**	14. **powerful**
12. **without**	15. **cloudless**
13. **cowboy**	

* Words from "A Chair for My Mother" and "Saving Money"

Word Building

READ A SPELLING WORD Write the word *town* on the board. Ask children to identify the letters that stand for the /ou/ sound. Remind children that the letters *ow* and *ou* can stand for the /ou/ sound. Then read the word and have children repeat.

BUILD SPELLING WORDS Ask children which letter you should change to make *town* become *down*. (Change *t* to *d*.) Write the word *down* on the board and have children read it. Continue building spelling words in this manner. Say:

- **Which letter do I have to change to make the word *crown*?** (Change *d* to *cr*.)
- **Which letters do I have to change to make the word *crowd*?** (Change *n* to *d*.)
- **Which letters do I have to change to make the word *count*?** (Take away the *r*, change *w* to *u*, and change *d* to *nt*.)
- **Which letters do I have to change to make the word *found*?** (Change *c* to *f*, and *t* to *d*.)

town
down
crown
crowd
count
found

Continue building the remaining spelling words in this manner.

BELOW-LEVEL	ADVANCED
Sort Spelling Words List the spelling words on the board. Have children make word cards for the words. Then have children sort the words into two piles: /ou/ spelled *ou* and /ou/ spelled *ow*. Read the words in each pile with children.	**Spelling Riddles** Challenge children to write a riddle for each of the spelling words, such as: **What is the opposite of *up*?** *(down)* Have children share their riddles with classmates to review the spelling words.

5-DAY PHONICS/SPELLING

DAY I	Pretest
DAY 2	**Word Building**
DAY 3	State the Generalization
DAY 4	Review
DAY 5	Posttest

Read Words in Context

APPLY PHONICS   Write the following sentences on the board or on chart paper. Have children read each sentence silently. Then track the print as children read the sentence aloud.

> Juan <u>found</u> a dime on the <u>ground</u>.
>
> My dog barks when she wants to go <u>out</u>.
>
> Tess and her mother rode the bus to <u>town</u>.

WRITE   Dictate several spelling words. Have children write the words in their notebook or on a dry-erase board.

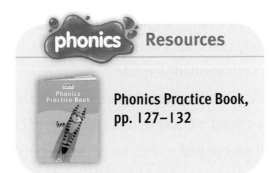

phonics **Resources**

**Phonics Practice Book,
pp. 127–132**

MONITOR PROGRESS

Vowel Diphthong /ou/*ou, ow*

IF children have difficulty building and reading words with vowel diphthong /ou/*ou, ow*	**THEN** help them blend and read the words *cow, how, down, frown, out, loud, mound,* and *round*.

Small-Group Instruction, pp. S2–S3:

● **BELOW-LEVEL:** Reteach
● **ON-LEVEL:** Reinforce
● **ADVANCED:** Extend

BELOW-LEVEL   **ON-LEVEL**   **ADVANCED**

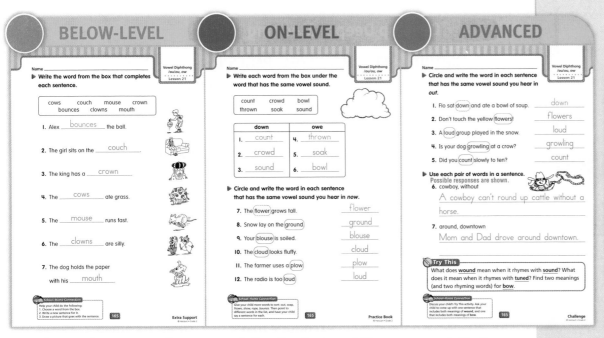

▲ **Extra Support, p. 165**   ▲ **Practice Book, p. 165**   ▲ **Challenge, p. 165**

E L L

- Group children according to academic levels, and assign one of the pages on the left.

- Clarify any unfamiliar concepts as necessary. See *ELL Teacher Guide* Lesson 21 for support in scaffolding instruction.

Build Robust Vocabulary

Words from the Selection

Objectives

- *To build robust vocabulary*
- *To build and expand word meanings*

 INTRODUCE ✓ Tested

Vocabulary: Lesson 21

bargain	**boost**
spoiled	**exchanged**
comfortable	**delivered**

Student-Friendly Explanations

bargain	If you didn't have to pay much to buy something good, you got a bargain.
spoiled	If you spoiled something, you damaged or ruined it.
comfortable	When you are comfortable, you feel good just as you are.
boost	If you give someone a boost, you lift him or her up to reach something.
exchanged	When you exchanged things, you gave something to someone and you got something else in return.
delivered	If you deliver something, you take it from one place and bring it to another.

Grade 2, Lesson 21   **R112**   Vocabulary

Transparency R112

Word Detective

Make Lists Tell children to look and listen for Vocabulary Words in places outside of their classroom.

HOMEWORK/INDEPENDENT PRACTICE

Teach/Model

Routine Card 4

INTRODUCE ROBUST VOCABULARY Introduce the words, using the following steps.

❶ Display Transparency R112 and read the word and the **Student-Friendly Explanation.**

❷ Have children **say the word** with you.

❸ Have children **interact with the word's meaning** by asking them the appropriate question below.

- Would you be getting a **bargain** if you paid $5 for a candy bar that usually costs 50 cents? Explain.
- Is a torn shirt **spoiled**? Explain.
- Would you be **comfortable** sitting on a soft chair? Explain.
- Would you need a **boost** to touch the ceiling? Explain.
- Have you **exchanged** money for something else? Explain.
- What kinds of things might be **delivered** to our school?

Develop Deeper Meaning

EXPAND WORDS' MEANINGS: PAGES 164–165 Have children read the passage. Then read the passage aloud, pausing at the end of page 164 to ask children questions 1–3. Read page 165, and then discuss children's answers to questions 4–6.

1. Was the **bargain** advertised in the shop window a good one? Explain.
2. What was **delivered** just in time for the sale?
3. What did Taylor think **spoiled** the shoes?
4. Why do you think Mom had to **boost** Taylor up?
5. How would **comfortable** shoes feel on your feet? Would they feel tight or could you wiggle your toes in them?
6. What did Mom **exchange** to get new shoes for Taylor?

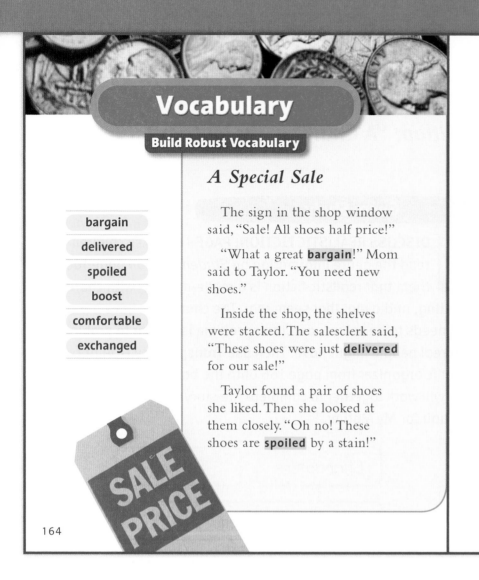

Vocabulary

Build Robust Vocabulary

bargain

delivered

spoiled

boost

comfortable

exchanged

A Special Sale

The sign in the shop window said, "Sale! All shoes half price!"

"What a great **bargain**!" Mom said to Taylor. "You need new shoes."

Inside the shop, the shelves were stacked. The salesclerk said, "These shoes were just **delivered** for our sale!"

Taylor found a pair of shoes she liked. Then she looked at them closely. "Oh no! These shoes are **spoiled** by a stain!"

164

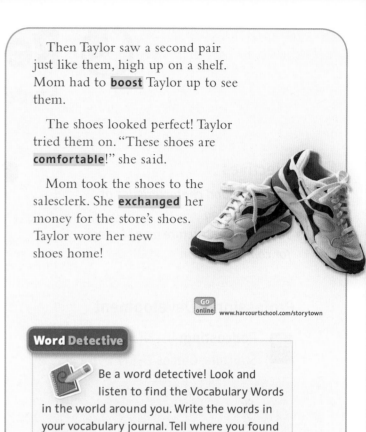

Then Taylor saw a second pair just like them, high up on a shelf. Mom had to **boost** Taylor up to see them.

The shoes looked perfect! Taylor tried them on. "These shoes are **comfortable**!" she said.

Mom took the shoes to the salesclerk. She **exchanged** her money for the store's shoes. Taylor wore her new shoes home!

www.harcourtschool.com/storytown

Word Detective

Be a word detective! Look and listen to find the Vocabulary Words in the world around you. Write the words in your vocabulary journal. Tell where you found them.

165

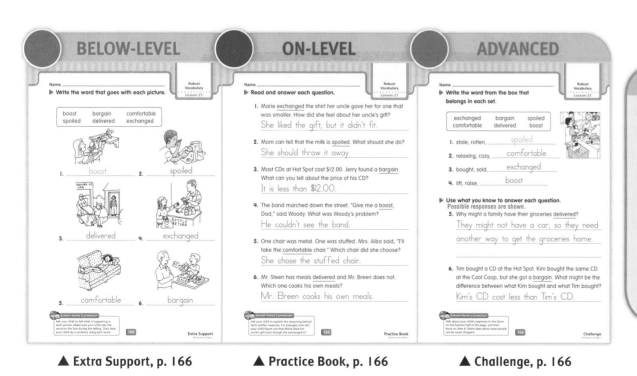

▲ Extra Support, p. 166   ▲ Practice Book, p. 166   ▲ Challenge, p. 166

E L L

• Group children according to academic levels, and assign one of the pages on the left.

• Clarify any unfamiliar concepts as necessary. See *ELL Teacher Guide* Lesson 21 for support in scaffolding instruction.

 Reading

Student Edition: **"A Chair for My Mother"**

Objectives

- *To understand characteristics of realistic fiction*
- *To use story structure as a strategy for comprehension*

Professional Development

 Podcasting: Use Story Structure, Grades 2–6

Options for Reading

● BELOW-LEVEL

Preview Have children preview the story by looking at the illustrations. Guide them to predict what the problem in the story is. Read each page of the story to children, and have them read it after you.

● ON-LEVEL

Monitor Comprehension Have children read the story aloud, page by page. Ask the Monitor Comprehension questions as you go.

● ADVANCED

Independent Reading Have children read each page silently, looking up when they finish a page. Ask the Monitor Comprehension questions as you go.

Genre Study

 DISCUSS REALISTIC FICTION: PAGE 166 Ask children to read the genre information on *Student Edition* page 166. Tell them that realistic fiction is a made-up story with characters, a setting, and a plot that seem real. The characters have a problem that needs to be solved, and their problem is similar to problems that real people might have. Then use **Transparency GO4** or copy the graphic organizer from page 166 onto the board. Tell children that they will work together to complete the story map as they read "A Chair for My Mother."

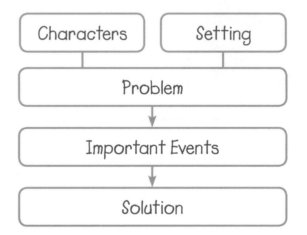

Comprehension Strategies

 USE STORY STRUCTURE: PAGE 166 Tell children that good readers use strategies to help them understand and remember what they read. Have children read the Comprehension Strategy information on page 166. Readers can use the story structure to help them understand fiction stories. They can think about the characters, setting, problem, important events, and solution. As they read, they can complete a story map to help them keep track of these story elements. Remind children that they will work together to use a story map as they read "A Chair for My Mother."

Vera B. Williams
A CHAIR FOR MY MOTHER

Realistic Fiction

Genre Study
Realistic fiction is a story that could really happen. Look for

• a plot that could be real.
• a problem that needs to be solved.

Characters	Setting

Problem
↓
Important Events
↓
Solution

Comprehension Strategy
 Use story structure to help you think about the important events in the plot.

166

A CHAIR FOR MY MOTHER

by
Vera B. Williams

167

Build Background

DISCUSS SAVING MONEY Tell children that they are going to read a story about a family that is saving money to buy something special. Ask children whether they know someone who has saved money to buy something. Invite them to share what they know.

Routine Card 6 **SET A PURPOSE AND PREDICT** Tell children that this is a story they will read to enjoy and to satisfy their curiosity about what the family is saving up to buy.

• Have children read the title and author's name.

• Identify the girl and her mother in the family and the diner. Ask children why they think the girl and her mother are at a diner.

• List predictions on the board.

• Have children read the story to find out what the family is saving up to buy.

TECHNOLOGY

 GO online **eBook** "A Chair for My Mother" is available in an eBook.

 Audiotext "A Chair for My Mother" is available on *Audiotext Grade 2*, CD 5 for subsequent readings.

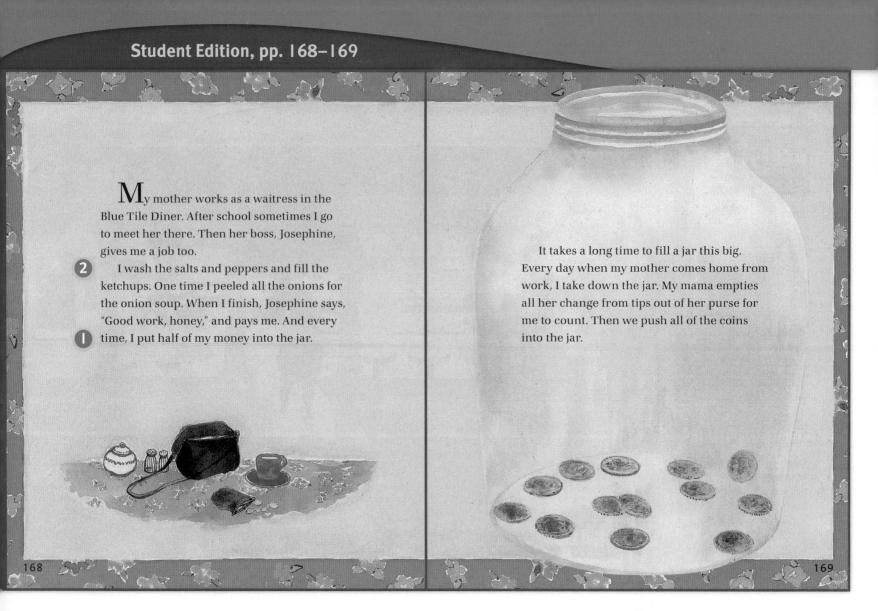

My mother works as a waitress in the Blue Tile Diner. After school sometimes I go to meet her there. Then her boss, Josephine, gives me a job too.

2   I wash the salts and peppers and fill the ketchups. One time I peeled all the onions for the onion soup. When I finish, Josephine says, "Good work, honey," and pays me. And every **1** time, I put half of my money into the jar.

It takes a long time to fill a jar this big. Every day when my mother comes home from work, I take down the jar. My mama empties all her change from tips out of her purse for me to count. Then we push all of the coins into the jar.

168   169

Monitor Comprehension

PAGES 168–169   Say: **I wonder why there are coins at the bottom of the big jar on page 169. Read to find out.**

1 **SPECULATE**   **Why do you think the girl and her mother are saving coins in the big jar?** (Possible response: They are saving up to spend the money on something special.)

2 **NOTE DETAILS**   **What does the narrator—the person who is telling the story—do at the diner?** (She washes the salt and pepper shakers and fills the ketchup bottles. Once she peeled onions.)

SOCIAL STUDIES

SUPPORTING STANDARDS

Producers and Consumers   Explain that a *producer* is a person who makes goods or provides services. A waitress is a producer because she provides a service: serving meals to customers. A customer is a *consumer*, a person who buys and uses goods, such as food and services. Explain that producers and consumers rely on each other. Consumers depend on producers for goods and services, and producers depend on consumers for money, just as the waitress in the story depends on customers for tips. Have children name other examples of producers, consumers, goods, and services.

Sometimes my mama is laughing when she comes home from work. Sometimes she's so tired she falls asleep while I count the money out into piles. Some days she has lots of tips. Some days she has only a little. Then she looks worried. But each evening every single shiny coin goes into the jar.

We sit in the kitchen to count the tips. Usually Grandma sits with us too. While we count, she likes to hum. Often she has money in her old leather wallet for us. Whenever she gets a good bargain on tomatoes or bananas or something she buys, she puts by the savings and they go into the jar.

170

171

Monitor Comprehension

PAGES 170–171 Say: **I wonder who the women in the illustration are. Read to find out.**

1 **CHARACTERS** **Who are the women in the illustration on page 170? How do you know?** (The sleeping woman is Mama; the woman with the wallet is Grandma. I know because it says that the girl's mama falls asleep and Grandma sits with them.)

2 **MAKE INFERENCES** **Who is telling the story? How do you know?** (The girl in the illustration is telling the story. The text says *I count the money,* and in the picture the girl is counting the money.)

3 **PLOT** **What has happened so far in the story?** (Possible response: The girl, her mama, and her grandma are saving money in a big jar.)

Apply
Comprehension Strategies

Use Story Structure
Demonstrate how to complete the story map to keep track of story structure. Use **Transparency GO4** to guide children.

Think Aloud I can use the story map to keep track of what is happening in the story. I will add *Josephine, Mama, Grandma,* and *girl* to the Characters box. I will also add an event, such as Mama, Grandma, and the girl filling a big jar with coins, to the box labeled Important Events.

Lesson 21 (*Student Edition*, pages 170–171) **T49**

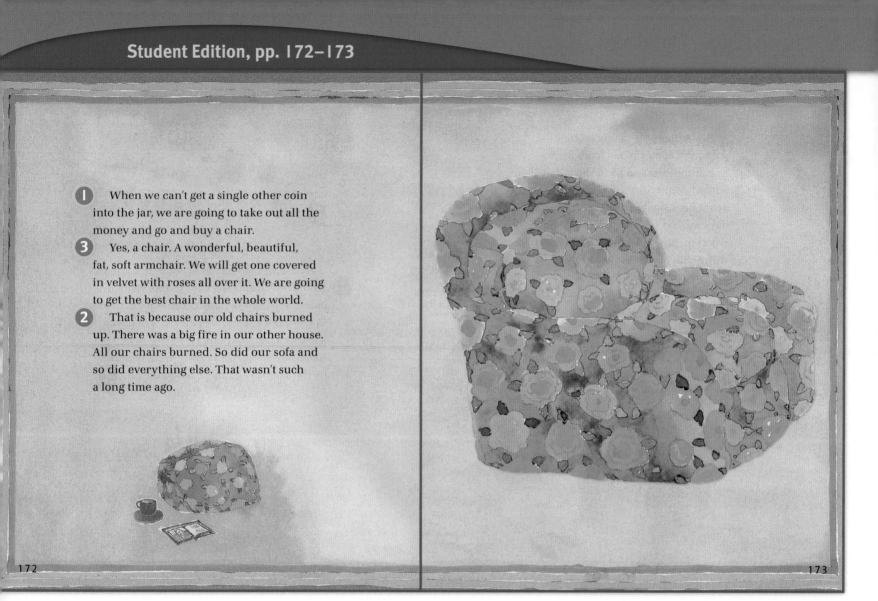

①   When we can't get a single other coin into the jar, we are going to take out all the money and go and buy a chair.

③   Yes, a chair. A wonderful, beautiful, fat, soft armchair. We will get one covered in velvet with roses all over it. We are going to get the best chair in the whole world.

②   That is because our old chairs burned up. There was a big fire in our other house. All our chairs burned. So did our sofa and so did everything else. That wasn't such a long time ago.

172

173

Monitor Comprehension

PAGES 172–173   Say: **I see a big picture of a chair. I wonder if the narrator will tell us why this chair is important. Read to find out.**

① **NOTE DETAILS**   **What are the characters going to do when the jar is full of coins?** (They are going to take out all the money and go to buy an armchair.)

② **CAUSE AND EFFECT**   **Why are they going to buy an armchair?** (All their old chairs burned up in a big fire in their other house.)

③ **EXPRESS PERSONAL OPINIONS**   **Would you like an armchair such as the one the author describes? Why or why not?** (Possible response: Yes, because it sounds comfortable.)

Apply
Comprehension Strategies

Use Story Structure

(Focus Strategy)

Demonstrate how to update the story map by adding another important event and the problem.

Think Aloud   We've learned the problem in the story: the family has no armchairs because of a fire. We will add these details to our story map.

My mother and I were coming home from buying new shoes. I had new sandals. She had new pumps. We were walking to our house from the bus. We were looking at everyone's tulips. She was saying she liked red tulips and I was saying I liked yellow ones. Then we came to our block.

174

175

Monitor Comprehension

PAGES 174–175   Say: **The girl and her mother look happy in the picture on page 174. Read to find out why they are happy.**

1 **DRAW CONCLUSIONS**   **Why do you think the girl and her mother are happy?** (Possible responses: They've just bought new shoes. They're enjoying looking at the tulips.)

2 **SETTING**   **Where does the story take place? How can you tell?** (Possible response: In a city, because there are apartment buildings in the illustrations.)

3 **MAKE INFERENCES**   **What time of year do you think it is? How do you know?** (Possible response: It is spring because there are tulips blooming. Also, the girl just bought new sandals, and she is wearing them.)

BELOW-LEVEL

Multiple-Meaning Words   Say: The word *pumps* has many meanings. What does *pumps* mean in the third sentence on page 175? (a kind of woman's shoe with a heel) Ask children what they could do if they didn't know what *pumps* meant. As needed, explain that children could use context and the illustrations to figure out that pumps are a kind of shoe. Guide children to name a dictionary as another place to look and guide them in looking up *pump* in the dictionary and choosing the correct definition.

Right outside our house stood two big fire engines. I could see lots of smoke. Tall orange flames came out of the roof. All the neighbors stood in a bunch across the street. Mama grabbed ② my hand and we ran. My Uncle Sandy saw us and ran to us. Mama yelled, "Where's Mother?" I yelled, "Where's my grandma?" My Aunt Ida waved and shouted, "She's here, she's here. She's O.K. Don't worry." ①

176

Grandma was all right. Our cat was safe too, though it took a while to find her. But everything else in our whole house ③ was spoiled.

177

Monitor Comprehension

PAGES 176–177   Say: **I see that there's a fire and that the girl and her mother look scared. Read to find out what is burning.**

① **NOTE DETAILS**   **What was burning?** (the girl's house)

② **CHARACTERS' EMOTIONS**   **How did Mama and the girl feel when they saw the fire? How can you tell?** (Possible response: They were upset and worried about Grandma. Mama grabbed the girl's hand, and they ran toward their house, yelling for Grandma.)

③ **MAKE INFERENCES**   **How do you think the characters felt when they saw that their house was spoiled? Why do you think so?**
(Possible response: Sad; I would feel sad if my house was spoiled.)

Use Multiple Strategies

Monitor Comprehension: Reread
Say: Sometimes rereading helps me understand text that is confusing. When I read page 177, I was confused. I thought the girl's house had already burned down a while ago. I decided to reread the first part of the story, paying more attention to time and sequence. Now I understand that at the beginning of the story, the girl is talking about things that are happening now. Most of the verbs are in the present tense. Then, on page 175, she talks about what happened in the past, on the day of the fire.

What was left of the house was turned to charcoal and ashes.

We went to stay with my mother's sister **1** Aunt Ida and Uncle Sandy. Then we were able to move into the apartment downstairs. We painted the walls yellow. The floors were all **2** shiny. But the rooms were very empty.

178   179

Monitor Comprehension

PAGES 178–179   Say: **The house is spoiled. Read to find out where the characters will live.**

1 **PLOT**   **Where do the characters go to live?** (First they stay with Aunt Ida and Uncle Sandy. Then they move into the apartment downstairs from Aunt Ida and Uncle Sandy.)

2 **MAKE PREDICTIONS**   **How do you think the characters will fill the empty rooms of the new apartment?** (Possible response: They will buy some furniture, and friends will give them some furniture.)

180

1   The first day we moved in, the neighbors brought pizza and cake and ice cream. And they brought a lot of other things too.

2   The family across the street brought a table and three kitchen chairs. The very old man next door gave us a bed from when his children were little.

My other grandpa brought us his beautiful rug. My mother's other sister, Sally, had made us red and white curtains. Mama's boss, Josephine, brought pots and pans, silverware and dishes. My cousin brought me her own stuffed bear.

Everyone clapped when my grandma made

3   a speech. "You are all the kindest people," she said, "and we thank you very, very much. It's lucky we're young and can start all over."

181

Monitor Comprehension

PAGES 180–181   Say: **A lot of people are bringing furniture, toys, and other things to one of the houses. Read to find out who they are.**

1   **NOTE DETAILS**   **Who brought pizza, cake, ice cream, and other things to the girl and her family?** (the neighbors)

2   **CONFIRM PREDICTIONS**   **Were your predictions correct about how the family filled the empty rooms of the apartment?** (Responses will vary.)

3   **SPECULATE**   **Why do you think neighbors and family members brought food, furniture, toys, and other things to the girl, Mama, and Grandma?** (Possible response: They knew the girl, Mama, and Grandma had lost all their belongings in the fire and wanted to help them.)

ELL

Word Meanings   Use the illustration to clarify the meanings of *pizza, cake, table, kitchen chair,* and *stuffed bear.* Read aloud the sentences in which the words appear, and point to the corresponding illustration. Then ask children questions such as *Where is the table?* Have children point to the correct detail in the illustration to answer the question. Encourage children to repeat the words after you.

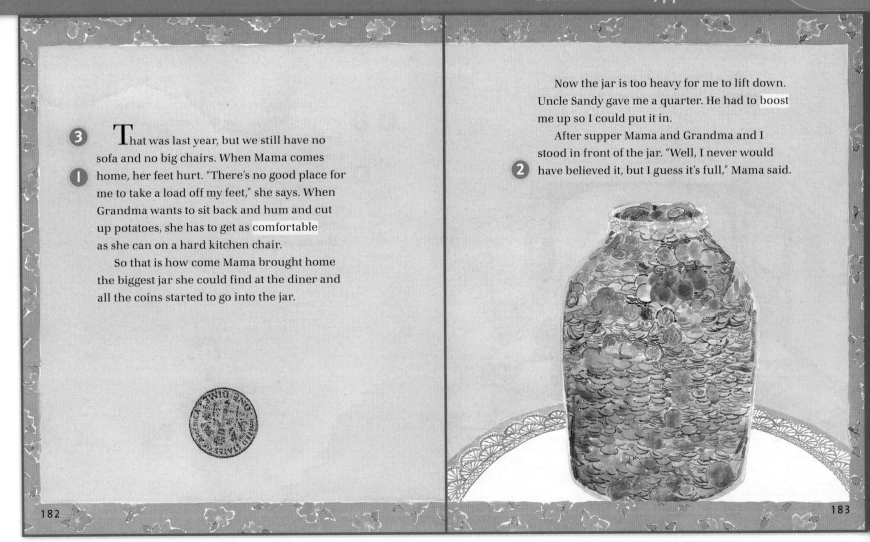

182

3 **1** That was last year, but we still have no sofa and no big chairs. When Mama comes home, her feet hurt. "There's no good place for me to take a load off my feet," she says. When Grandma wants to sit back and hum and cut up potatoes, she has to get as comfortable as she can on a hard kitchen chair.

So that is how come Mama brought home the biggest jar she could find at the diner and all the coins started to go into the jar.

Now the jar is too heavy for me to lift down. Uncle Sandy gave me a quarter. He had to me up so I could put it in.

After supper Mama and Grandma and I stood in front of the jar. **2** "Well, I never would have believed it, but I guess it's full," Mama said.

183

Monitor Comprehension

PAGES 182–183 Say: **It looks as if the jar is almost full. Read to find out what the family will do with it.**

1 CAUSE AND EFFECT **Why did Mama bring the big jar home?** (Possible response: Mama brought the jar home so they would start saving for a comfortable chair.)

2 MAKE PREDICTIONS **What do you think will happen now that the jar is almost full?** (Possible response: The family will use the money from the jar to pay for a comfortable armchair.)

3 DRAW CONCLUSIONS **When does this part of the story take place? How do you know?** (Possible response: It takes place in the present, or now. I know because the girl says the fire was last year and now they still have no sofa or big chairs.)

ELL

Clarify Meaning Explain that *"There's no good place for me to take a load off my feet"* means "There's no good place for me to sit down."

My mother brought home little paper wrappers for the nickels and the dimes and the quarters. I counted them all out and wrapped them all up.

On my mother's day off, we took all the coins to the bank. The bank exchanged them for ten-dollar bills. Then we took the bus downtown to shop for our chair.

We shopped through four furniture stores. We tried out big chairs and smaller ones, high chairs and low chairs, soft chairs and harder ones. Grandma said she felt like Goldilocks in "The Three Bears" trying out all the chairs.

184

185

Monitor Comprehension

PAGES 184–185   Say: **It looks as if Mama and the girl are at the bank. Read to find out what they are doing there.**

1 NOTE DETAILS   **Why did the family go to the bank?** (to exchange the coins for ten-dollar bills)

2 USE PRIOR KNOWLEDGE   **Why might someone want ten-dollar bills instead of the coins?** (Possible response: Paper bills are lighter and easier to carry than rolls of coins.)

3 MAKE PREDICTIONS   **Do you think the girl, her mother, and her grandma will find a chair that they want to buy? Explain.** (Possible response: No. They've already shopped through four furniture stores and they haven't found a chair just like the one the girl described earlier.)

BELOW-LEVEL

Read Aloud and Role-Play   Read aloud page 185. Then have children take turns reading it aloud. Provide feedback and guidance as children read. Then invite groups of three children to role-play the events on page 185. Remind children to make sure to keep events in order.

1 Finally we found the chair we were all dreaming of. And the money in the jar was enough to pay for it. We called Aunt Ida and Uncle Sandy. They came right down in their pickup truck to drive the chair home for us. They knew we couldn't wait for it to be delivered.

2 I tried out our chair in the back of the truck. Mama wouldn't let me sit there while we drove. But they let me sit in it while they carried it up to the door.

186   187

Monitor Comprehension

PAGES 186–187   Say: **I see that the girl is sitting on a chair in the back of a pickup truck. Read to find out why the chair is in the truck.**

1 **PLOT   What problem has the family solved?** (The family finally found and bought the chair each member had been dreaming of.)

2 **MAKE INFERENCES   How do you think the girl feels? How can you tell?** (Possible response: Happy because her family finally found the chair each person had been dreaming of. She's probably excited, too, because she sits in the chair in the back of the truck, and then she gets to sit in it while the grown-ups carry it up to the door.)

Apply
Comprehension Strategies

Use Story Structure
Demonstrate how to add the solution to the story map. Then have children use the story map to identify the problem and solution in the story.

Think Aloud   At last the family buys the armchair each person has been dreaming of. We'll add that information to the Solution box of our story map.

2 We set the chair right beside the window with the red and white curtains. Grandma and Mama and I all sat in it while Aunt Ida took our picture.

1 Now Grandma sits in it and talks with people going by in the daytime. Mama sits down and watches the news on TV when she comes home from her job. After supper, I sit with her and she can reach right up and turn out the light if I fall asleep in her lap.

188

189

Monitor Comprehension

PAGES 188–189 Say: **It looks as if everyone in the family is already using the new armchair. Read to find out how the family uses it.**

1 **NOTE DETAILS   How does the family use the armchair?** (Grandma sits in it and talks with people going by in the daytime. Mama sits in it to watch the news after work. The girl sits on Mama's lap after supper and sometimes falls asleep in her lap.)

2 **MAKE INFERENCES   Why do you think Aunt Ida takes a picture of the family sitting in the armchair?** (Possible response: Buying the armchair is a big, happy occasion, and they want a photo to remember the occasion.)

ANALYZE AUTHOR'S PURPOSE

Author's Purpose Remind children that authors have a purpose, or reason, for writing. After children have finished reading "A Chair for My Mother," ask:

Why did the author write "A Chair for My Mother"?

• to persuade readers that they should save money in a jar rather than in a bank

• to entertain readers with a story about a family that could be real

• to inform readers that there are many kinds of comfortable chairs

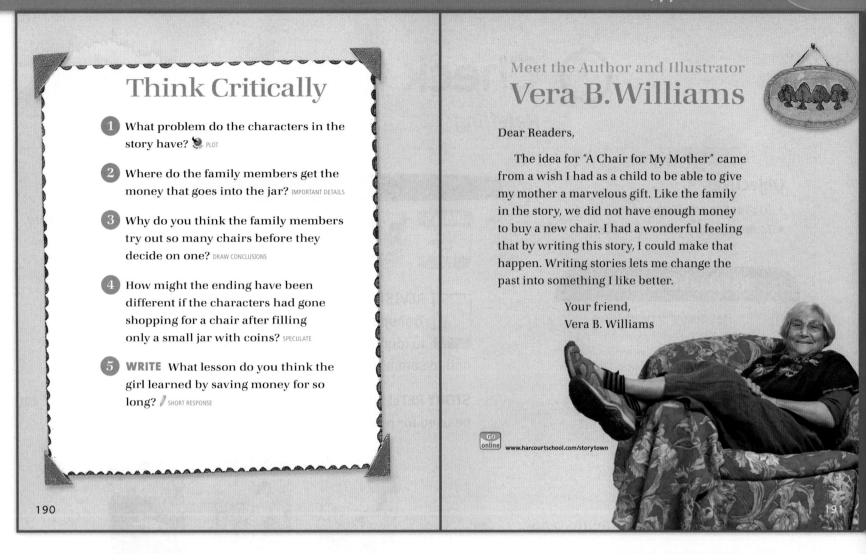

Think Critically

1 What problem do the characters in the story have? PLOT

2 Where do the family members get the money that goes into the jar? IMPORTANT DETAILS

3 Why do you think the family members try out so many chairs before they decide on one? DRAW CONCLUSIONS

4 How might the ending have been different if the characters had gone shopping for a chair after filling only a small jar with coins? SPECULATE

5 **WRITE** What lesson do you think the girl learned by saving money for so long? SHORT RESPONSE

190

Meet the Author and Illustrator
Vera B. Williams

Dear Readers,

The idea for "A Chair for My Mother" came from a wish I had as a child to be able to give my mother a marvelous gift. Like the family in the story, we did not have enough money to buy a new chair. I had a wonderful feeling that by writing this story, I could make that happen. Writing stories lets me change the past into something I like better.

Your friend,
Vera B. Williams

Go online www.harcourtschool.com/storytown

191

Think Critically

Respond to the Literature

1 They have to fill a jar with coins to save money to buy an armchair, because their old chairs burned in a fire. **PLOT**

2 Mama's tips go into the jar. The girl adds money she makes. Grandma adds what she saves from shopping. **IMPORTANT DETAILS**

3 Possible response: They want to find one that is just right. **DRAW CONCLUSIONS**

4 Possible response: There might not have been enough money for the chair. **SPECULATE**

5 **WRITE** Possible response: If you save your money, you can eventually buy what you want. **SHORT RESPONSE**

Meet the Author/ Illustrator

PAGE 191 Tell children that Vera B. Williams is the author and illustrator of "A Chair for My Mother." Ask children to read her letter on page 191. Then discuss how writing stories can let a person change the past into something he or she likes better.

Check Comprehension
Retelling

Objectives
- *To practice retelling a story*
- *To read a story with expression*

RETELLING RUBRIC

4	Uses details to clearly retell the story
3	Uses some details to retell the story
2	Retells the story with some inaccuracies
1	Is unable to retell the story

Professional Development

 Podcasting: Auditory Modeling

Retell

  PLOT Ask children to tell the problem in the story. (A family is saving money to buy a chair to replace the ones that burned.)

REVISIT THE GRAPHIC ORGANIZER Display completed **Transparency GO4.** Guide children to use the story map to identify the main characters and the setting in the story, and to summarize the problem, important events, and solution.

STORY RETELLING CARDS The cards for "A Chair for My Mother" can be used for retelling or as an aid to completing the chart.

▲ Story Retelling Cards 1–6, "A Chair for My Mother"

 # Fluency
Expression

Teach/Model

 USING EXPRESSION Explain that good readers use their voice to show the story's mood and the characters' feelings. Have children turn to *Student Edition* pages 175–177 and track the print as you read with expression.

Practice/Apply

Routine Card 8 **ECHO-READ** Read aloud the rest of the story, one page at a time, modeling expression. Have children echo-read each page after you.

Build Robust Vocabulary
Words About the Selection

Teach/Model

 Routine Card 3

INTRODUCE THE WORDS Use *Routine Card 3* to introduce the words.

❶ Put the word in **selection context**.
❷ Display Transparency R111 and read the word and the **Student-Friendly Explanation.**
❸ Have children **say the word** with you.
❹ Use the word in other contexts, and have children **interact with the word's meaning**.
❺ Remove the transparency. Say the Student-Friendly Explanation again, and ask children to **name the word** that goes with it.

❶ **Selection Context:** Grandma was **thrifty** so she always looked for a good bargain on the things she bought.
❹ **Interact with Word Meaning:** Are you thrifty if you don't care about the price or if you look for sales? Explain.

❶ **Selection Context:** The girl was **industrious** because she worked hard at the diner after school.
❹ **Interact with Word Meaning:** Industrious workers make sure to get their work done. Would you be an industrious worker if you worked hard or if you were lazy? Explain.

Practice/Apply

GUIDED PRACTICE Ask children to do the following:
• Think of someone you know who is *thrifty*. Tell how you know the person is thrifty.
• Think of someone you know who is *industrious*. Tell how you know the person is industrious.

Objective
• *To develop robust vocabulary*

 **Tested**

INTRODUCE ✓
Vocabulary: Lesson 21
thrifty   **industrious**

"Research Says"

Vocabulary "Teachers teaching word meanings should introduce the new word in an appropriate contextual setting. An attempt should be made to insure that this contextual setting is familiar."
—Gipe & Arnold (1979)

▼ **Student-Friendly Explanations**

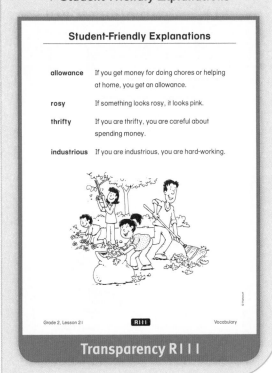

Student-Friendly Explanations

allowance	If you get money for doing chores or helping at home, you get an allowance.
rosy	If something looks rosy, it looks pink.
thrifty	If you are thrifty, you are careful about spending money.
industrious	If you are industrious, you are hard-working.

Grade 2, Lesson 21   R111   Vocabulary

Transparency R111

Grammar *Quick Write*

Present-Tense Action Verbs

5-DAY GRAMMAR

DAY 1	Introduce Present-Tense Action Verbs
DAY 2	Present-Tense Endings: *-s, -es*
DAY 3	Combining Sentences with the Same Verb
DAY 4	Apply to Writing
DAY 5	Weekly Review

Objectives

- *To identify and read present-tense action verbs*
- *To use the present-tense verb endings -s and -es correctly*

Daily Proofreading

Dad asked Jane, "Will you help I bake cookies."

(me; cookies?)

Writing Trait

Strengthening Conventions

Verbs Use this short lesson with children's own writing to build a foundation for revising/editing longer connected text on Day 5. See also *Writer's Companion*, Lesson 21.

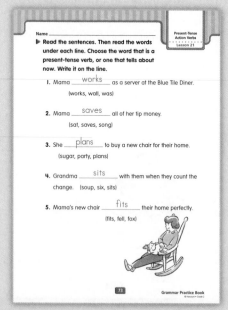

Name _____

► Read the sentences. Then read the words under each line. Choose the word that is a present-tense verb, or one that tells about now. Write it on the line.

Present-Tense Action Verbs
Lesson 21

1. Mama ___works___ as a server at the Blue Tile Diner.
   (works, wall, was)

2. Mama ___saves___ all of her tip money.
   (sat, saves, song)

3. She ___plans___ to buy a new chair for their home.
   (sugar, party, plans)

4. Grandma ___sits___ with them when they count the change. (soup, six, sits)

5. Mama's new chair ___fits___ their home perfectly.
   (fits, fell, fox)

73

Grammar Practice Book

▲ **Grammar Practice Book, p. 73**

Review

IDENTIFY PRESENT-TENSE ACTION VERBS Write these sentences on the board:

> I see Ryan. He stands on his tiptoes.
>
> Ryan reaches up to the jar.
>
> Mom and I both watch him.

Read aloud the sentences. Tell children that each sentence contains a present-tense action verb. Reread the first sentence and identify the present-tense verb. (*see*) Work together to identify the verbs in the other sentences. (*stands, reaches, watch*) Share these rules:

- Add the ending *-s* to most present-tense action verbs when the naming part of the sentence tells about one.

- Add the ending *-es* when a present-tense action verb ends in *s, x, sh, ch,* or *tch* and the naming part tells about one.

- Do not add an *-s* or *-es* to a verb when the naming part tells about *I, you,* or more than one.

Practice/Apply

GUIDED PRACTICE Write the following incomplete sentences on the board. Model how to complete the first sentence with the correct present-tense action verb. Elicit responses from children to complete the remaining sentences.

> You _____ the wagon. (push, pushes) (push)
>
> One wheel _____ off. (fall, falls) (falls)
>
> Dad _____ the wheel. (fix, fixes) (fixes)

INDEPENDENT PRACTICE Have children write three sentences using present-tense action verbs. Have partners check for correct usage.

Writing
Personal Narrative

5-DAY WRITING	
DAY 1	Introduce
DAY 2	Prewrite
DAY 3	Draft
DAY 4	Revise
DAY 5	Revise

Prewrite

GENERATE IDEAS Have children look again at the sentences they wrote on Day 1 (page T39) about a personal experience. Ask them to think of other details that tell more about the setting, people, objects, and events.

SENTENCE FLUENCY As children write additional sentences to tell more about their experiences, ask them to vary the subject of their sentences to avoid having each sentence start with *I*. Remind them that varying the subject will make their writing more interesting to read.

MODEL PREWRITING Copy the graphic organizer below. Model writing sentences based on the information in the chart.

My Feelings
excited, nervous

Who Went
my friends Jan and Pat and I

MY FIRST TIME CAMPING

What Happened
crunching sound woke me up, an animal howled and scared me

What We Did
set up camp at the campsite, cooked dinner over a campfire

Practice/Apply

GUIDED PRACTICE Tell children to brainstorm details and sentences for their personal narrative. Have volunteers share their ideas and add them to a graphic organizer.

INDEPENDENT PRACTICE Have children use their sentence from Day 1 and the graphic organizer to brainstorm more ideas for their personal narrative. Have them save these items to use on Days 3–5.

Objectives

- *To develop ideas and topics for writing*
- *To use a graphic organizer for prewriting*
- *To vary sentence structure*

Writing Prompt

Independent Writing Have children record what makes a personal narrative different from a story.

Demonstrate Meaning If children have difficulty understanding the information in the chart, use gestures and role-play to help them comprehend each section.

Day at a Glance
Day **3**

phonics and Spelling
- Review: Vowel Diphthong /ou/*ou*, *ow*
- State the Generalization

Fluency
- Expression
- "A Chair for My Mother," *Student Edition*, pp. 166–191

Comprehension

Review: Plot

- Introduce: Compare and Contrast

Reading
- "Saving Money," *Student Edition*, pp. 192–195

Robust Vocabulary
- Review: *allowance, rosy, bargain, spoiled, comfortable, boost, exchanged, delivered, thrifty, industrious*

Grammar [Quick Write]
- Review: Present-Tense Action Verbs

Writing
- Personal Narrative

Warm-Up Routines

Oral Language

Objective *To listen attentively and respond appropriately to oral communication*

> ## Question of the Day
>
> **What are some ways people show their feelings?**

Use the following prompts to help children brainstorm ways that people show their feelings, and list children's responses on the board under the columns "Good Feelings" or "Bad Feelings" as appropriate.

- **What are some ways people show they are happy?**
- **What are some ways people show they are sad?**
- **What are some ways people show they are nervous?**
- **What are some ways people show they are excited?**
- **What are some ways people show they are lonely?**

Read Aloud

Objective *To identify rhymes in poetry*

BIG BOOK OF RHYMES AND POEMS Display "Grown-Ups" on page 37, and ask children to tell what they remember about the poem. Read aloud the poem, emphasizing the rhyming words (*lonely, be, me* in lines 1, 3, and 4; *sad, glad* in lines 2 and 5). Ask a volunteer to point to and read the words that rhyme. Then reread the poem, encouraging children to join in.

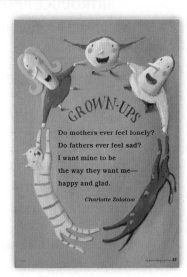

▲ Big Book of Rhymes and Poems, p. 37

Word Wall

Objective *To read high-frequency words*

REVIEW HIGH-FREQUENCY WORDS Review the following words from the Word Wall: *everything, young, finally, cheer, believe,* and *enough.* Have children begin clapping to keep time. Point to each word and have children spell and read the word to the beat of the claps. Repeat several times.

everything	young	finally
cheer	believe	enough

Vowel Diphthong /ou/ ou, ow  and Spelling

5-DAY PHONICS	
DAY 1	Introduce /ou/*ou, ow*
DAY 2	Word Building with /ou/*ou, ow*
DAY 3	Word Building with /ou/*ou, ow*
DAY 4	Abbreviations; Review /ou/*ou, ow*
DAY 5	Abbreviations; Review /ou/*ou, ow*

Objectives

- *To use common spelling patterns to build and read words*
- *To read and write common word families*
- *To recognize spelling patterns*

Skill Trace

 Tested **Vowel Diphthong /ou/*ou, ow***

Introduce	Grade 1
Reintroduce	T30–T33
Reteach	S2–S3
Review	T42–T43, T66–T67, T394–T395
Test	Theme 5
Maintain	Theme 6, T360

Vowel Diphthong /ou/*ou, ow*

Jess and Dad went to fish for trout.
Dad had a brown pouch filled with bait.
Jess asked, "Can we crouch by the lake to fish?"
Soon Jess gave a loud howl as her rod dipped down.
"Reel it in now!" shouted Dad.
"Wow! What a big trout!" said Jess proudly.

Grade 2, Lesson 21   **R108**   Phonics

Transparency R108

Work with Patterns

INTRODUCE PHONOGRAMS Write the following phonograms at the top of six columns.

-ouch	-oud	-out	-ow	-owl	-own

Tell children that these are the endings of some words. Slide your hand under the letters as you read each phonogram. Repeat, having children read the phonograms with you.

BUILD AND READ WORDS Write the letter *c* in front of the phonograms -ouch and -ow. Guide children to read each word: /c/ -ouch, *couch*; /c/ -ow, *cow*. Have children identify the letters that stand for the /ou/ sound. (*ou, ow*) Adapt the process, writing *cl* in front of -oud and -own to make *cloud* and *clown*, and *sc* in front of -out and -owl to make *scout* and *scowl*.

Then have children name other words that end with -ouch, -oud, -out, -ow, -owl, and -own. Have them tell which letter or letters to add to build each word, and write it on the board in the appropriate column. Have children read each column of words. Then point to words at random and have children read them.

Read Words in Context

READ SENTENCES Display **Transparency R108** or write the sentences on the board or on chart paper. Have children choral-read the sentences as you track the print. Then ask volunteers to read each sentence aloud and identify the words with the /ou/ sound. Invite volunteers to add words from the transparency to the appropriate columns of phonograms.

5-DAY SPELLING

DAY 1	Pretest
DAY 2	Word Building
DAY 3	**State the Generalization**
DAY 4	Review
DAY 5	Posttest

Review Spelling Words

STATE THE GENERALIZATION FOR /ou/*ou* AND /ou/*ow* List spelling words 1–10 on chart paper or on the board. Circle the words with /ou/ spelled *ou*, and have children read them. Ask: **What is the same in each word?** (Each word has the /ou/ sound and the letters *ou*.) Then, using a different color, circle the words with /ou/ spelled *ow*, and repeat the procedure.

WRITE Have children write the spelling words in their notebooks. Remind them to use their best handwriting and to use the chart to check their spelling.

Handwriting

LETTER SIZE Remind children to make sure their handwriting is neat and that their lowercase letters are all the same size, neither too large nor too small.

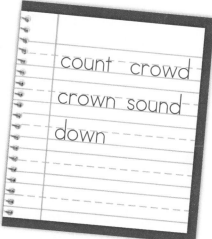

count crowd
crown sound
down

Spelling Words

1.	out*	6.	now*
2.	town	7.	found*
3.	count*	8.	crown
4.	crowd	9.	sound
5.	ground	10.	down*

Challenge Words

11.	surround	14.	powerful
12.	without	15.	cloudless
13.	cowboy		

* Words from "A Chair for My Mother" and "Saving Money"

Decodable Books

Additional Decoding Practice

- **Phonics**
  Vowel Diphthong /ou/*ou, ow*
- **Decodable Words**
- **High-Frequency Words**
  See the lists in *Decodable Book 17*.

  See also *Decodable Books*, online (Take-Home Version).

▲ Decodable Book 17
"Found in the Ground!"

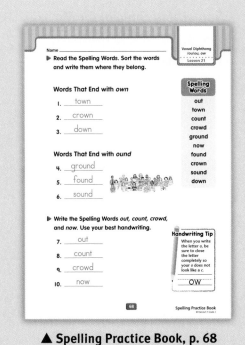

▲ Spelling Practice Book, p. 68

Fluency
Expression

Objectives

- *To build fluency through rereading*
- *To read fluently and with expression*

BELOW-LEVEL

Fluency Practice   Have children reread *Decodable Book 17*, Story 21 in the *Strategic Intervention Interactive Reader*, or the appropriate *Leveled Reader* (pp. T102–T105). Have them practice reading the text several times.

Additional Related Reading

- *Living in a Small Town* by Lisa Trumbauer. Capstone, 2005. **EASY**
- *Making Money* by Abby Jackson. Yellow Umbrella, 2004. **AVERAGE**
- *Something Special for Me* by Vera B. Williams. HarperTrophy, 1986. **CHALLENGE**

Review

▲ Student Edition, pp. 166–191

DIBELS Oral Reading Fluency **ORF**

MODEL READING WITH EXPRESSION   Remind children that good readers read with expression, or feeling. Tell children to

- think about the mood of the story and the characters' feelings as they read.

- use their voice to show the mood of the story and the characters' feelings.

Think Aloud   I'm going to reread part of "A Chair for My Mother" aloud. I'll use my voice to show the mood of the story and the characters' feelings. When I read a part of the story in which the characters feel sad, I'll make my voice sound sad. When I read a serious part of the story, I'll make my voice sound serious.

Practice/Apply

Routine Card 9

GUIDED PRACTICE   Read pages 178–181 aloud. Then have partners take turns reading aloud the same pages several times. Circulate among children, listening for children who are reading without expression. As needed, demonstrate reading a passage with expression, and have the child echo-read the same passage.

INDEPENDENT PRACTICE   Have partners choose a page to read aloud two or three times. Have the partner who is listening follow along in the *Student Edition* and alert the reader to adjust his or her voice when a particular emotion should be shown.

 # Plot
Comprehension

Review

REVIEW PLOT Ask children to tell what *plot* is. (Plot is what happens during the beginning, middle, and end of a story.) Review that the beginning of the story introduces the characters and tells about a problem they have. The middle tells how the characters deal with their problem, and the end tells how they solve it.

Practice/Apply

GUIDED PRACTICE Work with children to revisit "A Chair for My Mother" to recall the problem and how it is solved. Guide them to identify what happens at the beginning, in the middle, and at the end of the story. Ask:

- **What happens at the beginning of the story?** (A girl, her mother, and her grandma are saving coins so they can buy a chair.)

- **What happens in the middle of the story?** (First, the girl tells about the fire from a year before. Then, the family fills the jar and takes the coins to the bank. Then they shop for a chair.)

- **What happens at the end?** (They find and buy a chair)

- **What was the problem and the solution of the story?** (Problem: The family needed to save money to buy a chair. Solution: They saved enough money and bought a chair.)

INDEPENDENT PRACTICE Have children complete a story map (*Teacher Resource Book*, p. 97) for a previously read *Student Edition* story. Ask volunteers to use their completed story map to summarize the plot.

Objectives
- *To identify the plot of a story*
- *To identify the problem and solution in a story*

Skill Trace
 Plot

Introduce	T34–T35
Reteach	S6–S7
Review	T69, T85, T97, T136–T137, T171, T187, T197, T397, T414
Test	Theme 5
Maintain	Theme 6, T86

BELOW-LEVEL

Identify *Beginning, Middle, End* Explain that the beginning of "A Chair for My Mother" extends from *Student Edition* pages 166–173. The middle is on pages 174–185, and the end is on pages 186–189. Flip through the selection with children, identifying the sections of the selection that correspond to the three parts of the plot. Use the illustrations to discuss what happens in each part.

Compare and Contrast
Comprehension

Objective

- *To understand how to compare and contrast*

Skill Trace

 Tested **Compare and Contrast**

Introduce	T70–T71
Reteach	S12–S13
Review	T172–T173, T415, T425
Test	Theme 5

MONITOR PROGRESS

Compare and Contrast

IF children have difficulty comparing and contrasting,	**THEN** help them compare and contrast the girl and her mother from "A Chair for My Mother."

Small-Group Instruction, pp. S12–S13:

- ● **BELOW-LEVEL:** Reteach
- ● **ON-LEVEL:** Reinforce
- ● **ADVANCED:** Extend

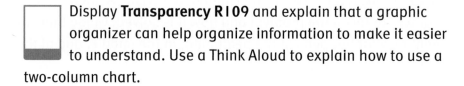 Teach/Model

INTRODUCE COMPARE AND CONTRAST Tell children that good readers know how to compare and contrast.

- Explain that when you *compare* two things, you tell how they are alike. When you *contrast* two things, you tell how they are different.

- Explain that knowing how to compare and contrast story elements can help children better understand what they read.

Display **Transparency R109** and explain that a graphic organizer can help organize information to make it easier to understand. Use a Think Aloud to explain how to use a two-column chart.

> **Think Aloud** **I can use a two-column chart to compare and contrast two things, such as two characters in a story, two characters from different stories, or even two stories. I write how the two things are different in one column and how they are the same in other column.**

Guided Practice

PRACTICE COMPARING Demonstrate how to complete a graphic organizer to compare and contrast Jill in "A Present for Mom" on *Student Edition* page 163 and the girl in "A Chair for My Mother" on *Student Edition* pages 166–191. Discuss the item listed in the first column. Have children continue to compare and contrast the two characters. Ask:

1. **What are some other ways Jill and the girl are alike?** (Both do work to get money. Both save money.)

2. **How are they different?** (Jill wants to buy flowers. The girl wants to buy a chair. The girl's house was in a fire. Jill has a lemonade stand.)

Practice/Apply

COMPARE AND CONTRAST ▶ Have children use a two-column chart either to compare and contrast two main characters from a previously read fiction story or to compare and contrast two different versions of the same story, such as Cinderella stories from different cultures. Have children use their completed charts to explain how the two characters or stories are the same and how they are different.

Compare and Contrast

How Jill and the girl are alike	How Jill and the girl are different
both are girls	

Grade 2, Lesson 21   R109   Comprehension

Transparency R109

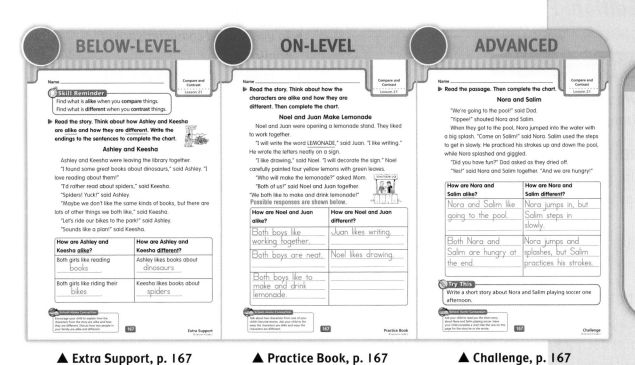

BELOW-LEVEL

Name _____

Compare and Contrast
Lesson 21

Skill Reminder
Find what is **alike** when you **compare** things.
Find what is **different** when you **contrast** things.

▶ Read the story. Think about how Ashley and Keesha are alike and how they are different. Write the endings to the sentences to complete the chart.

Ashley and Keesha

Ashley and Keesha were leaving the library together.
"I found some great books about dinosaurs," said Ashley. "I love reading about them!"
"I'd rather read about spiders," said Keesha.
"Spiders! Yuck!" said Ashley.
"Maybe we don't like the same kinds of books, but there are lots of other things we both like," said Keesha.
"Let's ride our bikes to the park!" said Ashley.
"Sounds like a plan!" said Keesha.

How are Ashley and Keesha **alike**?	How are Ashley and Keesha **different**?
Both girls like reading books	Ashley likes books about dinosaurs
Both girls like riding their bikes	Keesha likes books about spiders

School-Home Connection
Encourage your child to explain how the characters from the story are alike and how they are different. Discuss how two people in your family are alike and different.

167

Extra Support

▲ **Extra Support, p. 167**

ON-LEVEL

Name _____

Compare and Contrast
Lesson 21

▶ Read the story. Think about how the characters are alike and how they are different. Then complete the chart.

Noel and Juan Make Lemonade

Noel and Juan were opening a lemonade stand. They liked to work together.
"I will write the word LEMONADE," said Juan. "I like writing." He wrote the letters neatly on a sign.
"I like drawing," said Noel. "I will decorate the sign." Noel carefully painted four yellow lemons with green leaves.
"Who will make the lemonade?" asked Mom.
"Both of us!" said Noel and Juan together.
"We both like to make and drink lemonade!"
Possible responses are shown below.

How are Noel and Juan alike?	How are Noel and Juan different?
Both boys like working together.	Juan likes writing.
Both boys are neat.	Noel likes drawing.
Both boys like to make and drink lemonade.	

School-Home Connection
Talk about two characters from one of your child's favorite stories. Ask your child to list ways the characters are alike and ways the characters are different.

167

Practice Book

▲ **Practice Book, p. 167**

ADVANCED

Name _____

Compare and Contrast
Lesson 21

▶ Read the passage. Then complete the chart.

Nora and Salim

"We're going to the pool!" said Dad.
"Yippee!" shouted Nora and Salim.
When they got to the pool, Nora jumped into the water with a big splash. "Come on Salim!" said Nora. Salim used the steps to get in slowly. He practiced his strokes up and down the pool, while Nora splashed and giggled.
"Did you have fun?" Dad asked as they dried off.
"Yes!" said Nora and Salim together. "And we are hungry!"

How are Nora and Salim alike?	How are Nora and Salim different?
Nora and Salim like going to the pool.	Nora jumps in, but Salim steps in slowly.
Both Nora and Salim are hungry at the end.	Nora jumps and splashes, but Salim practices his strokes.

Try This
Write a short story about Nora and Salim playing soccer one afternoon.

School-Home Connection
Ask your child to read you the short story about Nora and Salim playing soccer. Have your child complete a chart like the one on this page for the story he or she wrote.

167

Challenge

▲ **Challenge, p. 167**

E L L

- Group children according to academic levels, and assign one of the pages on the left.

- Clarify any unfamiliar concepts as necessary. See *ELL Teacher Guide* Lesson 21 for support in scaffolding instruction.

Social Studies
Saving Money
by Mary Firestone

Nonfiction

Saving Money
BY MARY FIRESTONE

Putting money aside before you spend it helps you save. **Earnings** are money that you are paid or given. **Costs** are money you spend buying things. To save money, your earnings must be more than costs.

Dora is a second grader who wants to save her money. She spends only part of her earnings so she can save the rest.

Saving lets you buy more costly items without borrowing from others. Dora saves a little of her money each week. In time, she will save enough for a scooter.

192

193

Reading
Student Edition: Paired Selection

Genre Study

DISCUSS NONFICTION   Explain to children that "Saving Money" is a nonfiction selection.

NONFICTION FEATURES   Tell children that nonfiction
- gives facts and information about a subject or topic.
- often has photographs and captions to help explain the text.
- includes specialized or technical vocabulary to discuss the subject.

USE PRIOR KNOWLEDGE/SET A PURPOSE   Read aloud the title of the nonfiction selection. Guide children to use prior knowledge to set a purpose for listening. Then ask children to read the selection aloud.

Objectives
- *To understand characteristics of nonfiction*
- *To apply word knowledge to the reading of a text*

Small amounts of money add up over time. If you put $2 in a jar each week, you will have $8 at the end of the month. After saving for a year, you would have more than $100.

You can keep your savings at a bank. Banks pay **interest**. Interest is a little bit of money the bank gives you for keeping money at their bank.

Dora writes what she brings to the bank in a passbook. When she wants to spend her money, the bank will give it back with interest.

194

Saving money is a good choice. Saving money now will help you buy things you will need and want later. Dora saved enough to buy her own scooter. Saving money helps you plan for the future.

195

Respond to Nonfiction

MONITOR COMPREHENSION   As children read, ask:

- **NOTE DETAILS   What has to happen for people to save money?** (Their earnings must be more than their costs.)

- **PERSONAL RESPONSE   Do you think it is better to keep savings in a jar or at a bank? Why do you think so?** (Possible response: At a bank so the money will earn interest. In time, a person will have more money than they first put in the bank.)

- **GENRE   Why do you think the author included the smaller photograph on *Student Edition* page 194?** (Possible response: It helps explain the sentence *Dora writes what she brings to the bank in a passbook*. It shows a passbook. It also shows how much money Dora has in the bank.)

E L L

Role-Play   Use role-playing to reinforce the meanings of *earnings* and *costs*. Give a volunteer play money. Say: **These are your earnings, which is money you are paid.** Have the child use the "earnings" to buy a sheet of paper. Say: **You used your earnings to buy this paper. That is your** *cost*.

Writing Prompt

Write Your Ideas   Write your opinion about whether saving money is a good idea or a bad idea. Give reasons for your opinion.

Connections

Objectives

- *To compare texts*
- *To connect texts to personal experiences*

Comparing Texts

1. The characters in "A Chair for My Mother" save money in a big jar. In "Saving Money," Dora first saves money in a jar and then saves money in a bank. **TEXT TO TEXT**

2. Answers will vary. Possible response: I would travel around the world. **TEXT TO SELF**

3. Possible response: Some people save money to buy things they want or need. They may save to buy expensive objects. Other people save money to go places or to do fun things. **TEXT TO WORLD**

Connections

Comparing Texts

1. How do the characters save money in "A Chair for My Mother" and "Saving Money"?

2. What would you do with money you save?

3. What are some reasons people save money?

Phonics

Read a Sentence

List five words in which *ou* or *ow* stand for the vowel sound in *cloud*. Trade lists with a partner. Then write a sentence using as many of the words as you can. Draw a picture for it. Read the sentence to your partner.

196

Fluency Practice

Read with Feeling

Take turns reading parts of the story with a partner. Use your voices to show how the characters feel. Practice until you agree that the pages sound right.

Writing

Write a Story

What would you save money to buy? Use a story map to plan a story. Then write your story.

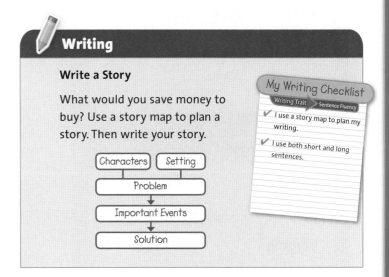

```
Characters  Setting
      |
   Problem
      ↓
Important Events
      ↓
   Solution
```

My Writing Checklist
Writing Trait > Sentence Fluency
✓ I use a story map to plan my writing.
✓ I use both short and long sentences.

197

PHONICS

Read a Sentence Have children make a list of five words in which the letters *ou* or *ow* stand for the vowel sound /ou/. After children write their sentence, remind them to draw a picture to illustrate it.

I found a brown hound dressed as a clown.

FLUENCY

Read with Feeling Group children into pairs. Assign one child to read aloud *Student Edition* pages 175–176 while the partner follows along and listens. Then tell children to swap roles. Remind children to use their voice in a way that shows how the characters feel.

WRITING

Write a Story Remind children to use the graphic organizer to plan their story. Tell children to describe the setting, characters, objects, and events in their story in detail. Have them check that the events are in time-order and that their writing makes sense. Have children revise their writing to improve sentence variety and to provide more descriptive details.

 Build Robust Vocabulary

Objectives

- *To review robust vocabulary*
- *To figure out a word's meaning based on the context*

REVIEW ☑ Tested

Vocabulary: Lesson 21

allowance	boost
rosy	exchanged
bargain	delivered
spoiled	thrifty
comfortable	industrious

Review Robust Vocabulary

USE VOCABULARY IN DIFFERENT CONTEXTS Remind children of the Student-Friendly Explanations of the Vocabulary Words introduced on Days 1 and 2. Then discuss each word using the following examples:

allowance

- **What are some things you might do at home to earn an allowance?**
- **What are some things you would like to spend your allowance on?**

rosy

- **How would you look if you had rosy cheeks?**
- **Tell about a time when your cheeks might not be rosy but might look pale instead.**

bargain

- **When you shop for a present, should you try to find just the right present for the person or should you look for a bargain? Explain.**
- **How can you tell if something is a bargain?**

spoiled

- **Describe what spoiled fruit looks and smells like.**
- **What might cause a picnic or a party to be spoiled?**

comfortable

- **What kind of bed do you think is comfortable to sleep in? Why?**
- **Are you more comfortable in a soft chair at home or in a chair at school? Explain.**

boost

- When might you need to give someone a boost?

- When might it not be a good idea to give someone a boost?

exchanged

- You were given a sweater that looks exactly like a sweater your best friend has. Is this something you would have exchanged? Why or why not?

- Which word has almost the same meaning as *exchanged*: *swapped* or *tore*?

delivered

- Which word has almost the same meaning as *delivered*: *brought* or *kept*? Explain.

- What kinds of things are delivered by postal workers?

thrifty

- Do you think it is better to be a thrifty person or a person who spends a lot of money? Why?

- How can you tell if someone is a thrifty person?

industrious

- Would you like to be described as industrious? Explain.

- What are some things an industrious student is most likely to do?

▼ Student-Friendly Explanations

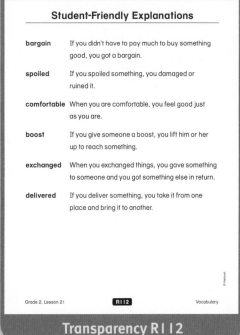

Student-Friendly Explanations

allowance	If you get money for doing chores or helping at home, you get an allowance.
rosy	If something looks rosy, it looks pink.
thrifty	If you are thrifty, you are careful about spending money.
industrious	If you are industrious, you are hard-working.

Grade 2, Lesson 21   R111   Vocabulary

Transparency R111

Student-Friendly Explanations

bargain	If you didn't have to pay much to buy something good, you got a bargain.
spoiled	If you spoiled something, you damaged or ruined it.
comfortable	When you are comfortable, you feel good just as you are.
boost	If you give someone a boost, you lift him or her up to reach something.
exchanged	When you exchanged things, you gave something to someone and you got something else in return.
delivered	If you deliver something, you take it from one place and bring it to another.

Grade 2, Lesson 21   R112   Vocabulary

Transparency R112

Grammar *Quick Write*

Present-Tense Action Verbs

5-DAY GRAMMAR	
DAY 1	Introduce Present-Tense Action Verbs
DAY 2	Present-Tense Endings −s, −es
DAY 3	**Combining Sentences with the Same Verb**
DAY 4	Apply to Writing
DAY 5	Weekly Review

Objective

- *To combine sentences that have the same verb*

Daily Proofreading

Molly gave Mrs brown some flowers.

(Mrs. Brown)

TECHNOLOGY

 www.harcourtschool.com/ storytown
Grammar Glossary

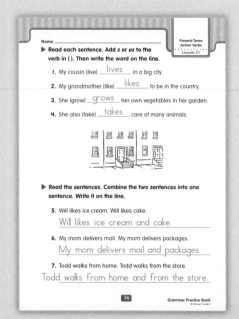

▲ **Grammar Practice Book, p. 74**

Review

COMBINING SENTENCES WITH THE SAME VERB   Write these sentences on the board.

Kate shops.

Bill shops.

Read the sentences aloud, and point out their naming parts. (Kate, Bill) Have children identify the present-tense action verb in the sentences. (shops) Explain to children that since both sentences have the same action verb, they can be combined to make one sentence. On the board, write *Kate and Bill shop.* Point out that the word *and* was used to combine the naming parts *Kate* and *Bill*. Explain that *Kate* and *Bill* tells about more than one, so you should complete the sentence with *shop*, not *shops*. Read the sentence aloud.

Kate and Bill shop.

Practice / Apply

GUIDED PRACTICE   Write these sentences on the board. Guide children to combine the pairs of sentences into one sentence.

Mr. Burns teaches. I teach. (Mr. Burns and I teach.)

Leslie swims. Henry swims. (Leslie and Henry swim.)

Miguel fishes. Anna fishes. (Miguel and Anna fish.)

INDEPENDENT PRACTICE   Have children write a pair of sentences that use the same verb. Have partners switch papers and correctly combine the pair of sentences into one sentence.

5-DAY WRITING	
DAY 1	Introduce
DAY 2	Prewrite
DAY 3	**Draft**
DAY 4	Revise
DAY 5	Revise

Writing
Personal Narrative

Draft a Personal Narrative

REVIEW A LITERATURE MODEL   Have children open their *Student Edition* to page 175. Read aloud the text on pages 175–177 as children follow along. Point out the following, and tell children to use the literature as a model for their own writing:

- The author writes about an important experience.
- The author uses the words *I* and *my*.
- The author avoids starting every sentence with *I* and uses different types of sentences and sentence beginnings.
- The author uses clear details and specific words to describe the setting, characters, objects, and events.
- The ending tells how things work out.

DRAFT PERSONAL NARRATIVE   Have children use their sentences and filled-in graphic organizers to write their personal narrative. Suggest that they write events in an order that makes sense and use details and specific words in their descriptions.

WRITING TRAIT   **SENTENCE FLUENCY**   As children write their personal narrative, remind them to vary their sentence beginnings to make their writing more interesting and flow smoothly. Explain that beginning every sentence with the word *I* may make their writing sound choppy.

CONFER WITH CHILDREN   Meet with individual children, helping them as they write personal narratives. Offer encouragement for what they are doing well, and make constructive suggestions for improving an aspect of writing, as needed.

Objectives

- *To draft a personal narrative*
- *To write events in a logical sequence*

Writing Prompt

Rewrite an Ending   Have children think and write about a different way that "A Chair for My Mother" might have ended. Have them explain what might have caused the story to end differently from the way it did.

▲ **Writer's Companion, Lesson 21**

   ADVANCED

Develop Vivid Images   Write these sentences on the board: *I held my mom's hand. I clutched my mom's hand.* Point out that the word *clutched* makes the second sentence more exciting and easier to visualize. Encourage children to use precise words in their writing to develop vivid images.

Day at a Glance

Day 4

phonics and Spelling

- Introduce: Abbreviations
- Review: Vowel Diphthong /ou/*ou*, *ow*

Fluency

- Expression
- "A Chair for My Mother," *Student Edition*, pp. 166–191

Read!

Comprehension

 Focus Skill Review: Plot

- Maintain: Make Predictions
- Maintain: Setting

Robust Vocabulary

- Review: *allowance, rosy, bargain, spoiled, comfortable, boost, exchanged, delivered, thrifty, industrious*

Grammar [Quick Write]

- Review: Present-Tense Action Verbs

Writing

- Personal Narrative

Warm-Up Routines

 Oral Language

Objective *To listen attentively and respond appropriately to oral communication*

Question of the Day

What words would you use to describe how you'd like things to be at home?

Help children brainstorm words to describe what being at home should be like, and record their ideas in a web. Use the following prompts:

- **What kinds of sounds do you hear in your home?**
- **What special things do you see, smell, or touch?**
- **What is your favorite place at home?**
- **What do you like best about being at home?**

Read Aloud

Objective *To listen for a purpose*

BIG BOOK OF RHYMES AND POEMS   Display
the poem "Home" on page 38 and read the
title. Tell children to listen to the poem for
the words that describe home. Then read the
poem aloud. Discuss with children the ideas
expressed in the poem and the feeling the
poem creates. Then invite children to name
the words that describe this home. (*quiet,
peaceful, lasting, all around me*)

▲ **Big Book of Rhymes
and Poems, p. 38**

Word Wall

Objective *To read high-frequency words*

REVIEW HIGH-FREQUENCY WORDS
Display the following words on the board
in two columns: *everything*, *guess*, *short*,
prove, *though*, and *exercise*. Divide the
class into two groups. Have the first group
choral read the first column of words,
snapping their fingers to keep time. Have
the second group do the same with the
second column of words. Then have the
groups switch columns and repeat.

everything	prove
guess	though
short	exercise

Abbreviations
phonics

5-DAY PHONICS	
DAY 1	Introduce /ou/*ou*, *ow*
DAY 2	Word Building with /ou/*ou*, *ow*
DAY 3	Word Building with /ou/*ou*, *ow*
DAY 4	**Abbreviations; Review /ou/*ou*, *ow***
DAY 5	Abbreviations; Review /ou/*ou*, *ow*

Objectives

- *To understand that an abbreviation is a short way to write a word*
- *To recognize and read abbreviations*
- *To match words to their abbreviations*

Skill Trace

 Tested **Abbreviations**

Introduce	T82
Review	T94
Test	Theme 5

Abbreviations

Please come to my birthday party on Sun., Oct. 23.

Shelly goes to Dr. Chow when she is sick.

My mom and Mr. Fowler work downtown.

Grant is going to visit his Grandmother in July, and he will return home in Aug.

Grade 2, Lesson 21   **R110**   Phonics

Transparency R110

Teach/Model

INTRODUCE ABBREVIATIONS   Write these words and their abbreviations on the board: *Mister*, *Mr.*, *February*, *Feb.*, *Tuesday*, *Tues.* Point to each abbreviation, and remind children that an abbreviation is a short way to write a word. Discuss the following points.

- Begin most abbreviations with a capital letter and end them with a period.

- Use abbreviations for some titles, such as *Dr., Mr., Mrs., Ms.*

- Use abbreviations for the names of days and some months.

MODEL READING ABBREVIATIONS

Model how to read abbreviations. Pronounce *Mister* and *Mr.* as you point to them. Tell children that when they see the abbreviation *Mr.*, they should say the word as though it were written without the abbreviation: *Mister*. Point to each word and its abbreviation and have children pronounce them out loud.

Guided Practice

MATCH ABBREVIATIONS   Write the following words on the board. Read them aloud with children. Then guide children to match them to their correct abbreviation.

September	Sept.	sept.	Sept
Doctor	Doc	dctr.	Dr.
Thursday	Thurs	Thurs.	thurs

READ ABBREVIATIONS   Display **Transparency R110** or write the sentences on the board or chart paper. Have children read the sentences aloud. Remind them to use what they have learned about abbreviations to help them read accurately.

Vowel Diphthong /ou/
OU, OW  and Spelling

5-DAY SPELLING	
DAY 1	Pretest
DAY 2	Word Building
DAY 3	State the Generalization
DAY 4	Review
DAY 5	Posttest

Build Words

REVIEW THE WORDS   Have the children open their notebooks to the spelling words they wrote on Day 3. Have them read the words several times and then close their notebooks.

MAP LETTERS TO SOUNDS   Have children follow your directions to change letters in each of the following words to spell a spelling word. Have them write the word on a sheet of paper or in their notebooks. Then have a volunteer change the spelling of the word on the board so that children can self-check their spelling.

- Write *at* on the board. Ask: **Which spelling word can you make by changing the first letter to letters that stand for the /ou/ sound?** (*out*)

- Write *mount* on the board. Ask: **Which spelling word can you make by changing the first letter?** (*count*)

- Write *cried* on the board. Ask: **Which spelling word can you make by changing the vowel sound?** (*crowd*)

out
count
crowd

Follow similar procedures for *tan* (*town*), *grand* (*ground*), *fund* (*found*), *not* (*now*), *clown* (*crown*), *sand* (*sound*), and *din* (*down*).

CHALLENGE WORDS   Write the first or second syllable of each challenge word on the board. Ask children to spell each word in its entirety and write the missing letters.

BELOW-LEVEL

Focus on Vowel Diphthong /ou/   Write the spelling words on the board, with blanks where the letters that stand for the /ou/ sound should be. Ask questions such as "What letters can you add to *t _ _ n* to make *town*?" Have children spell each word.

Objective

- *To use /ou/ou, ow, and other known letter-sounds to spell and write words.*

Spelling Words

1.	**out***	6.	**now***
2.	**town**	7.	**found***
3.	**count***	8.	**crown**
4.	**crowd**	9.	**sound**
5.	**ground**	10.	**down***

Challenge Words

11.	**surround**	14.	**powerful**
12.	**without**	15.	**cloudless**
13.	**cowboy**		

* Words from "A Chair for My Mother"
and "Saving Money"

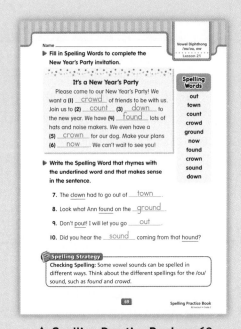

▲ Spelling Practice Book, p. 69

Fluency
Expression

Objectives

• *To build fluency through rereading a story*

• *To read fluently and with expression*

BELOW-LEVEL

Echo-Read   On the board, write sentences from the story that children have trouble reading fluently and with expression. Read each sentence aloud and have children repeat, matching your speed, phrasing, and expression. Repeat until children can read each sentence effortlessly.

MONITOR PROGRESS

Fluency

IF children have difficulty reading with expression,	**THEN** help them identify words that should show emotion. Read the words and have children repeat.

Small-Group Instruction, pp. S4–S5:

● **BELOW-LEVEL:** Reteach

● **ON-LEVEL:** Reinforce

● **ADVANCED:** Extend

Review

DIBELS
Oral Reading Fluency
ORF

MODEL USING EXPRESSION
Remind children that when good readers read, they think about the mood of each part of the story and use their voice to show emotion. Read aloud page 182 of "A Chair for My Mother." Point out the quotation marks on page 182.

▲ Student Edition, pp. 166–191

Think Aloud   When I saw the quotation marks as I was reading, I knew that I should read the words the way that Mama would say them. I had just read that when Mama comes home, her feet hurt. When I read what Mama was going to say, I knew she would speak in a complaining tone of voice. So I read the words inside the quotation marks as though Mama were complaining.

Practice/Apply

GUIDED PRACTICE   Guide children to read aloud pages 182–183 with you, matching your expression and pronunciation.

INDEPENDENT PRACTICE   Have children read along with "A Chair for My Mother" on *Audiotext* 5. Have them practice reading the story several times until they are able to read it fluently and with expression.

Plot
Comprehension

Review

EXPLAIN PLOT   Ask children to explain what the plot of a story is. (Plot is what happens during the beginning, in the middle, and at the end of a story. It includes a problem the characters have and tells how they solve it.) Remind children that the beginning of a story introduces characters and tells about a problem they have. The middle tells how the characters deal with the problem, and the end tells how they solve it.

Practice/Apply

☐ **GUIDED PRACTICE**   Display **Transparency R106.** Reread the story aloud to children, and ask them to identify the characters. (Miss Cline, Peng, the class, Principal Sanchez) Then guide children to think about the beginning, the middle, and the end of the story. Ask:

- **What problem is introduced at the beginning of the story?** (Miss Cline asks her students to think of a plan to make their old school look cheerful.)

- **What happens in the middle of the story?** (Peng suggests that they grow flowers in the schoolyard and tells what they could do to raise money for the supplies.)

- **What happens at the end of the story?** (Peng's plan is success-ful and the school looks cheerful.)

INDEPENDENT PRACTICE   Ask children to tell what problem is introduced at the beginning of "A Chair for My Mother." (A girl, her mother, and her grandma don't have any chairs because their house burned up in a fire.) Then have children tell what happens in the middle and at the end of the story. (Middle: The girl, her mother, and her grandma are saving money in a big jar so they can buy an armchair. When they finally fill the jar with coins, they shop for an armchair. End: They find and buy just the right armchair.)

Objectives

- *To identify the plot of a story*
- *To identify the problem and solution in a story*

Skill Trace

 Plot

Introduce	T34–T35
Reteach	S6–S7
Review	T69, T85, T97, T136–T137, T171, T187, T197, T397, T414
Test	Theme 5
Maintain	Theme 6, T86

Plot

Peng's Plan

Winter was almost over. At the Carver School, Miss Cline and her class were thinking of ways to make their old school look cheerful. Everyone agreed that the school looked kind of gloomy.

"We could plant flowers in the schoolyard!" said Peng. "We could earn money for the supplies by having a bake sale and doing a talent show."

"We like Peng's plan!" said everyone in the class.

"Well, then, let's get to work," said Miss Cline.

In the next two months, the class held two bake sales. In late March, the students held a big talent show with the rest of the school. Many people paid two dollars for a ticket.

By early April, the class had earned a lot of money. Miss Cline took them to a garden supply store to get supplies.

Two weeks later, the school looked beautiful. The class had worked hard to plant flowers all around the building.

"Thank you," Principal Sanchez said to the class. "The school looks cheerful!"

Grade 2, Lesson 21   R106   Comprehension

Transparency R106

Make Predictions
Comprehension

Objective

- *To use prior knowledge and story clues to make and explain predictions*

Skill Trace

 Tested **Make Predictions**

Introduce	Theme 2, T34–T35
Reteach	Theme 2, S6–S7
Review	Theme 2, T68–T69, T86, T94, T132–T133, T166–T167, T182, T192, T389, T406
Test	Theme 2
Maintain	T86

Reinforce the Skill

REVIEW MAKE PREDICTIONS   Remind children that good readers make predictions as they read. They use their own knowledge and clues from the text and pictures to make predictions. As they read, they confirm whether their predictions were correct. Have children turn to *Student Edition* pages 168–169. Model making predictions.

> **Think Aloud**   Before I read pages 168–169, I had read the story title "A Chair for My Mother" and looked at the illustrations on pages 168–169. I wondered what the change in the large jar was for. I know that many people save change in jars, so I used the illustration and what I know from real life to predict that one of the characters was saving money to buy something. I wanted to keep reading to find out whether I was right and to learn what the character might buy. The title of the story is "A Chair for My Mother," so I predicted someone was saving money to buy a chair for her mother.

Practice/Apply

GUIDED PRACTICE   Display a fiction book that children have not read. Guide children in using clues from the title, illustrations, and text to make predictions about the story. First, read aloud the title and show the cover illustration. Ask:

- **What do you predict the story might be about? What did you use to make your prediction?**

Next, read aloud the first page of the story and show any accompanying illustrations. Ask:

- **What do you predict will happen next? What did you use to make your prediction?**

INDEPENDENT PRACTICE   Have partners read an unfamiliar fiction story together. Have children make and explain predictions as they read.

Setting
Comprehension

Reinforce the Skill

REVIEW SETTING Remind children that the setting of a story is when and where a story takes place and that a story can have more than one setting. A story can take place in the past, present, or future. Draw the following chart on the board. Have children turn to *Student Edition* page 168. Read aloud the first two paragraphs on page 168 as children follow along. Then model how to identify the setting of those two paragraphs in "A Chair for My Mother" and how to complete the chart with information about them.

Setting	
When	**Where**
present	Blue Tile Diner

Think Aloud The events in the first two paragraphs of page 168 take place at the Blue Tile Diner. I will add *Blue Tile Diner* to the "Where" column of the Setting chart. The narrator uses present-tense action verbs to describe what she, her mother, and her mother's boss are doing, so I know the story takes place in the present. I will add *present* to the "When" column of the chart.

Practice/Apply

GUIDED PRACTICE Have a volunteer read aloud *Student Edition* page 169. Guide children to identify the setting, and add their responses to the Setting chart. Ask:

- **Where does this part of the story take place?** (in the home of the girl and her mother)

- **When does this part of the story take place?** (in the present)

- **What is the setting of this paragraph?** (in the present, in the home of the girl and her mother)

INDEPENDENT PRACTICE Have children identify other settings in "A Chair for My Mother," and add the information to the Setting chart.

Objective
- *To identify and describe the setting of a story*

Skill Trace
 Setting

Introduce	Theme 4, T34–T35
Reteach	Theme 4, S6–S7
Review	Theme 4, T67, T87, T95, T134–T135, T171, T187, T197, T389, T406
Test	Theme 4
Maintain	T87

Build Robust Vocabulary

Objectives

- *To review robust vocabulary*
- *To demonstrate knowledge of word meaning*

Tested

REVIEW ✓

Vocabulary: Lesson 21

allowance	spoiled
rosy	comfortable
thrifty	boost
industrious	exchanged
bargain	delivered

Extend Word Meanings

USE VOCABULARY IN DIFFERENT CONTEXTS   Remind children of the Student-Friendly Explantions of the Vocabulary Words. Then discuss each word in a new context, asking children to explain their responses:

allowance   Tell children that you will name some things that people do at home. Tell children to raise their hand if they think the activity is something a person would get an allowance for doing. If not, they should shake their head back and forth.

washing floors   eating food

dirtying clothes   cooking meals

rosy   Tell children that you will name some times when people are outside. Tell children to raise their hand if they think a time is one during which people's cheeks might get rosy. If not, they should do nothing.

ice skating on a chilly day

walking in the evening

gardening on a sunny day

thrifty   Explain that you will make some statements. If children think someone who is thrifty might make the statement, they should sit on their hands. If not, children should raise their hands above their head and shake them about.

I spent $20 for a toothbrush.

I own one shirt, and that's enough.

I save every rubber band I find.

industrious   Tell children that you will describe some things animals might do. If they think the animals are being industrious, they should stand up. If not, they should do nothing.

bees gathering nectar

cows lazily chewing their cud

ants carrying food to their nest

Word Relationships

SYNONYMS Tell children that a synonym is a word that means the same or almost the same as another word. Write these sentences on the board, underlining the words as shown.

1. Five shirts for $5 is a great <u>deal</u>! (bargain)
2. My fuzzy slippers are <u>cozy</u>. (comfortable)
3. Debbie <u>traded</u> her apple for some grapes. (exchanged)
4. The bus driver <u>transported</u> us to school. (delivered)

Ask children to read the sentences aloud and replace the underlined word with a Vocabulary Word that is a synonym.

▼ Student-Friendly Explanations

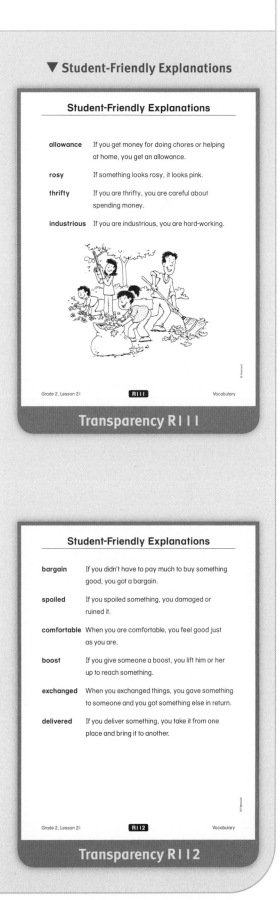

Student-Friendly Explanations

allowance	If you get money for doing chores or helping at home, you get an allowance.
rosy	If something looks rosy, it looks pink.
thrifty	If you are thrifty, you are careful about spending money.
industrious	If you are industrious, you are hard-working.

Grade 2, Lesson 21   R111   Vocabulary

Transparency R111

Student-Friendly Explanations

bargain	If you didn't have to pay much to buy something good, you got a bargain.
spoiled	If you spoiled something, you damaged or ruined it.
comfortable	When you are comfortable, you feel good just as you are.
boost	If you give someone a boost, you lift him or her up to reach something.
exchanged	When you exchanged things, you gave something to someone and you got something else in return.
delivered	If you deliver something, you take it from one place and bring it to another.

Grade 2, Lesson 21   R112   Vocabulary

Transparency R112

Grammar *Quick Write*

Present-Tense Action Verbs

5-DAY GRAMMAR	
DAY 1	Introduce Present-Tense Action Verbs
DAY 2	Present-Tense Endings –s, –es
DAY 3	Combining Sentences with the Same Verb
DAY 4	**Apply to Writing**
DAY 5	Weekly Review

Objective

• *To recognize and write present-tense action verbs in sentences*

Daily Proofreading

The shorter month of all is february.

(shortest; February.)

Writing Trait

Strengthening Conventions

Grammar   Use this short lesson with children's own writing to build a foundation for revising/editing longer connected text on Day 5. See also *Writer's Companion*, Lesson 21.

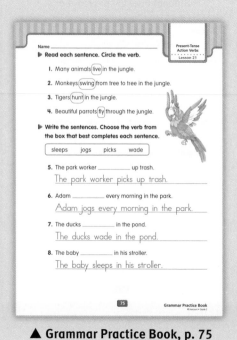

▲ **Grammar Practice Book, p. 75**

Review

DISCUSS PRESENT-TENSE ACTION VERBS   Review with children that a present-tense action verb tells about an action that is happening now. Remind them of the following:

• Add the ending -*s* to most present-tense action verbs when the naming part of the sentence tells about one.

• Add the ending -*es* when a present-tense action verb ends in *s, x, sh, ch,* or *tch* and the naming part of the sentence tells about one.

• Do not add an -*s* or -*es* to a verb when the naming part tells about *I, you,* or more than one.

Write the following sentences on the board and read them aloud:

Jemma tosses a ball to me.

Rusty and Spot jumps for it.

I throws the ball.

Explain that the present-tense action verb is used correctly in only the first sentence. Point to *tosses*. Explain that -*es* has been added to the verb *toss* because it ends in *s* and the naming part, Jemma, tells about one. Work through the second and third sentences to correct the present-tense action verbs.

Practice/Apply

GUIDED PRACTICE   Tell children that you are going to write three sentences about things people do with money and that you will use a present-tense action verb in each sentence. Write the first sentence and elicit additional sentence ideas from children. After you write each sentence, model orally how to check that the present-tense action verb is used correctly.

INDEPENDENT PRACTICE   Ask children to write three sentences about things they do with money. Tell children to use a present-tense action verb in each sentence. Have partners exchange sentences and check that present-tense action verbs are used correctly.

Writing
Personal Narrative

5-DAY WRITING	
DAY 1	Introduce
DAY 2	Prewrite
DAY 3	Draft
DAY 4	**Revise**
DAY 5	Revise

Write a Personal Narrative

WRITE   Children continue writing their personal narrative. Remind them that their personal narrative should be about an experience they really had. Encourage them to write events in the order in which they happened.

WRITING TRAIT   **SENTENCE FLUENCY**   Tell children to vary their sentence beginnings and avoid beginning each sentence with the word *I*. Remind them that having a variety of sentence beginnings will make their writing less choppy and more interesting.

REVISE   Have children read their personal narrative to a partner and check that they have used present-tense action verbs correctly. Children can use the list of criteria for a personal narrative to improve their writing.

Personal Narrative

- A personal narrative tells about an important experience the writer really had.

- The beginning tells what the personal narrative is about.

- The writer uses the words *I* and *me*.

- Details and words describe the setting, characters, objects, events, and feelings.

- The ending tells how things work out.

Have children revise their personal narrative. Let them work together to make sure they use present-tense action verbs correctly, and that they have a variety of sentence beginnings. Encourage children to use Editor's Marks to revise their writing. Save children's personal narratives so they can continue revising on Day 5.

Objectives

- *To draft a personal narrative*
- *To revise a personal narrative*
- *To use present-tense action verbs correctly*

Writing Prompt

Evaluate   Have children find something they wrote earlier in the year and compare it to something they recently wrote. Ask them to write an evaluation telling how their writing has changed. They should note ways in which their writing is better and any areas in which they feel they still need improvement.

BELOW-LEVEL

Improve Sequence   Have children tell you the events in their personal narrative. List the events as children speak. To clarify order, ask questions such as **What happened first? What happened next?** Help children number events in the order they occurred. Have children refer to the list as they revise their drafts.

Day at a Glance

Day 5

phonics and Spelling
- Review: Abbreviations
- Posttest: Vowel Diphthong /ou/*ou*, *ow*

Fluency
- Expression
- "A Chair for My Mother," *Student Edition*, pp. 166–191

Read!

Comprehension

Focus Skill
- Review: Plot

- *Read-Aloud Anthology:* "The Just-Right Gift"

Robust Vocabulary
- Cumulative Review

Grammar   *Quick Write*
- Review: Present-Tense Action Verbs

Writing
- Personal Narrative

Warm-Up Routines

Oral Language

Objective *To listen attentively and respond appropriately to oral communication*

Question of the Day

What makes a home quiet, peaceful, and lasting?

Invite children to speculate about what makes a home quiet, peaceful, and lasting. Use the following prompts.

- **Why might a quiet home be peaceful?**
- **How would someone growing up in a home like this feel?**
- **What are some other words that might describe a home like this?**
- **Can noisy, busy homes be fun to grow up in, too? Why?**

Write the following sentence frame and have children complete the sentences.

> I think that _____ makes a home quiet, peaceful, and lasting because _____.

Read Aloud

Objective *To identify repeated phrases in poetry*

BIG BOOK OF RHYMES AND POEMS Display the poem "Home" on page 38. Ask children to listen for the words that are repeated. Then read aloud the poem. Invite children to tell which words are repeated. *(All around me)* Discuss how the repeating of these words gives the poem a steady rhythm. Then read the poem again, telling children to join in.

▲ **Big Book of Rhymes and Poems, p. 38**

Word Wall

Objective *To read high-frequency words*

REVIEW HIGH-FREQUENCY WORDS Point to the following words in random order: *already, police, short, lose, half,* and *care.* Have children read the words quickly. Point to the words again and have volunteers use each word in a sentence.

already	police	short
lose	half	care

Abbreviations

phonics

5-DAY PHONICS	
DAY 1	Introduce /ou/*ou, ow*
DAY 2	Word Building with /ou/*ou, ow*
DAY 3	Word Building with /ou/*ou, ow*
DAY 4	Abbreviations; Review /ou/*ou, ow*
DAY 5	Abbreviations; Review /ou/*ou, ow*

Objectives

- *To read abbreviations*
- *To sort abbreviations for months, days, and titles*

Skill Trace

Tested **Abbreviations**

Introduce	T82
Review	T94
Test	Theme 5

Review

READ ABBREVIATIONS Write the abbreviation *Feb.* on the board. Have children read and explain what *Feb.* is. (the abbreviation for *February*) Explain that *Feb.* is the abbreviation of a proper noun, so it begins with a capital letter. Point out the period at the end of *Feb.*, and remind children that many abbreviations end with a period.

Practice/Apply

GUIDED PRACTICE Write the following abbreviations on the board and have children read them: *Mar., Mon., Mr., Nov., Sat.,* and *Dec.* Then make a chart as shown. Guide children in sorting the words by type and adding them to the chart.

Days	Months	Titles of People

INDEPENDENT PRACTICE Have children think of other abbreviations to add to the chart. Then point to the abbreviations at random and have children read them.

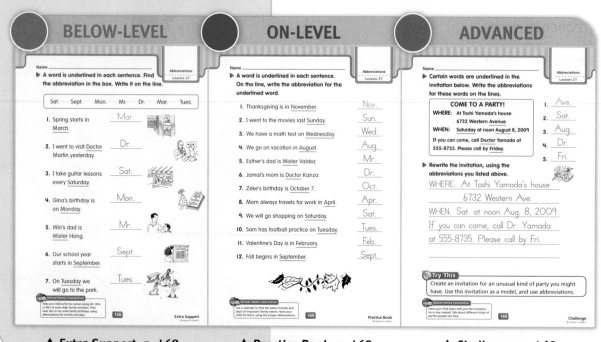

BELOW-LEVEL

▲ Extra Support, p. 168

ON-LEVEL

▲ Practice Book, p. 168

ADVANCED

▲ Challenge, p. 168

E L L

- Group children according to academic levels, and assign one of the pages on the left.

- Clarify any unfamiliar concepts as necessary. See *ELL Teacher Guide* Lesson 21 for support in scaffolding instruction.

Vowel Diphthong /ou/ *ou*, *ow* phonics *and Spelling*

5-DAY SPELLING

DAY I	Pretest
DAY 2	Word Building
DAY 3	State the Generalization
DAY 4	Review
DAY 5	**Posttest**

Assess

POSTTEST Assess children's progress. Use the dictation sentences from Day I.

Words with Vowel Diphthong /ou/*ou* or *ow*

I.	out	Bree goes **out** to play after school.
2.	town	Tamara was born in a **town** in Russia.
3.	count	Belin can **count** to a thousand.
4.	crowd	Carlos joined the **crowd** in front of the pet shop.
5.	ground	Ashley's mitten fell to the **ground**.
6.	now	You are writing spelling words **now**.
7.	found	Tran **found** a quarter.
8.	crown	The princess wore a sparkling **crown** on her head.
9.	sound	The **sound** of soft music is relaxing.
I0.	down	David watched the water swirl **down** the drain.

ADVANCED

Challenge Words   Use the challenge words in these dictation sentences.

I I.	surround	Fences **surround** the zoo.
I2.	without	Myra wanted a cake **without** frosting.
I3.	cowboy	The **cowboy** rounded up the cattle.
I4.	powerful	A **powerful** ox can haul heavy loads.
I5.	cloudless	A sky without clouds is **cloudless.**

WRITING APPLICATION   Have children write and illustrate a riddle using one of the spelling words.

Objective

• *To use /ou/ou, ow, and other known letter-sounds to spell and write words*

Spelling Words

I.	**out***	6.	**now***
2.	**town**	7.	**found***
3.	**count***	8.	**crown**
4.	**crowd**	9.	**sound**
5.	**ground**	I0.	**down***

Challenge Words

I I.	**surround**	I4.	**powerful**
I2.	**without**	I5.	**cloudless**
I3.	**cowboy**		

* Words from "A Chair for My Mother" and "Saving Money"

Mr. Brown lost something when he stood up. He found it again when he sat down. What did he find? (Answer: He found his lap.)

Fluency
Expression

Objective

• *To read fluently with accuracy and appropriate expression*

ASSESSMENT

Monitoring Progress Periodically, take a timed sample of children's oral reading and record the number of words read correctly per minute. Children should accurately read approximately 90–100 words per minute at the end of Grade 2.

Fluency Support Materials

Fluency Builders, Grade 2, Lesson 21

Audiotext *Student Edition* selections are available on *Audiotext Grade 2*, CD 5.

Strategic Intervention Teacher Guide, Lesson 21

Readers' Theater

DIBELS
Oral Reading Fluency
ORF

PERFORM "A CHAIR FOR MY MOTHER" To help children improve their fluency, have them perform "A Chair for My Mother" as Readers' Theater. Use the following procedures:

▲ **Student Edition, pp. 166–191**

• Discuss with children what the mood of the story is and how the characters might feel and sound throughout the story.

• Have groups of two children read the story together. One child should take the part of the narrator, and the other child should take the parts of Josephine, Mama, Aunt Ida, and Grandma. Encourage the child who has multiple parts to vary his or her voice for each character.

• Listen to the groups read. Provide feedback and support.

• Invite the groups to read the story to classmates. Remind them to focus on reading accurately and with expression.

E L L

Develop Vocabulary As you discuss the mood of the story and how characters in the story might feel, point out and read aloud words that indicate emotion, such as when Aunt Ida shouts, "Don't worry." Provide a model for reading these sections, and then have children read the sections with you.

Plot
Comprehension

Review

REVIEW THE SKILL Remind children that they have learned that *plot* is what happens during the beginning, middle, and end of a story. The beginning of a story introduces the characters and tells about a problem they have. The middle tells how the characters deal with the problem, and the end tells how they solve it.

 ▲ **Read-Aloud Anthology,** **"The Just-Right Gift," p. 76**

SET A PURPOSE FOR LISTENING Have children set a purpose for listening to the "Just-Right Gift" that includes

- listening to enjoy the story.
- listening to find out the problem of the story and how it is solved.

Practice/Apply

GUIDED PRACTICE As you read aloud "The Just-Right Gift," fill in a story map to tell about the plot.

> ### Problem
> Every time Gina finds something she thinks is just right for Mama, Donny points out there's something wrong with it.

⬇

> ### Important Events
> Gina buys a scarf that she thinks is just right for Mama. Donny says that Mama doesn't know what to do with it. Gina seems worried that she bought the wrong gift.

⬇

> ### Solution
> Mama loves the scarf. It is just right.

INDEPENDENT PRACTICE Have children use the graphic organizer to summarize the problem and solution in "The Just-Right Gift."

Objectives
- *To identify the plot of a story*
- *To identify the problem and solution in a story*

Skill Trace
Tested ✓ **Plot**

Introduce	T34–T35
Reteach	S6–S7
Review	T69, T85, T97, T136–T137, T171, T187, T197, T397, T414
Test	Theme 5
Maintain	Theme 6, T86

E L L

Build Background If children have difficulty understanding the concepts of problem and solution, describe problems and solutions as you act them out. For example, try to reach something that is too high up. Say: **I cannot reach the (object). That is a problem.** Stand on a step stool to reach the object, and say: **I can stand on a step stool to reach (object). That is the solution.**

Build Robust Vocabulary

Objectives
- *To review robust vocabulary*
- *To demonstrate knowledge of word meaning*

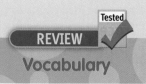

Tested

REVIEW

Vocabulary

Lesson 19	Lesson 21
brew	allowance
snug	rosy
supplies	bargain
crop	spoiled
provide	comfortable
earn	boost
committee	exchanged
experiments	delivered
innovation	thrifty
edible	industrious

Cumulative Review

SORT WORDS On the board, list the Vocabulary Words for Lessons 19 and 21. Then display **Transparency GO10**, and write the following categories at the top of the columns: *Money, Eating and Drinking,* and *Work.* Tell children to sort the Vocabulary Words into the categories. Explain that some words may apply to more than one category while other words may not be used at all. As children categorize the words, guide them to explain their choices.

Money	Eating and Drinking	Work
allowance	brew	supplies
earn	crop	committee
thrifty	edible	delivered
bargain	spoiled	industrious

REINFORCE MEANINGS Discuss children's answers to these questions.

1. What might an **industrious** child do to **earn** money? (Possible response: do extra chores around the house)

2. Suppose you found peaches for $0.30 a pound. Would that price be a **bargain** if the fruit was not **edible**? Why or why not? (Possible response: No, because if the fruit was spoiled, I wouldn't be able to eat it and the money would have been wasted.)

3. If a **committee** was reviewing the latest **innovation** in the growing of a **crop,** would its members want to see some **experiments**? Explain. (Possible response: To find out if the innovation would really work, the committee would most likely want to see experiments.)

4. If something was **delivered** to you by mail and it turned out to be **snug,** how could you get it **exchanged**? (Possible response: I would have to send it back by mail for something else that was not too tight.)

5. If you had been **thrifty** and saved your **allowance** to buy your mom a blouse as a gift, would you be upset to find that the blouse was **spoiled?** Why or why not? (Possible response: Yes, because I would have worked hard to save my money to buy my mom a blouse, so I would be upset to find that the blouse was ruined.)

6. Would someone have to **provide** you with a **boost** if you wanted to reach some **supplies** that were on the top shelf of a cabinet? Explain. (Possible response: Yes, because I am not tall enough to reach the top shelf without help.)

 MONITOR PROGRESS

Build Robust Vocabulary

IF children do not demonstrate understanding of the words and have difficulty using them,	**THEN** model using each word in several sentences, and have children repeat each sentence.

Small-Group Instruction, pp. S10–S11:

● **BELOW-LEVEL:** Reteach
● **ON-LEVEL:** Reinforce
● **ADVANCED:** Extend

Grammar Quick Write
Present-Tense Action Verbs

5-DAY GRAMMAR	
DAY 1	Introduce Present-Tense Action Verbs
DAY 2	Present Tense Endings -s, -es
DAY 3	Combining Sentences with the Same Verb
DAY 4	Apply to Writing
DAY 5	Weekly Review

Objectives

- *To identify present-tense action verbs, and use them correctly*
- *To combine two sentences that have the same present-tense action verb*

Daily Proofreading

Does Sheenas grandmother live in richmond?

(Sheena's; Richmond?)

 Language Arts Checkpoint

If children have difficulty with the concepts, see pages S12–S13 to reteach.

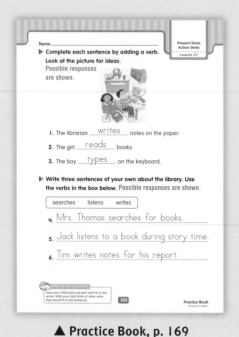

▲ Practice Book, p. 169

Review

REVIEW PRESENT-TENSE ACTION VERBS   Review what children have learned about present-tense action verbs.

- Add the ending -s to most present-tense action verbs when the naming part of the sentence tells about one.

- Add the ending -es when a present-tense action verb ends in s, x, sh, ch, or tch and the naming part of the sentence tells about one.

- Do not add an -s or -es to a verb when the naming part tells about I, you, or more than one.

- Combine two sentences that have the same present-tense action verb with *and*. Do not add an ending to the verb.

Practice/Apply

GUIDED PRACTICE   Write the following sentences on the board. Ask volunteers to help you revise sentences 1–2 to correct the present-tense verb and to combine the two sentences in item 3.

1. **My brothers plays games.** (My brothers play games.)
2. **Sam teach me one.** (Sam teaches me one.)
3. **Sam misses a turn. Jay misses a turn.**
   (Sam and Jay miss a turn.)

INDEPENDENT PRACTICE   Have children write sentences using present-tense action verbs. Have partners check their sentences to be sure the present-tense action verbs are used correctly.

Writing
Personal Narrative

5-DAY WRITING

DAY 1	Introduce
DAY 2	Prewrite
DAY 3	Draft
DAY 4	Revise
DAY 5	Revise

Revise

REVISE A PERSONAL NARRATIVE   Have children continue revising their personal narrative. As they read their writing to a partner, have the partner ask questions for clarification. Remind partners to tell what they like about the writing and to make helpful suggestions about how to improve it, including improving sequence. Tell writers to respond courteously to questions and suggestions. Remind children to use the criteria for personal narrative (see Day 4, *Teacher's Edition* page T91) to improve their writing.

REVIEW CONVENTIONS   Remind children to make sure they have capitalized abbreviations and proper nouns and that they have used present-tense verbs correctly. They should also check that each sentence ends with a period. Remind them also to check that their writing is neat and their handwriting is clear.

SENTENCE FLUENCY   Remind children to revise their personal narratives so that all sentences do not begin with the word *I*.

NOTE: A 4-point rubric appears on page R8.

SCORING RUBRIC

	6	5	4	3	2	1
FOCUS	Completely focused, purposeful.	Focused on topic and purpose.	Generally focused on topic and purpose.	Somewhat focused on topic and purpose.	Related to topic but does not maintain focus.	Lacks focus and purpose.
ORGANIZATION	Ideas progress logically; paper conveys sense of completeness.	Organization mostly clear; paper gives sense of completeness.	Organization mostly clear, but some lapses occur; may seem unfinished.	Some sense of organization; seems unfinished.	Little sense of organization.	Little or no sense of organization.
SUPPORT	Strong, specific details; clear, exact language; freshness of expression.	Strong, specific details; clear, exact language.	Adequate support and word choice.	Limited supporting details; limited word choice.	Few supporting details; limited word choice.	Little development; limited or unclear word choice.
CONVENTIONS	Varied sentences; few, if any, errors.	Varied sentences; few errors.	Some sentence variety; few errors.	Simple sentence structures; some errors.	Simple sentence structures; many errors.	Unclear sentence structures; many errors.

REPRODUCIBLE RUBRICS for specific writing purposes and presentations are available on pages R2–R8.

Objective
• *To revise a personal narrative*

Writing Prompt

Independent Writing   Have children generate a list of ideas about a new topic of their choice for writing.

WEEKLY LESSON TEST

▲ Weekly Lesson Tests, pp. 217–228

• Selection Comprehension with Short Response
• Phonics and Spelling
• Focus Skill
• Compare and Contrast
• Robust Vocabulary
• Grammar
• Fluency Passage  *FRESH READS*

 For prescriptions, see pp. A2–A6. Also available electronically on StoryTown Online Assessment and Exam View®.

 Podcasting: Assessing Fluency

Leveled Readers

Reinforcing Skills and Strategies

BELOW-LEVEL

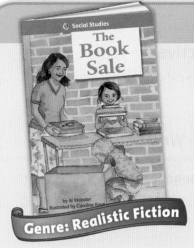

Genre: Realistic Fiction

The Book Sale

SUMMARY To help the town library buy more children's books, Cassie plans a used-book sale. It is a big success. At the end, she and her friend prepare to enjoy the library's new children's books.

- phonics **Vowel Diphthong /ou/***ou*, *ow*
- **Vocabulary**

    Focus Skill **Plot**

Before Reading

BUILD BACKGROUND/SET PURPOSE Ask for children's ideas about how a public library gets the money for new books. Then guide children to preview the story and set a purpose for reading it.

Reading the Book

PAGES 3–5 🎯 **PLOT** **What problem does Cassie want to solve? What is her idea for solving it?** (She wants to read new books, but there's no money to buy them. Her idea is to raise money from a used-book sale.)

PAGES 6–10 **SEQUENCE** **What are the steps in planning the book sale?** (Possible response: First, set up a box for used books with a sign. Then, sort through the books. Next, make a sign to advertise the sale. Last, set up the sale outside the library.)

REREAD FOR FLUENCY Have partners take turns reading the story a page at a time. Remind them to express the character's feelings.

Think Critically *(See inside back cover for questions.)*

1 🎯 **PLOT** Cassie's idea was to have a used-book sale. The library where Cassie's mom worked needed money to buy new library books.

2 **NOTE DETAILS** He made a sign telling about the sale.

3 **SEQUENCE** They sorted the books and took out any that had spoiled pages. Then they sold books at the sale.

4 **PERSONAL RESPONSE** Answers will vary.

5 **CHARACTER'S TRAITS** Possible responses: caring, clever

LEVELED READERS TEACHER GUIDE

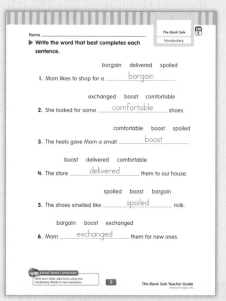

▲ Vocabulary, p. 5

▲ Comprehension, p. 6

Genre: Realistic Fiction

by Al Webster
illustrated by Richard

ON-LEVEL

Jackson's Tree

SUMMARY With the help of neighbors, Jackson carries out his idea to plant trees in the vacant lots next to his building. Then the owner of the lots contributes a large tree and names it Jackson's Tree.

- **phonics** **Vowel Diphthong /ou/** *ou, ow*
- **Vocabulary**

   Plot

Before Reading

BUILD BACKGROUND/SET PURPOSE Ask children why people who live in cities might want to plant trees. Then guide children to preview the story and set a purpose for reading it.

Reading the Book

PAGES 3–7 **PLOT** **What problem does Jackson want to solve, and what is his solution?** (Possible response: He wants to turn two vacant lots into a place more like a park by planting trees.)

PAGES 6, 11–13 **CHARACTER'S TRAITS** **What kind of person is Mr. Miro? Why do you think so?** (Possible response: He is generous. He agrees to the plan and contributes the biggest tree.)

REREAD FOR FLUENCY Have partners take turns reading pages of the story. Remind them to express the narrator's feelings.

Think Critically
(See inside back cover for questions.)

1 **PLOT** He decides that there should be trees in the vacant lots, and he and his mom organize some tree planting.

2 **STORY RESOLUTION** After everyone had planted trees, the vacant lots looked just like a park.

3 **CAUSE/EFFECT** Jackson and Mom wrote and passed out a letter.

4 **PERSONAL RESPONSE** Answers will vary.

5 **NOTE DETAILS** He found a two-for-the-price-of-one sale.

LEVELED READERS TEACHER GUIDE

Name _____

▶ Write the Vocabulary Word from the box that best completes each sentence.

| bargain | comfortable |
| boost | delivered |

1. We had a party to make our new friends feel ___comfortable___
2. We bought balloons for a ___bargain___ price.
3. My mom gave me a ___boost___ up the ladder to hang signs.
4. The store ___delivered___ a cake to our house.

▶ Write a sentence using each Vocabulary Word.
Accept reasonable responses.
5. exchanged _____
6. spoiled _____

Jackson's Tree Teacher Guide

▲ **Vocabulary, p. 5**

Name _____

▶ Complete the sentences to tell what happens in *Jackson's Tree*. Possible responses are shown.

1. Jackson asked Mr. Miro to ___plant trees in the vacant lots___
2. Mr. Miro thought Jackson had ___a great idea___
3. Jackson and his mom ___wrote a letter to the neighbors___
4. The neighbors brought ___trees to plant___
5. Mr. Miro had a big tree planted called ___Jackson's Tree___

Jackson's Tree Teacher Guide

▲ **Comprehension, p. 6**

Leveled Readers

Reinforcing Skills and Strategies

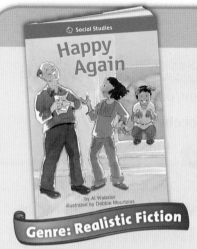

by Al Webster
illustrated by Debbie Mourtzios

Genre: Realistic Fiction

ADVANCED

Happy Again

SUMMARY   Lisa, Toby, Mom, and Dad help Mr. Cowan, whose home flooded from heavy rains. Lisa and Toby even cheer him up with a comical performance at a neighborhood party for him.

- **phonics**   Vowel Diphthong /ou/*ou*, *ow*
- **Vocabulary**

  Focus Skill   Plot

LEVELED READERS TEACHER GUIDE

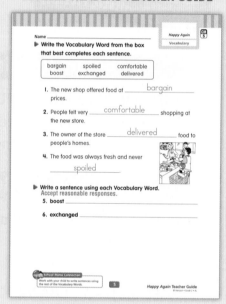

▲ Vocabulary, p. 5

Before Reading

BUILD BACKGROUND/SET PURPOSE   Ask children what they know about flooding. Ask how they might feel if their neighbor's house flooded but theirs stayed dry. Then guide children to preview the story and set a purpose for reading it.

Reading the Book

PAGES 5–8   DRAW CONCLUSIONS   Why do the parents and children try to help Mr. Cowan? (They know he is upset and want to help him.)

PAGE 14   PLOT   Why does Mr. Cowan feel better at the end of the story? (Possible responses: His neighbors have helped him. He has another house to move to, away from the river.)

REREAD FOR FLUENCY   Have partners take turns reading the story. Remind them to express the feelings of the character who is speaking.

Think Critically   *(See inside back cover for questions.)*

1 **PLOT**   His house was flooded. Toby's family decided to have a party for him. During the party, Mr. Cowan received a letter from the mayor offering him a new house away from the river.

2 **COMPARE/CONTRAST**   After the flood, he was feeling sad, unhappy, disappointed. After the party, he was feeling happy, excited, glad.

3 **CHARACTERS' TRAITS**   Possible responses: kind, helpful, caring

4 **CONTEXT CLUES**   Possible responses: swapped, shared

5 **PERSONAL RESPONSE**   Answers will vary.

▲ Comprehension, p. 6

www.harcourtschool.com/storytown

GO online

★ Leveled Readers Online Database
  Searchable by Genre, Skill, Vocabulary, Level, or Title
★ Student Activities and Teacher Resources, online

E L L

Social Studies

In Our Neighborhood
by Al Webster,
illustrated by Anna Godwin

Genre: Realistic Fiction

In Our Neighborhood

SUMMARY The young narrator introduces the new boy in the neighborhood, Jake, to neighbors and sights.

- Build Background
- Concept Vocabulary
- Scaffolded Language Development

Before Reading

BUILD BACKGROUND/SET PURPOSE Write the word *neighborhood*, and have children read it and tell what it means. Have them imagine that they are moving to a new neighborhood. What would they like to find there? Then guide children to preview the story and set a purpose for reading it.

Reading the Book

PAGES 4–6 DRAW CONCLUSIONS Why does the narrator think that Jake should get to know the neighborhood? (Possible responses: He and Jake are friends. He wants Jake to feel at home in the new neighborhood.)

PAGE 14 PLOT What has made Jake more comfortable in the neighborhood? (Possible responses: He has met people and seen places with his friend. He has a map to show his family what he has learned.)

REREAD FOR FLUENCY Have partners take turns reading the story a page at a time. Remind children to try to sound natural, like the boy who is telling about a walk through the neighborhood.

Scaffolded Language Development

(See inside back cover for teacher-led activity.)

Provide additional examples and explanation as needed.

LEVELED READERS TEACHER GUIDE

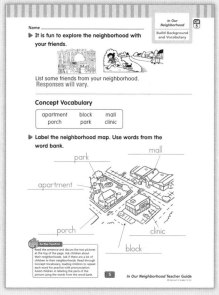

▲ Build Background and Vocabulary, p. 5

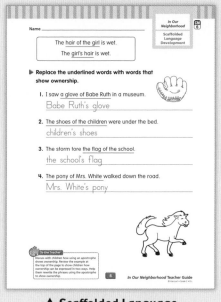

▲ Scaffolded Language Development, p. 6

THEME WRITING OVERVIEW

Reading-Writing Connection → Description

LESSON	FORM	TRAIT
21	Personal Narrative	Sentence Fluency
22	Fantasy Story	Sentence Fluency
23	Paragraph of Information	Word Choice
24	Paragraph That Compares	Word Choice
25	Student Choice: Revise and Publish	Sentence Fluency and Word Choice

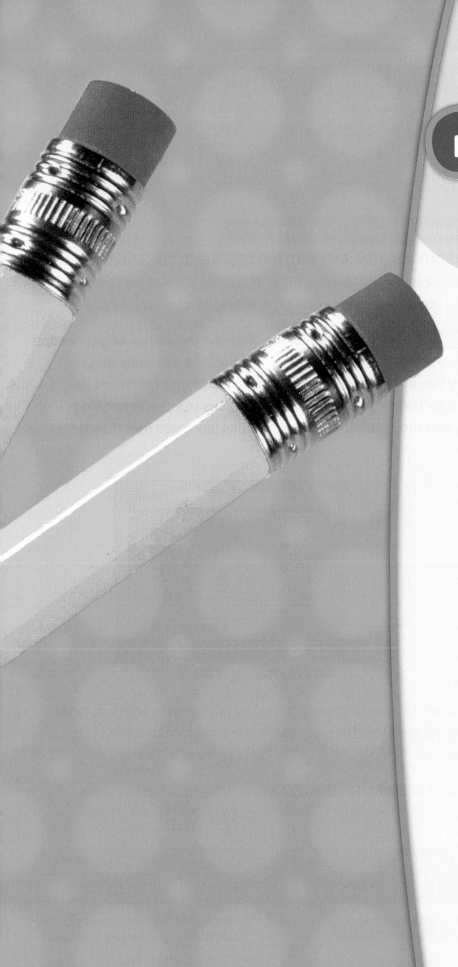

Reading-Writing Connection

Description

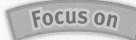
Focus on

Reading

Children will

- Use a literature model to generate ideas

- Select a topic

- Plan and draft a description

- Revise the description for word choice by replacing verbs with more lively action verbs

- Proofread the description for spelling of word endings, as well as for other conventions

- Publish a final version of the description

Set the Stage
Description

Objectives

- *To write a description*
- *To generate ideas for writing*
- *To learn about sensory details in a description*
- *To organize a descriptive paragraph*
- *To improve word choice using lively action verbs*
- *To combine sentences*
- *To spell word endings correctly*

Introduce the Writing Form

TALK ABOUT READING AND WRITING DESCRIPTIONS Tell children that they will be learning how to write a description. Point out the description in a familiar story by saying the following:

Think Aloud In "A Chair for My Mother," the author helped readers picture things clearly—the big jar of coins, the soft armchair, the scary fire, and more. The author chose words and sentences that describe clearly. Authors write descriptions to show what things look like, how they sound, what they feel like, and even how they taste and smell.

▲ *Student Edition, pp. 166–167*

Ask children to think of other stories they have read in which authors describe things. Have them share what they recall about the descriptions.

STAGES OF THE WRITING PROCESS Adjust pacing to meet children's needs. Guide them back and forth between the stages until the final product meets established criteria.

PREWRITE, p. T112

Writing Trait > Ideas
- Generating Ideas

Writing Trait > Word Choice
- Generating Sensory Details

DRAFT, p. T113

Writing Trait > Organization
- Drafting with a Plan

Writing Trait > Sentence Fluency
- Combining Sentences

Description

Use Text as a Model

DISCUSS DESCRIPTIVE LANGUAGE Tell children you will re-read page 171 of "A Chair for My Mother." Ask them to listen for words that help them see, hear, and touch the different things in the scene. After reading the page, draw a web on the board or use **Transparency GO9** to guide children in filling in a web like the one be-low. They may list sensory details from the description and add more based on what they can imagine.

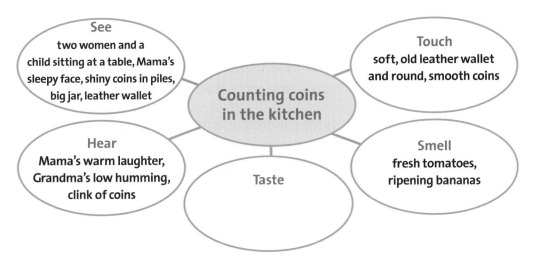

See
two women and a child sitting at a table, Mama's sleepy face, shiny coins in piles, big jar, leather wallet

Touch
soft, old leather wallet and round, smooth coins

Counting coins in the kitchen

Hear
Mama's warm laughter, Grandma's low humming, clink of coins

Taste

Smell
fresh tomatoes, ripening bananas

Tell children that when they plan their own descriptions, they should think about words that will help readers see, hear, touch, smell, and taste what is being described.

E L L

Clarify Concepts Use realia or pictures in magazines to focus on sensory details. Ask questions about what children can see, hear, touch, taste, and smell in selected pictures. Use adjectives in questions such as these: "Does this food taste spicy?" "Is the sky cloudy or bright?" "Is this a shiny table?" "Is this a noisy car?" Encourage children who can to respond with complete sentences.

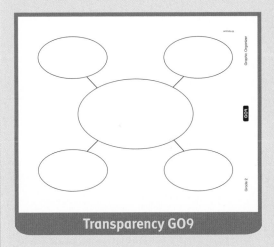

Transparency GO9

REVISE, p. T114	PROOFREAD, p. T114	PUBLISH, p. T115
Writing Trait ▶ Word Choice	**Writing Trait ▶ Conventions**	**Writing Trait ▶ Presentation**
• Revising a Draft for Lively Action Verbs	• Checking for Spelling	• Sharing the Description

Student Writing Model

Objective

To understand the stages of the writing process

Discuss the Model

READ PAGES 198–199 Have children open their *Student Editions* to page 198. Explain that this page shows a description that a child wrote. Have children read the description. Talk with them about what the writer described through seeing, hearing, touching, and smelling or tasting. Discuss the writing traits and how the writer made the writing strong and flowing using lively action verbs and sentence combining. Then have children read page 199.

Point out that Kaley, the writer, chose the topic of Grandma's rocking chair and then used a web to jot down ideas for her description. Tell children that they will choose a topic, generate ideas using a web, and make a plan before they write their descriptions.

READ PAGES 200–201 Have children turn to and read page 200 of their *Student Editions*. Explain that the plan on that page shows what the writer did next before beginning to write. Elicit that the writer planned her opening, middle, and closing.

Tell children they will follow the same steps that the writer did— making a web and a three-part plan, writing a draft, and revising the draft. Emphasize that writers often go through these stages to make sure the final description is as good as it can be. Then have children read page 201 and talk about the items in the checklist. Discuss why each one is important. Tell children to keep the checklist in mind as they write.

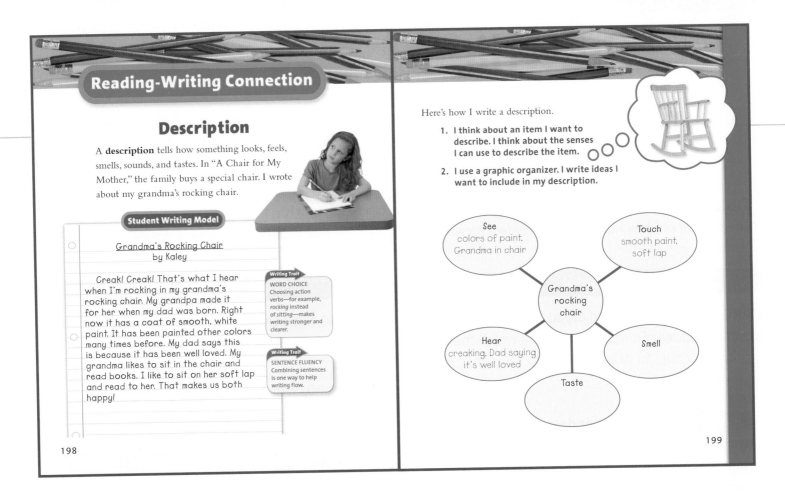

Reading-Writing Connection

Description

A **description** tells how something looks, feels, smells, sounds, and tastes. In "A Chair for My Mother," the family buys a special chair. I wrote about my grandma's rocking chair.

Student Writing Model

Grandma's Rocking Chair
by Kaley

Creak! Creak! That's what I hear when I'm rocking in my grandma's rocking chair. My grandpa made it for her when my dad was born. Right now it has a coat of smooth, white paint. It has been painted other colors many times before. My dad says this is because it has been well loved. My grandma likes to sit in the chair and read books. I like to sit on her soft lap and read to her. That makes us both happy!

Writing Trait
WORD CHOICE
Choosing action verbs—for example, *rocking* instead of *sitting*—makes writing stronger and clearer.

Writing Trait
SENTENCE FLUENCY
Combining sentences is one way to help writing flow.

198

Here's how I write a description.

1. I think about an item I want to describe. I think about the senses I can use to describe the item.

2. I use a graphic organizer. I write ideas I want to include in my description.

- See
colors of paint, Grandma in chair
- Touch
smooth paint, soft lap
- Grandma's rocking chair
- Hear
creaking, Dad saying it's well loved
- Smell
- Taste

199

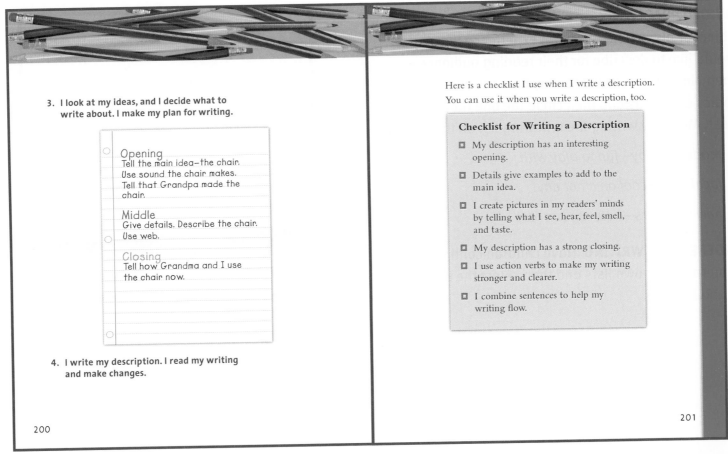

3. I look at my ideas, and I decide what to write about. I make my plan for writing.

Opening
Tell the main idea—the chair.
Use sound the chair makes.
Tell that Grandpa made the chair.

Middle
Give details. Describe the chair.
Use web.

Closing
Tell how Grandma and I use the chair now.

4. I write my description. I read my writing and make changes.

200

Here is a checklist I use when I write a description. You can use it when you write a description, too.

Checklist for Writing a Description

☐ My description has an interesting opening.

☐ Details give examples to add to the main idea.

☐ I create pictures in my readers' minds by telling what I see, hear, feel, smell, and taste.

☐ My description has a strong closing.

☐ I use action verbs to make my writing stronger and clearer.

☐ I combine sentences to help my writing flow.

201

Prewrite

GENERATING IDEAS
Writing Trait ➤ Ideas

Objective
To use what children know to generate ideas for writing

Teach/Model

USING EXPERIENCES Read aloud the second paragraph on *Student Edition* page 172, in which the author of *A Chair for My Mother,* describes the chair. Then say:

> **Think Aloud** The author describes a special armchair. Maybe it was a chair she had seen and remembered. Maybe it was like a chair she herself once sat in. Writers' own experiences help them describe things vividly for readers.

Apply to Writing

GUIDED PRACTICE Have children think about an object or place from their own experience that they would like to describe for their reading audience— their classmates. Children may find it useful to list topics and ideas and then circle the one they like best. Model by writing the following list on the board.

modeling clay—fun to play with

local pool—cool on a hot day

new sneakers—help me run fast

INDEPENDENT WRITING Have children continue to generate their own lists and then select the final topic of their choice.

GENERATING SENSORY DETAILS
Writing Trait ➤ Word Choice

Objective
To plan writing using sensory details

Teach/Model

USING THE SENSES Tell children that once they have chosen the object or place they will describe, they should fill in a web with sensory words. Say:

> **Think Aloud** I picture myself with what I am describing. What do I see, hear, feel, taste, smell?

Apply to Writing

GUIDED PRACTICE Remind children to keep to the topic they chose. Guide them to complete a web with sensory details for a class pet or plant, using **Transparency GO9.**

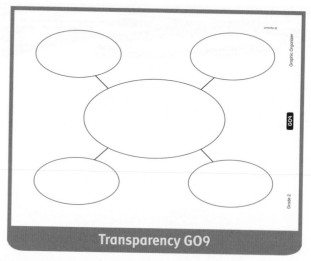

Transparency GO9

INDEPENDENT PRACTICE Confer with children as they generate sensory details for their own topic.

CONFERENCE

Use a Graphic Organizer Check that children understand that a web will help them identify details that appeal to the senses. Model for children, as necessary.

Draft

DRAFTING WITH A PLAN
Writing Trait > Organization

Objective
To draft using a plan

Teach/Model

USING A PLAN Display the web from p. T109 that you filled in with details from "A Chair for My Mother." Use it to talk about organizing details. Say:

Think Aloud If I were writing a description of this scene, I might begin like this: "The shiny coins gleam on the kitchen table. I like to hear them *clink clink clink* as I put them in piles."

Have children turn to and again skim the plan on page 200. Point out that the three main parts of a description are: (1) an opening that grabs readers' attention and tells what is described; (2) middle sentences with descriptive details; (3) a closing that will make the description memorable.

Apply to Writing

GUIDED PRACTICE Have children think of an interesting beginning for their description. Direct them to use their completed webs to draft a paragraph with an opening, a middle, and a closing.

INDEPENDENT PRACTICE Have children use their plan to begin drafting their description.

CONFERENCE

Drafting a Beginning Check that children understand how to take sensory details from their web and use them to write the beginning of their drafts.

COMBINING SENTENCES
Writing Trait > Sentence Fluency

Objective
To combine sentences

Teach/Model

LISTENING TO WRITING Tell children that writers listen for the sounds of their own words and sentences. Write the following sentences on the board and read them aloud:

The clay feels cool.
The clay feels smooth.

Think Aloud Short sentences with repeated words can sound choppy. I can combine ideas with the word *and* as I draft and later as I revise.

The clay feels cool and smooth.

Apply to Writing

GUIDED PRACTICE Guide children to combine two sentences they generate orally that have the same subject and verb.

INDEPENDENT PRACTICE Tell children to read their sentences softly to themselves as they write and ask themselves, "Can I combine these sentences to make the writing flow?"

E L L

Support Drafting Suggest that children draw a picture of something they like. Ask this question to help them get started writing: "Why do you like this [thing]?"

Revise/Proofread

REVISING A DRAFT
Writing Trait ▸ Word Choice

Objective
To revise for lively action verbs

Teach/Model

USING LIVELY VERBS Read aloud these sentences from the Read-Aloud story "The Just-Right Gift.":

> **Think Aloud** **Her shoulders drooped. Her head drooped. Then thump! She whammed right into a display table.**

Talk with children about how the lively action verbs *drooped* and *whammed* help readers imagine the scene.

Apply to Writing

GUIDED PRACTICE Read and discuss **Transparency LA43's** examples with children.

INDEPENDENT PRACTICE Have children reread their drafts to a partner and revise for livelier verbs.

Revise

Good
I hit the clay hard. I put a big piece between my hands. Then I make the clay into a long shape.

Better
I pound and smash the clay until it flattens. I break off a piece and squeeze it between my hands. Then I rub my hands fast. The clay warms and stretches. It grows into a long snake.

Grade 2, Theme 5   LA43   Reading-Writing Connection

Transparency LA43

CHECKING FOR SPELLING
Writing Trait ▸ Conventions

Objective
To spell word endings correctly

Review

PROOFREADING Discuss proofreading and the importance of checking for spelling errors.

Apply to Writing

GUIDED PRACTICE Review the spelling rules as you make these corrections together:

> happiest   sitting
> I am ~~happyest~~ when I am ~~siting~~ at a table
>
> shaping striped snakes
> ~~shapeing striped snaks~~ with clay.

INDEPENDENT PRACTICE Have children reread their descriptions to make sure words are spelled correctly. Tell them to proofread their drafts, mark corrections, and share their corrections with partners. Circulate and offer guidance as needed.

CONFERENCE

Proofreading Conference with children to be sure that they are checking for spelling errors in words ending in *-ed*, *-d*, *-s*, *-es*, *-er*, and *-est*.

Editing Marks

✗	delete text
∧	insert text
↶	move text
¶	new paragraph

Evaluate/Publish

PUBLISHING

Writing Trait > **Presentation**

Objective
To use available resources, including technology, to publish a description

Share the Writing

SHARE A CLEAN COPY Have children make and share a clean copy of their description. After children read their writing to the class, display it on a class bulletin board for others to read.

> I love to play with clay. I like the smooth, cool feeling of a bar of clay fresh from the box. It warms and softens in my hands. I can shape it into a perfect ball that rolls into a long curling snake.

GO online TECHNOLOGY

USE A COMPUTER Encourage children to use a computer to publish and share their final drafts. Show children the spell-checking feature of word-processing software. Explain that the software will show them most spelling errors.

PORTFOLIO OPPORTUNITY
Place children's descriptions in their portfolios as a record of their developing writing skills.

ASSESSMENT

SELF-ASSESSMENT CHECKLIST Talk about the checklist children used to write their description. Then have them self-assess their own writing in small groups and discuss with each other how they met each of the points. Discuss how each of these points supports the traits of writing and appears on rubrics.

- Includes an interesting opening, middle, and closing.
- Includes sensory words and other descriptive details.
- Includes action verbs.
- Combines sentences, when appropriate.

CONFERENCE

Using Rubrics Check that children are accurately self-assessing their descriptions. Help them find areas for improvement.

NOTE: A 4-point rubric appears on p. R8.

SCORING RUBRIC

	6	5	4	3	2	1
FOCUS	Completely focused, purposeful.	Focused on topic and purpose.	Generally focused on topic and purpose.	Somewhat focused on topic and purpose.	Related to topic but does not maintain focus.	Lacks focus and purpose.
ORGANIZATION	Ideas progress logically; paper conveys sense of completeness.	Organization; mostly clear, paper gives sense of completeness.	Organization mostly clear, but some lapses occur; may seem unfinished.	Some sense of organization; seems unfinished.	Little sense of organization.	Little or no sense of organization.
SUPPORT	Strong, specific details; clear, exact language; freshness of expression.	Strong, specific details; clear, exact language.	Adequate support and word choice.	Limited supporting details; limited word choice.	Few supporting details; limited word choice.	Little development; limited or unclear word choice.
CONVENTIONS	Varied sentences; few, if any, errors.	Varied sentences; few errors.	Some sentence variety; few errors.	Simple sentence structures; some errors.	Simple sentence structures; many errors.	Unclear sentence structures; many errors.

REPRODUCIBLE STUDENT RUBRICS for specific writing purposes and presentations are available on pp. R2–R8.

Writing on Demand

PREPARATION

Objectives
- *To write in response to an expository prompt*
- *To organize ideas using graphic organizers*
- *To revise and proofread for grammar, punctuation, capitalization, and spelling*

Prepare to Write

DISCUSS TIMED WRITING Tell children that in this theme they have written or are writing a description. Tell children that on a writing test, however, they may have only 30–45 minutes to write a description. Explain that on a timed test, they may be given an expository prompt directing them to define and describe something. Tell children that they will now practice writing a timed expository essay.

ANALYZE THE PROMPT Display **Transparency LA44.** Read the prompt with children. Explain that the topic of the prompt is something on a playground.

Elicit that the first part of this prompt tells them to limit themselves to a playground object. Something in the gym or their home would not be a topic for this essay. The prompt directs them to describe one thing. They must tell what the thing is and help their readers picture it clearly.

DISCUSS ORGANIZATION Tell children that to do well on a timed writing test such as this one, they must include the features of good writing:

- A sentence that tells what you are writing about.
- Other sentences that give details about the topic.
- Exact, vivid words that make the details clear to readers.
- A closing that sums up.

DISCUSS BUDGETING TIME Remind children that this timed writing allows 30 minutes to write. Recommend that they budget their time as follows:

Budgeting Time	
Prewrite	5 minutes
Draft	20 minutes
Revise & Proofread	5 minutes

Use the sample prompt on **Transparency LA44** to talk about what children might do in the Prewrite step to narrow their topic and make a plan. Then review what they would do in each of the other steps.

Explain that each writer might need to adjust the schedule and use more or less time for each step. Ask children to think about how much time they will need to complete each step.

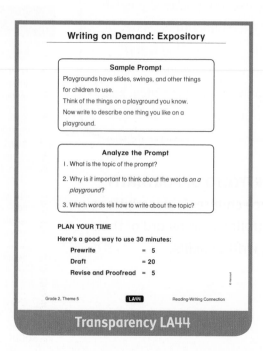

Transparency LA44

EXPOSITORY WRITING

Write to the Prompt

RESPOND TO A PROMPT Write the following prompt on the board and have children begin writing. Remind them when the first 5 minutes have passed. At the end of 30 minutes, ask children to stop writing.

> *Parks have trees, fields, benches, sidewalks, and sometimes playgrounds.*
>
> *Think of things in a park you know.*
>
> *Now write to describe one thing you like in a park.*

DISCUSSED TIMED WRITING Ask children to discuss their experiences during the timed writing assignment. Ask questions such as the following:

- Were you able to finish on time?
- Did you stick to your budgeted time for each step of the writing process?
- Does your writing do all the things the prompt asked you to do?
- In what ways was your prewriting helpful as you wrote your draft?
- What changes did you make?
- Did you have time to proofread to look for errors in punctuation, capitalization, grammar, and spelling?
- What could you do better the next time you write a timed essay?

EVALUATE Display the rubric on page R7 and discuss what is necessary for receiving a score of 6. Provide copies of the rubric for children who may have misplaced theirs, and have them work independently or in pairs to evaluate their papers.

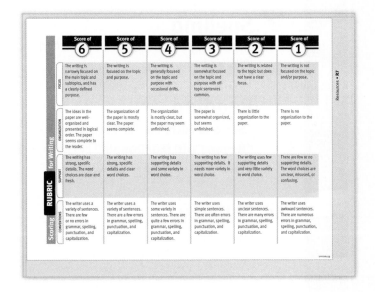

PORTFOLIO OPPORTUNITY
Children may keep their writing in portfolios and compare them with earlier expository writing to assess their progress.

Lesson 22

WEEK AT A GLANCE

 Phonics
r-Controlled Vowel /ôr/*or, ore, our*
Syllable Patterns V/CV and VC/V

 Spelling
store, fork, pour, score, your, chore, short, more, four, sore

Reading
"Serious Farm" by Tim Egan FANTASY
"Beyond Old MacDonald" by Charley Hoce POETRY

 Fluency
Expression

 Comprehension
 Plot
Compare and Contrast
 Use Story Structure

 Robust Vocabulary
acquired, assumed, serious, extremely, admit, barely, hilarious, witty, absurd, attempt

 Grammar [Quick Write]
Subject-Verb Agreement

Writing
Form: Fantasy
Trait: Sentence Fluency

Weekly Lesson Test

 = Focus Skill   = Focus Strategy   = Tested Skill

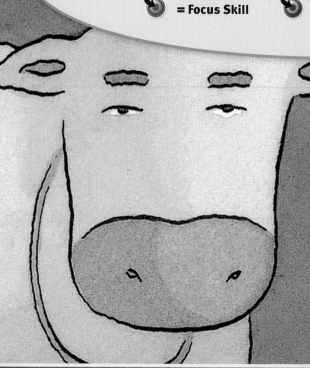

One stop *for all* *your* **Digital** *needs*

Lesson 22
Digital
CLASSROOM

GO online www.harcourtschool.com/storytown
To go along with your print program

FOR THE TEACHER

Prepare Professional Development

 Videos for Podcasting

Plan & Organize Online TE & Planning Resources*

Teach Transparencies

access from Online TE

Assess Online Assessment*

with Student Tracking System and Prescriptions

FOR THE STUDENT

Read  Student eBook*

 Strategic Intervention Interactive Reader

 Leveled Readers

Practice & Apply Splash into Phonics CD-ROM

 Also available on CD-ROM

Literature Resources

STUDENT EDITION

 eBook STUDENT EDITION

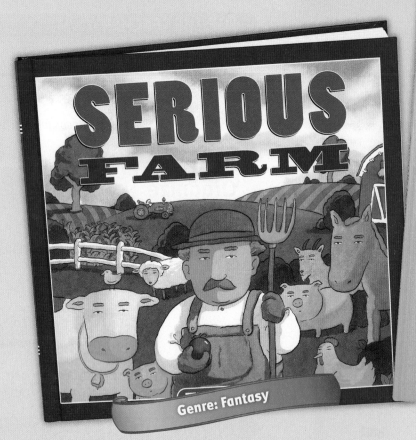

Genre: Fantasy

Beyond Old MacDonald
Funny Poems from Down on the Farm

By Charley Hoce

Genre: Poetry

 ◀ **Audiotext** *Student Edition selections are available on Audiotext Grade 2, CD 5*

 **Accelerated Reader** ◀ *Practice Quizzes for the Selection*

THEME CONNECTION: BETTER TOGETHER
Comparing Fantasy and Poetry

Paired Selections

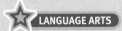 **SOCIAL STUDIES** **Serious Farm, pp. 208–233**

SUMMARY Farmer Fred takes his work on the farm very seriously. The animals decide to try to make the farm more fun and set out to find ways to make Farmer Fred laugh.

⭐ **LANGUAGE ARTS** **Beyond Old MacDonald, pp. 234–235**

SUMMARY Humorous poems about life on the farm

Support for Differentiated Instruction

 LEVELED READERS

   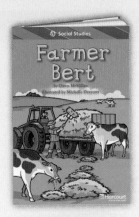

● **BELOW-LEVEL**　　● **ON-LEVEL**　　● **ADVANCED**　　**ELL**

LEVELED PRACTICE

◀ **Strategic Intervention Resource Kit, Lesson 22**

◀ **Strategic Intervention Interactive Reader, Lesson 22**

Strategic Intervention Interactive Reader Online

◀ **ELL Extra Support Kit, Lesson 22**

◀ **Challenge Resource Kit, Lesson 22**

● **BELOW-LEVEL**
Extra Support Copying Masters, pp. 170, 172–176

● **ON-LEVEL**
Practice Book, pp. 170–177

● **ADVANCED**
Challenge Copying Masters, pp. 170, 172–176

ADDITIONAL RESOURCES

cow　farm

• Decodable Book 18
• Spelling Practice Book, pp. 70–72
• Grammar Practice Book, pp. 77–80
• Reading Transparencies R113–R119
• Language Arts Transparencies LA45–LA46
• Test Prep System
◀ **Literacy Center Kit, Cards 106–110**
• Sound/Spelling Cards
◀ **Fluency Builders**
◀ **Picture Card Collection**
• Read-Aloud Anthology, p. 80–83

ASSESSMENT

✓ **Monitor Progress**

✓ **Weekly Lesson Tests, Lesson 22**
• Comprehension　• Robust Vocabulary
• Phonics and Spelling　• Grammar
• Focus Skill　• Compare and Contrast

 www.harcourtschool.com/ storytown
Online Assessment
Also available on CD-ROM—Exam View®

Suggested Lesson Planner

GO online Online TE & Planning Resources

	Day 1	Day 2
Step 1 Whole Group		
Daily Routines • Oral Language • Read Aloud • High-Frequency Words	**QUESTION OF THE DAY,** p. T130 *Which do you like better—serious stories or funny stories?* **READ ALOUD,** p. T131 *Transparency R113: Max and Ted* **WORD WALL,** p. T131	**QUESTION OF THE DAY,** p. T142 *What would you do if you saw a purple cow?* **READ ALOUD,** p. T143 *Big Book of Rhymes and Poems, "The Purple Cow"* **WORD WALL,** p. T143
Word Work • phonics • Spelling	, p. T132 Introduce: *r-Controlled Vowel /ôr/or, ore, our* **SPELLING,** p. T135 Pretest: *store, fork, pour, score, your, chore, short, more, four, sore*	, p. T144 Review: *r-Controlled Vowel /ôr/or, ore, our* **WORDS IN CONTEXT,** p. T145 Apply Phonics
Skills and Strategies • Reading • Fluency • Comprehension • Build Robust Vocabulary	**READING/COMPREHENSION,** p. T136 Introduce: Plot **LISTENING COMPREHENSION,** p. T138 Read-Aloud: "The Rooster That Crowed at Nightfall" **FLUENCY,** p. T138 Focus: Expression **BUILD ROBUST VOCABULARY,** p. T139 *Words from the Read-Aloud*	**BUILD ROBUST VOCABULARY,** p. T146 *Words from the Selection* Word Champion, p. T147 **READING,** p. T148 "Serious Farm" *Options for Reading* **COMPREHENSION,** p. T148 Introduce: Use Story Structure ▲ Student Edition **RETELLING/FLUENCY,** p. T162 Expression **BUILD ROBUST VOCABULARY,** p. T163 *Words About the Selection*

 Step 2 Small Groups

Suggestions for Differentiated Instruction (See pp. T124–T125.)

 Step 3 Whole Group

Language Arts
• Grammar *Quick Write*
• Writing

GRAMMAR, p. T140 Introduce: Subject–Verb Agreement ***Daily Proofreading*** Tims apple is the smaller of all. (Tim's, smallest) **WRITING,** p. T141 Introduce: Fantasy Writing Trait: Sentence Fluency *Writing Prompt* Write a sentence about an animal that you would like to talk to and tell why.	**GRAMMAR,** p. T164 Review: Subject–Verb Agreement ***Daily Proofreading*** Madison got two new puppys? (puppies.) **WRITING,** p. T165 Review: Fantasy Writing Trait: Sentence Fluency *Writing Prompt* Tell about a favorite fantasy story that you have read.

 = Focus Skill   = Focus Strategy    = Tested Skill

Skills at a Glance

phonics	Comprehension	Fluency	Vocabulary
• *r*-Controlled Vowel /ôr/or, ore, our • Syllable Patterns V/CV and VC/V	**Focus Skill** Plot **Focus Strategy** Use Story Structure	Expression	**ROBUST:** *acquired, assumed, serious, extremely, admit, barely, hilarious, witty, absurd, attempt*

Day 3

QUESTION OF THE DAY, p. T166
What could make something turn purple?

READ ALOUD, p. T167
Big Book of Rhymes and Poems, "The Purple Cow"

WORD WALL, p. T167

  , p. T168
Review: *r*-Controlled Vowel /ôr/or, ore, our

 SPELLING, p. T169
State the Generalization

FLUENCY, p. T170
Expression: "Serious Farm"

 COMPREHENSION, p. T171
 Review: Plot
Review: Compare and Contrast
Paired Selection: "Beyond Old MacDonald"

▲ Student Edition

CONNECTIONS, p. T176

 BUILD ROBUST VOCABULARY, p. T178
Review

Day 4

QUESTION OF THE DAY, p. T182
What might surprise a farmer after he or she planted seeds?

READ ALOUD, p. T183
Big Book of Rhymes and Poems, "A Young Farmer of Leeds"

WORD WALL, p. T183

 , p. T184
Introduce: Syllable Patterns V/CV and VC/V

 SPELLING, p. T185
Review Spelling Words

FLUENCY, p. T186
Expression: "Serious Farm"

 COMPREHENSION, p. T187
Review: Plot

▲ Student Edition

BUILD ROBUST VOCABULARY, p. T188
Review

Day 5

QUESTION OF THE DAY, p. T192
How can you tell if a poem is meant to be silly?

READ ALOUD, p. T193
Big Book of Rhymes and Poems, "A Young Farmer of Leeds"

WORD WALL, p. T193

 , p. T194
Review: Syllable Patterns V/CV and VC/V

 SPELLING, p. T195
Posttest

FLUENCY, p. T196
Expression: "Serious Farm"

COMPREHENSION, p. T197
Review: Plot
Read-Aloud: "The Rooster That Crowed at Nightfall"

▲ Student Edition

BUILD ROBUST VOCABULARY, p. T198
Cumulative Review

● BELOW-LEVEL ● ON-LEVEL ● ADVANCED 🅔🅛🅛

 GRAMMAR, p. T180
Review: Subject–Verb Agreement

Daily Proofreading
Ms. Greens birthday is in march.
(Green's, March)

 WRITING, p. T181
Review: Fantasy
Writing Trait: Sentence Fluency

Writing Prompt *Write a sentence to tell what part of "Serious Farm" seems the most unreal to you.*

 GRAMMAR, p. T190
Review: Subject–Verb Agreement

Daily Proofreading
my mother rushs to work.
(My, rushes)

 WRITING, p. T191
Review: Fantasy
Writing Trait: Sentence Fluency

Writing Prompt *Write about how you got the idea for your main character or characters in your story.*

 GRAMMAR, p. T200
Review: Subject–Verb Agreement

Daily Proofreading
Did you see Karlas new book.
(Karla's, book?)

 WRITING, p. T201
Review: Fantasy
Writing Trait: Sentence Fluency

Writing Prompt *Write a list of ideas about a new topic of your choice for writing.*

Suggested Small-Group Planner

45-60+ Minutes

	Day 1	Day 2

  BELOW-LEVEL
15-20+ Minutes

Day 1

Teacher-Directed
Leveled Reader:
"No More Fish!,"
p. T202
Before Reading

Independent
⭐ Listening/Speaking Center,
p. T128
Extra Support Copying Masters, pp. 170, 172

▲ Leveled Reader

Day 2

Teacher-Directed
Student Edition:
"Serious Farm,"
p. T148

Independent
⭐ Reading Center,
p. T128
Extra Support Copying Masters, pp. 173–174

▲ Student Edition

  ON-LEVEL
15-20+ Minutes

Day 1

Teacher-Directed
Leveled Reader:
"Monkey Business,"
p. T203
Before Reading

Independent
⭐ Reading Center, p. T128
Practice Book, pp. 170, 172

▲ Leveled Reader

Day 2

Teacher-Directed
Student Edition:
"Serious Farm,"
p. T148

Independent
⭐ Letters and Sounds
Center, p. T129
Practice Book, pp. 173–174

▲ Student Edition

  ADVANCED
15-20+ Minutes

Day 1

Teacher-Directed
Leveled Reader:
"Puppy Tricks,"
p. T204
Before Reading

Independent
⭐ Letters and Sounds Center,
p. T129
Challenge Copying Masters, pp. 170, 172

▲ Leveled Reader

Day 2

Teacher-Directed
Leveled Reader:
"Puppy Tricks,"
p. T204
Read the Book

Independent
⭐ Word Work Center, p. T129
Challenge Copying Masters, pp. 173–174

▲ Leveled Reader

 ELL

English-Language Learners

In addition to the small-group instruction above, use the ELL Extra Support Kit to promote language development.

LANGUAGE DEVELOPMENT SUPPORT
Teacher-Directed
ELL TG, Day 1
Independent
ELL Copying Masters, Lesson 22

▲ ELL Student Handbook

LANGUAGE DEVELOPMENT SUPPORT
Teacher-Directed
ELL TG, Day 2
Independent
ELL Copying Masters, Lesson 22

▲ ELL Student Handbook

Intervention

▲ Strategic Intervention Resource Kit

▲ Strategic Intervention Interactive Reader

Strategic Intervention TG, Day 1
Strategic Intervention Practice Book, Lesson 22

Strategic Intervention TG, Day 2
Strategic Intervention Interactive Reader, Lesson 22

▲ Strategic Intervention Interactive Reader

MONITOR PROGRESS

Small-Group Instruction

Comprehension	Phonics	Comprehension	Fluency	Robust Vocabulary	Language Arts Checkpoint
Focus Skill Plot pp. S18–S19	*r*-Controlled Vowel /ôr/*or*, *ore* pp. S14–S15	Compare and Contrast pp. S20–S21	Expression pp. S16–S17	*acquired, assumed, serious, extremely, admit, barely, hilarious, witty, absurd, attempt* pp. S22–S23	**Grammar:** Subject-Verb Agreement **Writing:** Story: Fantasy pp. S24–S25

Day 3

Teacher-Directed
Leveled Reader:
"No More Fish!,"
p. T202
Read the Book

Independent
 Word Work Center, p. T129
Extra Support Copying Masters, p. 175

▲ Leveled Reader

Teacher-Directed
Leveled Reader:
"Monkey Business,"
p. T203
Read the Book

Independent
 Writing Center, p. T129
Practice Book, p. 175

▲ Leveled Reader

Teacher-Directed
Leveled Reader:
"Puppy Tricks,"
p. T204
Think Critically

Independent
 Listening/Speaking Center,
p. T128
Challenge Copying Masters, p. 175

▲ Leveled Reader

LANGUAGE DEVELOPMENT SUPPORT

Teacher-Directed
Leveled Reader: "Farmer Bert,"
p. T205
Before Reading; Read the Book
ELL TG, Day 3

Independent
ELL Copying Masters, Lesson 22

▲ Leveled Reader

Strategic Intervention TG, Day 3
Strategic Intervention Interactive Reader, Lesson 22
Strategic Intervention Practice Book, Lesson 22

▲ Strategic Intervention Interactive Reader

Day 4

Teacher-Directed
Leveled Reader:
"No More Fish!,"
p. T202
Reread for Fluency

Independent
 Letters and Sounds Center,
p. T129

▲ Leveled Reader

Teacher-Directed
Leveled Reader:
"Monkey Business,"
p. T203
Reread for Fluency

Independent
 Word Work Center, p. T129

▲ Leveled Reader

Teacher-Directed
Leveled Reader:
"Puppy Tricks," p. T204
Reread for Fluency

Independent
 Writing Center, p. T129
Self-Selected Reading:
Classroom Library Collection

▲ Leveled Reader

LANGUAGE DEVELOPMENT SUPPORT

Teacher-Directed
Leveled Reader: "Farmer Bert,"
p. T205
Reread for Fluency
ELL TG, Day 4

Independent
ELL Copying Masters, Lesson 22

▲ Leveled Reader

Strategic Intervention TG, Day 4
Strategic Intervention Interactive Reader, Lesson 22

▲ Strategic Intervention Interactive Reader

Day 5

Teacher-Directed
Leveled Reader:
"No More Fish!,"
p. T202
Think Critically

Independent
 Writing Center, p. T129
Leveled Reader: Reread for Fluency
Extra Support Copying Masters, p. 176

▲ Leveled Reader

Teacher-Directed
Leveled Reader:
"Monkey Business," p. T203
Think Critically

Independent
 Listening/Speaking Center,
p. T128
Leveled Reader: Reread for Fluency
Practice Book, p. 176

▲ Leveled Reader

Teacher-Directed
Leveled Reader:
"Puppy Tricks," p. T204
Reread for Fluency

Independent
 Reading Center, p. T128
Leveled Reader: Reread for Fluency
Self-Selected Reading:
Classroom Library Collection
Challenge Copying Masters, p. 176

▲ Leveled Reader

LANGUAGE DEVELOPMENT SUPPORT

Teacher-Directed
Leveled Reader: "Farmer Bert,"
p. T205
Think Critically
ELL TG, Day 5

Independent
Leveled Reader: Reread for Fluency
ELL Copying Masters, Lesson 22

▲ Leveled Reader

Strategic Intervention TG, Day 5
Strategic Intervention Interactive Reader, Lesson 22

▲ Strategic Intervention Interactive Reader

Leveled Readers & Leveled Practice
Reinforcing Skills and Strategies

LEVELED READERS SYSTEM

- **Leveled Readers**
- **Leveled Readers, CD**
- **Leveled Readers Teacher Guides**
  - *Comprehension*
  - *Vocabulary*
  - *Oral Reading Fluency Assessment*
- **Response Activities**
- **Leveled Readers Assessment**

See pages T202–T205 for lesson plans.

BELOW-LEVEL

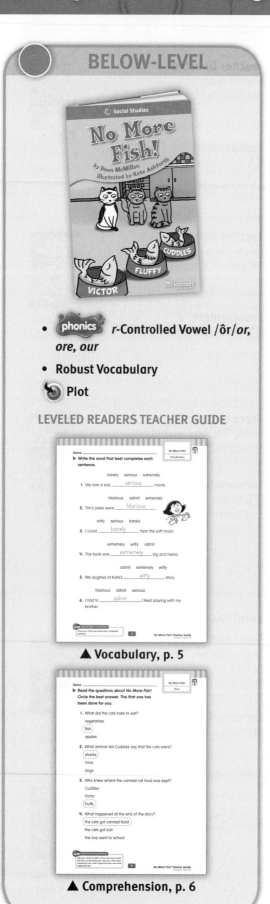

- **phonics** *r*-Controlled Vowel /ôr/*or, ore, our*
- **Robust Vocabulary**
- Plot

LEVELED READERS TEACHER GUIDE

▲ Vocabulary, p. 5

▲ Comprehension, p. 6

ON-LEVEL

- **phonics** *r*-Controlled Vowel /ôr/*or, ore, our*
- **Robust Vocabulary**
- Plot

LEVELED READERS TEACHER GUIDE

▲ Vocabulary, p. 5

▲ Comprehension, p. 6

www.harcourtschool.com/storytown

GO online

★ **Leveled Readers, Online Database**
Searchable by Genre, Skill, Vocabulary, Level, or Title
★ **Student Activities and Teacher Resources, online**

ADVANCED

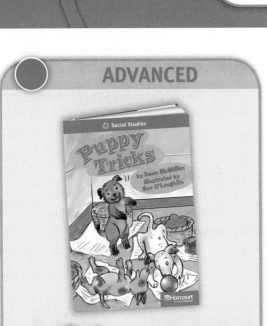

- **phonics** *r*-Controlled Vowel /ôr/*or, ore, our*
- **Robust Vocabulary**
- 🔄 **Plot**

LEVELED READERS TEACHER GUIDE

▲ **Vocabulary, p. 5**

▲ **Comprehension, p. 6**

ELL

- **Build Background**
- **Concept Vocabulary**
- **Scaffolded Language Development**

LEVELED READERS TEACHER GUIDE

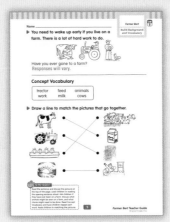

▲ **Build Background, p. 5**

▲ **Scaffolded Language Development, p. 6**

CLASSROOM LIBRARY

for Self-Selected Reading

EASY
▲ *Treasure Map* **by Stuart J. Murphy.**
FICTION

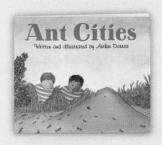

AVERAGE
▲ *Ant Cities* **by Arthur Dorros.**
NONFICTION

CHALLENGE
▲ *A Log's Life* **by Wendy Pfeffer.**
NONFICTION

▲ **Classroom Library Books**
Teacher Guide, Lesson 22

Literacy Centers

15 Min. each

Management Support

While you provide direct instruction to individuals or small groups, other children can work on literacy center activities.

▲ **Literacy Center Pocket Chart**

My Activities

✓ Put a check mark next to the activities you complete.

Literacy Activities
- ☐ Listening/Speaking Read with a Recording
- ☐ Reading Read and Respond
- ☐ Writing Plan a Fantasy Story
- ☐ Word Work Alphabetize Words
- ☐ Letters and Sounds Write Rhymes

Leveled Readers
- ☐ Rereading for Fluency
- ☐ Activities (See inside back cover.)

Practice Pages
- ☐ pages 170–177

Lesson 22   55   Teacher Resource Book

▲ **Teacher Resource Book, p. 55**

Homework for the Week

TEACHER RESOURCE BOOK, PAGE 25

The *Homework Copying Master* provides activities to complete for each day of the week.

GO online www.harcourtschool.com/ storytown

LISTENING/SPEAKING

Read with a Recording

Objective
To develop fluency by reading and recording a familiar story

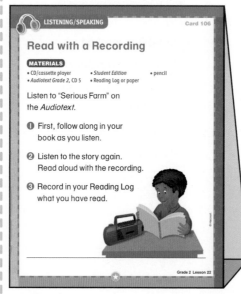

LISTENING/SPEAKING   Card 106

Read with a Recording

MATERIALS
- CD/cassette player
- *Student Edition*
- pencil
- *Audiotext Grade 2, CD 5*
- Reading Log or paper

Listen to "Serious Farm" on the *Audiotext*.

❶ First, follow along in your book as you listen.

❷ Listen to the story again. Read aloud with the recording.

❸ Record in your Reading Log what you have read.

Grade 2 Lesson 22

⭐ **Literacy Center Kit • Card 106**

READING

Read and Respond

Objective
To develop comprehension by rereading familiar stories and responding to them

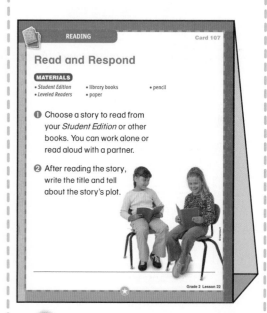

READING   Card 107

Read and Respond

MATERIALS
- *Student Edition*
- library books
- pencil
- *Leveled Readers*
- paper

❶ Choose a story to read from your *Student Edition* or other books. You can work alone or read aloud with a partner.

❷ After reading the story, write the title and tell about the story's plot.

Grade 2 Lesson 22

⭐ **Literacy Center Kit • Card 107**

WRITING
Plan a Fantasy Story

Objective
To generate ideas for a fantasy story

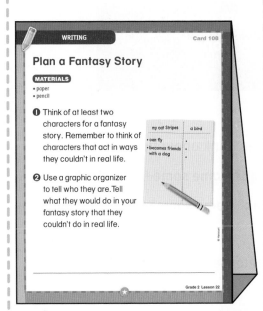

WRITING — Card 108

Plan a Fantasy Story

MATERIALS
• paper
• pencil

❶ Think of at least two characters for a fantasy story. Remember to think of characters that act in ways they couldn't in real life.

❷ Use a graphic organizer to tell who they are. Tell what they would do in your fantasy story that they couldn't do in real life.

Grade 2 Lesson 22

⭐ **Literacy Center Kit** • Card 108

my cat Stripes	a bird
• can fly	• helps animals escape from zoo
• becomes friends with a dog	• can talk

WORD WORK
Alphabetize Words

Objective
To practice using Vocabulary Words

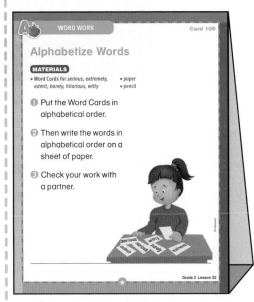

WORD WORK — Card 109

Alphabetize Words

MATERIALS
• Word Cards for *serious, extremely, admit, barely, hilarious, witty*
• paper
• pencil

❶ Put the Word Cards in alphabetical order.

❷ Then write the words in alphabetical order on a sheet of paper.

❸ Check your work with a partner.

Grade 2 Lesson 22

⭐ **Literacy Center Kit** • Card 109

serious

extremely

admit

barely

hilarious

witty

LETTERS AND SOUNDS
Write Rhymes

Objective
To read and write words using known letter/sound correspondences

LETTERS AND SOUNDS — Card 110

Write Rhymes

MATERIALS
• paper
• pencils

❶ With a partner, write a list of words that use *or, ore,* or *our* to stand for the vowel sound that you hear in *store*.

❷ Work together to write some rhymes. Have each line end with one of the words on your list.

❸ Share your rhymes with another pair of partners.

Grade 2 Lesson 22

⭐ **Literacy Center Kit** • Card 110

When I am done doing this chore,
I'm sure my mother will think of more!
When I was only four,
I went to my first toy store.

Day at a Glance

Day 1

 phonics and Spelling
- Introduce: *r*-Controlled Vowel /ôr/ *or, ore, our*
- Pretest

Reading/ Comprehension

 Review: Plot, *Student Edition*, pp. 204–205
- *Read-Aloud Anthology:* "The Rooster That Crowed At Nightfall"

Fluency
- Model Oral Fluency

Robust Vocabulary
Words from the Read-Aloud
- Introduce: *acquired, assumed*

Grammar [Quick Write]
- Introduce: Subject-Verb Agreement

Writing
- Fantasy

Warm-Up Routines

 Oral Language

Objective *To listen attentively and respond appropriately to oral communication*

Question of the Day

Which do you like better—serious stories or funny stories?

Use the following prompts to help children think about fiction stories.

- **Do you like stories that make you laugh? Name some funny stories.**

- **Do you like stories that make you think? Name some stories that made you think about things.**

Have children complete the following sentence frame to tell about stories they like.

I like _____ stories because _____.

Read Aloud

Objective *To listen for a purpose*

TRANSPARENCY Read aloud the story "Max and Ted" on **Transparency R113**. Use the following steps:

- **Set a purpose for listening.** Tell children to listen to find out who Max and Ted are, and what problem they have.

- **Model fluent reading.** Read the story aloud. Tell children that good readers use their voices to add expression as they read.

- **Discuss the article.** Ask: **Why does Max go on a cruise?** (He is unhappy because Ted is too busy for him.)

Plot

Max and Ted

Max and Ted were best friends. They played in the park together and went on long hikes. They talked about everything. There was one thing that made Ted and Max's friendship different, though. Max was Ted's dog.

Max helped Ted with his homework, and brought it to school when Ted left it at home. He even made sure Ted remembered to brush his teeth. There came a time, though, when Ted forgot what a good friend Max was. Ted got so busy with soccer that he didn't have time for Max. Max was lonely and unhappy.

Max took off on a two-week cruise. He had the time of his life, but he remembered to send a postcard to Ted.

Ted had no idea where Max went. He searched everywhere. Then, one day, he got Max's postcard. It said: "Miss me yet? I'll see you soon. Your best buddy, Max."

When Max came home Ted hugged Max. Max wagged his tail.

"Max!" Ted cried. "I'm so glad you're back! How can I make it up to you?"

"Don't worry about it," said Max. "Let me tell you about my trip."

Grade 2, Lesson 22 **R113** Comprehension

Transparency R113

Word Wall

Objective *To read high-frequency words*

REVIEW HIGH-FREQUENCY WORDS Review the words *woods, idea, laughed, though, worry, care, sign,* and *brought* as well as other previously learned high-frequency words. Hold up a word card at random, and ask children to read the word. Flip through the word cards several times.

woods idea laughed though

worry care sign brought

r-Controlled Vowel /ôr/ *or, ore*

our  *and Spelling*

Objectives

- *To recognize and blend the r-controlled vowel sound /ôr/*
- *To read words with /ôr/or, ore, our, and other known letter-sounds*
- *To use /ôr/ or, ore, our, and other known letter-sounds to spell words*

Skill Trace

 Tested **r-Controlled Vowel /ôr/ or, ore, our**

Introduce	Grade 1
Reintroduce	**T132–T135**
Reteach	S14–S15
Review	T144–T145, T168–T169, T412
Test	Theme 5
Maintain	Theme 6, T268

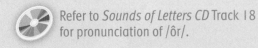 Refer to *Sounds of Letters CD* Track 18 for pronunciation of /ôr/.

Connect Letters to Sounds

WARM UP WITH PHONEMIC AWARENESS   Say the words *fork, court,* and *horse.* Have children say the words. Say: **The words *fork, court,* and *horse* have the /ôr/ sound in the middle.** Then say the words *more, your,* and *store,* and have children repeat. Say: **The words *more, your,* and *store* have the /ôr/ sound at the end.** Have children say /ôr/ several times.

Routine Card 1 **CONNECT LETTERS AND SOUNDS**   Display the *Sound/Spelling Card* for /ôr/ *or, ore, our.* Point to the letters *or* and review their letter/sound correspondence. Say: **The letters *or* can stand for the /ôr/ sound, the sound in *corn*.** Touch the letters several times, and have children say /ôr/ each time. Repeat with *ore* and *our.*

▲ **Sound/Spelling Card**

5-DAY PHONICS

DAY 1	Introduce /ôr/ *or, ore, our*
DAY 2	Word Building with /ôr/ *or, ore, our*
DAY 3	Word Building with /ôr/ *or, ore, our*
DAY 4	V/CV and VC/V; Review /ôr/ *or, ore, our*
DAY 5	V/CV and VC/V; Review /ôr/ *or, ore, our*

Work with Patterns

REINFORCE /ôr/or Write the following words on the board. Point out that each word has the letters *or*. Read each word, and then have children read it with you.

pork	sort
port	cork
fort	torn
scorn	born

REINFORCE /ôr/ore Repeat the procedure with the following words that have the letters *ore*.

shore	bore
core	sore
ignore	explore

REINFORCE /ôr/our Repeat the procedure with the following words that have the letters *our*.

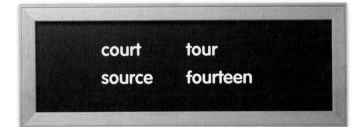

court	tour
source	fourteen

ADVANCED

Explore Rhyming Words Invite children to explore words with the /ôr/ sound. Point out that some rhyming words with the /ôr/ sound may have very different spellings, such as *cord, chord, bored,* and *board*.

r-Controlled Vowel /ôr/ *or, ore, our*

 *phonics* and Spelling

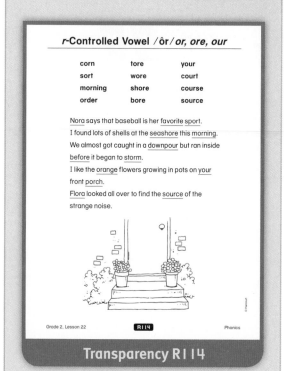

r-Controlled Vowel /ôr/ *or, ore, our*

corn	tore	your
sort	wore	court
morning	shore	course
order	bore	source

Nora says that baseball is her favorite sport.

I found lots of shells at the seashore this morning.

We almost got caught in a downpour but ran inside before it began to storm.

I like the orange flowers growing in pots on your front porch.

Flora looked all over to find the source of the strange noise.

Grade 2, Lesson 22   **R114**   Phonics

Transparency R114

Reading Words

GUIDED PRACTICE   Display **Transparency R114** or write the words and sentences on the board. Point to the word *corn.* Read the word, and then have children read it with you.

INDEPENDENT PRACTICE   Point to the remaining words in the top portion and have children read them. Then have children read aloud the sentences and identify words with /ôr/*or*, /ôr/*ore*, or/ôr/*our*.

Decodable Books

Additional Decoding Practice

- **Phonics**
  r-Controlled Vowel /or/*or, ore, our*
- **Decodable Words**
- **High-Frequency Words**
  See lists in *Decodable Book 18.*

  See also *Decodable Books,*
  online (Take-Home Version).

▲ **Decodable Book 18**
"Mort's Sports Store"
and "Courtyards"

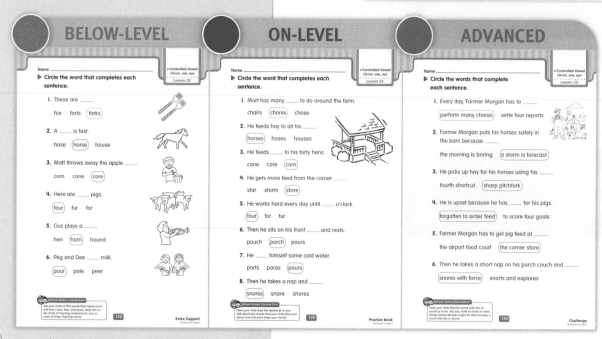

▲ **Extra Support, p. 170**   ▲ **Practice Book, p. 170**   ▲ **Challenge, p. 170**

ELL

- Group children according to academic levels, and assign one of the pages on the left.

- Clarify any unfamiliar concepts as necessary. See *ELL Teacher Guide* Lesson 22 for support in scaffolding instruction.

5-DAY SPELLING

DAY 1	Pretest
DAY 2	Word Building
DAY 3	State the Generalization
DAY 4	Review
DAY 5	Posttest

Introduce Spelling Words

PRETEST Say the first word and read the dictation sentence. Repeat the word as children write it. Write the word on the board and have children check their spelling. Tell them to circle the word if they spelled it correctly or write it correctly if they did not. Repeat for words 2–10.

Words with /ôr/ *or, ore, our*

1.	store	Margo bought lemons at the grocery **store.**
2.	fork	Please use a **fork** to eat your meat.
3.	pour	Will you **pour** a cup of milk for Rob?
4.	score	It's exciting to watch the players **score** a goal.
5.	your	Can I borrow **your** sunglasses?
6.	chore	Making my bed is my least favorite **chore.**
7.	short	When I was three, I was too **short** to reach the table.
8.	more	May I have some **more** ice cream?
9.	four	We need **four** people to play this game.
10.	sore	My feet were **sore** after the long hike.

ADVANCED

Challenge Words Use the challenge words in these dictation sentences.

11.	ignore	I had to **ignore** the noise to do my homework.
12.	important	Mr. Mitchell has something **important** to say.
13.	factory	We visited the jellybean **factory** on our vacation.
14.	explore	Manny likes to take hikes to **explore** the forest.
15.	fourteen	Next week, my sister will be **fourteen** years old.

Spelling Words

1.	store	6.	chore
2.	fork	7.	short
3.	pour	8.	more*
4.	score	9.	four
5.	your	10.	sore

Challenge Words

11.	ignore	14.	explore
12.	important	15.	fourteen
13.	factory		

* Word from "Serious Farm"

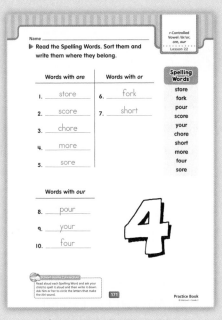

▲ Practice Book, p. 171

Plot

Comprehension

Objective

• *To identify the plot of a story*

Daily Comprehension

 Plot

DAY 1:	Review Plot *Student Edition*
DAY 2:	Review Plot *Student Edition*
DAY 3:	Review Plot *Student Edition*
DAY 4:	Review Plot *Transparency*
DAY 5:	Review Plot *Read-Aloud Anthology*

✓ MONITOR PROGRESS

Plot

IF children have difficulty identifying plot,	**THEN** guide them to identify the plot of a familiar story.

Small-Group Instruction, pp. S18–S19:

● **BELOW-LEVEL:** Reteach
● **ON-LEVEL:** Reinforce
● **ADVANCED:** Extend

Review

REVIEW PLOT   Have children read *Student Edition* page 204. Model how to determine a story's plot.

(Think Aloud)   **As I read a story, I think about what the problem is that the characters face. What events show how the characters solve their problem? Identifying important events helps me understand the story.**

Practice/Apply

GUIDED PRACTICE   Display a story that children have read. Guide them to tell what happens in the beginning, middle, and end. Then have them read the passage on page 205 and compare Jill's problem to that of the characters in "A Chair for My Mother."

(Try This)   **INDEPENDENT PRACTICE**   Have children determine ways in which the stories are alike and different. (Possible responses: The plots are alike because the characters don't have money to buy what they want. They save their money. The plots are different because what the characters want to buy are different.) Discuss children's responses.

E L L

Practice Comparing Provide practice in using correct words to compare by using real objects. Use objects that are alike in some ways but different in others, such as an apple and an orange or a pencil and a crayon. Guide children to tell how the objects are alike (both an apple and an orange are fruit; they are both sweet) and how they are different (they have different colors and textures; you eat the skin of an apple but not of an orange).

Focus Skill

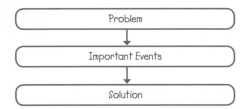

Plot

The **plot** is what happens in a story. At the beginning, the characters have a problem. During the middle of the story, they try to find a solution. At the end, the characters usually solve the problem.

```
Problem
   ↓
Important Events
   ↓
Solution
```

You can compare the plots of two stories. Think about these questions as you read.

- How are the characters' problems alike? How are they different?

- Do the characters solve their problems in the same way?

204

Read the story below again. How is Jill's problem like the characters' problem in "A Chair for My Mother"?

A Present for Mom

Mom's birthday was coming. Jill wanted to buy her flowers, but she had saved only $1.89. That wasn't enough for the flowers.

Then Jill had an idea. She would make some lemonade and set up a lemonade stand. After one day, Jill had made ten dollars. Now she could buy her mom flowers for her birthday.

A Present for Mom	A Chair for My Mother
Problem	Problem The family doesn't have enough money to buy a comfortable chair.
Important Events	Important Events
Solution	Solution

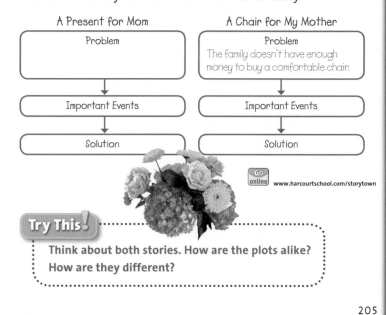

GO online www.harcourtschool.com/storytown

Try This!

Think about both stories. How are the plots alike? How are they different?

205

BELOW-LEVEL

Name _____

Plot
Lesson 22

Skill Reminder
A plot starts as a problem that the characters work to solve by the end of the story.

▶ Read the stories. Then circle the correct answers to complete the chart.

Nellie Eats

Nellie the cow was tired of eating grass. She put a note on the farmer's door. It said "I want something else to eat."
The next day her food bin was full of broccoli.
"Yuck!" said Nellie. She went back to eating grass.

Billy the Parrot

Billy the parrot was tired of eating seeds. He flew to the table and pecked at a nut. It almost broke his beak!
"I guess I'll go back to seeds," said Billy.

How the Stories Are Alike	How the Stories Are Different
Problems	**Events**
Nellie and Billy are both tired of their normal food.	Nellie writes a note. Billy flies to the table.
Nellie and Billy don't like their homes.	Nellie likes broccoli and Billy likes nuts.
Solutions	**The ending**
Billy and Nellie go back to eating their old foods.	Nellie and Billy eat new food.
Nellie and Billy eat nuts.	Nellie eats grass. Billy eats seeds.

School-Home Connection
Discuss the problem, the important events, and the solution of each story. Then ask your child what might happen in a story with both Nellie and Billy in it.

172   Extra Support

▲ **Extra Support, p. 172**

ON-LEVEL

Name _____

Plot
Lesson 22

▶ Read the two stories. Then answer the questions to complete the chart.

Freddie Tries a Worm

Freddie the frog was tired of eating flies. "I want to eat worms!" he said. Freddie tried a worm, but it got tangled in his tongue. "Help!" said Freddie. It tickled his throat. "Yuck!" said Freddie. Freddie went back to eating flies.

Wriggly Flies!

Wriggly the worm was tired of crawling on the ground. "I wish I could fly!" he said. Just then Wriggly spotted a bubble. He slithered into it, and the bubble carried him high into the air. "Wow!" cried Wriggly. "I'm flying! I'm really flying!"
Possible responses are shown.

How the Stories Are Alike	How the Stories Are Different
How are the story problems alike? Freddie and Wriggly are tired of the same old thing.	How are the events in the story different? Freddie eats a worm. Wriggly flies in a bubble.
How are the story solutions alike? Freddie and Wriggly both try something new.	How are the story solutions different? Freddie doesn't like the worm. Wriggly likes to fly.

School-Home Connection
For each story, help your child break it into the problem, important events, and the solution. Then discuss how the stories are alike and how they are different.

172   Practice Book

▲ **Practice Book, p. 172**

ADVANCED

Name _____

Plot
Lesson 22

Write a New Solution

▶ Write a new ending with a new solution for your favorite picture book.

What You Need
- a picture book • pencil
- paper

What to Do

1. Reread your favorite picture book. Think about the plot.

2. Fold a sheet of paper in three even parts. Write the titles Problem, Important Events, and Solution at the top of each section.

3. Write the problem, the important events, and the solution of the story.

4. Think of a different way the problem might be solved. Use your ideas to write a new ending to the story.

5. Read the picture book to your classmates using the new ending that you wrote.

172   Challenge

▲ **Challenge, p. 172**

E L L

- Group children according to academic levels, and assign one of the pages on the left.

- Clarify any unfamiliar concepts as necessary. See *ELL Teacher Guide* Lesson 22 for support in scaffolding instruction.

Listening Comprehension
Read Aloud

Objectives
- *To set a purpose for listening*
- *To identify plot in a story*

Build Fluency

Focus: Expression Tell children that good readers use their voices to give an idea of what different characters might sound like.

Before Reading

CONNECT TO PRIOR KNOWLEDGE Tell children that they will listen to a story in the form of a poem that tells about how the animals on a farm solve a problem.

Routine Card 2 **GENRE STUDY: FANTASY POEM** Tell children that the story poem "The Rooster That Crowed at Nightfall" is a fantasy. Remind children of the characteristics of this genre:

Think Aloud In a fantasy, the characters usually behave in ways that they cannot in real life.

▲ Read-Aloud Anthology, "The Rooster That Crowed at Nightfall," p. 82

After Reading

RESPOND Work with children to create a chart that shows the sequence of important events in the story poem. Record the events on the board.

> The old rooster who crows in the morning dies.
>
> ↓
>
> The new rooster prefers to crow at nightfall. This causes trouble at the farm.
>
> ↓
>
> The Wise Old Sow explains that things are often done in a different way.
>
> ↓
>
> A tiny piglet announces the day with "OINK-A-DOODLE!"

ELL

Connect to Prior Knowledge
As you read "The Rooster That Crowed at Nightfall" aloud, use vocal expression, gestures, and body movements to indicate different animals and characters.

REVIEW PLOT Have children summarize the plot of "The Rooster That Crowed at Nightfall."

Build Robust Vocabulary

Words from the Read-Aloud

Teach/Model

Routine Card 3

INTRODUCE THE WORDS   Use *Routine Card 3* to introduce the words.

❶ Put the word in **selection context**.
❷ Display Transparency R118 and read the word and the **Student-Friendly Explanation**.
❸ Have children **say the word** with you.
❹ Use the word in other contexts, and have children **interact with the word's meaning**.
❺ Remove the transparency. Say the Student-Friendly Explanation again, and ask children to **name the word** that goes with it.

❶ **Selection Context:** The people on the farm **acquired** a new rooster after the first one died.

❹ **Interact with Word Meaning:** I acquired a new lunchbox before school started. Would you have acquired a new backpack or a new suitcase to carry things to school?

❶ **Selection Context:** The people on the farm **assumed** that the rooster would crow early in the morning.

❹ **Interact with Word Meaning:** Would you have assumed that you would have breakfast or lunch when you got up this morning?

Practice/Apply

GUIDED PRACTICE   Guide children to tell about things they *assume* will happen on a daily basis. Begin with: *I assumed the sun would come up this morning.*

Objective

• *To develop robust vocabulary through discussing a literature selection*

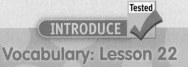

Tested

INTRODUCE ✓

Vocabulary: Lesson 22

acquired   **assumed**

▼ **Student-Friendly Explanations**

Student-Friendly Explanations	
acquired	If you own or buy something, you have acquired it.
assumed	If you assumed something, you believed something without thinking about it.
absurd	If something is absurd, it is crazy or silly.
attempt	If you attempt to do something, you try to do it.

Grade 2, Lesson 22   **R118**   Vocabulary

Transparency R118

Grammar *Quick Write*

Subject-Verb Agreement

5-DAY GRAMMAR

DAY 1	Introduce Subject-Verb Agreement
DAY 2	Practice Agreement
DAY 3	Use Agreement in Sentences
DAY 4	Apply to Writing
DAY 5	Weekly Review

Objective

- *To recognize subject-verb agreement*

Daily Proofreading

Tims apple is the smaller of all.

(Tim's; smallest)

Writing Trait

Strengthening Conventions

Agreement   Use this short lesson with children's writing to build a foundation for revising/editing longer connected text on Day 5. See also *Writer's Companion*, Lesson 22.

Subject-Verb Agreement

1. The chicken pecks at the corn.
   (naming part: chicken; verb: pecks)
2. The chickens peck at the corn.
   (naming part: chickens; verb: peck)
3. You gather the eggs.
   (naming part: You; verb: gather)
4. Tricia gathers the eggs.
   (naming part: Tricia; verb: gathers)
5. The children gather the eggs.
   (naming part: children; verb: gather)

Rules for Verbs That Tell About Now

Naming Part	Rule	Example
Names One	Add -s to most verbs.	The dog laps the water. Karl drinks lemonade.
Names More Than One	Do not add an ending.	The cows chew hay. The kittens drink the milk.
I or You	Do not add an ending.	I munch on popcorn. You bake muffins.

6. The children (wave, waves) goodbye to the farmer.
7. The farmer (smile, smiles) at the children.

Grade 2, Lesson 22   LA45   Grammar

Transparency LA45

Teach/Model

INTRODUCE SUBJECT-VERB AGREEMENT   Explain that when the naming part (subject) in a sentence tells about one person, place, or thing, an *-s* is usually added to the verb so it will agree, or match. Then tell children that when the naming part of the sentence tells about more than one thing, they do not add an *-s* to the verb. Write the following sentences on the board about "The Rooster That Crowed at Nightfall" (*Read-Aloud Anthology,* p. 82):

> **A rooster crows at nightfall to welcome the moon.**
> **The animals worry that they won't be fed.**

Read aloud the sentences. Ask: **What is the naming part of each sentence?** (*A rooster; The animals*) **Which naming part names one?** (*A rooster*) **Which naming part names more than one?** (*The animals*) **What is the action verb in each sentence?** (*crows; worry*) **What is the difference between these verbs?** (One has an s; the other does not.)

Guided Practice

IDENTIFY VERBS   Display **Transparency LA45**. Read aloud the first sentence. Explain that since the naming part tells about one chicken, an *−s* is added to the verb *pecks*. Ask volunteers to read the remaining items. Guide children to identify the naming part and the verb, and point out whether there is an *-s* at the end of the verb. Read aloud the rules from the chart and the examples.

Practice/Apply

INDEPENDENT PRACTICE   Have children work with partners to write sentences using the rules for verbs. Have children share their sentences.

Writing
Fantasy

5-DAY WRITING

DAY 1	Introduce
DAY 2	Prewrite
DAY 3	Draft
DAY 4	Revise
DAY 5	Revise

Teach/Model

INTRODUCE FANTASY Display **Transparency LA46,** and explain that this story was written by a child to tell about something that couldn't happen in real life. Read aloud the story to children, and discuss how the writer tells about an adventure that could not really happen. Together, develop a list of characteristics for a fantasy. Keep it on display for use on Days 3–5.

Fantasy

- A fantasy tells about something that could not take place in real life.
- A fantasy includes characters that behave in ways that they couldn't in real life.
- A fantasy should have a problem, important events, and a solution.

 Sure, what would you like to play?

Can we please go out and play?

WRITING TRAIT **SENTENCE FLUENCY** Read aloud this sentence: *When it was time to go, Pedro told me I could visit anytime.* Explain that it combines two ideas that could have been written as two sentences. Explain that by combining the two ideas into one sentence, the ideas flow more smoothly.

Guided Practice

DRAFT A SENTENCE Model writing a sentence, such as "The sparrow told Kerri he could help her get out of the forest." Discuss how it tells about something that could not happen.

Practice/Apply

WRITE AN OPENING SENTENCE Have children write a sentence that tells about something that could not happen in real life. They may want to save their sentences for use on Days 2–5.

Objectives

- *To read and respond to a fantasy story as a model for writing*
- *To develop an understanding of a fantasy story*
- *To write a sentence for a fantasy story*

Writing Prompt

Write Fantasy Sentence Have children write a sentence about an animal they would like to talk to, and tell why.

Student Model: Fantasy

A Very Cool Day

It was going to be another hot day. I glared at Pedro Penguin, the cartoon character on the cereal box. He looked nice and cool on his block of ice.

"Hey, pal, too hot for you?"

I looked around. Who said that?

"It's me, Pedro. Just close your eyes and jump! You'll be here in a flash!"

I stared at the box. It was Pedro, and he was talking to me!

I did what he said. When I opened my eyes, there I was with Pedro! Everything was a cartoon! It was nice and cool!

Pedro and I played cool games all day. We swam, slid down icebergs, and went ice fishing. When it was time to go, Pedro told me I could visit anytime. I think I'll go back tomorrow!

Grade 2, Lesson 22   LA46   Writing

Transparency LA46

Day at a Glance

Day 2

 phonics and Spelling
- Review: *r*-Controlled Vowel /ôr/*or*, *ore, our*
- Build Words

Robust Vocabulary
Words from the Selection
- Introduce: *extremely, barely, admit, serious, hilarious, witty*

Comprehension
 Focus Strategy Use Story Structure

Focus Skill Plot

Reading
- "Serious Farm," *Student Edition*, pp. 208–233

 Read!

Fluency
- Expression

Robust Vocabulary
Words About the Selection
- Introduce: *absurd, attempt*

Grammar Quick Write
- Review: Subject-Verb Agreement

Writing 🖉
- Fantasy

Warm-Up Routines

 ## Oral Language

Objective *To listen attentively and respond appropriately to oral communication*

Question of the Day

What would you do if you saw a purple cow?

Invite children to speculate about what they might do if they saw a purple cow. Use the following prompts:

- **What color cows have you seen?**
- **Why do you think a cow might be purple?**
- **Would you try to talk to a purple cow? What would you say to it?**

Then have children complete the following sentence frame:

If I saw a purple cow, I'd _____.

Read Aloud

Objective *To listen to and enjoy a nonsense poem*

BIG BOOK OF RHYMES AND POEMS Display the poem "The Purple Cow" on page 39 and read the title aloud. Explain that *nonsense* means "silly" or "without meaning," and tell children to listen for why this poem is called a nonsense poem. Then read the poem aloud. Ask children to tell what makes this a nonsense poem. (It is silly and fun to listen to.) Reread the poem several times, inviting children to join in when they are able.

▲ **Big Book of Rhymes and Poems, p. 39**

Word Wall

Objective *To read high-frequency words*

REVIEW HIGH-FREQUENCY WORDS Review the words *sweat, woman, popular, draw, clear, curve, lose,* and *covered* as well as other previously learned high-frequency words. Point to each word, and then have children read it, spell it, and read it again. Then point to words at random and have children read them.

sweat   woman   popular   draw

clear   curve   lose   covered

r-Controlled Vowel /ôr/ or, ore, our and Spelling

Objectives

- *To blend sounds into words*
- *To spell words that include the /ôr/ sound using or, ore, our*

Skill Trace

 r-Controlled Vowel /ôr/ or, ore, our

Introduce	Grade 1
Reintroduce	T132–T135
Reteach	S14–S15
Review	T144–T145, T168–T169, T412
Test	Theme 5
Maintain	Theme 6, T268

Spelling Words

1.	store	6.	chore
2.	fork	7.	short
3.	pour	8.	more*
4.	score	9.	four
5.	your	10.	sore

Challenge Words

11.	ignore	14.	explore
12.	important	15.	fourteen
13.	factory		

* Word from "Serious Farm"

Word Building

READ A SPELLING WORD Write the word *sore* on the board. Ask children to identify the letters that stand for the /ôr/ sound. Then read the word, and have children do the same.

BUILD SPELLING WORDS Ask children which letter you should add to make *sore* become *score*. (Add *c* between *s* and *o*.) Write the word *score* on the board. Point to the word, and have children read it. Continue building the spelling words in this manner. Say:

- **Which letter do I have to change to make the word *store*?** (Change the *c* to *t*.)
- **Which letters do I have to change to make the word *chore*?** (Change *st* to *ch*.)
- **Which letters do I have to change to make the word *short*?**
  (Change *c* to *s* and *e* to *t*.)
- **Which letters do I have to change to make the word *fork*?**
  (Change *sh* to *f* and *t* to *k*.)

sore
score
store
chore
short
fork

Continue building the remaining spelling words in this manner.

BELOW-LEVEL

Chart Words List the spelling words on the board. Make a three-column chart with the headings *or, ore,* and *our*. Point to each word and have a volunteer write the word under its heading. Have children say and spell each word aloud.

ADVANCED

Build New Words Have children make a list of more words that use *or, ore,* and *our* to stand for the /ôr/ sound. Tell children to use a dictionary to check spellings and pronunciation. Have children share their lists with a partner.

5-DAY PHONICS/SPELLING

DAY 1	Pretest
DAY 2	Word Building
DAY 3	State the Generalization
DAY 4	Review
DAY 5	Posttest

Read Words in Context

APPLY PHONICS   Write the following sentences on the board or on chart paper. Have children read each sentence silently. Then track the print as children read the sentence aloud.

> Will you <u>pour</u> a glass of water for everyone?
> Lena's legs were <u>sore</u> because she jumped rope.
> I like all the different colors in <u>your</u> painting.
> Josh got the highest <u>score</u> on the math test.
> Ethan's <u>chore</u> is to wipe the tables after lunch.

 WRITE   Dictate several spelling words. Have children write the words in their notebook or on a dry-erase board.

phonics Resources

Phonics Practice Book,
pp. 133–138

MONITOR PROGRESS

r*-Controlled Vowel /ôr/ *or*, *ore, our

IF children have difficulty building and reading words with *r*-controlled vowel /ôr/ *or, ore, our,*	THEN help them blend and read the words *fork, your, short, more,* and *store.*

Small-Group Instruction, pp. S14–S15:

- **BELOW-LEVEL:** Reteach
- **ON-LEVEL:** Reinforce
- **ADVANCED:** Extend

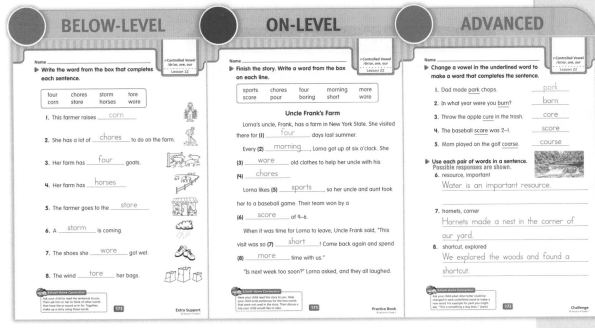

BELOW-LEVEL

▲ Extra Support, p. 173

ON-LEVEL

▲ Practice Book, p. 173

ADVANCED

▲ Challenge, p. 173

E L L

- Group children according to academic levels, and assign one of the pages on the left.

- Clarify any unfamiliar concepts as necessary. See *ELL Teacher Guide* Lesson 22 for support in scaffolding instruction.

Build Robust Vocabulary
Words from the Selection

Objective
• *To build robust vocabulary*

INTRODUCE ✓ *Tested*

Vocabulary: Lesson 22

extremely	serious
barely	hilarious
admit	witty

Student-Friendly Explanations

serious	When something is serious, it is important and not at all funny.
extremely	Something that is extremely a certain way is very much that way.
admit	When you admit something, you agree that it is true even though you might not want to.
barely	When you can barely do something, you almost can't do it at all.
hilarious	When you think something is hilarious, you think it is very, very funny.
witty	If you are witty, you say things in a clever and funny way.

Grade 2, Lesson 22   **R119**   Vocabulary

Transparency R119

Word Champion

Provide Context   Encourage children to tell how people respond when they use each word. HOMEWORK/ INDEPENDENT PRACTICE

Teach/Model

Routine Card 4

INTRODUCE ROBUST VOCABULARY   Use *Routine Card* 4 to introduce the words.

❶ Display Transparency R119 and read the word and the **Student-Friendly Explanation**.
❷ Have children **say the word** with you.
❸ Have children **interact with the word's meaning** by asking them the appropriate question below.

• If you were **extremely** sick, would you go to a party? Explain.

• If you can **barely** reach something, is it easy to reach? Explain.

• Would you **admit** it if you forgot to do your homework? Explain.

• Would you laugh while you were telling about something that was **serious**? Explain.

• How do you react when see something that is **hilarious**?

• Why do people laugh when someone tells a **witty** joke?

Develop Deeper Meaning

EXPAND WORD MEANINGS: PAGES 206–207   Have children read the passage on pages 206–207. Then read the passage aloud, pausing at the end of page 206 to ask children questions 1–4. Read page 207 and then discuss children's answers to questions 5–6.

1. Do you think it was **extremely** hard for Alyssa to have to get up so early? Why or why not?

2. How would you act if you were **barely** awake?

3. Why didn't Alyssa want to **admit** that she was tired?

4. Why would Aunt Abby worry that Alyssa was so **serious**?

5. Would Aunt Abby have thought it was **hilarious** if Alyssa had said she was homesick? Why or why not?

6. Why was it hard for Alyssa to be **witty** when she first got up?

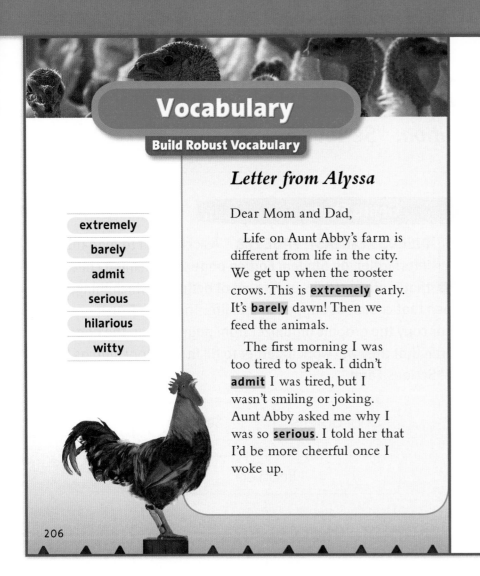

Vocabulary

Build Robust Vocabulary

Letter from Alyssa

extremely

barely

admit

serious

hilarious

witty

Dear Mom and Dad,

Life on Aunt Abby's farm is different from life in the city. We get up when the rooster crows. This is **extremely** early. It's **barely** dawn! Then we feed the animals.

The first morning I was too tired to speak. I didn't **admit** I was tired, but I wasn't smiling or joking. Aunt Abby asked me why I was so **serious**. I told her that I'd be more cheerful once I woke up.

206

Then I said something Aunt Abby thought was **hilarious**. I asked if we could put the rooster in a dark closet. This way he wouldn't crow in the morning. She laughed and said she was glad I was waking up. I guess I was back to my **witty** self.

I'll write more later, but now we're going horseback riding.

Love,
Alyssa

GO online www.harcourtschool.com/storytown

Word Champion

Your challenge this week is to use the Vocabulary Words while talking to others. For example, you might ask a friend to tell you a **witty** and **hilarious** story. Each day, write in your vocabulary journal the sentences you spoke.

207

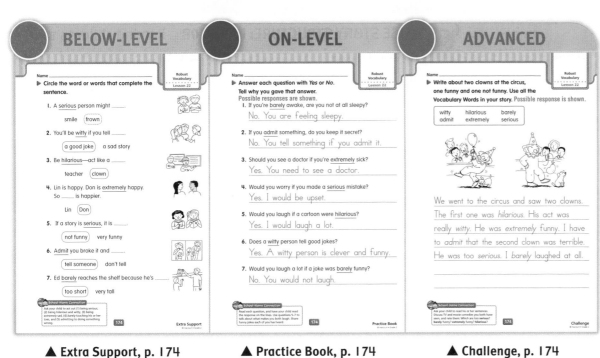

▲ Extra Support, p. 174   ▲ Practice Book, p. 174   ▲ Challenge, p. 174

ELL

- Group students according to academic levels, and assign one of the pages on the left.

- Clarify any unfamiliar concepts and vocabulary. See *ELL Teacher Guide* Lesson 22 for support in scaffolding instruction.

Reading

Student Edition: **"Serious Farm"**

Objectives

- *To understand characteristics of fantasy*
- *To use story structure as a strategy for comprehension*

Professional Development

 Podcasting: Use Story Structure, Grades 2–6

Options for Reading

 BELOW-LEVEL

Preview Have children preview the story by looking at the illustrations. Guide them to predict what the problem will be. Read each page of the story to children, and have them read it after you.

 ON-LEVEL

Monitor Comprehension Have children read the story aloud, page by page. Ask them the Monitor Comprehension questions as you go.

 ADVANCED

Independent Reading Have children read each page silently, looking up each time they finish a page. Ask them the Monitor Comprehension questions as you go.

Genre Study

DISCUSS FANTASY: PAGE 208 Ask children to read the genre information on *Student Edition* page 208. Remind children that fantasy stories are a kind of fiction in which things happen that could not happen in real life. Then use **Transparency GO4** or copy the graphic organizer from page 208 on the board. Tell children that they will work together to fill in the story map as they read "Serious Farm."

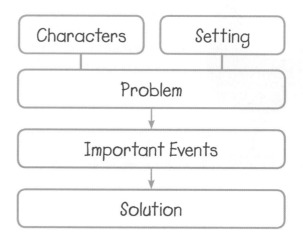

Comprehension Strategies

USE STORY STRUCTURE: PAGE 208 Remind children that good readers use strategies to help them understand what they read. Explain that one strategy readers can use is story structure. Have children read aloud the Comprehension Strategy information on page 208. Provide information about story structure.

> **Think Aloud** When I read a fantasy such as "Serious Farm," I identify story problem. Then I look for events that have to do with how the characters try to solve the problem. Finally, I find the solution.

Point out that by completing the story map, they will use story structure to help them understand what they read.

SERIOUS FARM

Fantasy

Genre Study

A **fantasy** is a story that could not really happen. Look for

• made-up characters.

• a make-believe plot.

Characters → Setting
↓
Problem
↓
Important Events
↓
Solution

Comprehension Strategy

Use **story structure** to think about how characters solve their problem.

208

SERIOUS FARM

by
TIM EGAN

209

Build Background

DISCUSS HAVING A SENSE OF HUMOR   Tell children that they are going to read a story about what happens when the animals on a farm try to help a farmer who is too serious. Ask volunteers to tell about a time when having a sense of humor helped make people feel better.

 Routine Card 6

SET A PURPOSE AND PREDICT   Tell children that this is a story they will read to enjoy.

• Have children read the title.

• Identify Farmer Fred and have children name the different farm animals they see. Ask children to predict what they think Farmer Fred will be like.

• List their predictions on the board.

• Have children read the story to find out what life is like on Farmer Fred's farm.

TECHNOLOGY

 **eBook**   "Serious Farm" is available in an eBook.

 Audiotext   "Serious Farm" is available on *Audiotext Grade 2,* CD 5 for subsequent readings.

Farmer Fred never smiled much. He wasn't a sad fellow, just very serious. "Farmin' is serious business," he'd say. "Nothing funny about corn."

Now, because it was Farmer Fred's farm, all the animals acted the way he did, so they were very serious, too. **1**

210

When he would say, "There's no humor in tomatoes," they'd all agree.

The pigs, the cows, the horses, the chickens, the rabbit, the sheep. All extremely serious. **2**

211

Monitor Comprehension

PAGES 210–211 Say: **Farmer Fred and the animals look very serious. Read to find out why.**

1 **CHARACTERS** **Why are Farmer Fred and the animals so serious?** (Possible response: Farmer Fred thinks that running a farm is serious business. The animals act serious because Farmer Fred is in charge.)

2 **EXPRESS PERSONAL OPINIONS** **Would you like to visit Farmer Fred's farm? Why or why not?** (Possible response: No; they don't look like they are enjoying themselves.)

Apply
Comprehension Strategies

Focus Strategy **Use Story Structure** Demonstrate how to use story structure to comprehend the story to this point.

Think Aloud I'll fill in what I know so far—the characters and setting. Since Farmer Fred thinks everything is serious, this might be the problem. I'll read to find out.

Characters	Setting
Farmer Fred, animals	Farmer Fred's farm

One night, Edna, the cow, said, "We've got to get Farmer Fred to laugh. I mean, it's okay to be serious, but not all the time. We need some laughter."

"Must admit," said Bernie, the goat, "I wouldn't mind smilin' again."

212

He stretched his mouth and showed all his teeth. It wasn't a very convincing smile. They all decided they needed a plan to make the farm more fun. ②

213

Monitor Comprehension

PAGES 212–213 Say: **It looks like the animals are having a meeting. Read to find out what they talk about.**

① **PLOT** **What is the problem the animals are having?** (Possible response: They aren't happy because they think Farmer Fred is too serious.)

② **GENRE** **How can you tell that this story is a fantasy?** (The animals can talk.)

The next morning, as the sun came up, Edna was standing on the fence where Cormac, the rooster, usually stood.

She was barely able to keep her balance.

She tried to yell, "Cock-a-doodle-do," but since she was a cow, it didn't come out like that at all. It was the first time anyone had done anything funny in months, so it made all the animals laugh. ① ②

214

Farmer Fred just looked out the window and said, "You're not a rooster," and shut the window and went back to sleep.

"Wow," said Edna, "this is gonna be tougher than I thought." ③

215

Monitor Comprehension

PAGES 214–215 Say: **I can see that Edna the cow is standing on a fence! Read to find out why she is there.**

① **CAUSE/EFFECT** **Why does Edna decide to stand on the fence?** (Possible response: She thinks that if she acts like a rooster Farmer Fred and the other animals will laugh.)

② **COMPARE/CONTRAST** **How do the animals' faces look different in this illustration?** (Possible response: They are not serious. They are laughing and smiling.)

③ **RETELL** **How does Farmer Fred react to Edna's joke?** (Possible response: He doesn't think it is funny.)

Use Multiple Strategies

Use Prior Knowledge Remind children that they can use what they already know to help them better understand a story. Say: **I'm not too surprised that Farmer Fred doesn't think Edna's joke is funny. I learned earlier in the story that he is very serious and doesn't seem to have much of a sense of humor.**

That morning was serious as usual, with Farmer Fred saying things like "Broccoli's no fun" and "I never laugh at bell peppers."

"Okay," said Edna to the others, "let's try another idea."

When Farmer Fred went to feed the pigs that afternoon, they started barking like dogs. Everyone thought it was hilarious but Farmer Fred.

216

"That's more weird than funny," he said as he walked away.

"All right," said Edna, "this isn't working. Let's try something new."

They sneaked into the house and took some clothes from Farmer Fred's closet and put them on. It wasn't as easy as it sounds. **①②**

217

Monitor Comprehension

PAGES 216–217   Have children describe what they see on these pages. Say: **Read to find out what's going on.**

① **PLOT   Why are the animals doing all these silly things?** (Possible response: They are trying to make Farmer Fred laugh to make life on the farm more fun.)

②AUTHOR'S CRAFT   How does the author help make his ideas seem funny? (Possible response: He uses funny expressions like "It wasn't as easy as it sounds." He uses humor in his illustrations.)

That evening, as the moon lit up the field, Bernie rang the doorbell. Farmer Fred came out onto the porch and said, "What in the world?" The animals were all dancing around in Farmer Fred's clothes.

218

They were terrible dancers, which actually made it funnier. But Farmer Fred just said, "Better not get my clothes dirty." ❶ He walked back inside without smiling. ❷

219

Monitor Comprehension

PAGES 218–219 Say: **It looks like the animals are trying another plan. Read to see if it works.**

❶ **GENRE** **What is happening on pages 218–219 that could not happen in real life?** (Possible response: The animals are wearing human clothing and are dancing.)

❷ **MAKE PREDICTIONS** **What do you think will happen next?** (Possible response: The animals will try something else to make Farmer Fred become less serious.)

Use Multiple Strategies

Monitor Comprehension: Read Ahead
Say: The animals have tried some different ways to try to make Farmer Fred laugh but none of them seem to be working. I know that in stories like this something unexpected often happens. If I read ahead, maybe I will find out what the animals can do to make Farmer Fred laugh.

For the next two weeks, the animals tried everything they could to make Farmer Fred smile a little, but nothing worked. **1**

220

It got to be very discouraging. **2** **3**

221

Monitor Comprehension

PAGES 220–221   Say: **I can see that the animals are trying lots of new ideas. Read to find out how Farmer Fred reacts.**

1 SUMMARIZE   **How does Farmer Fred react to all the things the animals do?** (He still doesn't smile at all.)

2 EXPRESS PERSONAL OPINIONS   **Which of the things that the animals do is the funniest? Tell why.** (Possible response: I like the picture of the cow doing a handstand, because it looks so silly.)

3 CONFIRM/MAKE PREDICTIONS   **Were your predictions correct? What do you think might happen next?** (Possible response: Yes, the animals did lots of things to try to make Farmer Fred smile. Now, I think the animals will give up trying to make him smile.)

One night, the animals met in the barn.
"Well, I don't know about you," said Edna, "but
I can't take it anymore. I have to live somewhere
more fun than this. I'm leaving."

They all agreed with Edna and packed up
their stuff, which wasn't much, and headed
out into the night.

222

223

Monitor Comprehension

PAGES 222–223 Say: **I wonder where the animals are going. Read to find out.**

① **PLOT** **Why are the animals leaving? Do you think this is a good solution to their problem?** (Possible response: They want to live someplace else where they can be happier. It may not be a good solution, because they don't know where they are going to go.)

② **CONFIRM/MAKE PREDICTIONS** **Were your predictions correct? How do you think Farmer Fred will react when he finds that the animals are gone?** (Possible response: Yes, the animals are giving up trying to make Farmer Fred smile. Now, I think he will just get new animals.)

Apply
Comprehension Strategies

Use Story Structure Model how to recognize story events.

Think Aloud Now I know the problem and that the animals haven't solved it yet. Something else must still have to happen.

Characters	Setting
Farmer Fred, animals	Farmer Fred's farm

Problem
Farmer Fred won't smile.

Important Events
Animals try to make Farmer Fred laugh. They leave the farm.

He got into his truck and drove down the road in search of his friends.

He went about four miles, but there was no sign of them anywhere. Then he heard some laughter in the distance.

He followed the sound and saw the animals walking through the woods.

The next morning, there was no sound of a rooster or even a cow. Farmer Fred looked outside and saw that all the animals were gone.

"Oh no," he said, "all the animals are gone."

Farmer Fred became sad immediately. Now, it was one thing to be serious, but it was another thing to be sad. **①** **②**

Farmer Fred didn't like the feeling at all.

224

225

Monitor Comprehension

PAGES 224–225   Say: **I see Farmer Fred driving in his truck. Read to find out where he is going.**

① CHARACTERS' EMOTIONS   **How does Farmer Fred feel when he finds that the animals are gone?** (He is very sad.)

② DRAW CONCLUSIONS   **What do you think it means when the author says, "it was one thing to be serious, but it was another thing to be sad"?** (Possible response: I think it means that Farmer Fred is serious about his important job of growing vegetables, but he hasn't been sad and unhappy until the animals left.)

 **SOCIAL STUDIES**

SUPPORTING STANDARDS

Farming and Agriculture   Explain to children that since the beginnings of farming and agriculture, humans have relied upon animals for food production and help in completing tasks that farmers could not do by themselves. Ask children to tell about ways farmers care for and need animals to help them in their work.

He got out of his truck, walked into the forest, and asked, "What's going on here?"

"We couldn't stand it," said Edna. "We've tried to cheer you up, but nothing's worked, so we're running away. Well, walking away."

The other animals nodded in agreement.

226

"Well, that's no way to solve a problem," said Farmer Fred. "You don't just leave. I mean, sure, I'm serious, but that doesn't mean you have to be. And, besides, we're family. I take care of you. I need you.

"Not to mention that you're safe on the farm. You'd probably be eaten by lions in a day or two  out here in the woods."

227

Monitor Comprehension

PAGES 226–227 Say: **I wonder what Farmer Fred and the animals are talking about. Read to find out.**

❶ GENERALIZE **What does Farmer Fred mean when he says that running away is "no way to solve a problem"? Do you agree with him?** (Possible response: He means that the problems will still be there, even if the animals run away. I think he's right; you have to figure out a way to solve your problems, not run away.)

❷ MAKE INFERENCES **Why do you think the animals look frightened in the illustration on page 227?** (Possible response: They look frightened because they probably hadn't thought about the possibility of being eaten by lions.)

Punctuation and Dialogue
Remind children that writers use quotations when they write dialogue. Ask children to read the dialogue on pages 226–227 and tell about the punctuation. Then point out the missing quotation mark at the end of paragraph one on page 227. Explain that there is no ending quotation mark because the speaker doesn't change, although a new paragraph is needed.

The animals thought about this for a moment.
As they whispered to one another about the lion
issue, Farmer Fred mumbled, "Cows and chickens
runnin' wild in the woods, heh, heh." ❶

Edna turned quickly and said, "What was that?"

"I think he laughed a little," said Bernie. ❷

228

"Yes," said a chicken, "I heard it. It wasn't
much, but he did laugh."

"Well," said Edna, "in that case, you're witty
enough for us, Farmer Fred. And we care about
you, too. I guess we can go back to the farm."

229

Monitor Comprehension

PAGES 228–229 Say: **I can see that the animals are talking to each other. Read to find out what they think.**

❶ **PLOT What happens to make the animals decide that they would go back to the farm?** (Farmer Fred laughed a little. The animals found out that Farmer Fred did have a sense of humor after all.)

❷ **MAKE JUDGMENTS Are you surprised to find out that Farmer Fred has a sense of humor after all? Tell why.** (Possible response: I am surprised, because all along, Farmer Fred never thinks that anything is funny.)

ANALYZE AUTHOR'S PURPOSE

Author's Purpose Remind children that authors have a purpose, or reason, for writing. As children read "Serious Farm," ask:

Why did the author write "Serious Farm"?

- to persuade readers that they should never leave home because they might face danger
- to inform readers that some kinds of animals talk
- to entertain readers with a fantasy story that shows the importance of having a sense of humor

The other animals nodded their heads and said things like "I agree" and "Good idea" and "Let's go back."

They hopped onto the truck and Farmer Fred drove them home.

230

From that day forward, they were able to make Farmer Fred laugh a little more, especially by bringing up the idea of cows and chickens running wild, although he still doesn't see anything funny about corn.

231

Monitor Comprehension

PAGES 230–231 Say: **I see that the animals are back on the farm. Read to find out what life is like now on the farm.**

① **COMPARE AND CONTRAST** **How is Farmer Fred different from the way he was at the beginning of the story? How is he the same?** (Farmer Fred now is less serious than he used to be. He shows that he does have a sense of humor, but he is still pretty serious.)

② **EXPRESS PERSONAL OPINIONS** **Which part of the story did you enjoy the most? Tell why.** (Possible response: I liked the part when the animals had a talk about "the lion issue" because they looked so scared.)

Apply
Comprehension Strategies

Focus Strategy

Use Story Structure Model how to summarize the ending.

Think Aloud Since the animals have solved their problem, I can complete the story map.

> **Important Events**
> Animals try to make Farmer Fred laugh. They leave the farm. He follows them.

> **Solution**
> Animals agree to go home after Farmer Fred laughs a little.

T160 Grade 2, Theme 5 (*Student Edition*, pages 230–231)

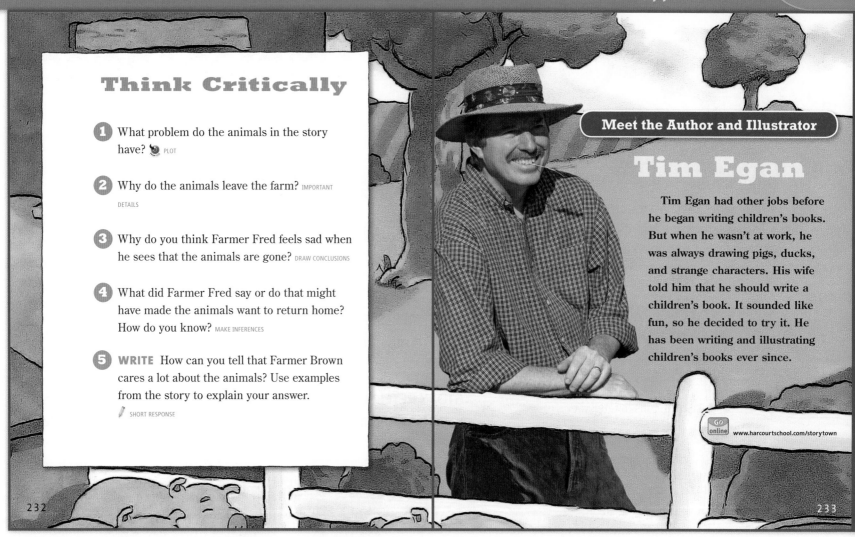

Think Critically

Respond to the Literature

1. The animals want life to be less serious, but Farmer Fred has no sense of humor. **PLOT**

2. They leave because all their efforts to make Farmer Fred laugh fail. **IMPORTANT DETAILS**

3. Possible response: He feels sad because he likes the animals. **DRAW CONCLUSIONS**

4. Possible response: When he laughs, the animals decide they can go back. **MAKE INFERENCES**

5. **WRITE** He goes after them when they leave, he explains why he needs them, he feeds them, he cares about whether they are happy. **SHORT RESPONSE**

Meet the Author and Illustrator

PAGE 233 Read page 233 aloud. Explain that Tim Egan has written and illustrated a number of humorous books for children. One of his books was even performed as an opera. He lives in California with his wife and their two boys. He enjoys giving presentations to kids to tell about how books are made.

Check Comprehension
Retelling

Objectives
- *To practice retelling a story*
- *To use expression to read in a manner that sounds like natural speech*

RETELLING RUBRIC

4	Uses details to clearly retell the story
3	Uses some details to retell the story
2	Retells story with some inaccuracies
1	Is unable to retell the story

Professional Development

 Podcasting: Auditory Modeling

BELOW-LEVEL

Fluency Practice For fluency practice, have children read *Decodable Book 18*, the appropriate *Leveled Reader* (pp. T202–T205), or Story 22 in the *Strategic Intervention Interactive Reader*.

Retell

  PLOT Ask children to tell how the characters in "Serious Farm" solve their problem. (When the animals run away, Farmer Fred follows them and shows he can laugh.)

REVISIT THE GRAPHIC ORGANIZER Display completed **Transparency GO4**. Children can use it to retell the story.

STORY RETELLING CARDS The cards for "Serious Farm" can be used for retelling or as an aid to completing the graphic organizer.

▲ Story Retelling Cards 1–6, "Serious Farm"

Fluency
Expression

Teach/Model

 USING EXPRESSION Explain that good readers use expression to bring the characters to life. Have children open to pages 228–229 and track the print as you model using your voice to express what characters say.

Practice/Apply

 ECHO-READ Read aloud the rest of the story, modeling using expression. Have children echo-read each page with you.

Routine Card 8

Build Robust Vocabulary

Words About the Selection

Teach/Model

Routine Card 3 INTRODUCE ROBUST VOCABULARY   Use *Routine Card 3* to introduce the words.

❶ Put the word in **selection context**.
❷ Display Transparency R118 and read the word and the **Student-Friendly Explanation**.
❸ Have children **say the word** with you.
❹ Use the word in other contexts, and have children **interact with the word's meaning**.
❺ Remove the transparency. Say the Student-Friendly Explanation again, and ask children to **name the word** that goes with it.

❶ **Selection Context:** It is **absurd** for a cow to try to act like a rooster.
❹ **Interact with Word Meaning:** My dog looked absurd when my sister dressed him in doll clothes and wheeled him in a baby carriage. Would you expect to see something absurd at school or at the circus? Explain.

❶ **Selection Context:** The animals **attempt** to make Farmer Fred laugh by dressing up in his clothes.
❹ **Interact with Word Meaning:** My brother wanted to attempt to break a record for jumping rope longer than anyone else. If you tell someone that you are going to attempt to do something, are you certain that you will be able to do it or do you think that you might be unable to do it?

Practice/Apply

GUIDED PRACTICE   Guide children to come up with things they could *attempt* to do that would be *absurd*. Ask volunteers to share their ideas. Then have children write in their notebooks which idea they think would be the most absurd to attempt, and why.

Objective

• *To develop robust vocabulary through discussing a literature selection*

Tested

INTRODUCE ✓

Vocabulary: Lesson 22

absurd   **attempt**

▼ **Student-Friendly Explanations**

Student-Friendly Explanations

acquired	If you own or buy something, you have acquired it.
assumed	If you assumed something, you believed something without thinking about it.
absurd	If something is absurd, it is crazy or silly.
attempt	If you attempt to do something, you try to do it.

Grade 2, Lesson 22   R118   Vocabulary

Transparency R118

Grammar
Subject-Verb Agreement

Quick Write

5-DAY GRAMMAR

DAY 1	Introduce Subject-Verb Agreement
DAY 2	Practice Agreement
DAY 3	Use Agreement in Sentences
DAY 4	Apply to Writing
DAY 5	Weekly Review

Objective
- *To recognize and use subject-verb agreement*

Daily Proofreading

Madison got two new puppys?

(puppies.)

Agreement   Subject-verb agreement in children's home language may differ from English. Model and reinforce that, in English, a verb must agree with its subject. Help children by providing them with partial statements such as *He says, They say, I go, She goes, We go.* Point out when *−s* is added.

Name _____

▶ Look at the verb in ( ). On the line, write the form of the verb that agrees with the subject.

Subject-Verb
Agreement
Lesson 22

1. Edna ____wants____ to make Farmer Fred laugh. (want)

2. She ____decides____ to make a plan. (decide)

3. The animals ____bark____ like dogs. (bark)

4. Then they ____dress____ in Farmer Fred's clothes. (dress)

5. The cows and chickens ____walk____ away from the farm. (walk)

6. Farmer Fred ____drives____ the animals back to the farm. (drive)

7. Edna's plan ____works____ well. (work)

8. The animals ____sleep____ soundly all night. (sleep)

77

Grammar Practice Book

▲ **Grammar Practice Book, p. 77**

Review

PRACTICE SUBJECT-VERB AGREEMENT   Write the following sentences on the board:

> I feed the animals.
> Marco feeds the animals.
> The children feed the animals.

Read aloud the sentences and explain that in each sentence the subjects and verbs agree. Remind them that an *-s* is added to most verbs when the naming part of the sentence tells about one and that there is no *-s* when the naming part tells about more than one or when it tells about *I* or *you.*

Practice/Apply

GUIDED PRACTICE   Write the following verb pairs on the board: *pick/picks, water/waters, plant/plants.* Model how to use each verb in a sentence about being on a farm. Then guide children to use the rest of the verbs in sentences.

Think Aloud   I know that if the naming part of a sentence tells about one, I usually add *-s* to the verb. So I say: *Farmer Fred picks some peppers.* If the naming part tells about more than one, I do not add *-s* to the verb. So I say: *The helpers pick some peppers.*

INDEPENDENT PRACTICE   Write these verbs on the board: *eat, ride, give, race.* Have children use the correct form of one of the verbs to write sentences. Then have children generate more verbs and use the correct forms to write new sentences.

Writing
Fantasy

5-DAY WRITING	
DAY 1	Introduce
DAY 2	**Prewrite**
DAY 3	Draft
DAY 4	Revise
DAY 5	Revise

Prewrite

GENERATE IDEAS   Ask children to think about ideas for a fantasy story. Children may wish to refer back to their sentences from Day 1. Suggest that children make a quick list to record their ideas.

 SENTENCE FLUENCY   Suggest that children begin to think about how using different kinds of sentences will make the ideas in their fantasy more interesting.

MODEL PREWRITING   Copy on the board the story map below. Tell children that they can use a graphic organizer such as this one to develop their ideas for a fantasy story. Model writing ideas for a problem, important events, and a solution for a fantasy story. Point out instances where two sentences or ideas might be combined.

> #### Problem
> A girl wants to travel throughout the world, but she has no way to get where she wants to go.

> #### Important Events
> The girl meets and talks to an eagle. The eagle lets the girl fly on its back. They fly all over.

> #### Solution
> The eagle gives the girl a majic feather. She can use it to fly with him again.

Practice/Apply

GUIDED PRACTICE   Ask children to brainstorm ideas for a fantasy story. Invite volunteers to describe their ideas. Record their ideas in a new story map.

INDEPENDENT PRACTICE   Have children use the story map to brainstorm details for their fantasies. Have children save their story maps for use on Days 3–5.

Objectives

- *To develop ideas and topics for writing a fantasy*
- *To use a graphic organizer for prewriting*

Writing Prompt

Independent Writing   Have children tell about a favorite fantasy story they have read.

Work With a Partner   Have children draw illustrations that tell about their ideas. Then have then work with an English-proficient peer to generate and write details about their pictures. Children may wish to later include their illustrations with their completed story.

Day at a Glance

Day 3

 phonics and Spelling

- Review: *r*-Controlled Vowel /ôr/*or*, *ore*, *our*
- State the Generalization

Fluency

- Expression
- "Serious Farm," *Student Edition*, pp. 208–233

Comprehension

 **Review: Plot**

- Introduce: Compare and Contrast

Reading

- "Beyond Old MacDonald," *Student Edition*, pp. 234–235 **Read!**

Robust Vocabulary

- Review: *acquired, assumed, extremely, barely, admit, serious, hilarious, witty, absurd, attempt*

Grammar *Quick Write*

- Review: Subject-Verb Agreement

Writing

- Fantasy

Warm-Up Routines

Oral Language

Objective *To listen attentively and respond appropriately to oral communication*

Question of the Day

What could make something turn purple?

Use the following prompts to help children speculate as to what could make something change color.

- **Name some foods that are purple.**

- **What are some other things that are purple?**

- **How could you change the color of clothing such as a shirt or a sweater?**

- **What would you need to do to add some purple color to a drawing or a painting?**

Record a list of children's ideas on the board.

Read Aloud

Objective *To identify rhymes in poetry*

BIG BOOK OF RHYMES AND POEMS   Display "The Purple Cow" on page 39. Read the poem aloud, emphasizing the rhyming words. Ask volunteers to point to and read the words that rhyme. (*Cow, anyhow*; *see one, be one*) Then reread the poem aloud several times as a class. Emphasize the rhythm and rhyme of the poem by reading with expression.

▲ **Big Book of Rhymes and Poems, p. 39**

Word Wall

Objective *To read high-frequency words*

REVIEW HIGH-FREQUENCY WORDS   Remove from the Word Wall the cards for *ears, knee, sure, expensive, young, picture, quite,* and *ago* as well as other previously learned high-frequency words. Have children begin snapping their fingers to keep time. Hold up each card and have children spell and read the word to the beat of the snaps. Flip through the word cards several times.

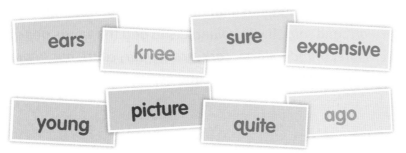

r-Controlled Vowel /ôr/ or, ore, our *and Spelling*

5-DAY PHONICS	
DAY 1	Introduce /ôr/ *or, ore, our*
DAY 2	Word Building with /ôr/ *or, ore, our*
DAY 3	**Word Building with /ôr/ *or, ore, our***
DAY 4	V/CV and VC/V; Review /ôr/ *or, ore, our*
DAY 5	V/CV and VC/V; Review /ôr/ *or, ore, our*

Objectives

• *To read and write common word families*
• *To recognize spelling patterns*

Skill Trace

Tested ✓ *r*-**Controlled Vowel /ôr/ or, ore, our**

Introduce	Grade 1
Reintroduce	T132–T135
Reteach	S14–S15
Review	**T144–T145, T168–T169, T412**
Test	Theme 5
Maintain	Theme 6, T268

---

r-**Controlled Vowel /ôr/ *or, ore, our***

Lisa munched on popcorn while she watched the juggler perform.
I could hear my dad snore all through the thunderstorm!
I know a cork can float, but I don't think an acorn will.
There were only four players on the basketball court for our game.
We heard a weather report that said we would get a huge snowstorm!
I heard a foghorn warn boats to come in to shore.
I heard the newborn baby crying before we got to the house.

Grade 2, Lesson 22   R115   Phonics

Transparency R115

Work with Patterns

INTRODUCE PHONOGRAMS Write the following phonograms at the top of six columns.

-ore	-ork	-orn	-orm	-ort	-our

Tell children that these are the endings of some words. Slide your hand under the letters as you read each phonogram. Repeat, and have children read the phonograms with you.

BUILD AND READ WORDS Write the letter *c* in front of the phonograms *-ore*, *-ork*, and *-orn*. Guide children to read each word: /k/-*ore*, *core*; /k/-*ork*, *cork*; /k/-*orn*, *corn*. Repeat the procedure for the phonograms *-orm*, *-ort*, and *-our* using the letter *f* to build *form*, *fort*, and *four*.

Then have children name other words that end with *-ore*, *-ork*, *-orn*, *-orm*, *-ort*, and *-our*. Have them tell which letter or letters to add to build each word, and write the word in the appropriate column. Have children read each column of words. Then point to words at random and have children read them.

Read Words in Context

READ SENTENCES Display **Transparency R115** or write the sentences on the board. Have children choral-read the sentences as you track the print. Then have volunteers read each sentence aloud and underline words with *-ore*, *-ork*, *-orn*, *-orm*, *-ort*, and *-our*. Invite volunteers to add the words *popcorn*, *perform*, *snore*, *thunderstorm*, *cork*, *acorn*, *four*, *court*, *our*, *report*, *snowstorm*, *foghorn*, *shore*, *newborn*, and *before* to the appropriate columns.

5-DAY SPELLING	
DAY 1	Pretest
DAY 2	Word Building
DAY 3	**State the Generalization**
DAY 4	Review
DAY 5	Posttest

Review Spelling Words

STATE THE GENERALIZATION FOR /ôr/ or, ore, our List spelling words 1–10 on chart paper or on the board. Circle the words *fork* and *short*, and have children read them aloud. Ask: **What is the same in each word?** (The letters *or* stand for the /ôr/ sound.) Repeat the procedure for *ore* (*store, score, shore, more, sore*). Circle the words, using a different color. Repeat for *our* (*pour, your, four*), using another color to circle the words.

 WRITE Have children write the spelling words in their notebooks. Remind them to use their best handwriting.

Handwriting

LETTER SPACING Remind children that their letters should not be too close together or too far apart.

Spelling Words

1. **store**	6. **shore**
2. **fork**	7. **short**
3. **pour**	8. **more***
4. **score**	9. **four**
5. **your**	10. **sore**

Challenge Words

11. **ignore**	14. **explore**
12. **important**	15. **fourteen**
13. **factory**	

* Word from "Serious Farm"

Decodable Books

Additional Decoding Practice

- **Phonics**
  r-Controlled Vowel /ôr/ or, ore, our
- **Decodable Words**
- **High-Frequency Words**
  See lists in *Decodable Book 18*.

  See also *Decodable Books*, online (Take-Home Version).

▲ Decodable Book 18
"Not Your Normal Fish!" and
"Courtney's Plans"

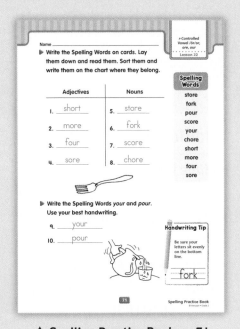

▲ Spelling Practice Book, p. 71

Fluency
Expression

Objectives
- *To build fluency through rereading*
- *To read with expression*

BELOW-LEVEL

Fluency Practice For fluency practice, have children read *Decodable Book 18*, the appropriate *Leveled Readers* (pp. T202–T205), or Story 22 in the *Strategic Intervention Interactive Reader*.

Review

▲ Student Edition, pp. 208–233

DIBELS
Oral Reading Fluency
ORF

MODEL USING EXPRESSION
Remind children that good readers use expression when they read to make the story come to life. Tell children to

- think about the meaning of the words and what the author is trying to express.

- think about what the characters are like and how they feel when they are saying something.

- match the pace at which they read aloud with the speed of the action or speech.

(Think Aloud) **I'm going to read aloud the beginning of "Serious Farm." I know the beginning of the story tells about how serious life on the farm is, so I'm going to try to show that by using my voice.**

Practice/Apply

GUIDED PRACTICE Read pages 210–211 aloud. Then have children practice reading aloud the same two pages several times with a partner. Circulate among the pairs, listening for appropriate expression and providing feedback as needed.

Routine Card **9**

INDEPENDENT PRACTICE Have small groups reread "Serious Farm" aloud together two or three times. Have members read two pages and then give other members a turn. Remind them to think about what is happening, what the characters are like, and how they are feeling when they speak.

Additional Related Reading

- ***Millie Wants to Play!*** by Janet Pedersen. Candlewick, 2004. **EASY**

- ***The Cow in the House*** by Harriet Ziefert. Puffin, 1997. **AVERAGE**

- ***Farmer Dale's Red Pickup Truck*** by Lisa Wheeler. Harcourt, 2006. **CHALLENGE**

Plot
Comprehension

Review

REVIEW PLOT Remind children that the plot of a story involves the problem the characters face and the events that show how they solve it. Explain that sometimes characters have to try different solutions until they find the one that solves their problem.

Practice/Apply

GUIDED PRACTICE Display completed **Transparency GO4** for "Serious Farm." Ask questions such as the following to discuss the important events:

- **What was the first way that the animals tried to solve their problem? Did it work? Why or why not?** (Edna the cow pretended to be a rooster. It didn't work, because Farmer Fred didn't think it was funny.)

- **What caused the animals to run away?** (They tried many different ways to get Farmer Fred to laugh. However, nothing worked so they got very discouraged.)

INDEPENDENT PRACTICE Have children complete a chart like the one on **Transparency GO4** for a story they have read, such as "Mr. Putter and Tabby Write the Book," "Annie's Gifts," or a fantasy story from the classroom library. After they are done, discuss the story's plot.

Objective
- *To identify and analyze the plot of a story*

Skill Trace
Tested **Plot**

Introduce	T34–T35
Reteach	S18–S19
Review	T69, T85, T97, T136–T137, T171, T187, T197, T397, T414
Test	Theme 5
Maintain	Theme 6, T86

"Research Says"

Direct Instruction "This project clearly demonstrates that children can be taught about the existence and use of reading strategies through informal, direct instructions in their regular classrooms."

—Paris, et. al (1984), p. 1248

Compare and Contrast
Comprehension

Objectives

- *To understand how to compare and contrast*
- *To compare and contrast across texts*

Skill Trace

 Compare and Contrast

Introduce	T70–T71
Reteach	S24–S25
Review	T172–T173, T415, T425
Test	Theme 5

 MONITOR PROGRESS

Compare and Contrast

IF children have difficulty understanding how to compare and contrast,	**THEN** display two similar objects, such as a baseball and a basketball, and have children compare and contrast them.

Small-Group Instruction, pp. S20–S21:

- **BELOW-LEVEL:** Reteach
- **ON-LEVEL:** Reinforce
- **ADVANCED:** Extend

Review

REVIEW COMPARE AND CONTRAST Tell children that good readers can get a better understanding of what they read by thinking about how stories or parts of stories are alike and different. Explain the following points:

- When you compare two things, you tell how they are alike.
- When you contrast two things, you tell how they are different.

Practice/Apply

GUIDED PRACTICE Display **Transparency R116.**

> Think Aloud **I can use a chart to compare and contrast two things, such as a real cow and the cow in "Serious Farm." To compare, I think about the ways both cows act and decide how they are alike. To contrast, I decide how their actions are different.**

Have a volunteer read aloud how the cows are alike. Guide children to determine other comparisons. Use these questions:

- **What color are real cows? What color is Edna?** (Real cows can be brown and white; Edna is brown and white.)
- **What do real cows eat? What do you think Edna eats?** (They both probably eat grass and hay.)

Add the comparisons to the chart. Then have a volunteer read aloud how the cows are different. Guide children to determine other contrasts. Use these questions:

- **How does Edna get the other animals to do what she says? Could a real cow do that?** (Possible response: Edna has lots of ideas so she gets the other animals to follow her. A real cow could not do this.)
- **When Edna leaves the farm, she packs her stuff. Would a real cow have anything to pack?** (No.)

Add the contrasts to the chart.

INDEPENDENT PRACTICE Have children use a chart to compare and contrast two characters in one story, such as Annie and Patty in "Annie's Gifts." Then have children use a chart to compare and contrast Farmer Fred and a character from a previously read story, such as the mother in "A Chair for My Mother" or Mr. Putter in "Mr. Putter and Tabby Write the Book." Have volunteers use their completed charts to explain how the two characters are the same and how they are different.

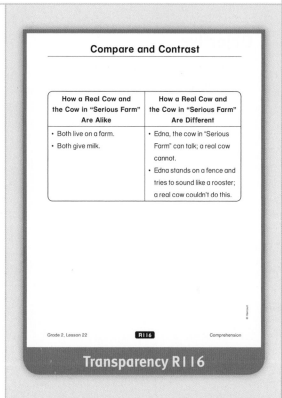

Transparency R116

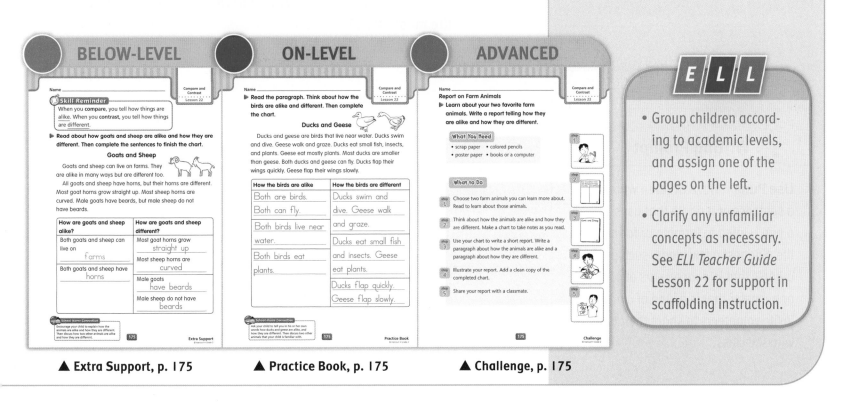

▲ Extra Support, p. 175   ▲ Practice Book, p. 175   ▲ Challenge, p. 175

E L L

- Group children according to academic levels, and assign one of the pages on the left.

- Clarify any unfamiliar concepts as necessary. See *ELL Teacher Guide* Lesson 22 for support in scaffolding instruction.

Reading

Student Edition: Paired Selection

Objective

- *To understand characteristics of poetry*

Genre Study

DISCUSS POETRY   Tell children that they will read three poems from a collection called "Beyond Old MacDonald," written by Charley Hoce. Remind children that some poems, called nonsense poems, also have a silly topic and are meant to be funny. Explain that each of these poems ends with a pun, or a phrase that is funny because of words that can have more than one meaning.

USE PRIOR KNOWLEDGE/SET A PURPOSE   Remind children of the silly picture of life on a farm that they read about in "Serious Farm." Invite children to examine the illustrations in the poems and tell what they think the poems will be about. Guide them to set a purpose for reading. Then have children read the poems.

Respond to the Poems

MONITOR COMPREHENSION   Have children reread each poem. Ask:

- **GENRE**   **What are the words used as puns in the last two poems?** (*calves, sows*)

- **PERSONAL RESPONSE**   **Which of the three poems did you enjoy the most? Why?** (Possible response: I liked "When My Cow Goes Dancing," because it is funny to picture a cow dancing.)

Writing Prompt

Use Puns   Have children write a sentence or a riddle that uses a pun related to farming or farm life. Suggest a few ideas, such as a *horse* that is *hoarse*, *ears* of corn, or a rooster that is a kind of *chicken*. Invite volunteers to share their puns with the class.

Poetry

Beyond Old MacDonald

poems by Charley Hoce
illustrated by Eugenie Fernandes

When My Cow Goes Dancing

When my cow goes dancing
At the weekly fashion ball,
She always wears a muumuu
Since it makes her calves look small.

Mischievous Goat

The baby goat was scolded
For the mischievous things he did.
But no one got too angry
After all, he's just a kid.

Farm Family

My mother patches all my jeans
My grandma makes my clothes
But when he's on a tractor
My dad's the one who sows.

234

235

SOCIAL STUDIES

SUPPORTING STANDARDS

Trends in Food Consumption   Explain to children that the kinds and amounts of food produced by farmers change over time. Tell children that by 1996, people consumed more vegetables, fruits, poultry, and low-fat milk than they did in 1970.

Explain that they also consumed much less red meat, eggs, and whole milk than they did in 1970.

Use these facts to discuss why our eating habits might have changed, and how these changes affect farmers and farming.

ELL

Clarify Puns and Multiple-Meaning Words   Explain the puns in the first two poems by using the illustrations to help clarify and define the multiple meanings of *kid* and *calves*. For the poem "Farm Family," write the words *sows* and *sews* on the board. Point out how the poem makes a joke by discussing sewing and sowing. Use miming gestures to help define the words. Have children repeat the words with you.

Connections

Objectives

- *To compare texts*
- *To connect texts to personal experiences*

Comparing Texts

1. In "When My Cow Goes Dancing" and "Serious Farm," the cows dance and dress in human clothes. In "Serious Farm," the cow also imitates a rooster and does a handstand. **TEXT TO TEXT**

2. Possible response: I laugh at things that are unexpected and when people tell good jokes. **TEXT TO SELF**

3. They talk to people and other animals, they put on clothes, and act in ways that real animals cannot. **TEXT TO WORLD**

Connections

Comparing Texts

1 What do the cows do in "Serious Farm" and "When My Cow Goes Dancing"?

2 What kinds of things make you laugh?

3 How are the animals in "Serious Farm" different from real animals?

Phonics

Make Picture Cards

Write words in which the letters *or*, *ore*, or *our* stand for the vowel sound in *fork*. Draw a picture for each. Share your words with a partner.

storm

pour

core

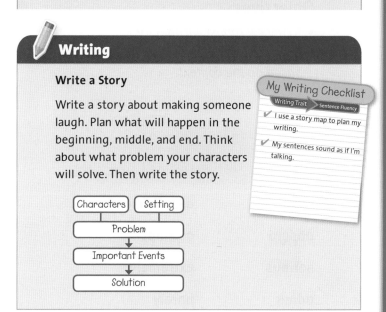

Fluency Practice

Readers' Theater

Work with a group to read "Serious Farm" as Readers' Theater. Think about how the characters should sound. Make the sounds that the animals make!

Writing

Write a Story

Write a story about making someone laugh. Plan what will happen in the beginning, middle, and end. Think about what problem your characters will solve. Then write the story.

My Writing Checklist

Writing Trait ▸ Sentence Fluency

✔ I use a story map to plan my writing.

✔ My sentences sound as if I'm talking.

Characters → Setting
↓
Problem
↓
Important Events
↓
Solution

236

237

PHONICS

Make Picture Cards Suggest that children use this week's spelling words as a starting point, but explain that they should think of additional words with /ôr/ for their cards. Have children later meet with a small group and compare their cards.

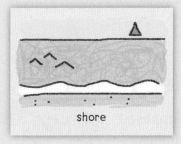

shore

FLUENCY

Readers' Theater Have children work in small groups, and assign roles to each child. As needed, provide examples of what Farmer Fred's deadpan expression might sound like, as well as how Edna the cow's expression might change when she is hopeful, frustrated, or pleased. Encourage children to use expression to help convey meaning as they read their lines.

WRITING

Write a Story Explain that children may use an event from their own life in their stories, or they can use an event that they make up. Have children use a chart like the one on page 237 to plan their stories. After they are done, invite volunteers to read their stories aloud.

Once my brother was sad because he was too sick to go to a party. I decided to try to make him laugh

Build Robust Vocabulary

Objectives

- *To review robust vocabulary*
- *To figure out a word's meaning based on the context*

REVIEW [Tested ✓]

Vocabulary: Lesson 22

acquired	assumed
absurd	attempt
serious	extremely
admit	barely
hilarious	witty

Review Robust Vocabulary

USE VOCABULARY IN DIFFERENT CONTEXTS Remind children of the Student-Friendly Explanations of the Vocabulary Words introduced on Days 1 and 2. Then discuss each word, using the following prompts:

acquired

- **What is something that we acquired recently for the classroom? Why did we acquire it?**
- **What questions would you ask if a friend told you he or she had acquired a new pet?**

assumed

- **Tell about something that you assumed about second grade when you were in first grade.**
- **Name some things you assumed would happen when you had your last music class.**

absurd

- **Is it absurd to eat dessert before dinner? Why or why not?**
- **Do absurd things happen every day? Explain.**

attempt

- **What would you have to do before you could attempt to walk on the moon?**
- **Would you want to attempt to do third grade work while in second grade? Why or why not?**

serious

- **Is a clown usually serious? Explain.**
- **Tell what it's like when you are supposed to be serious but you have the giggles.**

extremely

- Tell about something that you tried to do that was extremely hard.
- Name a sound that is extremely loud. Name a sound that is extremely soft.

admit

- If you made a mistake and no one knew about it, would you keep it secret or would you admit it?
- What might someone say if they were going to admit that they made a mistake?

barely

- Name some kinds of weather when you can barely see outside.
- Would someone who is barely sick have to go to the hospital? Tell why or why not.

hilarious

- Tell about the most hilarious thing that has ever happened to you.
- How can you tell if people coming out of a movie have just seen something that is hilarious?

witty

- Would someone who is witty be fun to play with? Tell why or why not.
- Would you rather sit next to someone who is witty or someone who is serious? Explain your answer.

▼ **Student-Friendly Explanations**

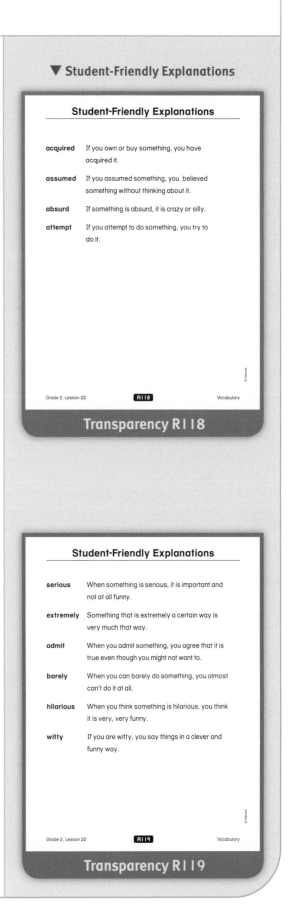

Student-Friendly Explanations

acquired	If you own or buy something, you have acquired it.
assumed	If you assumed something, you believed something without thinking about it.
absurd	If something is absurd, it is crazy or silly.
attempt	If you attempt to do something, you try to do it.

Grade 2, Lesson 22   **R118**   Vocabulary

Transparency R118

Student-Friendly Explanations

serious	When something is serious, it is important and not at all funny.
extremely	Something that is extremely a certain way is very much that way.
admit	When you admit something, you agree that it is true even though you might not want to.
barely	When you can barely do something, you almost can't do it at all.
hilarious	When you think something is hilarious, you think it is very, very funny.
witty	If you are witty, you say things in a clever and funny way.

Grade 2, Lesson 22   **R119**   Vocabulary

Transparency R119

Grammar Quick Write

Subject-Verb Agreement

5-DAY GRAMMAR	
DAY 1	Introduce Subject-Verb Agreement
DAY 2	Practice Agreement
DAY 3	**Use Agreement in Sentences**
DAY 4	Apply to Writing
DAY 5	Weekly Review

Objective

• *To use correct subject-verb agreement in sentences*

Daily Proofreading

Ms. Greens birthday is in march.

(Green's; March)

TECHNOLOGY

GO online www.harcourtschool.com/
storytown
Grammar Glossary

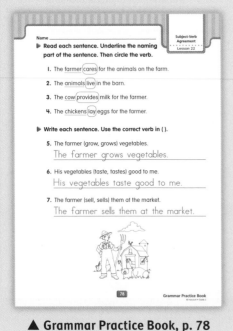

▲ **Grammar Practice Book, p. 78**

Review

SUBJECT-VERB AGREEMENT   Write the following sentences on the board, and have children read them aloud.

> Sonia pops a balloon.
>
> I pop a balloon.
>
> All the children pop a balloon.

Tell children that in the first sentence, *pops* ends with an *-s* because the naming part tells about one, *Sonia*. Explain that in the second and third sentences, *pop* does not end with an *-s* because the naming parts tell about *I* and more than one.

Practice/Apply

GUIDED PRACTICE   Write the following sentences on the board. Model how to correct the agreement in the first sentence. Guide children to correct the remaining sentences.

> **Tito laugh at the clown.** (laughs)
>
> **The kittens plays with some yarn.** (play)
>
> **The factory worker fill the boxes.** (fills)
>
> **Kendra and I skips rope together.** (skip)

INDEPENDENT PRACTICE   Have children write sentences using correct subject-verb agreement. Have partners switch papers to check for correct usage.

Writing
Fantasy

5-DAY WRITING	
DAY 1	Introduce
DAY 2	Prewrite
DAY 3	**Draft**
DAY 4	Revise
DAY 5	Revise

Draft a Fantasy Story

REVIEW WITH A LITERATURE MODEL   Remind children that "Serious Farm" is a fantasy. Have children turn to pages 214–215 in their *Student Edition*. Point out the following:

> • Edna the cow is standing on a fence. This could not take place in real life.
>
> • All the animals laugh. In a fantasy, characters behave in ways that they couldn't in real life.
>
> • Farmer Fred doesn't see the humor in Edna's actions. He's too serious. This is the problem. A fantasy has a problem, important events, and a solution.

DRAFT A FANTASY   Have children use their ideas, their graphic organizers, and what they now know to write a draft of a fantasy story.

SENTENCE FLUENCY   As children write their drafts, remind them that they can combine short sentences into a longer sentence to help make ideas flow more smoothly. Tell them they will also be able to do this when they revise.

CONFER WITH CHILDREN   Meet with children, helping them as they write their fantasy stories. Offer encouragement for what they are doing well and make constructive suggestions for improving an aspect of the writing, as needed.

Objectives
• *To write a draft of a fantasy story*
• *To use correct subject-verb agreement*

Writing Prompt

Evaluate Fantasy   Have children write a sentence that tells what part of "Serious Farm" seems most unreal to them.

▲ Writer's Companion, Lesson 22

Write Short Sentences   Encourage children to write short sentences to jot their ideas down. Emphasize that they will have time to revise later, and can work to create more detailed sentences then.

Day at a Glance

Day 4

 **phonics and Spelling**

- Review: Syllable Pattern V/CV and VC/V
- Review: *r*-Controlled Vowel /ôr/*or, ore, our*

Fluency

- Expression
- "Serious Farm," *Student Edition,* pp. 208–233

 Read!

Comprehension

Focus Skill Review: Plot

Robust Vocabulary

- Review: *acquired, assumed, extremely, barely, admit, serious, hilarious, witty, absurd, attempt*

Grammar Quick Write

- Review: Subject-Verb Agreement

Writing

- Fantasy

Warm-Up Routines

 Oral Language

Objective *To listen attentively and respond appropriately to oral communication*

> ## Question of the Day
>
> **What might surprise a farmer after he or she planted seeds?**

Discuss possible mistakes or unusual happenings that might occur after planting seeds. Use the following prompts:

- **What do seeds look like? Do you think it is easy to tell seeds apart?**

- **What might happen if a farmer mixed up the seeds for different kinds of crops?**

Have children brainstorm other unusual things that might cause surprises for farmers. List their ideas on the board.

Read Aloud

Objective *To listen for enjoyment*

BIG BOOK OF RHYMES AND POEMS Display "A Young Farmer of Leeds" on page 40 and read the title aloud. Tell children to listen for enjoyment. Then read the poem aloud. Invite children to tell what had happened to the farmer, and explain what parts they especially enjoyed. Reread the poem several times, inviting children to join in when they are able.

▲ **Big Book of Rhymes and Poems, p. 40**

Word Wall

Objective *To read high-frequency words*

REVIEW HIGH-FREQUENCY WORDS Arrange the words *sugar, half, believe, year, shoes, father, impossible,* and *coming* in two columns. Divide the class into two groups. Have children in the first group choral-read the first column of words, snapping their fingers or clapping to keep time. Have the second group do the same with the second column of words. Then have the groups switch columns and repeat.

Syllable Patterns V/CV and VC/V phonics

5-DAY PHONICS	
DAY 1	Introduce /ôr/or, ore, ou
DAY 2	Word Building with /ôr/or, ore, our
DAY 3	Word Building with /ôr/or, ore, our
DAY 4	V/CV and VC/V; Review /ôr/or, ore, our
DAY 5	V/CV and VC/V; Review /ôr/or, ore, our

Objectives

- *To identify V/CV and VC/V syllable patterns*
- *To read longer words with V/CV and VC/V syllable patterns*

Skill Trace

Tested Syllable Patterns V/CV and VC/V

Introduce	Theme 4, T184, T350
Review	T184, T194

Syllable Patterns V/CV and VC/V

Marcus will use a shovel to make the hole wider.

The tulip is starting to lose its petals.

My toy robot is made out of metal.

Your shadow grows longer later in the day.

Grade 2, Lesson 22   R117   Phonics

Transparency R117

Teach/Model

Routine Card 11

REVIEW V/CV AND VC/V Write the word *tulip* on the board. Ask: **Is the vowel sound in *tulip* long or short?** (long) Write *tu-lip* on the board and read it aloud. Say: **In a word with a vowel-consonant-vowel, if the vowel sound is long, divide before the consonant.** Then write the word *petal* on the board. Ask: **Is the vowel sound in *petal* long or short?** (short) Write *pet-al* on the board and read it aloud. Say: **In a word with a vowel-consonant-vowel, if the vowel sound is short, divide after the consonant.**

MODEL DECODING LONGER WORDS Model how to blend the syllables together to read *tulip*.

- Cover the second syllable and have children read /tū/.
- Cover the first syllable and have children read /lip/.
- Then have children read the word *tulip*.

Distribute Syllabication Cards 11 and 12 (Teacher Resource Book, p. 92) and read them aloud.

Guided Practice

DIVIDING WORDS Write the words *palace*, *moment*, *decoy*, *broken*, *shadow*, and *rejoice* on the board. Guide children to identify the V/CV or VC/V pattern in each word, to divide the word into syllables, and to blend the syllables to read each word. Ask children to identify the words that have the diphthong /oi/ to maintain the skill.

Practice/Apply

INDEPENDENT PRACTICE Display **Transparency R117** or write the sentences on the board or on chart paper. Have children read the sentences aloud. Remind them to use what they have learned about V/CV and VC/V to help them read accurately. Ask children to identify and read the word that uses the diphthong /oi/.

r-Controlled Vowel
/ôr/ or, ore, our  and Spelling

5-DAY SPELLING	
DAY 1	Pretest
DAY 2	Word Building
DAY 3	State the Generalization
DAY 4	Review
DAY 5	Posttest

Build Words

REVIEW THE WORDS Have children open their notebooks to the spelling words that they wrote on Day 3. Have them read the words several times and then close their notebooks.

MAP LETTERS TO SOUNDS Have children follow your directions to change one letter in each of the following words to make a spelling word. Have them write the spelling word on a sheet of paper. Then have a volunteer write the word on the board so that children can self-check their spelling.

- Write *scare* on the board. Ask:
  Which spelling word can you make by changing the third letter? *(score)*

- Write *shore* on the board. Ask:
  Which spelling word can you make by changing the first letter? *(chore)*

- Write *fort* on the board. Ask:
  Which spelling word can you make by changing the last letter? *(fork)*

scare
score
shore
chore
fort
fork

Follow a similar procedure with the following words: *bore* (more), *stare* (store), *tore* (sore), *pound* (pour), *you* (your), *shout* (short), *for* (four).

CHALLENGE WORDS Write the five challenge words on the board in random order. Have children write the words in a list in alphabetical order. *(explore, factory, fourteen, ignore, important)*

Objective

- *To use /ôr/or, ore, our and other known letter-sounds to spell and write words*

Spelling Words

1.	**store**	6.	**chore**
2.	**fork**	7.	**short**
3.	**pour**	8.	**more***
4.	**score**	9.	**four**
5.	**your**	10.	**sore**

Challenge Words

11.	**ignore**	14.	**explore**
12.	**important**	15.	**fourteen**
13.	**factory**		

* Word from "Serious Farm"

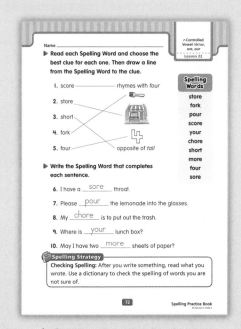

▲ Spelling Practice Book, p. 72

 Fluency
Expression

Objectives

- *To build fluency through rereading a fantasy story*
- *To read with expression*

 BELOW-LEVEL

Reread for Confidence Children may need to practice reading text until they feel comfortable with the words. Have children choose two or more pages of "Serious Farm" that they especially enjoy, and practice reading them aloud until they can read accurately and confidently. Then have them work to include expression in their voices as they read aloud.

 MONITOR PROGRESS

Fluency

IF children have difficulty reading with expression,	THEN model reading with expression as you have the children echo-read the story with you.

Small-Group Instruction, pp. S16–S17:

- **BELOW-LEVEL:** Reteach
- **ON-LEVEL:** Reinforce
- **ADVANCED:** Extend

Review

 MODEL USING EXPRESSION Read aloud pages 216–217 of "Serious Farm." Tell children to listen to your expression.

▲ Student Edition, pp. 208–233

Think Aloud I tried to make my expression as serious as Farmer Fred when I read, "Broccoli's no fun," and "I never laugh at bell peppers." When I read what Edna said, I wanted my expression to show that she was hopeful when she said, "Let's try another idea." In this story, even the narrator, who tells the story, has a voice. I used expression to show what the narrator is like when I read a line like, "It wasn't as easy as it sounds."

Practice/Apply

 GUIDED PRACTICE Have children echo-read pages 216–217 with you, matching your expression and pace.

INDEPENDENT PRACTICE Have children read along as they listen to "Serious Farm" on *Audiotext Grade 2,* CD 5. Stop the recording periodically to note how the reader uses expression. Have children practice reading aloud at these points.

Plot
Comprehension

Review

DEFINE PLOT   Ask children to define what the plot of a story is. (the problem the characters face and the events that tell how they solve it) Explain that the problem usually appears at the beginning of a story, that the important events show how the characters work to solve the problem, and the solution usually comes near the end of the story.

Practice /Apply

GUIDED PRACTICE   Display **Transparency R113**. Reread the story aloud to children and ask them to identify the characters. (Max and Ted) Guide children to identify elements of the story's plot. Ask:

- **What is the problem in the story?** (Max feels lonely and unhappy.)

- **What caused this problem?** (Ted got so busy with soccer that he forgot about Max.)

- **What events in the story tell how Max tries to solve the problem?** (He decides to go on a two-week cruise. He sends Ted a postcard.)

- **Do you think this was a good solution? Tell why.** (Possible response: Yes, because Max has a good time, and it helps Ted realize that he has not paid enough attention to Max.)

INDEPENDENT PRACTICE   Have partners review the plot of "Serious Farm." Ask partners to explain whether they thought the animals' idea to run away was a good solution. (Possible response: It is not a good solution, because they don't really have a plan to go anywhere in particular. But since it does make Farmer Fred realize that they are unhappy, it leads to making life on the farm much better.)

Objective

- *To identify the plot of a story*

Skill Trace

 Plot

Introduce	T34–T35
Reteach	S18–S19
Review	T69, T85, T97, T136–T137 T171, T187, T197, T397, T414
Test	Theme 5
Maintain	Theme 6, T86

Plot

Max and Ted

Max and Ted were best friends. They played in the park together and went on long hikes. They talked about everything. There was one thing that made Ted and Max's friendship different, though. Max was Ted's dog.

Max helped Ted with his homework, and brought it to school when Ted left it at home. He even made sure Ted remembered to brush his teeth. There came a time, though, when Ted forgot what a good friend Max was. Ted got so busy with soccer that he didn't have time for Max. Max was lonely and unhappy.

Max took off on a two-week cruise. He had the time of his life, but he remembered to send a postcard to Ted.

Ted had no idea where Max went. He searched everywhere. Then, one day, he got Max's postcard. It said: "Miss me yet? I'll see you soon. Your best buddy, Max."

When Max came home Ted hugged Max. Max wagged his tail.

"Max!" Ted cried. "I'm so glad you're back! How can I make it up to you?"

"Don't worry about it," said Max. "Let me tell you about my trip."

Grade 2, Lesson 22   R113   Comprehension

Transparency R113

Build Robust Vocabulary

Objectives

- *To review robust vocabulary*
- *To understand vocabulary in new contexts*

Tested

REVIEW ✓

Vocabulary: Lesson 22

acquired	assumed
serious	extremely
admit	barely
hilarious	witty
absurd	attempt

Extend Word Meanings

USE VOCABULARY IN DIFFERENT CONTEXTS Remind children of the Student-Friendly Explanations of the Vocabulary Words. Then discuss the words, using the following activities:

serious, hilarious Tell children that you will describe some things. If children think the thing is serious, they should make a somber expression and say, "Now, that's serious." If they think it sounds hilarious, they should laugh and say, "Now, that's hilarious!"

your neighbor has broken his arm

a cream pie throwing contest

a severe thunderstorm is coming

a clown splitting his pants

attempt Tell children that you will describe some things you might try to do. If children think your attempt will succeed, they should say, "Go for it!" If not, they should say, "Don't attempt it!"

balance a raw egg on your nose

carry five big boxes all at once

climb a ladder to clean a window

learn to speak a new language

absurd Tell children that you will tell about some pictures they might see in a book. If children think the picture sounds absurd, they should stand up. If not, they should shake their heads back and forth.

a mother pig and her piglets

a mother pig teaching her piglets to fly

a barber giving a boy a haircut

a barber giving a porcupine a haircut

Word Relationships

SYNONYMS   Tell children that a synonym is a word that means about the same as another word. Write these sentences on the board, underlining words as shown. Then read the sentences aloud and have children replace each underlined word with its Vocabulary Word synonym.

I <u>believed</u> that we would have fruit salad at lunch. (assumed)

Giorgio will <u>try</u> to walk on his hands. (attempt)

I think that making a sweater for a pig is <u>silly</u>. (absurd)

I <u>confess</u> that I should have asked before eating the rest of the berries. (admit)

A cheetah can run <u>very</u> fast. (extremely)

My Aunt Diana told me a <u>clever</u> joke. (witty)

Ms. Jackson said that I <u>got</u> my sense of humor from my father. (acquired)

Please speak louder—I can <u>hardly</u> hear you. (barely)

She is very <u>thoughtful</u> and dedicated to her school work. (serious)

When my brother dressed up like a taco shell, it was really <u>funny</u>. (hilarious)

▼ **Student-Friendly Explanations**

Student-Friendly Explanations

acquired	If you own or buy something, you have acquired it.
assumed	If you assumed something, you believed something without thinking about it.
absurd	If something is absurd, it is crazy or silly.
attempt	If you attempt to do something, you try to do it.

Grade 2, Lesson 22   R118   Vocabulary

Transparency R118

Student-Friendly Explanations

serious	When something is serious, it is important and not at all funny.
extremely	Something that is extremely a certain way is very much that way.
admit	When you admit something, you agree that it is true even though you might not want to.
barely	When you can barely do something, you almost can't do it at all.
hilarious	When you think something is hilarious, you think it is very, very funny.
witty	If you are witty, you say things in a clever and funny way.

Grade 2, Lesson 22   R119   Vocabulary

Transparency R119

Grammar *Quick Write*
Subject-Verb Agreement

5-DAY GRAMMAR

DAY 1	Introduce Subject-Verb Agreement
DAY 2	Practice Agreement
DAY 3	Use Agreement in Sentences
DAY 4	**Apply to Writing**
DAY 5	Weekly Review

Objective

• *To use correct subject-verb agreement in sentences*

Daily Proofreading

my mother rushs to work.

(My; rushes)

Writing Trait ➤

Strengthening Conventions

Verbs Use this short lesson with children's own writing to build a foundation for revising/editing longer connected text on Day 5. See also *Writer's Companion*, Lesson 22.

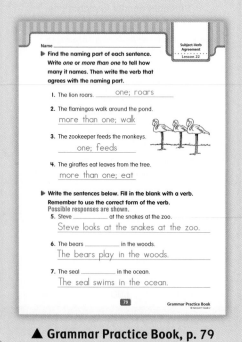

▲ **Grammar Practice Book, p. 79**

Review

DISCUSS SUBJECT-VERB AGREEMENT Review what children have learned about subject-verb agreement, using the following points:

• Add an *-s* to most verbs when the naming part of the sentence tells about one.

• Do not add an *-s* when the naming part tells about more than one.

• Do not add an *-s* to a verb when the naming part is *I* or *you*.

Write the following sentence frames and verb choices on the board. Read the first one aloud. Work with children to identify the correct verb. Guide them to tell which form of the verb to use in the remaining sentences.

> Sarah _____ her soup. (stir, stirs)
>
> You _____ your juice. (slurp, slurps)
>
> Frank _____ an egg into the bowl. (break, breaks)
>
> I _____ some carrots. (peel, peels)

Practice/Apply

GUIDED PRACTICE Tell children that you will work together to write sentences to tell about the class making a giant pizza. Begin by writing the following sentences on the board.

> I grate cheese to put on the pizza.
>
> Anna slices some mushrooms.

Elicit sentence ideas that include toppings and related verbs. Have children write the sentence on the board.

INDEPENDENT PRACTICE Invite children to write three sentences that tell about foods that come from a farm. Children could begin sentences with subjects such as: Some foods, A food. Tell children that they should use action verbs, and the verb should agree with the naming part. Invite volunteers to share their sentences.

5-DAY WRITING	
DAY 1	Introduce
DAY 2	Prewrite
DAY 3	Draft
DAY 4	Revise
DAY 5	Revise

Writing
Fantasy

Write and Revise

WRITE Have children continue writing their fantasy stories. Remind them that their stories should have a plot with a problem, important events, and a solution.

WRITING TRAIT **SENTENCE FLUENCY** Remind children to think about combining two short sentences to create one longer, smoother sentence. Write the following sentences on the board: *Peter Pig cut a piece of the cake. He gave it to Peggy.* Read the sentences aloud, and explain that the ideas can be put together in one sentence, such as *Peter Pig cut a piece of the cake and gave it to Peggy.* Point out that this sentence does not sound as choppy as the two sentences.

REVISE Have children read their fantasy story to a partner. They can use the list of criteria for a fantasy to check and improve their writing.

Fantasy

- A fantasy tells about something that could not take place in real life.

- A fantasy includes characters that behave in ways that they couldn't in real life.

- A fantasy should have a problem, important events, and a solution.

Tell children to make notes on their drafts of the changes they will make. Encourage them to use Editor's Marks. Remind children to check that they have used correct subject-verb agreement in their sentences. Have children continue to work on revising their drafts. Tell them that they will continue revising on Day 5.

Editor's Marks

∧	Add
℘	Take out
⌒	Change
⊙	Add a period
≡	Capitalize
⬭	Check Spelling

Objectives

- *To revise a draft of a fantasy*
- *To edit a draft for appropriate grammar*

Writing Prompt

Explain Have children write about how they got the idea for the main character or characters for their stories.

Confer with Children Encourage children to share their revisions with you. Invite children to tell what they would like to change, and provide support.

phonics and Spelling

- Review: Syllable Patterns V/CV and VC/V
- Posttest: *r*-Controlled Vowel /ôr/ *or, ore, our*

Fluency

- Expression
- "Serious Farm," *Student Edition*, pp. 208–233

Read!

Comprehension

 Review: Plot

Focus Skill

- *Read-Aloud Anthology:* "The Rooster That Crowed At Nightfall"

Robust Vocabulary

- Cumulative Review

Grammar Quick Write

- Review: Subject-Verb Agreement

Writing

- Fantasy

Warm-Up Routines

 Oral Language

Objective *To listen attentively and respond appropriately to oral communication*

Question of the Day

How can you tell if a poem is meant to be silly?

Invite children to explain how they know whether a poem is meant to be silly or realistic. Use the following prompts:

- **Name some poems we've heard that are meant to be silly.**
- **What clues told you that the things in these poems couldn't really happen?**
- **Why do you think people write silly poems?**

Write the following sentence frame and have children complete it.

I can tell that a poem is meant to be silly when _____ .

Read Aloud

Objective *To identify structure and rhymes in poetry*

BIG BOOK OF RHYMES AND POEMS Display "A Young Farmer of Leeds" on page 40. Tell children that this is a special kind of poem called a *limerick*, and that it follows a special pattern. Read the poem aloud. Have children identify the rhymes. *(Leeds, seeds, weeds; pass, grass)* Point out the limerick pattern. Say: **A limerick is five lines, and has a special rhythm. Lines one, two, and five rhyme with each other. Lines three and four rhyme with each other, too.** Point out the pattern for children. Then read the poem aloud. Invite children to read along or to chime in on the last line of the limerick.

▲ Big Book of Rhymes and Poems, p. 40

Word Wall

Objective *To read high-frequency words*

REVIEW HIGH-FREQUENCY WORDS Review the words *brother, world, minute, cook, touch, board, enjoy,* and *straight*. Point to a card at random, and ask children to read the word.

Syllable Patterns V/CV and VC/V phonics

5-DAY PHONICS	
DAY 1	Introduce /ôr/ *or, ore, our*
DAY 2	Word Building with /ôr/ *or, ore, our*
DAY 3	Word Building with /ôr/ *or, ore, our*
DAY 4	V/CV and VC/V; Review /ôr/ *or, ore, our*
DAY 5	V/CV and VC/V; Review /ôr/ *or, ore, our*

Objectives

- *To identify V/CV and VC/V syllable patterns*
- *To read words with V/CV and VC/V syllable patterns*

Skill Trace

Tested **Syllable Patterns V/CV and VC/V**

Introduce	Theme 4, T184, T350
Review	T184, T194

Review

READ V/CV AND VC/V WORDS Write the words *robot* and *metal* on the board. Guide children to label *robot* and *metal* with the V/CV and the VC/V syllable patterns and read the words aloud.

Practice/Apply

GUIDED PRACTICE Write the following words on the board: *hotel, student, river, seven, raven,* and *melon.* Then make a chart as shown. Guide children to sort the words and add them to the chart.

V/CV Pattern	VC/V Pattern
hotel	river
student	seven
raven	melon

INDEPENDENT PRACTICE Have children read aloud the words in the chart.

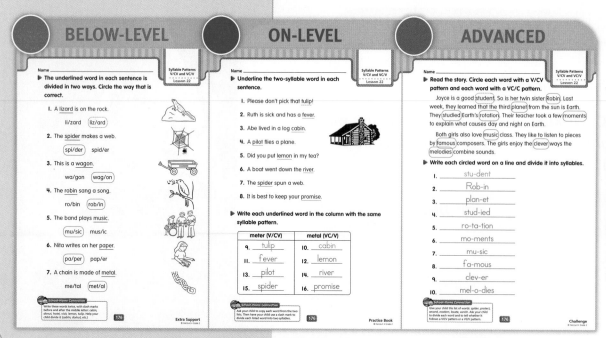

▲ **Extra Support, p. 176**   ▲ **Practice Book, p. 176**   ▲ **Challenge, p. 176**

ELL

- Group children according to academic levels and assign one of the pages on the left.
- Clarify any unfamiliar concepts as necessary. See *ELL Teacher Guide* Lesson 22 for support in scaffolding instruction.

r-Controlled Vowel /ôr/ or, ore, our phonics *and Spelling*

5-DAY SPELLING
DAY 1 Pretest
DAY 2 Word Building
DAY 3 State the Generalization
DAY 4 Review
DAY 5 Posttest

Assess

POSTTEST Assess children's progress. Use the dictation sentences from Day 1.

Words with /ôr/ *or, ore, our*

1.	store	Margo bought lemons at the grocery **store.**
2.	fork	Please use a **fork** to eat your meat.
3.	pour	Will you **pour** a cup of milk for Rob?
4.	score	It's exciting to watch the players **score** a goal.
5.	your	Can I borrow **your** sunglasses?
6.	chore	Making my bed is my least favorite **chore.**
7.	short	When I was three, I was too **short** to reach the table.
8.	more	May I have some **more** ice cream?
9.	four	We need **four** people to play this game.
10.	sore	My feet were **sore** after the long hike.

ADVANCED

Challenge Words Use the challenge words in these dictation sentences.

11.	ignore	I had to **ignore** the noise to do my homework.
12.	important	Mr. Mitchell has something **important** to say.
13.	factory	We visited the jellybean **factory** on our vacation.
14.	explore	Manny likes to take hikes to **explore** the forest.
15.	fourteen	Next week, my sister will be **fourteen** years old.

WRITING APPLICATION
Have children use one of the spelling words to write and illustrate a sentence about something they say or do at mealtime.

Objective

• *To use /ôr/or, ore, our and other known letter-sounds to spell and write words*

Spelling Words

1.	store	6.	chore
2.	fork	7.	short
3.	pour	8.	more*
4.	score	9.	four
5.	your	10.	sore

Challenge Words

11.	ignore	14.	explore
12.	important	15.	fourteen
13.	factory		

* Word from "Serious Farm"

May I have some more milk?

Fluency
Expression

Objective

• *To read fluently with expression*

 Readers' Theater

DIBELS
Oral Reading Fluency
ORF

PERFORM "SERIOUS FARM"
To help children improve their fluency, have them perform "Serious Farm" as Readers' Theater. Use the following procedures:

▲ **Student Edition, pp. 208–233**

• Discuss with children how the characters and the narrator might feel and sound throughout the story.

• Have the class prepare to perform the story for another class. Assign the roles of Farmer Fred, Edna, Bernie, and a chicken. Split the part of the narrator among several children. Children who are not reading at a given time may play the part of a farm animal.

• Have groups practice reading the story several times, paying particular attention to expression. Point out that characters who are not speaking may use body and facial expression to show how they are feeling.

• Once they are ready, have the class perform the story for another class.

ASSESSMENT

Monitoring Progress
Periodically, take a timed sample of children's oral reading and record the number of words read correctly per minute. Children should accurately read approximately 90–100 words per minute at the end of Grade 2.

Fluency Support Materials

 Fluency Builders, Grade 2, Lesson 22

 Audiotext *Student Edition* selections are available on *Audiotext Grade 2*, CD 5.

 Strategic Intervention Teacher Guide, Lesson 22

Develop Vocabulary   Point out words that tell how characters might be feeling or acting, such as *serious, hilarious, discouraging,* and *sad.* Say each word, modeling an expression that matches its meaning, and have children repeat it with you. Have children practice saying each word and using their voices and bodies to express the feeling.

Plot

Comprehension

Review

REVIEW THE SKILL Remind children that the plot of a story is the problem the characters face and the events that show how they solve the problem.

▲ **Read-Aloud Anthology, "The Rooster That Crowed at Nightfall," p. 82**

SET A PURPOSE FOR LISTENING Guide children to set a purpose for listening that includes

- noticing the problem, important events, and the solution.

- thinking about how the plot compares to that of "Serious Farm."

Practice/Apply

GUIDED PRACTICE As you read aloud "The Rooster That Crowed at Nightfall," record information about the plot in a story map.

```
┌─────────────────────┐   ┌─────────────────────┐
│     Characters      │   │       Setting       │
│   rooster, sheep,   │   │       a farm        │
│   cow, sow, piglet  │   │                     │
└──────────┬──────────┘   └─────────────────────┘
           │
┌──────────┴──────────────────────────┐
│              Problem                 │
│  When the old rooster dies, the new  │
│   rooster crows only at nightfall.   │
└──────────────────┬───────────────────┘
                   │
┌──────────────────┴───────────────────┐
│           Important Events            │
│  No one wakes up on time. The animals │
│   ask the Wise Old Sow for advice.    │
└──────────────────┬───────────────────┘
                   │
┌──────────────────┴───────────────────┐
│               Solution                │
│   A little piglet does the job, with an│
│           "Oink-a-doodle!"            │
└───────────────────────────────────────┘
```

INDEPENDENT PRACTICE Have children review the story map for "Serious Farm." Then have them tell how the plots are alike and different.

Objectives

- *To identify the plot of a story*
- *To compare the plots of two stories*

Skill Trace

Tested **Plot**

Introduce	T34–T35
Reteach	S18–S19
Review	T69, T85, T97, T136–T137, T171, T187, T197, T397, T414
Test	Theme 5
Maintain	Theme 6, T86

BELOW-LEVEL

Clarify Plot Events If children have difficulty identifying the plot in "The Rooster That Crowed at Nightfall," pause each time an event takes place and ask, "What just happened?" and have children restate the event.

 Build Robust Vocabulary

Objectives

- *To review robust vocabulary*
- *To organize word meanings to understand word relationships*

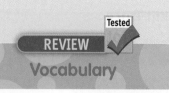

REVIEW [Tested]
Vocabulary

Lesson 21	Lesson 22
allowance	acquired
rosy	assumed
thrifty	absurd
industrious	attempt
bargain	serious
spoiled	extremely
comfortable	admit
boost	barely
exchanged	hilarious
delivered	witty

Cumulative Review

SORT WORDS   Guide children in sorting into three groups all the Vocabulary Words except *extremely* and *barely*. Display **Transparency GO10** or draw a chart like the following on the board. Have children consider the meaning and use of each word as they identify words as nouns, verbs, or adjectives.

Nouns	Verbs	Adjectives
allowance	spoiled	rosy
bargain	exchanged	thrifty
boost	delivered	industrious
	acquired	comfortable
	assumed	absurd
	attempt	serious
	admit	hilarious
		witty

Then have small groups use the chart to play a game. Have children take turns creating a sentence that includes at least one word from each column of the chart. Have groups play until each member has had several turns.

DEMONSTRATE WORD MEANING Discuss children's answers to these questions.

1. **If a friend told you that his or her allowance was one hundred dollars a week, would you say that was absurd? Why or why not?** (Possible response: Yes, because that is too much money for a young child.)

2. **Would someone admit that they were thrifty?** (Accept reasonable responses.)

3. **Name some things that are extremely tasty and some things that barely have any taste.** (Possible responses: a fresh carrot or apple, a potato chip, ice cream; water, cauliflower, lettuce)

4. **If someone is industrious, are they always serious?** (Possible response: Not always; someone who is industrious doesn't have to be serious all the time.)

5. **Would you attempt to give a grownup a boost by yourself? Why or why not?** (No, because a grownup would probably be too heavy for me.)

6. **Would someone who had acquired something that was a bargain be unhappy about it? Why or why not?** (Possible response: Probably not, since they got what they felt was a good deal.)

MONITOR PROGRESS

Build Robust Vocabulary

IF children have difficulty understanding the relationships between these pairs of words,	THEN work with children to identify synonyms for each word.

Small-Group Instruction, pp. S22–S23:

● **BELOW-LEVEL:** Reteach
● **ON-LEVEL:** Reinforce
● **ADVANCED:** Extend

Grammar

Subject-Verb Agreement

5-DAY GRAMMAR	
DAY 1	Introduce Subject-Verb Agreement
DAY 2	Practice Agreement
DAY 3	Use Agreement in Sentences
DAY 4	Apply to Writing
DAY 5	Weekly Reveiw

Objective

- *To use correct subject-verb agreement*

Daily Proofreading

Did you see Karlas new book.

(Karla's; book?)

 Language Arts Checkpoint

If children have difficulty with the concepts, see pages S24–S25 to reteach.

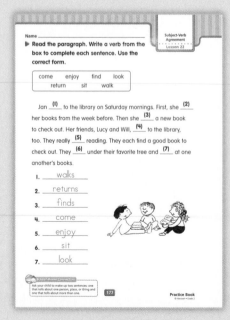

▲ **Practice Book, p. 177**

Review

REVIEW SUBJECT-VERB AGREEMENT Use these questions to review what children have learned about subject-verb agreement. Have volunteers write answers on the board as they are provided. Ask:

- When the naming part of the sentence tells about one, what is added to most verbs?

- When the naming part tells about more than one, how is the verb spelled?

- When the naming part tells about *I* or *you*, how is the verb spelled?

Practice/Apply

GUIDED PRACTICE Write the following sentences on the board. Then guide children to underline the action verb and to tell whether the naming part tells about one or more than one.

The mail carrier delivers the mail in the morning. (one)

Deena and Mario walk to the park. (more than one)

My neighbors wave when they drive by.
   (more than one)

A squirrel hides acorns in a hole in the big tree. (one)

INDEPENDENT PRACTICE Have children write a short paragraph. Tell them to pay attention to subject-verb agreement. Then have partners switch papers to check for agreement.

Writing
Fantasy

5-DAY WRITING	
DAY 1	Introduce
DAY 2	Prewrite
DAY 3	Draft
DAY 4	Revise
DAY 5	Revise

Revise

REVISE DRAFTS   Tell children that writers often look back after a day or so to see if they need to revise to improve their stories. Suggest that they ask themselves questions such as the following:

- Does my story move smoothly from the problem to the important events to the solution?

- Have I clearly described the events in the story?

WRITING TRAIT   **SENTENCE FLUENCY**   Ask volunteers to share an example of a place where they combined two shorter sentences to make one longer sentence. Discuss how combining sentences makes for smoother, more interesting writing.

Encourage children to revise their writing to clarify events and strengthen descriptions, and to make any changes they had noted from Day 4.

NOTE: A 4-point rubric appears on page R8.

SCORING RUBRIC

	6	5	4	3	2	1
FOCUS	Completely focused, purposeful.	Focused on topic and purpose.	Generally focused on topic and purpose.	Somewhat focused on topic, purpose.	Related to topic but does not maintain focus.	Lacks focus and purpose.
ORGANIZATION	Ideas progress logically; story conveys sense of completeness.	Organization mostly clear, story gives sense of completeness.	Organization mostly clear, but some lapses occur; may seem unfinished.	Some sense of organization; seems unfinished.	Little sense of organization.	Little or no sense of organization
SUPPORT	Strong, specific details; clear, exact language; freshness of expression.	Strong, specific details; clear, exact language.	Adequate support and word choice.	Limited supporting details; limited word choice.	Few supporting details; limited word choice.	Little development, limited or unclear word choice.
CONVENTIONS	Varied sentences; few, if any, errors.	Varied sentences; few errors.	Some sentence variety; few errors.	Simple sentence structures; some errors.	Simple sentence structures; many errors.	Unclear sentence structures; many errors.

REPRODUCIBLE RUBRICS for specific writing purposes and presentations are available on pages R2–R8.

Objective
- *To revise a fantasy story*

 ## Writing Prompt

Independent Writing   Have children generate a list of ideas about a new topic.

WEEKLY LESSON TEST

▲ **Weekly Lesson Tests, pp. 229–240**

- Selection Comprehension with Short Response
- Phonics and Spelling
- Focus Skill
- Compare and Contrast
- Robust Vocabulary
- Grammar
- Fluency Practice *FRESH READS*

 For prescriptions, see pp. A2–A6. Also available electronically on StoryTown Online Assessment and Exam View®.

 Podcasting: Assessing Fluency

Leveled Readers

Reinforcing Skills and Strategies

BELOW-LEVEL

No More Fish!

SUMMARY   Three pet cats are fed up with meals of fresh fish. They decide to reveal to the boy of the family that they can talk. They express their wish for canned cat food, and their wish is granted.

Genre: Fantasy

- **phonics**   *r*-Controlled Vowel /ôr/*or, ore, our*
- **Vocabulary**

  Plot

  Focus Skill

LEVELED READERS TEACHER GUIDE

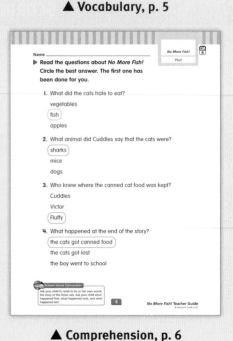

▲ Vocabulary, p. 5

Before Reading

BUILD BACKGROUND/SET PURPOSE   Ask children what might happen if animals could talk to people. Then guide children to preview the story and set a purpose for reading it.

Reading the Book

PAGES 3–5   **PLOT**   **What is the problem that the cats want to solve?** (They are sick of the fresh fish that they are always fed.)

PAGES 8–10   **CAUSE/EFFECT**   **Why do the cats decide to give their secret away?** (Possible response: Sitting by the cupboard did not get them the canned food they wanted, so they decide to ask directly.)

REREAD FOR FLUENCY   Have groups of five take the parts of the three cats, the boy, and the narrator, and read the story aloud, Readers' Theater style. Remind them to express their character's feelings.

Think Critically   *(See inside back cover for questions.)*

1 **PROBLEM/SOLUTION**   The cats are tired of being given fish to eat. They get the boy to ask his mom to buy canned cat food instead.

2 **PLOT**   The cats decide they will have to give away their secret and talk to the boy.

3 **CAUSE/EFFECT**   He is shocked when he hears the cats talk.

4 **IDENTIFY WITH CHARACTERS**   Possible response: shocked.

5 **PERSONAL RESPONSE**   Answers will vary.

▲ Comprehension, p. 6

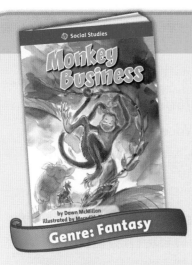

by Dawn McMillan
illustrated by Meredith

Genre: Fantasy

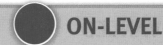

ON-LEVEL

Monkey Business

SUMMARY When Giraffe's sore throat lands her in a soft hospital bed, Monkey tricks the zookeeper into sending him to the hospital, too. The doctor is not fooled, however, and Monkey apologizes to all.

• **phonics** *r*-Controlled Vowel /ôr/*or, ore, our*

• **Vocabulary**

  Plot

Focus Skill

Before Reading

BUILD BACKGROUND/SET PURPOSE Have children tell what they know of the expression *monkey business*. After discussion, tell them that monkeys in stories often try to do tricky or mischievous things. Then guide children to preview the story and set a purpose for reading it.

Reading the Book

PAGE 6   MAKE PREDICTIONS   How can you tell that Monkey is going to do something tricky? (He sees how comfortable Giraffe is, and when he sits on his hard bed, he thinks of a "clever plan.")

PAGE 12   PLOT   What goes wrong with Monkey's plan? (The doctor realizes Monkey's leg isn't broken, so he can't stay.)

REREAD FOR FLUENCY Have partners take turns reading pages of the story. Remind them to express each character's feelings.

Think Critically   *(See inside back cover for questions.)*

①   PLOT Monkey pretended to be injured in front of the other animals so that he would be taken to the hospital to a comfortable bed.

②   CHARACTER'S EMOTIONS Possible responses: embarrassed, guilty

③   COMPARE/CONTRAST Giraffe was really sick with a sore throat. Monkey was just pretending to have a broken leg.

④   RETELL Monkey told all the animals he was sorry.

⑤   PERSONAL RESPONSE Answers will vary.

LEVELED READERS TEACHER GUIDE

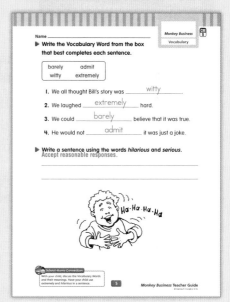

▲ Vocabulary, p. 5

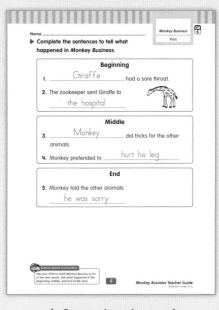

▲ Comprehension, p. 6

Leveled Readers

Reinforcing Skills and Strategies

ADVANCED

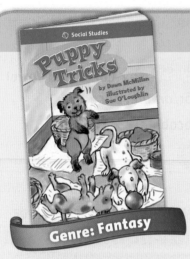

Genre: Fantasy

Puppy Tricks

SUMMARY Three puppies in a pet shop want to stay together. When a girl and her parents come into the shop, the puppies use cute antics to persuade the family to take them all home.

- **phonics** *r*-Controlled Vowel /ôr/*or, ore, our*
- **Vocabulary**
- **Plot**

Focus Skill

Before Reading

BUILD BACKGROUND/SET PURPOSE Ask children who have pet dogs to share stories about how the dog came to their home. Then guide children to preview the story and set a purpose for reading it.

Reading the Book

PAGES 3–4 **PLOT** **What problem are the puppies going to try to solve?** (Possible response: They want to leave the pet shop but worry about going to separate homes.)

PAGES 10–12 **CAUSE/EFFECT** **Why does the last part of the puppies' plan work?** (Possible response: They act so adorable together that Eleanor and Mom can't resist them.)

REREAD FOR FLUENCY Have partners take turns reading. Remind them to read using their voices to express feelings.

Think Critically
(*See inside back cover for questions.*)

1. **PLOT** The puppies howl at the same time, do tricks, and blink at Eleanor. They want to look cute, and they do.

2. **MAKE COMPARISONS** At the start, she is feeling sad and lonely because her friend has moved overseas. At the end, she is feeling happy and excited because she has three new puppies.

3. **NOTE DETAILS** Mom thinks the puppies could help on the farm.

4. **MAKE PREDICTIONS** Possible responses: herd sheep, be guard dogs

5. **PERSONAL RESPONSE** Answers will vary.

LEVELED READERS TEACHER GUIDE

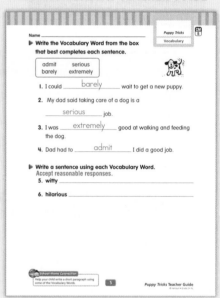

▲ Vocabulary, p. 5

▲ Comprehension, p. 6

E L L

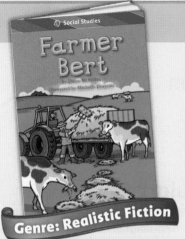

Genre: Realistic Fiction

Farmer Bert

SUMMARY   Farmer Bert starts his work day before dawn, calling to his dog to join him. He takes care of his dairy cows and plows his fields. At the end of a long day, he and his dog return home together.

- **Build Background**
- **Concept Vocabulary**
- **Scaffolded Language Development**

Before Reading

BUILD BACKGROUND/SET PURPOSE   Ask children where the milk they drink comes from. Have children share any knowledge of milking cows, and add information about small dairy farms. Then guide children to preview the story and set a purpose for reading it.

Reading the Book

PAGES 10–11   **CAUSE/EFFECT**   **What do hay and turnips have to do with getting milk from cows?** (Possible response: The cows make milk from eating food, so Farmer Bert feeds them hay and turnips.)

PAGES 3 AND 14   **PLOT**   **How does the story begin? How does it end?** (Possible response: At the beginning, Farmer Bert gets up early to milk the cows. At the end, he walks back home from the field.)

REREAD FOR FLUENCY   Have partners take turns reading the story one page at a time. Remind children that if they see an exclamation point, they should make their voices express strong feeling.

Scaffolded Language Development

(See inside back cover for teacher-led activity.)

Provide additional examples and explanation as needed.

LEVELED READERS TEACHER GUIDE

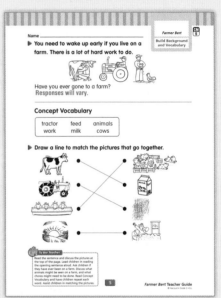

▲ **Build Background and Vocabulary, p. 5**

▲ **Scaffolded Language Development, p. 6**

Lesson 23

WEEK AT A GLANCE

 Phonics
Vowel Variant /o͞o/oo, ew, ue, ui, ou
Prefixes mis-, re-, un-

 Spelling
true, grew, suit, smooth, clue, soup, stew, food, group, fruit

Reading
"The Bee" by Sabrina Crewe NONFICTION
"California Bee Business" by Dimarie Santiago NONFICTION

 Fluency
Reading Rate

 Comprehension
 Use Graphic Aids
Synonyms
 Summarize

 Robust Vocabulary
thickens, plentiful, crowd (v.), sealed, carefully, attack, pattern, disappear, role, diligent

 Grammar
Past-Tense Verbs

Writing
Form: Paragraph of Information
Trait: Word Choice

Weekly Lesson Test

 = Focus Skill   = Focus Strategy   = Tested Skill

One stop
for all
your Digital *needs*

Lesson 23

Digital
CLASSROOM

 www.harcourtschool.com/storytown
To go along with your print program

FOR THE TEACHER

Prepare Professional Development

 Videos for Podcasting

Plan & Organize Online TE & Planning Resources*

Teach Transparencies

access from Online TE

Assess Online Assessment*

with Student Tracking System and Prescriptions

FOR THE STUDENT

Read  Student eBook*

 Strategic Intervention Interactive Reader

 Leveled Readers

Practice & Apply Splash into Phonics CD-ROM

 Also available on CD-ROM

Literature Resources

STUDENT EDITION

GO online eBook STUDENT EDITION

The Bee

Genre: Nonfiction

California
Bee Business
by Dimarie Santiago

Genre: Nonfiction

 ◀ **Audiotext** *Student Edition selections are available on Audiotext Grade 2, CD 5.*

 Accelerated Reader® ◀ *Practice Quizzes for the Selection*

THEME CONNECTION: BETTER TOGETHER
Comparing Two Nonfiction Selections

Paired Selections

 SCIENCE **The Bee, pp. 244–273**

SUMMARY Children will learn about the life cycle of a bee.

 SCIENCE **California Bee Business, pp. 274–275**

SUMMARY Children will discover how bees affect the production of almonds and honey in the state of California.

Support for Differentiated Instruction

 LEVELED READERS

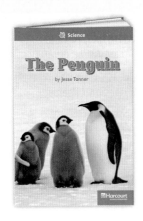   

● **BELOW-LEVEL** ● **ON-LEVEL** ● **ADVANCED** **E L L**

LEVELED PRACTICE

◄ **Strategic Intervention Resource Kit, Lesson 23**

◄ **Strategic Intervention Interactive Reader, Lesson 23**

Strategic Intervention Interactive Reader Online

◄ **ELL Extra Support Kit, Lesson 23**

◄ **Challenge Resource Kit, Lesson 23**

● **BELOW-LEVEL**

Extra Support Copying Masters, pp. 178, 180–184

● **ON-LEVEL**

Practice Book, pp. 178–185

● **ADVANCED**

Challenge Copying Masters, pp. 178, 180–184

ADDITIONAL RESOURCES

insects
flower

• Decodable Book 19
• Spelling Practice Book, pp. 73–75
• Grammar Practice Book, pp. 81–84
• Reading Transparencies R120–R126
• Language Arts Transparencies LA47–LA48
• Test Prep System
◄ **Literacy Center Kit, Cards 111–115**
• Sound/Spelling Cards
◄ **Fluency Builders**
◄ **Picture Card Collection**
• Read-Aloud Anthology, pp. 84–87

ASSESSMENT

✓ **Monitor Progress**

✓ **Weekly Lesson Tests, Lesson 23**
• Comprehension   • Robust Vocabulary
• Phonics and Spelling • Grammar
• Focus Skill   • Synonyms

 www.harcourtschool.com/ storytown
Online Assessment
Also available on CD-ROM—Exam View®

Suggested Lesson Planner

 Online TE & Planning Resources

Day 1

Step 1 | Whole Group

Daily Routines
- Oral Language
- Read Aloud
- High-Frequency Words

QUESTION OF THE DAY, p. T218
What insects do you find interesting? Why?

READ ALOUD, p. T219
Transparency R120: Leafcutter Bees

WORD WALL, p. T219

Word Work
- phonics
- Spelling

 phonics, p. T220
Introduce: Vowel Variant /o͞o/oo, ew, ue, ui, ou

SPELLING, p. T223
Pretest: *true, grew, suit, smooth, clue, soup, stew, food, group, fruit*

Skills and Strategies
- Reading
- Fluency
- Comprehension
- Build Robust Vocabulary

 READING, Words with *oo, ew, ue, ui, ou,* p. T221

 COMPREHENSION, p. T224
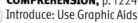 Introduce: Use Graphic Aids

LISTENING COMPREHENSION, p. T226
Read-Aloud: "Brilliant Bees"

FLUENCY, p. T226
Focus: Reading Rate

 BUILD ROBUST VOCABULARY, p. T227
Words from the Read-Aloud

Day 2

QUESTION OF THE DAY, p. T230
What do you like or dislike about bees?

READ ALOUD, p. T231
Big Book of Rhymes and Poems,
"Bumblebees"

WORD WALL, p. T231

 phonics, p. T232
Review: Vowel Variant /o͞o/oo, ew, ue, ui, ou

 SPELLING, p. T234
Word Building

BUILD ROBUST VOCABULARY, p. T234
Words from the Selection
Word Scribe, p. T235

 READING, p. T236
"The Bee"
Options for Reading

 COMPREHENSION,
p. T236
Introduce: Summarize

▲ Student Edition

RETELLING/FLUENCY,
p. T252
Reading Rate

 BUILD ROBUST VOCABULARY, p. T253
Words About the Selection

Step 2 | Small Groups

Suggestions for Differentiated Instruction (See pp. T212–T213.)

Step 3 | Whole Group

Language Arts
- Grammar *Quick Write*
- Writing

 GRAMMAR, p. T228
Introduce: Past-Tense Verbs

Daily Proofreading
the Beekeeper opens the hive.
(The beekeeper)

 WRITING, p. T229
Introduce: Paragraph of Information
Writing Trait: Word Choice

Writing Prompt *Draw a picture and write sentences about something that is important to you.*

 GRAMMAR, p. T254
Review: Past-Tense Verbs

Daily Proofreading
gary saw a gren frog.
(Gary, green)

 WRITING, p. T255
Review: Paragraph of Information
Writing Trait: Word Choice

Writing Prompt *Write about what you learned from reading a paragraph of information recently.*

 = Focus Skill    = Focus Strategy    = Tested Skill

Skills at a Glance

phonics
- Vowel Variant /oo/oo, ew, ue, ui, ou
- Prefixes mis-, re-, un-

Comprehension
 Focus Skill
Use Graphic Aids

Focus Strategy
Summarize

Fluency
Reading Rate

Vocabulary
ROBUST: *thickens, plentiful, crowd (v.), sealed, carefully, attack, pattern, disappear, role, diligent*

Day 3

QUESTION OF THE DAY, p. T256
Imagine that you are a bee. What words could you use so that other people would be able to guess what you are?

READ ALOUD, p. T257
Big Book of Rhymes and Poems, "Bumblebees"

WORD WALL, p. T257

 phonics, p. T258
Review: Vowel Variant /oo/oo, ew, ue, ui, ou

 SPELLING, p. T259
State the Generalization

FLUENCY, p. T260
Reading Rate: "The Bee"

COMPREHENSION, p. T261
Review: Use Graphic Aids
Paired Selection: "California Bee Business"

▲ Student Edition

CONNECTIONS, p. T264

 BUILD ROBUST VOCABULARY, p. T266
Review
Introduce: Synonyms, p. T268

 GRAMMAR, p. T270
Review: Past-Tense Verbs

Daily Proofreading
the clown juggled three orange.
(The, oranges)

WRITING, p. T271
Review: Paragraph of Information
Writing Trait: Word Choice

Writing Prompt *Write about what you find easy or difficult about writing paragraphs.*

Day 4

QUESTION OF THE DAY, p. T272
What are some ways you could learn more about bees?

READ ALOUD, p. T273
Big Book of Rhymes and Poems, "The Swarm of Bees"

WORD WALL, p. T273

 phonics, p. T274
Introduce: Prefixes mis-, re-, un-

 SPELLING, p. T275
Review Spelling Words

FLUENCY, p. T276
Reading Rate: "The Bee"

COMPREHENSION, p. T277
Review: Use Graphic Aids
Maintain: Author's Purpose
Maintain: Locate Information

▲ Student Edition

BUILD ROBUST VOCABULARY, p. T280
Review

 GRAMMAR, p. T282
Review: Past-Tense Verbs

Daily Proofreading
Last week, I hikd in the woods
(hiked, woods.)

 WRITING, p. T283
Review: Paragraph of Information
Writing Trait: Word Choice

Writing Prompt *Write about what you like about your paragraph of information and what you would like to improve.*

Day 5

QUESTION OF THE DAY, p. T284
What would you do if you saw a swarm of bees?

READ ALOUD, p. T285
Big Book of Rhymes and Poems, "The Swarm of Bees"

WORD WALL, p. T285

 phonics, p. T286
Review: Prefixes mis-, re-, un-

 SPELLING, p. T286
Posttest

FLUENCY, p. T288
Reading Rate: "The Bee"

COMPREHENSION, p. T289
Review: Use Graphic Aids
Read-Aloud: "Brilliant Bees"

▲ Student Edition

BUILD ROBUST VOCABULARY, p. T290
Cumulative Review

 GRAMMAR, p. T292
Review: Past-Tense Verbs

Daily Proofreading
Lori yellid on the playground?
(yelled; playground.)

 WRITING, p. T293
Review: Paragraph of Information
Writing Trait: Word Choice

Writing Prompt *Write ideas about a new topic of your choice for writing.*

 BELOW-LEVEL ON-LEVEL ADVANCED ELL

Suggested Small-Group Planner

45-60+ Minutes

	Day 1	Day 2

15-20+ Minutes

BELOW-LEVEL

Day 1

Teacher-Directed
Leveled Reader:
"The Penguin," p. T294
Before Reading

Independent
⭐ Listening/Speaking Center, p. T216
Extra Support Copying Masters, pp. 178, 180

▲ Leveled Reader

Day 2

Teacher-Directed
Student Edition:
"The Bee," p. T236

Independent
⭐ Reading Center, p. T216
Extra Support Copying Masters, pp. 181–182

▲ Student Edition

15-20+ Minutes

ON-LEVEL

Day 1

Teacher-Directed
Leveled Reader:
"The Ant," p. T295
Before Reading

Independent
⭐ Reading Center, p. T216
Practice Book, pp. 178, 180

▲ Leveled Reader

Day 2

Teacher-Directed
Student Edition:
"The Bee," p. T236

Independent
⭐ Letters and Sounds Center, p. T217
Practice Book, pp. 181–182

▲ Student Edition

15-20+ Minutes

ADVANCED

Day 1

Teacher-Directed
Leveled Reader:
"The Prairie Dog," p. T296
Before Reading

Independent
⭐ Letters and Sounds Center, p. T217
Challenge Copying Masters, pp. 178, 180

▲ Leveled Reader

Day 2

Teacher-Directed
Leveled Reader:
"The Prairie Dog," p. T296
Read the Book

Independent
⭐ Word Work Center, p. T217
Challenge Copying Masters, pp. 181–182

▲ Leveled Reader

English-Language Learners

In addition to the small-group instruction above, use the ELL Extra Support Kit to promote language development.

Day 1

LANGUAGE DEVELOPMENT SUPPORT
Teacher-Directed
ELL TG, Day 1
Independent
ELL Copying Masters, Lesson 23

▲ ELL Student Handbook

Day 2

LANGUAGE DEVELOPMENT SUPPORT
Teacher-Directed
ELL TG, Day 2
Independent
ELL Copying Masters, Lesson 23

▲ ELL Student Handbook

Intervention

▲ Strategic Intervention Resource Kit

▲ Strategic Intervention Interactive Reader

Day 1

Strategic Intervention TG, Day 1
Strategic Intervention Practice Book, Lesson 23

Day 2

Strategic Intervention TG, Day 2
Strategic Intervention Interactive Reader, Lesson 23

▲ Strategic Intervention Interactive Reader

Comprehension	Phonics	Comprehension	Fluency	Robust Vocabulary	Language Arts Checkpoint
Focus Skill Use Graphic Aids pp. S30–S31	Vowel Variant /o͞o/oo, ew, ue, ui, ou pp. S26–S27	Synonyms pp. S32–S33	Reading Rate pp. S28–S29	*thickens, plentiful, crowd, sealed, carefully, attack, pattern, disappear, role, diligent* pp. S34–S35	**Grammar:** Past-Tense Verbs **Writing:** Paragraph of Information pp. S36–S37

Day 3

Teacher-Directed
Leveled Reader: "The Penguin," p. T294
Read the Book

Independent
⭐ Word Work Center, p. T217
Extra Support Copying Masters, p. 183

▲ Leveled Reader

Teacher-Directed
Leveled Reader: "The Ant," p. T295
Read the Book

Independent
⭐ Writing Center, p. T217
Practice Book, p. 183

▲ Leveled Reader

Teacher-Directed
Leveled Reader: "The Prairie Dog," p. T296
Think Critically

Independent
⭐ Listening/Speaking Center, p. T216
Challenge Copying Masters, p. 183

▲ Leveled Reader

LANGUAGE DEVELOPMENT SUPPORT

Teacher-Directed
Leveled Reader: "Insects," p. T297
Before Reading; Read the Book
ELL TG, Day 3

Independent
ELL Copying Masters, Lesson 23

▲ Leveled Reader

Strategic Intervention TG, Day 3
Strategic Intervention Interactive Reader, Lesson 23
Strategic Intervention Practice Book, Lesson 23

▲ Strategic Intervention Interactive Reader

Day 4

Teacher-Directed
Leveled Reader: "The Penguin," p. T294
Reread for Fluency

Independent
⭐ Letters and Sounds Center, p. T217

▲ Leveled Reader

Teacher-Directed
Leveled Reader: "The Ant," p. T295
Reread for Fluency

Independent
⭐ Word Work Center, p. T217

▲ Leveled Reader

Teacher-Directed
Leveled Reader: "The Prairie Dog," p. T296
Reread for Fluency

Independent
⭐ Writing Center, p. T217
Self-Selected Reading: Classroom Library Collection

▲ Leveled Reader

LANGUAGE DEVELOPMENT SUPPORT

Teacher-Directed
Leveled Reader: "Insects," p. T297
Reread for Fluency
ELL TG, Day 4

Independent
ELL Copying Masters, Lesson 23

▲ Leveled Reader

Strategic Intervention TG, Day 4
Strategic Intervention Interactive Reader, Lesson 23

▲ Strategic Intervention Interactive Reader

Day 5

Teacher-Directed
Leveled Reader: "The Penguin," p. T294
Think Critically

Independent
⭐ Writing Center, p. T217
Leveled Reader: Reread for Fluency
Extra Support Copying Masters, p. 184

▲ Leveled Reader

Teacher-Directed
Leveled Reader: "The Ant," p. T295
Think Critically

Independent
⭐ Listening/Speaking Center, p. T216
Leveled Reader: Reread for Fluency
Practice Book, p. 184

▲ Leveled Reader

Teacher-Directed
Leveled Reader: "The Prairie Dog," p. T296
Reread for Fluency

Independent
⭐ Reading Center, p. T216
Leveled Reader: Reread for Fluency
Self-Selected Reading: Classroom Library Collection
Challenge Copying Masters, p. 184

▲ Leveled Reader

LANGUAGE DEVELOPMENT SUPPORT

Teacher-Directed
Leveled Reader: "Insects," p. T297
Think Critically
ELL TG, Day 5

Independent
Leveled Reader: Reread for Fluency
ELL Copying Masters, Lesson 23

▲ Leveled Reader

Strategic Intervention TG, Day 5
Strategic Intervention Interactive Reader, Lesson 23

▲ Strategic Intervention Interactive Reader

Leveled Readers & Leveled Practice
Reinforcing Skills and Strategies

LEVELED READERS SYSTEM

- **Leveled Readers**
- **Leveled Readers, CD**
- **Leveled Readers Teacher Guides**
  - *Comprehension*
  - *Vocabulary*
  - *Oral Reading Fluency Assessment*
- **Response Activities**
- **Leveled Readers Assessment**

See pages T294–T297 for lesson plans.

BELOW-LEVEL

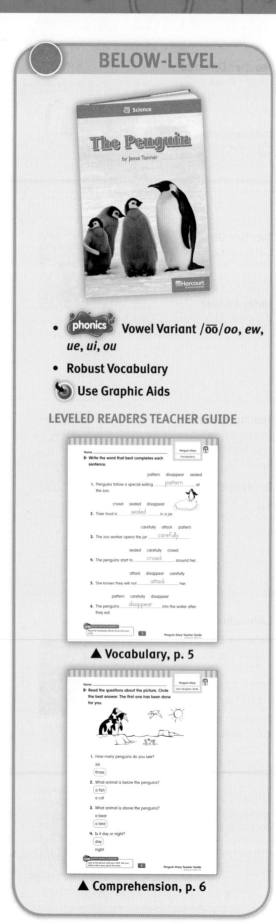

The Penguin
by Jesse Tanner

- **phonics** Vowel Variant /o͞o/*oo, ew, ue, ui, ou*
- **Robust Vocabulary**
- **Use Graphic Aids**

LEVELED READERS TEACHER GUIDE

▲ Vocabulary, p. 5

▲ Comprehension, p. 6

ON-LEVEL

The Ant
by Betsy Samuels

- **phonics** Vowel Variant /o͞o/*oo, ew, ue, ui, ou*
- **Robust Vocabulary**
- **Use Graphic Aids**

LEVELED READERS TEACHER GUIDE

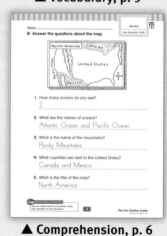

▲ Vocabulary, p. 5

▲ Comprehension, p. 6

ADVANCED

- **phonics** Vowel Variant /ōo/*oo, ew, ue, ui, ou*
- **Robust Vocabulary**
- **Use Graphic Aids**

LEVELED READERS TEACHER GUIDE

▲ Vocabulary, p. 5

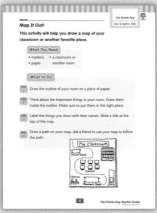

▲ Comprehension, p. 6

ELL

- **Build Background**
- **Concept Vocabulary**
- **Scaffolded Language Development**

LEVELED READERS TEACHER GUIDE

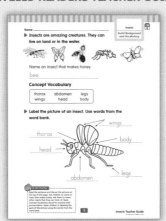

▲ Build Background, p. 5

▲ Scaffolded Language Development, p. 6

CLASSROOM LIBRARY

for Self-Selected Reading

EASY
▲ *Treasure Map* by Stuart J. Murphy.
FICTION

AVERAGE
▲ *Ant Cities* by Arthur Dorros.
NONFICTION

CHALLENGE
▲ *A Log's Life* by Wendy Pfeffer.
NONFICTION

▲ Classroom Library Books
Teacher Guide, Lesson 23

Literacy Centers

15 Min. each

Management Support

While you provide direct instruction to individuals or small groups, other children can work on literacy center activities.

▲ **Literacy Center Pocket Chart**

My Activities
✓ Put a check mark next to the activities you complete.

Literacy Activities
- Listening/Speaking Read with a Recording
- Reading Read and Respond
- Writing Paragraph of Information
- Word Work Read and Write Words
- Letters and Sounds Write Rhymes

Leveled Readers
- Rereading for Fluency
- Activities (See inside back cover.)

Practice Pages
- pages 178–185

Lesson 23 · 56 · Teacher Resource Book

▲ **Teacher Resource Book, p. 56**

 ## Homework for the Week

TEACHER RESOURCE BOOK, PAGE 26

The *Homework Copying Master* provides activities to complete for each day of the week.

GO online **www.harcourtschool.com/storytown**

 ### LISTENING/SPEAKING
Read with a Recording

Objective
To develop fluency by listening to familiar selections and reading them aloud

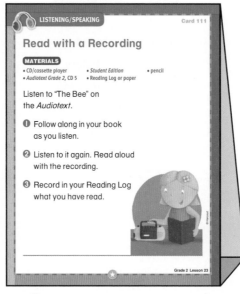

LISTENING/SPEAKING Card 111

Read with a Recording

MATERIALS
- CD/cassette player
- Audiotext Grade 2, CD 5
- Student Edition
- Reading Log or paper
- pencil

Listen to "The Bee" on the *Audiotext*.

1. Follow along in your book as you listen.
2. Listen to it again. Read aloud with the recording.
3. Record in your Reading Log what you have read.

Grade 2 Lesson 23

⭐ **Literacy Center Kit • Card 111**

READING
Read and Respond

Objective
To develop comprehension by reading and responding to nonfiction selections

READING Card 112

Read and Respond

MATERIALS
- Student Edition
- nonfiction books from the classroom library
- paper
- pencil

1. Choose two nonfiction selections from your *Student Edition* or choose other nonfiction books.
2. Meet with a small group and read them aloud.
3. Look for graphic aids and talk about how they help you understand what you read.
4. Write down the titles of the books you read and the types of graphic aids you found in them.

Grade 2 Lesson 23

⭐ **Literacy Center Kit • Card 112**

WRITING

Paragraph of Information

Objective
To practice writing a paragraph of information

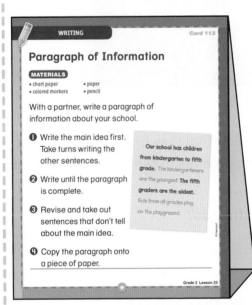

Literacy Center Kit • Card 113

WORD WORK

Read and Write Words

Objective
To practice using Vocabulary Words

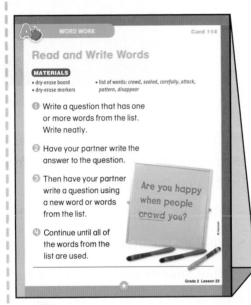

Literacy Center Kit • Card 114

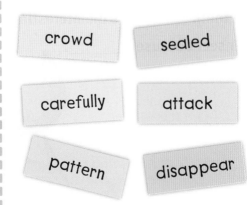

ABC LETTERS AND SOUNDS

Write Rhymes

Objective
To read and write words using known letter/sound correspondences

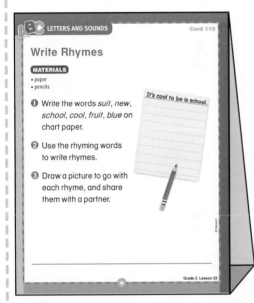

Literacy Center Kit • Card 115

Day at a Glance

Day 1

 phonics and Spelling
- Introduce: Vowel Variant /o͞o/oo, ew, ue, ui, ou
- Pretest

Reading
- Words with *oo, ew, ue, ui, ou*, *Student Edition*, pp. 240–241

Comprehension
 Introduce: Use Graphic Aids

- *Read-Aloud Anthology:* "Brilliant Bees"

Fluency
- Model Oral Fluency

Robust Vocabulary
Words from the Read-Aloud
- Introduce: *thickens, plentiful*

Grammar [Quick Write]
- Introduce: Past-Tense Verbs

Writing
- Paragraph of Information

Warm-Up Routines

 ## Oral Language

Objective *To listen attentively and respond appropriately to oral communication*

Question of the Day

What insects do you find interesting? Why?

Invite children to brainstorm names of insects that they find interesting. List their ideas on the board. Use the following prompts to compare and contrast the insects they name.

- **What insects have you seen? What did they do?**
- **What do the insects look like?**
- **What sounds do insects make?**
- **What is the biggest insect you have seen? The smallest?**
- **What insect would you most like to be? Why?**

Then have children complete the following sentence frame.

I think _____ is an interesting insect because _____.

Read Aloud

Objective *To listen for information*

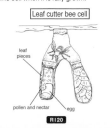

TRANSPARENCY Read aloud the passage "Leafcutter Bees" on **Transparency R120**. Use the following steps:

- **Set a purpose for listening.** Tell children to listen for information about leafcutter bees.

- **Model fluent reading.** Read the passage aloud. Remind children that when good readers read nonfiction, they read more slowly so listeners can pay attention to the main ideas and details.

- **Discuss the passage.** Ask: **How does the diagram help you understand the passage?** (Possible response: It shows the parts of a leafcutter's cell.)

Use Graphic Aids

Leafcutter Bees

Many bees that you see on flowers are honeybees. But some may be leafcutter bees. Leafcutters collect pollen and nectar, but they do not make honey. They cut leaves to build nests.

The female leafcutter bee lives about two months. During that time, she cuts leaves, builds a nest in rotten wood or in the ground, and lays eggs.

Inside her nest, she makes walls out of the leaf pieces. The walls form a cell, or container. She lines the walls with pollen and nectar. The bee lays an egg in each cell and closes it. After the larva hatches, it eats the food and in time it turns into a bee. It comes out of the cell when it is fully grown.

Leaf cutter bee cell

leaf pieces

pollen and nectar   egg

Grade 2, Lesson 23   R120   Comprehension

Transparency R120

Word Wall

Objective *To read high-frequency words*

REVIEW HIGH-FREQUENCY WORDS Review the words *police, sugar, sometimes, world, though, understand, wear,* and *interesting* as well as other previously learned high-frequency words. Hold up a word card at random, and ask children to read the word. Flip through the word cards several times.

police   sugar   sometimes   world

though   understand   wear   interesting

Vowel Variant /o͞o/
oo, ew, ue, ui, ou phonics and Spelling

Objectives

- *To recognize and blend the vowel variant /o͞o/oo, ew, ue, ui, ou*
- *To read words with the vowel variant /o͞o/oo, ew, ue, ui, ou, and other known letter-sounds*
- *To use the vowel variant /o͞o/oo, ew, ue, ui, ou and other known letter-sounds to spell words*

Skill Trace

 Tested Vowel Variant /o͞o/oo, ew, ue, ui, ou

Introduce	Grade I
Reintroduce	**T220–T223**
Reteach	S26–S27
Review	T232–T233, T258–T259, T422
Test	Theme 5
Maintain	Theme 6, T360

 Refer to *Sounds of Letters CD* Track 19 for pronunciation of /o͞o/.

Connect Letters to Sounds

WARM UP WITH PHONEMIC AWARENESS Say the words *grew* and *zoo*. Have children say the words. Say: **The words *grew* and *zoo* have the /o͞o/ sound at the end.** Then say the words *food* and *suit*, and have children repeat. Say: **The words *food* and *suit* have the /o͞o/ sound in the middle.** Then have children say /o͞o/ several times.

Routine Card 1 **CONNECT LETTERS AND SOUNDS** Display the *Sound/Spelling Card* for long *u*. Point to the letters *oo* and explain their letter/sound correspondence. Say: **The letters *oo* can stand for the /o͞o/ sound, the sound at the end of *too*.** Touch the letters several times, and have children say /o͞o/ each time. Repeat with *ew*, *ue*, *ui*, and *ou*.

▲ **Sound/Spelling Card**

Phonics Skill

Words with *oo, ew, ue, ui, ou*

The letters *oo*, *ew*, *ue*, *ui*, and *ou* can stand for the same sound. Read the words below.

spoon   dew   glue

fruit   soup

Do you hear the same vowel sound in each word?

240

Read each word on the left. Tell which word on the right has the same sound.

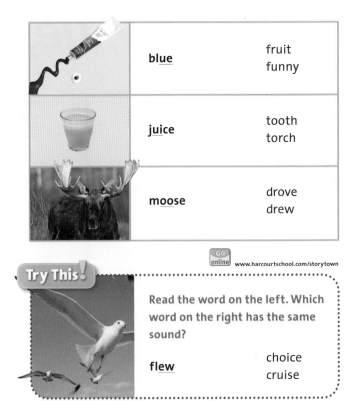

	blue	fruit funny
	juice	tooth torch
	moose	drove drew

GO online www.harcourtschool.com/storytown

Try This!

Read the word on the left. Which word on the right has the same sound?

flew	choice cruise

241

Reading Words

GUIDED PRACTICE Have children read *Student Edition* page 240. Ask volunteers to read aloud the words below the pictures, and have children repeat. Then read aloud the word *blue* and the two answer choices in the right-hand column of *Student Edition* page 241, as children follow along. Have children read the words with you. Elicit from children that the word *fruit* has the same /ōō/ sound that they hear in *blue*. Repeat for the remaining words.

Try This! Have children use what they have learned to identify the word that has the same sound as *flew*. (cruise)

Vowel Variant /o͞o/
oo, ew, ue, ui, ou and Spelling

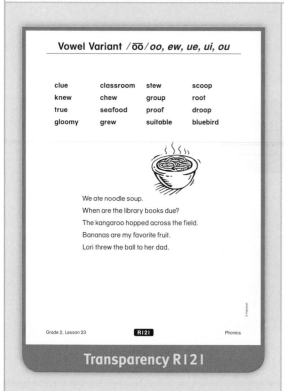

Vowel Variant /o͞o/oo, ew, ue, ui, ou

clue	classroom	stew	scoop
knew	chew	group	root
true	seafood	proof	droop
gloomy	grew	suitable	bluebird

We ate noodle soup.
When are the library books due?
The kangaroo hopped across the field.
Bananas are my favorite fruit.
Lori threw the ball to her dad.

Grade 2, Lesson 23   R121   Phonics

Transparency R121

Reading Words

INDEPENDENT PRACTICE Display **Transparency R121** or write the words and sentences on the board. Point to the words in the top portion and have children read them. Then have children read aloud the sentences and identify words with the /o͞o/ sound.

Decodable Books

Additional Decoding Practice

- **Phonics**
  Vowel Variant /o͞o/oo, ew, ue, ui, ou
- **Decodable Words**
- **High-Frequency Words**
  See lists in *Decodable Book 19*.
  See also *Decodable Books*, online (Take-Home Version).

▲ Decodable Book 19: "How to Groom Your Dog," "Sue Hunts for Clues," and "Soup Tale"

BELOW-LEVEL · ON-LEVEL · ADVANCED

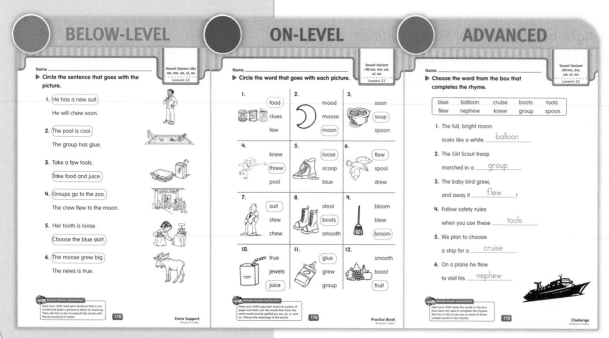

▲ Extra Support, p. 178   ▲ Practice Book, p. 178   ▲ Challenge, p. 178

ELL

- Group children according to academic levels, and assign one of the pages on the left.
- Clarify any unfamiliar concepts as necessary. See *ELL Teacher Guide* Lesson 23 for support in scaffolding instruction.

5-DAY SPELLING

DAY 1 Pretest
DAY 2 Word Building
DAY 3 State the Generalization
DAY 4 Review
DAY 5 Posttest

Introduce Spelling Words

PRETEST Say the first word and read the dictation sentence. Repeat the word as children write it. Write the word on the board and have children check their spelling. Tell them to circle the word if they spelled it correctly or write it correctly if they did not. Repeat for words 2–10.

Words with /o͞o/oo, ew, ue, ui, ou

1.	true	Is the story **true** or is it made up?
2.	grew	The sunflower **grew** tall in July.
3.	suit	Please wear a **suit** to the wedding.
4.	smooth	I spread the **smooth** icing on the cake.
5.	clue	Would you please give me a **clue** to the answer?
6.	soup	Diana made a spicy **soup**.
7.	stew	Are you going to add beans to the **stew**?
8.	food	We placed the **food** on the picnic table.
9.	group	The children in the **group** held hands and danced.
10.	fruit	Add bananas and berries to the **fruit** salad.

ADVANCED

Challenge Words Use the challenge words in these dictation sentences.

11.	nephew	Aunt Jean sent a present to her **nephew**.
12.	classroom	We listen to stories in our **classroom**.
13.	cartoon	Jerome drew a **cartoon** about his cat.
14.	juicy	The plums are **juicy** and sweet.
15.	newspaper	Do you read the comics in the **newspaper**?

Spelling Words

1.	true	6.	soup
2.	grew	7.	stew
3.	suit	8.	food*
4.	smooth	9.	group
5.	clue	10.	fruit

Challenge Words

11.	nephew	14.	juicy
12.	classroom	15.	newspaper
13.	cartoon		

* Word from "The Bee"

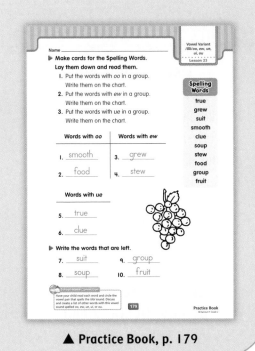

▲ Practice Book, p. 179

Use Graphic Aids
Comprehension

Objective

• *To use graphic aids to understand nonfiction selections*

Daily Comprehension

Use Graphic Aids

DAY 1:	Introduce Graphic Aids *Student Edition*
DAY 2:	Review Graphic Aids *Student Edition*
DAY 3:	Review Graphic Aids *Student Edition*
DAY 4:	Review Graphic Aids *Transparency*
DAY 5:	Review Graphic Aids *Read-Aloud Anthology*

✓ MONITOR PROGRESS

Use Graphic Aids

IF children have difficulty using graphic aids,	**THEN** ask them yes/no questions about a familiar graphic aid.

Small-Group Instruction, pp. S30–S31

● **BELOW-LEVEL:** Reteach
● **ON-LEVEL:** Reinforce
● **ADVANCED:** Extend

Teach/Model

INTRODUCE GRAPHIC AIDS   Display **Transparency R120** and point out the diagram. Ask children to describe what the diagram shows. (a leafcutter bee's cell) Explain that the diagram helps readers understand the text. Tell children that diagrams are one kind of graphic aid. Explain that nonfiction selections may include graphic aids such as diagrams, time lines, maps, charts, and graphs. Model how to use the diagram on the transparency to find information.

Think Aloud   As I read the information, I look at the diagram to help me know what a leafcutter bee's cell looks like. It helps me know what the leafcutter bee does inside her nest.

E L L

Clarify Graphic Aids   Some children may think that the graphic aids mentioned here are totally different from the graphic organizers they use during the writing process. Explain that all graphic aids/organizers help organize information and make it easier to find and understand. Have children tell about graphic aids/organizers they use, such as a web, Venn diagram, and chart.

PRACTICE/APPLY

GUIDED PRACTICE   Have children look at a time line in their *Student Edition* (Volume One), pages 378–379. Ask them to describe what a time line shows and what they can learn from a time line. (Dates and events over a period of time; you can tell which event happened first.) Then display a map, such as the one on *Student Edition* (Volume Two) pages 354–355, "South Korea." Guide children in recognizing that a map shows where places are located. Have children look at the chart found on *Student Edition* (Volume Two) pages 118–119. Elicit that a chart shows information in rows, columns, and headings. Draw a simple bar graph on the board. Ask: **What do the bars in the graph help you do?** (Possible response: They help you compare information.)

INDEPENDENT PRACTICE   Have partners work together to create a simple diagram of something they are learning in science such as how Earth moves around the sun or the parts of a plant. Remind them to label their diagram. Ask volunteers to share their diagrams. Discuss the information provided in each diagram and how it makes finding that information easier.

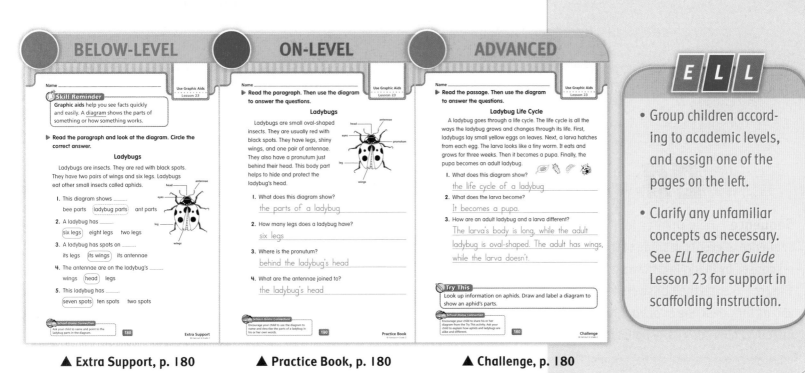

▲ Extra Support, p. 180   ▲ Practice Book, p. 180   ▲ Challenge, p. 180

ELL

• Group children according to academic levels, and assign one of the pages on the left.

• Clarify any unfamiliar concepts as necessary. See *ELL Teacher Guide* Lesson 23 for support in scaffolding instruction.

Listening Comprehension
Read Aloud

Objectives
- *To set a purpose for listening*
- *To use graphic aids in a nonfiction selection*

Build Fluency

Focus: Reading Rate   Tell children that good readers change their reading rate based on the type of writing they are reading. They might slow down as they read nonfiction so they can pay attention to the main ideas and details.

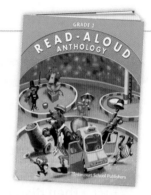

Before Reading

CONNECT TO PRIOR KNOWLEDGE   Tell children that they will listen to a nonfiction selection that answers common questions about honeybees.

Routine Card 2   **GENRE STUDY: NONFICTION**   Tell children that "Brilliant Bees" is nonfiction. Remind them of the characteristics of this genre:

▲ Read-Aloud Anthology, "Brilliant Bees," p. 84

Think Aloud   **Nonfiction writing has facts and details about a topic.**

After Reading

RESPOND   Have children summarize the nonfiction selection by restating in their own words what they learned. Write a group summary on the board.

 REVIEW USING GRAPHIC AIDS   Have children name graphic aids such as charts, maps, and diagrams. Display "Brilliant Bees" and ask children what the diagram shows.

Build Robust Vocabulary

Words from the Read-Aloud

Teach/Model

Routine Card 3

INTRODUCE ROBUST VOCABULARY   Use *Routine Card 3* to introduce the words.

❶ Put the word in **selection context**.
❷ Display Transparency R125 and read the word and the **Student-Friendly Explanation**.
❸ Have children **say the word** with you.
❹ Use the word in other contexts, and have children **interact with the word's meaning**.
❺ Remove the transparency. Say the Student-Friendly Explanation again, and ask children to **name the word** that goes with it.

❶ **Selection Context:** In the hive, the nectar **thickens** into honey.
❹ **Interact with Word Meaning:** Whipped cream thickens into butter. What thickens into fudge?

❶ **Selection Context:** Sometimes flowers are **plentiful** on cherry trees.
❹ **Interact with Word Meaning:** Books are plentiful in this classroom. What is plentiful in a forest—cars or leaves?

Practice/Apply

GUIDED PRACTICE   Ask children to discuss the following questions:
• When an ice cube melts, does it *thicken*? How do you know?
• Imagine that you are in a garden. What would be *plentiful*?

Objective
• *To develop robust vocabulary through discussing a literature selection*

Tested

INTRODUCE ✓

Vocabulary: Lesson 23

thickens   **plentiful**

▼ Student-Friendly Explanations

Student-Friendly Explanations

thickens	If something thickens, it becomes more gooey.
plentiful	If something is plentiful, there is a lot of it.
role	If you have a role, there are certain things you have to do.
diligent	If you are diligent, you keep working until you're done.

Grade 2, Lesson 23   R125   Vocabulary

Transparency R125

Grammar *Quick Write*

Past-Tense Verbs

5-DAY GRAMMAR	
DAY 1	Introduce Past-Tense Verbs
DAY 2	Verbs that Take *-ed*
DAY 3	Verbs that Take *-d*
DAY 4	Apply to Writing
DAY 5	Weekly Review

Objectives

- *To recognize that some verbs tell about the past*
- *To identify past-tense verbs in sentences*

Daily Proofreading

the Beekeeper opens the hive.

(The beekeeper)

Writing Trait ➤

Strengthening Conventions

Parts of Speech   Use this short lesson with children's own writing to build a foundation for revising/editing longer connected text on Day 5.

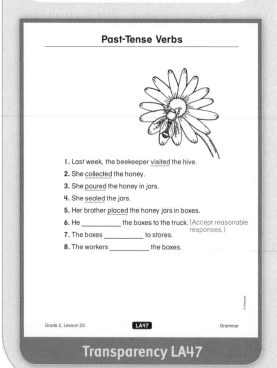

Past-Tense Verbs

1. Last week, the beekeeper <u>visited</u> the hive.
2. She <u>collected</u> the honey.
3. She <u>poured</u> the honey in jars.
4. She <u>sealed</u> the jars.
5. Her brother <u>placed</u> the honey jars in boxes.
6. He _____ the boxes to the truck. (Accept reasonable responses.)
7. The boxes _____ to stores.
8. The workers _____ the boxes.

Grade 2, Lesson 23   LA47   Grammar

Transparency LA47

Teach/Model

INTRODUCE PAST-TENSE VERBS   Explain that a verb can tell about an action that happened in the past. Many verbs that tell about the past end in *-ed* or *-d*. Write this sentence on the board from "Brilliant Bees" (*Read-Aloud Anthology*, p. 84). Then write the past-tense form of the sentence below it:

Present: Baby bees <u>hatch</u> from small white eggs.

Past: Baby bees <u>hatched</u> from small white eggs.

Read aloud the first sentence. Explain that it tells about the present, or something that happens now. Then read aloud the second sentence. Explain how the word *hatched* tells about an action in the past. Point out that it ends with *-ed*.

Guided Practice

IDENTIFY VERBS   Display **Transparency LA47**. Explain that each sentence has a past-tense verb. Read the first sentence aloud, and identify the past-tense verb (visited). Explain that the verb *visited* tells about an action the beekeeper did in the past. Complete remaining items together.

Practice/Apply

WRITE SENTENCES   Have children write three sentences about what they did in class yesterday. Have partners switch papers to check for correct verb usage.

Writing
Paragraph of Information

5-DAY WRITING

DAY 1	Introduce
DAY 2	Prewrite
DAY 3	Draft
DAY 4	Revise
DAY 5	Revise

Teach/Model

INTRODUCE PARAGRAPH OF INFORMATION Display **Transparency LA48,** and explain that this paragraph was written by a child to give information about ants. Read aloud the paragraph, and discuss how it is organized. Work together to develop a list of characteristics for a paragraph of information.

Paragraph of Information

- The paragraph gives information about one topic.
- The title explains what the paragraph is about.
- The topic sentence tells about the main idea.
- The other sentences give more details about the main idea.
- Sometimes, the writer does research to find facts and information for the paragraph.

WRITING TRAIT **WORD CHOICE** Discuss how the writer uses action words such as *walking* and *carry*. Point out that action words make it easier to picture and understand the information in a paragraph.

Guided Practice

PLAN A PARAGRAPH Model how you would begin to write a paragraph of information with an example, such as, "I want to give information about birds. First, I write a title. Then I think of a topic sentence that tells the main idea. The main idea is that birds are good fliers."

Practice/Apply

IDENTIFY TOPICS Have children generate their own topic ideas. Ask them to make a list of ideas that they can use on Days 2–5.

Objectives

- *To read and respond to a paragraph that gives information as a model for writing*
- *To develop ideas and topics for writing*

 ## Writing Prompt

Write and Illustrate Have children draw a picture of something that is important to them and write a few sentences to explain why.

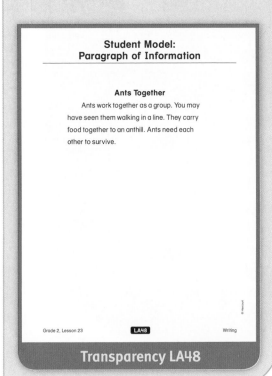

Student Model:
Paragraph of Information

Ants Together

Ants work together as a group. You may have seen them walking in a line. They carry food together to an anthill. Ants need each other to survive.

Grade 2, Lesson 23 LA48 Writing

Transparency LA48

Day at a Glance

Day 2

phonics and Spelling

- Review: Vowel Variant /ōō/oo, ew, ue, ui, ou
- Build Words

Robust Vocabulary

Words from the Selection

- Introduce: *crowd, sealed, carefully, attack, pattern, disappear*

Comprehension

Focus Strategy Summarize

Focus Skill Use Graphic Aids

Reading

- "The Bee," *Student Edition*, pp. 244–273

Read!

Fluency

- Reading Rate

Robust Vocabulary

Words About the Selection

- Introduce: *role, diligent*

Grammar Quick Write

- Review: Past-Tense Verbs

Writing

- Paragraph of Information

Warm-Up Routines

Oral Language

Objective *To listen attentively and respond appropriately to oral communication*

Question of the Day

What do you like or dislike about bees?

Organize children into two groups. Ask one group to give reasons why they like bees, and ask the other group to give reasons why they don't like bees. Use the following prompts:

- **Do you like the honey that bees make? Why?**

- **Why do you think bees sometimes sting?**

- **What do bees look like when they visit flowers?**

- **What would you do if you had a pet bee?**

Then have children complete the following sentence frame to explain the reasons for their choice.

I _____ bees because _____.

Read Aloud

Objective *To listen for enjoyment*

BIG BOOK OF RHYMES AND POEMS Display the poem "Bumblebees" on page 41 and read aloud the title. Ask children to listen for enjoyment. Then read the poem aloud. Reread the poem several times, asking children to chime in when they are able. Model how to raise your voice for the words in all capital letters. Invite volunteers to say why the poem was fun to read and listen to.

▲ **Big Book of Rhymes and Poems, p. 41**

Word Wall

Objective *To read high-frequency words*

REVIEW HIGH-FREQUENCY WORDS Review the words *cook, tough, young, worry, board, woman, impossible,* and *ago* as well as other previously learned high-frequency words. Point to each word, and then have children read it, spell it, and use it in a sentence.

cook	tough	young	worry
board	woman	impossible	ago

Vowel Variant /o͞o/ oo, ew, ue, ui, ou phonics and Spelling

Objectives
- *To blend sounds into words*
- *To spell two- and three-syllable words*

Skill Trace

 Tested **Vowel Variant /o͞o/ oo, ew, ue, ui, ou**

Introduce	Grade 1
Reintroduce	T220–T223
Reteach	S26–S27
Review	T232–T233, T258–T259, T422
Test	Theme 5
Maintain	Theme 6, T360

Spelling Words

1. true	6. soup
2. grew	7. stew
3. suit	8. food*
4. smooth	9. group
5. clue	10. fruit

Challenge Words

11. nephew	14. juicy
12. classroom	15. newspaper
13. cartoon	

* Word from "The Bee"

Word Building

READ A SPELLING WORD Write the word *suit* on the board. Ask children to identify the letters that stand for the /o͞o/ sound. Then read the word and have children do the same.

BUILD SPELLING WORDS Ask children which letters you should change to make *suit* become *fruit*. (Change *s* to *fr*.) Write the word *fruit* on the board. Point to the word, and have children read it. Continue building spelling words in this manner. Say:

- **Which letters do I have to change to make the word *food*?** (Change *ruit* to *ood*.)

- **Which letters do I have to change to make the word *smooth*?** (Change *f* to *sm* and *d* to *th*.)

- **Which letters do I have to change to make the word *stew*?** (Change *mooth* to *tew*.)

- **Which letters do I have to change to make the word *soup*?** (Change *tew* to *oup*.)

Continue building the remaining spelling words in this manner.

suit
fruit
food
smooth
stew
soup

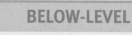 **BELOW-LEVEL**

Focus on Vowel Variants Write the spelling words in five columns according to their vowel variants (*ue, ew, ui, oo, ou*). Ask volunteers to circle the letters that stand for the /o͞o/ sound in each word and say the sound.

 ADVANCED

Rhyming Words Write the words *clue* and *stew* on the board. Point out that the words rhyme even though the /o͞o/ sound is spelled differently in each word. Have children think of other rhyming words and list them on the board. (Possible responses: *blue, dew, Sue, new*)

5-DAY PHONICS/SPELLING

DAY 1	Pretest
DAY 2	Word Building
DAY 3	State the Generalization
DAY 4	Review
DAY 5	Posttest

Read Words in Context

APPLY PHONICS Write the following sentences on the board or on chart paper. Have children read each sentence silently. Then track the print as children read the sentence aloud.

Last year my dad <u>grew</u> tomatoes.

The <u>group</u> found seats on the train.

Maria ate <u>fruit</u> after lunch.

Paul solved the <u>clue</u>.

 WRITE Dictate several spelling words. Have children write the words in their notebook or on a dry-erase board.

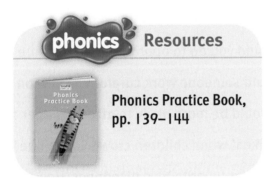

phonics Resources

Phonics Practice Book, pp. 139–144

MONITOR PROGRESS

Vowel Variant /ōō/oo, ew, ue, ui, ou

IF children have difficulty building and reading words with the vowel variant /ōō/oo, ew, ue, ui, ou,

THEN write oo, ew, ue, ui, ou on index cards and the first and last letters of words on other index cards. Use the cards to help children blend and read *fruit*, *group*, *grew*, *clue*, and *smooth*.

Small-Group Instruction, pp. S26–S27:

● **BELOW-LEVEL:** Reteach
● **ON-LEVEL:** Reinforce
● **ADVANCED:** Extend

ELL

- Group children according to academic levels, and assign one of the pages on the left.
- Clarify any unfamiliar concepts as necessary. See *ELL Teacher Guide* Lesson 23 for support in scaffolding instruction.

BELOW-LEVEL | **ON-LEVEL** | **ADVANCED**

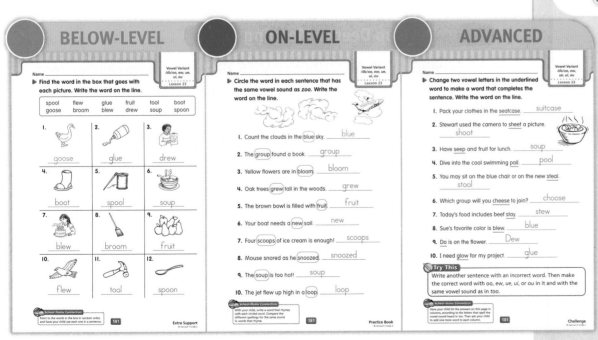

▲ Extra Support, p. 181   ▲ Practice Book, p. 181   ▲ Challenge, p. 181

Build Robust Vocabulary

Words from the Selection

Objective

• *To build robust vocabulary*

Tested

INTRODUCE ✓

Vocabulary: Lesson 23

pattern	sealed
carefully	attack
crowd	disappear

Student-Friendly Explanations

pattern	When you see a design in something, you are seeing a pattern.
sealed	If you sealed something, you closed it up tightly.
carefully	When you do something carefully, you pay close attention to what you are doing so that you don't make a mistake.
attack	If you attack something, you use great force to try to cause it harm.
crowd	When people or animals gather in large numbers, they crowd together.
disappear	When something disappears, you can't see it anymore.

Grade 2, Lesson 23   R126   Vocabulary

Transparency R126

Word Scribe

Writing   Provide children with sentence frames to complete, such as "When _____ crowd me, I _____."
Have children share the sentences.
HOMEWORK/INDEPENDENT PRACTICE

Teach/Model

Routine Card 4

INTRODUCE ROBUST VOCABULARY   Use *Routine Card 4* to introduce the words.

❶ Display **Transparency R126** and read the word and the **Student-Friendly Explanation**.
❷ Have children **say the word** with you.
❸ Have children **interact with the word's meaning** by asking them the appropriate question below.

• What colors would you paint in a striped **pattern**?

• What would you do to open a **sealed** treasure chest? Explain.

• Why would someone work **carefully** to sew on a button?

• Which would be more likely to **attack**: a tiger or a rabbit? Why?

• Do you like it when children **crowd** you in line? Why or why not?

• Imagine your favorite toys **disappear**. How would you feel?

Develop Deeper Meaning

EXPAND WORD MEANINGS: PAGES 242–243   Have children read the passage. Then read it aloud, pausing at the end of page 242 to ask children questions 1–3. Read page 243 and ask questions 4–6.

1. Why would someone make a **pattern** on toast? (Possible response: to make eating toast more fun)

2. What can be **sealed** in a jar? (Possible response: peanut butter)

3. Why do beekeepers raise their bees **carefully**? (to keep the bees healthy)

4. What are some reasons that bees might **attack**? (Possible response: if they thought the hive was in danger)

5. Imagine that bees **crowd** around you. How would you feel? (Possible responses: afraid; worried that they would sting)

6. If bees **disappear,** what do they do? (They go away.)

Vocabulary

Build Robust Vocabulary

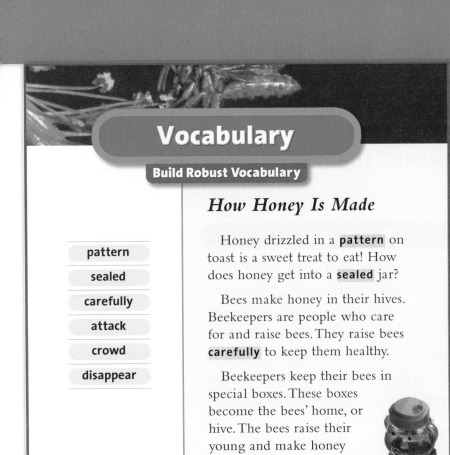

How Honey Is Made

- pattern
- sealed
- carefully
- attack
- crowd
- disappear

Honey drizzled in a **pattern** on toast is a sweet treat to eat! How does honey get into a **sealed** jar?

Bees make honey in their hives. Beekeepers are people who care for and raise bees. They raise bees **carefully** to keep them healthy.

Beekeepers keep their bees in special boxes. These boxes become the bees' home, or hive. The bees raise their young and make honey there. The honey is the bees' food.

Beekeepers must be careful when they gather honey from a hive. Most bees can sting. They **attack** anyone or anything that disturbs their hive. Many beekeepers wear a bee suit. A bee suit helps keep a beekeeper safe when angry bees **crowd** around him or her. The bee suit doesn't make the bees **disappear**. It just makes it hard for them to sting the person.

 www.harcourtschool.com/storytown

Word Scribe

This week your task is to use the Vocabulary Words in your writing. For example, you might write a note to your teacher that says "Last night I saw a star **pattern** in the sky." At the end of each day, write in your vocabulary journal the sentences that had Vocabulary Words.

242

243

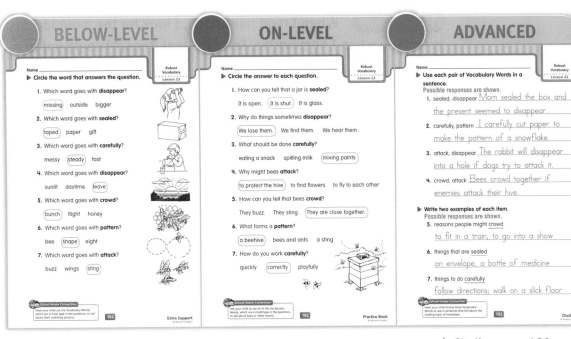

▲ **Extra Support, p. 182**   ▲ **Practice Book, p. 182**   ▲ **Challenge, p. 182**

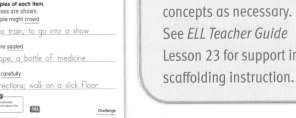

- Group children according to academic levels, and assign one of the pages on the left.

- Clarify any unfamiliar concepts as necessary. See *ELL Teacher Guide* Lesson 23 for support in scaffolding instruction.

 Reading

Student Edition: **"The Bee"**

Objectives

- *To recognize features of nonfiction*
- *To summarize as a strategy for comprehension*
- *To represent main ideas and details in a chart*
- *To apply word knowledge to the reading of a text*

Options for Reading

 BELOW-LEVEL

Preview Have children preview the selection by looking at the headings and photographs. Guide them to predict what the selection will be about. Read each page of the selection to children, and have them read it after you.

 ON-LEVEL

Monitor Comprehension Have children read the selection aloud, page by page. Ask them the Monitor Comprehension questions as you go.

 ADVANCED

Independent Reading Have children read each page silently, looking up each time they finish a page. Ask them the Monitor Comprehension questions as you go.

Genre Study

DISCUSS NONFICTION: PAGE 244 Ask children to read the genre information on *Student Edition* page 244. Remind children that nonfiction gives information about topics, and that it can have graphic aids, which give more facts. Then use **Transparency GO6** or copy the graphic organizer from page 244 on the board. Tell children that they will work together to complete the main idea and details chart as they read "The Bee."

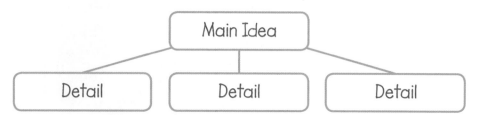

Comprehension Strategies

SUMMARIZE: PAGE 244 Remind children that good readers use strategies such as summarizing to help them remember what they read. Read aloud the Comprehension Strategy information on page 244.

Think Aloud When I read nonfiction, I look for the main ideas to include when I summarize. For "Brilliant Bees," I could write: "There are thousands of honeybees in one hive and each one has a specific job to do."

Point out that as they read, children can keep track of the main idea and details by summarizing the important information in their own words.

Genre Study

Nonfiction gives information about the world. Look for

- graphic aids, such as diagrams, that give more facts.
- paragraphs with main ideas and details.

Main Idea

Detail   Detail   Detail

Comprehension Strategy

Summarize a selection to help you think about the most important ideas.

The Bee

by Sabrina Crewe

Build Background

DISCUSS BEES   Tell children that they are going to read a non-fiction selection about the lives of honeybees. Ask them to share what they know about honeybees.

SET A PURPOSE AND PREDICT   Tell children that this is a nonfiction selection that they will read to gain information.

- Have children read the title.

- Ask children to tell what they see in the photograph. Elicit that it shows a close-up of a bee. Explain that there are different kinds of bees, and that this is a honeybee. Ask what they might learn about honeybees.

- List their predictions on the board.

- Have children read the selection to find out about the life of a honeybee.

TECHNOLOGY

 eBook   "The Bee" is available in an eBook.

 Audiotext   "The Bee" is available on *Audiotext Grade 2*, CD 5 for subsequent readings.

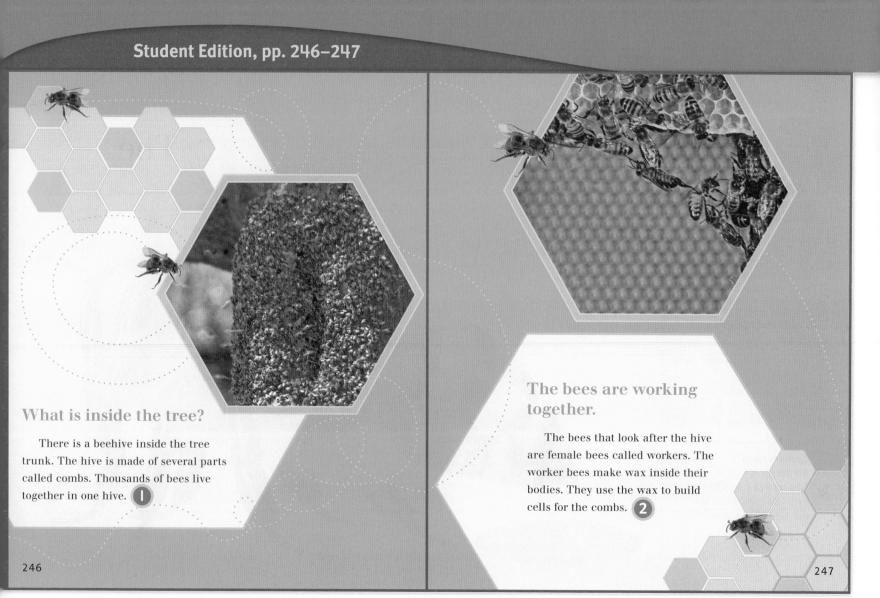

What is inside the tree?

There is a beehive inside the tree trunk. The hive is made of several parts called combs. Thousands of bees live together in one hive. ❶

246

The bees are working together.

The bees that look after the hive are female bees called workers. The worker bees make wax inside their bodies. They use the wax to build cells for the combs. ❷

247

Monitor Comprehension

PAGES 246–247 Say: **The heading on page 246 reads, "What is inside the tree?" Read to find out if there is a beehive inside the tree and what it is like.**

❶ **NOTE DETAILS** **Are beehives crowded or not crowded? Explain.**
(They are crowded—thousands of bees live in one hive.)

❷ **DRAW CONCLUSIONS** **Why is *worker bees* a good name for the female bees that look after the hive?** (Possible response: They work hard by building cells in the hive.)

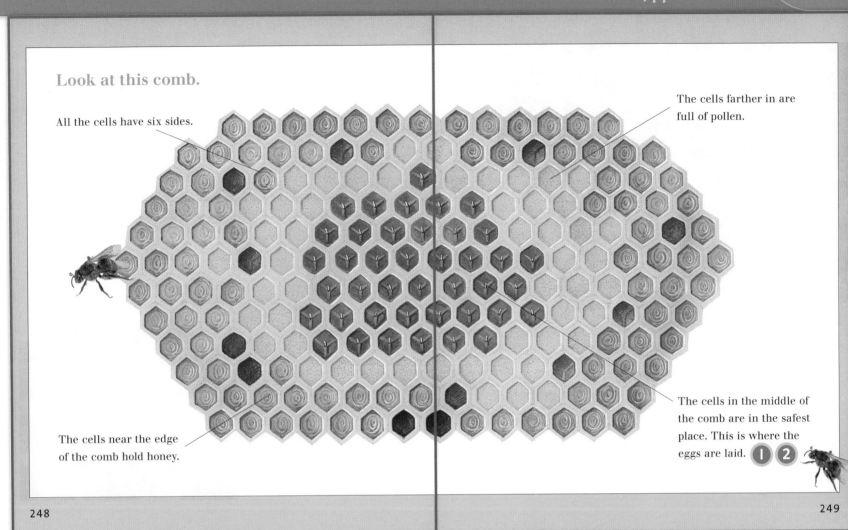

Look at this comb.

All the cells have six sides.

The cells farther in are full of pollen.

The cells near the edge of the comb hold honey.

The cells in the middle of the comb are in the safest place. This is where the eggs are laid. ❶ ❷

248

249

Monitor Comprehension

PAGES 248–249 Say: **The heading reads, "Look at this comb." I see a diagram. I think the diagram will explain what is inside a comb. Read to find out.**

❶ **USE GRAPHIC AIDS** **What do you learn about cells in this diagram?** (They have six sides; the ones near the edge hold honey; the ones farther in hold pollen; the ones in the middle hold eggs.) **What parts of the diagram helped you picture what a cell looks like?** (Accept reasonable responses.)

❷ **CAUSE/EFFECT** **Why are eggs laid in the middle of the comb?** (It is the safest place.)

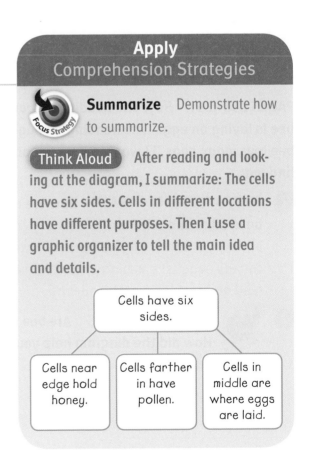

Apply
Comprehension Strategies

Summarize Demonstrate how to summarize.

Think Aloud After reading and looking at the diagram, I summarize: The cells have six sides. Cells in different locations have different purposes. Then I use a graphic organizer to tell the main idea and details.

Cells have six sides.

Cells near edge hold honey.

Cells farther in have pollen.

Cells in middle are where eggs are laid.

The queen bee is laying an egg.

Only one bee in the hive can lay eggs. She is called the queen bee, and she is bigger than the worker bees. The workers feed her and take good care of her. They crowd around the queen bee when she lays her eggs. ❶

250

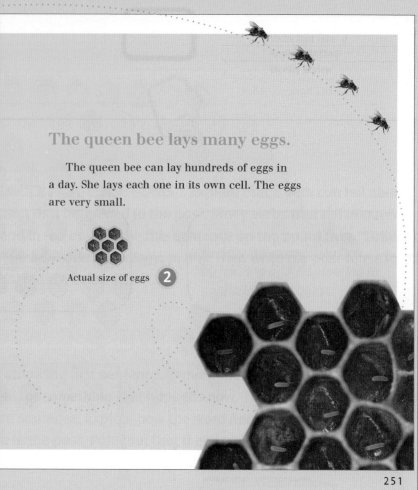

The queen bee lays many eggs.

The queen bee can lay hundreds of eggs in a day. She lays each one in its own cell. The eggs are very small.

Actual size of eggs ❷

251

Monitor Comprehension

PAGES 250–251 Say: **The heading on page 250 reads, "The queen bee is laying an egg." The heading on page 251 reads, "The queen bee lays many eggs." I want to know what the queen bee is. Read to find out.**

❶ **COMPARE AND CONTRAST How are queen bees and worker bees alike and different?** (Possible response: Alike: they all live in the hive and are female bees. Different: only the queen bee can lay eggs; she is bigger than worker bees; the worker bees feed and take care of the queen.)

❷ *Focus Skill* **USE GRAPHIC AIDS Are bee eggs big or small?** (small) **How did the diagram help you answer the question?** (It showed the actual size of the egg.)

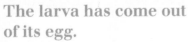

The larva has come out of its egg.

After three days, the larvae that are **1** inside the eggs hatch. A larva comes out of each egg. The larvae stay inside their cells. They are looked after by worker bees.

The larva is being fed.

The worker bee feeds the larva to make it grow. **2** For the first three days, the larva eats royal jelly. For the next three days, it feeds on pollen and honey. **3**

252

253

Monitor Comprehension

PAGES 252–253 Have children read the headings and describe what they see. Say: **Read to find out what is being described.**

1 SEQUENCE **What happens to the larvae first?** (They hatch from the eggs.) **Where did you find the answer?** (in the first sentence.)

2 CAUSE AND EFFECT **Why does the worker bee feed the larva?** (to make it grow)

3 MAKE PREDICTIONS **What do you think the larvae will do next?** (Possible response: turn into bees)

Use Multiple Strategies

Use Graphic Organizers Demonstrate how to use a flowchart to describe the life cycle of a bee.

Think Aloud After reading, I know about the first few stages in a bee's life cycle.

> First
> The queen lays an egg.

> Next
> After three days, the larva hatches.

> Then
> The larva stays in the cell and eats royal jelly and pollen and honey.

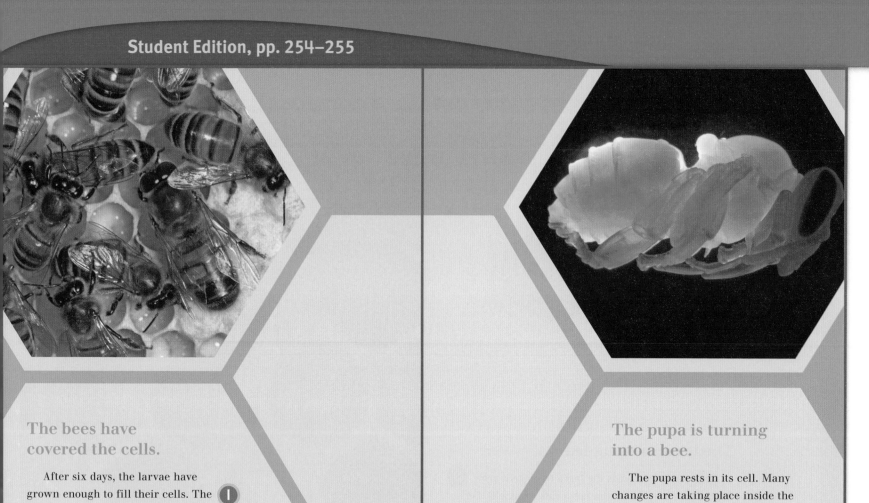

The bees have covered the cells.

After six days, the larvae have grown enough to fill their cells. The **1** cells are sealed with wax by worker bees. Now the larvae turn into pupae. **2**

254

The pupa is turning into a bee.

The pupa rests in its cell. Many changes are taking place inside the pupa. After 12 days, the pupa will become a bee. **3**

255

Monitor Comprehension

PAGES 254–255   Have children read the headings and tell what they see. Say: **Read to find out what happens next in the bee's life cycle.**

1 SEQUENCE   What happens after the larvae fill their cells?
(The worker bees seal the cells and the larvae turn into pupae.)

2 MAKE INFERENCES   Why do you think the worker bees seal the cells? (Possible response: They don't need to feed the pupae.)

3 NOTE DETAILS   How long does it take for the pupa to become a bee? (12 days) **Can you show where you found the answer?**
(Children should point out the last sentence on page 255.)

BELOW-LEVEL

Singular and Plural Nouns
Help children understand some of the scientific terms in the lesson. Write on the board two columns: *One* and *More Than One*. In the first column, list *larva* and *pupa*. In the second column, list *larvae* and *pupae*. Explain that the letter *e* at the end of *larvae* and *pupae* shows that each word names more than one.

The bee is coming out.

The bee chews through the wax. At first, the bee is very soft, and its new wings are wet. Older workers share their nectar with young bees until they are ready to find their own food. **1**

The new bee starts to work.

The bee's first job is to clean empty cells. It climbs into the cells and cleans them carefully. The clean cells can be used for new eggs. **2**

256

257

Monitor Comprehension

PAGES 256–257 Say: **The heading on page 257 reads, "The new bee starts to work." I wonder what life is like for the new bee. Read to find out.**

1 DRAW CONCLUSIONS **Why do you think the new bees are not ready at first to find their own food?** (Possible response: They need to fly but their wings are too wet.)

2 CAUSE AND EFFECT **Think about what happens in the cells. Why do you think the cells need to be clean and empty?** (Possible response: so the queen can lay an egg in them and there is room for the larva and pupa to grow.)

Worker bees look after drones.

Young workers feed the male bees when they come out of their cells. Male bees are called drones. Drones are bigger than worker bees, and they have larger eyes. They do not work at all in the hive. **1**

The bees are guarding the hive.

When worker bees are two weeks old, they start work around the edge of the hive. They clean and fix the hive, and watch out for enemies. The bees will sting any enemies who attack the hive. **2**

258

259

Monitor Comprehension

PAGES 258–259 Have children read the headings and ask them to predict why the bees guard the hive. Say: **Read to find out more about bees.**

1 COMPARE AND CONTRAST **How are worker bees different from drones?** (Possible response: Worker bees are female and drones are male; drones are bigger and have larger eyes; the worker bees work, but the drones do not.)

2 CAUSE/EFFECT **What happens if enemies attack the hive?** (They get stung.)

Apply
Comprehension Strategies

Summarize Model how to summarize and fill in the main idea and details chart.

Think Aloud I can summarize what I read on page 258: Worker bees care for male bees. Then I add details to the chart.

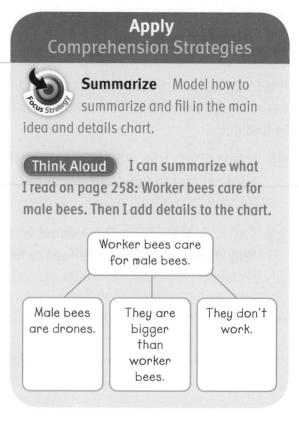

Worker bees care for male bees.

| Male bees are drones. | They are bigger than worker bees. | They don't work. |

The bee flies out of the hive.

Bees make their first flight when they are three weeks old. They fly around their hive to learn its shape and where it is. Then they are ready to search for food. **①** **②**

The bee visits a flower.

Bees suck nectar from flowers with their proboscis. They carry the nectar in a special stomach. The bee must get nectar from many flowers before its stomach is full. **③**

260

261

Monitor Comprehension

PAGES 260–261 Have children read the headings and describe what they see. Say: **Read to find out what the bee does.**

① **SEQUENCE** **What does the bee do before she searches for food?** (She flies around the hive to learn its shape and where it is.)

② **DRAW CONCLUSIONS** **Why do you think the bee needs to learn about the hive?** (Possible response: She needs to find her way back; it's where she lives.)

③ **NOTE DETAILS** **What does the bee do with its proboscis?** (sucks nectar from flowers) **Show on the photo on page 260 where you think the bee's proboscis is.** (Children should point to mouth.)

E L L

Role-Play Invite children to act out the movements of a bee during its first flights and its search for nectar in flowers. Explain their actions using key words from the text, and then ask them yes/no questions to reinforce comprehension. Encourage them to add action words related to bees, such as *fly*, *search*, and *carry* to their notebook.

The bee is carrying pollen.

Pollen from flowers sticks to the bee's body while it is getting nectar. The bee packs the pollen onto the pollen baskets on its back legs. Then it carries the pollen back to its hive. **1**

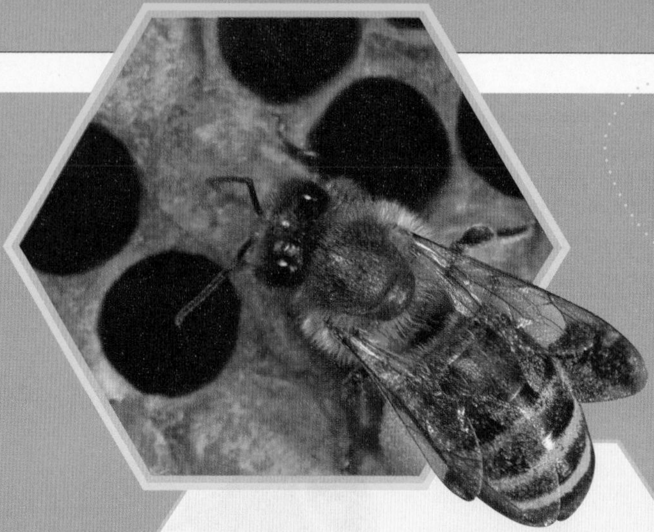

The bees bring food for the hive.

The bees find cells to store their pollen. Then they feed some nectar to young workers and drones. The nectar that is left over is given to other workers, who turn it into honey. The honey is stored in cells, too. **2**

3

262

263

Monitor Comprehension

PAGES 262–263 Have children read the headings. Say: **Read to find out how the bee helps feed the hive.**

1 SEQUENCE   **What does the bee do with the pollen after it packs it onto pollen baskets?** (It takes the pollen to the hive.)

2 DRAW CONCLUSIONS   **Why is nectar important to the hive?** (Possible response: The young workers and drones eat it. The other workers turn it into honey.)

3 EXPRESS PERSONAL OPINIONS   **Has the information in this selection changed how you feel about bees? Why or why not?** (Accept reasonable responses.)

264

The bee is dancing.

The bee with the pollen is showing the other bees where it found its nectar. The dance shows the other bees which way to go. The bee dances very fast in a circle if the flowers are close. If the flowers are far away, it slowly makes a pattern like an 8.

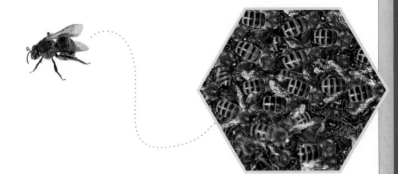

The hive is getting crowded.

The queen bee has laid many eggs. The hive is full of bees. It is time for some of the bees to leave.

265

Monitor Comprehension

PAGES 264–265 Say: **The headings make me wonder why a bee dances and what happens when the hive gets crowded. Read to find out.**

1 **MAKE INFERENCES** **Why is it important for bees to share information about the location of the pollen?** (Possible response: The bees all need the pollen to survive.)

2 **DRAW CONCLUSIONS** **Why do you think the author says that the bee is dancing?** (Possible response: The bee is moving in a particular pattern, as if it were doing a dance.)

SCIENCE

SUPPORTING STANDARDS

Map a Bee's Movements Ask children to recall the movements bees make when they are showing that a flower is either close or far away. Have children imagine that they are observing a bee collecting honey. Have them draw the paths that the bee makes to and from a hive and then explain the movements made by the bee.

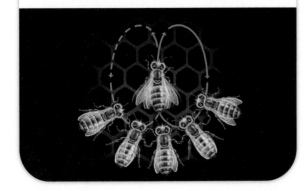

The bees are swarming.

Some of the bees are leaving their hive in a swarm. The queen bee goes with them. The swarm gathers on a branch while a few bees look for a good place to make a new hive. ❶

A new queen takes over.

A new queen bee has been born in the old hive. She starts laying eggs. ❷

266

267

Monitor Comprehension

PAGES 266–267 Have children read the headings and discuss the pictures. Say: **Read to find out why the bees are swarming and why a new queen takes over.**

❶ **DRAW CONCLUSIONS** **Why do you think that the bees wait on a branch until a new place for a hive is found?** (Possible response: They might get tired or lost if they travel as a swarm.)

❷ **SPECULATE** **What kinds of bees do you think will be needed in the new hive?** (Possible response: female workers and male drones)

ANALYZE AUTHOR'S PURPOSE

Author's Purpose Remind children that authors have a purpose, or reason, for writing. After children have finished reading "The Bee," ask:

Why did the author write "The Bee"?

• to persuade readers that bees are the best insects in the world

• to provide readers with information about bees

• to entertain readers with a story about a queen bee and her drones

The honey cells are full.

By the end of the summer, the bees have filled the hive with honey. They start to cover the honey cells with wax. There won't be any nectar in the fall and the winter. The bees will live on the honey stored in the honey cells. **1**

The bees are keeping warm.

When winter comes, the bees disappear. They shut themselves in their hive. They stay together in the hive until spring comes and they can gather nectar. **2**

268

269

Monitor Comprehension

PAGES 268–269   Say: **The heading on page 268 reads, "The honey cells are full." The heading on page 269 reads, "The bees are keeping warm." Read to find out about what happens when bee cells are full and warm.**

1 **NOTE DETAILS**   **What do the bees cover honey cells with?** (wax)
How do they survive? (They live on honey stored in honey cells.)

2 **CAUSE AND EFFECT**   **What causes the bees to disappear?**
(winter)

Parts of a Bee

Bees are insects. All insects have three parts to their body. These are the head, the thorax, and the abdomen. All insects have six legs, too. Insects such as bees also have wings and can fly.

Wings
Pair on each side of body

Abdomen
Rear part of body

Pollen baskets
Long hairs on legs to carry pollen

Stinger
Sharp point used to fight enemies ❶

Head
Front part of body

Antennae
Used to smell and sense things around them ❷

Compound eyes
Made of hundreds of tiny eyes that each see a part of the whole picture

Proboscis
Mouth that sucks in water and nectar

Thorax
Middle part of body

270

271

Monitor Comprehension

PAGES 270–271   Have children read the heading and describe what they see. Say: **Read about the parts of the bee.**

❶ **USE GRAPHIC AIDS**   **What do you learn about a bee's stinger in this diagram?** (It is sharp.) **What parts of the diagram helped you learn about the wings and abdomen?** (Accept reasonable responses.)

❷ **NOTE DETAILS**   **What part of a bee is used to smell things?** (antennae)

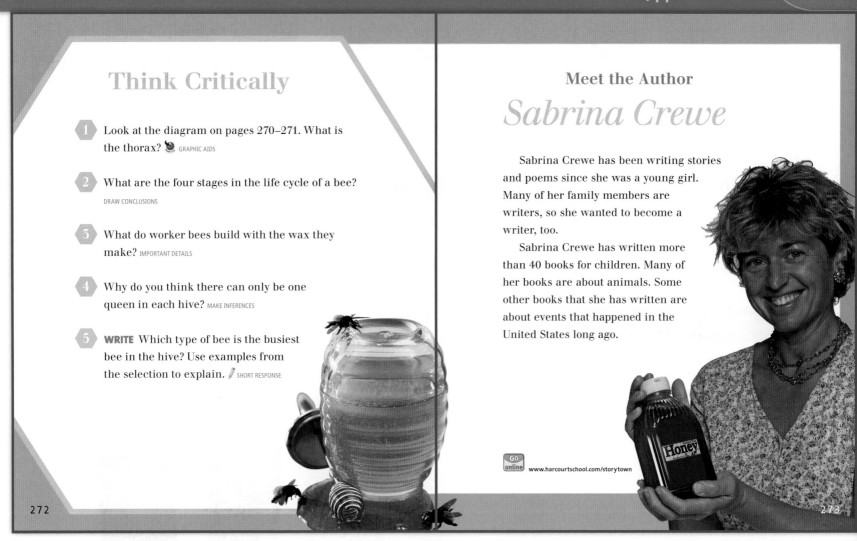

Think Critically

1. Look at the diagram on pages 270–271. What is the thorax? GRAPHIC AIDS

2. What are the four stages in the life cycle of a bee? DRAW CONCLUSIONS

3. What do worker bees build with the wax they make? IMPORTANT DETAILS

4. Why do you think there can only be one queen in each hive? MAKE INFERENCES

5. **WRITE** Which type of bee is the busiest bee in the hive? Use examples from the selection to explain. SHORT RESPONSE

Meet the Author
Sabrina Crewe

Sabrina Crewe has been writing stories and poems since she was a young girl. Many of her family members are writers, so she wanted to become a writer, too.

Sabrina Crewe has written more than 40 books for children. Many of her books are about animals. Some other books that she has written are about events that happened in the United States long ago.

GO online www.harcourtschool.com/storytown

272

273

Think Critically

Respond to the Literature

1. the middle part of the body **GRAPHIC AIDS**

2. pupa, larva, new bee, bee **DRAW CONCLUSIONS**

3. cells for the honeycomb **IMPORTANT DETAILS**

4. Possible response: The hive needs only one queen to lay eggs. **MAKE INFERENCES**

5. **WRITE** Possible response: The worker bees are the busiest. They build cells, feed the queen, drones, larvae, and young bees. They protect the hive and collect nectar and pollen. **SHORT RESPONSE**

Meet the Author

PAGE 273 Ask children to read page 273. Explain that Sabrina Crewe has written many nonfiction books about the life cycles of animals. Help them recall the life cycle of the bee. Then discuss what they might learn about the life cycles of other animals in Sabrina Crewe's books, such as *The Alligator*, *The Ladybug*, or *The Butterfly*.

Check Comprehension
Summarizing

Objectives

- *To practice summarizing a nonfiction selection*
- *To read at the appropriate rate for a nonfiction selection*

RETELLING RUBRIC

4	Uses details to clearly summarize the selection
3	Uses some details to summarize the selection
2	Summarizes selection with some inaccuracies
1	Is unable to summarize the selection

Professional Development

 Podcasting: Auditory Modeling

BELOW-LEVEL

Fluency Practice For fluency practice, have children read *Decodable Book 19*, the appropriate *Leveled Readers* (pp. 294–297), or Story 23 in the *Strategic Intervention Interactive Reader*.

Summarize

 DIBELS Oral Reading Fluency ORF **USE GRAPHIC AIDS** Ask children to tell what they learned from the diagram of the bee. (the parts of a bee's body and what they are used for)

 REVISIT THE GRAPHIC ORGANIZER Display completed **Transparency GO6**. Guide children to identify the main idea and details in "The Bee."

STORY RETELLING CARDS The cards for "The Bee" can be used for retelling or as an aid to completing the graphic organizer.

▲ Story Retelling Cards 1–6, "The Bee"

 # Fluency
Reading Rate

Teach/Model

DIBELS Oral Reading Fluency ORF **USING READING RATE** Explain that good readers slow down or speed up depending on what they are reading. Read pages 268–269 aloud, modeling an appropriate rate.

Practice/Apply

 Routine Card 7 **CHORAL-READ** Read aloud the rest of the selection, one page at a time, modeling using an appropriate reading rate for nonfiction. Have children choral-read each page with you.

Build Robust Vocabulary

Words About the Selection

Teach/Model

Routine Card 3

INTRODUCE THE WORDS Use *Routine Card 3* to introduce the words.

---

❶ Put the word in **selection context**.
❷ Display Transparency R125 and read the word and the **Student-Friendly Explanation**.
❸ Have children **say the word** with you.
❹ Use the word in other contexts, and have children **interact with the word's meaning**.
❺ Remove the transparency. Say the Student-Friendly Explanation again, and ask children to **name the word** that goes with it.

---

❶ **Selection Context:** The **role** of the worker bees is to look after the hive.

❹ **Interact with Word Meaning:** My role in the classroom is to teach. What is the role of a firefighter—to drive a bus or to put out fires?

❶ **Selection Context:** The worker bees are **diligent** about cleaning the cells.

❹ **Interact with Word Meaning:** I am diligent when I grade homework. If you are diligent at practicing a musical instrument, would you be more likely to perform well or perform poorly during a recital?

Practice/Apply

GUIDED PRACTICE Ask children to do the following:

• Imagine that you are a doctor. What would your *role* be?

• Imagine that you have to take care of a garden. Would you be *diligent* about weeding? Why or why not?

Objective

• *To develop robust vocabulary through discussing a literature selection*

INTRODUCE ✓ | Tested

Vocabulary: Lesson 23

role   diligent

▼ **Student-Friendly Explanations**

Student-Friendly Explanations

thickens	If something thickens, it becomes more gooey.
plentiful	If something is plentiful, there is a lot of it.
role	If you have a role, there are certain things you have to do.
diligent	If you are diligent, you keep working until you're done.

Grade 2, Lesson 23   **R125**   Vocabulary

Transparency R125

Grammar Quick Write

Past-Tense Verbs

5-DAY GRAMMAR	
DAY 1	Introduce Past-Tense Verbs
DAY 2	Verbs that Take -*ed*
DAY 3	Verbs that Take -*d*
DAY 4	Apply to Writing
DAY 5	Weekly Review

Objective

- *To identify and use past-tense verbs*

Daily Proofreading

gary saw a gren frog.

(Gary; green)

Using *When* Words Instruct children that they should use words that tell *when* to show exactly when an action happened in the past. Provide some examples such as *long ago* and *yesterday*. Ask students to name other words.

Grammar Practice Book, p. 81

Name _____

▶ Read each sentence. Circle the verb. If the verb tells about the past, write *past*. If the verb tells about now, write *now*.

Past-Tense Verbs
Lesson 23

1. The bees (worked) together. ___past___
2. The queen bee (lays) the eggs. ___now___
3. Other bees in the colony (created) cells inside the hive. ___past___
4. The eggs (hatched) ___past___
5. The worker bees (collect) pollen and nectar. ___now___
6. The nectar (turns) into honey. ___now___
7. My mom (picked) out two kinds of honey. ___past___
8. I (liked) the honey in the comb the best. ___past___

81   Grammar Practice Book

▲ **Grammar Practice Book, p. 81**

Review

FORM PAST-TENSE VERBS USING -*ed*   Write these words on the board.

rush	talk	walk
add	laugh	start

Have children read aloud the words. Model how to add -*ed* to *rush* so that it tells about an action that happened in the past. Use the word in a sentence such as, "This morning I rushed to the bus stop." Call on volunteers to come to the board and add -*ed* to the remaining words so they tell about the past. Then ask children to use the words in sentences. Provide this example: "Yesterday, I talked to my grandmother."

Practice/Apply

GUIDED PRACTICE   Write the following incomplete sentences on the board. Have a volunteer read the first sentence aloud. Model how to add -*ed* to the verb in parentheses so that it tells about the past. *(fished)* Work with children to rewrite the remaining sentences using a past-tense verb.

Lori _____ in the pond. (fish)

Her dad _____ the boat. (row)

A frog _____ in the water. (jump)

A dragonfly _____ on a lily pad. (land)

INDEPENDENT PRACTICE   Have children write three sentences about animals using past-tense verbs. Remind them that past-tense verbs end in -*ed*.

Writing
Paragraph of Information

5-DAY WRITING	
DAY 1	Introduce
DAY 2	**Prewrite**
DAY 3	Draft
DAY 4	Revise
DAY 5	Revise

Prewrite

GENERATE IDEAS Ask children to look at the list of ideas they wrote on Day 1. Tell them to think of sentences that might give more information about one of their ideas.

 WORD CHOICE Suggest that children brainstorm a list of action words that tell more about their topic.

MODEL PREWRITING Copy on the board the chart below. Tell children that they can use a graphic organizer such as this one to organize their ideas for their paragraph of information. Model filling in the main idea and details chart.

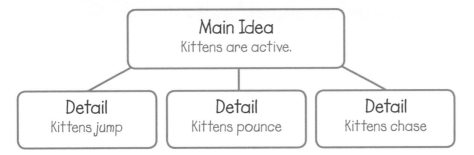

Main Idea
Kittens are active.

Detail
Kittens *jump*

Detail
Kittens *pounce*

Detail
Kittens *chase*

Practice/Apply

GUIDED PRACTICE Ask children to brainstorm several ideas that tell more about the main idea in your graphic organizer. Call on volunteers to share their ideas with classmates. As children respond, add their ideas to the chart in the appropriate boxes.

 INDEPENDENT PRACTICE Have children use their lists and make a new chart to brainstorm ideas for writing their paragraphs. Tell children to save their charts to use on Days 3–5.

Objectives

- *To develop ideas and topics for writing*
- *To use a graphic organizer for prewriting*

 ### Writing Prompt

Independent Writing Have children write several sentences about what they learned from reading a paragraph of information recently.

BELOW-LEVEL

Use Pictures If children have difficulty completing their main idea and details chart, work with them to choose a topic familiar to them, such as playing soccer. Then have them sketch their supporting ideas and dictate captions for them.

Day at a Glance
Day 3

phonics and Spelling
- Review: Vowel Variant /o͞o/oo, ew, ue, ui, ou
- State the Generalization

Fluency
- Reading Rate
- "The Bee," *Student Edition*, pp. 244–273

Comprehension

Review: Use Graphic Aids

Reading
- "California Bee Business," *Student Edition*, pp. 274–275

Read!

Robust Vocabulary
- Review: *thickens, plentiful, crowd, sealed, carefully, attack, pattern, disappear, role, diligent*
- Introduce: Synonyms

Grammar *Quick Write*
- Review: Past-Tense Verbs

Writing
- Paragraph of Information

Warm-Up Routines

Oral Language

Objective *To listen attentively and respond appropriately to oral communication*

Question of the Day

Imagine that you are a bee. What words could you use so that other people would be able to guess what you are?

Use the following prompts to help children think about the characteristics of bees.

- **How do bees fly?**
- **What sounds do bees make?**
- **What do bees look like?**
- **How do bees sting?**

Have children complete the following sentence frames to tell how they would describe bees.

I have _____ and _____. I also _____. I am a bee.

Read Aloud

Objective *To identify rhymes in poetry*

BIG BOOK OF RHYMES AND POEMS Display "Bumblebees" on page 41 and read aloud the title. Then read the poem aloud. Ask children to identify the pairs of rhyming words. (teensy-weensy, itty-bitty, wings/ stings) Ask how these rhyming words are different from rhyming words in some other poems they have read. (Some of the rhyming words are in the middle of lines and not just at the end of lines.)

▲ **Big Book of Rhymes and Poems, p. 41**

Word Wall

Objective *To read high-frequency words*

REVIEW HIGH-FREQUENCY WORDS Remove from the Word Wall the cards for *already*, *woods*, *ears*, *short*, *lose*, *clear*, *draw*, and *shoes* as well as other previously learned high-frequency words. Have children begin snapping their fingers to keep time. Hold up each card and have children spell and read the word to the beat of the snaps. Flip through the cards several times.

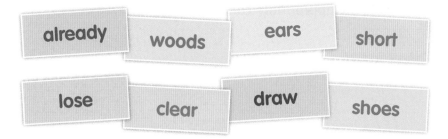

Vowel Variant /ōō/
oo, ew, ue, ui, ou and Spelling

5-DAY PHONICS

DAY 1	Introduce /ōō/oo, ew, ue, ui, ou
DAY 2	Word Building with /ōō/oo, ew, ue, ui, ou
DAY 3	**Word Building with /ōō/oo, ew, ue, ui, ou**
DAY 4	Prefixes mis-, re-, un-; Review /ōō/oo, ew, ue, ui, ou
DAY 5	Prefixes mis-, re-, un-; Review /ōō/oo, ew, ue, ui, ou

Objectives

- To read phonetically regular words
- To read and write common word families
- To recognize spelling patterns

Skill Trace

 Tested Vowel Variant
/ōō/oo, ew, ue, ui, ou

Introduce	Grade 1
Reintroduce	T220–T223
Reteach	S26–S27
Review	**T232–T233, T258–259, T422**
Test	Theme 5
Maintain	Theme 6, T360

Work with Patterns

INTRODUCE PHONOGRAMS   Write the following phonograms at the top of six columns.

-oo	-ool	-ue	-ew	-uit	-oup

Tell children that these are the endings of some words. Slide your hand under the letters as you read each phonogram. Repeat, having children read the phonograms with you.

BUILD AND READ WORDS   Write the letter *t* in front of *-oo* and *-ool*. Guide children to read each word: /t/-*oo*, *too*; /t/-*ool*, *tool*. Continue in the same manner with *bl* in front of *-ue* and *-ew* and with *s* in front of *-uit* and *-oup*. Then have children name other words that end with *-oo*, *-ool*, *-ue*, *-ew*, *-uit*, and *-oup*. Have them tell which letter or letters to add to build each word, and write the word in the appropriate column. Have children read each column of words. Then point to words at random and have children read them.

Read Words in Context

READ SENTENCES   Display **Transparency R122** or write the sentences on the board. Have children echo-read the sentences as you track the print. Then ask volunteers to read each sentence aloud and to underline words with the phonograms *-oo*, *-ool*, *-ue*, *-ew*, *-uit*, and *-oup*. Invite volunteers to add the words *school, group, cool, new, Sue, fruit,* and *zoo* to the appropriate columns.

Vowel Variant /ōō/oo, ew, ue, ui, ou

Our school group went to the farm.
It was a cool, windy day.
We looked at Kendra's new beehives.
Sue wore a mask by the hives.
The honey smelled like fruit.
Next week, we will go to the zoo.

Grade 2, Lesson 23   R122   Phonics

Transparency R122

5-DAY SPELLING
DAY 1	Pretest
DAY 2	Word Building
DAY 3	**State the Generalization**
DAY 4	Review
DAY 5	Posttest

Review Spelling Words

STATE THE GENERALIZATION FOR /o͞o/oo, ew, ue, ui, ou List spelling words 1–10 on chart paper or on the board. Circle the words in which the letters *ue* stand for the /o͞o/ sound, and have children read them aloud. Ask: **What is the same in each word?** (The letters *ue* stand for the /o͞o/ sound.) Repeat the procedure for *ew, oo, ui,* and *ou,* circling the words using a different color.

WRITE Have children write the spelling words in their notebooks. Remind them to use their best handwriting and to check the position of their paper to make sure it is positioned correctly as they write.

Handwriting

PENCIL GRIP Remind children to make sure they are holding their pencils correctly.

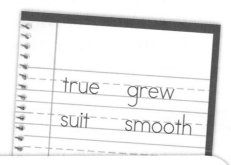

Decodable Books

Additional Decoding Practice

- **Phonics**
  Vowel Variant /o͞o/oo, ew, ue, ui, ou
- **Decodable Words**
- **High-Frequency Words**
  See the list in *Decodable Book 19.*

  See also *Decodable Books,*
  online (Take-Home Version).

▲ Decodable Book 19: "Seafood Stew," "True Buddies," and "Ouzels"

Spelling Words

1.	**true**	6.	**soup**
2.	**grew**	7.	**stew**
3.	**suit**	8.	**food***
4.	**smooth**	9.	**group**
5.	**clue**	10.	**fruit**

Challenge Words

11.	**nephew**	14.	**juicy**
12.	**classroom**	15.	**newspaper**
13.	**cartoon**		

* Word from "The Bee"

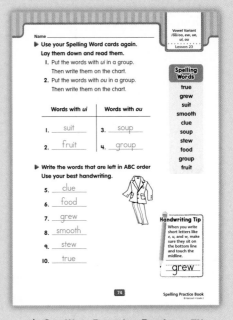

▲ Spelling Practice Book, p. 74

⏱ Fluency
Reading Rate

Objective

- *To read fluently at a rate appropriate to the genre*

BELOW-LEVEL

Fluency Practice Have children reread using *Decodable Book 19*, Story 23 in the *Strategic Intervention Interactive Reader*, or the appropriate *Leveled Reader* (see pp. T294–T297). Have them practice reading the text several times.

Additional Related Reading

- ***Bees (Creepy Creatures)*** by Sue Barraclough. Raintree, 2005. **EASY**
- ***From Flower to Honey*** by Robin Nelson. Lerner, 2002 **AVERAGE**
- ***The Bumblebee Queen*** by April Pulley Sayre. Charlesbridge, 2006. **CHALLENGE**

"Research Says"

Fluency Instruction "Based on acknowledged reading theory, fluency instruction holds promise for improving reading for all students in the 'real world' of classrooms."
—Rasinski, et. al. (1994)

Review

DIBELS
Oral Reading Fluency
ORF

MODEL USING READING RATE Remind children that good readers change their reading rate depending on what they are reading. Tell children to

▲ Student Edition, pp. 244–273

- read nonfiction at a rate that is slow enough for the listener to understand the information.

- read slowly if they are reading scientific or technical words.

Think Aloud I'm going to read part of "The Bee" aloud. Since it is nonfiction, I'll read more slowly than I would read a fiction story to make sure everyone understands the information that I am reading. If I come to a science or technical word, I'll slow down a little bit so listeners pay attention to that key word.

Practice/Apply

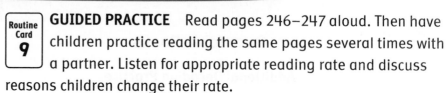

Routine Card 9

GUIDED PRACTICE Read pages 246–247 aloud. Then have children practice reading the same pages several times with a partner. Listen for appropriate reading rate and discuss reasons children change their rate.

INDEPENDENT PRACTICE Have partners reread sections of "The Bee" aloud two or three times. Remind them to slow down, yet still make the reading sound smooth and natural. Have the partner who is listening follow along in the *Student Edition* and alert the reader when he or she is pausing too often or reading too slowly.

Use Graphic Aids

Comprehension

Review

REVIEW GRAPHIC AIDS   Remind children of types of graphic aids such as diagrams, maps, charts, and time lines. Ask what types of information they can learn from each graphic aid. (diagram–facts related to parts of something; maps–where places are found; charts–information that can be compared; time lines–dates and events over time) Then model for children using a graphic aid to learn more about a nonfiction topic.

> **Think Aloud**   **When I look at a graphic aid, first I figure out what kind of information it gives me. A diagram, for example, can show the parts of something or how something works. The diagram will make it easier for me to understand the information because parts are labeled.**

Practice/Apply

GUIDED PRACTICE   Have children study the diagram on *Student Edition* pages 270–271. Ask children to use the lines from the captions to help them figure out what each part of the bee's body is used for. Remind them to pay attention to key words, which are in dark type.

Ask children the following questions about the diagram, and have them point to where they found their answers.

- **Where is the abdomen?** (in the rear of the bee's body)

- **How many legs does a bee have?** (six)

- **Why does a bee have a stinger?** (to fight enemies)

INDEPENDENT PRACTICE   Have children meet with a partner to study the diagram on pages 270–271. Have them jot down on index cards three new questions and answers based on the diagram. Then have children meet with other pairs of children to share their questions and answers. Circulate among children to hear their discussions. Ask children to tell how the diagram helped them understand bees. (It explains the parts of a bee and shows what the parts look like.)

Objective

- *To use graphic aids to understand nonfiction selections*

Skill Trace

Tested   Use Graphic Aids

Introduce	T224–T225
Reteach	S30–S31
Review	T261, T277, T289, T316–T317, T345, T361, T371, T424, T445
Test	Theme 5
Maintain	Theme 6, T272

Reading

Student Edition: **Paired Selection**

Objectives

- *To understand characteristics of nonfiction selections*
- *To apply word knowledge to the reading of a text*

Writing Prompt

Reflect Ask children to write three of the most interesting facts about bees in "California Bee Business." Then have children compare those facts to their three favorite facts in "The Bee."

Genre Study

DISCUSS NONFICTION Explain to children that "California Bee Business" is a nonfiction selection. It gives facts and information about a topic.

TEXT FEATURES Tell children that most nonfiction selections have certain features that can help them understand and enjoy what they read. These features may include

- photographs and captions.
- facts and details about a subject or topic.
- graphic aids such as charts, maps, or diagrams.

USE PRIOR KNOWLEDGE/SET A PURPOSE Guide children to use prior knowledge and set a purpose for listening. Then have children read the feature.

Respond to the Article

MONITOR COMPREHENSION Ask children to reread the feature. Ask:

- **TEXT STRUCTURE** **What sentence in paragraph 2 tells the main idea?** (the first sentence) **What do the other sentences tell more about?** (the main idea)

- **PERSONAL RESPONSE** **What did you learn about honey in California that you found most interesting?** (Responses will vary.)

- **GENRE** **Do you like reading about real insects in real places? Explain.** (Possible response: Yes; I like knowing about the foods I eat.)

Science

California

Bee Business

by **Dimarie Santiago**

Nonfiction

More than 300 kinds of honey are made in the United States. The kind of honey a bee makes depends on the flowers it visits. Bees that visit almond flowers are important in California. Why?

California produces almost half the world's almonds. When bees visit almond flowers, they spread the flowers' pollen that makes almonds grow. It takes almost a million hives of bees to keep California's almonds growing!

Bees are attracted to the fragrant flowers on almond trees.

When caring for a hive, beekeepers use smoke to calm the bees.

California is one of the top producers of honey in the nation. In a recent year, California produced about 15 million pounds of honey! That's almost enough for every person in California to have half a pound of honey. How much honey do you eat?

274

275

SOCIAL STUDIES

SUPPORTING STANDARDS

Use a Map Ask children to locate California on a map of the United States. Tell them that other top honey-producing states include North and South Dakota, Florida, Minnesota, Montana, and Texas. Then guide children to locate each of these states on the map.

Connections

Objectives
- *To compare texts*
- *To connect texts to personal experiences*

Comparing Texts

1 Possible response: "The Bee" describes how the bee sucks nectar from flowers and carries both pollen and nectar to the hive. "California Bee Business" states that the kind of honey a bee produces depends on the flower it visits. **TEXT TO TEXT**

2 Responses will vary but should be based on the information gathered from the selections. **TEXT TO SELF**

3 Possible response: They might not be able to produce honey in a place with few or no flowering plants. **TEXT TO WORLD**

Connections

Comparing Texts

1. What do "The Bee" and "California Bee Business" tell you about how flowers help bees make honey?

2. What else would you like to know about bees?

3. In what places might bees be unable to make honey?

Phonics

Word Clues

List words in which the letters *oo*, *ew*, *ue*, *ui*, or *ou* stand for the vowel sound in *tooth*. Write clues for your words. Take turns with a partner to guess each other's words.

> This word names apples, oranges, and bananas.
>
> fr**ui**t

Fluency Practice

Partner Reading

Read the selection again with a partner. Take turns reading one or two pages at a time. Try to read at a pace that sounds like you are talking to a friend.

Writing

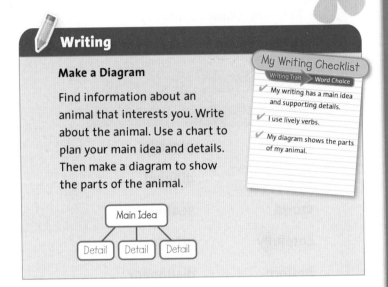

Make a Diagram

Find information about an animal that interests you. Write about the animal. Use a chart to plan your main idea and details. Then make a diagram to show the parts of the animal.

> **My Writing Checklist**
> Writing Trait > Word Choice
> ✓ My writing has a main idea and supporting details.
> ✓ I use lively verbs.
> ✓ My diagram shows the parts of my animal.

```
              Main Idea
          /      |      \
      Detail  Detail  Detail
```

276

277

⏱ PHONICS

Word Clues Draw a five-column chart on the board. Help children generate rhyming words or words with the same vowel sound and spelling as those in the columns, and add them to the correct column of the chart. Have children use the chart as they write their clues. Invite them to share their clues after meeting with a partner.

t**oo**th	ch**ew**	d**ue**	fr**ui**t	s**ou**p
booth	dew	Sue	suit	toucan
boot	new	clue		

⏱ FLUENCY

Timed Reading With a volunteer, model how to use a stopwatch to time your reading of pages 246–247 of "The Bee." Suggest that children choose two pages to read aloud, such as pages 250–251. Ask partners to take turns reading or using the stopwatch. Have them do at least two readings before switching roles.

⏱ WRITING

Make a Diagram Help children brainstorm ideas for a diagram, such as the parts of a cat or a dog. List their ideas on the board. Provide a model, such as the bee diagram on pages 270–271. Invite children to share their finished diagram and read aloud what they wrote.

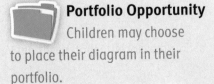 **Portfolio Opportunity** Children may choose to place their diagram in their portfolio.

Build Robust Vocabulary

Objective

- *To review robust vocabulary*

REVIEW Tested ✓

Vocabulary: Lesson 23

thickens	plentiful
role	diligent
crowd	sealed
carefully	attack
pattern	disappear

Review Robust Vocabulary

USE VOCABULARY IN DIFFERENT CONTEXTS   Remind children of the Student-Friendly Explanations of the Vocabulary Words introduced on Days 1 and 2. Then discuss each word, using the following prompts:

thickens

- If frosting thickens, is it easier or harder to spread on cake?
- If you add flour to water, do you think it thickens? Why?

plentiful

- Where is snow most likely to be plentiful?
- Where are books plentiful in your school?

role

- What is the role of a mother bear?
- What is the role of a coach of a sports team?

diligent

- Does a diligent police officer stop speeding drivers or let them go?
- Does a diligent painter stop before the painting is done? Why or why not?

crowd

- When might children crowd you on the playground— at recess or during class?
- If you had bread crumbs, would ducks crowd you at a pond? Why or why not?

sealed

- Would you rather get a sealed birthday present or an open one? Why?
- If a magician were in a sealed box, how could he or she escape?

carefully

- Why does a dentist need to work carefully on his or her patients?
- Do you study for tests carefully? Why or why not?

attack

- What can a mouse do if an owl swoops down to attack it?
- Why might large animals in the jungle attack smaller animals?

pattern

- What pattern do you see in a rainbow?
- What pattern has circles: polka dots or stripes?

disappear

- What makes snow disappear—the sun or the moon?
- If you laugh, does a frown disappear? Show this.

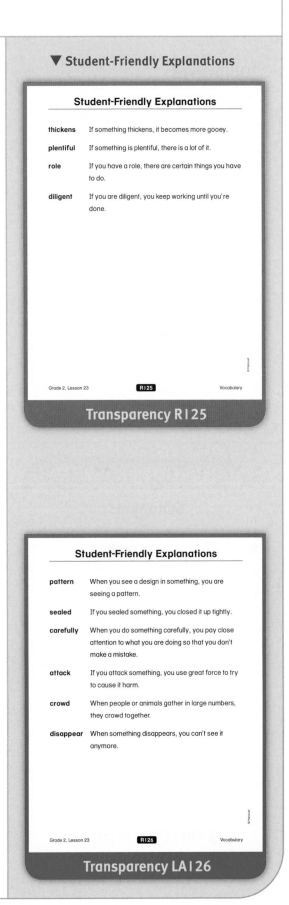

▼ Student-Friendly Explanations

Student-Friendly Explanations

thickens	If something thickens, it becomes more gooey.
plentiful	If something is plentiful, there is a lot of it.
role	If you have a role, there are certain things you have to do.
diligent	If you are diligent, you keep working until you're done.

Grade 2, Lesson 23   R125   Vocabulary

Transparency R I 25

Student-Friendly Explanations

pattern	When you see a design in something, you are seeing a pattern.
sealed	If you sealed something, you closed it up tightly.
carefully	When you do something carefully, you pay close attention to what you are doing so that you don't make a mistake.
attack	If you attack something, you use great force to try to cause it harm.
crowd	When people or animals gather in large numbers, they crowd together.
disappear	When something disappears, you can't see it anymore.

Grade 2, Lesson 23   R126   Vocabulary

Transparency LA I 26

Synonyms
Vocabulary

Objectives

- *To identify synonyms*
- *To use a dictionary and a thesaurus to locate synonyms*

Skill Trace

 Tested **Synonyms**

Introduce	T268–T269
Reteach	S32–S33
Review	T352–T353, T437, T446
Test	Theme 5

 MONITOR PROGRESS

Synonyms

IF children have difficulty identifying and locating synonyms,	**THEN** create a list of familiar verbs and show them how to use a dictionary or thesaurus to find other words that mean about the same thing.

Small-Group Instruction, pp. S32–S33:

- **BELOW-LEVEL:** Reteach
- **ON-LEVEL:** Reinforce
- **ADVANCED:** Extend

Teach/Model

INTRODUCE SYNONYMS Tell children the following about synonyms:

- Synonyms are words that have the same, or almost the same, meanings.

- Use the context and what you already know to figure out if the words are synonyms.

- Use a dictionary or thesaurus to check if the words are synonyms or to find a synonym for a word.

Model how to identify synonyms:

> **Think Aloud** I want to know a synonym for *sealed*. I know that the word means "closed up tightly." I can use a dictionary or a thesaurus to find a synonym. I look in the *s* section to find *sealed*. Some synonyms are *closed, shut, locked, secured*, and *fastened*.

Guided Practice

IDENTIFY SYNONYMS   Display **Transparency R123**. Read the first sentence with children. Work with them to choose the word in parentheses that has a similar meaning to the word *attack*. *(strike)* Repeat for the word *disappear* in sentence 2. *(vanish)* Model how to use a dictionary or thesaurus to check the answers. Then guide children to choose the synonym for sentence 3.

Practice/Apply

IDENTIFY SYNONYMS   Have children work with partners to choose the synonyms for sentences 4, 5, and 6. Call on children to share their answers with the class and to check their answers in a dictionary or thesaurus.

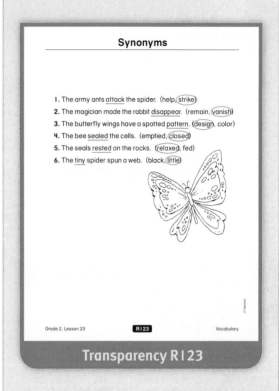

Synonyms

1. The army ants attack the spider. (help, strike)
2. The magician made the rabbit disappear. (remain, vanish)
3. The butterfly wings have a spotted pattern. (design, color)
4. The bee sealed the cells. (emptied, closed)
5. The seals rested on the rocks. (relaxed, fed)
6. The tiny spider spun a web. (black, little)

Grade 2, Lesson 23   R123   Vocabulary

Transparency R123

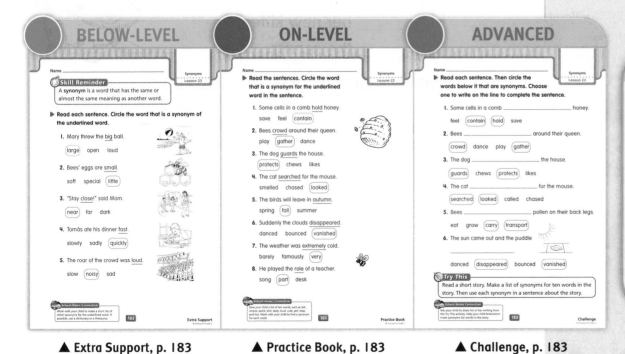

BELOW-LEVEL

▲ Extra Support, p. 183

ON-LEVEL

▲ Practice Book, p. 183

ADVANCED

▲ Challenge, p. 183

ELL

• Group children according to academic levels, and assign one of the pages on the left.

• Clarify any unfamiliar concepts as necessary. See *ELL Teacher Guide* Lesson 23 for support in scaffolding instruction.

Grammar Quick Write

Past-Tense Verbs

5-DAY GRAMMAR

DAY 1 Introduce Past-Tense Verbs
DAY 2 Verbs that Take -ed
DAY 3 Verbs that Take -d
DAY 4 Apply to Writing
DAY 5 Weekly Review

Objective

- *To form sentences with past-tense verbs*

Daily Proofreading

the clown juggled three orange.

(The; oranges)

TECHNOLOGY

GO online www.harcourtschool.com/storytown
Grammar Glossary

Name _____

▶ Read each verb. Add *ed* so that the verb tells about the past.

Past-Tense Verbs
Lesson 23

1. laugh — *laughed*
2. jump — *jumped*
3. soar — *soared*
4. glue — *glued*
5. collect — *collected*

▶ Write three sentences that tell about something you did in the past. Use verbs from the list above. Possible responses shown.

6. We laughed at my baby brother.
7. The plane soared over the canyon.
8. We collected rocks today.

82   Grammar Practice Book

▲ **Grammar Practice Book, p. 82**

Review

PAST-TENSE VERBS WITH -d Write these words on the board.

like	pile	giggle
smile	hope	care

Read aloud the words with children. Model how to add *-d* to *like* to form a verb that tells about the past. *(liked)* Elicit from children that when a word ends in a silent *e*, they should add a *d* so it tells about an action in the past. Use *liked* in an oral sentence: "I <u>liked</u> the pancakes I had for breakfast yesterday." Then call on volunteers to add *-d* to the remaining words and use the words in sentences.

Practice/Apply

GUIDED PRACTICE Write these sentences on the board. For the first sentence, model how to add the letter *d* to the verb so it tells about an action in the past. Work with children to complete the remaining sentences.

Marti _____ the boat in the water. (place)

Ted _____ a space for me. (save)

Kim _____ her new kitten. (name)

Ben _____ the carrots. (slice)

INDEPENDENT PRACTICE Have children write sentences that tell about the past. Then have them read the sentences aloud.

Writing
Paragraph of Information

5-DAY WRITING	
DAY 1	Introduce
DAY 2	Prewrite
DAY 3	**Draft**
DAY 4	Revise
DAY 5	Revise

Draft a Paragraph of Information

REVIEW WITH A LITERATURE MODEL   Have children open their *Student Edition* to "The Bee," page 250. Invite them to read the heading and the first sentence. Explain that this is the first sentence of a paragraph of information. Have children read the rest of the paragraph. Point out the following:

> • The heading tells what the paragraph is about.
>
> • The topic sentence tells the main idea.
>
> • The paragraph gives information about the queen bee.
>
> • The other sentences give more details about the queen bee.

DRAFT A PARAGRAPH OF INFORMATION   Have children use their lists and filled-in main idea and details charts to write a draft of a paragraph of information. Remind them to use proper indentation at the beginning of their paragraph. Direct them to simple reference materials in the classroom, such as a children's encyclopedia article, if they want to research additional facts about their topic.

WORD CHOICE   As children write their sentences, remind them to include action verbs to tell what is happening. Remind them that verbs that tell about the past often end in *-ed* or *-d*.

CONFER WITH CHILDREN   Meet with children, helping them draft their paragraph of information. Encourage them for their efforts and make constructive suggestions for improving an aspect of the writing, as needed. Remind them that their first sentence should state the main idea and the other sentences should tell more about the main idea.

Objectives

• *To write a draft of a paragraph of information*
• *To use past-tense verbs correctly in writing*

 Writing Prompt

Evaluate   Have children jot down what they find easy or difficult about writing paragraphs.

▲ Writer's Companion, Lesson 23

ADVANCED

Conduct Research   If children wish to take notes for any research they do, provide them with index cards. Model how to write the title of the source, the page number, and key facts that relate to their topic. Remind them when they write their paragraphs, they should not copy the information, but write their sentences using their own words.

Day at a Glance

Day 4

 phonics and Spelling

- Introduce: Prefixes *mis-, re-, un-*
- Review: Vowel Variant /ōō/*oo*, *ew, ue, ui, ou*

Fluency

- Reading Rate
- "The Bee," *Student Edition,* pp. 244–273

Read!

Comprehension

 Review: Use Graphic Aids

- Maintain: Author's Purpose
- Maintain: Locate Information

Robust Vocabulary

- Review: *thickens, plentiful, crowd, sealed, carefully, attack, pattern, disappear, role, diligent*

Grammar [Quick Write]

- Review: Past-Tense Verbs

Writing

- Paragraph of Information

Warm-Up Routines

 Oral Language

Objective *To listen attentively and respond appropriately to oral communication*

Question of the Day

What are some ways you could learn more about bees?

Discuss with children some sources that they could use to learn more about bees. Use the following prompts:

- **What source could you use that has articles about topics?**
- **What computer sources could you use to find pictures of bees?**
- **What other sources could you use to read more about bees?**

Record their responses on a chart. Display the chart for children to revisit through the lesson.

Read Aloud

Objective *To identify patterns in poetry*

BIG BOOK OF RHYMES AND POEMS Display the poem "The Swarm of Bees" on page 42 and read aloud the title. Ask children to listen to the details in the poem and to form in their mind a picture of what is happening. Then read the poem aloud. Reread the poem several times, asking children to chime in when they are able. Invite children to identify the number pattern in the poem. (Every second line begins with one higher number—one, two, three, four, five.)

▲ **Big Book of Rhymes and Poems, p. 42**

Word Wall

Objective *To read high-frequency words*

REVIEW HIGH-FREQUENCY WORDS Arrange the words *caught, eight, exercise, finally, guess, sure, thumb,* and *wash* in two columns. Divide the class into two groups. Have children in the first group choral-read the first column of words, snapping their fingers to keep time. Have the second group do the same thing with the second column of words. Then have groups switch columns and repeat.

caught	guess
eight	sure
exercise	thumb
finally	wash

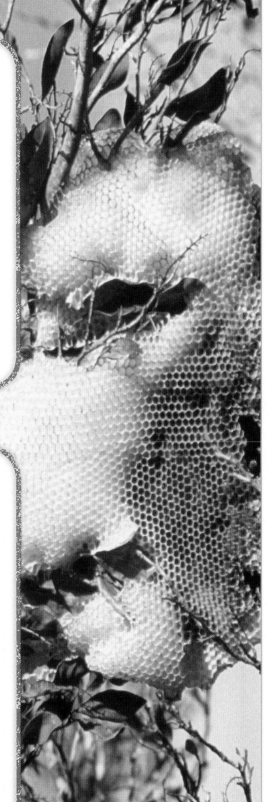

Prefixes mis-, re-, un- *phonics*

5-DAY PHONICS	
DAY 1	Introduce /o͞o/oo, ew, ue, ui, ou
DAY 2	Word Building with /o͞o/oo, ew, ue, ui, ou
DAY 3	Word Building with /o͞o/oo, ew, ue, ui, ou
DAY 4	Prefixes mis-, re-, un-; Review /o͞o/
DAY 5	Prefixes mis-, re-, un-; Review /o͞o/

Objectives

- *To identify the prefixes* mis-, re-, *and* un- *in two-syllable words*
- *To know the meanings of the prefixes* mis-, re-, *and* un-
- *To read longer words with the prefixes* mis-, re-, *and* un-

Skill Trace

 Tested **Prefixes *mis-, re-, un-***

Introduce	T274
Review	T286
Test	Theme 5

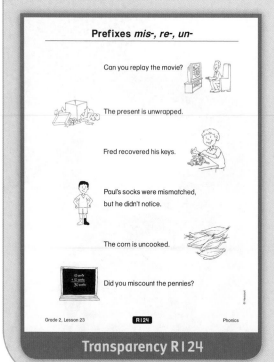

Prefixes *mis-, re-, un-*

Can you replay the movie?

The present is unwrapped.

Fred recovered his keys.

Paul's socks were mismatched, but he didn't notice.

The corn is uncooked.

Did you miscount the pennies?

Grade 2, Lesson 23   R124   Phonics

Transparency R124

Teach/Model

INTRODUCE PREFIXES Write *spell* on the board and have children read it. Then write *misspell* and underline *mis-*. Explain that *mis-* is a word part added to the beginning of a word that changes the meaning. Repeat the procedure with *redo* and *unhappy*. Draw the following chart, and explain each prefix's meaning.

Prefix	Meaning	Word/Meaning
mis–	bad, wrong	misspell: spell wrongly
re–	again	redo: do again
un–	not	unhappy: not happy

MODEL DECODING LONGER WORDS Model how to blend the syllables together to read *refuel*.

- Cover the second syllable and have children read /rē/.
- Cover the first syllable and have children read /fyo͞ol/.
- Then have children read the word—*refuel*.

Distribute Syllabication Card 13 (*Teacher Resource Book*, p. 93) and have children read the example words (*reread, unkind*).

Guided Practice

NONSENSE WORDS Write these nonsense words: *unphane, reknown, miswrite, miswrap,* and *untough* on the board to maintain /n/kn, /r/wr, /f/gh, ph. Explain that these words are made-up and have no meaning. Guide children to identify the prefixes and blend the syllables to read each word.

Practice/Apply

INDEPENDENT PRACTICE Display **Transparency R124** or write the sentences on the board. Have children read the sentences aloud.

Vowel Variant /oō/oo, ew, ue, ui, ou phonics *and Spelling*

5-DAY SPELLING	
DAY 1	Pretest
DAY 2	Word Building
DAY 3	State the Generalization
DAY 4	Review
DAY 5	Posttest

Build Words

REVIEW THE WORDS Have children open their notebooks to the spelling words that they wrote on Day 3. Have them read the words several times and then close their notebooks.

MAP LETTERS TO SOUNDS Have children follow your directions to change one or more letters in each of the following words to spell a spelling word. Have them write the spelling word on a sheet of paper. Then have a volunteer change the spelling of the word on the board so that children can self-check their spelling.

- Write *club* on the board. Ask: **Which spelling word can you make by changing the last letter?** *(clue)*

- Write *foot* on the board. Ask: **Which spelling word can you make by changing the last letter?** *(food)*

- Write *growl* on the board. Ask: **Which spelling word can you make by changing the last two letters?** *(group)*

club
clue
foot
food
growl
group

Follow a similar procedure for *front (fruit)*, *truck (true)*, *stem (stew)*, *smog (smooth)*, *sour (soup)*, *drew (grew)*, *sun (suit)*.

CHALLENGE WORDS Write each challenge word on the board, omitting the first two letters. Ask volunteers to spell each word in its entirety and write the missing letters.

BELOW-LEVEL

Focus on Consonant Blends Write the following word endings on the board, with a blank where the initial consonant sounds should be: _ _ue, _ _ew, _ _ooth, _ _oup, _ _uit. Then prompt children to build spelling words by asking questions such as, "What letters can you add to *ue* to make *true*?" Have children spell each completed word.

Objective

- *To use vowel variant /oō/oo, ew, ue, ui, ou and other known letter-sounds to spell and write words*

Spelling Words

1.	true	6.	soup
2.	grew	7.	stew
3.	suit	8.	food*
4.	smooth	9.	group
5.	clue	10.	fruit

Challenge Words

11.	nephew	14.	juicy
12.	classroom	15.	newspaper
13.	cartoon		

* Word from "The Bee"

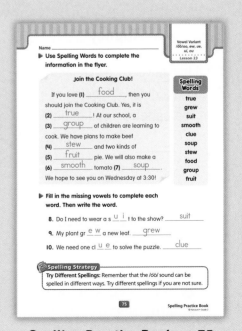

Spelling Practice Book, p. 75

Fluency
Reading Rate

Objective

• *To read fluently at an appropriate rate for nonfiction*

BELOW-LEVEL

Chunk Text Write the text on page 254 in large printing on chart paper so that each sentence is on a separate line. Work with children to chunk the text so that their reading rate is the appropriate speed, yet also fluid. Make sure they have extra practice pronouncing *larvae* and *pupae* correctly, and that they know each word's meaning.

MONITOR PROGRESS

Fluency

IF children have difficulty reading at an appropriate rate,	**THEN** model reading at an appropriate rate as you have children echo-read with you.

Small-Group Instruction, pp. S28–S29:

● **BELOW-LEVEL:** Reteach
● **ON-LEVEL:** Reinforce
● **ADVANCED:** Extend

Review

DIBELS
Oral Reading Fluency
ORF

MODEL READING RATE
Read aloud pages 254–255 of "The Bee." Point out the word *pupae* in the sentence *Now the larvae turn into pupae.*

▲ **Student Edition, pp. 244–273**

(Think Aloud) **On this page, I see the word *pupae* in the sentence *Now the larvae turn into pupae.* Since the word *pupae* is a science word, I slow my reading rate to make sure I understand what this word means.**

Practice/Apply

Routine Card 8

GUIDED PRACTICE Have children echo-read pages 254–255 with you, matching your reading rate.

INDEPENDENT PRACTICE Have children read along as they listen to "The Bee" on *Audiotext Grade 2,* CD 5. Have them practice reading the selection several times until they can read it in "one voice," at the same reading rate.

Use Graphic Aids
Comprehension

Review

DESCRIBE USING GRAPHIC AIDS   Remind children that there are different types of graphic aids. Ask: **How could you use a diagram to help understand a nonfiction selection such as "The Bee"?** (look at the picture and read the captions) Explain that good readers use graphic aids such as charts, diagrams, maps, and time lines to understand more about the topic or subject.

Practice/Apply

GUIDED PRACTICE   Display **Transparency R120**. Reread the passage aloud to children and ask them to identify the graphic aid. (diagram) Guide children to think about what the diagram tells them about leafcutter bees. Ask:

- **Where is the egg?** (in the cell)

- **What else is in the cell?** (pollen and nectar)

- **What is the cell made of?** (leaves)

INDEPENDENT PRACTICE   Ask children to tell how the diagram helped them understand the topic. (Possible response: It showed the shape of the leafcutter cell.)

Objective

- *To use graphic aids to understand nonfiction selections*

Skill Trace

 Tested **Use Graphic Aids**

Introduce	T224–T225
Reteach	S30–S31, S42–S43
Review	T261, T277, T289, T316–317, T345, T361, T371, T424, T445
Test	Theme 5
Maintain	Theme 6, T272

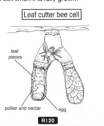

Use Graphic Aids

Leafcutter Bees

Many bees that you see on flowers are honeybees. But some may be leafcutter bees. Leafcutters collect pollen and nectar, but they do not make honey. They cut leaves to build nests.

The female leafcutter bee lives about two months. During that time, she cuts leaves, builds a nest in rotten wood or in the ground, and lays eggs.

Inside her nest, she makes walls out of the leaf pieces. The walls form a cell, or container. She lines the walls with pollen and nectar. The bee lays an egg in each cell and closes it. After the larva hatches, it eats the food and in time it turns into a bee. It comes out of the cell when it is fully grown.

Leaf cutter bee cell

leaf pieces

pollen and nectar   egg

Grade 2, Lesson 23   R120   Comprehension

Transparency R120

Lesson 23   **T277**

Author's Purpose
Comprehension

Objective

- *To identify an author's purpose for writing*

Skill Trace
 Tested **Author's Purpose**

Introduce	Theme 3, T34–T35
Reteach	Theme 3, S6–S7
Review	Theme 3, T68, T82, T92, T130–T131, T162, T176, T186, T379, T394
Test	Theme 3
Maintain	T278

Reinforce the Skill

REVIEW AUTHOR'S PURPOSE   Remind children that authors have a purpose, or reason, for writing. Reread *Student Edition* pages 246–247 ("The Bee") and model how to identify the author's purpose.

Think Aloud   **I know that I am reading nonfiction. Authors often write nonfiction to tell how to make something or to give information. These pages tell me about bees and beehives. I think the author's purpose is to give information.**

Practice/Apply

GUIDED PRACTICE   Draw a two-column chart on the board. Then work with children to identify what type of writing "Bee Business" is and the author's purpose. Add the information to the chart. Ask: **How does knowing the author's purpose help you as you read?** (Possible responses: It helps me know that I should read some selections more carefully.)

Kind of Writing	Author's Purpose
nonfiction selection about the state's honey business	to give information

INDEPENDENT PRACTICE   Ask children to review the selections in Theme 4 to determine the type of writing and the author's purpose for each one. (Possible response: "Mr. Putter and Tabby Write the Book," fiction, to entertain; "Annie's Gifts," fiction, to entertain; "Ah, Music," nonfiction, to give information; "The Life of George Washington Carver," nonfiction, to give information.)

Locate Information
Comprehension

Reinforce the Skill

REVIEW LOCATE INFORMATION   Remind children that good readers understand how to use the parts of a book. Elicit that nonfiction books are organized so that readers can find information quickly and easily. Have children open their *Student Editions* to pages 4–9. Model how to locate information.

> **Think Aloud**   I want to know on which page "The Bee" starts. I can skim the table of contents for the selection title. Then I can find the page number.

Practice/Apply

GUIDED PRACTICE   Write the following questions on the board. Then work with children to decide where they could find the answer to each question.

- **Where can I find an explanation of the meaning for the word *upbeat*?** (glossary)

- **Where can I look to find out where the story "Serious Farm" begins?** (table of contents)

- **What heading in "The Bee" would I look under to find information about the queen bee laying an egg?** ("The queen bee is laying an egg," page 250)

INDEPENDENT PRACTICE   Ask children to tell where they would look to locate information about Sabrina Crewe, the author of "The Bee." (in the Index of Titles and Authors) Lead them to determine that this is an appropriate circumstance to skim and scan the index in order to find a page with information about Sabrina Crewe. Ask them to name the page with the author infomation. (page 273)

Objective

- *To use the parts of a book to locate information*

Skill Trace

 Tested   **Locate Information**

Introduce	Theme 4, T224–T225
Reteach	Theme 4, S30–S31
Review	Theme 4, T253, T269, T281, T308–T309, T337, T353, T363, T416, T437
Test	Theme 4
Maintain	**T279**

Build Robust Vocabulary

Objective

• *To review robust vocabulary*

Tested
REVIEW ✓

Vocabulary: Lesson 23

thickens	plentiful
role	diligent
crowd	sealed
carefully	attack
pattern	disappear

Extend Word Meanings

USE VOCABULARY IN DIFFERENT CONTEXTS   Remind children of the Student-Friendly Explanations of the Vocabulary Words. Then discuss the words, using the following activities:

diligent   Tell children that you will make some statements a person might say while studying for a spelling test. If they think the person is being diligent, they should say, "Good work." If not, they should say, "Study harder."

> I'm going to have a snack.
> I'm going to quiz myself again.
> I'm going to read the words twice.
> I'm going to read a comic book.

crowd   Tell children that you will name some places. If they think people might crowd them in the place, they should hold their arms tightly around them. If not, they should stand and open their arms wide.

> a busy city bus   a schoolyard at night
> an empty lake   a sold-out soccer game

role   Tell children that you will name some activities. If they think an activity is part of a nurse's role, they should say, "Yes." If not, they should say, "No."

> take a temperature   give medicine
> carry a birthday cake   race across a field

pattern   Tell children that you will name some animals. If they think the animal has a pattern on it, they should raise their hand. If not, they should do nothing.

> a striped zebra
> a black dog
> a polka-dotted butterfly
> an orange snake

Word Relationships

ANTONYMS Tell children that an antonym is a word that means the opposite of another word. Suggest some common antonym pairs, such as *tall/short, day/night,* and *black/white* to reinforce the concept. Then write the following sentences on the board, underlining the words *few, open, carelessly, appear,* and *play*.

Frogs in the pond were <u>scarce</u>. (plentiful)

The letter was in the <u>open</u> envelope. (sealed)

Bernie <u>carelessly</u> watered the plants. (carefully)

The sun will <u>appear</u> behind the mountain. (disappear)

The lion and the hyena <u>defend</u> other animals. (attack)

Ask children to read the sentences aloud and replace each underlined word with its Vocabulary Word antonym. Provide help as needed.

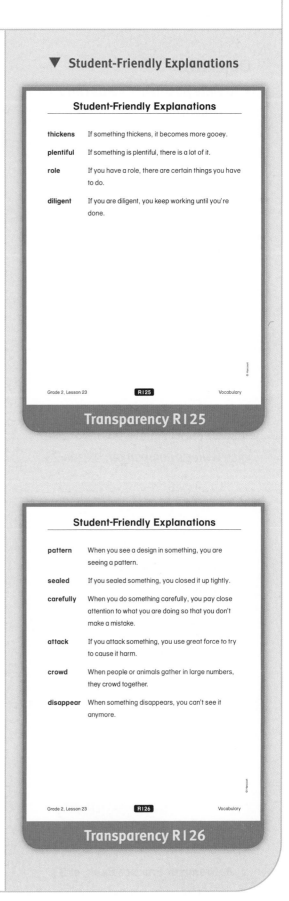

▼ **Student-Friendly Explanations**

Student-Friendly Explanations

thickens	If something thickens, it becomes more gooey.
plentiful	If something is plentiful, there is a lot of it.
role	If you have a role, there are certain things you have to do.
diligent	If you are diligent, you keep working until you're done.

Grade 2, Lesson 23   R125   Vocabulary

Transparency R125

Student-Friendly Explanations

pattern	When you see a design in something, you are seeing a pattern.
sealed	If you sealed something, you closed it up tightly.
carefully	When you do something carefully, you pay close attention to what you are doing so that you don't make a mistake.
attack	If you attack something, you use great force to try to cause it harm.
crowd	When people or animals gather in large numbers, they crowd together.
disappear	When something disappears, you can't see it anymore.

Grade 2, Lesson 23   R126   Vocabulary

Transparency R126

Grammar *Quick Write*

Past-Tense Verbs

5-DAY GRAMMAR	
DAY 1	Introduce Past-Tense Verbs
DAY 2	Verbs that Take *-ed*
DAY 3	Verbs that Take *-d*
DAY 4	**Apply to Writing**
DAY 5	Weekly Review

Objective

- *To write past-tense verbs correctly in sentences*

Daily Proofreading

Last week, I hikd in the woods

(hiked; woods.)

Writing Trait

Strengthening Conventions

Verbs   Use this short lesson with children's own writing to build a foundation for revising/editing longer connected text on Day 5. See also *Writer's Companion*, Lesson 23.

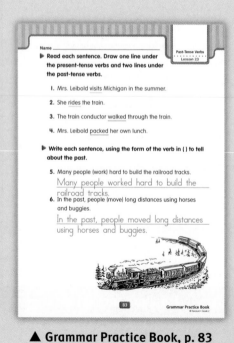

▲ **Grammar Practice Book, p. 83**

Review

DISCUSS PAST-TENSE VERBS   Review what children have learned about past-tense verbs. Write these rules on the board.

- Add an *-ed* to most verbs to tell about an action that happened in the past.

- Add a *-d* to verbs that end in a silent *e* to tell about an action that happened in the past.

Write the following on the board:

phone	print
wipe	sniff

Point to and read aloud *phone*. Rewrite the word as *phoned* and underline the *-d*. Use it in a sentence: "Yesterday, I <u>phoned</u> my best friend." Work together to add *-d* or *-ed* to each remaining verb.

Practice/Apply

GUIDED PRACTICE   Tell children that you are going to use past-tense verbs to write three sentences about insects. Model writing the first sentence. Call on volunteers to suggest additional sentences. After you write each sentence, model orally how to check that it is complete, uses past-tense verbs correctly, begins with a capital letter, and ends with a period.

INDEPENDENT PRACTICE   Tell children to write three complete sentences that include past-tense verbs that tell about insects. Have partners exchange sentences and check that their sentences use past-tense verbs correctly.

Writing

Paragraph of Information

5-DAY WRITING	
DAY 1	Introduce
DAY 2	Prewrite
DAY 3	Draft
DAY 4	**Revise**
DAY 5	Revise

Write and Revise

WRITE   Have children continue writing their paragraphs of information. Remind them that their sentences should all tell more about the main idea.

WRITING TRAIT   **WORD CHOICE**   Remind children that they can make their paragraph more interesting by replacing verbs such as *was* or *is* with action verbs.

REVISE   Have children read their paragraph of information to a partner. They can use the list of criteria for a paragraph of information to check and improve their writing.

Paragraph of Information

- The paragraph gives information about one topic.

- The title explains what the paragraph is about.

- The topic sentence tells about the main idea.

- The other sentences give more details about the main idea.

- Sometimes, the writer does research to find facts and information for the paragraph.

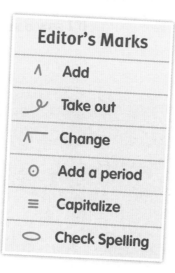

Tell children to make notes on their drafts of the changes they will make. Encourage them to use Editor's Marks. Then have children begin revising their drafts. Tell them that they will make more revisions on Day 5.

Editor's Marks

∧	Add
℘	Take out
⌃	Change
⊙	Add a period
≡	Capitalize
⌒	Check Spelling

Objectives

- *To revise a paragraph of information*
- *To use past-tense verbs correctly in writing*

Writing Prompt

Evaluate   Have children jot down what they like about their paragraph of information and what they want to improve.

Use Picture Cards   Suggest that children use Picture Cards on a familiar topic to help them draft and revise their paragraphs. For example, they can use *Picture Card 69* to write about familiar insects. Ask them questions requiring yes/no answers as they draft and revise their sentences.

Day at a Glance
Day 5

phonics and Spelling
- Review: Prefixes *mis-, re-, un-*
- Posttest: Vowel Variant /$\overline{oo}$/*oo, ew, ue, ui, ou*

Fluency
- Reading Rate
- "The Bee," *Student Edition,* pp. 244–273

Read!

Comprehension

- Review: Use Graphic Organizers
- *Read-Aloud Anthology:* "Brilliant Bees"

Robust Vocabulary
- Cumulative Review

Grammar   *Quick Write*
- Review: Past-Tense Verbs

Writing
- Paragraph of Information

Warm-Up Routines

Oral Language

Objective *To listen attentively and respond appropriately to oral communication*

> ### Question of the Day
>
> What would you do if you saw a swarm of bees?

Ask children to recall why bees swarm. Use the following prompts:

- **What happens when a bee hive becomes too crowded?**
- **Why do you think bees swarm when they look for a new hive?**
- **What do you think the swarm would do if the bees thought they were being attacked?**
- **What could you do to be safe from a swarm of bees?**

Then have children complete the following sentence frame to explain what they would do if they saw a swarm of bees.

If I saw a swarm of bees, I'd _____.

Read Aloud

Objective *To identify repeated sounds and rhythm*

BIG BOOK OF RHYMES AND POEMS Display "The Swarm of Bees" on page 42 and read aloud the title. Ask children to recall what the poem is about. Then read the poem aloud, inviting children to join in. Help children identify the repeated phrase. *(then there were ‹number›)* Discuss how the repeated phrase gives the poem its rhythm. Do a choral reading of the poem, clapping out its beat.

▲ **Big Book of Rhymes and Poems, p. 42**

Word Wall

Objective *To read high-frequency words*

REVIEW HIGH-FREQUENCY WORDS Review the words *prove, bicycle, cheer, idea, believe, draw, care,* and *sweat.* Point to a card at random, and ask children to read the word.

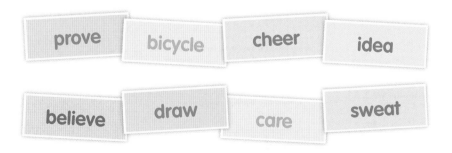

Prefixes mis-, re-, un-

5-DAY PHONICS	
DAY 1	Introduce /o͞o/oo, ew, ue, ui, ou
DAY 2	Word Building with /o͞o/oo, ew, ue, ui, ou
DAY 3	Word Building with /o͞o/oo, ew, ue, ui, ou
DAY 4	Prefixes mis-, re-, un-; Review /o͞o/
DAY 5	Prefixes mis-, re-, un-; Review /o͞o/

Objectives

- *To identify and decode the prefixes* mis-, re-, *and* un- *in two-syllable words*
- *To read longer words with the prefixes* mis-, re-, *and* un-

Skill Trace

Tested **Prefixes *mis-, re-, un-***

Introduce	T274
Review	T286
Test	Theme 5

Review

READ WORDS WITH PREFIXES Write the word *misread* on the board. Guide children to identify the prefix and tell its meaning. Repeat with the words *restate* and *unknown*.

Practice/Apply

GUIDED PRACTICE Write the following words on the board: *unswirl, unfriendly, misheard, return, relearn,* and *misstep.* Then make a chart as shown. Guide children to sort the words and add them to the chart. Have children point to words that use /ûr/ to maintain the skill.

Words with Prefix and Suffix	Words with Prefix only	
unswirl	misheard	relearn
unfriendly	return	misstep

INDEPENDENT PRACTICE Have children read aloud the words in the chart.

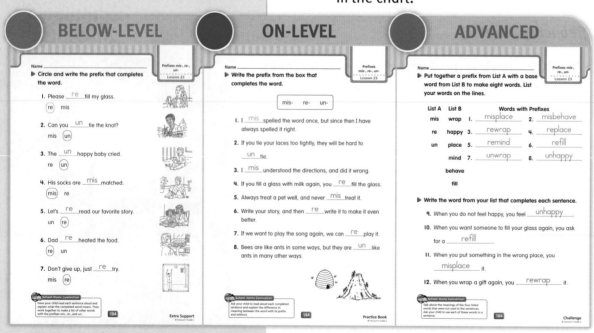

▲ Extra Support, p. 184   ▲ Practice Book, p. 184   ▲ Challenge, p. 184

- Group children according to academic levels, and assign one of the pages on the left.

- Clarify any unfamiliar concepts as necessary. See *ELL Teacher Guide* Lesson 23 for support in scaffolding instruction.

Vowel Variant /o͞o/oo, ew, ue, ui, ou phonics *and Spelling*

5-DAY SPELLING	
DAY 1	Pretest
DAY 2	Word Building
DAY 3	State the Generalization
DAY 4	Review
DAY 5	Posttest

Assess

POSTTEST   Assess children's progress. Use the dictation sentences from Day 1.

Words with /o͞o/oo, ew, ue, ui, ou

1.	true	Is the story **true** or is it made up?
2.	grew	The sunflower **grew** tall in July.
3.	suit	Please wear a **suit** to the wedding.
4.	smooth	I spread the **smooth** icing on the cake.
5.	clue	Would you please give me a **clue** to the answer?
6.	soup	Diana made a spicy **soup.**
7.	stew	Are you going to add beans to the **stew?**
8.	food	We placed the **food** on the picnic table.
9.	group	The children in the **group** held hands and danced.
10.	fruit	Add bananas and berries to the **fruit** salad.

ADVANCED

Challenge Words   Use the challenge words in these dictation sentences.

11.	nephew	Aunt Jean sent a present to her **nephew.**
12.	classroom	We listen to stories in our **classroom.**
13.	cartoon	Jerome drew a **cartoon** about his cat.
14.	juicy	The plums are **juicy** and sweet.
15.	newspaper	Do you read the comics in the **newspaper?**

WRITING APPLICATION   Have children write a silly sentence about animals using two or more of the spelling words.

The dog wore a fancy suit and a top hat.

Objective

- *To use the vowel variant /o͞o/oo, ew, ue, ui, ou and other known letter-sounds to spell and write words*

Spelling Words

1.	**true**	6.	**soup**
2.	**grew**	7.	**stew**
3.	**suit**	8.	**food***
4.	**smooth**	9.	**group**
5.	**clue**	10.	**fruit**

Challenge Words

11.	**nephew**	14.	**juicy**
12.	**classroom**	15.	**newspaper**
13.	**cartoon**		

* Word from "The Bee"

 Fluency
Reading Rate

Objective

- *To read fluently at an appropriate rate*

 ASSESSMENT

Monitoring Progress Periodically, take a timed sample of children's oral reading and record the number of words read correctly per minute. Children should accurately read approximately 90–100 words per minute at the end of Grade 2.

Fluency Support Materials

   Fluency Builders, Grade 2, Lesson 23

 Audiotext *Student Edition* selections are available on *Audiotext Grade 2*, CD 5.

 Strategic Intervention Teacher Guide, Lesson 23

Readers' Theater

 DIBELS Oral Reading Fluency **ORF**

PERFORM "THE BEE" To help children improve their ability to adjust their reading rate to a nonfiction selection, have them perform "The Bee" as Readers' Theater. Use the following procedures:

▲ **Student Edition, pp. 244–273**

- Discuss with children how they can adjust their reading rate to make sure that their listeners understand the key words and ideas. Remind them to chunk the words to make the reading sound like natural speech.

- Have groups of three children read the selection together. Children should alternate sections or pages.

- Monitor groups as they read. Provide feedback and support, paying attention to the rate at which they read.

E L L

Use Illustrations As you discuss how to adjust the reading rate for nonfiction, also focus on images in the photographs that correspond to key words, such as *cells, worker bees*, and *pupae* on page 254. Ask children to point to the words and the picture and say the words or answer yes/no questions about them. Then have children model your reading the words in context, matching your reading rate.

Use Graphic Aids
Comprehension

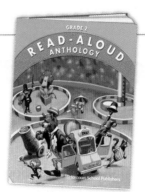

▲ *Read-Aloud Anthology*
"Brilliant Bees," p. 84

Review

REVIEW THE SKILL Remind children that good readers use graphic aids to understand ideas and information quickly and easily. Point out examples of graphic aids, including charts, maps, diagrams, graphs, and time lines.

SET A PURPOSE FOR LISTENING Guide children to set a purpose for listening that includes

- listening to gain information about the topic.

- listening to understand what the diagram shows them about the topic.

Practice/Apply

GUIDED PRACTICE As you read aloud "Brilliant Bees," record information about the diagram.

Type of Graphic Aid	What It Explains
diagram	stages of a bee's life

INDEPENDENT PRACTICE Have children tell how the diagram helped them understand the stages of a bee's life. (Possible response: The pictures show how the bee changes at each stage.) Then have them find additional examples of graphic aids in their *Student Edition*.

Objective

- *To use graphic aids to understand nonfiction selections*

Skill Trace
 Tested **Use Graphic Aids**

Introduce	T224–T225
Reteach	S30–S31, S42–S43
Review	T261, T277, T289, T316–T317, T345, T361, T371, T424, T445
Test	Theme 5
Maintain	Theme 6, T272

Use Graphic Aids Focus attention on the diagram's labels. Read each label aloud, and connect the text to the appropriate portion of the diagram. Ask children questions about the diagram so that they can answer with one word or a short phrase.

Build Robust Vocabulary

Objective

- *To review robust vocabulary*

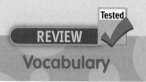

Vocabulary

Lesson 22	Lesson 23
acquired	thickens
assumed	plentiful
serious	role
extremely	diligent
admit	crowd
barely	sealed
hilarious	carefully
witty	attack
absurd	pattern
attempt	disappear

Cumulative Review

CHARACTER CHART   Guide children to sort words based on whether they describe what a story character can do or what a story character is like. Draw a two-column chart like the one below on the board. Then read the following words aloud: *disappear, serious, absurd, hilarious, witty, crowd, attack,* and *diligent.* After each one, pause to ask children which column in the chart they think the word belongs in. Encourage children to use the words in sentences to tell about the characters. Provide this model: "The witty monkey told a joke to the other animals."

What a Character Does	What a Character Is Like
disappear	serious
crowd	absurd
attack	hilarious
	witty
	diligent

DEMONSTRATE WORD MEANING   Discuss children's answers to these questions.

1. **What are some roles that you have seen people play in movies that are hilarious, witty, or absurd?** (Accept reasonable responses.)

2. **Would it be safe to assume that every pattern you see can be repeated?** (Possible response: Probably not. Some patterns in nature might be impossible to repeat.)

3. **Name some animals that are extremely plentiful and some animals that there are barely any of.** (Possible responses: Insects are plentiful and birds are plentiful. Some animals that there are barely any of are endangered ones such as manatees.)

4. **If someone is diligent, do you think the person would admit that he or she is serious about what he or she is doing?** (Possible response: Yes, because the person is a hard worker and takes his or her responsibility seriously and being diligent is not something to be ashamed of.)

5. **Would you attempt to open a sealed envelope that is not addressed to you?** (Possible response: No, because it belongs to someone else, and it would be wrong to open it.)

6. **Would someone who had acquired something very valuable handle it carefully? Why or why not?** (Possible response: Yes, because something valuable needs to be handled carefully so it doesn't break, get lost, or stolen.)

 MONITOR PROGRESS

Build Robust Vocabulary

IF children do not demonstrate understanding of the words and have difficulty using them,	**THEN** model using each word in several sentences, and have children repeat each sentence.

Small-Group Instruction, pp. S34–S35:

● **BELOW-LEVEL:** Reteach
● **ON-LEVEL:** Reinforce
● **ADVANCED:** Extend

Grammar *Quick Write*

Past-Tense Verbs

5-DAY GRAMMAR

DAY 1 Introduce Past-Tense Verbs
DAY 2 Verbs that Take *-ed*
DAY 3 Verbs that Take *-d*
DAY 4 Apply to Writing
DAY 5 Weekly Review

Objectives

- *To write past-tense verbs correctly in sentences*
- *To speak in complete, coherent sentences*

Daily Proofreading

Lori yellid on the playground?

(yelled, playground.)

Language Arts Checkpoint

If children have difficulty with the concepts, see pages S36–S37 to reteach.

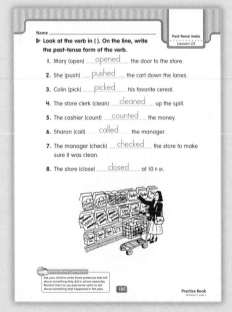

▲ **Practice Book, p. 185**

Review

REVIEW PAST-TENSE VERBS Use the following questions to review what children have learned about past-tense verbs. Have volunteers write answers on the board as they are provided. Ask:

- What kind of verb tells about an action that did not happen in the present or future? (past-tense verb)

- What is added to most verbs to tell about an action that already took place? (-ed)

- What is added to verbs that end in a silent *e* to tell about something that already happened? (-d)

Practice/Apply

GUIDED PRACTICE Write the following sentences on the board. Ask volunteers to help you change the word in parentheses so that it tells about an action that happened in the past.

Cornell _____ the circle. (trace)

Mika _____ the ball. (roll)

Ashley _____ the train. (board)

 INDEPENDENT PRACTICE Have children write sentences that include past-tense verbs. Ask volunteers to read aloud their sentences.

Writing
Paragraph of Information

5-DAY WRITING
DAY 1	Introduce
DAY 2	Prewrite
DAY 3	Draft
DAY 4	Revise
DAY 5	Revise

Revise

REVISE A PARAGRAPH OF INFORMATION   Explain that good writers look back after a day or so to see if their writing is clear and to add any new ideas they have thought of. Tell children to reread their paragraphs and ask themselves these questions:

- Does my paragraph give information on one topic?

- Have I included a main idea?

- Have I included details that tell about the main idea?

- Have I used past-tense verbs correctly?

WRITING TRAIT   **WORD CHOICE**   Ask children to identify interesting action verbs in their writing. Discuss how these words make the information easier to understand.

Encourage children to revise their paragraphs of information to focus on the topic and add new information they want to include.

NOTE: A 4-point rubric appears on page R8.

SCORING RUBRIC

	6	5	4	3	2	1
FOCUS	Completely focused, purposeful.	Focused on topic and purpose.	Generally focused on topic and purpose.	Somewhat focused on topic and purpose.	Related to topic but does not maintain focus.	Lacks focus and purpose.
ORGANIZATION	Ideas progress logically; paper conveys sense of completeness.	Organization mostly clear; paper gives sense of completeness.	Organization mostly clear, but some lapses occur; may seem unfinished.	Some sense of organization; seems unfinished.	Little sense of organization.	Little or no sense of organization.
SUPPORT	Strong, specific details; clear, exact language; freshness of expression.	Strong, specific details; clear, exact language.	Adequate support and word choice.	Limited supporting details; limited word choice.	Few supporting details; limited word choice.	Little develop-ment; limited or unclear word choice.
CONVENTIONS	Varied sentences; few, if any, errors.	Varied sentences; few errors.	Some sentence variety; few errors.	Simple sentence structures; some errors.	Simple sentence structures; many errors.	Unclear sentence structures; many errors.

REPRODUCIBLE STUDENT RUBRICS for specific writing purposes and presentations are available on pages R2–R8.

Objective

- *To revise paragraphs to improve organization and word choice*

Writing Prompt

Independent Writing   Have children generate ideas about a new topic for writing.

WEEKLY LESSON TEST

▲ **Weekly Lesson Tests, pp. 241–252**

- Selection Comprehension with Short Response
- Phonics and Spelling
- Focus Skill
- Synonyms
- Robust Vocabulary
- Grammar
- Fluency Passage  **FRESH READS**

 GO online   For prescriptions, see pp. A2–A6. Also available electronically on StoryTown Online Assessment and Exam View®.

 Podcasting: Assessing Fluency

Leveled Readers
Reinforcing Skills and Strategies

BELOW-LEVEL

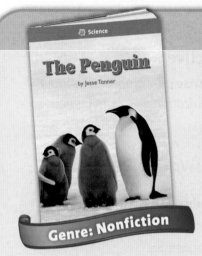

The Penguin

SUMMARY A year in the life of emperor penguins of Antarctica includes months at sea and months at a crowded nesting site. Male and female penguins both care for their egg and chick.

Genre: Nonfiction

- **phonics** Vowel Variant /o͞o/*oo, ew, ue, ui, ou*
- **Vocabulary**
   Use Graphic Aids

Before Reading

BUILD BACKGROUND/SET PURPOSE Talk about the traits animals would need to survive winters in Antarctica. Then guide children to preview the book and set a purpose for reading it.

Reading the Book

PAGE 3 **USE GRAPHIC AIDS** **What can you tell about Antarctica from the map?** (Possible responses: It is big; it includes the South Pole.)

PAGES 6–9 SEQUENCE **What do the male and female penguins do during the three winter months?** (The female lays one egg and then leaves. The male looks after the egg until the chick hatches. Then the female returns with food for the chick, and the male leaves to find food.)

REREAD FOR FLUENCY Have partners read their favorite page(s) aloud several times. Remind children to read at just the right speed.

Think Critically

(See inside back cover for questions.)

1. **NOTE DETAILS** The male looks after the egg for sixty-six days.

2. **USE GRAPHIC AIDS** Possible response: The photographs show that it is very cold, because the ground is covered in snow and ice.

3. **SEQUENCE** In June, the female penguin has found her mate. She lays an egg and then goes back into the sea to find food.

4. **PERSONAL RESPONSE** Answers will vary.

5. **AUTHOR'S PURPOSE** Possible responses: to show what happens to the penguins at different times in a year.

LEVELED READERS TEACHER GUIDE

▲ Vocabulary, p. 5

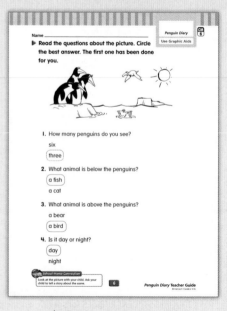

▲ Comprehension, p. 6

www.harcourtschool.com/storytown
★ Leveled Readers Online Database
Searchable by Genre, Skill, Vocabulary, Level, or Title
★ Student Activities and Teacher Resources, online

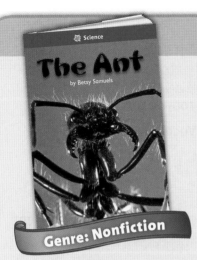

Genre: Nonfiction

ON-LEVEL

The Ant

SUMMARY Ants are insects with six legs and three body parts. Ants live in a colony with a queen that produces all the eggs. Eggs turn into larvae that may become worker ants, males, or new queens.

 phonics **Vowel Variant** /oo/*oo, ew, ue, ui, ou*

- **Vocabulary**

  Use Graphic Aids

Before Reading

BUILD BACKGROUND/SET PURPOSE Ask children what is interesting about ants. Then guide children to preview the book and set a purpose for reading it.

Reading the Book

PAGES 4–5 **USE GRAPHIC AIDS** **What does the diagram of the ant show you that you could not see in a photograph?** (Possible response: the different parts of an ant's body in a clear way, with the name of each part)

PAGES 8 AND 13 **COMPARE AND CONTRAST** **How is the information on page 13 like the information on page 8?** (Both tell how the queen ant lays eggs for the colony. On page 13, a queen has just started a new colony.)

REREAD FOR FLUENCY Have partners take turns reading the book, a page or a section at a time. Remind children to read at a rate that is just right to convey meaning—neither too fast nor too slow.

Think Critically
(See inside back cover for questions.)

① **NOTE DETAILS** A group of ants living in a nest is a colony.

② **SEQUENCE** After the eggs hatch, larvae come out. They get bigger and shed their skin. Then they build cocoons around themselves. They grow into adult ants and come out of the cocoons.

③ **USE GRAPHIC AIDS** head, thorax, and abdomen

④ **MAKE JUDGMENTS** Answers will vary.

⑤ **PERSONAL RESPONSE** Answers will vary.

LEVELED READERS TEACHER GUIDE

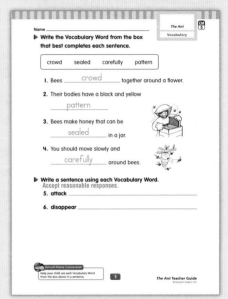

▲ Vocabulary, p. 5

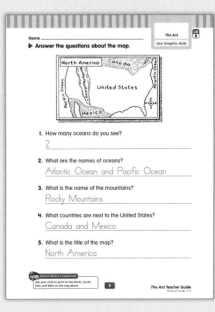

▲ Comprehension, p. 6

Leveled Readers

Reinforcing Skills and Strategies

 **ADVANCED**

The Prairie Dog

SUMMARY   Prairie dogs are members of the squirrel family and are native to western North America. Family groups, or coteries, dig burrows with chambers and tunnels. They share and defend their territory.

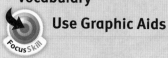 **phonics**   Vowel Variant
/o͞o/*oo, ew, ue, ui, ou*

• **Vocabulary**

   Use Graphic Aids

Before Reading

BUILD BACKGROUND/SET PURPOSE   Ask children about animals that live in groups. Guide them to preview the book and set a purpose for reading.

Reading the Book

PAGE 7   **USE GRAPHIC AIDS**   **Why is the diagram on page 7 helpful to readers?** (Possible responses: The diagram shows the chambers.)

PAGES 12–13   **MAIN IDEA**   **What is the most important idea in the section called "Defending the Territory"?** (Possible responses: Prairie dogs defend themselves by attacking prairie dogs from other coteries and barking to warn each other about predators.)

REREAD FOR FLUENCY   Have partners take turns choosing an interesting picture and reading the accompanying text. Remind them to read at a speed that makes the information clear.

Think Critically   *(See inside back cover for questions.)*

1 **CONTEXT CLUES**   Possible response: They like to do things together.

2 **SEQUENCE**   It gets fur when it is three weeks old. It opens its eyes at five weeks. It goes outside the burrow at about six weeks. It drinks milk from its mother for the first seven weeks.

3 **CAUSE/EFFECT**   Prairie dogs bark to warn others of danger.

4 **USE GRAPHIC AIDS**   how the chambers and tunnels in a burrow are connected; what the different chambers are used for

5 **PERSONAL RESPONSE**   Answers will vary.

LEVELED READERS TEACHER GUIDE

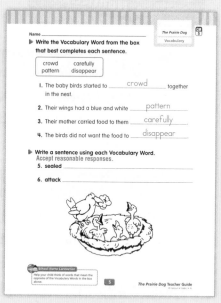

▲ Vocabulary, p. 5

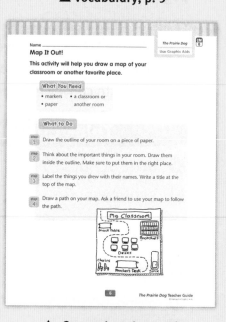

▲ Comprehension, p. 6

www.harcourtschool.com/storytown

★ **Leveled Readers Online Database**
Searchable by Genre, Skill, Vocabulary, Level, or Title
★ **Student Activities and Teacher Resources, online**

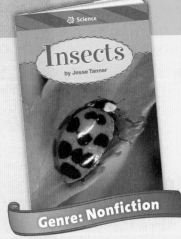

Genre: Nonfiction

Insects

SUMMARY Insects' bodies, ways of moving, growth, homes, and defenses are shown and described.

- **Build Background**
- **Concept Vocabulary**
- **Scaffolded Language Development**

Before Reading

BUILD BACKGROUND/SET PURPOSE List the words *moth, butterfly, ant, beetle, bee,* and *wasp.* Read the words with children, and talk about how all these animals are alike. During discussion, add the label *insects* above the list. Then guide children to preview the book and set a purpose for reading it.

Reading the Book

PAGE 4 USE GRAPHIC AIDS **What are the three body parts shown in the diagram?** (head, thorax, abdomen)

PAGES 11–13 CAUSE/EFFECT **How does an insect's color or shape keep it safe?** (Possible responses: A bright, colorful body warns animals not to eat the insect, maybe because it will taste bad or sting. Bodies that look like part of a plant make insects hard to find and eat.)

REREAD FOR FLUENCY Have partners take turns choosing a favorite picture and reading the accompanying text aloud. Remind children to practice until they can read at a just-right speed.

Scaffolded Language Development

(See inside back cover for teacher-led activity.)

Provide additional examples and explanation as needed.

LEVELED READERS TEACHER GUIDE

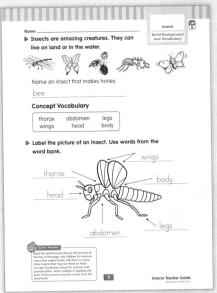

▲ Building Background and Vocabulary, p. 5

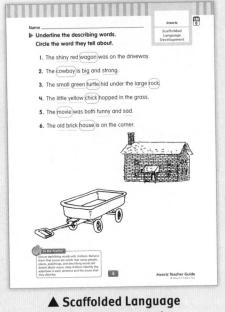

▲ Scaffolded Language Development, p. 6

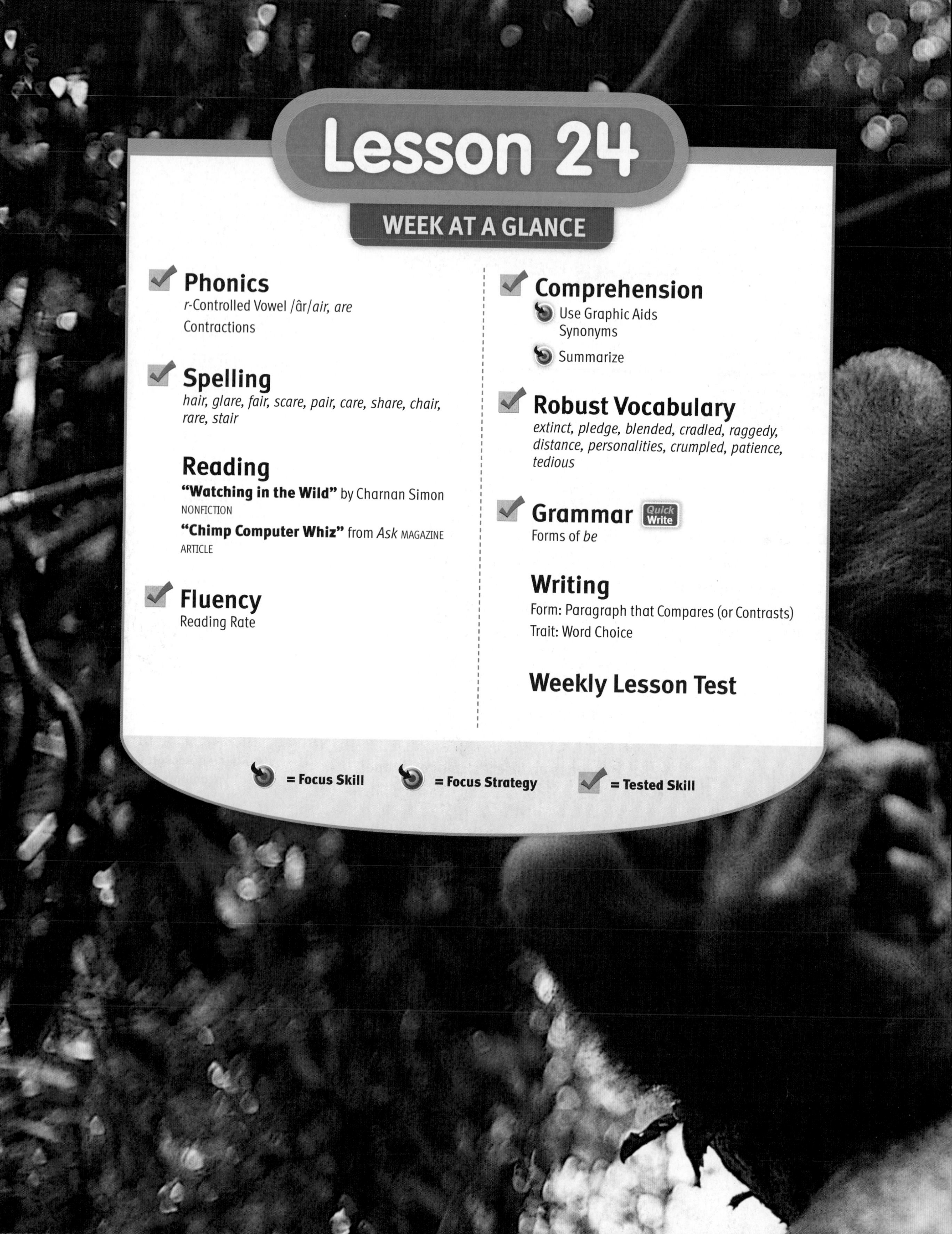

Lesson 24

WEEK AT A GLANCE

 **Phonics**
r-Controlled Vowel /âr/*air, are*
Contractions

Spelling
hair, glare, fair, scare, pair, care, share, chair, rare, stair

Reading
"Watching in the Wild" by Charnan Simon
NONFICTION

"Chimp Computer Whiz" from *Ask* MAGAZINE
ARTICLE

Fluency
Reading Rate

Comprehension
 Use Graphic Aids
Synonyms
 Summarize

Robust Vocabulary
extinct, pledge, blended, cradled, raggedy, distance, personalities, crumpled, patience, tedious

Grammar Quick Write
Forms of *be*

Writing
Form: Paragraph that Compares (or Contrasts)
Trait: Word Choice

Weekly Lesson Test

 = Focus Skill   = Focus Strategy   = Tested Skill

One stop *for all* your **Digital** *needs*

Lesson 24

Digital
CLASSROOM

 www.harcourtschool.com/storytown
To go along with your print program

FOR THE TEACHER

Prepare | Professional Development

 Videos for Podcasting

Plan & Organize | Online TE & Planning Resources*

Teach |  Transparencies

access from Online TE

Assess | Online Assessment*

with Student Tracking System and Prescriptions

FOR THE STUDENT

Read |  Student eBook*

 Strategic Intervention Interactive Reader

 Leveled Readers

Practice & Apply | Splash into Phonics CD-ROM

 Also available on CD-ROM

Literature Resources

STUDENT EDITION

GO online
eBook STUDENT EDITION

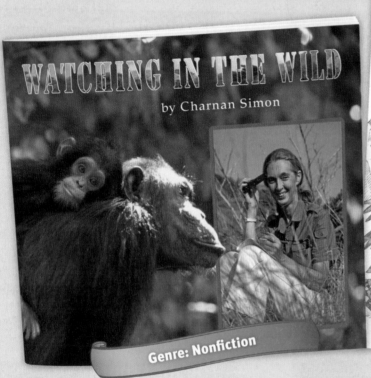

WATCHING IN THE WILD
by Charnan Simon

Genre: Nonfiction

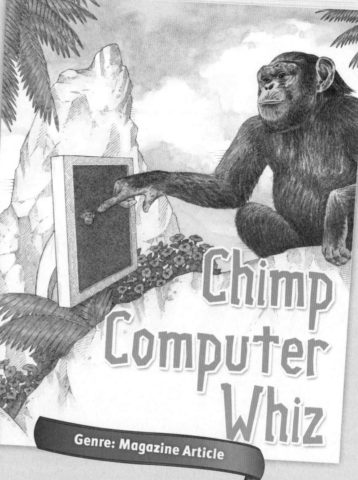

Chimp Computer Whiz

Genre: Magazine Article

 ◄ **Audiotext** *Student Edition selections are available on Audiotext Grade 2, CD 5.*

 ◄ *Practice Quizzes for the Selection*

THEME CONNECTION: BETTER TOGETHER
Comparing Nonfiction and a Magazine Article

Paired Selections

 SCIENCE   **Watching in the Wild, pp. 284–297**

SUMMARY   Children will learn about Jane Goodall and her research on chimpanzees in their native habitat.

 SCIENCE   **Chimp Computer Whiz, pp. 298–299**

SUMMARY   Scientists watch apes using special computers as a way to learn more about how animals think.

Support for Differentiated Instruction

 LEVELED READERS

  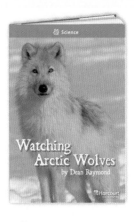 

BELOW-LEVEL   **ON-LEVEL**   **ADVANCED**   **ELL**

LEVELED PRACTICE

◀ **Strategic Intervention Resource Kit, Lesson 24**

◀ **Strategic Intervention Interactive Reader, Lesson 24**

Strategic Intervention Interactive Reader Online

◀ **ELL Extra Support Kit, Lesson 24**

◀ **Challenge Resource Kit, Lesson 24**

BELOW-LEVEL
Extra Support Copying Masters, pp. 186, 188–192

ON-LEVEL
Practice Book, pp. 186–193

ADVANCED
Challenge Copying Masters, pp. 186, 188–192

ADDITIONAL RESOURCES

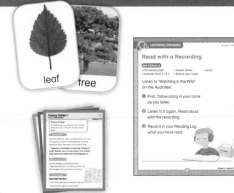

- Decodable Book 20
- Spelling Practice Book, pp. 76–78
- Grammar Practice Book, pp. 85–88
- Reading Transparencies R127–R133
- Language Arts Transparencies LA49–LA50
- Test Prep System
◀ **Literacy Center Kit, Cards 116–120**
- Sound/Spelling Card
◀ **Fluency Builders**
◀ **Picture Card Collection**
- Read-Aloud Anthology, pp. 88–89

ASSESSMENT

✓ **Monitor Progress**

✓ **Weekly Lesson Tests, Lesson 24**
- Comprehension   • Robust Vocabulary
- Phonics and Spelling   • Grammar
- Focus Skill   • Synonyms

 www.harcourtschool.com/ storytown
Online Assessment
Also available on CD-ROM—Exam View®

Suggested Lesson Planner

GO online Online TE & Planning Resources

Day 1 | Day 2

Step 1 Whole Group

Daily Routines
- Oral Language
- Read Aloud
- High-Frequency Words

Day 1

QUESTION OF THE DAY, p. T310
Why are maps important?

READ ALOUD, p. T311
Transparency R127: Africa

WORD WALL, p. T311

Day 2

QUESTION OF THE DAY, p. T322
What is your favorite kind of jungle animal?

READ ALOUD, p. T323
Big Book of Rhymes and Poems,
"Chimpanzee"

WORD WALL, p. T323

Word Work
- phonics
- Spelling

Day 1

 phonics, p. T312
Introduce: *r*-Controlled Vowel /âr/*air, are*

 SPELLING, p. T315
Pretest: *hair, glare, fair, scare, pair, care, share, chair, rare, stair*

Day 2

 phonics, p. T324
Review: *r*-Controlled Vowel /âr/*air, are*

 SPELLING, p. T325
Word Building

Skills and Strategies
- Reading
- Fluency
- Comprehension
- Build Robust Vocabulary

Day 1

 READING/COMPREHENSION, p. T316
Introduce: Use Graphic Aids

LISTENING COMPREHENSION, p. T318
Read-Aloud: "Hanging On"

FLUENCY, p. T318
Focus: Reading Rate

BUILD ROBUST VOCABULARY, p. T319
Words from the Read-Aloud

Day 2

 BUILD ROBUST VOCABULARY, p. T326
Words from the Selection
Word Detective, p. T327

READING, p. T328
"Watching in the Wild"
Options for Reading

COMPREHENSION, p. T328
Introduce: Summarize

RETELLING/FLUENCY, p. T336
Reading Rate

BUILD ROBUST VOCABULARY, p. T337
Words About the Selection

 Read!
▲ Student Edition

Step 2 Small Groups

Suggestions for Differentiated Instruction (See pp. T304–T305.)

Step 3 Whole Group

Language Arts
- Grammar *Quick Write*
- Writing

Day 1

 GRAMMAR, p. T320
Introduce: Forms of *be*

Daily Proofreading
I playd with Emilys ball.
(played, Emily's)

 WRITING, p. T321
Introduce: Paragraph That Compares
(or Contrasts)
Writing Trait: Word Choice

Writing Prompt *Write sentences to compare and contrast two of your favorite toys.*

Day 2

 GRAMMAR, p. T338
Review: Forms of *be*

Daily Proofreading
Ari washes clothes Yesterday. (washed, yesterday)

 WRITING, p. T339
Review: Paragraph That Compares
(or Contrasts)
Writing Trait: Word Choice

Writing Prompt *Write about something you learned when you watched somebody or something for a long period of time.*

 = Focus Skill    = Focus Strategy    = Tested Skill

Skills at a Glance

phonics
- *r*-Controlled Vowel /âr/*air, are*
- Contractions

Comprehension
Focus Skill
Use Graphic Aids

Focus Strategy
Summarize

Fluency
Reading Rate

Vocabulary
ROBUST: *extinct, pledge, blended, cradled, raggedy, distance, personalities, crumpled, patience, tedious*

Day 3

QUESTION OF THE DAY, p. T340
What do you think you would see if you watched a chimpanzee?

READ ALOUD, p. T341
Big Book of Rhymes and Poems, "Chimpanzee"

WORD WALL, p. T341

, p. T342
Review: *r*-Controlled Vowel /âr/*air, are*

 SPELLING, p. T343
State the Generalization

FLUENCY, p. T344
Reading Rate:
"Watching in the Wild"

COMPREHENSION,
p. T345
Review: Use Graphic Aids
Paired Selection:
"Chimp Computer Whiz"
▲ Student Edition

CONNECTIONS, p. T348

BUILD ROBUST VOCABULARY, p. T350
Review

VOCABULARY
Synonyms, T352

Day 4

QUESTION OF THE DAY, p. T356
What do you like about playing hide-and-seek?

READ ALOUD, p. T357
Big Book of Rhymes and Poems, "Hide-and-Seek"

WORD WALL, p. T357

, p. T358
Introduce: Contractions

 SPELLING, p. T359
Review Spelling Words

FLUENCY, p. T360
Reading Rate:
"Watching in the Wild"

COMPREHENSION,
p. T361
Review: Use Graphic Aids
▲ Student Edition

BUILD ROBUST VOCABULARY,
p. T362
Review

Day 5

QUESTION OF THE DAY, p. T366
Is a tree a good place to hide? Why or why not?

READ ALOUD, p. T367
Big Book of Rhymes and Poems, "Hide-and-Seek"

WORD WALL, p. T367

, p. T368
Review: Contractions

 SPELLING, p. T369
Posttest

FLUENCY, p. T370
Reading Rate:
"Watching in the Wild"

COMPREHENSION,
p. T371
Review: Use Graphic Aids
Read-Aloud: "Hanging On"
▲ Student Edition

BUILD ROBUST VOCABULARY,
p. T372
Cumulative Review

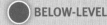 BELOW-LEVEL ON-LEVEL ADVANCED ELL

 GRAMMAR, p. T354
Review: Forms of *be*

Daily Proofreading
All the childs ran in the race on labor day.
(children, Labor Day)

 WRITING, p. T355
Review: Paragraph That Compares (or Contrasts)
Writing Trait: Word Choice

Writing Prompt *Write a poem about Jane Goodall and the chimpanzees in "Watching in the Wild."*

 GRAMMAR, p. T364
Review: Forms of *be*

Daily Proofreading
When did those familys move.
(families, move?)

 WRITING, p. T365
Review: Paragraph That Compares (or Contrasts)
Writing Trait: Word Choice

Writing Prompt *Write one or more funny sentences about two unlike objects.*

 GRAMMAR, p. T374
Review: Forms of *be*

Daily Proofreading
People says the funiest things.
(say, funniest)

 WRITING, p. T375
Review: Paragraph That Compares (or Contrasts)
Writing Trait: Word Choice

Writing Prompt *Write a list of ideas about a new topic of your choice for writing.*

Suggested Small-Group Planner

45-60+ Minutes

	Day 1	Day 2

BELOW-LEVEL
15-20+ Minutes

Day 1

Teacher-Directed
Leveled Reader:
"Mountain Gorillas,"
p. T376
Before Reading

Independent
⭐ Listening/Speaking Center,
p. T308
Extra Support Copying Masters, pp. 186, 188

▲ Leveled Reader

Day 2

Teacher-Directed
Student Edition:
"Watching in the Wild,"
p. T328

Independent
⭐ Reading Center,
p. T308
Extra Support Copying Masters, pp. 189–190

▲ Student Edition

ON-LEVEL
15-20+ Minutes

Teacher-Directed
Leveled Reader:
"Orangutans," p. T377
Before Reading

Independent
⭐ Reading Center, p. T308
Practice Book, pp. 186, 188

▲ Leveled Reader

Teacher-Directed
Student Edition:
"Watching in the Wild,"
p. T328

Independent
⭐ Letters and Sounds
Center, p. T309
Practice Book, pp. 189–190

▲ Student Edition

ADVANCED
15-20+ Minutes

Teacher-Directed
Leveled Reader:
"Watching Arctic Wolves," p. T378
Before Reading

Independent
⭐ Letters and Sounds Center,
p. T309
Challenge Copying Masters, pp. 186, 188

▲ Leveled Reader

Teacher-Directed
Leveled Reader: "Watching
Arctic Wolves," p. T378
Read the Book

Independent
⭐ Word Work Center, p. T309
Challenge Copying Masters,
pp. 189–190

▲ Leveled Reader

ELL

English-Language Learners

In addition to the small-group instruction above, use the ELL Extra Support Kit to promote language development.

LANGUAGE DEVELOPMENT SUPPORT
Teacher-Directed
ELL TG, Day 1
Independent
ELL Copying Masters, Lesson 24

▲ ELL Student Handbook

LANGUAGE DEVELOPMENT SUPPORT
Teacher-Directed
ELL TG, Day 2
Independent
ELL Copying Masters, Lesson 24

▲ ELL Student Handbook

Intervention

▲ Strategic Intervention Resource Kit   ▲ Strategic Intervention Interactive Reader

Strategic Intervention TG, Day 1
Strategic Intervention Practice Book, Lesson 24

Strategic Intervention TG, Day 2
Strategic Intervention Interactive
Reader, Lesson 24

▲ Strategic Intervention Interactive Reader

MONITOR PROGRESS

Small-Group Instruction

Comprehension	Phonics	Comprehension	Fluency	Robust Vocabulary	Language Arts Checkpoint
Focus Skill Use Graphic Aids pp. S42–S43	*r*-Controlled Vowel /âr/*air*, *are* pp. S38–S39	Synonyms pp. S44–S45	Reading Rate pp. S40–S41	*extinct, pledge, blended, cradle, raggedy, distance, personalities, crumpled, patience, tedious* pp. S46–S47	**Grammar:** Forms of *be* **Writing:** Paragraph that Compares (or Contrasts) pp. S46–S47

Day 3

Teacher-Directed
Leveled Reader:
"Mountain Gorillas,"
p. T376
Read the Book

Independent
⭐ Word Work Center, p. T309
Extra Support Copying Masters, p. 191

▲ Leveled Reader

Teacher-Directed
Leveled Reader:
"Orangutans," p. T377
Read the Book

Independent
⭐ Writing Center, p. T309
Practice Book, p. 191

▲ Leveled Reader

Teacher-Directed
Leveled Reader:
"Watching Arctic Wolves," p. T378
Think Critically

Independent
⭐ Listening/Speaking Center,
p. T308
Challenge Copying Masters, p. 191

▲ Leveled Reader

LANGUAGE DEVELOPMENT SUPPORT

Teacher-Directed
Leveled Reader: "A Wild Animal Tour,"
p. T379
Before Reading; Read the Book
ELL TG, Day 3

Independent
ELL Copying Masters, Lesson 24

▲ Leveled Reader

Strategic Intervention TG, Day 3
Strategic Intervention Interactive
Reader, Lesson 24
Strategic Intervention Practice Book,
Lesson 24

▲ Strategic Intervention Interactive Reader

Day 4

Teacher-Directed
Leveled Reader:
"Mountain Gorillas,"
p. T376
Reread for Fluency

Independent
⭐ Letters and Sounds Center,
p. T309

▲ Leveled Reader

Teacher-Directed
Leveled Reader:
"Orangutans," p. T377
Reread for Fluency

Independent
⭐ Word Work Center, p. T309

▲ Leveled Reader

Teacher-Directed
Leveled Reader:
"Watching Arctic Wolves," p. T378
Reread for Fluency

Independent
⭐ Writing Center, p. T309
Self-Selected Reading:
Classroom Library Collection

▲ Leveled Reader

LANGUAGE DEVELOPMENT SUPPORT

Teacher-Directed
Leveled Reader: "A Wild Animal Tour,"
p. T379
Reread for Fluency
ELL TG, Day 4

Independent
ELL Copying Masters, Lesson 24

▲ Leveled Reader

Strategic Intervention TG, Day 4
Strategic Intervention Interactive
Reader, Lesson 24

▲ Strategic Intervention Interactive Reader

Day 5

Teacher-Directed
Leveled Reader:
"Mountain Gorillas,"
p. T376
Think Critically

Independent
⭐ Writing Center, p. T309
Leveled Reader: Reread for Fluency
Extra Support Copying Masters, p. 192

▲ Leveled Reader

Teacher-Directed
Leveled Reader:
"Orangutans," p. T377
Think Critically

Independent
⭐ Listening/Speaking Center,
p. T308
Leveled Reader: Reread for Fluency
Practice Book, p. 192

▲ Leveled Reader

Teacher-Directed
Leveled Reader:
"Watching Arctic Wolves," p. T378
Reread for Fluency

Independent
⭐ Reading Center, p. T308
Leveled Reader: Reread for Fluency
Self-Selected Reading:
Classroom Library Collection
Challenge Copying Masters, p. 192

▲ Leveled Reader

LANGUAGE DEVELOPMENT SUPPORT

Teacher-Directed
Leveled Reader: "A Wild Animal Tour,"
p. T379
Think Critically
ELL TG, Day 5

Independent
Leveled Reader: Reread for Fluency
ELL Copying Masters, Lesson 24

▲ Leveled Reader

Strategic Intervention TG, Day 5
Strategic Intervention Interactive
Reader, Lesson 24

▲ Strategic Intervention Interactive Reader

Leveled Readers & Leveled Practice
Reinforcing Skills and Strategies

LEVELED READER SYSTEM

- **Leveled Readers**
- **Leveled Readers, CD**
- **Leveled Readers Teacher Guides**
  - *Comprehension*
  - *Vocabulary*
  - *Oral Reading Fluency Assessment*
- **Response Activities**
- **Leveled Readers Assessment**

See pages T376–T379 for lesson plans.

BELOW-LEVEL

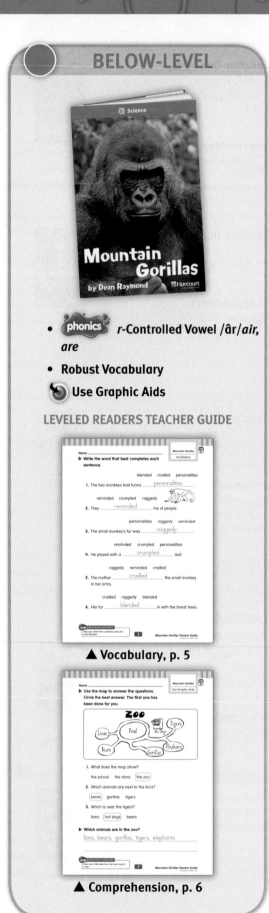

-  **phonics** *r*-Controlled Vowel /âr/*air*, *are*
- **Robust Vocabulary**
- **Use Graphic Aids**

LEVELED READERS TEACHER GUIDE

▲ **Vocabulary, p. 5**

▲ **Comprehension, p. 6**

ON-LEVEL

- **phonics** *r*-Controlled Vowel /âr/*air*, *are*
- **Robust Vocabulary**
- **Use Graphic Aids**

LEVELED READERS TEACHER GUIDE

▲ **Vocabulary, p. 5**

▲ **Comprehension, p. 6**

www.harcourtschool.com/storytown

GO online

★ Leveled Readers, Online Database
Searchable by Genre, Skill, Vocabulary, Level, or Title
★ Student Activities and Teacher Resources, online

ADVANCED

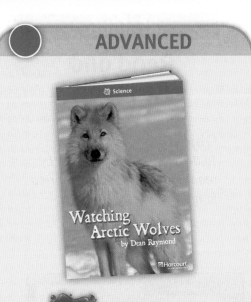

- **phonics** *r*-Controlled Vowel /âr/*air*, *are*
- **Robust Vocabulary**
- **Use Graphic Aids**

LEVELED READERS TEACHER GUIDE

▲ Vocabulary, p. 5

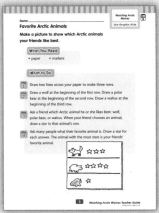

▲ Comprehension, p. 6

ELL

- **Build Background**
- **Concept Vocabulary**
- **Scaffolded Language Development**

LEVELED READERS TEACHER GUIDE

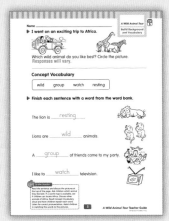

▲ Build Background p. 5

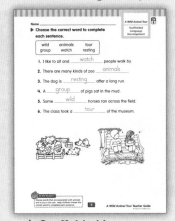

▲ Scaffolded Language Development, p. 6

CLASSROOM LIBRARY

for Self-Selected Reading

EASY
▲ *Treasure Map* by Stuart J. Murphy.
FICTION

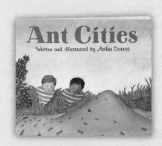

AVERAGE
▲ *Ant Cities* by Arthur Dorros.
NONFICTION

CHALLENGE
▲ *A Log's Life* by Wendy Pfeffer.
NONFICTION

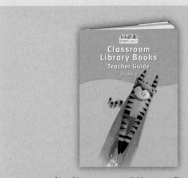

▲ **Classroom Library Books
Teacher Guide, Lesson 24**

Literacy Centers

15 Min. each

Management Support

While you provide direct instruction to individuals or small groups, other children can work on literacy center activities.

▲ **Literacy Center Pocket Chart**

▲ **Teacher Resource Book, p. 57**

 ## Homework for the Week

TEACHER RESOURCE BOOK, PAGE 27

The *Homework Copying Master* provides activities to complete for each day of the week.

GO online www.harcourtschool.com/storytown

 ## LISTENING/SPEAKING

Read with a Recording

Objective
To develop fluency by listening to and reading familiar stories

⭐ **Literacy Center Kit • Card 116**

 ## READING

Read and Respond

Objective
To develop comprehension by reading silently and comparing familiar stories

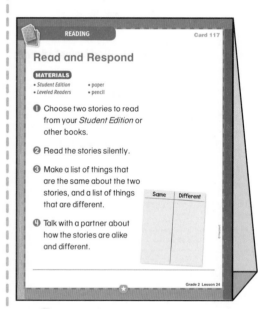

⭐ **Literacy Center Kit • Card 117**

WRITING
Write a Paragraph

Objective
To practice writing a paragraph that compares or contrasts

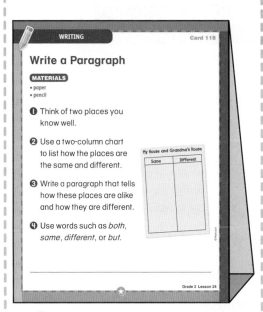

WRITING — Card 118

Write a Paragraph

MATERIALS
- paper
- pencil

❶ Think of two places you know well.

❷ Use a two-column chart to list how the places are the same and different.

My House and Grandma's House
Same	Different

❸ Write a paragraph that tells how these places are alike and how they are different.

❹ Use words such as *both, same, different,* or *but.*

Grade 2 · Lesson 24

⭐ **Literacy Center Kit** • Card 118

WORD WORK
Use a Computer

Objective
To practice using Vocabulary Words

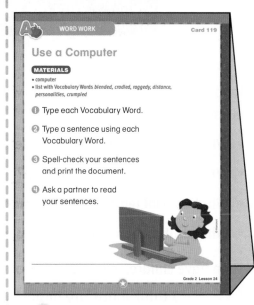

WORD WORK — Card 119

Use a Computer

MATERIALS
- computer
- list with Vocabulary Words *blended, cradled, raggedy, distance, personalities, crumpled*

❶ Type each Vocabulary Word.

❷ Type a sentence using each Vocabulary Word.

❸ Spell-check your sentences and print the document.

❹ Ask a partner to read your sentences.

Grade 2 · Lesson 24

⭐ **Literacy Center Kit** • Card 119

The girl cradled her doll.

LETTERS AND SOUNDS
Complete Words

Objective
To read and write words using known letter/sound correspondences

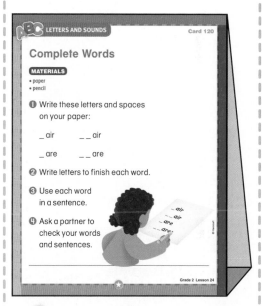

LETTERS AND SOUNDS — Card 120

Complete Words

MATERIALS
- paper
- pencil

❶ Write these letters and spaces on your paper:

_ air   _ _ air

_ are   _ _ are

❷ Write letters to finish each word.

❸ Use each word in a sentence.

❹ Ask a partner to check your words and sentences.

Grade 2 · Lesson 24

⭐ **Literacy Center Kit** • Card 120

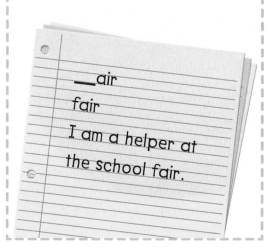

___air
fair
I am a helper at
the school fair.

Day at a Glance

Day 1

phonics **and Spelling**
- Introduce: *r*-Controlled Vowel /âr/*air, are*
- Pretest

Reading/ Comprehension

 Use Graphic Aids
Student Edition,
pp. 280–281
- *Read-Aloud Anthology:* "Hanging On"

Fluency
- Model Oral Fluency

Robust Vocabulary
Words from the Read-Aloud
- Introduce: *extinct, pledge*

Grammar [Quick Write]
- Introduce: Forms of *Be*

Writing ✏
- Paragraph That Compares (or Contrasts)

Warm-Up Routines

 Oral Language

Objective *To listen attentively and respond appropriately to oral communication*

Question of the Day

Why are maps important?

Help children brainstorm reasons why maps are important. Use the following prompts:

- **What map or maps have you used?**

- **Why did you need to use a map?**

- **What special features did the map have?**

- **When is it a good idea to carry a map? Why?**

Then have children complete the following sentence frame.

I think maps are important because _____.

Read Aloud

Objective *To listen for a purpose*

TRANSPARENCY   Read aloud the description of Africa as you point out each region on the map on **Transparency R127**. Use the following steps:

- **Set a purpose for listening.** Tell children to listen to learn about some of Africa's geographical features.

- **Model fluent reading.** Read the passage aloud. Remind children that good readers vary their reading rate depending on what they are reading. They slow down to pronounce unfamiliar vocabulary or when they read new information. They speed up when they recognize words and understand the content.

- **Discuss the passage.** Ask: **What different kinds of regions does Africa have?** (desert, savannah plains, jungle)

Use Graphic Aids

Africa

Africa is the second largest continent in the world. The northern half of Africa is hot and dry with mostly desert land. Africa's central and southern regions are also hot, but these areas receive more rain. They contain savannah plains and dense jungles. Each region contains many different kinds of wild animals. The jungles of Africa, for example, are home to a variety of primates, including chimpanzees.

Grade 2, Lesson 24   R127   Comprehension

Transparency R127

Word Wall

Objective *To read high-frequency words*

REVIEW HIGH-FREQUENCY WORDS   Review the words *already, guess, hundred, learn, curve,* and *fair,* as well as other previously learned high-frequency words. Hold up a word card at random, and ask children to read the word. Flip through the word cards several times.

already	guess	hundred
learn	curve	fair

r-Controlled Vowel /âr/ *air, are*

 phonics *and Spelling*

Objectives

- *To recognize and blend the r-controlled vowel sound of /âr/air, are*
- *To read words with /âr/air, are, and other known letter-sounds*
- *To use /âr/air, are, and other known letter-sounds to spell words*

Skill Trace

Tested **r-Controlled Vowel /âr/*air, are***

Introduce	T312–T315
Reteach	S38–S39
Review	T324–T325, T342–T343, T432
Test	Theme 5
Maintain	Theme 6, T360

 Refer to *Sounds of Letters CD* Track 20 for pronunciation of /air/.

"Research Says"

Word Recognition "Research, grounded in a common theoretical framework, now provides evidence that instruction that heightens phonological awareness and that emphasizes the connections to the alphabetic code promotes greater skill in word recognition—a skill essential to becoming a proficient reader."

—Blachman (2000)

Connect Letters to Sounds

WARM UP WITH PHONEMIC AWARENESS Say the words *fair* and *care.* Have children say the words. Say: **The words *fair* and *care* have the /âr/ sound at the end.** Then say the words *stair* and *share,* and have children repeat. Say: **The words *stair* and *share* also have the /âr/ sound.** Have children say /âr/ several times.

Routine Card 1 **CONNECT LETTERS AND SOUNDS** Display the *Sound/Spelling Card* for *air* and *are.* Point to the letter patterns *air* and *are* and review their letter/sound correspondence. Say: **The letters *air* can stand for the /âr/ sound, the sound in *chair*. The letters *are* can also stand for the /âr/ sound, the sound in *care*.** Touch the letter patterns several times, and have children say the /âr/ sound each time.

_air

_are

chair

▲ Sound/Spelling Card

5-DAY PHONICS

DAY 1	Introduce /âr/*air, are*
DAY 2	Word Building with /âr/*air, are*
DAY 3	Word Building with /âr/*air, are*
DAY 4	Contractions; Review /âr/*air, are*
DAY 5	Contractions; Review /âr/*air, are*

Work with Patterns

REINFORCE /âr/*air* Write the following words on the board. Point out that each word ends with the letters *air*. Read each word, and then have children read the words with you.

hair   fair

pair   chair

stair   repair

REINFORCE /âr/*are* Repeat the procedure with the following words that end with the letters *are*.

rare   glare

dare   share

stare   square

E L L

Reinforce Spelling As you read each word, point out whether it is spelled with *air* or *are*. Help children begin a list of words for each spelling in their notebooks, using the words in the lesson. Encourage them to add words they hear or read throughout the week.

ADVANCED

Extend Point out that the /âr/ sound can also be spelled with *ear*, as in *bear*. Have children work with partners to list as many words as they can that rhyme with *bear*. Then have partners sort their lists according to each word's spelling, *air, are,* or *ear*.

r-Controlled Vowel /âr/ *air, are*

 phonics *and Spelling*

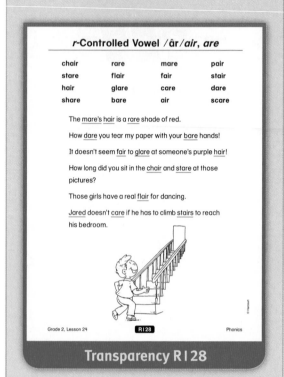

r-Controlled Vowel /âr/ *air, are*

chair	rare	mare	pair
stare	flair	fair	stair
hair	glare	care	dare
share	bare	air	scare

The mare's hair is a rare shade of red.

How dare you tear my paper with your bare hands!

It doesn't seem fair to glare at someone's purple hair!

How long did you sit in the chair and stare at those pictures?

Those girls have a real flair for dancing.

Jared doesn't care if he has to climb stairs to reach his bedroom.

Grade 2, Lesson 24   R128   Phonics

Transparency R128

Reading Words

GUIDED PRACTICE   Display **Transparency R128** or write the words and sentences on the board. Point to the word *chair*. Read the word, and then have children read it with you.

INDEPENDENT PRACTICE   Point to the remaining words in the top portion and have children read them. Then have children read aloud the sentences and identify words with *air* and *are*.

Decodable Books

Additional Decoding Practice

- **Phonics**
  r-Controlled Vowel /âr/*air, are*
- **Decodable Words**
- **High-Frequency Words**
  See lists in *Decodable Book 20.*
  See also *Decodable Books,* online (Take-Home Version).

▲ **Decodable Book 20** "Blair and His Lair"

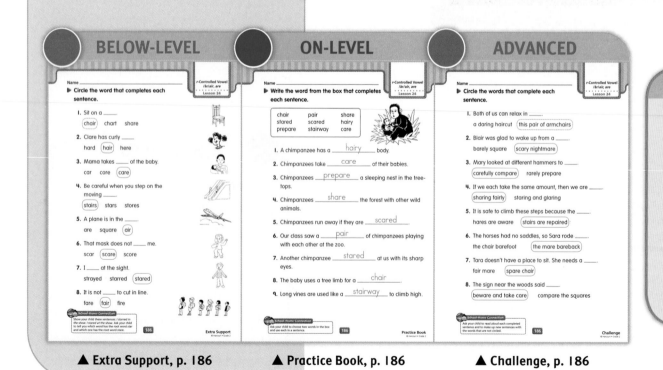

BELOW-LEVEL

ON-LEVEL

ADVANCED

▲ **Extra Support, p. 186**   ▲ **Practice Book, p. 186**   ▲ **Challenge, p. 186**

ELL

- Group children according to academic levels, and assign one of the pages on the left.

- Clarify any unfamiliar concepts as necessary. See *ELL Teacher Guide* Lesson 24 for support in scaffolding instruction.

5-DAY SPELLING	
DAY 1	Pretest
DAY 2	Word Building
DAY 3	State the Generalization
DAY 4	Review
DAY 5	Posttest

Introduce Spelling Words

PRETEST Say the first word and read the dictation sentence. Repeat the word as children write it. Write the word on the board and have children check their spelling. Tell them to circle the word if they spelled it correctly or write it correctly if they did not. Repeat for words 2–10.

Words with /âr/ air, are

1.	hair	The puppy has curly black **hair**.
2.	glare	The **glare** of the sun is blinding.
3.	fair	A referee follows rules so the game is **fair** for both teams.
4.	scare	Sharp teeth **scare** me!
5.	pair	Robby lost a **pair** of blue socks.
6.	care	The vet will **care** for the injured bird.
7.	share	Would you like to **share** this muffin with me?
8.	chair	That old **chair** is missing a leg.
9.	rare	It is **rare** that I don't want ice cream for dessert!
10.	stair	Josie skipped every other **stair**.

ADVANCED

Challenge Words Use the challenge words in these dictation sentences.

11.	airplane	The **airplane** flew through the sky.
12.	repair	Who will **repair** the broken window?
13.	downstairs	Leda keeps her art supplies **downstairs**.
14.	haircut	Charlie's **haircut** is too short.
15.	careful	Be **careful** when you use scissors.

Spelling Words

1.	hair	6.	care
2.	glare	7.	share
3.	fair	8.	chair
4.	scare	9.	rare
5.	pair	10.	stair

Challenge Words

11.	airplane	14.	haircut
12.	repair	15.	careful
13.	downstairs		

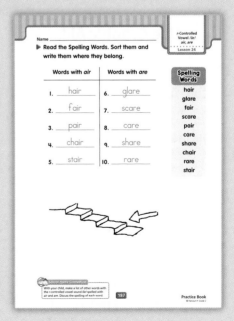

▲ Practice Book, p. 187

Use Graphic Aids
Comprehension

Objectives
- *To identify graphic aids*
- *To read and interpret information in graphic aids*

Daily Comprehension
Use Graphic Aids

DAY 1:	Review Graphic Aids *Student Edition*
DAY 2:	Review Graphic Aids *Student Edition*
DAY 3:	Review Graphic Aids *Student Edition*
DAY 4:	Review Graphic Aids *Transparency*
DAY 5:	Review Graphic Aids *Read-Aloud Anthology*

MONITOR PROGRESS

Use Graphic Aids

IF children have difficulty identifying the features of specific graphic aids,	**THEN** show them examples of each graphic aid, using additional books and resources in the classroom.

Small-Group Instruction, pp. S42–S43:

- ● **BELOW-LEVEL:** Reteach
- ● **ON-LEVEL:** Reinforce
- ● **ADVANCED:** Extend

Review

REVIEW GRAPHIC AIDS   Have children read *Student Edition* page 280. List on the board the different kinds of graphic aids discussed in the passage: diagram, chart, map, and graph. Next to each type of graphic aid, list its main features. Model how to read the diagram of a plant on page 280.

> **Think Aloud**   **The diagram shows me the parts of a plant. As I read each label, I follow the arrow to the part of the plant that is being described.**

Practice/Apply

GUIDED PRACTICE   Display a nonfiction book that contains graphic aids. Share them with children. Guide them to identify any graphic aids. Then point out the diagram on *Student Edition* page 281. Explain that this is a diagram of a chimpanzee. Then read aloud the passage with children. As parts of the chimpanzee are mentioned, ask children to touch each part on the diagram.

Try This   **INDEPENDENT PRACTICE**   Ask children to look at the diagram and tell what it explains. Then ask: **How does the diagram help you understand the information in the passage?** (Accept reasonable answers.)

Clarify Graphic Aids   Display an example of each graphic aid introduced on page 280. Review each graphic aid's distinct features and what it is used for. To check comprehension, have children point to the correct graphic aid when you say its name.

Focus Skill

 ## Use Graphic Aids

Nonfiction often uses **graphic aids** to help explain information quickly. Some examples of graphic aids are diagrams, charts, maps, and graphs.

- A diagram is a drawing with labels. It shows the parts of something or how something works.

- A chart has rows, columns, and headings.

- A map is a picture that shows where places are.

- A graph is a drawing that gives information about the amounts of things.

Diagram of a Plant

flower

stem   leaves

roots

280

Read the passage. Look at the diagram. Tell which information in the passage is made clear in the diagram.

A chimpanzee spends much of its time in trees. Its thumbs and big toes help it grab things. Its long arms are useful for swinging through trees. When a chimpanzee walks, it usually leans on its knuckles and walks on all fours.

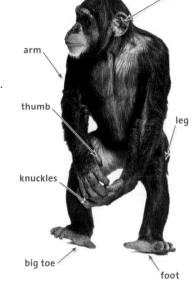

ear

arm

thumb

leg

knuckles

big toe

foot

GO online www.harcourtschool.com/storytown

Try This!

Look back at the diagram. What does it explain?

281

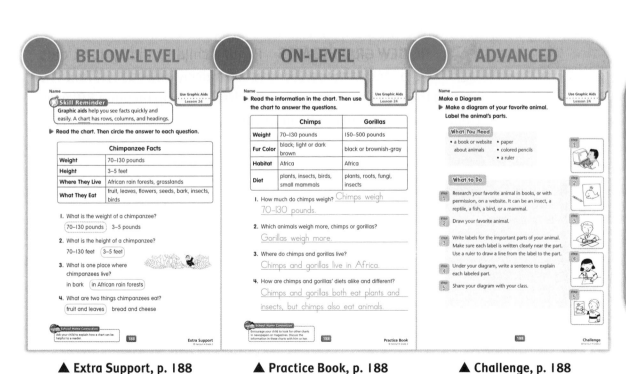

BELOW-LEVEL

Name _____

Skill Reminder
Graphic aids help you see facts quickly and easily. A chart has rows, columns, and headings.

▶ Read the chart. Then circle the answer to each question.

Chimpanzee Facts	
Weight	70–130 pounds
Height	3–5 feet
Where They Live	African rain forests, grasslands
What They Eat	fruit, leaves, flowers, seeds, bark, insects, birds

1. What is the weight of a chimpanzee?
   70–130 pounds   3–5 pounds

2. What is the height of a chimpanzee?
   70–130 feet   3–5 feet

3. What is one place where chimpanzees live?
   in bark   in African rain forests

4. What are two things chimpanzees eat?
   fruit and leaves   bread and cheese

School-Home Connection
Ask your child to explain how a chart can be helpful to a reader.   188

Extra Support

ON-LEVEL

Name _____

▶ Read the information in the chart. Then use the chart to answer the questions.

	Chimps	Gorillas
Weight	70–130 pounds	150–500 pounds
Fur Color	black; light or dark brown	black or brownish-gray
Habitat	Africa	Africa
Diet	plants, insects, birds, small mammals	plants, roots, fungi, insects

1. How much do chimps weigh? Chimps weigh 70–130 pounds.

2. Which animals weigh more, chimps or gorillas?
   Gorillas weigh more.

3. Where do chimps and gorillas live?
   Chimps and gorillas live in Africa.

4. How are chimps and gorillas' diets alike and different?
   Chimps and gorillas both eat plants and insects, but chimps also eat animals.

School-Home Connection
Encourage your child to look for other charts in newspapers or magazines. Discuss the information in these charts with him or her.   188

Practice Book

ADVANCED

Name _____

Make a Diagram
▶ Make a diagram of your favorite animal. Label the animal's parts.

What You Need
- a book or website about animals
- paper
- colored pencils
- a ruler

What to Do
1. Research your favorite animal in books, or with permission, on a website. It can be an insect, a reptile, a fish, a bird, or a mammal.
2. Draw your favorite animal.
3. Write labels for the important parts of your animal. Make sure each label is written clearly near the part. Use a ruler to draw a line from the label to the part.
4. Under your diagram, write a sentence to explain each labeled part.
5. Share your diagram with your class.

188

Challenge

ELL

- Group children according to academic levels, and assign one of the pages on the left.

- Clarify any unfamiliar concepts as necessary. See *ELL Teacher Guide* Lesson 24 for support in scaffolding instruction.

▲ Extra Support, p. 188   ▲ Practice Book, p. 188   ▲ Challenge, p. 188

Listening Comprehension

Read Aloud

Objectives

- *To set a purpose for listening*
- *To discuss the genre of nonfiction articles*
- *To use graphic aids*

Build Fluency

Focus: Reading Rate   Tell children that good readers vary their reading rate when they need to. They slow down to pronounce unfamiliar words and speed up when they recognize words. Good readers work to increase their reading speed and still understand what they are reading.

Use Graphic Aids   Use a world map or a globe to point out the continents named in the article: Asia and Africa. Then point to New York City, and explain that the United Nations Building is in New York City. Ask children to take turns putting a finger on each place when you name it. Have them repeat the names with you.

Before Reading

CONNECT TO PRIOR KNOWLEDGE   Tell children that they will listen to an article about the great apes and how their survival in Asia and Africa depends on an international pledge to keep them alive.

▲ Read-Aloud Anthology, "Hanging On," p. 88

Routine Card 2

GENRE STUDY: NONFICTION ARTICLE   Tell children that "Hanging On" is a nonfiction article that gives information on a topic. Remind children of the characteristics of this genre:

Think Aloud   **In a nonfiction article, sections are divided with headings. Photos and captions are usually included. Sometimes quotations from experts are used to present the information in an interesting way.**

After Reading

RESPOND   Have children identify the names of the great apes in "Hanging On." List them on the board. (gorillas, chimpanzees, orangutans, and bonobos)

REVIEW GRAPHIC AIDS   Remind children that graphic aids help readers understand ideas quickly and easily. Walk around the classroom and show children the map on page 89. Ask children to explain what the map shows. (where great apes can be found)

Build Robust Vocabulary
Words from the Read-Aloud

Teach/Model

INTRODUCE ROBUST VOCABULARY Use *Routine Card 3* to introduce the words.

❶ Put the word in **selection context**.
❷ Display Transparency R132 and read the word and the **Student-Friendly Explanation**.
❸ Have children **say the word** with you.
❹ Use the word in other contexts, and have children **interact with the word's meaning**.
❺ Remove the transparency. Say the Student-Friendly Explanation again, and ask children to **name the word** that goes with it.

❶ **Selection Context:** The great apes are in danger of becoming **extinct**.
❹ **Interact with Word Meaning:** I know that the dodo bird is extinct. Would you be more likely to see an extinct animal at a museum or at a zoo? Why?

❶ **Selection Context:** Twenty countries have made a **pledge** to save the great apes.
❹ **Interact with Word Meaning:** I made a pledge to be kind to all living creatures. Which would you make a pledge to do—drive a car or clean your room?

Practice/Apply

GUIDED PRACTICE Guide children in naming animals that have become *extinct*. Write children's suggestions on the board. If necessary, use a search engine on the Internet to find a current website on extinct or endangered species.

Objective
• *To develop robust vocabulary through discussing a literature selection*

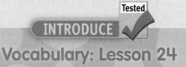

INTRODUCE ✓ Tested
Vocabulary: Lesson 24

extinct   pledge

▼ **Student-Friendly Explanations**

Student-Friendly Explanations	
extinct	If an animal is extinct, there are no more of that kind of animal alive.
pledge	When you make a pledge, you promise to do something.
patience	If you can wait for someone or something without complaining or getting restless, you have patience.
tedious	When something is boring and takes a long time to do, it is tedious.

Grade 2, Lesson 24   R132   Vocabulary

Transparency R132

Grammar Quick Write

Forms of Be

5-DAY GRAMMAR	
DAY 1	Introduce Forms of *Be: am, is, are*
DAY 2	Forms of *Be: was, were*
DAY 3	Subject-Verb Agreement
DAY 4	Apply to Writing
DAY 5	Weekly Review

Objective

• *To identify and use forms of the verb* be: am, is, are

Daily Proofreading

I playd with Emilys ball.

(played; Emily's)

Writing Trait ➤

Strengthening Conventions

Parts of Speech   Use this short lesson with children's own writing to build a foundation for revising/ editing longer connected text on Day 5. See also *Writer's Companion,* Lesson 24.

Forms of *be*

1. Gary is a gorilla.
2. I am glad Gary lives in the wild.
3. Great apes are special creatures.
4. They are almost extinct.
5. We are pleased about the pledge to save the great apes.
6. I am ready to help Gary survive.

Grade 2, Lesson 24   **LA49**   Grammar

Transparency LA49

Teach/Model

INTRODUCE FORMS OF *BE*   Explain that some verbs do not show action. They tell what someone or something is like. The verbs *am, is,* and *are* tell about the present.

Write this sentence on the board from "Hanging On" (*Read-Aloud Anthology,* p. 88):

> A pledge is a promise.

Read aloud the sentence. Then underline *is.* Say: **The verb *is* does not show action, but it does tell what something is like in the present time. In this sentence, it tells that a pledge is like a promise.** Then write these sentences on the board:

> Gorillas, chimpanzees, orangutans, and bonobos are great apes.

> I am concerned about the great apes.

Read aloud the first sentence. Underline *are.* Explain that *are* is used because there is more than one subject. Then read the next sentence and underline *am.* Explain that *am* and *is* are used with one subject.

Guided Practice

UNDERLINE THE FORM OF *BE*   Display **Transparency LA49.** Read the first sentence aloud and underline the verb *is.* Ask volunteers to tell what the sentence tells and to name the subject. Complete the remaining items together, eliciting responses from volunteers.

Practice/Apply

IDENTIFY FORM OF *BE*   Have children work with partners to write three sentences using *am, is,* or *are* as the verb. Have them write the verb and the subject or subjects of each sentence. Have partners share their sentences with the class.

Writing
Paragraph That Compares (or Contrasts)

5-DAY WRITING

DAY 1	Introduce
DAY 2	Prewrite
DAY 3	Draft
DAY 4	Revise
DAY 5	Revise

Teach/Model

INTRODUCE PARAGRAPH THAT COMPARES (OR CONTRASTS) Display **Transparency LA50**, and explain that these paragraphs were written by a child to compare and contrast a toy monkey with real monkeys. Read aloud the paragraphs. Together, develop a list of characteristics for these paragraphs. Ask children what they noticed about the author's use of the verb *to be*.

> ### Paragraph That Compares (or Contrasts)
>
> • A paragraph that compares tells how two things are alike and a paragraph that contrasts tells how two things are different.
>
> • The first sentence introduces the topic or one of the subjects.
>
> • Other sentences give examples of how another subject is the same or different from the first subject.
>
> • The paragraph uses words such as *like* and *different*.

WRITING TRAIT **WORD CHOICE** Tell children that good writers use signal words to help readers know that they are comparing or contrasting. Signal words include *similar, different,* and *unlike*.

Guided Practice

DRAFT SENTENCES Show children two classroom objects. Model writing a sentence that compares or contrasts the objects. Discuss the sentences. Ask volunteers to suggest other sentences.

Practice/Apply

WRITE SENTENCES Have children select two living things and write one sentence that shows how the living things are alike and one sentence that shows how they are different. Children should save their sentences for use on Days 2–5.

Objectives

• To read and respond to a paragraph that compares or contrasts as a model for writing
• To identify elements of a paragraph that compares or contrasts
• To write sentences that compare and contrast

Writing Prompt

Compare/Contrast Have children write sentences that compare and contrast two of their favorite toys.

Student Model: Paragraph That Compares (or Contrasts)

My Toy Monkey

I have a stuffed animal named Mickey. He is a monkey. I won him as a prize at the fair one summer. He has brown fur, brown eyes, and a red tongue. When I visit the monkeys at the animal park, I think of Mickey. Real monkeys are brown and furry like Mickey. They have long tails and round ears like him, too.

Real monkeys are also very different from Mickey. Real monkeys are bigger. They are busy and loud. They swing from tree to tree and scream at each other. Mickey is quiet and doesn't move unless I pick him up. He lets me hold him close. I know Mickey isn't a real monkey, but that's okay. He is real enough for me!

Grade 2, Lesson 24   **LA50**   Writing

Transparency LA50

phonics and Spelling
- Review: *r*-Controlled Vowel /âr/ *air, are*
- Build Words

Robust Vocabulary
Words from the Selection
- Introduce: *blended, cradled, raggedy, personalities, distance, crumpled*

Comprehension

 Summarize
Focus Strategy

 Use Graphic Aids
Focus Skill

Reading

- "Watching in the Wild," *Student Edition*, pp. 284–297

Read!

Fluency
- Rate

Robust Vocabulary
Words About the Selection
- Introduce: *patience, tedious*

Grammar Quick Write
- Forms of *Be*

Writing ✏️
- Paragraph That Compares

Warm-Up Routines

 ## Oral Language

Objective *To listen attentively and respond appropriately to oral communication*

Question of the Day
What is your favorite kind of jungle animal? Why?

Help children think about jungle animals that they like. Use the following prompts:

- **What is special about a jungle?**

- **What jungle animals do you know about? What ones would you like to know more about?**

- **Would a jungle animal make a good pet? Explain.**

Then have children complete the following sentence frame to explain the reasons for their choice.

My favorite jungle animal is the _____ because _____.

Read Aloud

Objective *To listen for a purpose*

BIG BOOK OF RHYMES AND POEMS
Display the poem "Chimpanzee" on page 43, and read the title aloud. Ask children to listen for details that tell about what chimpanzees do and where they live. Then track the print as you read the poem aloud. Invite volunteers to name details about the chimpanzee in the poem.

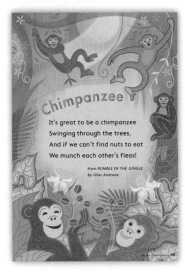

Chimpanzee

It's great to be a chimpanzee
Swinging through the trees,
And if we can't find nuts to eat
We munch each other's fleas!

*from RUMBLE IN THE JUNGLE
by Giles Andreae*

▲ **Big Book of Rhymes and Poems, p.** 43

Word Wall

Objective *To read high-frequency words*

REVIEW HIGH-FREQUENCY WORDS   Review the words *exercise, woods, prove, caught, world,* and *accept,* as well as other previously learned high-frequency words. Point to each word, and have children read it, spell it, and read it again. Then point to words at random and have children read them.

exercise	woods	prove
caught	world	accept

r-Controlled Vowel /âr/*air, are*

 phonics *and Spelling*

Objectives

- *To blend sounds into words*
- *To spell four- and five-letter r-controlled vowel /âr/ words*

Skill Trace

Tested ✔ **r-Controlled Vowel /âr/*air, are***

Introduce	T312–T315
Reteach	S38–S39
Review	T324–T325, T342–T343, T432
Test	Theme 5
Maintain	Theme 6, T360

Spelling Words

1.	hair	6.	care
2.	glare	7.	share
3.	fair	8.	chair
4.	scare	9.	rare
5.	pair	10.	stair

Challenge Words

11.	airplane	14.	haircut
12.	repair	15.	careful
13.	downstairs		

Word Building

READ SPELLING WORDS Write the word *pair* on the board. Ask children to identify the letters that stand for the /âr/ sound. Then read the word, and have children do the same.

BUILD SPELLING WORDS Ask children which letter you should change to make *pair* become *hair*. (Change *p* to *h*.) Write the word *hair* on the board. Point to the word, and have children read it. Continue building spelling words in this manner. Say:

- **Which letter do I have to change to make the word *fair*?** (Change *h* to *f*.)

- **Which letter do I have to change to make the word *chair*?** (Change *f* to *ch*.)

- **Which letters do I have to change to make the word *stair*?** (Change *ch* to *st*.)

- **Which letters do I have to change to make the word *share*?** (Change *t* to *h*, *ir* to *re*.)

Continue building the remaining spelling words in this manner.

pair
hair
fair
chair
stair
share

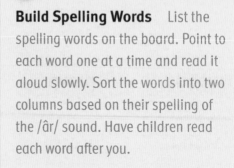

BELOW-LEVEL

Build Spelling Words List the spelling words on the board. Point to each word one at a time and read it aloud slowly. Sort the words into two columns based on their spelling of the /âr/ sound. Have children read each word after you.

ADVANCED

Word Constructions Have children combine the initial letters with the correct endings below to build all the spelling words.

Beginning	Ending
c, ch, f, gl, h, p, r, sc, sh, st	*air* *are*

5-DAY PHONICS/SPELLING

DAY 1	Pretest
DAY 2	Word Building
DAY 3	State the Generalization
DAY 4	Review
DAY 5	Posttest

Read Words in Context

APPLY PHONICS   Write the following sentences on the board or on chart paper. Have children read each sentence silently. Then track the print as children read the sentence aloud.

> Payton will <u>share</u> his sandwich with Aubrey.
>
> Erin needs a new <u>pair</u> of shoes.
>
> Is that <u>chair</u> already taken?
>
> Mr. Connor's treasure chest held a <u>rare</u> coin.
>
> What a <u>glare</u> that angry dog gave me!

WRITE   Dictate several spelling words. Have children write the words in their notebook or on a dry-erase board.

phonics Resources

Phonics Practice Book, pp. 145–150

MONITOR PROGRESS

r-Controlled Vowel /âr/*air*, *are*

IF children have difficulty building and reading words with *r*-controlled vowel /âr/*air*, *are*,

THEN write *air* and *are* on index cards and the beginning letters of the words *care*, *hair*, *fair*, *stair*, and *scare* on other index cards. Use the cards to help children blend and read the words.

Small-Group Instruction, pp. S38–S39:

● **BELOW-LEVEL:** Reteach
● **ON-LEVEL:** Reinforce
● **ADVANCED:** Extend

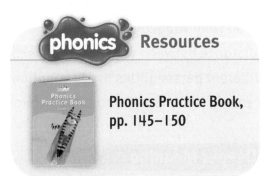

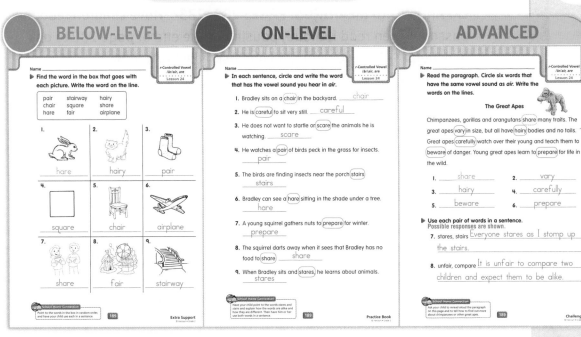

▲ Extra Support, p. 189   ▲ Practice Book, p. 189   ▲ Challenge, p. 189

E L L

• Group children according to academic levels, and assign one of the pages on the left.

• Clarify any unfamiliar concepts as necessary. See *ELL Teacher Guide* Lesson 24 for support in scaffolding instruction.

Build Robust Vocabulary

Words from the Selection

Objective

• *To build robust vocabulary*

Tested

INTRODUCE

Vocabulary: Lesson 24

blended	distance
cradled	personalities
raggedy	crumpled

Student-Friendly Explanations

blended	When things are blended, they are mixed together so you can't tell there are separate parts.
cradled	If you cradle something, you hold it closely as if you were taking care of it.
raggedy	When something is raggedy, it looks rough and torn at the edges, like a rag.
distance	Distance is how far away something is.
personalities	People's personalities are made up of all the ways they act, think, and feel that make them special.
crumpled	If you crumple something, you gently crush it or bunch it up.

Grade 2, Lesson 24   **R133**   Vocabulary

Transparency R133

Word Detective

Listen   Model how to listen closely to oral communication and then jot down any words from the lesson you may have heard.

HOMEWORK/INDEPENDENT PRACTICE

Teach/Model

Routine Card 4

INTRODUCE ROBUST VOCABULARY   Use *Routine Card 4* to introduce the words.

❶ Display Transparency R133 and read the word and the **Student-Friendly Explanation**.
❷ Have children **say the word** with you.
❸ Have children **interact with the word's meaning** by asking them the appropriate question below.

• What drinks with **blended** fruit do you like best?
• Have you ever **cradled** a baby? How did it feel?
• When might you wear **raggedy** clothes?
• What is the **distance** between your home and school?
• How many different **personalities** live in your home? Explain.
• What would you do if you found a **crumpled** dollar bill?

Develop Deeper Meaning

EXPAND WORD MEANINGS: PAGES 282–283   Have children read the passage. Then read it aloud, pausing at the end of page 282 to ask questions 1–2. Read page 283 and ask questions 3–6.

1. What surroundings do you think the deer **blended** into? Why? (woods; Their hides are brown.)

2. Why was Zoe's camera **cradled** in her lap? (Possible response: It is an expensive object, and Zoe wanted to keep it safe.)

3. Why might deer look **raggedy**? (They shed their fur, but not at once.)

4. How can Zoe tell the deer's **personalities**? (She watches them.)

5. How much **distance** might there be between Bashful and the other deers? (Possible response: several yards)

6. Why were Zoe's and Dad's clothes **crumpled**? (They'd been crouching, watching the deer for an hour.)

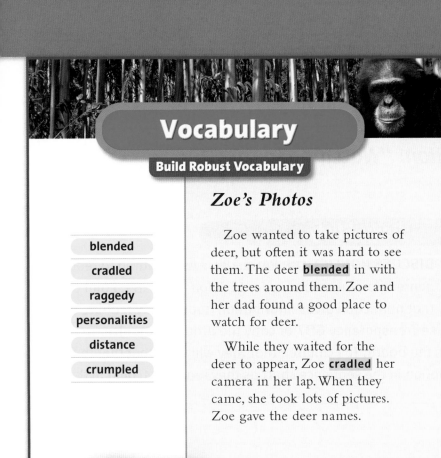

Vocabulary

Build Robust Vocabulary

Zoe's Photos

blended

cradled

raggedy

personalities

distance

crumpled

Zoe wanted to take pictures of deer, but often it was hard to see them. The deer **blended** in with the trees around them. Zoe and her dad found a good place to watch for deer.

While they waited for the deer to appear, Zoe **cradled** her camera in her lap. When they came, she took lots of pictures. Zoe gave the deer names.

Zoe named one deer Rags. He was shedding his thick fur and looked **raggedy**. Zoe named other deer by their **personalities**. She named a curious deer Nosy. One deer reminded Zoe of her shy cousin. Zoe named him Bashful. He always stayed at a **distance**.

After an hour of watching deer, Zoe and her dad stood up. Their clothes were all **crumpled**. Zoe wondered what the deer would name her and her dad!

www.harcourtschool.com/storytown

Word Detective

Where else can you find the Vocabulary Words? Look on billboards and signs around town. Listen to announcements and songs. When you see or hear one of the words, write it in your vocabulary journal and tell where you found it.

282

283

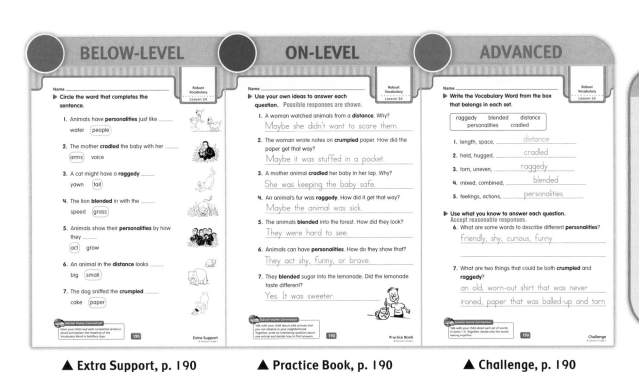

BELOW-LEVEL

Name _____
▶ Circle the word that completes the sentence.

1. Animals have **personalities** just like ___
   water (people)

2. The mother **cradled** the baby with her ___
   (arms) voice

3. A cat might have a **raggedy** ___
   yawn (tail)

4. The lion **blended** in with the ___
   speed (grass)

5. Animals show their **personalities** by how they ___
   (act) grow

6. An animal in the **distance** looks ___
   big (small)

7. The dog sniffed the **crumpled** ___
   cake (paper)

▲ Extra Support, p. 190

ON-LEVEL

Name _____
▶ Use your own ideas to answer each question. Possible responses are shown.

1. A woman watched animals from a **distance**. Why?
   Maybe she didn't want to scare them.

2. The woman wrote notes on **crumpled** paper. How did the paper get that way?
   Maybe it was stuffed in a pocket.

3. A mother animal **cradled** her baby in her lap. Why?
   She was keeping the baby safe.

4. An animal's fur was **raggedy**. How did it get that way?
   Maybe the animal was sick.

5. The animals **blended** into the forest. How did they look?
   They were hard to see.

6. Animals can have **personalities**. How do they show that?
   They act shy, funny, or brave.

7. They **blended** sugar into the lemonade. Did the lemonade taste different?
   Yes. It was sweeter.

▲ Practice Book, p. 190

ADVANCED

Name _____
▶ Write the Vocabulary Word from the box that belongs in each set.

| raggedy blended distance |
| personalities cradled |

1. length, space, _____ distance

2. held, hugged, _____ cradled

3. torn, uneven, _____ raggedy

4. mixed, combined, _____ blended

5. feelings, actions, _____ personalities

▶ Use what you know to answer each question. Accept reasonable responses.

6. What are some words to describe different **personalities**?
   friendly, shy, curious, funny

7. What are two things that could be both **crumpled** and **raggedy**?
   an old, worn-out shirt that was never ironed, paper that was balled-up and torn

▲ Challenge, p. 190

E L L

• Group children according to academic levels, and assign one of the pages on the left.

• Clarify any unfamiliar concepts as necessary. See *ELL Teacher Guide* Lesson 24 for support in scaffolding instruction.

Reading

Student Edition: "Watching in the Wild"

Objectives

- *To understand characteristics and features of nonfiction*
- *To summarize as a strategy for comprehension*
- *To apply word knowledge to the reading of a text*

Options for Reading

BELOW-LEVEL

Preview Have children preview the selection by looking at the photographs and time line. Guide them to predict what the selection will be about. Read each page of the selection to children, and have them read it after you.

ON-LEVEL

Monitor Comprehension Have children read the selection aloud, page by page. Ask them the Monitor Comprehension questions as you go.

ADVANCED

Independent Reading Have children read each page silently, looking up each time they finish a page. Ask them the Monitor Comprehension questions as you go.

Genre Study

DISCUSS NONFICTION: PAGE 284 Ask children to read the genre information on *Student Edition* page 284. Point out that nonfiction gives information about many real-life topics. Then use **Transparency GO7** or copy the graphic organizer from page 284 on the board. Tell children that they will work together to fill in information in the sequence chart as they read "Watching in the Wild."

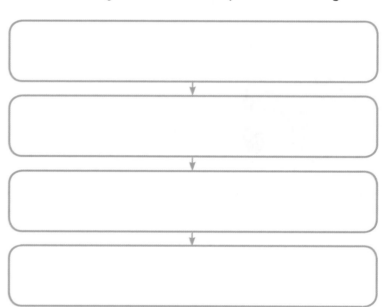

Comprehension Strategies

SUMMARIZE: PAGE 284 Remind children that good readers use strategies to make sense of what they read. Explain that one strategy readers can use is to summarize. Have children read aloud the Comprehension Strategy information on page 284. Provide information about a summary.

Think Aloud When I read a nonfiction article such as "Watching in the Wild," I look for the key points so I can use those ideas when I summarize.

Tell children that summarizing is a useful strategy to help them remember and understand what they read.

Genre Study

Nonfiction gives information about the world. Look for

- headings that tell what each section is about.

- graphic aids such as time lines.

Comprehension Strategy

 Summarize a selection to understand the main ideas.

284

Watching in the Wild

by
Charnan Simon

285

Build Background

DISCUSS CHIMPANZEES   Tell children that they are going to read a nonfiction selection about a famous scientist, Jane Goodall, who observed chimpanzees in the wild. Invite volunteers to name things that they already know about chimpanzees. List their responses on the board. Ask children to predict what Jane Goodall might learn by watching chimpanzees.

| Routine Card 6 | **SET A PURPOSE AND PREDICT**   Tell children that this is a selection they will read for information. Have them look at the photographs. |

- Have children read the title.

- Identify Jane Goodall on page 286. Ask children what they think she is holding in her hand and trying to do.

- List their predictions on the board.

- Invite children to read the selection to find out what Jane Goodall is doing.

TECHNOLOGY

 eBook   "Watching in the Wild" is available in an eBook.

 Audiotext   "Watching in the Wild" is available on *Audiotext Grade 2*, CD 5 for subsequent readings.

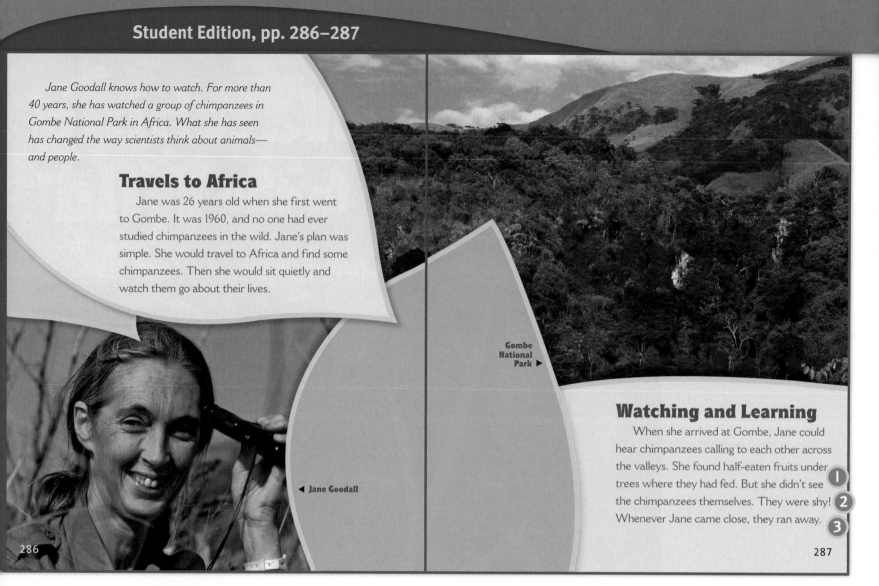

Jane Goodall knows how to watch. For more than 40 years, she has watched a group of chimpanzees in Gombe National Park in Africa. What she has seen has changed the way scientists think about animals—and people.

Travels to Africa

Jane was 26 years old when she first went to Gombe. It was 1960, and no one had ever studied chimpanzees in the wild. Jane's plan was simple. She would travel to Africa and find some chimpanzees. Then she would sit quietly and watch them go about their lives.

◄ Jane Goodall

Gombe National Park ►

Watching and Learning

When she arrived at Gombe, Jane could hear chimpanzees calling to each other across the valleys. She found half-eaten fruits under trees where they had fed. But she didn't see the chimpanzees themselves. They were shy! Whenever Jane came close, they ran away.

286

287

Monitor Comprehension

PAGES 286–287 Say: **I see Jane Goodall holding a pair of binoculars. Read to find out what she is looking at.**

① **NOTE DETAILS** **How did Jane know the chimpanzees were in the Gombe National Park?** (She watched them. She heard them calling and found food they left.)

② **MAKE INFERENCES** **Why does the author say the chimpanzees were shy? What else might they be?** (Possible response: They ran away whenever Jane came close. They could be afraid.)

③ **GRAPHIC AIDS** **How do the photographs help you understand what this selection is about?** (Possible response: They show the setting and subject that Jane is studying.)

Apply
Comprehension Strategies

Summarize Demonstrate how to summarize the main points of these opening pages.

Think Aloud Headings usually give the main idea of the text that follows. So, I can summarize these two pages by using the headings: Jane Goodall traveled to Africa in 1960 to watch and learn about how chimpanzees live in the wild.

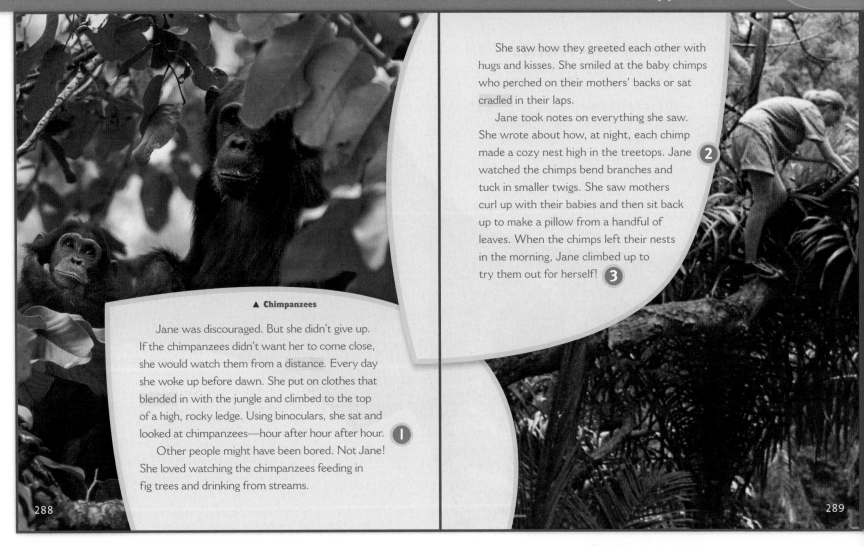

She saw how they greeted each other with hugs and kisses. She smiled at the baby chimps who perched on their mothers' backs or sat cradled in their laps.

Jane took notes on everything she saw. She wrote about how, at night, each chimp made a cozy nest high in the treetops. Jane  watched the chimps bend branches and tuck in smaller twigs. She saw mothers curl up with their babies and then sit back up to make a pillow from a handful of leaves. When the chimps left their nests in the morning, Jane climbed up to try them out for herself! ③

▲ Chimpanzees

Jane was discouraged. But she didn't give up. If the chimpanzees didn't want her to come close, she would watch them from a distance. Every day she woke up before dawn. She put on clothes that blended in with the jungle and climbed to the top of a high, rocky ledge. Using binoculars, she sat and looked at chimpanzees—hour after hour after hour.

Other people might have been bored. Not Jane! She loved watching the chimpanzees feeding in fig trees and drinking from streams.

288

289

Monitor Comprehension

PAGES 288–289   Say: **I see chimpanzee faces. Read to find out if Jane got to see them up close.**

① **MAIN IDEA AND DETAILS**   **How did Jane observe the chimps from a distance?** (She wore clothes that blended into the jungle, found a good observation post, and used binoculars.)

② **MAKE INFERENCES**   **Why did Jane take notes on everything she saw?** (Possible response: She was the first scientist to gather information on chimps in the wild and every detail was important.)

③ **DRAW CONCLUSIONS**   **Why did Jane climb up and try out the chimp nests?** (Possible response: She wanted to see for herself how the nests looked and felt.)

SCIENCE

SUPPORTING STANDARDS

Scientific Method and Tools   Explain that binoculars are designed to show things that are far away. They consist of two small telescopes joined with a single focusing device. Scientists use binoculars to observe objects from a distance. The records scientists make of their observations are called field notes. Ask children to name some other tools scientists might use.

Making New Friends

Slowly, the chimpanzees became used to Jane. They let her come closer and closer. Jane began naming the chimps she recognized. David Greybeard had a silvery beard and a calm manner. Old Flo was ugly, with a big nose and raggedy ears—but she was a wonderful mother. Mr. McGregor reminded Jane of the gardener in *The Tale of Peter Rabbit*.

▲ A chimpanzee and her baby

At the time, scientists thought that animals being studied should be given numbers, not names. But Jane didn't agree. She saw that the chimpanzees had real personalities. It made sense to give them real names. Today, many scientists name the animals they study in the wild.

290

291

Monitor Comprehension

PAGES 290–291   Have children describe what they see and predict what information they will learn. Say: **Read to find out what's going on.**

① **CHARACTERS' MOTIVATIONS   Why did the chimpanzees let Jane get closer to them?** (Possible response: They became used to her and, most likely, they felt that she would not harm them.)

② **MAIN IDEA AND DETAILS   Why did Jane give the chimpanzees names?** (Possible response: She wanted to give them names that fit their personalities.)

③ **MAKE CONNECTIONS   If you were studying an animal in the wild, would you name him or her? Why or why not?** (Answers will vary.)

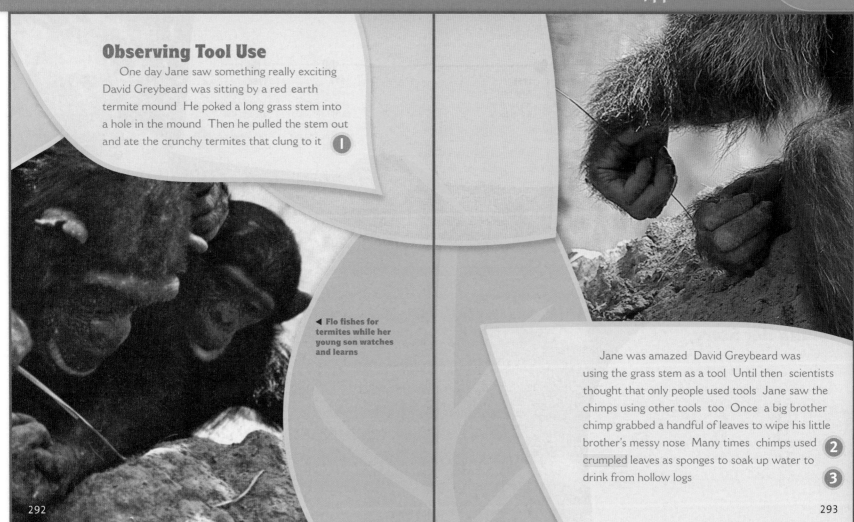

Observing Tool Use

One day Jane saw something really exciting David Greybeard was sitting by a red earth termite mound He poked a long grass stem into a hole in the mound Then he pulled the stem out and ate the crunchy termites that clung to it ❶

◀ Flo fishes for termites while her young son watches and learns

Jane was amazed David Greybeard was using the grass stem as a tool Until then scientists thought that only people used tools Jane saw the chimps using other tools too Once a big brother chimp grabbed a handful of leaves to wipe his little brother's messy nose Many times chimps used ❷ crumpled leaves as sponges to soak up water to drink from hollow logs ❸

292   293

Monitor Comprehension

PAGES 292–293   Say: **I see a chimpanzee holding a stem. Read to find out what he is doing with it.**

❶ **SUMMARIZE   What did Jane see David Greybeard do?** (David Greybeard used a long grass stem as a tool to pull termites out of a mound.)

Focus Skill

❷ **NOTE DETAILS   How did the chimps use leaves as tools?** (to wipe messy noses and soak up drinking water)

❸ **MAKE INFERENCES   Why were Jane's discoveries important?** (Possible response: Jane's discoveries proved that chimpanzees were intelligent creatures. Until that time, scientists thought that only people used tools.)

ANALYZE AUTHOR'S PURPOSE

Author's Purpose   Have children complete this sentence:

• The author wrote "Watching in the Wild" to _____. (provide information about chimpanzees)

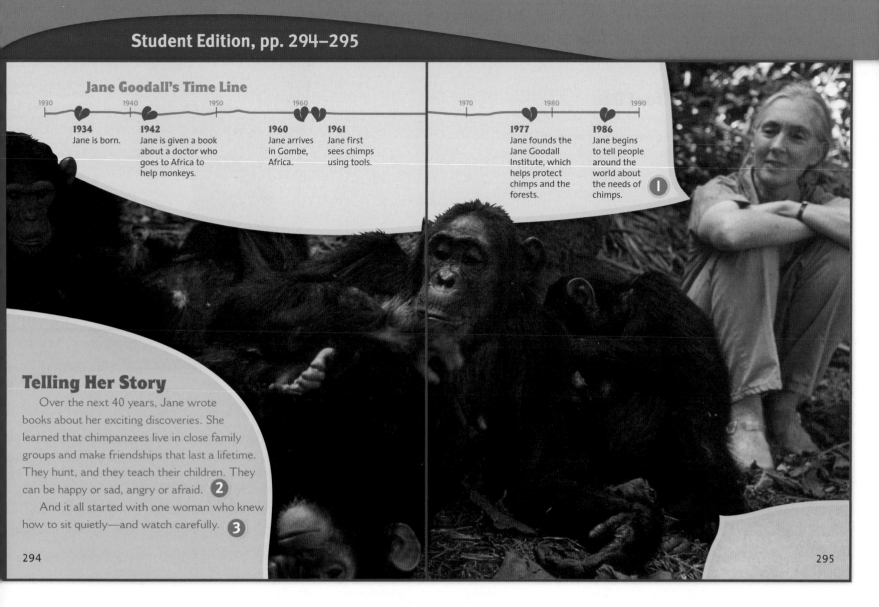

Jane Goodall's Time Line

| 1930 | 1940 | 1950 | 1960 | | 1970 | 1980 | 1990 |

1934
Jane is born.

1942
Jane is given a book about a doctor who goes to Africa to help monkeys.

1960
Jane arrives in Gombe, Africa.

1961
Jane first sees chimps using tools.

1977
Jane founds the Jane Goodall Institute, which helps protect chimps and the forests.

1986
Jane begins to tell people around the world about the needs of chimps. ①

Telling Her Story

Over the next 40 years, Jane wrote books about her exciting discoveries. She learned that chimpanzees live in close family groups and make friendships that last a lifetime. They hunt, and they teach their children. They can be happy or sad, angry or afraid. ②

And it all started with one woman who knew how to sit quietly—and watch carefully. ③

294   295

Monitor Comprehension

PAGES 294–295 Say: **I see a line labeled "Jane Goodall's Time Line." Read to find out what happens to Jane.**

①  **GRAPHIC AIDS How does the time line help you understand Jane's life?** (It shows important facts about her life in time order so it is easier to see at a glance what she has done and when she did it.)

② **MAKE COMPARISONS How are chimps like people?** (They live in family groups, make friendships, hunt, teach their children, and express emotions.)

③ **AUTHOR'S PURPOSE Why do you think Charnan Simon wrote about Jane Goodall?** (Possible response: to inform people about the important contributions Jane Goodall has made to science and our understanding of other living creatures)

BELOW-LEVEL

Graphic Aids Remind children that time lines arrange important dates in time order. Model how to read the time line. Tell children to begin at the left side of the time line on page 294 and read across to the end on page 295. Have children read the information.

Think Critically

Respond to the Literature

1. 1961 **USE GRAPHIC AIDS**

2. The chimpanzees were shy and ran away whenever she came close. **CAUSE/EFFECT**

3. Possible response: Scientists had never observed animals using tools before. They believed that only people used tools. **IMPORTANT DETAILS**

4. Possible response: So readers would know that Jane knew the chimps had individual personalities. **AUTHOR'S PURPOSE**

5. **WRITE** Scientists have learned that chimpanzees use tools, live in family groups, and make friendships. **EXTENDED RESPONSE**

Meet the Author

PAGE 297 Point to Charnan Simon and tell children that she has written many other biographies about the lives of interesting people. Among her subjects are Jane Addams, Andrew Carnegie, Rachel Carson, Walt Disney, Bill Gates, Jesse Jackson, Lady Bird Johnson, Janet Reno, and Martha Washington. Ask: **What are the author's favorite things to do?**

RUBRIC For additional support in scoring the WRITE item, see the rubric on p. R6.

Lesson 24 (*Student Edition*, pages 296–297) **T335**

Check Comprehension
Summarizing

Objectives

- *To practice summarizing the selection*
- *To read at a rate and in a manner that sounds like natural speech*

SUMMARIZE RUBRIC

4	Uses main points to clearly summarize the selection
3	Uses some main points to summarize the selection
2	Summarizes the selection with some inaccuracies
1	Is unable to summarize the selection

Professional Development

 Podcasting: Auditory Modeling

BELOW-LEVEL

Fluency Practice   For fluency practice, have children read *Decodable Book 20*, the appropriate *Leveled Reader* (pp. T376–T379), or Story 24 in the *Strategic Intervention Interactive Reader*.

Summarize

 DIBELS Oral Reading Fluency **ORF**

 USE GRAPHIC AIDS   Ask children to tell how the time line helped them understand the selection. (It shows what happened in Goodall's life before and after the time of the selection.)

REVISIT THE GRAPHIC ORGANIZER   Display completed **Transparency GO7**. Guide children to use the sequence chart to identify the main parts of "Watching in the Wild."

STORY RETELLING CARDS   The cards can be used for summarizing or as an aid to completing the graphic organizer.

▲ Story Retelling Cards 1–6, "Watching in the Wild"

Fluency
Rate

Teach/Model

 DIBELS Oral Reading Fluency **ORF**

USING RATE   Explain that good readers slow down their reading when they come to unfamiliar words and read at a faster rate when words are familiar. Have children open to pages 286–287 of "Watching in the Wild" and track the print as you model varying reading rate.

Practice/Apply

 Routine Card 7

CHORAL-READ   Assign groups alternating pages to read with you. Remind children to use the same rate as you do.

Build Robust Vocabulary

Words About the Selection

Objectives
- *To build robust vocabulary through discussing a literature selection*
- *To understand and use vocabulary in new contexts*

Teach/Model

Routine Card 3

INTRODUCE THE WORDS Use *Routine Card 3* to introduce the words.

❶ Put the word in **selection context**.
❷ Display Transparency R132 and read the word and the **Student-Friendly Explanation**.
❸ Have children **say the word** with you.
❹ Use the word in other contexts, and have children **interact with the word's meaning**.
❺ Remove the transparency. Say the Student-Friendly Explanation again, and ask children to **name the word** that goes with it.

❶ **Selection Context:** Jane shows **patience** when she watches the chimps for hours.
❹ **Interact with Word Meaning:** I have patience with children because I like being with them. Is it easier to have patience while waiting for your TV show to begin or while waiting for someone to shop?

❶ **Selection Context:** Jane didn't mind the **tedious** job of taking notes on everything the chimps were doing.
❹ **Interact with Word Meaning:** When I have to do a tedious job, I play music that I like. What do you do when you have a tedious job to do?

Practice/Apply

GUIDED PRACTICE Ask children to use the vocabulary to tell about situations in which it is important to have *patience*.

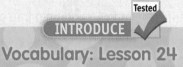

INTRODUCE ✓ Tested

Vocabulary: Lesson 24

patience   tedious

▼ Student-Friendly Explanations

Student-Friendly Explanations

extinct	If an animal is extinct, there are no more of that kind of animal alive.
pledge	When you make a pledge, you promise to do something.
patience	If you can wait for someone or something without complaining or getting restless, you have patience.
tedious	When something is boring and takes a long time to do, it is tedious.

Grade 2, Lesson 24   R132   Vocabulary

Transparency R132

Grammar *Quick Write*

Forms of Be

5-DAY GRAMMAR	
DAY 1	Introduce Forms of *Be*: *am, is, are*
DAY 2	**Forms of *Be*: *was, were***
DAY 3	Subject-Verb Agreement
DAY 4	Apply to Writing
DAY 5	Weekly Review

Objective

• *To identify forms of* Be: was, were

Daily Proofreading

Ari washes clothes Yesterday.

(washed, yesterday)

The Verb *Be* Forms of verbs in children's home language may not correspond to English. Model and reinforce that forms of the verb *be* link the subject to a word or words in the predicate. These forms must agree with the subject.

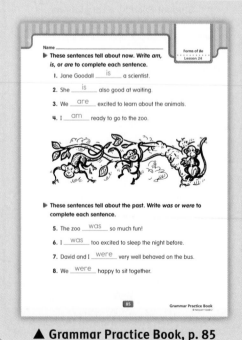

▲ **Grammar Practice Book, p. 85**

Review

FORMS OF *BE*: *was, were* Remind children that some verbs do not show action. They tell what someone or something is like. The verbs *was* and *were* tell about the past. Write these sentences on the board:

> Jane was discouraged when she didn't see the chimps.
>
> The chimpanzees were shy at first.

Read aloud the first sentence. Then underline *was*. Tell children: **The verb *was* does not show action, but it does tell how someone felt in the past. In this sentence, it tells that Jane was discouraged.** Point out that the verb *was* is used because the sentence tells about a singular subject, *Jane*. Read aloud the second sentence. Have children identify the verb. Explain or elicit that the verb *were* is used because it tells about the plural subject, *chimpanzees*.

Practice/Apply

GUIDED PRACTICE Write the following sentences on the board. Model how to underline the verb in the first sentence. Then work together to underline the verb in the remaining sentences and tell if the sentence is about the present or the past.

- **The chimp is near the tree.** (*is*, present)
- **Jane was excited about the chimps.** (*was*, past)
- **The chimps were happy to see Jane.** (*were*, past)

 INDEPENDENT PRACTICE Write these incomplete sentences on the board. Have children rewrite each sentence using *was* or *were*.

- Jane _____ 26 years old when she went to Gombe. (*was*)
- The chimpanzees _____ in family groups. (*were*)
- Old Flo _____ a wonderful mother. (*was*)
- Jane _____ amazed to see David Greybeard using a tool. (*was*)

Writing
Paragraph That Compares (or Contrasts)

5-DAY WRITING

DAY 1	Introduce
DAY 2	Prewrite
DAY 3	Draft
DAY 4	Revise
DAY 5	Revise

Prewrite

GENERATE IDEAS Have children look again at the sentences they wrote on Day 1 (page T321). Ask them to think of details that might tell more about the two living subjects they wrote about.

 WORD CHOICE Tell children that good writers choose words that create vivid pictures and avoid using the same words over and over again. Words that "show" rather than "tell" make writing more interesting.

MODEL PREWRITING Copy on the board the Venn diagram below. Tell children that they can use a graphic organizer such as this one to generate details about how two subjects are alike and different. Model filling out each part of the Venn diagram below with one detail about each classroom object compared and contrasted on Day 1.

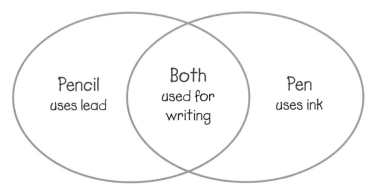

Pencil
uses lead

Both
used for
writing

Pen
uses ink

Practice/Apply

GUIDED PRACTICE Ask children to brainstorm details to include in their paragraphs. Have volunteers share their subjects and have the class ask questions to find out more. Record their ideas in a new Venn diagram.

INDEPENDENT PRACTICE Children can use the Venn diagram to brainstorm details about how the living things are alike and different. If children have difficulty doing this, encourage them to draw a picture of each living thing. Have children save their Venn diagrams to use on Days 3–5.

Objectives

• *To develop ideas and details for a paragraph that compares or contrasts*

• *To use a graphic organizer for prewriting*

Writing Prompt

Independent Writing Have children write about what they observed when they watched somebody or something for a long period of time.

Reinforce Comparisons
If children have difficulty with the language of comparing or contrasting, show them two *Picture Cards*. To compare and contrast the objects, ask children yes/no questions or questions that require a one-word response. Then talk about how the objects are alike and different. Repeat with other classroom objects.

Day at a Glance
Day 3

 phonics and Spelling
- Review: *r*-Controlled Vowel /âr/*air, are*
- State the Generalization

Fluency
- Rate
- "Watching in the Wild," *Student Edition*, pp. 284–297

Comprehension
 Review: Use Graphic Aids

Reading
- "Chimp Computer Whiz," *Student Edition*, pp. 298–299

 Read!

Robust Vocabulary
- Review: *extinct, pledge, blended, cradled, raggedy, personalities, distance, crumpled, patience, tedious*
- Synonyms

Grammar Quick Write
- Review: Forms of *Be*

Writing
- Paragraph That Compares

Warm-Up Routines

Oral Language

Objective *To listen attentively and respond appropriately to oral communication*

Question of the Day

What do you think you would see if you watched a chimpanzee?

Use the following prompts to help children think about what they associate with the word *chimpanzee*.

- **What picture pops into your head when you hear the word *chimpanzee*?**

- **What sounds do you hear? Why?**

- **What smells do you imagine? Why?**

Then have children complete the following sentence frame.

> **If I watched a chimpanzee, I would see _____.**

Read Aloud

Objective *To identify rhymes in poetry*

BIG BOOK OF RHYMES AND POEMS Display "Chimpanzee" on page 43, and ask children to tell what they remember about it. Read aloud the poem, emphasizing the rhyming words at the end of lines two and four. Ask children to identify which words rhyme. (trees, fleas) Point out that the words *chimpanzee* and *eat* also have the long *e* sound found in *trees* and *fleas*. Then reread the poem, adding gestures to reinforce the action of the poem. Ask children to join in, imitating or adding new gestures.

Chimpanzee

It's great to be a chimpanzee
Swinging through the trees,
And if we can't find nuts to eat
We munch each other's fleas!

*from RUMBLE IN THE JUNGLE
by Giles Andreae*

▲ **Big Book of Rhymes
and Poems, p. 43**

Word Wall

Objective *To read high-frequency words*

REVIEW HIGH-FREQUENCY WORDS Remove from the Word Wall the cards for *brought*, *bought*, *board*, *tough*, *thumb*, and *father*, as well as other previously learned high-frequency words. Have children begin snapping their fingers to keep time. Hold up each card and have children spell and read the word to the beat of the snaps. Flip through the word cards several times.

brought	bought	board
tough	thumb	father

r-Controlled Vowel /âr/ air, are *and Spelling*

5-DAY PHONICS	
DAY 1	Reintroduce /âr/*air, are*
DAY 2	Word Building with /âr/*air, are*
DAY 3	**Word Building with /âr/*air, are***
DAY 4	Contractions; Review /âr/*air, are*
DAY 5	Contractions; Review /âr/*air, are*

Objectives

- *To read phonetically regular words*
- *To read and write common word families*
- *To recognize spelling patterns*

Skill Trace

Tested *r-Controlled Vowel /âr/air, are*

Introduce	T312–T315
Reteach	S38–S39
Review	**T324–T325, T342–T343, T432**
Test	Theme 5
Maintain	Theme 6, T360

r-Controlled Vowel /âr/air, are

Blair's fair hair was long and shaggy.

A pair of Blair's pals dared him to get a haircut.

Blair was not scared, so he went to take care of his hair.

He went to a stylist who has a flair with hair.

Blair sat down in the stylist's chair for a haircut.

The stylist was careful with his pair of scissors.

Now Blair's pals stare at his shiny, bare head!

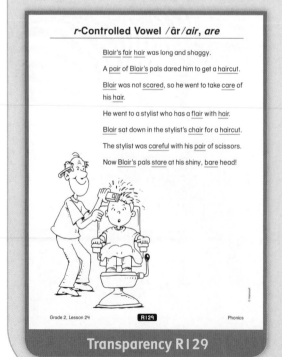

Grade 2, Lesson 24   R129   Phonics

Transparency R129

Work with Patterns

INTRODUCE PHONOGRAMS Write the following phonograms at the top of two columns.

-air   -are

Tell children that these are the endings of some words. Slide your hand under the letters as you read each phonogram. Repeat, having children read the phonograms with you.

BUILD AND READ WORDS Write the letter *f* in front of each phonogram. Guide children to read each word: /f/-*air, fair* and /f/-*are, fare*. Then have children name other words that end with *-air* and *-are*. Have them tell which letter or letters to add to build each word, and write the word in the appropriate column. Have children read each column of words. Then point to words at random and have children read them.

Read Words in Context

READ SENTENCES Display **Transparency R129** or write the sentences on the board. Have children choral-read the sentences as you track the print. Then ask volunteers to read each sentence aloud and to underline words with *-air* and *-are*. Invite volunteers to add the words *Blair, hair, pair, fair, dared, haircut, scared, care, flair, chair, careful, stare,* and *bare* to the appropriate columns.

5-DAY SPELLING
DAY 1 Pretest
DAY 2 Word Building
DAY 3 State the Generalization
DAY 4 Review
DAY 5 Posttest

Review Spelling Words

STATE THE GENERALIZATION FOR /âr/air, are   List spelling words 1–10 on chart paper or on the board. Circle the words *hair* and *chair*, and have children read them aloud. Ask: **What is the same in each word?** (The letters *air* stand for the /âr/ sound.) Ask children to name the other spelling words with *air*. (*fair, pair, stair*) Circle the words. Repeat the procedure for *are*, using a different color pen to circle the words.

Have children apply the generalization by naming other words with the /âr/ sound spelled with *air* or *are*. Write the words on the board to show whether they fit the generalization.

 WRITE   Have children write the spelling words in their notebooks. Remind them to use their best handwriting.

Handwriting

LETTER STROKE   Remind children to make their letters smooth and even. They should not be too light or too dark.

Spelling Words

1. **hair**	6. **care**
2. **glare**	7. **share**
3. **fair**	8. **chair**
4. **scare**	9. **rare**
5. **pair**	10. **stair**

Challenge Words

11. **airplane**	14. **haircut**
12. **repair**	15. **careful**
13. **downstairs**	

Decodable Books

Additional Decoding Practice

- **Phonics**
  r-Controlled Vowel /âr/*air, are*
- **Decodable Words**
- **High-Frequency Words**
  See lists in *Decodable Book 20.*
  See also *Decodable Books,*
  online (Take-Home Version).

▲ Decodable Book 20
"A Visit to the County Fair"

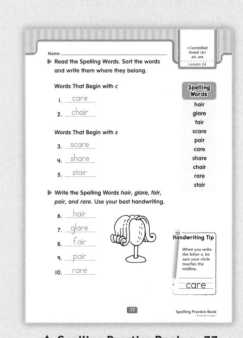

▲ Spelling Practice Book, p. 77

Fluency
Rate

Objectives

- *To build fluency through rereading*
- *To read at an appropriate rate in a manner that sounds like natural speech*

BELOW-LEVEL

Fluency Practice   Have children reread *Decodable Book 20*, Story 24 in the *Strategic Intervention Interactive Reader*, or the appropriate *Leveled Reader* (pp. T376–T379). Have them practice reading the text several times.

Additional Related Reading

- *Animals in the Wild (Animal Worlds)* by Sue Barraclough. Raintree, 2005. **EASY**
- *Good Morning, Africa! (Our Amazing Continents)* by April Pulley Sayre. Millbrook, 2003 **AVERAGE**
- *Dr. White* by Jane Goodall. North-South, 2003. **CHALLENGE**

Review

DIBELS Oral Reading Fluency **ORF**

MODEL USING RATE   Remind children that good readers vary the speed at which they read depending on the difficulty of the words or ideas. Tell children to:

▲ **Student Edition, pp. 284–297**

- read slowly when the words are unfamiliar or the ideas are complicated.
- think about the meaning and adjust their rate so they can understand what they are reading.
- try to increase their speed with each reading by doing timed readings.

(**Think Aloud**)   **I'm going to read part of "Watching in the Wild" aloud several times. The first time I read the text, I'll go slowly to make sure I recognize all the words and understand what the author is saying. The second time, I'll try to read faster without making any mistakes. The third time, I'll try to read even faster.**

Practice/Apply

Routine Card 9

GUIDED PRACTICE   Read page 288 aloud. Then have children practice reading aloud the same page several times with a partner. Circulate among the pairs, providing feedback and encouraging them to increase their speed with each reading.

INDEPENDENT PRACTICE   Have partners take turns reading "Watching in the Wild" aloud, a page at a time. Tell children to read several times, each time increasing their rate.

Use Graphic Aids
Comprehension

Review

REVIEW USING GRAPHIC AIDS Remind children that graphic aids help readers understand ideas and information quickly and easily. On the board, write the different kinds of graphic aids children might encounter when reading nonfiction. Discuss the specific features of each type of graphic aid.

- Chart—shows information in rows, columns, and headings
- Map—shows where places are located
- Diagram—shows parts of something or how something works
- Graph—shows amounts of things
- Time line—shows dates and events over a period of time

Practice/Apply

GUIDED PRACTICE Draw the following chart on the board. Invite children to help you fill in the names and gender of the chimpanzees found on page 290 of "Watching in the Wild." Elicit that the completed chart quickly and easily tells them some information about the chimps.

Name	Gender
David Greybeard	male
Old Flo	female
Mr. McGregor	male

INDEPENDENT PRACTICE Ask children to draw their own chart and add the headings *How It Looks* and *Personality*. Have them fill in the physical features and personality traits for each chimpanzee found on page 290. Have volunteers share their completed charts.

Objectives
- *To identify graphic aids*
- *To analyze and use graphic aids*

Skill Trace

Tested **Use Graphic Aids**

Introduce	T224–T225
Reteach	S30–S31, S42–S43
Review	T261, T277, T289, T316–T317, T345, T361, T371, T424, T445
Test	Theme 5
Maintain	Theme 6, T272

Reading

Student Edition: Paired Selection

Objective

- *To apply word knowledge to the reading of a magazine article*

Genre Study

DISCUSS MAGAZINE ARTICLES   Explain to children that "Chimp Computer Whiz" is a magazine article. Point out that the article was in the magazine shown in the upper left-hand corner of page 298.

TEXT FEATURES   Tell children that most magazine articles give real information about a topic. They have certain features to help readers understand and enjoy what they read. These features may include:

- the title of the article
- photographs with captions
- interesting or exciting beginnings
- facts that prove an idea

USE PRIOR KNOWLEDGE/SET A PURPOSE   Guide children to use prior knowledge and set a purpose for listening. Then ask volunteers to take turns reading the article aloud.

Respond to the Article

MONITOR COMPREHENSION   Ask children to reread the article. Ask:

- **PERSONAL RESPONSE   How well do you think you'd do at the computer game Keo plays?** (Responses will vary.)

- **GENRE   Is "Chimp Computer Whiz" a story or an article? How can you tell?** (The selection is an article because it gives information about a real topic. It uses numbers to prove a point.)

Writing Prompt

Reflect   Have children reflect on the idea of chimps using computers. Ask: **Is this a good thing for chimps to be doing? Why or why not?**

Science

Magazine Article

Chimp Computer Whiz

from *Ask*

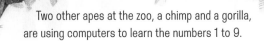

Keo never forgets a face.

Keo is a chimpanzee who lives at Lincoln Park Zoo in Chicago. Five times a week, he sits in front of a special computer screen. The screen flashes the face of a chimp he's never met. When Keo touches the picture of the chimp, he gets treats. Next, the screen flashes two pictures. One is of the first chimp, and one is of a new chimp. If Keo touches the picture of the first chimp, he gets another treat.

Keo plays this game 30 times each day. After months of practice, he can now run through all 30 new faces in just a few minutes.

298

Two other apes at the zoo, a chimp and a gorilla, are using computers to learn the numbers 1 to 9.

Working on the computer is voluntary. So far, only three of the nine apes that have tried it have stayed with it.

Scientists hope that all the apes at the zoo will soon use computer programs to tell which foods they like best and which activities they prefer. Watching the apes use computers should help scientists learn more about how the animals think.

299

SOCIAL STUDIES

SUPPORTING STANDARDS

Animal Training   Tell children that Ivan Pavlov (1849–1936) was a Russian scientist who conducted experiments on dogs. He sounded a bell while showing food to a dog. The dog would start to salivate. After he repeated this several times, Pavlov changed the procedure to see if the dog would do the same thing. Pavlov rang the bell, but did not present food. The dog still salivated. This experiment proved that if you train an animal to expect something, it will continue to expect it even when the event doesn't happen. Have children compare and contrast Pavlov's experiment to the experiments with Keo.

И. П. Павлов
1849–1936

E L L

Reinforce Meaning   Show relevant *Picture Cards* to children as you teach "Chimp Computer Whiz": *Picture Card 32* and *104*. You can also show number cards for 1, 2, 3, 5, 9, 30, and 47 to reinforce the numbers mentioned in the article.

 Connections

Objectives

- *To compare texts*
- *To connect texts to personal experiences*

Comparing Texts

1. The chimpanzees in both selections are being observed so scientists can learn what these animals are capable of doing.   **TEXT TO TEXT**

2. Responses will vary.   **TEXT TO SELF**

3. Possible response: They can conduct formal experiments on animals in captivity and plant life in laboratories.   **TEXT TO WORLD**

Connections

Comparing Texts

❶ How are the chimpanzees in "Watching in the Wild" and "Chimp Computer Whiz" alike?

❷ What animal would you like to observe? Tell why.

❸ What other methods can scientists use to learn about animals?

Phonics

Make a Chart

Write the words *hair* and *care* in a chart. Below each word, write three more words that have the same spelling and sound as the underlined letters. Read your lists to a partner.

hair	care
fair	glare

Fluency Practice

Read with a Partner

Read "Watching in the Wild" aloud with a partner. Take turns reading one page at a time. Work on reading each sentence at the speed in which you usually speak.

Writing

Write About an Event

Write about important events in your life. Tell about them in the order in which they happened. Use a chart to plan what you will tell about first, next, and last.

My Writing Checklist
Writing Trait ▸ Word Choice
- ✔ I use a chart to plan my writing in time order.
- ✔ I use words that help the reader picture what is happening.
- ✔ I use words like *first, next,* and *last.*

300

301

PHONICS

Make a Chart Suggest that children think of rhyming words to help them add words to their charts. Remind them that some words with different spellings rhyme and to be careful to place words in the correct column.

hair	care
chair	glare
stair	dare
fair	share
pair	rare

FLUENCY

Read with a Partner Remind partners to take turns reading one page at a time. Model how to read one sentence at a moderate speaking speed. Read the fifth sentence on *Student Edition* page 288 moderately, but slowing down for the phrase *blended in with the jungle.*

WRITING

Write About an Event Help children brainstorm important events. Encourage them to tell about the events in sequence. Remind children to use descriptive words to help the reader visualize what they are saying.

Portfolio Opportunity Children may choose to place their writing in their portfolios.

 Build Robust Vocabulary

Objectives

- *To review robust vocabulary*
- *To figure out a word's meaning based on the context*

REVIEW [Tested ✓]

Vocabulary: Lesson 24

extinct	cradled
pledge	raggedy
patience	personalities
tedious	distance
blended	crumpled

Review Robust Vocabulary

USE VOCABULARY IN DIFFERENT CONTEXTS Remind children of the Student-Friendly Explanations of the Vocabulary Words introduced on Days I and 2. Then discuss each word using the following examples:

extinct

- What could you do to help an endangered animal avoid becoming extinct?
- Why might scientists be interested in extinct plants and animals?

pledge

- What is something you might pledge to every day? Why do people make pledges?
- What kind of pledge might be hard to keep? Explain.

patience

- Why do you need patience when learning to do something?
- How can you tell if someone has patience?

tedious

- Tell about the most tedious task you have ever had to do.
- When might a fun activity become tedious?

blended

- Would it taste good if you blended peanut butter and broccoli? Why or why not?

- If someone said you blended into the environment, what might you be wearing?

cradled

- Why do both babies and puppies need to be cradled?

- Are you too old to be cradled? Why or why not?

raggedy

- What do you consider to be raggedy clothing?

- Would you get rid of a favorite shirt if it became raggedy? Why or why not?

distance

- Would you rather visit someone who lives close to your home, or someone who lives a distance away? Why?

- What stores are good to have only a short distance from home? Why?

personalities

- Would you rather be with people who have quiet or noisy personalities? Explain.

- Think about the personalities of some of your favorite book characters. What do you like about their personalities?

crumpled

- Would you read a crumpled note if you found it in the trash? Why or why not?

- Do you prefer your school clothes crumpled or neatly pressed? Explain.

▼ **Student-Friendly Explanations**

Student-Friendly Explanations

extinct	If an animal is extinct, there are no more of that kind of animal alive.
pledge	When you make a pledge, you promise to do something.
patience	If you can wait for someone or something without complaining or getting restless, you have patience.
tedious	When something is boring and takes a long time to do, it is tedious.

Grade 2, Lesson 24   **R132**   Vocabulary

Transparency R132

Student-Friendly Explanations

blended	When things are blended, they are mixed together so you can't tell there are separate parts.
cradled	If you cradle something, you hold it closely as if you were taking care of it.
raggedy	When something is raggedy, it looks rough and torn at the edges, like a rag.
distance	Distance is how far away something is.
personalities	People's personalities are made up of all the ways they act, think, and feel that make them special.
crumpled	If you crumple something, you gently crush it or bunch it up.

Grade 2, Lesson 24   **R133**   Vocabulary

Transparency R133

Synonyms
Vocabulary

Objectives

- *To identify and use synonyms*
- *To use reference books such as a thesaurus or dictionary to locate synonyms*

Skill Trace

 Tested **Synonyms**

Introduce	T268–T269
Reteach	S44–S45
Review	**T352–T353, T437, T446**
Test	Theme 5

 MONITOR PROGRESS

Synonyms

IF children have difficulty identifying and using synonyms,	**THEN** create a list of familiar verbs and show them how to use a dictionary or thesaurus to find other words that mean about the same thing.

Small-Group Instruction, pp. S44–S45:

- ● **BELOW-LEVEL:** Reteach
- ● **ON-LEVEL:** Reinforce
- ● **ADVANCED:** Extend

Review

IDENTIFY SYNONYMS Write these sentences on the board:

> Jane's plan was <u>simple.</u>
>
> Jane's plan was <u>easy.</u>

Ask: **How are the underlined words alike?** (They mean about the same thing.) Remind children that words that have the same or almost the same meaning are called synonyms. Explain that they can look up a word in a thesaurus or a dictionary to find synonyms for it.

Point out these words on page 286 of "Watching in the Wild": *find, sit, quietly,* and *watch.* Model how to think of and locate synonyms for *find:*

> **Think Aloud** After I read the word *find,* I'll list other words I know that mean the same or nearly the same thing: *locate, discover.* I'll also look up the word in a thesaurus or a dictionary to check my words and to see if there are any others. Here are three more synonyms: *come upon, recover, track down.*

Ask children to name synonyms for the rest of the words. Then ask them to read these sentences:

> Jane <u>found</u> that chimpanzees use tools.
>
> Jane <u>discovered</u> that chimpanzees use tools.

Point out that *found* and *discovered* are synonyms, but *discovered* is a stronger word than *found.* It is more descriptive, and it better explains the idea that Jane was the first scientist to realize that chimpanzees used tools. Write the following synonym pairs on the board. Guide children to identify the word that is more descriptive in each pair.

sit	squat	(squat)
quietly	noiselessly	(noiselessly)
watch	observe	(observe)

Practice/Apply

GUIDED PRACTICE Display **Transparency R130.** Read aloud the first set of words. Then have children read the words aloud with you. Identify the word in the second column that is a synonym for *mixed*. (*blended*) Ask volunteers to match the synonyms in the columns and tell which word is stronger. Then use one word in a sentence and ask a volunteer to repeat the sentence, inserting its synonym. Repeat with other words.

INDEPENDENT PRACTICE Have partners read the second set of words on **Transparency R130.** Then have partners match the synonyms in the two columns and identify which one is stronger. Then have children use a thesaurus or dictionary to find additional synonyms for each word.

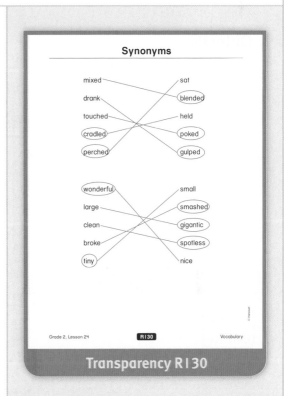

Transparency R130

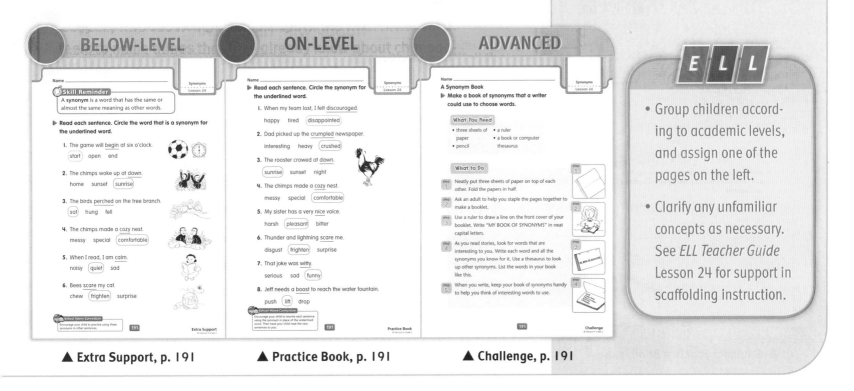

▲ Extra Support, p. 191   ▲ Practice Book, p. 191   ▲ Challenge, p. 191

ELL

• Group children according to academic levels, and assign one of the pages on the left.

• Clarify any unfamiliar concepts as necessary. See *ELL Teacher Guide* Lesson 24 for support in scaffolding instruction.

Grammar
Forms of Be

Quick Write

5-DAY GRAMMAR	
DAY 1	Introduce Forms of *Be*: *am, is, are*
DAY 2	Forms of *Be*: *was, were*
DAY 3	**Subject-Verb Agreement**
DAY 4	Apply to Writing
DAY 5	Weekly Review

Objective

• *To introduce subject-verb agreement with forms of* Be

Daily Proofreading

All the childs ran in the race on labor day.

(children; Labor Day.)

TECHNOLOGY

Go online www.harcourtschool.com/storytown
Grammar Glossary

▲ Grammar Practice Book, p. 86

Review

SUBJECT-VERB AGREEMENT WITH FORMS OF *Be*

Write these sentences on the board:

> I am a good student.
>
> Emily is a good student, too.
>
> Science and math are her favorite subjects.
>
> The science class was interesting.
>
> We were happy to learn about great apes.

Read aloud the first sentence and underline the verb. Elicit from children that *am* is used to tell about the present and about a singular subject. Repeat the procedure for the rest of the sentences, pointing out that *is* and *are* tell about the present, while *was* and *were* tell about the past. Say: **The verbs** *is, are, am, was,* **and** *were* **must agree with the subject of the sentence. Use the verbs** *are* **and** *were* **with plural subjects. Use** *is* **and** *am* **with singular subjects.**

Practice/Apply

GUIDED PRACTICE   Write these sentences on the board.

> Ken _____ happy with his drawing. (is/was)
>
> His drawings _____ amazing. (are/were)
>
> I _____ a good artist, too. (am)

Read the first sentence aloud and circle the subject.
Ask: **Does this noun tell about one or more than one?**
Ask children which form of *be* to use. Fill in the verb they suggest and read the sentence aloud. Ask: **Does this verb match the subject?** Complete the remaining sentences with children.

INDEPENDENT PRACTICE   Have children write sentences about their favorite animal using *is, are, am, was,* or *were*. Have them share their sentences with a partner to check for correct usage and subject/verb agreement.

Writing
Paragraph That Compares (or Contrasts)

5-DAY WRITING
DAY 1	Introduce
DAY 2	Prewrite
DAY 3	Draft
DAY 4	Revise
DAY 5	Revise

Draft a Paragraph

REVIEW WITH A LITERATURE MODEL Tell children that parts of "Watching in the Wild" use comparisons. Have children turn to page 293 in their *Student Edition*, and invite them to tell how chimpanzees are like people. Point out the following:

- Sentences give details about the humanlike things chimpanzees do.
- Words that "show" are used throughout the paragraph.
- Sentences directly and indirectly compare chimps to people.

Point out examples of forms of *be* used in the paragraph. Ask children to explain how they could use them in their own writing.

DRAFT A PARAGRAPH THAT COMPARES OR CONTRASTS Have children use their filled-in graphic organizers, pictures, and what they know about their subjects to write a paragraph that compares or contrasts two living things. Remind them that each sentence in their paragraph should be an example that supports the main idea sentence. Tell them to use forms of *be* when necessary.

WORD CHOICE As children write their paragraphs, remind them to include words that "show" rather than tell. Encourage them to use compare words and contrast words such as *alike, like, same as, similar, different,* and *unlike.*

CONFER WITH CHILDREN Meet with children, helping them as they write their comparison or contrast paragraphs. Offer encouragement for what they are doing well and make constructive suggestions for improving an aspect of the writing, as needed.

Objectives
- *To read and discuss a writing model*
- *To draft a paragraph that compares or contrasts*

Writing Prompt

Write a Poem Have children write a poem about Jane Goodall and the chimpanzees in "Watching in the Wild."

▲ Writer's Companion, Lesson 24

ADVANCED

Paragraph Organization Tell children that one way they can organize their paragraph is to write about the similarities or differences in the order of their importance: least important to most important.

Day at a Glance

Day 4

 **phonics** and Spelling

- Introduce: Contractions
- Review: *r*-Controlled Vowel /âr/*air*, *are*

Fluency

- Rate
- "Watching in the Wild," *Student Edition*, pp. 284–297

 Read!

Comprehension

 Review: Use Graphic Aids

Robust Vocabulary

- Review: *extinct, pledge, blended, cradled, raggedy, personalities, distance, crumpled, patience, tedious*

Grammar Quick Write

- Review: Forms of *Be*

Writing ✏️

- Paragraph That Compares (or Contrasts)

Warm-Up Routines

Oral Language

Objective *To listen attentively and respond appropriately to oral communication*

Question of the Day

What do you like about playing hide-and-seek?

Help children brainstorm ideas about what they like about playing the game of hide-and-seek. Record their ideas in a web. Use the following prompts:

- **When do you like to play hide-and-seek?**
- **Where do you most like to play hide-and-seek—inside or outside? Why?**
- **Whom do you like to play hide-and-seek with? Why?**
- **What are the best hiding places?**

Read Aloud

Objective *To listen for enjoyment*

BIG BOOK OF RHYMES AND POEMS Display the poem "Hide-and-Seek" on page 44, and read the title. Tell children to listen to the poem for enjoyment. Then read the poem aloud. Elicit that the speaker of the poem is hiding up in a tree. Explain that the words *limb*, *trunk*, and *leaves* describe different parts of a tree. Draw the outline of a tree on the board, and ask volunteers to label these parts. Then reread the poem and invite children to join in when they are able.

Hide-and-Seek

It's hide and seek.
I climb a tree
and from a leafy limb
I watch my seeker seeking me
and sneak a look at him.

The trunk is strong
to lean upon.
The leaves leave room to peek.
If it had apples for me, too,
I'd stay up here a week.

Constance Levy

▲ **Big Book of Rhymes and Poems, p. 44**

Word Wall

Objective *To read high-frequency words*

REVIEW HIGH-FREQUENCY WORDS Arrange the words *quite*, *picture*, *imagine*, *above*, *sweat*, and *early* in two columns. Divide the class into two groups. Have children in the first group choral-read the first column of words, snapping their fingers to keep time. The second group can do the same with the second column. Then have groups switch columns and repeat.

quite	above
picture	sweat
imagine	early

 Contractions

phonics

5-DAY PHONICS
DAY 1 Reintroduce /âr/*air, are*
DAY 2 Word Building with /âr/*air, are*
DAY 3 Word Building with /âr/*air, are*
DAY 4 Contractions; Review /âr/*air, are*
DAY 5 Contractions; Review /âr/*air, are*

Objectives

- *To identify and read contractions*
- *To identify words that contractions stand for*
- *To identify letters that are omitted from contractions*
- *To combine words into contractions*

Skill Trace

 Tested Contractions

Introduce	Grade 1
Reintroduce	**T358**
Review	T368
Test	Theme 5

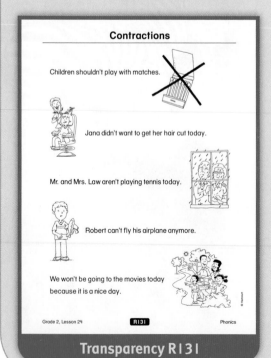

Contractions

Children shouldn't play with matches.

Jana didn't want to get her hair cut today.

Mr. and Mrs. Law aren't playing tennis today.

Robert can't fly his airplane anymore.

We won't be going to the movies today because it is a nice day.

Grade 2, Lesson 24   R131   Phonics

Transparency R131

Teach/Model

INTRODUCE CONTRACTIONS Write the following sentences on the board, underlining the words as shown.

I <u>did not</u> know the answer.

I <u>didn't</u> know the answer.

did not

didn't

Read the sentences, and guide children to notice the contraction. Tell children that a contraction is a shortened way of saying and writing one or more words. Explain that when a contraction is formed, one or more letters are left out and an apostrophe takes the place of the missing letter or letters. Then underline *o* in *not* to show the letter that is left out of *didn't*. Circle the apostrophe.

MODEL DECODING CONTRACTIONS Model how to blend and read the contraction *didn't*.

- Cover the *n't* and have children read /did/.
- Cover the first syllable and have children read /n't/.
- Then have children read the word *didn't*.

Guided Practice

READ WORDS Write the words *hasn't*, *isn't*, and *wasn't* on the board. Read each word, and have children read it after you.

Practice/Apply

READ SENTENCES Display **Transparency R131** or write the sentences on the board or on chart paper. Have children read the sentences aloud. Remind them to use what they have learned about contractions to help them read accurately.

r-Controlled Vowel /âr/ air, are

phonics *and Spelling*

5-DAY SPELLING

DAY 1	Pretest
DAY 2	Word Building
DAY 3	State the Generalization
DAY 4	Review
DAY 5	Posttest

Build Words

REVIEW THE WORDS   Have children open their notebooks to the spelling words that they wrote on Day 3. Have them read the words several times and then close their notebooks.

MAP LETTERS TO SOUNDS   Have children follow your directions to change, add, or take off one or two letters in each of the following words to spell a spelling word. Have them write the spelling word on a sheet of paper. Then have a volunteer change the spelling of the word on the board so that children can self-check their spelling.

- Write *stare* on the board. Ask: **Which spelling words can you make by changing one letter?** *(scare, share)*

- Write *air* on the board. Ask: **Which spelling words can you make by adding a letter to the beginning?** *(hair, fair, pair)*

- Write *flair* on the board. Ask: **Which spelling words can you make by changing the first two letters?** *(chair, stair)*

Follow a similar procedure with the following words: *flare (glare)*, *dare (care, rare)*.

CHALLENGE WORDS   Write the first or second syllable of each challenge word on the board. Ask children to spell each word in its entirety by providing the missing letters. Have them use a dictionary to locate the correct spelling of any word they are unsure how to spell. Then have children write each word two or three times until they know it.

Objective

- *To use /âr/air, are and other known letter-sounds to spell and write words*

Spelling Words

1.	**hair**	6.	**care**
2.	**glare**	7.	**share**
3.	**fair**	8.	**chair**
4.	**scare**	9.	**rare**
5.	**pair**	10.	**stair**

Challenge Words

11.	**airplane**	14.	**haircut**
12.	**repair**	15.	**careful**
13.	**downstairs**		

BELOW-LEVEL

Focus on Patterns Write the spelling words on the board, with a blank where the letters *air* or *are* should be. Then prompt children to complete each word by asking questions such as: **What letters can you add to *st___* to make *stair*?** Have children spell each completed word.

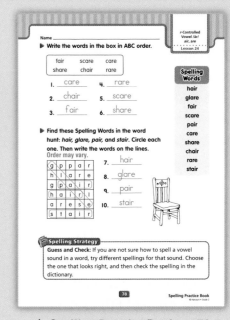

▲ Spelling Practice Book, p. 78

Fluency
Rate

Objectives

- *To build fluency through rereading*
- *To increase reading rate while reading in a manner that sounds like natural speech*

BELOW-LEVEL

Echo-Read On the board, write words and names from the selection that children have trouble reading fluently. Read each word or name aloud and have children repeat. Repeat until children can read the words and names effortlessly.

 MONITOR PROGRESS

Fluency

IF children have difficulty reading at an appropriate rate,	**THEN** model reading at an appropriate rate and have the children echo-read with you.

Small-Group Instruction, pp. S40–S41:

- **BELOW-LEVEL:** Reteach
- **ON-LEVEL:** Reinforce
- **ADVANCED:** Extend

Review

 DIBELS Oral Reading Fluency **ORF**

MODEL USING RATE
Read aloud pages 290–291 of "Watching in the Wild." Point out the words *silvery*, *raggedy*, *gardener*, and *personalities*.

▲ Student Edition, pp. 284–297

Think Aloud I am going to practice saying the words *silvery*, *raggedy*, *gardener*, and *personalities* before I read so that I can pronounce them easily. I know I'll be able to read faster if I can pronounce these challenging words correctly.

Practice /Apply

Routine Card 8 **GUIDED PRACTICE** Have children echo-read pages 290–291 with you, matching your reading rate.

INDEPENDENT PRACTICE Have children read along as they listen to "Watching in the Wild" on *Audiotext Grade 2*, CD 5. Have them practice reading the selection several times until they can read it in "one voice" at the rate established by the speaker on the recording.

Use Graphic Aids

Comprehension

Review

EXPLAIN GRAPHIC AIDS   Ask children to explain the purpose of graphic aids. (Graphic aids show information and help readers understand ideas and information quickly and easily.) Explain that maps can provide valuable visual information about specific places. Ask children to name other graphic aids they have studied, such as diagrams, charts, graphs, and time lines.

Practice /Apply

GUIDED PRACTICE   Display **Transparency R127**. Reread the paragraph aloud to children and ask them to identify the graphic aid. (a map) Ask:

- **What does the map show?** (The map shows the outlines of the countries in Africa. It also names the oceans on either side of Africa.)

- **How does the map help you understand what you are reading?** (It shows some of the wild animals in Africa.)

INDEPENDENT PRACTICE   Ask children to tell about a graphic aid in "Watching in the Wild." (Possible response: The time line of Jane Goodall's life helps me understand more easily when Jane lived and first did her important research on chimpanzees.)

Objectives

- *To identify graphic aids*
- *To analyze and use graphic aids*

Skill Trace

 Use Graphic Aids

Introduce	T224–T225
Reteach	S30–S31, S42–S43
Review	T261, T277, T289, T316–T317, T345, T361 T371, T424, T445
Test	Theme 5
Maintain	Theme 6, T272

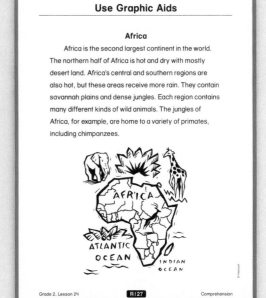

Use Graphic Aids

Africa

Africa is the second largest continent in the world. The northern half of Africa is hot and dry with mostly desert land. Africa's central and southern regions are also hot, but these areas receive more rain. They contain savannah plains and dense jungles. Each region contains many different kinds of wild animals. The jungles of Africa, for example, are home to a variety of primates, including chimpanzees.

Grade 2, Lesson 24   R127   Comprehension

Transparency R127

Build Robust Vocabulary

Objectives

- *To review robust vocabulary*
- *To understand vocabulary in new contexts*

REVIEW ✓ Tested

Vocabulary: Lesson 24

extinct	cradled
pledge	raggedy
patience	personalities
tedious	distance
blended	crumpled

Extend Word Meanings

USE VOCABULARY IN DIFFERENT CONTEXTS Remind children of the Student-Friendly Explanations of the Vocabulary Words. Then discuss the words, using the following activities:

distance Tell children that you will make some statements about traveling. If children think the statements have to do with traveling a short distance, they should say, "I traveled a short distance." If the statements have to do with traveling a long distance, they should say, "I traveled a long distance."

> It took 10 minutes to get to school.
> Sometimes, we drive for hours in the car.
> It's a quick trip to the grocery store.
> I fell asleep on the way to my cousin's house.

crumpled, raggedy Tell children that you will name some things that might be crumpled or raggedy. If children think the thing is crumpled or raggedy, they should slouch in their seat. If not, they should sit up very straight.

> a dancer's top hat and vest   recently pressed pants
> torn jeans   pieces of wrinkled paper

patience, tedious Tell children that you will name some tasks that might require them to have patience because the tasks are tedious. If children think they will need patience because the tasks are tedious, they should stand. If not, they should remain seated.

> running a race
> untangling shoelace knots
> answering math questions
> finding a book to read

Word Relationships

SYNONYMS Remind children that a synonym is a word that means the same, or almost the same, as another word. Write these sentences on the board, underlining the words as shown.

> The <u>characters</u> in that play are funny. (personalities)
>
> The dodo <u>died out</u> many years ago. (became extinct)
>
> Dad <u>held</u> the baby in his arms. (cradled)
>
> Kamaya made a <u>promise</u> to clean up the kitchen. (pledge)
>
> Roy sang the <u>tiresome</u> song over and over. (tedious)

Ask children to read the sentences aloud and replace each underlined word with its Vocabulary Word synonym.

ANTONYMS Tell children that an antonym is a word that means the opposite of another word. Write these sentences on the board, underlining the words as shown.

> Erin's <u>impatience</u> kept her from learning how to tie her shoes. (patience)
>
> The drink <u>separated</u> into two liquids. (blended)
>
> Myra's <u>neat</u> haircut looked nice. (raggedy)
>
> The <u>nearness</u> of her job made it easy for Ms. Tent to get there. (distance)
>
> John's shirt was clean and <u>pressed</u>. (crumpled)

Ask children to orally revise the sentences as needed to replace each underlined word with its Vocabulary Word antonym.

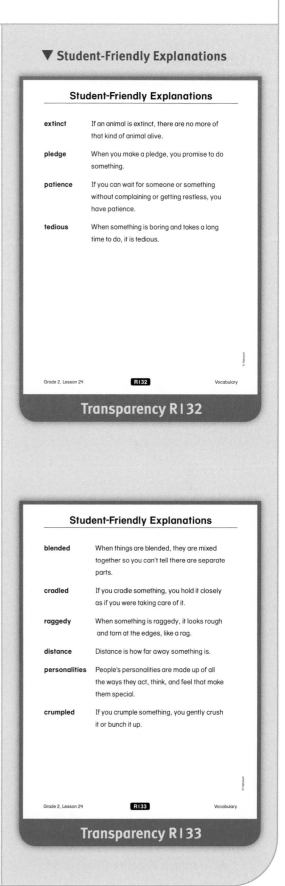

▼ Student-Friendly Explanations

Student-Friendly Explanations

extinct	If an animal is extinct, there are no more of that kind of animal alive.
pledge	When you make a pledge, you promise to do something.
patience	If you can wait for someone or something without complaining or getting restless, you have patience.
tedious	When something is boring and takes a long time to do, it is tedious.

Grade 2, Lesson 24   R132   Vocabulary

Transparency R132

Student-Friendly Explanations

blended	When things are blended, they are mixed together so you can't tell there are separate parts.
cradled	If you cradle something, you hold it closely as if you were taking care of it.
raggedy	When something is raggedy, it looks rough and torn at the edges, like a rag.
distance	Distance is how far away something is.
personalities	People's personalities are made up of all the ways they act, think, and feel that make them special.
crumpled	If you crumple something, you gently crush it or bunch it up.

Grade 2, Lesson 24   R133   Vocabulary

Transparency R133

Grammar *Quick Write*

Forms of *Be*

5-DAY GRAMMAR	
DAY 1	Introduce Forms of *Be*: *am*, *is*, *are*
DAY 2	Forms of *Be*: *was*, *were*
DAY 3	Subject-Verb Agreement
DAY 4	**Apply to Writing**
DAY 5	Weekly Review

Objective

• *To write using forms of* Be

Daily Proofreading

When did those familys move.
(families, move?)

Writing Trait

Strengthening Conventions

Verbs Use this short lesson with children's own writing to build a foundation for revising/editing longer connected text on Day 5. See also *Writer's Companion*, Lesson 24.

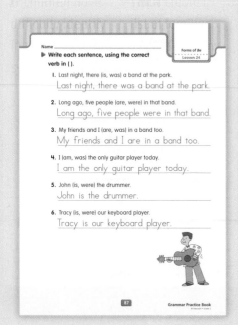

▲ **Grammar Practice Book, p. 87**

Review

DISCUSS FORMS OF *BE* Review what children have learned about the forms of *be*, using the following points:

• The verbs *am*, *is*, and *are* tell about the present.

• The verbs *was* and *were* tell about the past.

• The verbs *am*, *is*, and *was* tell about singular subjects.

• The verbs *are* and *were* tell about plural subjects.

• Verbs must agree with their subjects.

Write the following sentences on the board:

> They were happy to help.   They are happy to help.
>
> She is eight.   She was seven last year.

Have children identify the verb and tell if the subject is singular or plural.

Practice/Apply

GUIDED PRACTICE Tell children that you are going to write five sentences using the forms of *be*. Model writing the first sentence: *I am sorry about your accident.* Elicit additional sentence ideas from children using *is*, *are*, *was*, and *were*. After you write each sentence, ask a volunteer to underline the verb and circle the subject. Then have children check to make sure the verb and subject match.

 INDEPENDENT PRACTICE Ask children to write five sentences using the forms of *be*. Encourage them to use these sentence frames:

> _____ am a _____.
>
> _____ is _____ when _____.
>
> _____ and _____ are _____.
>
> _____ was a _____.
>
> _____ were _____ about _____.

Have partners exchange completed sentences and check that verbs match the subject.

Writing
Paragraph That Compares (or Contrasts)

5-DAY WRITING

DAY 1	Introduce
DAY 2	Prewrite
DAY 3	Draft
DAY 4	**Revise**
DAY 5	Revise

Write and Revise

WRITE   Have children continue writing their paragraphs that compare or contrast. Remind them to use words that show how their subjects are alike or different.

WORD CHOICE   Remind children that words that "show" rather than tell make writing more interesting. Words and phrases such as *like*, *the same as*, *share*, *unlike*, and *different from* make a paragraph that compares or contrasts easier to understand. Remind children to use synonyms in their writing so they avoid repeated words.

REVISE   Have children read their paragraphs to a partner. They can use the list of criteria for a paragraph that compares or contrasts to improve their writing.

Paragraph That Compares (or Contrasts)

- A paragraph that *compares* tells how two things are alike. A paragraph that *contrasts* tells how two things are different.

- The first sentence introduces the topic or one of the subjects.

- Other sentences give examples of how another subject is the same or different from the first subject.

- The paragraph uses words such as *like* or *different*.

Tell children to make notes on their drafts of the changes they will make. Encourage them to use Editor's Marks. Remind children to check that they have used the correct form of *be* in their writing. Save children's paragraphs to revise further on Day 5.

Objectives

- *To revise a draft of a paragraph that compares or contrasts*
- *To use forms of* be *correctly*

Writing Prompt

Compare/Contrast   Have children write one or more funny sentences about two unlike objects.

BELOW-LEVEL

Revise   If children are unsure of how to revise their paragraphs, review each point on the list of criteria with them. Suggest that they use it as a checklist to make sure their paragraphs follow the correct format.

Warm-Up Routines

Day at a Glance
Day 5

 **and Spelling**

- Review: Contractions
- Posttest: *r*-Controlled Vowel /âr/ *air, are*

Fluency

- Rate
- "Watching in the Wild," *Student Edition*, pp. 284–297

Read!

Comprehension

 Review: Use Graphic Aids

- *Read-Aloud Anthology:* "Hanging On"

Robust Vocabulary

- Cumulative Review

Grammar [Quick Write]

- Review: Forms of *Be*

Writing

- Paragraph That Compares (or Contrasts)

 Oral Language

Objective *To listen attentively and respond appropriately to oral communication*

> ### Question of the Day
>
> **Is a tree a good place to hide?**
> **Why or why not?**

Invite children to think about why a tree might or might not be a good place to hide. Use the following prompts.

- **Which animals can easily hide in a tree?**
- **Which animals can't hide in trees?**
- **Is a tree a safe or unsafe place for children to hide? Explain.**
- **Which kinds of trees might make the best hiding places? Explain.**

On the board, record children's ideas about why a tree is or isn't a good hiding place.

Read Aloud

Objective *To identify alliteration in poetry*

BIG BOOK OF RHYMES AND POEMS Display "Hide-and-Seek" on page 44. Ask children to listen for words that start with the same sound. Then read the poem aloud. Guide children to identify examples of alliteration in the poem. (hide, him; seek, seeker seeking, sneak; leafy limb, look, lean, leaves leave; tree, trunk) Then read the poem again, encouraging children to join in. Invite children to draw a picture of the poet's idea of playing hide-and-seek in a tree. Suggest to children that the "I" in the poem may not be a human.

Hide-and-Seek

It's hide and seek.
I climb a tree
and from a leafy limb
I watch my seeker seeking me
and sneak a look at him.

The trunk is strong
to lean upon.
The leaves leave room to peek.
If it had apples for me, too,
I'd stay up here a week.

Constance Levy

▲ **Big Book of Rhymes and Poems, p. 44**

Word Wall

Objective *To read high-frequency words*

REVIEW HIGH-FREQUENCY WORDS Review the words *already*, *finally*, *brother*, *clear*, *straight*, and *especially*. Point to a card at random, and ask children to read the words.

already	finally	brother
clear	straight	especially

Contractions

5-DAY PHONICS	
DAY 1	Reintroduce /âr/air, are
DAY 2	Word Building with /âr/air, are
DAY 3	Word Building with /âr/air, are
DAY 4	Contractions; Review /âr/air, are
DAY 5	Contractions; Review /âr/air, are

Objective

- *To identify and read contractions*

Skill Trace

| Tested | **Contractions** |

Introduce	Grade 1
Reintroduce	T358
Review	T368
Test	Theme 5

Review

READ CONTRACTIONS Write the words *have not* on the board. Cross out the letter *o* and insert an apostrophe (') to show how to write the contraction *haven't*. Repeat with the word *cannot*. Ask children to tell what letters *n't* stand for. *(not)*

Practice/Apply

GUIDED PRACTICE Write the following words on the board: *don't*, *hadn't*, *won't*, *shouldn't*, and *aren't*. Then make a chart as shown. Guide children to write the contractions and the two words they were shortened from.

Contraction	Two Words Formed From	
don't	do	not
hadn't	had	not

INDEPENDENT PRACTICE Have children read aloud the words in the chart.

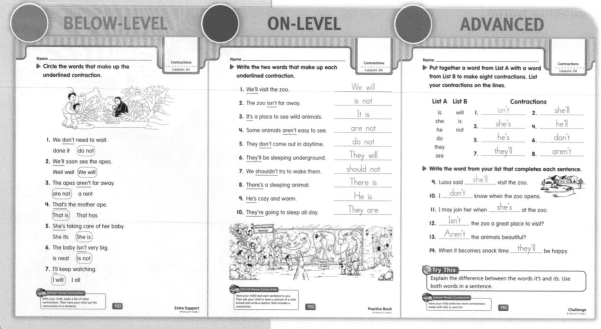

▲ Extra Support, p. 192   ▲ Practice Book, p. 192   ▲ Challenge, p. 192

- Group children according to academic levels, and assign one of the pages on the left.

- Clarify any unfamiliar concepts as necessary. See *ELL Teacher Guide* Lesson 24 for support in scaffolding instruction.

5-DAY SPELLING

DAY 1	Pretest
DAY 2	Word Building
DAY 3	State the Generalization
DAY 4	Review
DAY 5	Posttest

r-Controlled Vowel /âr/ *air, are* phonics *and Spelling*

Assess

POSTTEST   Assess children's progress. Use the dictation sentences from Day 1.

Words with /âr/ *air, are*

1.	hair	The puppy has curly black **hair**.
2.	glare	The **glare** of the sun is blinding.
3.	fair	A referee follows rules so the game is **fair** for both teams.
4.	scare	Sharp teeth **scare** me!
5.	pair	Robby lost a **pair** of blue socks.
6.	care	The vet will **care** for the injured bird.
7.	share	Would you like to **share** this muffin with me?
8.	chair	That old **chair** is missing a leg.
9.	rare	It is **rare** that I don't want ice cream for dessert!
10.	stair	Josie skipped every other **stair**.

ADVANCED

Challenge Words   Use the challenge words in these dictation sentences.

11.	airplane	The **airplane** flew through the sky.
12.	repair	Who will **repair** the broken window?
13.	downstairs	Leda keeps her art supplies **downstairs**.
14.	haircut	Charlie's **haircut** is too short.
15.	careful	Be **careful** when you use scissors.

   WRITING APPLICATION   Have children write riddles for two or more spelling words. Remind them to write neatly.

What has four legs, a seat, and a back? (a chair)

What do you step on to get to another floor? (a stair)

Objective

• *To use r-controlled vowel /âr/air, are and other known letter-sounds to spell and write words*

Spelling Words

1.	**hair**	6.	**care**
2.	**glare**	7.	**share**
3.	**fair**	8.	**chair**
4.	**scare**	9.	**rare**
5.	**pair**	10.	**stair**

Challenge Words

11.	**airplane**	14.	**haircut**
12.	**repair**	15.	**careful**
13.	**downstairs**		

 Fluency

Rate

Objective

• *To read fluently at an appropriate rate*

 ASSESSMENT

Monitoring Progress

Periodically, take a timed sample of children's oral reading and record the number of words read correctly per minute. Children should accurately read approximately 90–100 words per minute at the end of Grade 2.

Fluency Support Materials

    Fluency Builders, Grade 2, Lesson 24

 Audiotext *Student Edition* selections are available on *Audiotext Grade 2*, CD 5.

 Strategic Intervention Teacher Guide, Lesson 24

Readers' Theater

 DIBELS Oral Reading Fluency **ORF**

PERFORM "WATCHING IN THE WILD" To help children improve their fluency, have them perform "Watching in the Wild" as Readers' Theater. Use the following procedures:

 ▲ **Student Edition, pp. 284–297**

• Discuss with children how the different features of the selection might sound. Point out the italicized introduction, the headings, and the time line. Discuss how children might present each feature to set it apart from the main text. For example, you might suggest that children read the headings in a loud, crisp voice. Within the main text, point out words and punctuation that indicate a change in expression or intonation.

• Have groups of five children read the story together. Each child should read aloud one section of the selection.

• Monitor the groups as they read. Provide feedback and support, paying attention to the rate readers use.

E L L

Develop Vocabulary Model how to pronounce unfamiliar vocabulary in the section children will read aloud with their group. Have them imitate your expression, intonation, and the rate at which you read as they say the words after you. Provide feedback and support.

Use Graphic Aids
Comprehension

Review

REVIEW THE SKILL   Remind children that good readers pay attention to graphic aids. Review that graphic aids such as charts, maps, diagrams, graphs, and time lines help readers understand ideas and information quickly and easily.

▲ **Read-Aloud Anthology** "Hanging On," p. 88

SET A PURPOSE FOR LISTENING   Guide children to set a purpose for listening that includes

- listening for details about the great apes.

- listening for details about why the great apes are in danger.

Practice/Apply

GUIDED PRACTICE   As you read aloud "Hanging On," record in a chart the following information about the great apes. Then use the map to show the area of the world where each kind of ape is found.

GREAT APES			
gorilla	**chimpanzee**	**orangutan**	**bonobo**
largest great ape	uses tools	largest tree-dwelling animal	smallest great ape

INDEPENDENT PRACTICE   Have children review what they know about the great apes by looking at the chart. Then have them tell which of the great apes may be in the most danger and why. (Possible response: The gorilla may be in the most danger because it is the largest. It needs the most space to live and perhaps is the easiest target for hunters.)

Objectives

- *To identify graphic aids*
- *To use graphic aids*

Skill Trace

 Tested   Use Graphic Aids

Introduce	T224–T225
Reteach	S30–S31, S42–S43
Review	T261, T277, T289, T316–T317, T345, T361, T371, T424, T445
Test	Theme 5
Maintain	Theme 6, T272

Understand Graphic Aids   If children have difficulty recalling words related to graphic aids, model using the vocabulary as you discuss each kind. For example, after you have modeled how to use a map, have children repeat words you have used, such as *ocean, continent, north, south, east,* and *west.*

Build Robust Vocabulary

Objectives

- *To review robust vocabulary*
- *To organize word meanings in order to understand word relationships*

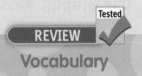

REVIEW Tested

Vocabulary

Lesson 23	Lesson 24
thickens	extinct
plentiful	pledge
role	patience
diligent	tedious
crowd	blended
sealed	cradled
carefully	raggedy
attack	distance
pattern	personalities
disappear	crumpled

Cumulative Review

RELATING WORDS Ask children the following questions:

- **Would you need a lot of patience to open a carefully wrapped present? Why or why not?**

- **Would a diligent person be more likely than a lazy person to finish a tedious job? Why or why not?**

- **How might a car or camel disappear in the distance? Explain.**

- **Is it possible for certain animals to go from being plentiful to being extinct? Explain.**

- **What kind of personalities do people who take roles in a play need to have?**

- **Would an animal with a pattern blend in with its environment? Why or why not?**

MAKE WORD WEBS Using **Transparency GO9,** guide children to complete word webs for *personalities* and *crumpled*. Write *personalities* in the center of a word web and have children name examples of different personalities that people have. Write their responses in the web.

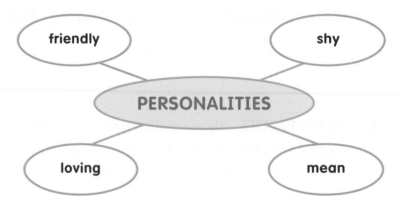

Then have children create their own web for *crumpled.* Have them fill the web with examples of things that can get crumpled in a backpack.

REINFORCE MEANINGS Discuss children's answers to the following questions:

1. **Would you wear crumpled and raggedy clothes to a friend's birthday party? Explain.** (Possible response: No. People usually dress nicely for a party.)

2. **Would you rather have people crowd around you in a dark room or disappear?** (Possible response: I'd rather people crowd around me, so I would know where they are.)

3. **Would a person with a lot of patience be likely to attack another person? Explain.** (Possible response: No. People with a lot of patience are usually calm, not angry.)

4. **Why do packages that come from a distance have to be sealed carefully?** (Possible response: so the package doesn't open accidentally during the trip)

5. **What animals could be cradled in your hand? Explain.** (Possible response: kitten, puppy, mouse, gerbil, frog)

6. **What is something that you might pledge never to do?** (Possible response: lie, steal, cheat)

7. **Do blended foods thicken? Explain.** (Possible response: Sometimes they do because you might combine things with different textures.)

MONITOR PROGRESS

Build Robust Vocabulary

IF children do not demonstrate understanding of the words and have difficulty using them,	**THEN** model using each word in several sentences, and have children repeat each sentence.

Small-Group Instruction, pp. S46–S47:

- **BELOW-LEVEL:** Reteach
- **ON-LEVEL:** Reinforce
- **ADVANCED:** Extend

Grammar *Quick Write*

Forms of Be

5-DAY GRAMMAR	
DAY 1	Introduce Forms of *Be: am, is, are*
DAY 2	Forms of *Be: was, were*
DAY 3	Subject-Verb Agreement
DAY 4	Apply to Writing
DAY 5	Weekly Review

Objectives

- *To recognize forms of* be: am, is, are, was, were
- *To recognize subject-verb agreement with* am, is, are, was, were

Daily Proofreading

People says the funiest things.

(say; funniest)

Language Arts Checkpoint

If children have difficulty with the concepts, see pages S48–S49 to reteach.

▲ **Practice Book, p. 193**

Review

REVIEW FORMS OF *BE* Use the following questions to review what children learned about forms of *be*. Have volunteers write answers on the board as they are provided. Ask:

- What do the verbs *am*, *is*, and *are* tell about? (present)
- What do the verbs *was* and *were* tell about? (past)
- Which verbs are used with singular subjects? (*am, is, was*)
- Which verbs are used with plural subjects? (*are, were*)

Practice/Apply

GUIDED PRACTICE Write the following sentences on the board. Ask volunteers to help you choose the correct form of *be*.

I (is/am) hopeful that the storm will pass. (am)

Yesterday, they (are/were) sad about losing the game. (were)

Mr. Goldman (was/were) glad we arrived safely. (was)

INDEPENDENT PRACTICE Have partners work together to write sentences with the correct form of *be* in each sentence. Have volunteers read aloud the sentences.

Writing
Paragraph That Compares (or Contrasts)

5-DAY WRITING	
DAY 1	Introduce
DAY 2	Prewrite
DAY 3	Draft
DAY 4	Revise
DAY 5	Revise

Revise

REVISE PARAGRAPH Explain that good writers look back after a day or so to see if their writing is clear and to add any new ideas. Tell children to reread their paragraphs and ask themselves these questions:

- Have I included examples that show how one subject is the same or different from another subject?

- Have I used words such as *like* or *different*?

WORD CHOICE Ask children to identify words that "show" rather than tell. Have them check that they have used synonyms so their writing is less repetitious.

NOTE: A 4-point rubric appears on page R8.

SCORING RUBRIC

	6	5	4	3	2	1
FOCUS	Completely focused, purposeful.	Focused on topic and purpose.	Generally focused on topic and purpose.	Somewhat focused on topic and purpose.	Related to topic but does not maintain focus.	Lacks focus and purpose.
ORGANIZATION	Ideas progress logically; paper conveys sense of completeness.	Organization mostly clear; paper gives sense of completeness.	Organization mostly clear, but some lapses occur; may seem unfinished.	Some sense of organization; seems unfinished.	Little sense of organization.	Little or no sense of organization.
SUPPORT	Strong, specific details; clear, exact language; freshness of expression.	Strong, specific details; clear, exact language.	Adequate support and word choice.	Limited supporting details; limited word choice.	Few supporting details; limited word choice.	Little development; limited or unclear word choice.
CONVENTIONS	Varied sentences; few, if any, errors.	Varied sentences; few errors.	Some sentence variety; few errors.	Simple sentence structures; some errors.	Simple sentence structures; many errors.	Unclear sentence structures; many errors.

REPRODUCIBLE STUDENT RUBRICS for specific writing purposes and presentations are available on pages R2–R8.

Objective
- *To revise a paragraph*

Writing Prompt

List ideas Have children generate a list of ideas about a new topic.

WEEKLY LESSON TEST

 **Weekly Lesson Tests, pp. 253–264**

- Selection Comprehension with Short Response
- Phonics and Spelling
- Focus Skill
- Synonyms
- Robust Vocabulary
- Grammar
- Fluency Passage **FRESH READS**

 For prescriptions, see pp. A2–A6. Also available electronically on StoryTown Online Assessment and Exam View®.

 Podcasting: Assessing Fluency

Leveled Readers

Reinforcing Skills and Strategies

BELOW-LEVEL

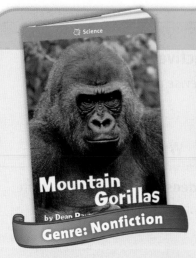

Mountain Gorillas

SUMMARY Dian Fossey studied the mountain gorillas of Congo and Rwanda by living among them until they became used to her.

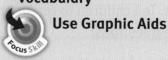 **r-Controlled Vowel /âr/ air, are**

- **Vocabulary**

  Use Graphic Aids

Before Reading

BUILD BACKGROUND/SET PURPOSE Ask children to share what they know about gorillas. Then guide children to preview the book and set a purpose for reading it.

Reading the Book

PAGES 5–7 USE GRAPHIC AIDS Why are two maps shown on pages 5 and 7? (The maps show where Congo and Rwanda are located in Africa—both places that Dian Fossey worked with gorillas.)

PAGES 10–13 CAUSE/EFFECT Why did Peanuts and Digit come over to touch Dian? (She had spent so much time sitting among them that they got used to her. Maybe they thought she was part of their group.)

REREAD FOR FLUENCY Have partners take turns reading the book a page at a time. Remind children to read at just the right speed to sound clear.

Think Critically *(See inside back cover for questions.)*

1. **NOTE DETAILS** In 1966 Dian Fossey went to the Congo and in 1967 she went to Rwanda.

2. **CAUSE AND EFFECT** Dian made noises like the gorillas and she walked near them on her hands and knees.

3. **USE GRAPHIC AIDS** Possible responses: It is in the center of Africa; a tiny part is on the coast.

4. **CHARACTER'S TRAITS** Possible responses: brave, amazing, clever

5. **PERSONAL RESPONSE** Answers will vary.

LEVELED READER TEACHER GUIDE

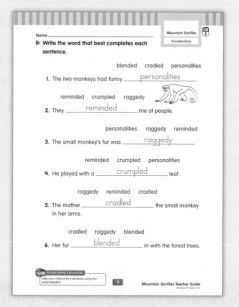

▲ Vocabulary, p. 5

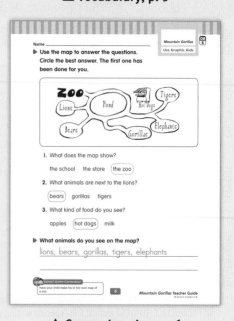

▲ Comprehension, p. 6

ON-LEVEL

Genre: Nonfiction

Orangutans

SUMMARY For more than thirty years, scientist Biruté Galdikas has studied endangered orangutans in their native forests of Sumatra and Borneo.

• **phonics** *r*-Controlled Vowel /âr/*air, are*

• **Vocabulary**

Use Graphic Aids

Before Reading

BUILD BACKGROUND/SET PURPOSE Tell children that the only great ape that lives in the wild outside of Africa is the orangutan of Asia. Have them tell what they know or can guess about orangutans. Then guide children to preview the book and set a purpose for reading it.

Reading the Book

PAGES 3–4 INTERPRET CHARACTER'S EMOTIONS How do you think Biruté felt after coming close to the orangutan? (scared, frightened)

PAGE 11 CAUSE/EFFECT Why do some orangutans live at Camp Leakey instead of in the wild? (Possible response: They lost their homes when parts of the rainforest were being cut down.)

REREAD FOR FLUENCY Have partners take turns reading, as if reading for an audience. They may point to details in the photograph.

Think Critically *(See inside back cover for questions.)*

1 NOTE DETAILS because the rainforests are being cut down

2 SPECULATE Possible response: The orangutan was her favorite.

3 MAKE INFERENCES Possible response: Yes, because Dr. Biruté lived among them.

4 AUTHOR'S PURPOSE Possible responses: to share information about orangutans; to protect endangered species

5 PERSONAL RESPONSE Answers will vary.

LEVELED READERS TEACHER GUIDE

Name _____

Orangutans — Vocabulary

▶ Write the Vocabulary Word from the box that best completes each sentence.

| blended | crumpled | distance | personalities |

1. My dogs had funny ____ **personalities**
2. They ran a long ____ **distance**
3. The dogs liked to roll in the **crumpled** ____ leaves.
4. Their brown fur ____ **blended** in with the trees.

▶ Write a sentence using each Vocabulary Word. **Accept reasonable responses.**
5. raggedy _____
6. cradled _____

School-Home Connection
Discuss the meanings of the Vocabulary Words with your child.

5 — Orangutans Teacher Guide

▲ **Vocabulary, p. 5**

Name _____

Orangutans — Use Graphic Aids

▶ Answer the questions about the map. **Possible responses are shown.**

Orangutan Forest
bridge
cave
trees
ropes
rocks
pond

1. How many orangutans do you see?
   4
2. What is the pond next to?
   trees and rocks
3. What goes between the caves?
   a bridge
4. What is the title of the map?
   Orangutan Forest

School-Home Connection
Have your child draw another object on the map. Ask your child to describe the new object's location in relation to the nearest object.

6 — Orangutans Teacher Guide

▲ **Comprehension, p. 6**

Leveled Readers

Reinforcing Skills and Strategies

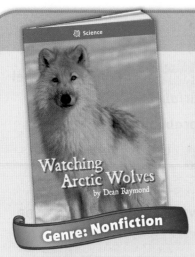

Genre: Nonfiction

ADVANCED

Watching Arctic Wolves

SUMMARY David Mech has studied wolves of the Arctic, especially one pack living on Ellesmere Island in Canada. He has written books to share his knowledge of how wolves live and hunt together.

- **phonics** *r*-Controlled Vowel /âr/*air, are*
- **Vocabulary**
  Use Graphic Aids

Before Reading

BUILD BACKGROUND/SET PURPOSE Have children tell what they know about wolves. Have them preview the book and set a purpose for reading.

Reading the Book

PAGE 5 **USE GRAPHIC AIDS** **Why is the map on page 5 helpful to readers?** (Possible response: It shows Ellesmere Island, Canada, where David Mech went to study Arctic wolves.)

PAGES 10–12 **CAUSE/EFFECT** **Why did several cold summers lead to the disappearance of the wolf pack?** (Several cold summers caused a food shortage, so the wolves did not have enough to eat.)

REREAD FOR FLUENCY Have partners take turns reading the book, a page at a time. Remind children to read at a rate that makes the sentences clear to listeners.

Think Critically
(See inside back cover for questions.)

1 **NOTE DETAILS** An arctic wolf has a thick coat and a long tail.

2 **SPECULATE** People can understand wolves better.

3 **USE GRAPHIC AIDS** Ellesmere Island is in the northernmost part of central Canada.

4 **FANTASY/REALITY** Possible response: The information in this book is true, but in fairy tales it's made up.

5 **PERSONAL RESPONSE** Answers will vary.

LEVELED READERS TEACHER GUIDE

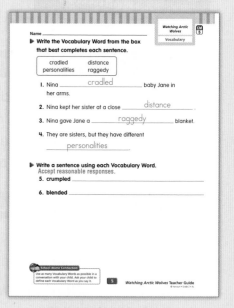

▲ Vocabulary, p. 5

▲ Comprehension, p. 6

www.harcourtschool.com/storytown

Go online

★ Leveled Readers Online Database
   Searchable by Genre, Skill, Vocabulary, Level, or Title
★ Student Activities and Teacher Resources, online

E L L

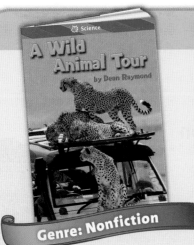

Genre: Nonfiction

A Wild Animal Tour

SUMMARY The narrator describes a safari tour in Kenya, in which tourists in a small truck watch the varied animals of the grasslands.

- Build Background
- Concept Vocabulary
- Scaffolded Language Development

Before Reading

BUILD BACKGROUND/SET PURPOSE Tell children that some countries in Africa have set aside lands where animals roam free. Talk about why tourists would want to visit these huge wildlife parks. Then guide children to preview the book and set a purpose for reading it.

Reading the Book

PAGE 3 USE GRAPHIC AIDS **What does the map show?** (the country of Kenya in Africa)

PAGES 11–13 DRAW CONCLUSIONS **How do the tourists probably feel when they see the lions?** (Possible responses: They are excited to see the cubs. They might be a little frightened when the male lion comes so close.)

REREAD FOR FLUENCY Have partners take turns choosing a favorite picture and reading the accompanying text aloud. Remind children to read at a rate that sounds like someone talking naturally.

Scaffolded Language Development

(See inside back cover for teacher-led activity.)

Provide additional examples and explanation as needed.

LEVELED READERS TEACHER GUIDE

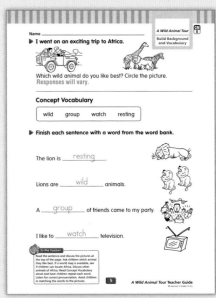

▲ Build Background and Vocabulary, p. 5

▲ Scaffolded Language Development, p. 6

Lesson 25
Theme Review and Vocabulary Builder

WEEK AT A GLANCE

 Phonics
REVIEW

- Vowel Diphthong /ou/*ou, ow*
- *r*-Controlled Vowel /ôr/*or, ore, our*
- Vowel Variant /o͞o/*oo, ew, ue, ui, ou*
- *r*-Controlled Vowel /âr/*air, are*

 Spelling
REVIEW

- Words with *ou* and *ow*
- Words with *or, ore,* and *our*
- Words with *oo, ew, ue, ui,* and *ou*
- Words with *air* and *are*

Reading

READERS' THEATER
"Town Hall" INTERVIEW

COMPREHENSION STRATEGIES
"A Time for Patience" FABLE

 Fluency
REVIEW

- Expression
- Reading Rate

 Comprehension
REVIEW

 Plot
Compare and Contrast

 Use Story Structure

 Use Graphic Aids
Synonyms

Summarize

 Robust Vocabulary
INTRODUCE *race, juggling, accomplish, feasible, attend, report, area, serve, preference, alternatives*

 Grammar
REVIEW

- Present-Tense Action Verbs
- Subject-Verb Agreement
- Past-Tense Verbs
- Forms of *be*

Writing: Revise and Publish
REVIEW Writing Trait: Sentence Fluency
REVIEW Writing Trait: Word Choice

Weekly Lesson Test

 = Focus Skill   = Focus Strategy   = Tested Skill

One stop *for all your* Digital *needs*

Digital
CLASSROOM

 www.harcourtschool.com/storytown
To go along with your print program

FOR THE TEACHER

Prepare Professional Development

 Videos for Podcasting

Plan & Organize Online TE & Planning Resources*

Teach Transparencies

access from Online TE

Assess Online Assessment*

with Student Tracking System and Prescriptions

FOR THE STUDENT

Read  Student eBook*

 Strategic Intervention Interactive Reader

 Leveled Readers

Practice & Apply Splash into Phonics CD-ROM

 Also available on CD-ROM

Literature Resources

STUDENT EDITION

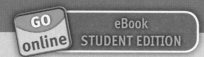
GO online eBook **STUDENT EDITION**

Town Hall

Readers' Theater
INTERVIEW

A Time for Patience

Reading a Fable

◀ **Audiotext** *Student Edition selections are available on Audiotext Grade 2, CD 5.*

REVIEW THEME CONCEPTS
Using Readers' Theater and a Fable

Paired Selections

SOCIAL STUDIES **Town Hall, pp. 304–315**

SUMMARY Students interview town leaders about a new park being built in the community.

SOCIAL STUDIES **A Time for Patience, pp. 316–319**

SUMMARY A hungry fox learns a lesson about the importance of patience.

Support for Differentiated Instruction

 LEVELED READERS

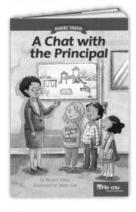

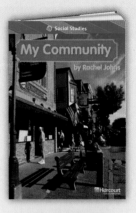

 BELOW-LEVEL

 ON-LEVEL

 ADVANCED

 E L L

LEVELED PRACTICE

◄ **Strategic Intervention Resource Kit, Lesson 25**

◄ **Strategic Intervention Interactive Reader, Lesson 25**

Strategic Intervention Interactive Reader Online

◄ **ELL Extra Support Kit, Lesson 25**

◄ **Challenge Resource Kit, Lesson 25**

● **BELOW-LEVEL**

Extra Support Copying Masters, pp. 194, 196–197, 199–202, 204–205

● **ON-LEVEL**

Practice Book, pp. 194–205

● **ADVANCED**

Challenge Copying Masters, pp. 194, 196–197, 199–202, 204–205

ADDITIONAL RESOURCES

- Teacher Resource Book, pp. 58, 116, 140–145
- Spelling Practice Book, pp. 79–82
- Grammar Practice Book, pp. 89–90
- Reading Transparencies R134–R135
- Test Prep System
- ◄ **Literacy Center Kit, Cards 121–125**
- Sound/Spelling Card
- ◄ **Fluency Builders**
- ◄ **Picture Card Collection**

ASSESSMENT

✔ **Weekly Lesson Tests, Lesson 25**
- Comprehension   • Robust Vocabulary

✔ **Rubrics, pp. R3–R8**

 www.harcourtschool.com/ storytown

Online Assessment
Also available on CD-ROM—Exam View®

Suggested Lesson Planner

GO online — Online TE & Planning Resources

	Day 1	**Day 2**
Step 1 — Whole Group **Daily Routines** • Oral Language • Read Aloud • High-Frequency Words	**QUESTION OF THE DAY,** p. T392 *What are some songs and sayings that have the word* home *in them?* **READ ALOUD,** p. T393 *Big Book of Rhymes and Poems,* "Home" **WORD WALL,** p. T393	**QUESTION OF THE DAY,** p. T410 *What would you plant if you could grow anything you wanted?* **READ ALOUD,** p. T411 *Big Book of Rhymes and Poems,* "A Young Farmer of Leeds" **WORD WALL,** p. T411

Word Work
• phonics
• Spelling

Day 1

 phonics, p. T394
Review: Vowel Diphthong /ou/*ou, ow*

 SPELLING, p. T396
Pretest: *found, down, store, four, smooth, grew, true, fruit, care, pair*

Day 2

 phonics, p. T412
Review: *r*-Controlled Vowel /ôr/*or, ore, our*

 READ IN CONTEXT, p. T413
Apply Phonics

Skills and Strategies
• Reading
• Fluency
• Comprehension
• Build Robust Vocabulary

Day 1

 COMPREHENSION, p. T397
Review: Plot

▲ Student Edition

BUILD ROBUST VOCABULARY, p. T398
Words from the Readers' Theater

 READING
READERS' THEATER
Read Aloud/Read Along: "Town Hall," p. T400

FLUENCY, p. T400 Model Oral Fluency

 BUILD ROBUST VOCABULARY, p. T407
Words About the Readers' Theater

Day 2

COMPREHENSION, p. T414
Review: Plot
Review: Compare and Contrast

▲ Student Edition

READING
READERS' THEATER
Read Together: "Town Hall" p. T416

FLUENCY, p. T416
Expression and Reading Rate

BUILD ROBUST VOCABULARY, p. T417
Words from the Read-Aloud

Step 2 — Small Groups

Suggestions for Differentiated Instruction (See pp. T386–T387.)

Step 3 — Whole Group

Language Arts
• Grammar *Quick Write*
• Writing

Day 1

 GRAMMAR, p. T408
Review: Present-Tense Action Verbs

Daily Proofreading
Fiona is tallest than her sister
(taller, sister.)

 WRITING, p. T409
Revise
Writing Trait: Word Choice

Writing Prompt *Write about which piece from Theme 5 you most enjoyed writing. Tell why.*

Day 2

 GRAMMAR, p. T418
Review: Subject-Verb Agreement

Daily Proofreading
my dog is noisiest than my cat.
(My, noisier)

 WRITING, p. T419
Revise
Writing Trait: Sentence Fluency

Writing Prompt *Write to tell how you came up with the idea for one of your writing pieces.*

 = Focus Skill   = Focus Strategy   ✓ = Tested Skill

Skills at a Glance

phonics REVIEW
• Lessons 21–24

Comprehension REVIEW
 Focus Skill
Plot, Use Graphic Aids
 Focus Strategy
Use Story Structure, Summarize

Fluency REVIEW
• Expression
• Reading Rate

Vocabulary INTRODUCE
ROBUST: *race, juggling, accomplish, feasible, attend, report, area, serve, preference, alternatives*

Day 3

QUESTION OF THE DAY, p. T420
What do you think would be the most fun about being a bee?

READ ALOUD, p. T421
Big Book of Rhymes and Poems, "Bumblebees"

WORD WALL, p. T421

 , p. T422
Review: Vowel Variant /o͞o/*oo, ew, ue, ui, ou*

SPELLING, p. T423
State the Generalization

COMPREHENSION, p. T424

Review: Use Graphic Aids
Review: Compare and Contrast

▲ Student Edition

FLUENCY
READERS' THEATER
Choose Roles/ Rehearse: "Town Hall," p. T426

BUILD ROBUST VOCABULARY, p. T427
Review

Day 4

QUESTION OF THE DAY, p. T430
What do you think a tree would say if it could talk?

READ ALOUD, p. T431
Big Book of Rhymes and Poems, "Hide-and-Seek"

WORD WALL, p. T431

 , p. T432
Introduce: *r*-Controlled Vowel /âr/*air, are*

SPELLING, p. T421
Review Spelling Words

READING 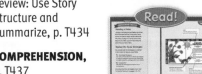 **COMPREHENSION STRATEGIES**
Review: Use Story Structure and Summarize, p. T434

COMPREHENSION, p. T437

VOCABULARY, p. T437
Review: Synonyms

▲ Student Edition

FLUENCY
READERS' THEATER
Rehearse Roles: "Town Hall," p. T438

BUILD ROBUST VOCABULARY, p. T439
Review

Day 5

QUESTION OF THE DAY, p. T442
What are some ways that people and bees are alike?

READ ALOUD, p. T443
Big Book of Rhymes and Poems, "The Swarm of Bees"

WORD WALL, p. T443

 , **SPELLING,** p. T444
Posttest

COMPREHENSION, p. T445
Review: Use Graphic Aids
Review: Synonyms

FLUENCY
READERS' THEATER
Perform: "Town Hall," p. T447

▲ Student Edition

● BELOW-LEVEL   ● ON-LEVEL   ● ADVANCED   **E L L**

GRAMMAR, p. T428
Review: Past-Tense Verbs

Daily Proofreading
Lindys sister is in Nebraska
(Lindy's, Nebraska.)

 WRITING, p. T429
Publish
Writing Trait: Presentation

Writing Prompt *Write a riddle based on a topic or selection in this theme.*

GRAMMAR, p. T440
Review: Forms of *Be*

Daily Proofreading
would you pass the cherry's?.
(Would, cherries?)

 WRITING, p. T441
Publish
Writing Trait: Conventions

Writing Prompt *Write about changes that you have made when you revised your writing.*

GRAMMAR, p. T448
Review: Lessons 21–24

Daily Proofreading
Dr Browns office is next door.
(Dr., Brown's)

 WRITING, p. T449
Present
Writing Trait: Sentence Fluency

Writing Prompt *Generate a list of ideas for a topic.*

Suggested Small-Group Planner

45-60+ Minutes

	Day 1	Day 2

15-20+ Minutes

BELOW-LEVEL

Day 1

Teacher-Directed
Leveled Reader:
"At the Library," p. T450
Before Reading

Independent
⭐ Listening/Speaking Center, p. T390
Extra Support Copying Masters, p. 194

▲ Leveled Reader

Day 2

Teacher-Directed
Student Edition:
"Town Hall," p. T401

Independent
⭐ Reading Center, p. T390
Extra Support Copying Masters, pp. 196–197

▲ Student Edition

15-20+ Minutes

ON-LEVEL

Day 1

Teacher-Directed
Leveled Reader:
"A Chat with the Principal," p. T451
Before Reading

Independent
⭐ Reading Center, p. T380
Practice Book, p. 194

▲ Leveled Reader

Day 2

Teacher-Directed
Student Edition:
"Town Hall," p. T401

Independent
⭐ Letters and Sounds Center, p. T391
Practice Book, pp. 196–197

▲ Student Edition

15-20+ Minutes

ADVANCED

Day 1

Teacher-Directed
Leveled Reader:
"At the Museum,"
p. T452
Before Reading

Independent
⭐ Letters and Sounds Center, p. T391
Challenge Copying Masters, p. 194

▲ Leveled Reader

Day 2

Teacher-Directed
Leveled Reader: "At the Museum,"
p. T454
Read the Book

Independent
⭐ Word Work Center, p. T391
Challenge Copying Masters, pp. 196–197

▲ Leveled Reader

ELL

English-Language Learners

In addition to the small-group instruction above, use the ELL Extra Support Kit to promote language development.

Day 1

LANGUAGE DEVELOPMENT SUPPORT
Teacher-Directed
ELL TG, Day 1
Independent
ELL Copying Masters, Lesson 25

▲ ELL Student Handbook

Day 2

LANGUAGE DEVELOPMENT SUPPORT
Teacher-Directed
ELL TG, Day 2
Independent
ELL Copying Masters, Lesson 25

▲ ELL Student Handbook

Intervention

▲ Strategic Intervention Resource Kit   ▲ Strategic Intervention Interactive Reader

Day 1

Strategic Intervention TG, Day 1
Strategic Intervention Practice Book, Lesson 25

Day 2

Strategic Intervention TG, Day 2
Strategic Intervention Interactive Reader, Lesson 25

▲ Strategic Intervention Interactive Reader

Day 3	Day 4	Day 5

Day 3

Teacher-Directed
Leveled Reader:
"At the Library,"
p. T450
Read the Book

Independent
⭐ Word Work Center, p. T391
Extra Support Copying Masters,
pp. 199–201

▲ Leveled Reader

Teacher-Directed
Leveled Reader:
"A Chat with the Principal," p. T451
Read the Book

Independent
⭐ Writing Center, p. T391
Practice Book, pp. 199–201

▲ Leveled Reader

Teacher-Directed
Leveled Reader:
"At the Museum,"
p. T452
Think Critically

Independent
⭐ Listening/Speaking Center,
p. T390
Challenge Copying Masters, pp. 199–201

▲ Leveled Reader

LANGUAGE DEVELOPMENT SUPPORT

Teacher-Directed
Leveled Reader: "My Community,"
p. T453
Before Reading; Read the Book
ELL TG, Day 3

Independent
ELL Copying Masters, Lesson 25

▲ Leveled Reader

Strategic Intervention TG, Day 3
Strategic Intervention Interactive Reader, Lesson 25
Strategic Intervention Practice Book, Lesson 25

▲ Strategic Intervention Interactive Reader

Day 4

Teacher-Directed
Leveled Reader:
"At the Library,"
p. T450
Reread for Fluency

Independent
⭐ Letters and Sounds Center,
p. T391
Extra Support Copying Masters, p. 202

▲ Leveled Reader

Teacher-Directed
Leveled Reader:
"A Chat with the Principal," p. T451
Reread for Fluency

Independent
⭐ Word Work Center,
p. T391
Practice Book, p. 202

▲ Leveled Reader

Teacher-Directed
Leveled Reader:
"At the Museum,"
p. T452
Reread for Fluency

Independent
⭐ Writing Center, p. T391
Challenge Copying Masters, p. 202
Self-Selected Reading: Classroom Library Collection

▲ Leveled Reader

LANGUAGE DEVELOPMENT SUPPORT

Teacher-Directed
Leveled Reader: "My Community,"
p. T453
Reread for Fluency
ELL TG, Day 4

Independent
ELL Copying Masters, Lesson 25

▲ Leveled Reader

Strategic Intervention TG, Day 4
Strategic Intervention Interactive Reader, Lesson 25

▲ Strategic Intervention Interactive Reader

Day 5

Teacher-Directed
Leveled Reader:
"At the Library,"
p. T450
Think Critically

Independent
⭐ Writing Center, p. T391
Leveled Reader: Reread for Fluency
Extra Support Copying Masters, pp. 204–205

▲ Leveled Reader

Teacher-Directed
Leveled Reader:
"A Chat with the Principal," p. T451
Think Critically

Independent
⭐ Listening/Speaking Center,
p. T390
Leveled Reader: Reread for Fluency
Practice Book, pp. 204–205

▲ Leveled Reader

Teacher-Directed
Leveled Reader:
"At the Museum,"
p. T452
Reread for Fluency

Independent
⭐ Reading Center, p. T390
Leveled Reader: Reread for Fluency
Challenge Copying Masters, p. 204–205
Self-Selected Reading: Classroom Library Collection

▲ Leveled Reader

LANGUAGE DEVELOPMENT SUPPORT

Teacher-Directed
Leveled Reader: "My Community,"
p. T453
Think Critically
ELL TG, Day 5

Independent
Leveled Reader: Reread for Fluency
ELL Copying Masters, Lesson 25

▲ Leveled Reader

Strategic Intervention TG, Day 5
Strategic Intervention Interactive Reader, Lesson 25

▲ Strategic Intervention Interactive Reader

Leveled Readers & Leveled Practice
Reinforcing Skills and Strategies

LEVELED READERS SYSTEM

- **Leveled Readers**
- **Leveled Readers, CD**
- **Leveled Readers Teacher Guides**
  - *Comprehension*
  - *Vocabulary*
  - *Oral Reading Fluency Assessment*
- **Response Activities**
- **Leveled Readers Assessment**

See pages T450–T453 for lesson plans.

BELOW-LEVEL

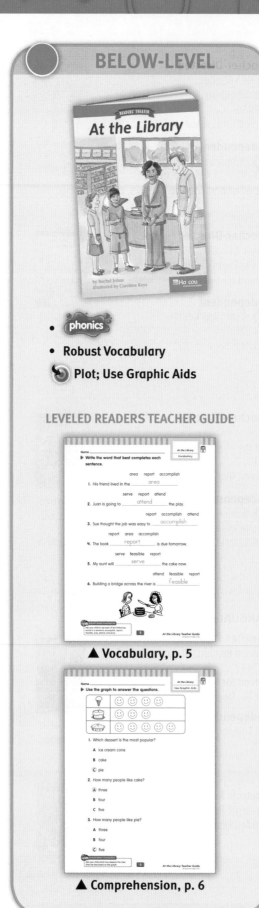

- phonics
- **Robust Vocabulary**
- **Plot; Use Graphic Aids**

LEVELED READERS TEACHER GUIDE

▲ Vocabulary, p. 5

▲ Comprehension, p. 6

ON-LEVEL

- phonics
- **Robust Vocabulary**
- **Plot; Use Graphic Aids**

LEVELED READERS TEACHER GUIDE

▲ Vocabulary, p. 5

▲ Comprehension, p. 6

ADVANCED

- **phonics**
- **Robust Vocabulary**
- **Plot; Use Graphic Aids**

LEVELED READERS TEACHER GUIDE

▲ **Vocabulary, p. 5**

▲ **Comprehension, p. 6**

ELL

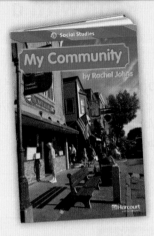

- **Build Background**
- **Concept Vocabulary**
- **Scaffolded Language Development**

LEVELED READERS TEACHER GUIDE

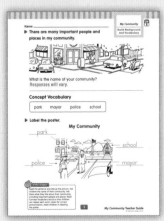

▲ **Build Background, p. 5**

▲ **Scaffolded Language Development, p. 6**

CLASSROOM LIBRARY
for Self-Selected Reading

EASY
▲ *Treasure Map* by Stuart J. Murphy.
FICTION

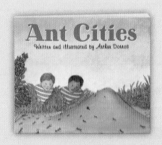

AVERAGE
▲ *Ant Cities* by Arthur Dorros.
NONFICTION

CHALLENGE
▲ *A Log's Life* by Wendy Pfeffer.
NONFICTION

▲ **Classroom Library Books Teacher Guide, Lesson 25**

Literacy Centers

15 Min. each

Management Support

While you provide direct instruction to individuals or small groups, other children can work on literacy center activities.

▲ **Literacy Center Pocket Chart**

My Activities

✓ Put a check mark next to the activities you complete.

Literacy Activities

☐ **Listening/Speaking** Read with a Recording
☐ **Reading** Read and Respond
☐ **Writing** Write to Compare
☐ **Word Work** Create Sentences
☐ **Letters and Sounds** Review Sounds and Spellings

Leveled Readers

☐ Rereading for Fluency
☐ Activities (See inside back cover.)

Practice Pages

☐ pages 194–205

▲ **Teacher Resource Book, p. 58**

Homework for the Week

TEACHER RESOURCE BOOK, PAGE 28

The *Homework Copying Master* provides activities to complete for each day of the week.

GO online www.harcourtschool.com/storytown

LISTENING/SPEAKING

Read with a Recording

Objective
To develop fluency by listening to familiar selections and reading them aloud

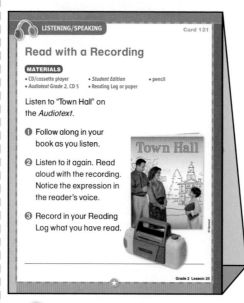

LISTENING/SPEAKING   Card 121

Read with a Recording

MATERIALS
• CD/cassette player   • Student Edition   • pencil
• Audiotext Grade 2, CD 5   • Reading Log or paper

Listen to "Town Hall" on the *Audiotext*.

❶ Follow along in your book as you listen.

❷ Listen to it again. Read aloud with the recording. Notice the expression in the reader's voice.

❸ Record in your Reading Log what you have read.

Grade 2 Lesson 25

⭐ **Literacy Center Kit • Card 121**

READING

Read and Respond

Objective
To develop comprehension by reading fiction selections and responding to them

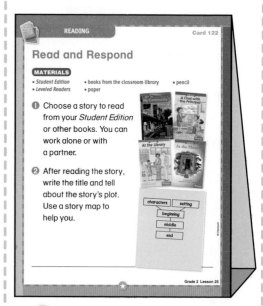

READING   Card 122

Read and Respond

MATERIALS
• Student Edition   • books from the classroom library   • pencil
• Leveled Readers   • paper

❶ Choose a story to read from your *Student Edition* or other books. You can work alone or with a partner.

❷ After reading the story, write the title and tell about the story's plot. Use a story map to help you.

characters   setting
beginning
middle
end

Grade 2 Lesson 25

⭐ **Literacy Center Kit • Card 122**

WRITING
Write to Compare

Objective
To practice writing to compare and contrast

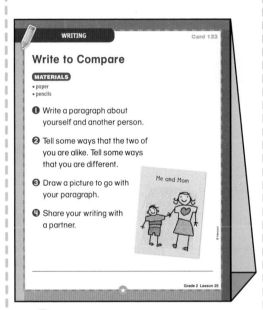

WORD WORK
Create Sentences

Objective
To practice using Vocabulary Words

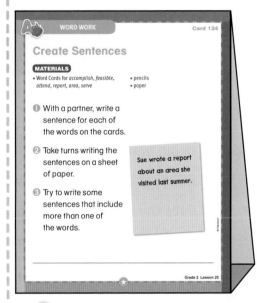

LETTERS AND SOUNDS
Review Sounds and Spellings

Objective
To read and write words using known letter/sound correspondences

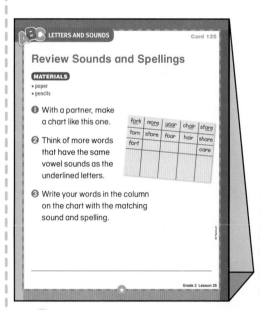

⭐ **Literacy Center Kit** • Card 123

⭐ **Literacy Center Kit** • Card 124

⭐ **Literacy Center Kit** • Card 125

Me and Mom

Sue wrote a report about an area she visited last summer.

fork	more	your	chair	stare
torn	store	four	hair	share
fort				

and Spelling

- Review: Vowel Diphthong /ou/*ou, ow*
- Pretest

Comprehension

 Review: Plot

 Monitor Comprehension

Robust Vocabulary

Words from Readers' Theater

- Introduce: *accomplish, feasible, attend, report, area, serve*

Words About the Readers' Theater

- Introduce: *preference, alternatives*

Fluency

READERS' THEATER

- Managing Readers' Theater
- Read Aloud/ Read Along

Model Fluent Reading "Town Hall," *Student Edition* pp. 304–315

Grammar [Quick Write]

- Review: Present-Tense Action Verbs

Writing

- Select and Revise

Warm-Up Routines

 Oral Language

Objective *To listen attentively and respond appropriately to oral communication*

Question of the Day

What are some songs and sayings that have the word *home* in them?

Use the following prompts to help children recall familiar songs and sayings about *home*:

- **What do you think people mean when they say, "Home, sweet home"?**
- **What does the song "Home on the Range" tell about?**
- **What does the saying "There's no place like home" mean?**

Encourage children to think of other songs and sayings, and list their responses on the board.

Read Aloud

Objective *To listen for enjoyment*

BIG BOOK OF RHYMES AND POEMS Display the poem "Home" on page 38 and read the title aloud. Then read the poem aloud. Ask children to think about how the poem makes them feel as you read it aloud again. Ask: **Does the poem make you feel excited or calm? Why do you say so?** Using a repeated gesture for the phrase "all around me," read the poem aloud again. Then repeat the gesture as you read the poem aloud together.

▲ Big Book of Rhymes
and Poems, p. 38

Word Wall

Objective *To read high-frequency words*

REVIEW HIGH-FREQUENCY WORDS Point to and read aloud words from the Word Wall: *impossible*, *children*, *learn*, *special*, *clear*, *imagine*, *favorite*, *young*, *fair*, and *exercise*. Point to words at random and have children read them together as a group. Then ask each child to read three words that you point to in quick succession. Continue until all children have had a chance to participate at least once.

impossible children learn special clear
imagine favorite young fair exercise

Vowel Diphthong /ou/*ou, ow*

 phonics *and Spelling*

Objectives

- *To recognize and blend the vowel diphthong /ou/ou, ow*
- *To read words with /ou/ou, ow, and other known letter-sounds*
- *To use /ou/ou, ow, and other known letter-sounds to spell words*

Skill Trace

Tested ✓ **Vowel Diphthong /ou/*ou, ow***

Introduce	Grade 1
Reintroduce	T30–T33
Reteach	S2–S3
Review	T42–T43, T66–T67, T394–T395
Test	Theme 5

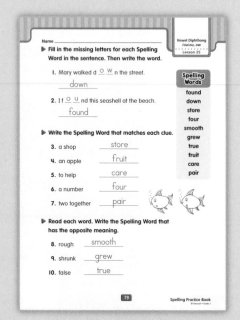

▲ **Spelling Practice Book, p. 79**

Review

REVIEW PHONICS ELEMENTS Explain to children that during this week they will review the phonics elements they learned in Theme 5. Tell them that they will focus on one phonics element each day, beginning with vowel diphthong /ou/*ou, ow.*

WARM UP WITH PHONEMIC AWARENESS Say the words *out* and *owl*. Have children repeat the words. Say: **The words *out* and *owl* have the /ou/ sound at the beginning.** Repeat with the words *pound* and *down*. Say: **The words *pound* and *down* have the /ou/ sound in the middle.** Have children say /ou/ several times.

Routine Card 1 **CONNECT LETTERS AND SOUNDS** Review the letter/sound correspondences for vowel diphthong /ou/*ou, ow.* Display the *Sound/Spelling Card* for /ou/*ou, ow.* Begin by pointing to *ou.* Ask children to say the sound that the letters stand for. Ask volunteers to name some words that use *ou* to stand for the /ou/ sound, and begin a list of the words they suggest on the board. In each word, ask children to identify the letters that stand for the /ou/ sound.

Follow a similar procedure for the vowel diphthong /ou/*ow.*

▲ **Sound/Spelling Card**

5-DAY PHONICS	
DAY 1	Review /ou/*ou, ow*
DAY 2	Review /ôr/*or, ore, our*
DAY 3	Review /o͞o/*oo, ew, ue, ui, ou*
DAY 4	Review /âr/*air, are*
DAY 5	Cumulative Review

Practice/Apply

GUIDED PRACTICE   Using the chart you have created, ask volunteers to read two words from each column. Then have the group choral-read words that you point to in each column. Finally, ask volunteers to suggest sentences using the words. Write their ideas on the board, underlining any words with the vowel diphthong /ou/*ou, ow.*

> The <u>owl</u> flew through the <u>clouds</u>.
> The <u>clown</u> is wearing a <u>frown</u>.
> Mr. <u>Brown</u> gave a <u>loud</u> <u>shout</u>.

INDEPENDENT PRACTICE   Have children work with partners to write sentences using words in which *ou* and *ow* stand for the /ou/ sound. Tell partners to exchange papers with another pair to read aloud each other's sentences.

ADVANCED

Multi-syllabic Words   Have children think of two-syllable words in which *ou* or *ow* stand for the /ou/ sound and add to the list begun on page T394. (Possible responses: *allow, somehow, around, amount*)

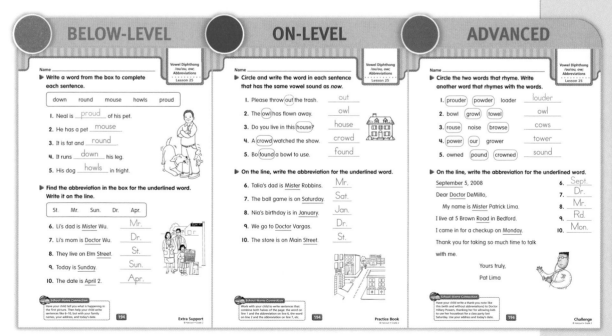

▲ **Extra Support, p. 194**   ▲ **Practice Book, p. 194**   ▲ **Challenge, p. 194**

ELL

- Group children according to academic levels and assign one of the pages on the left.

- Clarify any unfamiliar concepts as necessary. See *ELL Teacher Guide* Lesson 25 for support in scaffolding instruction.

Spelling
Review

5-DAY SPELLING

DAY 1 Pretest
DAY 2 Word Building
DAY 3 State the Generalization
DAY 4 Review
DAY 5 Posttest

Objective

• *To review spelling words from previous lessons*

Spelling Words

1. **found**	6. **grew**
2. **down**	7. **true**
3. **store**	8. **fruit**
4. **four**	9. **care***
5. **smooth**	10. **pair**

* Word from "Town Hall"

Reinforce the Skill

PRETEST Say the first word and read the dictation sentence. Repeat the word as children write it. Write the word on the board and have children check their spelling. Tell them to circle the word if they spelled it correctly or write it correctly if they did not. Repeat for words 2–10.

Words with /ou/*ou, ow;* /ôr/*or, ore, our;* /o͞o/*oo, ew, ue, ui, ou;* /âr/*air, are*

1.	found	Darla **found** her kitten hiding in the closet.
2.	down	We took the elevator **down** to the first floor.
3.	store	We need to go to the grocery **store** to get milk.
4.	four	I found **four** seashells at the beach.
5.	smooth	Dad's face feels **smooth** after he shaves.
6.	grew	Aunt Carol **grew** sunflowers in her garden.
7.	true	Is it **true** that you were born in Alaska?
8.	fruit	Have an apple or another **fruit** for a snack.
9.	care	Hank will **care** for our cat while we're away.
10.	pair	I will need a new **pair** of shoes soon!

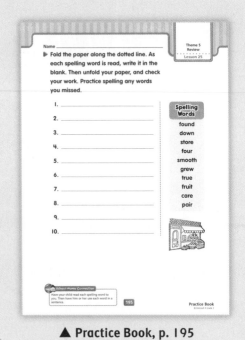

▲ Practice Book, p. 195

Plot

Comprehension: Review

Reinforce the Skill

DISCUSS PLOT   Have children reread *Student Edition* page 162. Model how to determine a story's plot.

Think Aloud   **I know that a plot is what happens in a story. When I begin reading a story, I look for the problem the main character faces. I know that the middle of a story tells about how the character tries to solve the problem. The ending of the story tells about the solution to the problem.**

Practice/Apply

GUIDED PRACTICE   Draw a chart similar to the one on *Student Edition* page 163. Then have children return to "Mr. Putter and Tabby Write the Book" from Theme 4, p. 22. Guide children to identify what happens at the beginning of the story, and add the information to the chart. Then lead them to tell what happens in the middle of the story, and add that information to the chart.

INDEPENDENT PRACTICE   On their own, have children write about what happens at the end of the story. Discuss how the end of the story tells about how Mr. Putter solves his problem.

> **Beginning**
> Mr. Putter wants to write a mystery novel.

> **Middle**
> Mr. Putter doesn't get much writing done, because he finds other things to do and think about. He writes a list called "Good Things."

> **Ending**
> Mrs. Teaberry helps Mr. Putter feel good about what he has written, and Mr. Putter looks forward to writing again.

Objectives

- *To identify the plot of a story*
- *To identify the problem and solution in a story*

Skill Trace
Tested **Plot**

Introduce	T34–T35
Reteach	S6–S7, S18–S19
Review	T69, T85, T97, T136–T137, T171, T187, T197, T397, T414
Test	Theme 5
Maintain	Theme 6, T86

Build Robust Vocabulary

Words from the Readers' Theater

Objective

- *To build robust vocabulary*

Tested ✓

INTRODUCE

Vocabulary: Lesson 25

accomplish	report
feasible	area
attend	serve

▼ **Student-Friendly Explanations**

Student-Friendly Explanations	
accomplish	When you accomplish a task, you have completed it with good results.
feasible	If something is feasible, it can be done.
attend	If you attend an event, you go to it.
report	When you make a report, you tell what you have learned or found out.
area	An area is an open space or a part of a place.
serve	When you serve people, you bring them food and drinks.

Grade 2, Lesson 25   **R135**   Vocabulary

Transparency R135

Teach/Model

 Routine Card 4

INTRODUCE ROBUST VOCABULARY Introduce the words using *Routine Card 4*.

❶ Display **Transparency R135** and have children read the word and the **Student-Friendly Explanation**.
❷ Have children **say the word** with you.
❸ Have children **interact with the word's meaning** by asking them the appropriate question below.

- How would you answer if someone asked what you plan to **accomplish** today? Explain.

- Is visiting a museum on Monday **feasible** if the museum is closed that day? Explain.

- Would someone plan a party for a day when most people could not **attend**? Explain.

- When someone is going to **report** to the class, what do you expect will happen?

- What other classes are in our **area** of the school?

- When someone's job is to **serve** others in a town, what might that person do?

Develop Deeper Meaning

EXPAND WORD MEANINGS Provide children with the following examples and questions.

1. If I asked you to **report** on a 500-page book tomorrow, do you think you could **accomplish** that task? Tell why or why not.
2. Would a field trip to an iceberg **area** be **feasible**? Explain.
3. Can you **attend** two parties and **serve** punch in both places at one time? Why or why not?

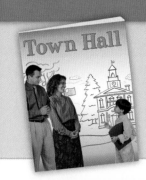

Managing **Readers' Theater**

"Town Hall"

Set the Stage

OVERVIEW Use the following suggestions to help children prepare a Readers' Theater presentation of "Town Hall."

Professional Development

 Podcasting: Readers' Theater

Day 1

MODEL FLUENT READING Model fluent, expressive reading by reading aloud the script on *Student Edition* pages 304–315 (pp. T401–T406) as children follow along. Then read the script again as children read along. Use the Monitor Comprehension questions to assess children's comprehension of the selection. Consider performance options for the end of the week. You may want to invite parents or other guests and allow children to create invitations.

▲ Teacher Resource Book, pp. 140–145

Day 2

READ TOGETHER Have children read the scripts on their own for the first time. Guide children to read with appropriate accuracy, reading rate, and expression. Encourage them to use the fluency tips to help them read more fluently.

Day 3

CHOOSE ROLES AND REHEARSE Distribute copies of the script (*Teacher Resource Book*, pp. 140–145). Assign children to groups and have them practice reading different roles aloud. After children read, assign roles or have children choose their own. Encourage children to highlight their part and to practice reading their script at home.

Day 4

REHEARSE Have children work in their assigned groups to read the script as many times as possible. Informally observe the groups and give feedback on children's accuracy and expression. You may want to have children rehearse while using the backdrop for "Town Hall" (*Teacher Resource Book*, p. 116).

Day 5

PERFORM Assign each group a scene to perform. Have children stand in a row at the front of the classroom and read the script aloud. Groups who are not performing become part of the audience. Encourage the audience to give feedback after the performances about each group's accuracy, reading rate, and expression.

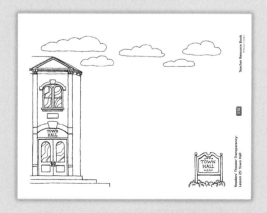

▲ Teacher Resource Book, p. 116

READERS' THEATER

5-DAY READERS' THEATER	
DAY 1	Read Aloud/Read Along
DAY 2	Read Together
DAY 3	Choose Roles/Rehearse
DAY 4	Rehearse Roles
DAY 5	Perform

Read Aloud/Read Along: "Town Hall"

Objectives

- *To identify the genre of a selection and its distinguishing characteristics*
- *To set a purpose for listening*

TECHNOLOGY

 eBook "Town Hall" is available in an eBook.

 Audiotext "Town Hall" is available on *Audiotext Grade 2,* CD 5 for subsequent readings.

Leveled Parts You may wish to assign the role of the Teacher to children needing ELL support. The role may be split among children as needed.

Build Background

DISCUSS GENRE Have children turn to *Student Edition* page 304. Explain that "Town Hall" is a Readers' Theater script that tells about how town leaders worked together to plan a new park. It is written as if students are interviewing town leaders.

PREVIEW READERS' THEATER WORDS Point to and read aloud the words on *Student Edition* page 304: *report, feasible, accomplish, serve, attend,* and *area.* Have children read the words aloud with you.

Reading for Fluency

DISCUSS FLUENCY TIPS Have children read the Reading for Fluency text on *Student Edition* page 304. Remind them that these are the two fluency strategies they learned to use in Lessons 21–24. Explain that throughout the Readers' Theater they will find fluency tips that will help them use expression and appropriate reading rate while reading aloud.

SET A PURPOSE Tell children to listen and read along as you read the selection aloud and to pay attention to the speed at which you read. Encourage children to notice that you try to read with expression to get ideas across.

READ ALOUD/READ ALONG Have children follow along as you read the script aloud. Remind them to pay close attention to whether you read lines quickly or more slowly, and to how you use your voice to show how a character might be feeling.

(Think Aloud) As I read "Town Hall" aloud, I will use my voice to express what the characters are feeling. If a character is enthusiastic or puzzled, I will try to show that with my voice. I may slow down if a character is trying to explain a new idea.

Read the script aloud a second time. This time, tell children to listen to what the selection tells about, because you will ask them questions.

READERS' THEATER

report

feasible

accomplish

serve

area

attend

Reading for Fluency

When you read a script aloud,

• think about how the characters feel to help you read with expression.

• read at the same speed as a speaker would say the lines.

304

Theme Review

① town hall

Town Hall

Roles

Teacher   Mayor

Kris   Town Leader 1

Robin   Town Leader 2

Setting

Town hall of a small town

Teacher: Good morning, Mayor. I'd like you to meet Kris and Robin, two of my students.

Kris: The students at our school have questions about the new park the town is building.

Robin: We'd like to ask you and some other town leaders our questions. Then we'll report back to our classmates. ②

Mayor: We'll be happy to answer your questions.

305

Monitor Comprehension

PAGES 304–305   Have children look at the illustrations. Ask them to tell what they see. Have them read to find out what is happening.

①  **USE GRAPHIC AIDS   How does the label "town hall" help tell about the setting?** (Possible response: It identifies the setting and shows what a town hall looks like.)

② **NOTE DETAILS   Why are the children and their teacher talking to the mayor?** (They want to find out about the plans for the new park so that they can tell their class about it.)

 SOCIAL STUDIES

SUPPORTING STANDARDS

Community Officials   Point out that in this Readers' Theater Script the mayor and town leaders discuss and develop plans, gather information, and make decisions about things that affect the town. Explain that a mayor is usually elected by citizens, and other leaders may also be elected or appointed. Discuss what children know about their community leaders, how these people gain office, and what they do to make and carry out laws.

Theme Review

Kris: Why did you decide to build a park?

Mayor: The people in our town need a place to go with their families.

Robin: What kinds of things will be at the park?

Mayor: I'm happy to tell you that there will be a playground! In a town the size of ours, people have many interests. Different people in our town want different things. ❶

Town Leader 1: We asked people to tell us what things they wanted in the new park.

306

Town Leader 2: People sent many letters to Town Hall, and we read all of them. ❷

Kris: So, are you building everything that the citizens asked for?

Mayor: No, that wouldn't be feasible.

Robin: How did you decide what to build?

Mayor: We looked carefully at everything that people asked for. We were very serious about building what people wanted, but we had to make choices.

307

Monitor Comprehension

PAGES 306–307 Ask children what they think the mayor is saying to the children. Have them read to find out.

❶ **MAIN IDEA AND DETAILS What problem did the mayor and the town leaders face?** (They had to plan a new park that would meet everyone's needs.)

❷ **SYNTHESIZE How can you tell that the mayor and the town leaders cared about what people wanted?** (They understood that the park should be for everyone, so they asked people in town to give them ideas, and then they discussed what was important.)

Reading for Fluency

Fluency Tip **Reading Rate**

Explain to children why a reader might speed up or slow down as he or she reads.

Think Aloud When the mayor and the town leaders are explaining new ideas, I slow down as I read to help make those ideas clear. When I am reading the parts of the children as they ask questions, I read at a slightly faster rate.

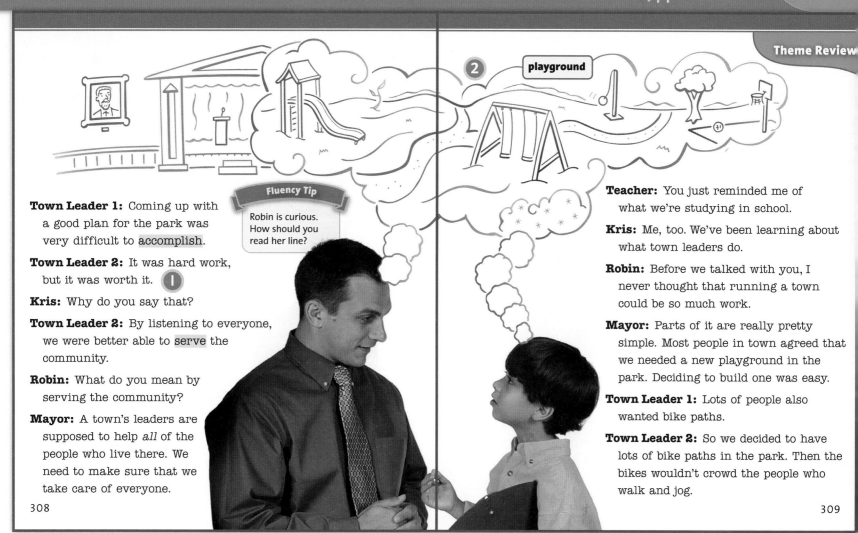

Theme Review

Town Leader 1: Coming up with a good plan for the park was very difficult to accomplish.

Town Leader 2: It was hard work, but it was worth it. ①

Kris: Why do you say that?

Town Leader 2: By listening to everyone, we were better able to serve the community.

Robin: What do you mean by serving the community?

Mayor: A town's leaders are supposed to help *all* of the people who live there. We need to make sure that we take care of everyone.

Fluency Tip
Robin is curious. How should you read her line?

308

② playground

Teacher: You just reminded me of what we're studying in school.

Kris: Me, too. We've been learning about what town leaders do.

Robin: Before we talked with you, I never thought that running a town could be so much work.

Mayor: Parts of it are really pretty simple. Most people in town agreed that we needed a new playground in the park. Deciding to build one was easy.

Town Leader 1: Lots of people also wanted bike paths.

Town Leader 2: So we decided to have lots of bike paths in the park. Then the bikes wouldn't crowd the people who walk and jog.

309

Monitor Comprehension

PAGES 308–309 Ask children what the town leader and the boy are thinking about. Have them read to find out.

① **DRAW CONCLUSIONS** **Why do you think that planning the new park was such hard work?** (The mayor and the town leaders had to try to serve everyone's needs while they made plans for the park.)

② **USE GRAPHIC AIDS** **How does the diagram help you to understand the plans for the playground?** (It shows the playground and how it might be set up with bike paths.)

Focus Skill

Reading for Fluency

Fluency Tip **Expression** Model using expression as you read aloud.

Think Aloud Robin wants the town leaders to explain something, so I will use my voice to express her interest and curiosity.

Robin: What else will be in the park?

Mayor: There will be a new soccer field.

Kris: What was wrong with the old one?

Town Leader 1: Nothing, but the town needed more than one.

Town Leader 2: So many children in our town play soccer that we needed a second field.

Robin: I can see that you are building lots of things for children, but what about for grown-ups?

Mayor: We're making a big picnic area for families who come to the park on weekends and holidays. We're also adding lots of park benches so people can sit and be comfortable.

310

soccer field

picnic area

Fluency Tip

The mayor is explaining something. Say these lines at a speed that others will be able to understand.

Town Leader 1: We also decided to make an area where people could let their dogs run. **1**

Town Leader 2: There are a lot of dog owners in our town. They told us that their dogs needed a place to play. The problem was that other people didn't like the idea of dogs running around.

Mayor: We thought about it and figured out a way to make everyone happy. Now we will have a special place where dogs can run and not bother other people. **2**

311

Monitor Comprehension

PAGES 310–311 Have children look at the illustrations. Ask what else might be part of the new park. Have them read along to find out.

1 MAIN IDEA AND DETAILS **What are some of the things that the town leaders will include so that everyone can enjoy the park?** (They will include bike paths, a soccer field, a picnic area, benches, and an area for dogs to run.)

2 MAKE JUDGMENTS **What do you think of the town leaders' ideas for the new park?** (Possible response: They have done a good job of trying to make the park a place for everyone.)

Reading for Fluency

Fluency Tip **Reading Rate**

Point out that the mayor is trying to make an idea clear. Explain to children that when they read these lines aloud, they should adjust their reading rate and read them more slowly because the mayor wants to make sure her idea is understood. If she said her ideas quickly, the listeners might not understand or trust what she was saying.

Kris: It sounds as if you put in something for everyone. Is there anything else you want to tell us about?

Mayor: Yes, there is. We will also have a place where we can have music shows.

Robin: What gave you that idea?

Town Leader 1: We knew that some other towns had music shows in the summer.

312

Town Leader 2: It seemed like a good idea to do it here, too.

Kris: Did people ask for it?

Mayor: No, they didn't, but we thought it was a good idea anyway.

Town Leader 1: When we started telling people about it, they all got excited.

Town Leader 2: We will have music shows and plays that people of all ages will want to attend. 1

313

bandstand  2

Monitor Comprehension

PAGES 312–313   Have children look at the illustration. Ask them if they can tell what is happening. Have them read to find out.

1 MAKE INFERENCES   How did the town leaders know that the people of their town would like a bandstand? (Possible response: They knew that the people wanted to have fun and have a place to meet and be with their family and friends.)

2 GRAPHIC AIDS   How does the diagram and label help you understand the dreams for the bandstand? (Possible response: It shows basically how it will look.)

Focus Skill

SOCIAL STUDIES

SUPPORTING STANDARDS

Explain to children that a city hall or town hall is the headquarters of a city and usually houses the city or town council, mayor, community departments and employees. It is also usually the base of the city or town.

In the United States, a hall is labeled a "city" or "town" hall depending on the size of the community it serves. City halls are usually found in larger cities and town halls in smaller urban areas.

Theme Review

Teacher: Thanks for answering all of our questions. I don't think that we have any more.

Robin: I do have one more question. When will the new park open?

Town Leader 1: Our plan is to open it on the Fourth of July.

Town Leader 2: We're going to have a big party.

314

Mayor: The whole town will be invited. We're going to have music and lots of games.

Kris: I know where I'm going for the Fourth of July!

Robin: Me, too. I can't wait! ❶❷

Fluency Tip
An exclamation point shows strong feeling. Read this line with feeling.

315

Monitor Comprehension

PAGES 314–315 Have children look at the pages. Have them read to find out what is happening.

❶ **SYNTHESIZE How did the problem of not having a park get solved?** (Possible response: The town leaders studied what the people in the community wanted and came up with a good plan as well as some things the people did not ask for.)

❷ **PERSONAL RESPONSE Do you think the problem was settled in the correct way?** (Yes. The town leaders worked hard and thought hard about serving everyone in the community. That seems fair.)

Reading for Fluency

Fluency Tip **Expression** Tell children to notice that the last two lines end in exclamation points. That means that the characters are feeling strongly about something, and are excited.

Think Aloud If I were reading the last two lines that end with exclamation points, I would speak with excitement in my voice. I would raise my voice slightly and say some of the words with more stress than others, like "*I* know where *I'm* going for the Fourth of July!" and "Me, *too*. I can't *wait!*"

Build Robust Vocabulary

Words About the Readers' Theater

Teach/Model

Routine Card 3

INTRODUCE ROBUST VOCABULARY   Use *Routine Card 3* to introduce the words.

❶ Put the word in **selection context**.

❷ Display Transparency R134 and read the word and the **Student-Friendly Explanation**.

❸ Have children **say the word** with you.

❹ Use the word in other contexts, and have children **interact with the word's meaning**.

❺ Remove the transparency. Say the Student-Friendly Explanation again, and ask children to **name the word** that goes with it.

❶ **Selection Context:** The town leaders' **preference** was to plan the new park so that it would be useful for everyone.

❹ **Interact with Word Meaning:** Would you name a food you didn't like if you were asked about your preference for lunch? Explain.

❶ **Selection Context:** The town leaders had to have **alternatives** while they worked on planning the new park.

❹ **Interact with Word Meaning:** Do you only have one choice if you know there are alternatives? Tell why.

Practice/Apply

GUIDED PRACTICE   Ask children to do the following:

- Tell about your *preference* for the best way to spend a Sunday afternoon. Do you know others who share the same preference? Explain.

- Imagine that you and your friends are tired of playing tag. Describe some *alternatives* to playing tag.

INDEPENDENT PRACTICE   Ask partners to list two alternatives for an art activity, and state their preference for which one they would like to do first.

Objective

- *To develop robust vocabulary through discussing a literature selection*

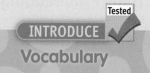

INTRODUCE ✓ **Tested**

Vocabulary

preference   **alternatives**

▼ Student-Friendly Explanations

Student-Friendly Explanations

race	If someone wants to be the president or a mayor, he or she runs in a political race.
juggling	If you say you are juggling many things, you are working on many projects at the same time.
preference	If you like one thing better than another, you have a preference.
alternatives	If you have several choices, then you have alternatives.

Grade 2, Lesson 25   R134   Vocabulary

Transparency R134

Grammar *Quick Write*

Review: Present-Tense Action Verbs

5-DAY GRAMMAR

DAY 1	Review Present-Tense Action Verbs
DAY 2	Review Subject-Verb Agreement
DAY 3	Review Past-Tense Verbs
DAY 4	Review Forms of *be*
DAY 5	Cumulative Review

Objective

- *To recognize and write present-tense action verbs in sentences*

Daily Proofreading

Fiona is tallest than her sister

(taller, sister.)

Writing Trait

Strengthening Conventions

Review Use these short daily lessons with children's own writing to continue building a foundation for revising/editing longer connected text. See also *Writer's Companion,* Lesson 25.

Reinforce the Skill

REVIEW PRESENT-TENSE ACTION VERBS Review what children have learned about present-tense action verbs, using the following points:

- Add the ending -*s* to most present-tense action verbs when the sentence tells about one.

- Add the ending -*es* when a present-tense action verb ends in *s, x, sh, ch,* or *tch* and the sentence tells about one.

- Do not add -*s* or -*es* to a verb when the sentence is about *I, you,* or more than one.

- To combine two sentences using the same present-tense action verb, use *and* to combine the naming parts. Add no ending to the verb.

Practice/Apply

GUIDED PRACTICE Write the following sentences on the board.

Mark and Miguel pulls the wagon.

Ellen pushes the stroller.

Lead children to identify the second sentence as the correct one. Have volunteers correct the present-tense action verbs in the other sentence. (pull) Then write these two sentences on the board:

Mark watches the baby. Miguel watches the baby.

Guide children to combine the two sentences into one. Ask a volunteer to correct the present-tense action verb. (Mark and Miguel watch the baby.)

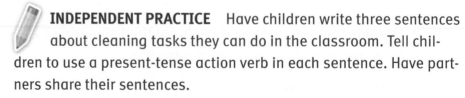 **INDEPENDENT PRACTICE** Have children write three sentences about cleaning tasks they can do in the classroom. Tell children to use a present-tense action verb in each sentence. Have partners share their sentences.

 # Writing
Revise

5-DAY WRITING	
DAY 1	Select a Piece and Revise
DAY 2	Revise
DAY 3	Publish
DAY 4	Publish
DAY 5	Present

Revise

SELECT WRITING Tell children to select one of the writing pieces they started earlier in this theme, such as the fantasy story, the description, or the paragraph that compares. Tell them to reread it and think about what they could do to improve it. Explain that they will revise the piece of writing that they select, and will decide on a way to publish their writing to share it with others.

Point out that when children reread their writing from earlier in the theme they may notice parts that are unclear, or descriptions that could be more interesting or livelier. Explain that as they revise, they will be able to take time to make any changes they like, and to make their writing stronger.

USE ACTIVE VERBS Remind children that reviewing and revising their verbs can help improve their writing. Write this sentence on the board: *The moth flew away*. Help children brainstorm more descriptive action verbs, such as *fluttered* or *floated*, and adjectives that would make the sentence more interesting.

 WORD CHOICE Remind children to use a thesaurus or dictionary to find alternatives for words.

GRAMMAR-WRITING CONNECTION Remind children to check that they have formed verb tenses correctly, and that the verb form matches the subject.

Objective

• *To revise a piece of writing*

 ## Writing Prompt

Independent Writing Have children write about a piece from Theme 5 they most enjoyed writing, and explain why.

E L L

Discuss Revisions Encourage children to tell or point out changes they might like to make, and help children note their ideas. If needed, ask questions about the piece to help generate ideas for revision.

Day at a Glance

Day 2

phonics and Spelling

- Review: *r*-Controlled Vowel /ôr/*or, ore, our*
- Build Words

Comprehension

 Review: Plot and Compare & Contrast

Fluency

READERS' THEATER

- Read Together: "Town Hall," *Student Edition*, pp. 304–315

Read!

Robust Vocabulary

- *Read-Aloud Anthology:* "From Study Hall to City Hall"
- *Words from the Read-Aloud:* Introduce: *race, juggling*

Grammar [Quick Write]

- Review: Subject-Verb Agreement

Writing

- Revise and Publish

Warm-Up Routines

Oral Language

Objective *To listen attentively and respond appropriately to oral communication*

Question of the Day

What would you plant if you could grow anything you wanted?

Invite children to generate ideas for crops they could grow, both realistic and imaginary. Use the following prompts:

- **What are some real crops you might like to grow?**
- **What are some silly things, like money or spaghetti, that would be fun to grow?**
- **What would you do with your crop?**

Have children complete the following sentence frame to explain their ideas.

I would grow _____ because _____.

Read Aloud

Objective *To listen for a purpose*

BIG BOOK OF RHYMES AND POEMS Display the poem "A Young Farmer of Leeds" on page 40 and read aloud the title. Remind children that they read this poem earlier in the theme. Tell them to listen for repeated sounds they hear as you read the poem aloud. Then read the poem. Ask children which sounds they heard most often. (/s/, /ē/) Then read the poem again and have children chime in on the last line.

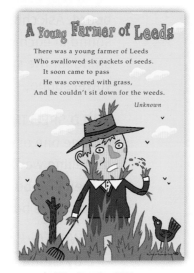

▲ **Big Book of Rhymes and Poems, p. 40**

Word Wall

Objective *To read high-frequency words*

REVIEW HIGH-FREQUENCY WORDS Point to the following words on the Word Wall: *impossible, children, learn, special, clear, imagine, favorite, young, fair,* and *exercise.* For each word, have children read it, spell it, and finally read it again. Point to a word, call on a child to use it in a sentence, and then read the word together again.

r-Controlled Vowel /ôr/
or, ore, our phonics and Spelling

Objectives

- *To recognize and blend the /ôr/ sound of or, ore, our*
- *To read words with /ôr/or, ore, our, and other known letter-sounds*
- *To use /ôr/or, ore, our, and other known letter-sounds to spell words*

Spelling Words

1. **found**	6. **grew**
2. **down**	7. **true**
3. **store**	8. **fruit**
4. **four**	9. **care***
5. **smooth**	10. **pair**

* Word from "Town Hall"

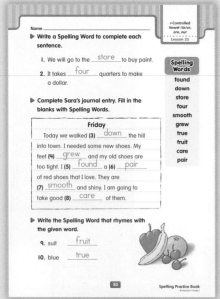

▲ **Spelling Practice Book, p. 80**

Review

READ A SPELLING WORD Write the words *store* and *four* on the board. Ask children to identify the letters that stand for the /ôr/ sound in each word. Remind children that *or, ore,* and *our* can stand for the short /ôr/ sound. Have them read the *r*-Controlled vowel sound.

BUILD SPELLING WORDS Have children follow your directions to change one or more letters in each of the following words to make a spelling word. Have them write the word on a sheet of paper or in their notebooks. Then have a volunteer change the spelling of the word on the board so that children can self-check their spelling.

- Write *fork* on the board. Ask: **Which spelling word can you make by changing the last two letters?** *(four)*

- Write *chore* on the board. Ask: **Which spelling word can you make by changing the first two letters?** *(store)*

Follow a similar procedure with the words *dawn* (down), *grow* (grew), *tooth* (smooth), *ground* (found), *pain* (pair), *stare* (care), *blue* (true), and *ruin* (fruit).

BELOW-LEVEL

Meanings and Sounds List the spelling words on the board. Provide a clue that tells each word's meaning, and have children identify and spell the word. Have children tell which letters stand for the vowel sound in each word.

ADVANCED

Form New Words Have children make a list of the spelling words. Have partners work together to replace the vowel or vowels in the middle of each word with different vowels to form new words. Have children use a dictionary as needed.

5-DAY PHONICS

DAY 1	Review /ou/ou, ow
DAY 2	**Review /ôr/or, ore, our**
DAY 3	Review /o͞o/oo, ew, ue, ui, ou
DAY 4	Review /âr/air, are
DAY 5	Cumulative Review

Read Words in Context

APPLY PHONICS Write the following sentences on the board or on chart paper. Have children read each sentence silently. Then track the print as children read the sentence aloud.

Lisa and Sam chose yellow roses for their mother at the flower <u>store</u>.

I need <u>four</u> stamps, but I have only three.

I don't think that story could be <u>true</u>.

Travis takes good <u>care</u> of his pet turtles.

Melanie <u>grew</u> two inches in two months!

WRITE Write the spelling words on the board or on chart paper. On their own, have children write the words in alphabetical order. Have partners check each other's work.

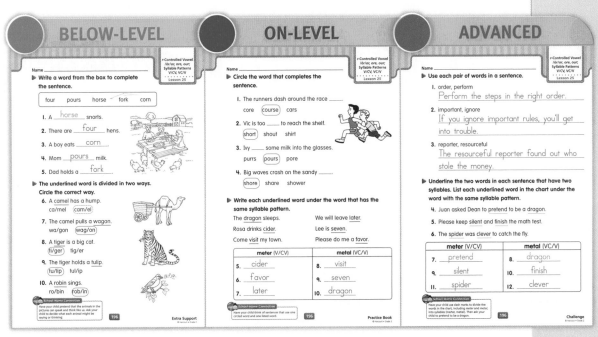

▲ **Extra Support, p. 196** ▲ **Practice Book, p. 196** ▲ **Challenge, p. 196**

ELL

- Group children according to academic levels, and assign one of the pages on the left.

- Clarify any unfamiliar concepts as necessary. See *ELL Teacher Guide* Lesson 25 for support in scaffolding instruction.

Plot

Comprehension: Review

Objectives

- *To identify the plot of a story*
- *To compare the plots of two stories*

Skill Trace

 Tested **Plot**

Introduce	T34–T35
Reteach	S6–S7, S18–S19
Review	T69, T85, T97, T136–T137, T171, T187, T197, T397, T414
Test	Theme 5
Maintain	Theme 6, T86

Review

DISCUSS COMPARING PLOTS Have children turn to *Student Edition* page 205. Remind children of what they know about identifying a story's plot, and describe how to compare the plots of two stories.

Think Aloud **By thinking about what happens in two stories, I can compare the plots to tell how they are alike and different.**

Practice/Apply

GUIDED PRACTICE Use a story map like the one on *Student Edition* page 205 to compare the plot of "Serious Farm" with the plot of "Click, Clack, Moo: Cows That Type."

Discuss the ways in which the stories are alike. (Both are set on farms and have farmers and cows as characters.)

INDEPENDENT PRACTICE On their own, have children write about what happens at the end of each story. Discuss their responses, and invite them to tell how the plots of the two stories are alike and different.

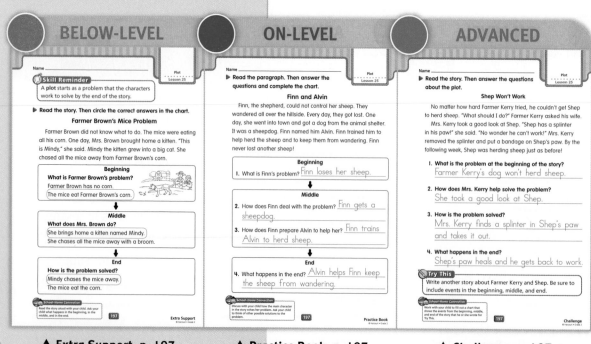

▲ Extra Support, p. 197   ▲ Practice Book, p. 197   ▲ Challenge, p. 197

E L L

- Group children according to academic levels, and assign one of the pages on the left.

- Clarify any unfamiliar concepts as necessary. See *ELL Teacher Guide* Lesson 25 for support in scaffolding instruction.

Compare and Contrast

Comprehension: Review

Review

EXPLAIN COMPARE AND CONTRAST   Remind children that when they compare two things, they tell how they are alike. When they contrast two things, they tell how they are different. Model the ways good readers can compare and contrast two selections:

> **Think Aloud**   When I compare and contrast two selections, I think about their topic or the kinds of illustrations or photographs they have.

Practice/Apply

GUIDED PRACTICE   Draw a Venn diagram like the following to compare and contrast "The Bee" and "Watching in the Wild." Work with children to fill in some information to show how the two selections are alike and different.

The Bee
tells about
honeybees

Both
tell details
about a
creature's
life

Watching
in the Wild
tells about
gorillas

INDEPENDENT PRACTICE   On their own, have children write another way in which the selections are alike or different. Have volunteers explain their ideas, and add the information to the chart. Children may suggest ideas about the illustrations and photographs, or the fact that "Watching in the Wild" includes a human "character" while "The Bee" does not.

Objective

• *To understand how to compare and contrast*

Skill Trace

Tested **Compare and Contrast**

Introduce	T70–T71
Reteach	S12–S13, S24–S25
Review	T172–T173, T415, T425
Test	Theme 5

READERS' THEATER

5-DAY READERS' THEATER	
DAY 1	Read Aloud/Read Along
DAY 2	Read Together
DAY 3	Choose Roles/Rehearse
DAY 4	Rehearse Roles
DAY 5	Perform

Read Together: "Town Hall"

Objective

- *To practice reading fluently with expression at an appropriate reading rate*

Fluency Support Materials

Fluency Builders, Grade 2, Lesson 25

Audiotext "Town Hall" is available on *Audiotext Grade 2*, CD 5.

Town Hall

Roles

Teacher	Robin	Town Leader 1
Kris	Mayor	Town Leader 2

Teacher: Good morning, Mayor. I'd like you to meet Kris and Robin, two of my students.

Kris: The students at our school have questions about the new park the town is building.

Robin: We'd like to ask you and some other town leaders our questions. Then we'll report back to our classmates.

Mayor: We'll be happy to answer your questions.

Kris: Why did you decide to build a park?

Mayor: The people in our town need a place to go with their families.

Robin: What kinds of things will be at the park?

Mayor: I'm happy to tell you that there will be a playground! In a town the size of ours, people have many interests. Different people in our town want different things.

Lesson 25: Town Hall · 140 · Teacher Resource Book

▲ **Teacher Resource Book, pp. 140–145**

Preview

GENRE Have children open their books to pp. 304–315, or distribute photocopies of the script from *Teacher Resource Book* pages 140–145. Help children recall that "Town Hall" is a Readers' Theater script about students interviewing town leaders.

Focus on Fluency

DISCUSS READING RATE AND EXPRESSION Remind children that in this theme they learned that good readers use expression and adjust their reading rate to help them read more fluently. Remind them that they should think about how they could use their voices to show how a character is feeling. They should think about whether certain lines should be read more slowly or more quickly.

Read Together

ORAL READING Have children take turns reading different parts in the Readers' Theater script. Point out that parts will be assigned later. Explain that, in this first reading, they should concentrate on using expression to make the characters come alive and on reading at a rate that will help them read more fluently. Then have small groups of children begin reading the script aloud. Tell children that they should think about what their character is feeling or trying to say and to use their voices to help express those ideas.

Visit the different groups, listening to children read. Offer encouragement, and model fluent reading as needed.

Think Aloud The town leaders and the mayor are trying to explain some new ideas. I will read those lines at a slower rate so that the other characters will understand the ideas.

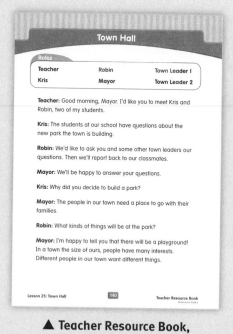

Build Robust Vocabulary

Words from the Read-Aloud

Teach/Model

Routine Card 3

INTRODUCE ROBUST VOCABULARY Use *Routine Card 3* to introduce the words after introducing and reading aloud the following selection.

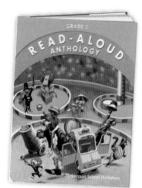

Read-Aloud Anthology, "From ▶ Study Hall to City Hall," p. 90

❶ Put the word in **selection context**.
❷ Display Transparency R134 and say the word and the **Student-Friendly Explanation**.
❸ Have children **say the word** with you.
❹ Use the word in other contexts, and have children **interact with the word's meaning**.
❺ Remove the transparency. Say the Student-Friendly Explanation again, and ask children to **name the word** that goes with it.

❶ **Selection Context:** Michael Sessions had to **race** home to get his homework done so that he could work on his campaign for mayor.
❹ **Interact with Word Meaning:** If you saw that the bus you wanted to take was coming, would you race to the bus stop? Why?

❶ **Selection Context:** Now that he's mayor but still in school, Michael finds that he is **juggling** a lot of responsibilities.
❹ **Interact with Word Meaning:** Would you be juggling your responsibilities if you had to finish your homework and take care of a baby brother or sister? Explain.

Practice/Apply

GUIDED PRACTICE   Ask children to do the following:
• Tell about a time when your family was juggling to get several chores done in one day.
• Describe a time when you had to race from one place to another.

Objective
• *To develop robust vocabulary through discussing a literature selection*

Tested

INTRODUCE ✔

Vocabulary

race   **juggling**

▼ Student-Friendly Explanations

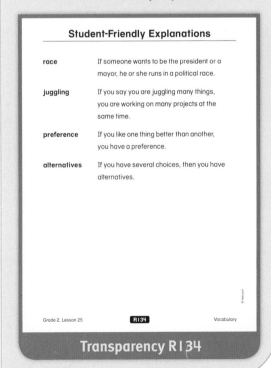

Student-Friendly Explanations	
race	If someone wants to be the president or a mayor, he or she runs in a political race.
juggling	If you say you are juggling many things, you are working on many projects at the same time.
preference	If you like one thing better than another, you have a preference.
alternatives	If you have several choices, then you have alternatives.

Grade 2, Lesson 25   R134   Vocabulary

Transparency R134

Grammar *Quick Write*

Review: Subject-Verb Agreement

5-DAY GRAMMAR

DAY 1	Review Present-Tense Action Verbs
DAY 2	**Review Subject-Verb Agreement**
DAY 3	Review Past-Tense Verbs
DAY 4	Review Forms of *be*
DAY 5	Cumulative Review

Objective
- *To use correct subject-verb agreement in sentences*

Daily Proofreading

my dog is noisiest than my cat.

(My, noisier)

Writing Trait ➤

Strengthening Conventions

Review Use these short daily lessons with children's own writing to continue building a foundation for revising/editing longer connected text. See also *Writer's Companion*, Lesson 25.

▲ Practice Book, p. 198

Reinforce the Skill

REVIEW SUBJECT-VERB AGREEMENT Review what children have learned about subject-verb agreement. Remind them of the following points:

- The naming part of a sentence must match the verb.
- Add *-s* to most verbs when the naming part of the sentence tells about one.
- Do not add *-s* when the naming part tells about more than one.
- Do not add *-s* to a verb when the naming part is *I* or *you*.

Write the following sentences on the board. For each one, have volunteers underline the action verb and tell whether the naming part tells about one or more than one.

The farmer milks the cows. (one)
Anna and Milo collect the eggs. (more than one)
A piglet squeezes under the gate. (one)

Practice/Apply

GUIDED PRACTICE Write the following incomplete sentences and verb choices on the board. Guide children to tell which form of the verb they should use in each sentence.

I _____ my hair. (comb, combs)
Miko _____ her teeth. (brush, brushes)
You _____ your backpack. (zip, zips)
We _____ out the door. (run, runs)

INDEPENDENT PRACTICE Have partners write four sentences about things they can do at recess or on the playground. Children should use the following four subjects: *I, You, We,* and the name of a classmate. Tell partners that they should use action verbs in each sentence, and the verb should agree with the naming part. Invite volunteers to share their sentences.

5-DAY WRITING	
DAY 1	Select a Piece and Revise
DAY 2	**Revise**
DAY 3	Publish
DAY 4	Publish
DAY 5	Present

Writing
Revise and Publish

Revise

REVISE Explain to children that good writers may revise their writing several times before they feel that their work is at its best.

Think Aloud **When I revise a draft, having someone read through it can be like getting a new set of eyes. Sometimes I know that certain parts could be improved, but I just don't know how to make them better, and this is a way to get help. It also really helps to have another person tell me what he or she likes about my writing.**

Have children conference with a partner to read each other's work as they continue to revise their drafts. Encourage readers to point out parts they enjoy or admire, and to provide clear, positive suggestions to help improve the piece.

SENTENCE FLUENCY Have children check that their sentences flow. Encourage them to check that they have not overused *I* and that they have combined sentences appropriately to avoid choppiness.

GRAMMAR-WRITING CONNECTION Remind children to check that the naming part of each sentence matches the verb used. Encourage them to use Editor's Marks to indicate changes.

CONFER WITH CHILDREN Meet with individual children, helping them as they revise their writing. Offer encouragement and suggestions for improving their writing, as needed.

Objectives

- *To progress through the stages of the writing process*
- *To revise a self-selected piece of assigned writing*

 ## Writing Prompt

Write about Ideas Have children write a few sentences to tell about how they came up with the idea for one of their writing pieces in this theme.

▲ Writer's Companion, Lesson 25

Day 3

phonics and Spelling

- Review: Vowel Variant /o͞o/ *oo, ew, ue, ui, ou*
- State the Generalization

Comprehension

Review: Use Graphic Aids and Compare and Contrast

Fluency

READERS' THEATER

- Choose Roles/ Rehearse: "Town Hall," *Student Edition*, pp. 304–315 **Read!**

 Town Hall

Robust Vocabulary

- Review: *accomplish, feasible, attend, report, area, serve*

Grammar *Quick Write*

- Review: Past-Tense Verbs

Writing ✏️

- Proofread and Publish

Warm-Up Routines

Oral Language

Objective *To listen attentively and respond appropriately to oral communication*

Question of the Day

What do you think would be the most fun about being a bee?

Invite children to recall what they learned about what bees do in a hive. Use the following prompts to generate ideas:

- **Where do bees live?**
- **Why do bees build honeycombs?**
- **What are some of the jobs that bees have in a hive?**
- **Which job would you like to have if you were a bee?**

Have children complete the following sentence frame to explain their choice.

If I were a bee, I would like to _____ because _____.

Read Aloud

Objective *To listen for a purpose*

BIG BOOK OF RHYMES AND POEMS Display the poem "Bumblebees" on page 41. Ask children to tell what they recall about the poem. Tell children to listen for the vowel sound that is repeated most often in the poem. Then read the poem aloud. Ask children which vowel sound they heard most often, and have them identify words with the sound. (long *e*; bees, teeny, teensy, weensy) Point out that this sound is the one they hear in the word *bee*. Invite children to join in as you reread the poem, emphasizing the words with the long *e* sound.

▲ **Big Book of Rhymes and Poems, p. 41**

Word Wall

Objective *To read high-frequency words*

REVIEW HIGH-FREQUENCY WORDS Point to the following words on the Word Wall: *impossible, children, learn, special, clear, imagine, favorite, young, fair,* and *exercise*. Choral-read the words with children, clapping out the number of syllables as you read each word. Then point to the words at random, and have volunteers read a word and clap out its syllables.

Vowel Variant /o͞o/ oo, ew, ue, ui, ou

 phonics and Spelling

5-DAY PHONICS	
DAY 1	Review /ou/ou, ow
DAY 2	Review /ôr/or, ore, ou
DAY 3	**Review /o͞o/oo, ew, ue, ui, ou**
DAY 4	Review /âr/air, are
DAY 5	Cumulative Review

Objectives

- *To recognize and blend the vowel variant /o͞o/oo, ew, ue, ui, ou*
- *To read words with /o͞o/oo, ew, ue, ui, ou, and other known letter-sounds*
- *To use /o͞o/oo, ew, ue, ui, ou, and other known letter-sounds to spell words*

Skill Trace

Tested ✓ **Vowel Variant /o͞o/oo, ew, ue, ui, ou**

Introduce	Grade 1
Reintroduce	T220–T223
Reteach	S26–S27
Review	**T232–T233, T258–T259, T422**
Test	Theme 5

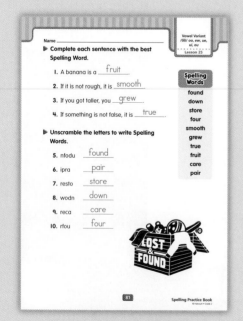

▲ Spelling Practice Book, p. 81

Review ⏱

 Routine Card 1

CONNECT LETTERS AND SOUNDS Remind children that they have learned that the letters *oo, ew, ue, ui,* and *ou* can all stand for the /o͞o/ sound. Display the *Sound/Spelling Card* for /o͞o/oo. Review the letter/sound correspondence for *oo, ew, ue, ui,* and *ou*.

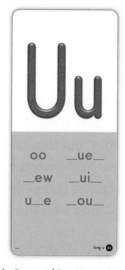

▲ Sound/Spelling Card

Read Words in Context ⏱

APPLY PHONICS Write the following sentences on the board or on chart paper. Have children read each sentence silently. Then track the print as children read the sentences aloud.

> We watched a <u>cartoon</u> about a <u>moose</u> and a <u>raccoon</u>.
>
> They wanted to make a <u>new</u> kind of <u>soup</u>.
>
> They put in <u>fruit</u> and <u>root</u> beer, and then they added some <u>glue</u>.
>
> When they <u>blew</u> on the <u>soup</u> to <u>cool</u> if off, it stuck to the <u>spoon</u>!

Day 3

5-DAY SPELLING
DAY 1 Pretest
DAY 2 Word Building
DAY 3 State the Generalization
DAY 4 Review
DAY 5 Posttest

Review Spelling Words

STATE THE GENERALIZATION FOR /o͞o/oo, ew, ue, ui, ou   List spelling words 1–10 on chart paper or on the board. Circle the word *smooth* and ask children to read it. Ask a volunteer to identify the letters that stand for the /o͞o/ sound and underline them. Then, repeat the process with the words *grew, true,* and *fruit,* leading children to identify the letters that stand for the /o͞o/ sound. Follow a similar procedure to identify the letters that stand for the following phonic elements:

- vowel diphthong /ou/*ou, ow*
- *r*-controlled vowel /ôr/*or, ore, our*
- *r*-controlled vowel /âr/*air, are*

WRITE   Have children write the spelling words in their note-books. Remind them to use their best handwriting and to use the chart to check their spelling.

Handwriting

LETTER SPACING   Remind children to make sure that they write the letters close together in each word, with proper spacing between words.

Spelling Words

1.	found	6.	grew
2.	down	7.	true
3.	store	8.	fruit
4.	fair	9.	care*
5.	smooth	10.	pair

* Word from "Town Hall"

BELOW-LEVEL

Make Flashcards   Have partners make flashcards for the spelling words. Have them take turns reading a card. The partner should spell the word and use it in a sentence.

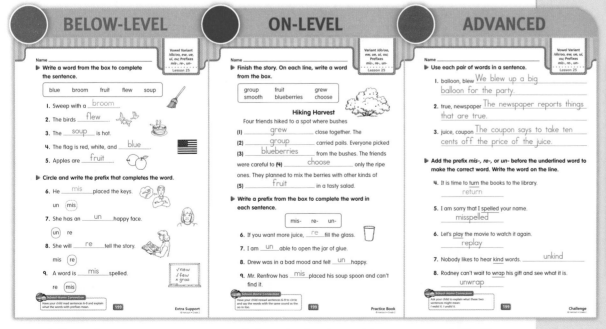

▲ Extra Support, p. 199   ▲ Practice Book, p. 199   ▲ Challenge, p. 199

E L L

- Group children according to academic levels, and assign one of the pages on the left.

- Clarify any unfamiliar concepts as necessary. See *ELL Teacher Guide* Lesson 25 for support in scaffolding instruction.

Use Graphic Aids
Comprehension: Review

Objective

- *To use graphic aids to understand nonfiction selections*

Skill Trace

 Use Graphic Aids

Introduce	T224–T225
Reteach	S30–S31, S42–S43
Review	T261, T277, T289, T316–T317, T345, T361, T371, T424, T445
Test	Theme 5
Maintain	Theme 6, T272

Reinforce the Skill

DISCUSS GRAPHIC AIDS Remind children that authors include pictures and other images to help readers see ideas and information quickly and easily. Discuss the following types of graphic aids with children. You may wish to display examples from science or social studies textbooks.

- A diagram shows parts of something or how something works.

- A time line shows dates and events over a period of time.

- A map shows where places are located.

- A chart shows information in rows, columns, and headings.

- A graph is a kind of picture that shows amounts of things.

Practice/Apply

GUIDED PRACTICE Have children turn to the diagram on pages 248–249 of "The Bee." Point out that, without the diagram, it might be hard for readers to understand what a honeycomb looks like. Review the information from the diagram. Ask: **How does the diagram help you understand how the comb is organized?** (It shows where honey, pollen, and eggs are stored.)

INDEPENDENT PRACTICE Have partners work together to find an example of a diagram, a time line, a map, a chart, or a graph in their science or social studies textbooks, in reference sources, or in nonfiction selections in the classroom. Invite volunteers to share and describe the graphic aids they find.

Compare and Contrast

Comprehension: Review

Reinforce the Skill

DISCUSS COMPARE AND CONTRAST   Remind children that good readers often compare and contrast stories. Elicit the meanings of the terms *compare* and *contrast*. (Comparing two things tells how they are alike. Contrasting them tells how they are different.)

Practice/Apply

GUIDED PRACTICE   Work together to complete a chart as you discuss how the genre and setting of "Annie's Gifts" and "Jamaica Louise James" are alike and different.

INDEPENDENT PRACTICE   On their own, have children write about how Annie and Jamaica are alike and different. Have them share their ideas and add them to the chart.

Objective
• *To compare and contrast story elements across texts*

Skill Trace

Tested   **Compare and Contrast**

Introduce	T70–T71
Reteach	S12–S13, S24–S25
Review	T172–T173, T415, T425
Test	Theme 5

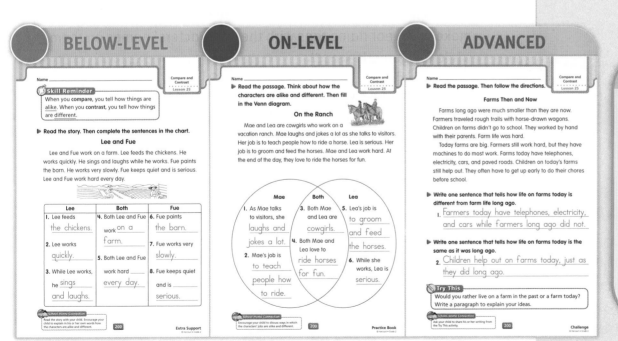

▲ **Extra Support, p. 200**   ▲ **Practice Book, p. 200**   ▲ **Challenge, p. 200**

ELL

• Group children according to academic levels, and assign one of the pages on the left.

• Clarify any unfamiliar concepts as necessary. See *ELL Teacher Guide* Lesson 25 for support in scaffolding instruction.

READERS' THEATER

Choose Roles: "Town Hall"

5-DAY READERS' THEATER	
DAY 1	Read Aloud/Read Along
DAY 2	Read Together
DAY 3	**Choose Roles/Rehearse**
DAY 4	Rehearse Roles
DAY 5	Perform

Objective

• *To practice using expression and appropriate reading rate to read fluently*

Fluency Support Materials

Fluency Builders, Grade 2, Lesson 25

Audiotext "Town Hall" is available on *Audiotext Grade 2*, CD5.

E L L

Choosing Roles   You may wish to assign the role of Teacher to children who need language development support. Children who need less support may choose their own roles.

Focus on Fluency

READ USING EXPRESSION AND APPROPRIATE RATE   Remind children that when they read aloud, their expression gives the audience an idea of what the character is like and how he or she is feeling. Point out that the characters should sound like they are having a conversation, so children should read at an even rate and speed up or slow down only when it makes sense to do so.

Practice Reading

CHOOSE/ASSIGN ROLES   Distribute copies of the script to the children if you have not already done so (*Teacher Resource Book*, pp. 140–145). Based on your observations on Day 2, assign or have children choose roles. Since the play is just one extended scene, you may wish to divide it into sections and split the roles among children so that everyone has a part. After you assign roles, encourage children to highlight the parts they will read aloud.

PRACTICE READING   You may wish to have children who are reading "scenes" together sit in groups. Read through the text one or two times. Have listeners follow along. Allow children time to become familiar with their lines. You may want to have children make and wear name tags with their characters' names on them while they practice reading.

Provide feedback to individuals and groups by modeling, encouraging, and praising children for their efforts and enthusiasm. Remind children to read at an even pace, and to use expression to bring their characters to life. Encourage children to give positive feedback to each other as they read their parts.

Monitor children's engagement with their own reading. Encourage them to note text they read fluently, as well as text they need to practice more.

Build Robust Vocabulary

Review

Reinforce Word Meanings

USE VOCABULARY IN DIFFERENT CONTEXTS   Remind children of the Student-Friendly Explanations of the Vocabulary Words introduced on Days I and 2. Then discuss each word in a new context.

accomplish, attend

- **Must you attend school to accomplish something?**

feasible

- **Is it more feasible to plan a party for 10 or for 200? Why?**

report

- **What would you do to report on today's weather?**

area

- **Describe the different areas in our classroom.**

serve

- **Tell about a job where the worker serves other people.**

Objectives

- *To review robust vocabulary*
- *To figure out a word's meaning based on its context*

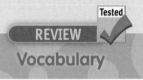

REVIEW | Tested ✓
Vocabulary

accomplish	report
feasible	area
attend	serve

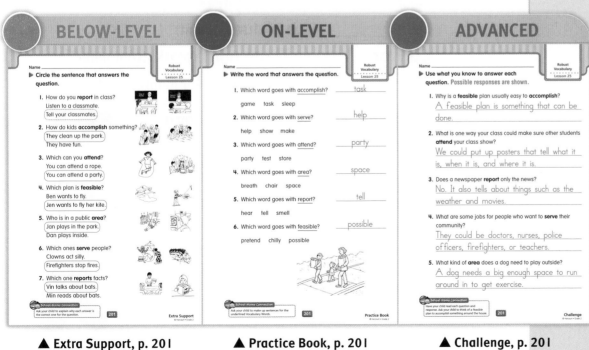

▲ Extra Support, p. 201   ▲ Practice Book, p. 201   ▲ Challenge, p. 201

E L L

- Group children according to academic levels, and assign one of the pages on the left.

- Clarify any unfamiliar concepts as necessary. See *ELL Teacher Guide* Lesson 25 for support in scaffolding instruction.

Grammar Quick Write

Review: Past-Tense Verbs

5-DAY GRAMMAR	
DAY 1	Review Present-Tense Action Verbs
DAY 2	Review Subject-Verb Agreement
DAY 3	Review Past-Tense Verbs
DAY 4	Review Forms of *be*
DAY 5	Cumulative Review

Objective

- *To write past-tense verbs correctly in sentences*

Daily Proofreading

Lindys sister is in nebraska

(Lindy's, Nebraska.)

Writing Trait

Strengthening Conventions

Review Use these short daily lessons with children's own writing to continue building a foundation for revising/editing longer connected text. See also *Writer's Companion,* Lesson 25.

Reinforce the Skill

REVIEW PAST-TENSE VERBS Review with children what they have learned about past-tense verbs. Discuss the following points:

- Some verbs tell about actions that happened in the past.
- Many past-tense verbs are formed by adding *-ed*.
- Verbs that end in silent *e* can tell about the past by adding *-d*.

Write the following verbs on the board:

laugh	giggle
frown	smile

Have volunteers tell whether *-ed* or *-d* should be added to each verb so it tells about an action in the past.

Practice/Apply

GUIDED PRACTICE Write the following sentences on the board. Work with children to change the verb in parentheses so it tells about an action that happened in the past.

Graham _____ playing trumpet. (practice)

Seth _____ a picture. (paint)

Candace _____ her homework. (complete)

Kate and Ayana _____ rope. (jump)

INDEPENDENT PRACTICE Brainstorm a list of regular verbs that tell about movement, and list the verbs on the board. Have children use verbs from the list to write three sentences that tell about something that happened in the past. Have partners share and check each other's work.

Writing
Publish

5-DAY WRITING	
DAY 1	Revise and Publish
DAY 2	Revise and Publish
DAY 3	**Publish**
DAY 4	Proofread and Publish
DAY 5	Present

Publish

CHOOSE A PUBLISHING IDEA   Have children choose a publishing idea that works well for the kind of writing they have chosen to revise and publish. You may wish to suggest the following options.

- **Make a Flap Frame:**   Have children glue or tape their writing to the upper half of a piece of construction paper. Have children cut a flap that will open like a door in the lower half of the paper. Have children place a piece of cardboard or card stock underneath and lightly trace the open space from the top sheet. Children will then create an illustration in this space. Children can then glue or staple the top sheet to the bottom sheet. Their illustration should appear when they lift the flap.

- **Create a Topic Frame:**   Have children tape or glue their writing to a piece of cardboard or card stock. They can then make a special frame that helps tell about the writing. Help children cut a frame from cardboard that will enclose their piece of writing. The frame should be at least two inches wide all around, so that children can draw, paint, or glue pictures or small items on it. Have children decorate their frames.

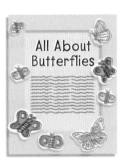

WRITING TRAIT **PRESENTATION**   Remind children that they should use their best handwriting in a published piece. Explain that writing should be neat and each letter should be clearly and correctly formed. Have them proofread their final draft carefully.

PREPARE FINAL WRITING   Once children have chosen their publishing idea, they can begin to work on the final version of their piece of writing. Children may either write on paper, using their best handwriting, or use available technology to type and print their writing.

Objectives

- *To progress through the stages of the writing process*
- *To publish a self-selected piece of assigned writing*

Writing Prompt

Reflect   Have children write about why they chose the piece they did to publish.

Day at a Glance
Day 4

phonics and Spelling

- *r*-Controlled Vowel /âr/*air, are*

COMPREHENSION STRATEGIES

- **Review: Use Story Structure, Summarize**
- **Review: Synonyms**

Reading

- Reading a Fable: "A Time for Patience," *Student Edition* pp. 316–319

Read!

Fluency

READERS' THEATER

- **Rehearse Roles: "Town Hall,"** *Student Edition*, pp. 304–315

Robust Vocabulary

- Review: *accomplish, feasible, attend, report, area, serve, preference, alternatives, race, juggling*

Grammar [Quick Write]

- Review: Forms of *be*

Writing

- **Proofread and Publish**

Warm-Up Routines

Oral Language

Objective *To listen attentively and respond appropriately to oral communication*

Question of the Day

What do you think a tree would say if it could talk?

Use the following prompts to discuss why trees are important to people and animals.

- **What are some ways that children enjoy trees?**
- **Why are trees important to animals?**
- **How do trees change during the year?**
- **What are some ways that people use trees?**

Have children complete the following sentence frame to tell what they think a tree might say if it could talk.

If a tree could talk, it would say, "_____."

Read Aloud

Objective *To listen for a purpose*

BIG BOOK OF RHYMES AND POEMS Display the poem "Hide-and-Seek" on page 44 and read the title. Ask children to recall how a tree is used in the poem. (as a place to play hide-and-seek) Then read the poem aloud. Tell children that as they listen they should think about what a tree would say to someone who was hiding in its limbs. Ask volunteers to share their ideas with the class. Then invite children to join in as you reread the poem.

Hide-and-Seek

It's hide and seek.
I climb a tree
and from a leafy limb
I watch my seeker seeking me
and sneak a look at him.

The trunk is strong
to lean upon.
The leaves leave room to peek.
If it had apples for me, too,
I'd stay up here a week.

Constance Levy

▲ **Big Book of Rhymes and Poems, p. 44**

Word Wall

Objective *To read high-frequency words*

REVIEW HIGH-FREQUENCY WORDS Point to the following words on the Word Wall: *impossible, children, learn, special, clear, imagine, favorite, young, fair,* and *exercise*. Ask volunteers to read each word and use it in a sentence. Repeat the procedure until all children have had a turn.

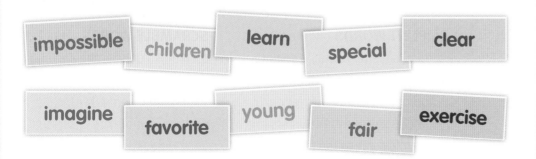

impossible   children   learn   special   clear

imagine   favorite   young   fair   exercise

r-Controlled Vowel /âr/ *air, are*

phonics *and Spelling*

Objectives

- *To recognize the sound /âr/air,* are
- *To read words with /âr/air,* are *and other known letter-sounds*
- *To use /âr/air,* are *and other known letter-sounds to spell words*

Spelling Words

1.	**found**	6.	**grew**
2.	**down**	7.	**true**
3.	**store**	8.	**fruit**
4.	**four**	9.	**care***
5.	**smooth**	10.	**pair**

* Word from "Town Hall"

Review

READ A SPELLING WORD   Write the word *care* on the board. Ask children to identify the letters that stand for the /âr/ sound. Remind them that the letters *air* and *are* can both stand for the /âr/ sound.

BUILD SPELLING WORDS   Have children follow your directions to change one or more letters in each of the following words to make a spelling word. Have them write the word on a sheet of paper or in their notebooks. Then have a volunteer change the spelling of the word on the board so that children can self-check their spelling.

- Write *chair* on the board. Ask: **Which spelling word can you make by changing the first two letters?** (pair)

- Write *share* on the board. Ask: **Which spelling word can you make by changing the first two letters?** (care)

Use a similar procedure for the rest of the spelling words: *foul* (found), *moon* (smooth), *flew* (grew), *clue* (true), *clown* (down), *stare* (store), *court* (four), *juice* (fruit).

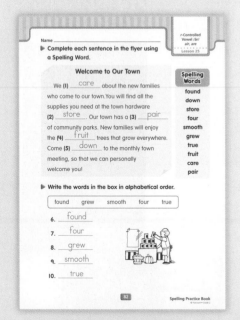

▲ Spelling Practice Book, p. 82

BELOW-LEVEL

COMPLETE WORDS   Write the first and last letter of each spelling word on the board, with blanks for the appropriate number of letters in the middle. Say one of the words and have a child come to the board and fill in the missing letters. Have the child say the word and spell it again.

ADVANCED

SCRAMBLE WORDS   Have children make a list of the spelling words and scramble the letters. Then have them switch papers with a partner and unscramble the letters to write each word.

5-DAY PHONICS	
DAY 1	Review /ou/*ou, ow*
DAY 2	Review /ôr/*or, ore, ou*
DAY 3	Review /ōō/*oo, ew, ue, ui, ou*
DAY 4	Review /âr/*air, are*
DAY 5	Cumulative Review

Read Words in Context

APPLY PHONICS   Write the following sentences on the board or on chart paper. Have children read each sentence silently. Then track the print as children read the sentence aloud.

> Farmer Johnson <u>grew</u> corn, tomatoes, and peppers.
>
> Tell me the <u>true</u> story about what happened.
>
> I like to watch the mother robin <u>care</u> for her babies.
>
> We saw a <u>pair</u> of chipmunks at the park.

WRITE   Have children use each spelling word in a new sentence.

BELOW-LEVEL

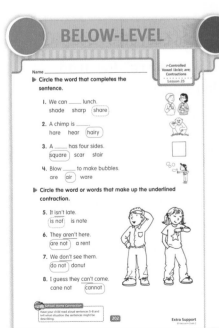

▲ Extra Support, p. 202

ON-LEVEL

▲ Practice Book, p. 202

ADVANCED

▲ Challenge, p. 202

E L L

- Group children according to academic levels, and assign one of the pages on the left.

- Clarify any unfamiliar concepts as necessary. See *ELL Teacher Guide* Lesson 25 for support in scaffolding instruction.

Comprehension Strategies
Review

Objectives

- *To analyze genre features*
- *To apply reading strategies to content-area reading*

Reading a Fable

PREVIEW PAGES 316–319 Have children scan the pages. Tell children that these pages provide information that will help them read fables. Point out that pages 318–319 show the same pages as those reduced on page 317, but that pages 318–319 are at full size.

SET A PURPOSE Tell children that as they read these pages, they should look for ways to read and better understand fables.

DISCUSS TEXT FEATURES Have children read the paragraph under Reading a Fable. Point out and explain the following features often found in fables, as shown on page 317:

- **TITLE** The title appears at the beginning of the fable and gives an idea of what the fable will be about.

- **PROBLEM AND SOLUTION** The plot of a fable includes a problem and solution. The problem is usually something a character has to do or figure out. The solution is how the character solves the problem.

- **MORAL** A fable usually includes a moral at the end. The moral is the lesson the reader is supposed to think about.

Review the Focus Strategies

DISCUSS COMPREHENSION STRATEGIES Have children read and discuss the information about using story structure and summarizing.

APPLY TO READING A FABLE Have children use the comprehension strategies as they read pages 318–319.

SET A PURPOSE AND READ Tell children that their purpose for reading pages 318–319 is to use comprehension strategies and what they now know about fables to read and understand the pages.

BELOW-LEVEL

Preview the Fable Explain that previewing a fable helps readers prepare for what it will be about. Guide children to use the illustrations to preview the fable. Have children identify the animals they see and predict the problem the animals might face.

Lesson 25

COMPREHENSION STRATEGIES
Review

Theme Review

Reading a Fable

Bridge to Reading Fiction Fables are stories that have been told for a long time. These stories are used to teach lessons about life. The notes on page 317 show some of the features of a fable. Look for these features each time you read a fable.

Review the Focus Strategies

You can also use the strategies you learned in this theme to help you read fables.

Use Story Structure
Use what you know about how stories are arranged to help you understand what you read. Think about the fable's characters, setting, problem, and solution.

Summarize
Tell about the most important ideas in one or two sentences.

Use comprehension strategies as you read "A Time for Patience" on pages 318–319.

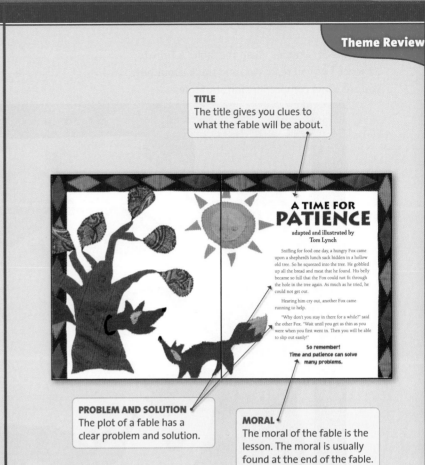

TITLE
The title gives you clues to what the fable will be about.

A TIME FOR PATIENCE

adapted and illustrated by
Tom Lynch

Sniffing for food one day, a hungry Fox came upon a shepherd's lunch sack hidden in a hollow old tree. So he squeezed into the tree. He gobbled up all the bread and meat that he found. His belly became so full that the Fox could not fit through the hole in the tree again. As much as he tried, he could not get out.

Hearing him cry out, another Fox came running to help.

"Why don't you stay in there for a while?" said the other Fox. "Wait until you get as thin as you were when you first went in. Then you will be able to slip out easily!"

**So remember!
Time and patience can solve
many problems.**

PROBLEM AND SOLUTION
The plot of a fable has a clear problem and solution.

MORAL
The moral of the fable is the lesson. The moral is usually found at the end of the fable.

316

317

Features of a Fable

Point out the special features of a fable noted on page 317.

TITLE Point out the fable's title, and read it aloud. Discuss with children what *patience* means. (waiting with understanding)

PROBLEM AND SOLUTION Explain that as in most other stories the beginning of the fable will tell about a problem a character has. Point out that the solution will be found at the end.

MORAL Point out the moral at the end. Explain that the moral is usually a lesson about life.

Apply the Strategies Read the fable "A Time for Patience." As you read, stop and think about how you are using comprehension strategies.

Stop and Think

How can you use story structure to help you understand? What parts of the fable would you use to summarize it?

A TIME FOR PATIENCE

adapted and illustrated by
Tom Lynch

Sniffing for food one day, a hungry Fox came upon a shepherd's lunch sack hidden in a hollow old tree. So he squeezed into the tree. He gobbled up all the bread and meat that he found. His belly became so full that the Fox could not fit through the hole in the tree again. As much as he tried, he could not get out.

Hearing him cry out, another Fox came running to help.

"Why don't you stay in there for a while?" said the other Fox. "Wait until you get as thin as you were when you first went in. Then you will be able to slip out easily!"

**So remember!
Time and patience can solve
many problems.**

318

319

Monitor Comprehension

PAGES 318–319 Have children use comprehension strategies as they read pages 318–319.

① PLOT **What problem does the fox face? What is the solution to his problem?** (Possible response: The fox ate so much of the food he found in a tree that he became too fat to get out. Another fox tells him he will just have to be patient and wait until he loses weight to get out.)

② USE GRAPHIC AIDS **How does the fable's illustration help you to understand what happens in the story?** (Possible response: It helps show the fox's problem at a glance.)

Stop and Think

Apply
Comprehension Strategies

Use Story Structure Model using story structure to clarify the story problem.

Think Aloud By thinking about the characters' problem, I recall that the fox found someone's lunch inside a hollow tree, and after he ate it all, he became stuck inside the tree.

Summarize Explain to children that to answer Question 1, they can summarize the plot by telling the problem and the solution in one or two sentences.

Synonyms
Vocabulary: Review

Reinforce the Skill

EXPLAIN SYNONYMS   Remind children that synonyms are words that have the same, or almost the same, meanings. Write the following sentences on the board:

> I <u>shut</u> the door quietly. I <u>closed</u> the door quietly.

Read the sentences aloud. Point to the words *shut* and *closed*. Elicit that the words mean about the same thing. Explain to children that they can use a dictionary or a thesaurus to find out if words are synonyms.

Practice/Apply

GUIDED PRACTICE   Write the following sentences on the board or on chart paper. Guide children to determine which word in parentheses is a synonym for the underlined word in each sentence. Model how to use a dictionary or thesaurus to check the answers.

> The caterpillar <u>nibbled</u> on a leaf. (chewed, tugged)
>
> Many spiders <u>produce</u> amazing webs. (create, eat)
>
> Some insects are <u>useful</u> to humans. (colorful, helpful)

INDEPENDENT PRACTICE   Write the following sentences on the board. Have children determine which word in the parentheses is a synonym for the underlined word in each sentence. Have children use a dictionary or thesaurus to check their answers.

> I was too scared to peek into the <u>unused</u> shed.
> (large, empty)
>
> The <u>glare</u> of the sun made it hard to see.
> (brightness, ashamed)
>
> Can you <u>repeat</u> the sound a dolphin makes?
> (hear, copy)

Objectives

- To understand and explain common synonyms
- To understand the purposes of a dictionary and a thesaurus

Skill Trace

 Tested **Synonyms**

Introduce	T268–T269
Reteach	S32–S33, S44–S45
Review	T352–T353, T437, T446
Test	Theme 5

READERS' THEATER

5-DAY READERS' THEATER	
DAY 1	Read Aloud/Read Along
DAY 2	Read Together
DAY 3	Choose Roles/Rehearse
DAY 4	**Rehearse Roles**
DAY 5	Perform

Rehearse Roles: "Town Hall"

Objective

- *To read with expression and at a rate that sounds like natural speech*

Fluency Support Materials

Fluency Builders, Grade 2, Lesson 25

Audiotext "Town Hall" is available on *Audiotext Grade 2, CD 5*

"Research Says"

Repeated Reading "Reading rate increased significantly from one to three readings, an occurence that brought instructional-level readers to near mastery-level performance."
—Rasinki, et al. (1994), p. 224

▲ **Teacher Resource Book, pp. 140–145**

Focus on Fluency

READING WITH EXPRESSION AT AN APPROPRIATE RATE   Have children continue to rehearse their parts. Explain to children that since they are going to perform the Readers' Theater tomorrow, they should imagine that their audience is watching them when they rehearse. Remind children to read at a rate that helps the audience understand what their character is saying. Tell children to use their voices to give an idea of what a character is like and what he or she is thinking or feeling.

Think Aloud   When I am reading the part of the Mayor or a Town Leader, I want to sound friendly and caring. These characters are excited and proud about the plans for the new park, and I want to read their lines with feeling so they sound that way.

Practice Reading

REHEARSE ROLES   Have the class read through the script, following their assigned parts. Encourage listeners to offer constructive criticism, focusing on positive aspects of the reading as well as areas for improvement.

Monitor children's reading, and model reading particular lines if children are having difficulties. If you copied pages 140–145 in the *Teacher's Resource Book* so that children have individual scripts, you may want to encourage them to mark those words or sections that they want to improve reading.

You may wish to prepare a simple set to approximate a conference room, with a table, chairs, and sample plans for the park. Children may wear nametags that tell their roles.

Have children practice one more time for their last rehearsal, as if their audience is listening to them read. You may wish to include the backdrop on page 116 of the *Teacher Resource Book.*

Build Robust Vocabulary

Review

Review Robust Vocabulary

USE VOCABULARY IN DIFFERENT CONTEXTS Remind children of the Student Friendly Explanations of the Vocabulary Words. Then discuss each word in a new context.

preference, alternatives Tell children that you will describe two things they could do after school. Read them once. Then read each one again, and have children raise their hand to show their preference. If children don't like either idea, they should say, "Are there any other alternatives?"

> **do homework OR do your chores**
>
> **fix a snack OR fix the family car**

accomplish, feasible Tell children you will name some things they could try to accomplish. If they think the thing is feasible, they should give a thumbs-up. If not, they should give a thumbs-down.

> **do your homework**   **build a treehouse**

attend Tell children you will name some events. If they think the thing is something they would like to attend, they should say, "I'd love to go!" If not, they should say, "I'll stay home, thanks."

> **an opera**   **a major hockey game**

report Tell children that you will name some things. If they think they could report on the thing, they should raise a hand. If not, they should do nothing.

> **explain why the sky is blue**
>
> **what life is like in New Zealand**

race Tell children you will describe some things they might have to do. If they would have to race to get the thing done, they should say, "Ready, set, go!" If not, they should say, "I've got plenty of time."

> **finish your homework in an hour**
>
> **clean your room in fifteen minutes**

Objectives
- *To review robust vocabulary*
- *To figure out a word's meaning based on its context*

REVIEW

Vocabulary

accomplish	serve
feasible	preference
attend	alternatives
report	race
area	juggling

Grammar *Quick Write*

Review: Forms of Be

5-DAY GRAMMAR	
DAY 1	Review Present-Tense Action Verbs
DAY 2	Review Subject-Verb Agreement
DAY 3	Review Past-Tense Verbs
DAY 4	**Review Forms of** *be*
DAY 5	Cumulative Review

Objectives

- *To recognize forms of* be: am, is, are, was, were
- *To write using forms of* be

Daily Proofreading

would you pass the cherry's?.

(Would, cherries?)

Writing Trait

Strengthening Conventions

Review Use these short daily lessons with children's own writing to continue building a foundation for revising/editing longer connected text.

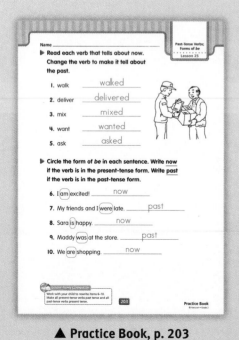

▲ **Practice Book, p. 203**

Reinforce the Skill

REVIEW FORMS OF *be* Remind children of what they have learned about the verb *be*. Review the following points:

- Verbs that are forms of *be* do not show action. They tell what someone or something is like. They also tell about one or more than one.

- The verbs *am, is,* and *are* tell about now.

- The verbs *was* and *were* tell about the past.

- The verbs *am, is,* and *was* tell about one.

- The verbs *are* and *were* tell about *you* and more than one.

Model revising the following sentence to use the correct form of *be*.

Our parents is coming to see the play. (Our parents are coming to see the play.)

Practice/Apply

GUIDED PRACTICE Write the following sentences on the board. Ask volunteers to help you choose the correct form of *be* to complete each sentence.

You (was/were) wearing your new boots. (were)

The stores (are/is) closed because of the holiday. (are)

INDEPENDENT PRACTICE Have children write sentences using the correct form of *be* in each sentence. Have volunteers share their completed sentences with the class.

Writing
Publish

5-DAY WRITING	
DAY 1	Revise and Publish
DAY 2	Revise and Publish
DAY 3	Publish
DAY 4	Proofread and Publish
DAY 5	Present

Publish

MODEL WRITING AN "ABOUT THE AUTHOR" NOTE   Tell children that published works often include a sentence or two about the author. Explain that readers enjoy knowing a little about the person who wrote the piece. Model how to think about what to include in an "About the Author" note.

Think Aloud   I could tell about myself, such as one or two things I enjoy doing. I might add a sentence about why the topic of my writing is interesting to me.

Using your own interests, write a few sentences using the third-person on the board. Have children add an "About the Author" feature to their finished work and evaluate it for logical thinking and consistent third-person point of view.

Handwriting

NEATNESS COUNTS   Remind children to use their best printing for any information that they add to their writing. Point out that neat printing makes their writing easier to read, which allows readers to enjoy it more.

WRITING TRAIT **CONVENTIONS**   Have children carefully proofread their writing one last time and ask themselves the following questions:

- Have I included my name? A title?

- Have I checked my spelling? Capitalization? Punctuation?

- Is my handwriting its neatest?

Allow children time to complete a final check of their work.

Learn About Hawaii

Our Fiftieth State, Hawaii, is a string of islands in the Pacific Ocean. Visitors to Hawaii see palm trees, mountains, waterfalls and volcanoes. Of course, there are also beautiful beaches! Hawaii produces sugar cane, pineapples, and beautiful flowers.

Objectives

- *To progress through the stages of the writing process*
- *To publish a self-selected piece of assigned writing*

Writing Prompt

Reflect   Have children write to tell about the changes they made when they revised their writing.

TECHNOLOGY

GO online   Children can use a word-processing program to produce and design their final piece of writing.

Warm-Up Routines

Day at a Glance

Day 5

 and Spelling
- Lessons 21–24 Review
- Postest

Comprehension

 Review: Use Graphic Aids
- Review: Synonyms

Fluency

READERS' THEATER
- Reading Using Expression and Rate
- Perform: "Town Hall," *Student Edition,* pp. 304–315

Read!

Grammar *Quick Write*
- Review: Lessons 21–24

Writing
- Present

Oral Language

Objective *To listen attentively and respond appropriately to oral communication*

> ### Question of the Day
> What are some ways that people and bees are alike?

Have children recall what they learned about bees in a hive. Use the following prompts to discuss how bees and people each form and live in communities.

- **What are some jobs that bees do in a hive? How are their jobs like the jobs people in a community have?**

- **Why do bees work together?**

- **How is a hive of bees like a human community?**

Read Aloud

Objective *To listen for rhyming words*

BIG BOOK OF RHYMES AND POEMS Display the poem "The Swarm of Bees" on page 42 and read the title. Ask children to recall what the poem is about. Then ask children to listen for rhyming words as you read the poem aloud. Call on volunteers to name the rhyming words they hear in the poem. (flew/two, tree/three, explore/four, hive/five, mix/six) Invite children to join in as you reread the poem.

▲ **Big Book of Rhymes and Poems, p. 42**

Word Wall

Objective *To read high-frequency words*

REVIEW HIGH-FREQUENCY WORDS Review the following words in two columns on the Word Wall: *impossible, children, learn, special, clear, imagine, favorite, young, fair,* and *exercise.* Divide the class into two groups and have each group alternate reading a column of words. Then have the groups switch columns and repeat the process.

impossible · children · learn · special · clear
imagine · favorite · young · fair · exercise

Lessons 21–24 Review

phonics *and Spelling*

Objective

- *To review spelling words from previous lessons*

Spelling Words

1.	found	6.	grew
2.	down	7.	true
3.	store	8.	fruit
4.	four	9.	care*
5.	smooth	10.	pair

* Word from "Town Hall"

Assess

POSTTEST Assess children's progress using the dictation sentences.

Words with /ou/ *ou, ow;* /ôr/ *or, ore, our;* /o͞o/ *oo, ew, ue, ui, ou;* /âr/ *air, are*

1.	found	Darla **found** her kitten hiding in the closet.
2.	down	We took the elevator **down** to the first floor.
3.	store	We need to go to the grocery **store** to get milk.
4.	four	I found **four** seashells at the beach.
5.	smooth	Dad's face feels **smooth** after he shaves.
6.	grew	Aunt Carol **grew** sunflowers in her garden.
7.	true	Is it **true** that you were born in Alaska?
8.	fruit	Have an apple or another **fruit** for a snack.
9.	care	Hank will **care** for our cat while we're away.
10.	pair	I will need a new **pair** of shoes soon!

Use Graphic Aids
Comprehension: Review

Reinforce the Skill

REVIEW GRAPHIC AIDS Ask children to name each type of graphic aid you describe. Say: **This graphic aid**

- **shows information in rows, columns, and headings.** (chart)

- **shows where places are located.** (map)

- **shows the parts of something or how it works.** (diagram)

- **shows amounts of things.** (graph)

- **shows dates and events over a period of time.** (time line)

Practice/Apply

GUIDED PRACTICE Have children turn to the timeline on *Student Edition* page 297 of "Watching in the Wild." Ask:

- **How old was Jane when she got Jubilee?** (2 years old)

INDEPENDENT PRACTICE Have children work in small groups. Assign each group to look for graphic aids in textbooks, encyclopedias, and other nonfiction books. Have them share what they find.

Objectives

- *To identify graphic aids*
- *To analyze and use graphic aids*

Skill Trace

Tested Use Graphic Aids

Introduce	T224–T225
Reteach	S30–S31, S42–S43
Review	T261, T277, T289, T316–T317, T345, T361, T371, T424, T445
Test	Theme 5
Maintain	Theme 6, T272

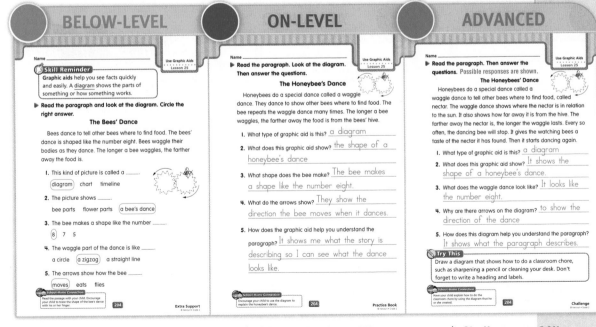

▲ Extra Support, p. 204   ▲ Practice Book, p. 204   ▲ Challenge, p. 204

E L L

- Group children according to academic levels, and assign one of the pages on the left.

- Clarify any unfamiliar concepts as necessary. See *ELL Teacher Guide* Lesson 25 for support in scaffolding instruction.

Synonyms
Vocabulary: Review

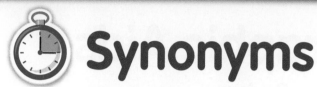

Objectives

- *To identify and use synonyms*
- *To use reference sources such as a thesaurus or dictionary to locate synonyms*

Skill Trace

 Tested **Synonyms**

Introduce	T268–T269
Reteach	S32–S33, S44–S45
Review	**T352–T353, T437, T446**
Test	Theme 5

Reinforce the Skill

REVIEW SYNONYMS Remind children that some words may have the same, or almost the same, meaning. Tell them that they can look up a word in a thesaurus or dictionary to find its synonyms. Model how to use synonyms.

Think Aloud I can use synonyms to make my writing and speaking more interesting. For example, instead of saying that my desk is *clean*, I could use a more interesting word, and say that my desk is *spotless*, *tidy*, or *sparkling*.

Practice/Apply

GUIDED PRACTICE Write the following sets of words on the board: *laughed, chuckled, walked, strolled*. Have children match the word in each set with its synonym. Work together, using the more interesting synonym to create sentences.

INDEPENDENT PRACTICE Have partners work together to find synonyms for the following words: *funny, think, pull, rude*.

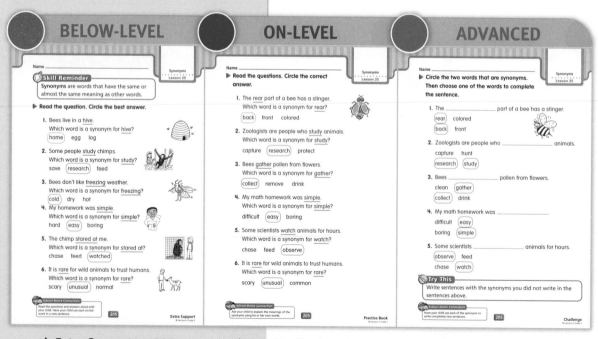

▲ **Extra Support, p. 205**   ▲ **Practice Book, p. 205**   ▲ **Challenge, p. 205**

ELL

- Group children according to academic levels, and assign one of the pages on the left.

- Clarify any unfamiliar concepts as necessary. See *ELL Teacher Guide* Lesson 25 for support in scaffolding instruction.

READERS' THEATER

Perform: "Town Hall"

5-DAY READERS' THEATER
DAY 1 Read Aloud/Read Along
DAY 2 Read Together
DAY 3 Choose Roles/Rehearse
DAY 4 Rehearse Roles
DAY 5 Perform

Performance Ideas

PRESENTATION STRATEGIES   Help children feel confident about performing by reminding them that they have practiced a number of times. Remind groups to enter and exit smoothly and quietly. Explain that the entire cast should take a bow at the end. Explain that while members are not reading, they become part of the audience and should listen attentively and quietly.

You may want to project the backdrop for "Town Hall" against a board or screen.

Focus on Fluency

READING WITH EXPRESSION AND AT AN APPROPRIATE RATE
Remind children to use the fluency tips they've been practicing this week.

- Use a natural speaking voice, and read more quickly or more slowly when it makes sense to do so.

- Use expression in your voice to make your character come alive.

Perform

SPEAKING AND LISTENING   Before children perform Readers' Theater, review good rules for reading and being part of an audience.

- **I look up occasionally at the audience as I read.**

- **I read clearly and with feeling.**

- **I listen quietly and politely as others read.**

RUBRIC See the rubric for Presentations on page R5.

EVALUATE   Invite children or others in the audience to comment positively about how the readers read.

Objectives
- *To self-evaluate oral reading for fluency*
- *To speak in complete sentences*

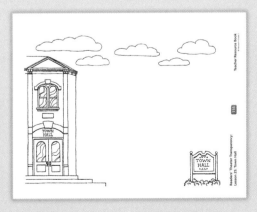

▲ **Teacher Resource Book, p. 116**

Grammar Quick Write

Review: Lessons 21–24

5-DAY GRAMMAR	
DAY 1	Review Present-Tense Verbs
DAY 2	Review Subject-Verb Agreement
DAY 3	Review Past-Tense Verbs
DAY 4	Review Forms of *be*
DAY 5	Cumulative Review

Objectives

- *To use present-tense action verbs correctly*
- *To use correct subject-verb agreement*
- *To form past-tense verbs correctly*
- *To use forms of* be *correctly*

Daily Proofreading

Dr Browns office is next door.

(Dr., Brown's)

Writing Trait

Strengthening Conventions

Review   Use these short daily lessons with children's own writing to continue building a foundation for revising/editing longer connected text. See also *Writer's Companion*, Lesson 25.

Reinforce the Skills

MIXED REVIEW   Discuss with children the following points:

- Most present-tense action verbs end with *-s* or *-es* unless the naming part tells about *I, you*, or more than one.

- Many verbs that end with *-ed* tell about something that happened in the past. Past-tense verbs with a final silent *e* end with *-d*.

- Some verbs tell what someone or something is like. The verbs *am, is*, and *are* tell about now. The verbs *was* and *were* tell about the past.

- The verbs *am, is*, and *was* are used to tell about one. The verbs *are* and *were* are used to tell about *you* and more than one.

Practice/Apply

GUIDED PRACTICE   Write the following sentences on the board. Ask a volunteer to complete the first sentence by choosing the correct verb in parentheses. Then guide children to form the present tense of the verb in parentheses to complete the remaining sentences.

Nick and Pete _____ at the beach now. (are, were)
(are)

The boys _____ buckets with water. (fill) (fill)

Brenda _____ them build a sandcastle. (watch)
(watches)

INDEPENDENT PRACTICE   Have children work on their own to rewrite the sentences to show that the actions happened in the past. Have volunteers share their sentences and have children check that they have formed the past tense of the verbs correctly.

Writing

Present

5-DAY WRITING	
DAY 1	Revise and Publish
DAY 2	Revise and Publish
DAY 3	Publish
DAY 4	Publish
DAY 5	**Present**

Share

CELEBRATE WRITING   Provide an opportunity for children to share their published pieces of writing. Encourage children to read aloud to the group, and to explain the reasons for the publishing ideas they chose. Later, display their framed writing pieces in a special hall exhibition. Have an "opening," inviting guests from other classrooms.

WRITING TRAIT ➤ **SENTENCE FLUENCY**   Take this opportunity to point out and praise examples of sentence fluency in finished writing, particularly for those children who exhibited significant efforts to improve their writing by avoiding the overuse of *I,* and by combining sentences so that their writing flows better.

LISTENING AND SPEAKING SKILLS   Remind children that when they are reading aloud they should speak clearly and at an appropriate pace. Remind listeners that they should

- listen quietly and politely.

NOTE: A 4-point rubric appears on page R8.

SCORING RUBRIC

	6	5	4	3	2	1
FOCUS	Completely focused, purposeful.	Focused on topic and purpose.	Generally focused on topic and purpose.	Somewhat focused on topic and purpose.	Related to topic but does not maintain focus.	Lacks focus and purpose.
ORGANIZATION	Ideas progress logically; paper conveys sense of completeness.	Organization mostly clear; paper gives sense of completeness.	Organization mostly clear, but some lapses occur; may seem unfinished.	Some sense of organization; seems unfinished.	Little sense of organization.	Little or no sense of organization.
SUPPORT	Strong, specific details; clear, exact language; freshness of expression.	Strong, specific details; clear, exact language.	Adequate support and word choice.	Limited supporting details; limited word choice.	Few supporting details; limited word choice.	Little development; limited or unclear word choice.
CONVENTIONS	Varied sentences; few, if any, errors.	Varied sentences; few errors.	Some sentence variety; few errors.	Simple sentence structures; some errors.	Simple sentence structures; many errors.	Unclear sentence structures; many errors.

REPRODUCIBLE RUBRICS for specific writing purposes and presentations are available on pages R2–R8.

Objectives

- *To listen attentively to oral presentations*
- *To speak clearly, using an appropriate pace and phrasing*

 Writing Prompt

Self-Selected Writing   Have children make a list of ideas for a new topic of their choice for writing.

WEEKLY LESSON TEST

▲ **Weekly Lesson Tests, pp. 265–269**

- Selection Comprehension with Short Response
- Robust Vocabulary

 For prescriptions, see pp. A2–A6. Also available electronically on StoryTown Online Assessment and Exam View®.

 Podcasting: Assessing Fluency

Leveled Readers
Reinforcing Skills and Strategies

Genre: Readers' Theater

BELOW-LEVEL

At the Library

SUMMARY Children interview local librarians about the library and a visiting author.

- **phonics** **Lessons 21–24 Review**
- **Vocabulary**

Plot; Use Graphic Aids

Before Reading

BUILD BACKGROUND/SET PURPOSE Ask children to tell about special events they have heard of or been to at their local library. Guide them to preview the play and set a purpose for reading it.

Reading the Book

PAGES 4–14 🔘 **PLOT** **How is the plot of the play similar to the one in "Town Hall"?** (Both are about people explaining how they made decisions to help the community.)

PAGE 14 🔘 **USE GRAPHIC AIDS** **What information does the poster give?** (It tells about the author visit.)

REREAD FOR FLUENCY Have partners or small groups read pages 9–14. Remind them to read more slowly if a character is trying to explain something and use their voice to express the characters' feelings.

Think Critically *(See inside back cover for questions.)*

1 **TEXT STRUCTURE AND FORMAT** Possible responses: the book has a list of characters; characters' names are in front of their speech

2 🔘 **PLOT** He was a visiting author that would bring more people to the library.

3 **NOTE DETAILS** There would be chairs, food, and drink.

4 **MAKE INFERENCES** Possible response: Yes, he is a popular author and everyone loves his books.

5 **PERSONAL RESPONSE** Answers will vary.

LEVELED READERS TEACHER GUIDE

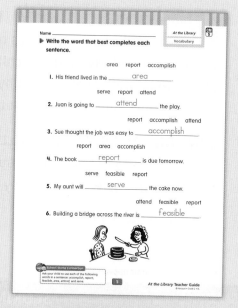

▲ Vocabulary, p. 5

▲ Comprehension, p. 6

www.harcourtschool.com/storytown

GO online

★ **Leveled Readers Online Database**
  Searchable by Genre, Skill, Vocabulary, Level, or Title
★ **Student Activities and Teacher Resources, online**

ON-LEVEL

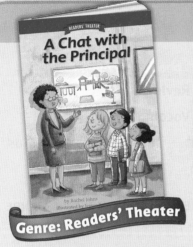

Genre: Readers' Theater

A Chat with the Principal

SUMMARY Children and their teacher interview the school principal about plans for the new school playground.

• **phonics** **Lessons 21–24 Review**

• **Vocabulary**

Focus Skill

Plot; Use Graphic Aids

Before Reading

BUILD BACKGROUND/SET PURPOSE Ask children to tell what they think a new playground should include. Guide them to preview the play and set a purpose for reading it.

Reading the Book

PAGES 4–14 🎯 **PLOT** **How did the plans for the new playground get developed?** (A group of teachers, parents, and students worked together to come up with a number of plans.)

PAGES 9–14 🎯 **USE GRAPHIC AIDS** **How does the diagram of the playground shown on page 14 help you picture what Mrs. North describes on page 9?** (The diagram shows where things like the slides, the sandpit, and the basketball court will be.)

REREAD FOR FLUENCY Have partners or small groups decide on roles and read pages 8–14 together. Remind children to use expression to make the characters come alive.

Think Critically

(See inside back cover for questions.)

1 **DESCRIBE CHARACTERS** Possible responses: helpful, friendly

2 **NOTE DETAILS** swings, a slide, a sandpit, a basketball court, benches, and trees

3 **CONTEXT CLUES** Possible responses: possible, achievable

4 🎯 **PLOT** the old playground wasn't big enough

5 **PERSONAL RESPONSE** Answers will vary.

LEVELED READERS TEACHER GUIDE

▲ Vocabulary, p. 5

▲ Comprehension, p. 6

Leveled Readers

Reinforcing Skills and Strategies

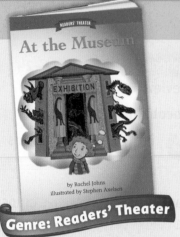

Genre: Readers' Theater

 **ADVANCED**

At the Museum

SUMMARY Two children and their teacher interview museum leaders about an upcoming exhibition on dinosaurs.

by Rachel Johns
illustrated by Stephen Axelsen

 phonics Lessons 21–24 Review

• **Vocabulary**

  Plot; Use Graphic Aids

Focus Skill

Before Reading

BUILD BACKGROUND/SET PURPOSE Ask children to tell about museum exhibitions they have visited. Guide them to preview the play and set a purpose for reading it.

Reading the Book

PAGES 4–14 **PLOT** Were the museum's ideas on how to put together an exhibition on dinosaurs successful? How do you know? (Yes; lots of museums contributed pieces to the exhibition.)

PAGES 12–13 **USE GRAPHIC AIDS** How is the skeleton of the *Tyrannosaurus rex* like a diagram? (it shows the different bones.)

REREAD FOR FLUENCY Have partners take turns reading pages 10–14. Suggest that they alternate roles on each page. Remind children to slow their reading rate if a character is explaining something and to use their voices to express how the characters are feeling.

Think Critically *(See inside back cover for questions.)*

1 **DESCRIBE CHARACTERS** Possible responses: helpful, friendly

2 **NOTE DETAILS** museums around the world

3 **TEXT STRUCTURE AND FORMAT** Possible responses: the book has a list of characters; characters' names are in front of their speech

4 **PLOT** the dinosaur exhibition at the museum

5 **PERSONAL RESPONSE** Answers will vary.

LEVELED READERS TEACHER GUIDE

Name _____

▶ Write the Vocabulary Word from the box that best completes each sentence.

| area | feasible | attend |
| accomplish | report | serve |

1. The chef will ___serve___ hot sandwiches for lunch.

2. Lisa hopes she will ___accomplish___ her work before it is due.

3. Mrs. Baker cleared the ___area___ so that she could mop up the spilled juice.

4. It is not ___feasible___ to fly by flapping your arms.

5. I would like to ___attend___ the party, but I have some place else to be.

6. The teacher asked the class to write a ___report___ about dinosaurs.

▶ Write a sentence using words from the box above.
Accept reasonable responses.

▲ **Vocabulary, p. 5**

Name _____

▶ Use the graph to answer the questions.

Favorite Animals No Longer Around

Brontosaurus	
Wooly Mammoth	
Moa Bird	
Tyrannosaurus Rex	

1. Which was liked by the most children?
   A Tyrannosaurus Rex
   B Brontosaurus
   C Moa Bird

2. How many more children liked the Tyrannosaurus Rex than the Brontosaurus?
   A one
   B four
   C two

3. Which did fewer children like?
   A Brontosaurus
   B Tyrannosaurus Rex
   C Moa Bird

▲ **Comprehension, p. 6**

E L L

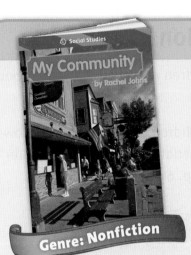

Social Studies

My Community
by Rachel Johns

Genre: Nonfiction

My Community

SUMMARY   A young girl tells about important places in her community and how they help people.

- Build Background
- Concept Vocabulary
- Scaffolded Language Development

Before Reading

BUILD BACKGROUND/SET PURPOSE   Ask children to tell about places they know in their community. Guide them to preview the book and set a purpose for reading it.

Reading the Book

PAGES 3–14   **PLOT**   **What are some places you learn about at the beginning of the selection? At the end?** (At the beginning, the selection tells about the town hall and the police station; at the end, it tells about the library and a museum.)

PAGES 3–14   **USE GRAPHIC AIDS**   **How might a map of the town help people who live there?** (It would help people find out how to get from one place to another.)

REREAD FOR FLUENCY   Have partners take turns reading the story a page at a time. Remind children to read at an even pace and use their voices to express what is important about each place.

Scaffolded Language Development

(See inside back cover for teacher-led activity.)

Provide additional examples and explanation as needed.

LEVELED READERS TEACHER GUIDE

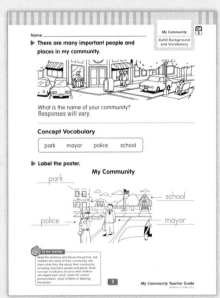

▲ Build Background and Vocabulary, p. 5

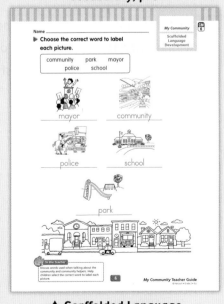

▲ Scaffolded Language Development, p. 6

Theme Wrap-up and Review

Discuss the Literature

Use the questions below to guide children in making connections across the texts in this theme.

- **In what way do the selections in this theme tell about communities?** (Possible response: All of the selections show a different type of community.)

- **Why were "Watching in the Wild" and "The Bee" included in this theme?** (Possible response: Animals are members of communities.)

- **Which selection best shows how members of a community can come together to solve a problem?** (Responses will vary but should include details from the selection chosen.)

Return to the Theme Connections

Complete a graphic organizer to show information compiled from the selections children have read in this theme.

Better Together	
Types of Communities	**How Communities Help Each Other**
• animal families • neighborhoods • farms	• helping people in need • look out for one another • share

Response Option

🖉 **REFLECT**　Have children reflect on and write about communities.

SELF-ASSESSMENT　Children can reflect on their own progress using the My Reading Log blackline master on *Teacher Resource Book,* p. 64.

▲ Teacher Resource Book, p. 64

LITERATURE CRITIQUE CIRCLES　Have children meet in small groups to discuss and reflect on the literature in this theme. Encourage children to share their likes and dislikes about the following:

- genres

- subjects/topics

- illustrations or photographs

Remind children to support their opinions with text-based reasons and details.

Children may also like to use this time to recommend to classmates any books they read and enjoyed during independent reading. Have them list promising titles for future reading.

School Community Mural

PRESENT THE MURAL Children may present their mural to an audience. Encourage them to demonstrate what they have learned in a creative way.

PRESENTATION IDEA Guide children in making up a poem about the school community shown in their mural. They may then recite the poem chorally.

- **Provide a structure for a poem.** For example, you might have children start each line with the same words about their school community and end each line with information about particular members of the community. Try to have a "refrain" in the poem that the whole group can say together.

- **Help children divide the poem** into lines that are spoken by partners or trios, and lines that are said by the whole group. Give children time to rehearse their choral reading.

To evaluate children's work, you may wish to use the Rubric for Presentations on page R5.

School-Home Connection

Theme Project Presentations
You may want to invite family members to see the completed mural and children's presentations. Guide children in writing an invitation for the event that includes the appropriate date, time, and location.

Everyone Works Together in Our School Community

Monitor Progress
at the end of Theme 5

THEME 5 TEST After instruction for Theme 5, assess student progress in the following areas:

- Comprehension of grade-level text
- Phonics
- Robust Vocabulary
- Grammar
- Writing to a prompt
- Fluency*

(*Note on Fluency: Assessment can be staggered to make sure all students can be individually assessed.)

 Podcasting: Assessing Fluency

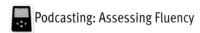

ONLINE ASSESSMENT

✓ Theme 5 Test
✓ Weekly Lesson Tests
✓ Student Profile System to track student growth
✓ Prescriptions for Reteaching

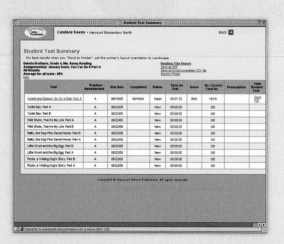

 www.harcourtschool.com/storytown

MONITOR PROGRESS

Use Data to Inform Instruction for Theme 6

IF performance is	THEN, in addition to core instruction, use these resources:
● **BELOW-LEVEL:** Reteach	• Below-Level Leveled Readers • Leveled Readers System • Extra Support Copying Masters • Strategic Intervention Resource Kit • Intervention Station, Primary
● **ON-LEVEL:** Reinforce	• On-Level Leveled Readers • Leveled Readers System • Practice Book
● **ADVANCED:** Extend	• Advanced Leveled Readers • Leveled Readers System • Challenge Copying Masters • Challenge Resource Kit

---

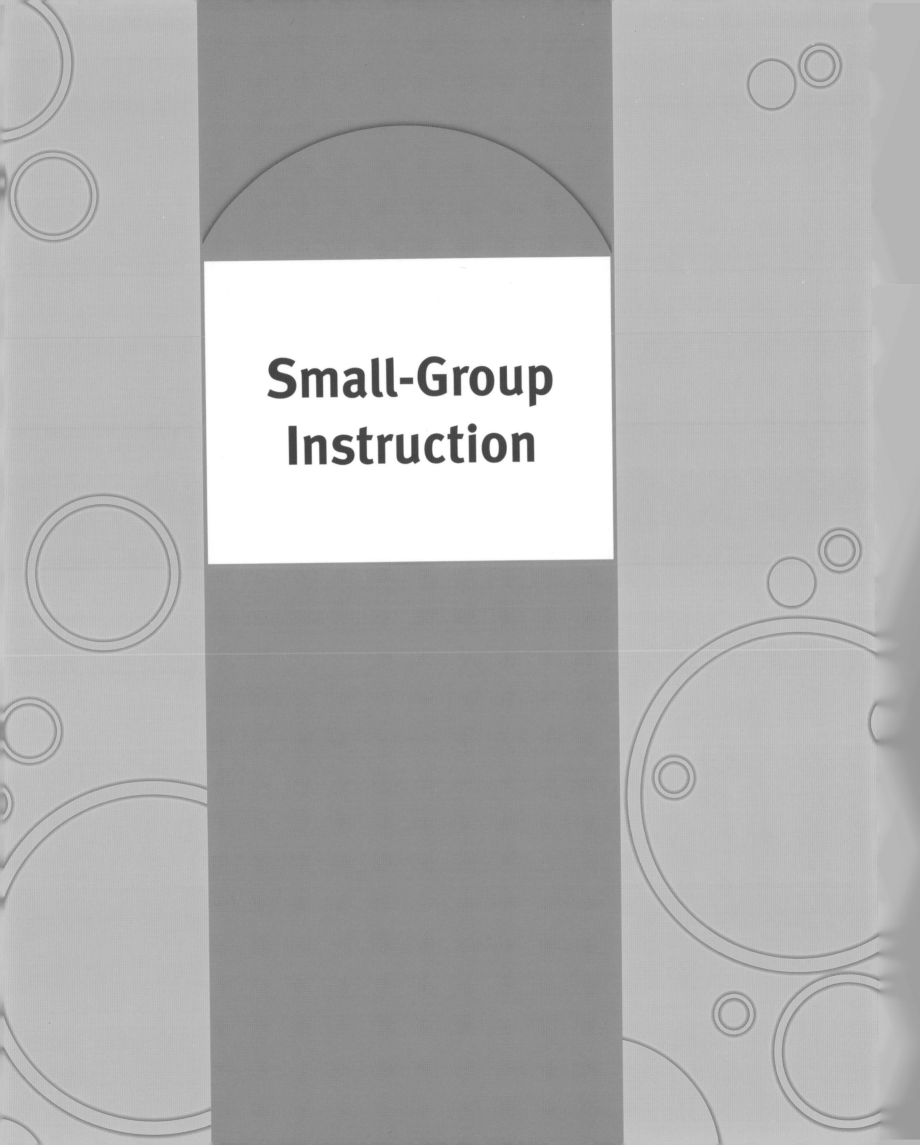

Small-Group Instruction

SMALL-GROUP INSTRUCTION

Lesson 21

Phonics..S2

Fluency...S4

🔧 Plot...S6

Compare and Contrast S8

Robust Vocabulary S10

Grammar and Writing S12

Lesson 22

Phonics... S14

Fluency... S16

🔧 Plot... S18

Compare and Contrast S20

Robust Vocabulary S22

Grammar and Writing S24

Lesson 23

Phonics... S26

Fluency... S28

🔧 Use Graphic Aids S30

Synonyms S32

Robust Vocabulary S34

Grammar and Writing S36

Lesson 24

Phonics... S38

Fluency... S40

🔧 Use Graphic Aids S42

Synonyms S44

Robust Vocabulary S46

Grammar and Writing S48

Phonics

Objective
To practice and apply knowledge of the vowel diphthong /ou/ou, ow

Decodable Book 17

"Meg and the Ground-hog" and "Found in the Ground!" ▶

MONITOR PROGRESS

Phonics After small-group instruction, are children able to read words with /ou/*ou* and *ow*?

If not, provide additional small-group practice with the sound. See the *Strategic Intervention Resource Kit* for additional support.

Strategic ▶
Intervention
Resource Kit

BELOW-LEVEL **RETEACH**

Connect Letters and Sounds

Routine Card 1 Using *Routine Card 1* and the corresponding *Sound/Spelling Card*, reintroduce the vowel diphthong /ou/*ou, ow*. Display the words *out, found*, and *loud*. As you read the words aloud, have children identify the vowel sound they hear in all these words. (/ou/) Then point to each word, and ask children to tell you what letters spell the /ou/ sound. (ou) Explain that the letters *ou* can stand for the /ou/ sound. Follow a similar procedure for *ow*, using the words *now, town*, and *howl*. Then have children read aloud *Decodable Book 17*. Pause at the end of each page to review any word that children struggled to read.

ON-LEVEL **REINFORCE**

Word Building

Build some word ladders: *ow* to *owl* to *howl*; *ouch* to *couch* to *crouch*; *out* to *pout* to *spout* to *sprout*. Begin by saying the first word aloud and asking children how to spell it. Write the word on the board. Then say the next word and ask children what letter you should add to spell it. Have children read each new word as it is built. Write it underneath as children dictate. Now ask children some rhyming riddles. Afterward, write the two rhymes on the board, and have volunteers underline the /ou/ spelling in each word.

> This *ow* word rhymes with *ground* and is something an angry person did. (frowned)
>
> This *ou* word rhymes with *crowd* and means "noisy." (loud)
>
> This *ow* word rhymes with *sour* and is something pretty that grows. (flower)

ADVANCED EXTEND

Play an /ou/ Memory Game

Have children brainstorm words in which the /ou/ sound is spelled *ou* or *ow*. Display the words on the board. Then tell children that they are going to play a game about things that might be found. Write the word *noun* on the board, and read it with children, eliciting that a noun names a person, animal, place, or thing. Tell children that their /ou/ list should just show nouns—people, animals, places, or things that could be found. Work together to eliminate any words that are not nouns from the list. Then begin the game by saying, "I found a crown." Move on to the next child, who should say, "I found a crown and a ___," adding something from the list, such as a *mouse*. The next child says, "I found a crown and a mouse and a ___," adding yet another /ou/ noun. Continue until every child has had a chance to participate at least twice.

Fluency

Objective
To read fluently and with proper expression

Expressing Emotions Have children show how they look when they're scared, happy, sad, or angry. Read aloud expressive sentences from the appropriate *Leveled Reader*. Use your face as well as your voice to communicate each emotion. Have children follow along and imitate you.

Fluency After small-group instruction, are children able to read their *Leveled Reader* expressively, capturing the story's mood?

If not, provide additional small-group practice. See the *Strategic Intervention Resource Kit* for additional support.

Strategic ▶ Intervention Resource Kit

BELOW-LEVEL RETEACH

Model Fluent Reading

Routine Card 8 Remind children that good readers read with expression, trying to match the mood of the story and the characters' feelings. List *scary, happy, sad,* and *angry* on the board and discuss these moods with children. Read aloud the following story openers (without the words in parentheses), and have children match your expressive reading to one of the displayed moods:

The poor little puppy had nowhere to go. (sad)

This is the best day of my whole life! (happy)

It was a dark and stormy night. (scary)

Today my baby brother wrecked my birthday party! (angry)

Distribute *The Book Sale.* As you read it aloud, stop to point out particularly expressive passages, having children echo-read them, matching your expression. Then have them read the book aloud with a partner.

ON-LEVEL REINFORCE

Partner Reading

 Routine Card 9 Remind children that good readers read with expression, matching their voices to the mood of the story. Display these moods: *scared, happy, sad, angry.* Have children demonstrate how they sound when they are experiencing each mood. Distribute *Jackson's Tree,* and explain that they will practice reading this story in a way that matches its mood. Read each page aloud, pausing when appropriate to draw attention to the way your voice matches the mood. Have children read aloud after you, imitating the way you use your voice to express mood. Afterward, direct children to practice reading the book with a partner, instructing listeners to alert their partners when their voices are flat and don't match the mood.

ADVANCED EXTEND

Partner Reading

Routine Card 10 Have children suggest words that express different moods, discussing how people act and sound when they're in that particular mood. Point out that good readers think about mood when they're reading a story aloud. Distribute *Happy Again* to children, and tell them that they will be practicing reading with expression, using their voices to capture the mood of the story. Group children in pairs, having one child read the book aloud while the other listens. After the first child is done, have the listener offer constructive feedback about what the reader did to express story mood. Then have children switch roles and repeat the read-aloud process.

LEVELED READERS

● BELOW-LEVEL

▲ The Book Sale

● ON-LEVEL

▲ Jackson's Tree

● ADVANCED

▲ Happy Again

Comprehension
Plot

Objective
To identify the plot of a story, including the problem and solution

Clarify Meaning Make sure children understand how *problem* is used when it is a plot element: Identify the problem in a few stories children know well. Each time you identify a problem, introduce it by saying: **This is the problem. It's what [main character's name] wants to do.**

Comprehension After small-group instruction, are children able to identify the beginning, middle, and end of a story, including the problem the main character faces and how it is solved?

If not, provide additional small-group practice with the skill. See the *Strategic Intervention Resource Kit* for additional support.

Strategic ▶
Intervention
Resource Kit

Guided Review

Have children turn to page 162 in their *Student Edition*. Read aloud the opening paragraph to review the elements of a plot. Go over the story map, and have children respond to the prompts in the second paragraph (What problem does Ashley have? How does she solve it?). Now read aloud the little story, "A Present for Mom," on page 163 as children follow along. Work together to complete the story map. Then prompt children to identify the problem in the story (Mike wants to buy Mom flowers but doesn't have enough money) and the solution (he sets up a lemonade stand and earns the money). Help children see that the problem the character faces comes at the beginning of the story, while the solution to the problem comes at the end.

Look back with children at some stories they have read in their *Student Editions*. Have them use the pictures to recall what happened at the beginning, in the middle, and at the end of a few stories. Guide them to identify the problem and solution in each story as well.

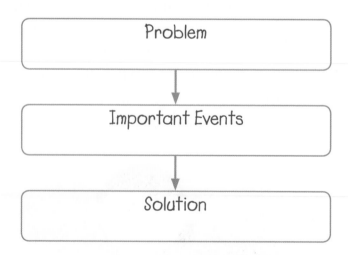

Identify Plot Elements

Remind children that the plot is what happens during a story—at the beginning, in the middle, and at the end. Point out that the beginning of the story includes a problem that the main character has to solve and that the solution to this problem comes at the end of the story. Reproduce the story map used on *Student Edition* page 162. Have partners work together, copying and filling out this story map for a story that both of them know well, such as one from the *Student Edition*. Afterward, have partners present their maps to the group.

Create an Outline for Plot

Have children think of a story they might tell. (You may want to give them a general idea related to "A Chair for My Mother:" Write a story about a special gift that someone wants to give to someone else.) Display a story map like the one below. Have children work alone or with a partner to fill out the story map with the general idea of their plot, including the story problem and solution. Invite children to share their story maps with the group, and encourage them to pursue this story at a later time, if it interests them.

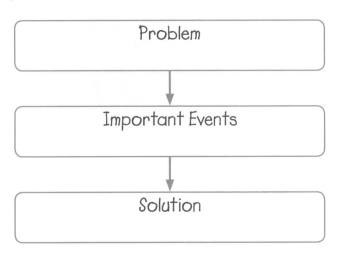

Problem

↓

Important Events

↓

Solution

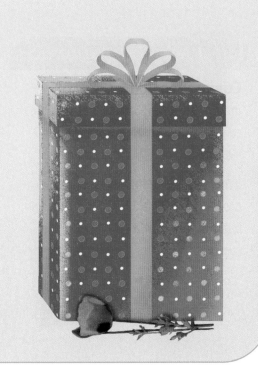

Comprehension
Compare and Contrast

Objective
To understand how to compare and contrast stories

BELOW-LEVEL **RETEACH**

Guided Review

Prompt children to recall the difference between comparing and contrasting:

> **When you compare things, do you tell how they are alike or how they are different?**

> **When you contrast things, do you tell how they are alike or how they are different?**

Display an orange ball and an orange (or two other objects that share a couple of obvious similarities and differences). Work with children to name ways in which the two objects are alike (both are orange; both are round) and ways in which they are different (you can eat one but not the other; you can bounce one but not the other). Then work with children to compare and contrast two characters in "A Chair for My Mother," using a Venn diagram. First prompt children to think of two ways in which the characters are alike. Then move on and prompt them to name two ways in which the characters are different.

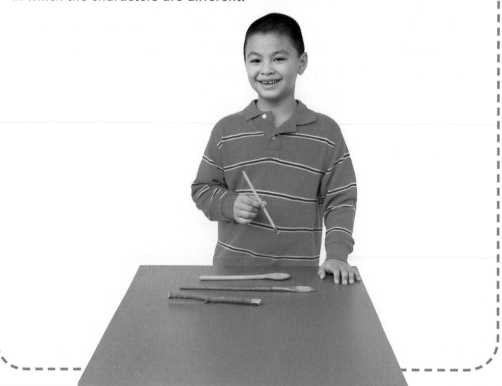

MONITOR PROGRESS

Comprehension After small-group instruction, are children able to compare and contrast two stories or two characters?

If not, provide additional small-group practice with the skill. See the *Strategic Intervention Resource Kit* for additional support.

Strategic ▶
Intervention
Resource Kit

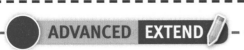

ON-LEVEL REINFORCE

Compare/Contrast Characters

Remind children that good readers will often compare and contrast stories and story characters to help them think about and understand stories. If necessary, review what it means to compare two things (tell how they are alike) and to contrast two things (tell how they are different). Look back through the *Student Edition* with children, and ask them to pick two characters from two different stories that they really liked. Guide them to fill in a Venn diagram with ways in which these two characters are alike and ways in which they are different.

ADVANCED EXTEND

Compare/Contrast Stories

Have children tell you what it means to compare two stories and what it means to contrast two stories. Point out that good readers compare and contrast stories to help them think more deeply about and better understand both stories. Brainstorm with children things you can compare in two stories, such as the setting, the characters, and the story solution. List these elements on the board. Reproduce the comparison chart shown below for children to use to record the similarities and differences between the two stories. Then ask children to each think of two stories that they really like. Direct them to copy the chart and fill it in with ways in which these two stories are similar and ways in which the two stories are different.

Compare/Contrast	Story 1:	Story 2:
Setting		
Characters		
How the characters solve their problem		

Clarify Meaning Give children practice with the concepts of *alike* and *different*, using classroom objects. Generate sentences that tell how these two things are alike or different, listing each sentence under the heading Compare or the heading Contrast.

Robust Vocabulary

Objective
To review robust vocabulary

Tested
REVIEW
Build Robust Vocabulary

allowance	spoiled
rosy	comfortable
thrifty	boost
industrious	exchanged
bargain	delivered

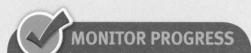

MONITOR PROGRESS

Robust Vocabulary After small-group instruction, are children able to use and understand the Vocabulary Words?

If not, provide additional small-group practice with the words. See the *Strategic Intervention Resource Kit* for additional support.

**Strategic ▶
Intervention
Resource Kit**

Reintroduce the Words

Routine Card 3 Use *Routine Card 3* and **Transparencies R111 and R112** to re-introduce the words to children. Review the Student-Friendly Explanations until children are familiar with the words. Then use prompts such as the following to check understanding. Be sure children explain their answers.

allowance — Which would a child most likely get an allowance for: raking leaves, eating lunch, or going to school?

rosy — If a child looks rosy, does he or she look sick or healthy?

thrifty — If you are thrifty, do you save lots of money or spend lots of money?

industrious — Which one is industrious — a lazy dog or a busy bee?

bargain — Who got a bargain? Pat bought a pair of socks for a dollar. Matt bought the same kind of socks for five dollars.

spoiled — If a bottle of milk is spoiled, is it good to drink it or bad to drink it?

comfortable — Which of these is a more comfortable place to sit: a big, stuffed sofa or a small, wooden bench?

boost — Who needs a boost at a parade: a little child who can't see or a grown-up who wants to sit down?

exchanged — If you exchanged a gift, did you like it or did you not like it?

delivered — If your family had a new bookcase delivered, did your family bring it home or did someone else bring it?

ON-LEVEL REINFORCE

Apply Word Knowledge

Review for children the Student-Friendly Explanation for each word, and use it in a sentence. Then combine two Vocabulary Words in a question that can be answered with *yes* or *no*. Have children respond and give reasons for their responses. Possible questions:

Does a *thrifty* person dislike *bargains*?

Should you *exchange* a bottle of *spoiled* milk?

Does an *industrious* person deserve an *allowance*?

Would it be *comfortable* to give a big dog a *boost*?

Can a *rosy* red sweater be *delivered*?

ADVANCED EXTEND

Word Categories

Display the Vocabulary Words, and ask children to think of oral sentences for each one. Then tell children that you are going to say two words that go together. They should tell you which Vocabulary Word completes the set. Provide these sets, leaving a blank line for the Vocabulary Word in parentheses:

bought, sold, (exchanged)

pretty, pink, (rosy)

money, pay, (allowance)

sale, deal, (bargain)

careful, saving, (thrifty)

mailed, sent, (delivered)

Help the group work together to develop their own sets of words for *spoiled, industrious, comfortable,* and *boost.*

Clarify Meaning Use a store scenario to enhance the meaning of several words. Give children paper money (*allowance*) and have them act out buying things at the store (finding *bargains, exchanging* goods, arranging to have things *delivered*), with you as sales associate/commentator.

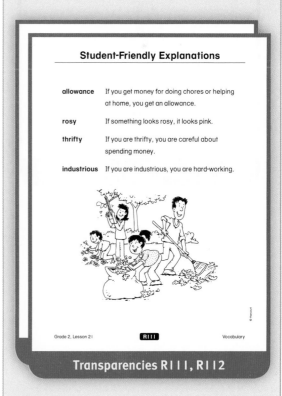

Student-Friendly Explanations

allowance	If you get money for doing chores or helping at home, you get an allowance.
rosy	If something looks rosy, it looks pink.
thrifty	If you are thrifty, you are careful about spending money.
industrious	If you are industrious, you are hard-working.

Grade 2, Lesson 21   R111   Vocabulary

Transparencies R111, R112

Grammar and Writing
Language Arts Checkpoint

Objectives

- *To identify and correctly use present-tense action verbs*
- *To write a personal narrative*

Present-Tense Action Verbs

1. Donny and Gina <u>go</u> to a store.
2. Gina <u>shops</u> for a birthday gift for Mom.
3. They <u>see</u> many goods for sale.
4. Gina <u>waves</u> a timer in the air.
5. She and her brother <u>smell</u> perfume.
6. At last, Gina <u>sees</u> a silky scarf.
7. She <u>wraps</u> it with pretty paper.
8. Mom <u>puts</u> the scarf around her neck.

Grade 2, Lesson 21   LA41   Grammar

Transparency LA41

BELOW-LEVEL   RETEACH

Review Present-Tense Action Verbs

Tell children that you are going to write a sentence on the board that tells what one of them is doing. Read the sentence with children, and then have the child in question do what the sentence says. Give each child an action to perform, using simple sentences like these:

(Child One's name) waves.

(Child Two's name) reads a book.

(Child Three's name) shakes (his/her) head.

Underline the verbs in each sentence (claps, reads, shakes), and remind children that an action verb is a word that tells what someone or something does. Point out that these sentences tell about an action that is happening now, in the present, so these are present-tense action verbs. Have each child act out his or her action as you read each displayed sentence together.

Display **Transparency LA41**, reminding children that they have seen it before. Work with children to find and underline the present-tense action verbs in sentences 2–8.

REVIEW PERSONAL NARRATIVE Remind children that a personal narrative tells about an important experience that the writer really had. Write a paragraph on the board that tells about something that happened to you when you were young. Identify the topic of your narrative in the first sentence. Use the pronouns *I, me,* and *my* in your text. Prompt children to use this paragraph to review important elements of a personal narrative:

Is this story real or made up? Who is it about?

Who can find the sentence that tells what this narrative is about?

What happened first? next? last? Are the events in time order?

Who can find the word *I*? the word *me*? the word *my*?

ON-LEVEL REINFORCE

Connect Grammar and Writing

Remind children that a personal narrative tells about an important experience that the writer really had. Point out that sometimes writers use a "you are there" approach with readers. The writing is in the present tense, as if events were happening now. Put this paragraph starter on the board:

> **I am five years old. Today is my first day of school.**

Have children discuss the kinds of things that happen on a child's first day of school. List some ideas on the board. Then have each child write a few sentences that tell about what his or her first day was like. Remind children to write in the present tense. Afterward, have children share their narratives. Display a sentence or two from each child's narrative that contains a present-tense action verb, and have the group identify it. Then use their sentences to show how *I*, *me*, and *my* occur in personal narratives.

ADVANCED EXTEND

Write a "You Are There" Personal Narrative

Have children tell you what a personal narrative is. Explain that sometimes writers use a "you are there" approach with their readers. They go back in time and pretend that everything is happening now. Tell children that this means that they write in the present tense. Display the following sentence as an example of an opening for a "you are there" personal narrative:

> **I am five years old. Today is my first day of school.**

Have children recall an event that happened to them when they were younger. Direct them to tell this event as if it is happening in the present, using present-tense verbs. Afterward, have children share their narratives. Also pick out and display sentences with present-tense action verbs, and have children come up to underline them.

Present Tense Endings Give children practice in figuring out when to add *-s* or *-es* to a present-tense verb. Write the verbs *sit, run, march,* and *mix* at the top of columns. For each verb, work together to form sentences for each pronoun. For example: *I sit. You sit. He sits. She sits. We sit. You sit. They sit.*

Phonics

Objective

To practice and apply knowledge of the r-Controlled vowel /ôr/or, ore, our

Decodable Book 18

"Mort's Sports Store,"
"Not Your Normal Fish!" "Courtyards,"
and "Courtney's Plans" ▶

MONITOR PROGRESS

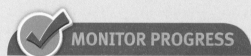

Phonics After small-group instruction, are children able to read words with *r*-Controlled vowel /ôr/or, ore, our?

If not, provide additional small-group practice with the sound. See the *Strategic Intervention Resource Kit* for additional support.

**Strategic ▶
Intervention
Resource Kit**

BELOW-LEVEL RETEACH

Connect Letters and Sounds

Routine Card 1 Using *Routine Card 1* and the corresponding *Sound/Spelling Card*, reintroduce the *r*-Controlled vowel /ôr/*or, ore, our*. Write the words *fork, short,* and *corn* on the board, underlining the *or*. Read the words aloud, and have children tell you what sound *or* stands for. (/ôr/) Explain that *or* can stand for the /ôr/ sound. Follow a similar procedure for *ore* using the words *more, chore,* and *score*. Then do the same for *our* using *pour, your,* and *four*. Elicit the three ways they have learned to spell the /ôr/ sound: *or, ore,* and *our*. Finish by having children read aloud *Decodable Book 18*. Pause at the end of each page to review any word that children struggled to read.

ON-LEVEL REINFORCE

Word Building

Write the word *storm* on the board. Build the words *store, sore, sort, fort, for, four,* and *pour* by directing children to change a letter, add a letter, or subtract a letter to make a word that fits in an oral sentence. For example, you might say, "Take away a letter from *fort* to make a word that fits in this sentence: *I'm having a sandwich ___ lunch.*" Have children read each word as it is built. Afterward, display these sentences for children to read aloud:

This store sort of looks like a fort in a storm.

I will pour four glasses for you, since you are sore.

Then have them read the stories in *Decodable Book 18* aloud. Ask questions about each one to check children's selection comprehension.

Hink Pinks

Have children brainstorm and list words that rhyme with *store, short, cord, form, horse, fork, corn, torch,* and *four.* (Children should not be restricted to *or, ore,* and *our* spellings. For example, *warm* rhymes with *form* and *board* rhymes with *cord.*) Then have each child think of two rhyming words that they could put together as the answer to a hink-pink clue. For example,

What's a racetrack? (a horse course)

What's something a tall bird uses to eat with? (a stork fork)

Give children index cards, directing them to write their clue on the front, along with a helpful picture, and the answer on the back. When children are ready, have them pose their hink-pink riddles to the rest of the group, displaying the front of their index card.

Fluency

Objective
To read fluently and with expression

Understand Dialogue   Make sure children understand how dialogue is punctuated in English. Put some dialogue from the appropriate *Leveled Reader* on the board. Work with children to identify, underline, and expressively read the characters' exact words.

MONITOR PROGRESS

Fluency   After small-group instruction, are children able to read the dialogue in their *Leveled Reader* in a way that expresses how the characters feel?

If not, provide additional small-group practice. See the *Strategic Intervention Resource Kit* for additional support.

**Strategic ▶
Intervention
Resource Kit**

BELOW-LEVEL   RETEACH

Echo-Reading

Routine Card 8   Remind children that good readers read with expression. Point out that one way to do this is through dialogue. A good reader thinks about what the characters are like and how they feel when they are saying something. Read aloud this dialogue between excited Sunny and gloomy Gus, asking children to listen to your voice and decide how each character feels.

> **"Wow! Just look at that sunset!" cried Sunny.**

> **"You look at it," said Gus. "I don't care."**

Point out that you used your voice to show how the characters feel, just as people do in real life when they speak. Distribute *No More Fish!* As you read it aloud, stop to comment on characters' feelings as they speak and draw attention to how you used your voice. Have children echo-read the dialogue, matching your expression. Then have them read aloud with a partner, monitoring one another's readings for accuracy and proper expression.

ON-LEVEL REINFORCE

Echo-Reading

Routine Card 8

Remind children that good readers read with expression, thinking about how a character feels as they read what the character says. Assign each child a different mood (happy, sad, scared, angry, bored, or sleepy) and give them a sentence to say, expressing their mood. Distribute *Monkey Business*, and explain that children will practice reading the dialogue in a way that expresses how the characters are feeling. Read each page aloud, pausing when you come to dialogue to draw attention to your expressiveness. Have children read aloud after you, imitating you. Afterward, direct them to practice reading the book with a partner, instructing listeners to pay particular attention to the reading of dialogue.

ADVANCED EXTEND

Partner-Reading

Routine Card 10

Elicit from children that thinking about how a character feels is useful when reading aloud that character's dialogue. Point out that a good reader wants the listener to hear the dialogue exactly as the character might have spoken it. Distribute *Puppy Tricks* to children, and tell them that they will practice reading dialogue with appropriate expression, using their voices to capture what a character is like and how that character is feeling as he or she speaks. Pair children, asking one child to read the book aloud while the other listens. After the first child is done, have the listener offer constructive feedback on how well the reader captured the feelings of the characters when reading aloud dialogue. Then have children switch roles and repeat the read-aloud process.

I don't think this is funny.

BELOW-LEVEL

▲ No More Fish!

ON-LEVEL

▲ Monkey Business

ADVANCED

▲ Puppy Tricks

Comprehension
Plot

Objective
To identify, analyze, and compare story plots

Use Comparison Frames   Display compare/contrast language frames such as the following:

___ is like ___. Both ___.

___ is not like ___. This one ___, but this one ___.

Have children use these frames to practice using appropriate language to compare and contrast various classroom objects.

Comprehension   After small-group instruction, are children able to identify the elements of a plot in a story and to compare the plots of two different stories?

If not, provide additional small-group practice with the skill. See the *Strategic Intervention Resource Kit* for additional support.

Strategic ▶
Intervention
Resource Kit

Guided Review

Have children open their *Student Editions* to pages 204–205. Read aloud the opening paragraph to review plot. Use the story map to remind children how to determine a story's plot. Point out that they should look at the beginning of the story to find the problem the characters face, they should look in the middle for events that show how the characters try to solve the problem, and they should read the end to see how the problem is solved. Then read the paragraph at the bottom of page 204, and go on to page 205. Briefly discuss with children what happened in "A Chair for My Mother," including the problem the family faced and how it was solved. Then read "A Present for Mom" to children, and work with them to complete the story map that compares the plots of these two stories.

Finally, help children compare the plot of "A Chair for My Mother" with "Frog and Toad All Year," another story in which characters try to do something nice for someone else. Use the prompts at the bottom of page 204 to guide children to compare the two plots.

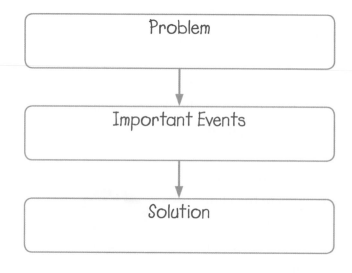

ON-LEVEL REINFORCE

Compare/Contrast Plots

Remind children how to determine the plot of a story: *As you begin, look for the problem the characters face. As you read on, look for events that show how the characters try to solve the problem. As the story ends, see how the problem is solved.* Divide the class into two groups, and give each team a story map like the one on page 204 of their *Student Edition.* Assign each team a story to map they've already read. (Make sure the plots of the two stories involve similar problems that the characters face.) Afterward, have the whole group use the maps to compare and contrast the two plots. Guide them to see that the story problems are similar but that the events and solutions are different.

ADVANCED EXTEND

Revise Plots

Have children discuss how to determine the plot of a story. Decide on a story that everyone knows well and discuss its plot. Together, complete a story map that includes the story problem, important story events, and the story solution. Then have children think of other stories they know in which characters face a similar problem. List the titles they suggest on the board, and have children settle on one that they all know. Together, fill out the same story map for this story's plot. Have children use these two maps to briefly discuss, compare, and contrast the two stories.

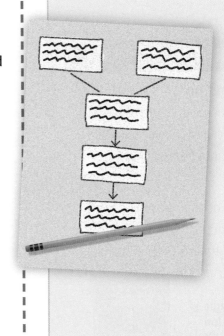

Now challenge each child (or pair of children, if you prefer) to think of a way to change the plot of one of the stories so that it is even more like the other story's plot. The whole plot can't be changed, only one thing that happens in the beginning, in the middle, or at the end. Have each child/pair fill out the same story map for the "revised" story. When everyone is done, have children compare their revised plots to see how many different possibilities they thought of.

Comprehension
Compare and Contrast

Objective
To compare story elements within a text and across texts

Guided Review

Remind children that good readers can get a better understanding of what they read by thinking about how stories or parts of stories are alike and different. Connect *alike* to comparing and *different* to contrasting. Have children recall two entertaining characters from a story they have recently read. Ask them how these two characters are alike. After children have responded, ask them how the two are different. Then draw this comparison chart on the board:

	Story 1:	Story 2:
Setting		
Characters		
How the characters try to solve their problem		

Use the story children have just discussed and another familiar story. Work together to fill in the chart, comparing and contrasting the two stories.

MONITOR PROGRESS

Comprehension   After small-group instruction, are children able to compare and contrast elements within a story and across texts, comparing two stories?

If not, provide additional small-group practice with the skill. See the *Strategic Intervention Resource Kit* for additional support.

**Strategic ▶
Intervention
Resource Kit**

ON-LEVEL REINFORCE

Compare/Contrast Stories

Remind children that good readers can get a better understanding of what they read by comparing and contrasting two stories. Have them tell you what it means to compare two things and what it means to contrast two things. Pair children up, and have each pair make a copy of the comparison chart shown on the previous page. Select the same two stories for all the pairs to compare and contrast, and direct them to record their results on their charts. Circulate as children work, helping them craft their ideas so that they fit in the chart. Afterward, have children use their charts to discuss as a group how the two stories are alike and different.

ADVANCED EXTEND

Compare/Contrast Three Story Elements

Have children tell you what it means to compare and contrast two things. Ask children what kinds of things they can compare in two stories. List these things on the board, making sure that setting, characters, story problem, and story solution are included. Then ask children to work alone or with a partner to pick one of the elements on the board to compare and contrast, challenging them to do this across three stories. Reproduce the chart shown below, and direct children to use it to record their ideas.

Story Element to Compare/Contrast:

	How are they all similar?	How are they different?
Story 1		
Story 2		

ELL

Use Comparison Frames   Use the language frames from the ELL note on page S18.

___ is like ___. Both _____.
___ is not like___. This one ___, but this one ___.

This time help children use them to compare and contrast two characters in the same story. Then help them compare and contrast two characters from two different stories.

Robust Vocabulary

Objective
To review robust vocabulary

REVIEW Tested ✓

Build Robust Vocabulary

acquired	extremely
assumed	admit
absurd	barely
attempt	hilarious
serious	witty

MONITOR PROGRESS

Robust Vocabulary After small-group instruction, are children able to use and understand the Vocabulary Words?

If not, provide additional small-group practice with the words. See the *Strategic Intervention Resource Kit* for additional support.

Strategic ▶
Intervention
Resource Kit

BELOW-LEVEL RETEACH

Reintroduce the Words

Routine Card 3 Use *Routine Card 3* and **Transparencies R118 and R119** to re-introduce the words to children. Review the Student-Friendly Explanations until children are familiar with the words. Then use prompts such as the following to check understanding. Be sure children explain their answers.

acquired   Where can an animal be acquired—at a zoo or at a pet store?

assumed   Which person assumed a movie was great? Rosa saw the movie. Ross didn't see it but knew his friends liked it.

absurd   Which of these is absurd—to fly on a plane or to think you can fly?

attempt   If you attempt to ride a bike, are you probably doing something you know how to do well or trying to do something for the first time?

serious   Which of these is serious—taking a test or going to a party?

extremely   If something is extremely funny, is it sort of funny or very funny?

admit   If someone says a book is great and you admit that this is so, did you like the book or dislike the book?

barely   Which of these can you barely hear—a crashing wave, a whisper, or a dog barking outside your window?

hilarious   If you think a movie is hilarious, are you happy, upset, or angry as you watch it?

witty   Is a witty person boring, smart or foolish?

ON-LEVEL **REINFORCE**

Word Associations

Display the Vocabulary Words, and review for children the Student-Friendly Explanations, using each word in an oral context sentence. Then tell children that you are going to say a word or phrase that goes with one or more of the Vocabulary Words. For each one, tell children how many of the Vocabulary Words can go with this association, and have children identify them: **funny** (*absurd, hilarious, witty*), **not funny** (*serious*), **try** (*attempt*), **a lot** (*extremely*), **a little** (*barely*), **bought** (*acquired*), **thinking about ideas** (*assumed, admit*).

 **ADVANCED** **EXTEND**

Determining Relationships

Display the Vocabulary Words. List and discuss different ways that words can be related:

Words can be synonyms, with similar meanings, such as *small* and *little*.

Words can be antonyms, with opposite meanings, such as *night* and *day*.

Words can have related meanings, such as *song* and *guitar* both having to do with music.

Ask children to brainstorm different ways that they can group the displayed Vocabulary Words, such as synonyms (*hilarious, absurd,* and *witty* as synonyms for *funny*) and antonyms (*hilarious* or *absurd* and *serious; extremely* and *barely*). For each of the remaining words, have children think of other words that could be grouped with this word, using one of the displayed grouping ideas. The word *acquired*, for example, could be grouped with synonyms (*bought*), antonyms (*lost*), or a category (*shopping*).

Clarify Meaning Use facial expressions that children imitate to demonstrate the difference between *barely serious* (e.g., try to keep a straight face), *serious,* and *extremely serious.* Do the same kind of thing for *hilarious.*

Student-Friendly Explanations

acquired	If you own or buy something, you have acquired it.
assumed	If you assumed something, you believed something without thinking about it.
absurd	If something is absurd, it is crazy or silly.
attempt	If you attempt to do something, you try to do it.

Grade 2, Lesson 22   R118   Vocabulary

Transparencies R118, R119

Grammar and Writing
Language Arts Checkpoint

Objectives
- *To recognize subject-verb agreement*
- *To write a fantasy*

Subject-Verb Agreement

1. The chicken pecks at the corn.
   (naming part: chicken; verb: pecks)
2. The chickens peck at the corn.
   (naming part: chickens; verb: peck)
3. You gather the eggs.
   (naming part: You; verb: gather)
4. Tricia gathers the eggs.
   (naming part: Tricia; verb: gathers)
5. The children gather the eggs.
   (naming part: children; verb: gather)

Rules for Verbs That Tell About Now

Naming Part	Rule	Example
Names One	Add -s to most verbs.	The dog laps the water. Karl drinks lemonade.
Names More Than One	Do not add an ending.	The cows chew hay. The kittens drink the milk.
I or *You*	Do not add an ending.	I munch on popcorn. You bake muffins.

6. The children (<u>wave</u>, waves) goodbye to the farmer.
7. The farmer (smile, <u>smiles</u>) at the children.

Grade 2, Lesson 22 **LA45** Grammar

Transparency LA45

BELOW-LEVEL **RETEACH**

Review Subject-Verb Agreement

Remind children that there are two parts to a sentence: The naming part, or subject, tells who or what the sentence is about. The telling part, including the verb, tells what this person, animal, place, or thing is or does. Point out that the subject and verb in a sentence have to match, or agree. Display **Transparency LA45,** and tell children that they have seen it before. Use the chart on this transparency to review the rules of subject-verb agreement. Then guide children in completing the items. For items 1–5, have them identify the subject (naming part) of the sentence and then identify the verb, telling whether this verb has an *-s* at the end or not. For items 6–7, children should choose the correct verb to complete the sentence. Begin by having them identify whether the subject of the sentence names one or more than one. Then have them identify the verb form that agrees with this subject.

REVIEW FANTASY Remind children that a fantasy story tells about something that could not happen in real life. Explain that in a fantasy, one or more of the characters does something that couldn't really happen. Have children listen to the beginning of two stories and tell you which one sounds like a fantasy.

> **Rita was going to visit her cousin, who had moved far away. It was time to go to the airport. She grabbed her backpack and headed out the door.**

> **Rita was going to visit her cousin, who had moved far away. She grabbed her backpack, ran outside, and hopped on her horse, Snow. He took off, his big wings beating, and flew toward the west.**

After children identify which one is the fantasy, discuss the difference between flying on an airplane and flying on a horse. Then have children brainstorm another way they might begin a fantasy about a girl named Rita who is about to go visit her cousin. What other fantasy form of travel might they have Rita use?

ON-LEVEL REINFORCE

Connect Grammar and Writing

Explain that in any story, including a fantasy, it is important for a writer to be sure that there is subject-verb agreement. Write the following opening to a fantasy story on the board, and read it aloud:

Marco points at the mirror. It grows gray and cloudy. He grabs his dog Po. They go inside the mirror together. I wave good-bye to them.

Have children tell you how they can tell that this story is going to be a fantasy. (A boy and his dog step into a mirror, something that can't happen in real life.) Then review each sentence with children to identify the subject and the verb. Have children note which verbs have -s added at the end. Use these sentences and the chart on **Transparency LA45** to review the rules for when to add -s to a verb so that it agrees with the subject.

ADVANCED EXTEND

Apply the Skill

Have children discuss how a fantasy story is different from a story that is realistic. Invite children to think of an interesting opening paragraph for a fantasy story. The paragraph should have a few sentences, perhaps three or four, and be written in the present tense—as if the story is happening now. When children are ready, have them share their paragraphs with the group. After each one is read, have children identify any fantasy elements that the paragraph contains. Then direct attention to sentences from children's paragraphs that have easily-identified subjects and action verbs. Make sure some verbs have the -s ending and some don't, modifying sentences as needed. Display the sentences, and have children identify the subjects and verbs. Finally, use all the sentences to review the rules (listed on **Transparency LA45**) for when to add -s to a verb so that it agrees with the subject.

Phonics

Objective

To practice and apply knowledge of the vowel variant /ōō/oo, ew, ue, ui, ou

Decodable Book 19

"How to Groom Your Dog," "Seafood Stew," "Sue Hunts for Clues," "True Buddies," "Soup Tale," and "Ouzels" ▶

MONITOR PROGRESS

Phonics After small-group instruction, are children able to read words with /ōō/oo, ew, ue, ui, and ou?

If not, provide additional small-group practice with the sound. See the *Strategic Intervention Resource Kit* for additional support.

Strategic ▶
Intervention
Resource Kit

BELOW-LEVEL RETEACH

Connect Letters and Sounds

Routine Card 1 Using *Routine Card 1* and the corresponding *Sound/Spelling Card*, reintroduce the vowel variant /ōō/oo, ew, ue, ui, and ou. Write the words *true, clue,* and *due* on the board. Read them aloud, and have children identify the vowel sound they hear. (/ōō/) Have them look at the words to identify the letters that stand for the vowel sound. (*ue*) Do the same for *oo* (*smooth, food, soon*), *ew* (*grew, stew, threw*), *ui* (*fruit, suit, juice*), and *ou* (*soup, group, you*). Elicit that *ue, oo, ew, ui,* and *ou* can all spell the /ōō/ sound. Finish by having children read aloud *Decodable Book 19.* Pause at the end of each page to review any word that children struggled to read.

ON-LEVEL REINFORCE

Word Building

Display the words in dark type, one at a time, and have children tell you what letter to change to spell the word in parentheses: **tree** (*true*), **now** (*new*), **skit** (*suit*), **top** (*too*), **die** (*due*), and **soap** (*soup*). Ask children to read each new word as it is built. Then write the following sentences on the board for children to read:

> **I am due to get a new suit.**

> **Is it true that we will have soup, too?**

Have children read aloud the stories in *Decodable Book 19.* Afterward, ask questions about each story to make sure that children have understood what they read.

Homophones

Remind children that some words can sound the same but be spelled differently and have different meanings, as in I _see_ the _sea_. Display the following words in sentences, with underlining as shown:

> The sky is <u>blue.</u>
>
> <u>Do</u> you like sports?
>
> She <u>brews</u> ice tea.
>
> Let's walk <u>through</u> the park.
>
> There are <u>crews</u> on ships.

For each one, ask a volunteer to read aloud the context sentence, and challenge children to think of another word (or words) that sounds like the underlined word. Write it on the board as children dictate its spelling. Target homophones are _blew, dew_ and _due, bruise, threw,_ and _cruise._ If necessary, provide a riddle whose answer is the targeted word. Then have children think of context sentences for each of the words they have spelled.

Fluency

Objective
To read fluently at a rate appropriate for nonfiction

Provide Scaffolding
Display difficult terms from the appropriate *Leveled Reader*, so children can practice reading them. Reproduce text in line-for-line chunks, to help children develop smoothness in their reading of the text. When they feel confident, have them read aloud from the *Leveled Reader*.

Fluency After small-group instruction, are children able to vary their reading rate as needed to read text fluently and accurately?

If not, provide additional small-group practice. See the *Strategic Intervention Resource Kit* for additional support.

Strategic ▶
Intervention
Resource Kit

BELOW-LEVEL **RETEACH**

Echo-Reading

Routine Card 8

Remind children that good readers change their reading rate depending on what they are reading. When they read nonfiction, they read it more slowly, so their listeners can understand what the text is about. Point out that good readers also slow down when they come to an unfamiliar or difficult word, to be sure they read it correctly. On the board, write an easy passage from an earlier fiction *Leveled Reader*. Then write a more dense passage from an earlier nonfiction one. Model reading the two aloud at appropriate speeds, have children echo-read with you, and discuss why you read at different rates. Distribute *The Penguins*. Read the book aloud to children, drawing their attention to your reading rate and to times when you slowed down for difficult terms. Have children echo-read with you, imitating your rate. Then ask them to read the book with a partner. Remind them to monitor each other's reading. Circulate and listen to readers, providing feedback on their reading rate and noting if they pause too often, read too slowly, or make a mistake.

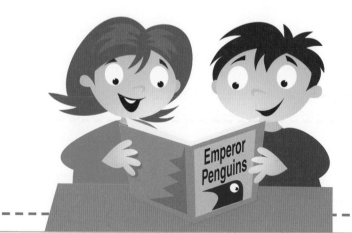

●―― ON-LEVEL REINFORCE ―――

Partner Reading

Routine Card **9**

Remind children that good readers read nonfiction more slowly than fiction so that their listeners can understand what the text is about. Distribute *The Ant*, and explain that they will practice reading this nonfiction text at a slower reading rate. Point out that even though they read more slowly, they should still make their reading sound smooth and natural. Read each page of *The Ant* aloud to children, modeling an appropriate rate and slowing down a bit when you come to a difficult term. Have children read after you, matching your reading rate. Then have them practice reading aloud with a partner. Instruct listeners to alert their partner if he or she pauses too often, reads too slowly, or makes a mistake.

●―― ADVANCED EXTEND ✏ ―――

Partner Reading

Routine Card **10**

Ask a volunteer to explain how a good reader changes his or her reading rate when reading aloud nonfiction and fiction. Distribute copies of *The Prairie Dog* to children, and tell them that they will practice slowing their reading rate as they read this book aloud to a partner. Remind them that they should only slow down enough so that their listener can understand what the text is about and so they can read it accurately. Point out that they should still make their reading sound smooth and natural. Have one partner read aloud while the other one listens and monitors the reading, providing constructive feedback about reading rate, naturalness, and accuracy. Then have children switch roles and repeat the read-aloud process.

The prairie dog is not really a dog. It belongs to the squirrel family.

Pete Prairie Dog poked his head out of his burrow and smiled.

LEVELED READERS

● BELOW-LEVEL

▲ The Penguin

● ON-LEVEL

▲ The Ant

● ADVANCED

▲ The Prairie Dog

Comprehension
Use Graphic Aids

Objective
To use graphic aids to understand nonfiction selections

Clarify Meaning Guide children through graphic aids that have brief labels or entries with words, such as articles, omitted. Note that this is done to save space. Work together to expand labels into oral sentences (*This is a ___.*) and to flesh out condensed entries into full sentences on the board.

Comprehension After small-group instruction, are children able to identify and find information in maps, time lines, diagrams, charts, and graphs?

If not, provide additional small-group practice with the skill. See the *Strategic Intervention Resource Kit* for additional support.

Strategic ▶ Intervention Resource Kit

Guided Review
Point out that nonfiction selections often include graphic aids that the author uses to help readers understand the information that is being presented about a topic. Have children turn to appropriate pages in their *Student Editions*, or in social studies, science, and math textbooks as you review the following graphic aids:

Map: shows where places are located

Diagram: shows the parts of something or how something works

Time line: shows dates and events for one period of time

Chart: shows lots of information in one place, in rows and columns

Graph: compares different amounts of things

For each graphic aid, prompt children to find certain information, such as identifying a label in a diagram, or an event that occurs on a certain date in a time line.

Identify Graphic Aids

Remind children that nonfiction selections often include graphic aids to help readers understand the information, and that graphic aids are quick, visual ways to present a lot of information. Have children take out their social studies, science, and math books. One at a time, review what one graphic aid (map, diagram, chart, time line, or graph) shows. Flip through the textbooks together to find examples of this kind of graphic aid. Elicit the kind of information generally found in this kind of graphic aid. Ask children to find particular information, to make sure they know how to use this graphic aid. Wrap up by encouraging children to study the graphic aids in a nonfiction selection to learn and understand more about the selection topic.

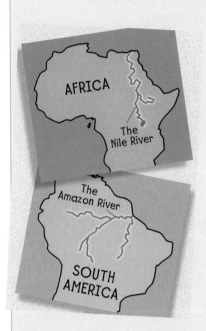

Analyze Graphic Aids

List these graphic aids on the board: maps, diagrams, time lines, charts, and graphs. Have children discuss the differences between and among them. Then have children take out their science, social studies, and math textbooks. Give them five index cards, and direct them to work independently to find an example of each kind of graphic aid. For each one, they should write a question on the front of the card that can be answered by studying the particular graphic aid that they have found. Their question should begin by identifying where the graphic aid is (which textbook, which page). On the back, they should write the answer to their question. When children are ready, have them pose their questions to the rest of the group.

Look at the chart on page 275 of our social studies text. Which river is longer—the Amazon or the Nile?

Vocabulary
Synonyms

Objective
To recognize and understand common synonyms

Guided Review

Remind children that synonyms are words that have the same, or almost the same, meanings. Write the following paragraph on the board:

> **Seahorses are tiny fish, not horses. Their heads look like the heads of horses. These small animals are found near the shore.**

Tell children that there are two words in this paragraph that are synonyms. (*tiny, small*) If necessary, identify the first word, and guide children to find the second. Ask them to think of another word that is a synonym for *tiny*. (*little*) List the three synonyms in a circle. Now write this sentence on the board: *The whale is a big animal.* Underline *big*, and have children think of other words that are synonyms for *big*. (*huge, large, giant*) List all these synonyms in another circle. Go through a similar procedure with these sentences, having children think of synonyms for the underlined words: *I get <u>scared</u> when I see a snake. Don't be <u>mean</u> to animals. Be <u>kind</u> to animals.*

Vocabulary After small-group instruction, are children able to identify or name synonyms?

If not, provide additional small-group practice with the skill. See the *Strategic Intervention Resource Kit* for additional support.

Strategic ▶
Intervention
Resource Kit

ON-LEVEL REINFORCE

Identify Synonyms

Remind children that synonyms are two words that mean the same or almost the same. Display the following pairs of words, inserting each in the sentence in parentheses. Have children identify if the words are synonyms or not. If so, have them think of another synonym. If not, have them think of a synonym for each word in the pair.

cold, chilly (The air feels ___.)

happy, noisy (This is a ___ party.)

yell, shout (The children ___ as they play.)

tiny, huge (This lake is ___.)

Clarify Meaning Use crayon colors to help children distinguish between the same, similar (almost the same), and different. Have them select crayons that are exactly the same color. Then help them find crayons that are similar in color. Contrast them with crayons quite different in color.

Generate Synonyms

Display a chart that is titled "A Better Way to Say It." Label the columns with several overused adjectives, such as *hot, cold, small, big, soft, scary, bad,* and *good.* Challenge children to work together to come up with interesting synonyms for each of these words, brainstorming at first and then consulting a dictionary or thesaurus as needed to find additional words. When they feel they have filled the chart with lots of interesting words, have them copy it neatly onto a piece of oak tag so that you can post it on the classroom wall or leave it in the Writing Center—for the class to consult when writing.

hot	cold	small	big	soft	scary	bad	laugh
burning	chilly	tiny	huge	mushy	frightening	nasty	giggle
steamy	nippy	miniature	gigantic	velvety	alarming	evil	chuckle

Robust Vocabulary

Objective
To review robust vocabulary

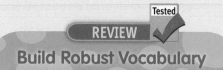

REVIEW Tested ✓

Build Robust Vocabulary

thickens	sealed
plentiful	carefully
role	attack
diligent	pattern
crowd	disappear

MONITOR PROGRESS

Robust Vocabulary After small-group instruction, are children able to use and understand the Vocabulary Words?

If not, provide additional small-group practice with the words. See the *Strategic Intervention Resource Kit* for additional support.

**Strategic ▶
Intervention
Resource Kit**

BELOW-LEVEL **RETEACH**

Reintroduce the Words

Routine Card 3
Use *Routine Card 3* and **Transparencies R125 and R126** to re-introduce the words to children. Review the Student-Friendly Explanations until children are familiar with the words. Then use prompts such as the following to check understanding. Be sure children explain their answers.

thickens — If soup thickens, is it easier or harder to stir?

plentiful — If hot dogs are plentiful at a party, will everyone get one or not?

role — Which one has a role in the park cleanup? Micky picks up trash around the pond. Nicky stops to watch everyone clean up the park.

diligent — Which worker is diligent at the park cleanup? Ling works for two hours and then goes home. Lina works all afternoon, until the park is all cleaned up.

crowd — Where would people be most likely to crowd together—in an elevator or at a park?

sealed — Which of these is sealed—an opened or an unopened cereal box?

carefully — Which person moves more carefully—a tightrope walker or a person walking a dog?

attack — Which animal is more likely to attack you—a cat or a lion?

pattern — Which curtain has a pattern—a plaid curtain or a white curtain?

disappear — Which disappears from sight—the rising sun or the setting sun?

ON-LEVEL REINFORCE

Apply Word Knowledge

Review the Student-Friendly Explanations with children. Have children tell you whether a statement is true or not, supplying reasons for their responses. For example, you might pose the following:

Cal was diligent, so he didn't finish cleaning his room. (false)

Sand is plentiful at the beach. (true)

If you lick the flap of an envelope and close it shut, the envelope is sealed. (true)

If you add lots of water to paste, it thickens. (false)

 ADVANCED EXTEND

Apply Word Knowledge

Display the Vocabulary Words, and have children suggest oral context sentences for each one.

Name two things that can <u>thicken</u>.

Name two places where trees are <u>plentiful</u>.

Find two <u>patterns</u> in the classroom.

Name two things a <u>diligent</u> reader does when reading a story.

Name two <u>roles</u> a student could have in a fire drill.

Name two things it's important to do <u>carefully</u>.

Name two things that can be <u>sealed</u>.

Name two animals that can <u>attack</u> people in the ocean.

Names two places where people might <u>crowd</u> together.

Name two things that can <u>disappear</u>.

Visualize Meaning   Use photographs or artwork from classroom materials to help children understand *plentiful*, *crowd*, and *pattern*. Use props and pantomime to enhance the meaning of *thickens*, *sealed*, *attack*, and *disappear*.

Student-Friendly Explanations

thickens	If something thickens, it becomes more gooey.
plentiful	If something is plentiful, there is a lot of it.
role	If you have a role, there are certain things you have to do.
diligent	If you are diligent, you keep working until you're done.

Grade 2, Lesson 23   R125   Vocabulary

Transparencies R125, R126

Grammar and Writing
Language Arts Checkpoint

Objectives

- *To identify past-tense verbs in sentences and to form sentences correctly with past-tense verbs*
- *To write a paragraph of information*

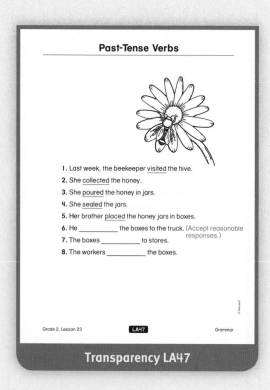

Transparency LA47

Past-Tense Verbs

1. Last week, the beekeeper <u>visited</u> the hive.
2. She <u>collected</u> the honey.
3. She <u>poured</u> the honey in jars.
4. She <u>sealed</u> the jars.
5. Her brother <u>placed</u> the honey jars in boxes.
6. He _____ the boxes to the truck. (Accept reasonable responses.)
7. The boxes _____ to stores.
8. The workers _____ the boxes.

Grade 2, Lesson 23   LA47   Grammar

BELOW-LEVEL   RETEACH

Review Past-Tense Verbs

Remind children that a verb can tell about an action that is happening now or an action that happened in the past. Guide children to find the action verbs in the following sentences. Then ask them to decide which tells about an action happening now and which tells about an action that happened in the past.

> **Today we play ball. Last week we played ball.**

> **Yesterday they painted. Now Gil paints.**

> **The twins dance in the show. They danced last year too.**

Point out how the verb in each pair changed when the sentence told about something in the past. Explain that many verbs have *-ed* added when they tell about the past, but that if a verb ends in a silent *e*, only *-d* is added. Display **Transparency LA47**, reminding children that they have seen it before. Guide children to identify and circle the verb in sentences 1–5 that tells about the past.

REVIEW A PARAGRAPH OF INFORMATION   Remind children that a paragraph can give information about a real subject or topic. Display this paragraph:

Odd Ostriches

> **The ostrich is a strange bird. It has wings, but it cannot fly. It is the tallest and biggest of all birds, but it is also very fast. An ostrich on the run can beat a racehorse.**

Read the paragraph aloud, and review that a paragraph of information has a title that tells what the paragraph is about, a main-idea sentence, and other sentences that tell more about the main idea. Guide children to locate the main-idea sentence, and note that this sentence often comes at the beginning of the paragraph. Have children find facts in the paragraph that tell more about the main idea.

ON-LEVEL **REINFORCE**

Connect Grammar and Writing

Explain that a paragraph that gives information often includes action verbs to make it easier for the reader to picture and understand the information. Display the following paragraph:

Dinosaurs Ruled

Huge dinosaurs once lived on Earth. Some hunted for food. Some snacked on plants. Dinosaurs soared through the sky, dived in the ocean, and walked across the land. Then millions of years ago, they disappeared.

Guide children to find the past-tense action words in this paragraph. Have them tell whether *-ed* or *-d* was added to the action verb to form the past tense. Then use classroom resources and children's general knowledge to work together to write another paragraph about dinosaurs or one kind of dinosaur. Guide children to include past-tense action verbs, drawing attention to them and how they are formed as the paragraph is composed.

 **ADVANCED** **EXTEND**

Write About an Insect

List some insects on the board. (Possible responses: mosquito, spider, honeybee, ant, wasp) Provide encyclopedias or library books that have information on the insects you list. Then direct children to work alone or with a partner to write a paragraph of information about one of the insects. As needed, review the elements of this kind of paragraph: *It gives information about a real subject or topic. The title explains what the paragraph is about. The main-idea sentence is written first. The other sentences tell more about this main idea.* Encourage children to include past-tense action verbs in their paragraphs that help their readers picture how these insects acted in a certain situation. Give children time to draft, revise, and edit their paragraphs. Then provide time for them to read their paragraphs aloud.

Extra Practice Display simple sentences with present-tense action words, and work with children to add *-ed* or *-d* to the verb to form past-tense sentences. Possible verbs: *play, walk, race, dance, hike, fix, count, join, wash, sail, wave, pass*

Phonics

Objective

To practice and apply knowledge of the r-Controlled vowel /âr/air, are

Decodable Book 20

"Blair and His Lair," "A Visit to the County Fair" ▶

Phonics   After small-group instruction, are children able to read words with /âr/*air, are*?

If not, provide additional small-group practice with the sound. See the *Strategic Intervention Resource Kit* for additional support.

Strategic ▶ Intervention Resource Kit

BELOW-LEVEL   RETEACH

Connect Letters and Sounds

Routine Card I   Using *Routine Card I* and the corresponding *Sound/Spelling Card*, reintroduce the *r*-Controlled vowel /âr/*air, are*. Write the words *hair, fair,* and *chair* on the board, and have children listen as you pronounce the words. Ask them to identify the common sound that they hear in all three. (/âr/) Then have them look at the displayed words and tell you what letters stand for the /âr/ sound in these words. (*air*) Follow a similar procedure for *are*, using the words *care, share,* and *scare*. Work with children to blend sounds to read each of the displayed words. Help them to see that the /âr/ sound can be spelled *air* or *are*. Finish by having children read aloud *Decodable Book 20*. Pause at the end of each page to review any word that children struggled to read.

ON-LEVEL   REINFORCE

Build Words

Display the words in dark type, one at a time, and have children tell you which letter to change or what letter to add to spell the word in parentheses: **car** (*care*), **pail** (*pair*), **shame** (*share*), **star** (*stair*), **dart** (*dare*), and **fir** (*fair*). Ask children to read each new word as it is built. Then write the following sentences on the board for children to read:

> **Take care as you put the pail on the stair.**

> **Be fair when you cut the cake, if you dare!**

Have children read aloud the stories in *Decodable Book 20*. Afterward, ask questions about each story to make sure that children have understood what they read.

Homophone Puzzles

List these words on the board: *hair, pair, flair, fare, stare,* and *bare.* For each word, have children think of a homophone, a word that sounds the same but has a different meaning and different spelling. (For *pair,* there are two homophones: *pare* and *pear.* Other homophones include *hare, flare, fair, stair,* and *bear.*) List these homophone pairs and triplets. Then have children, alone or with a partner, create and write a sentence that uses two of these homophones, leaving a blank for each one. Have them exchange papers with another child or pair and solve one another's puzzles.

We paid our bus _____ to go to the _____.

The _____ lost his fur, and now he's _____.

Fluency

Objective
To increase reading rate while reading in a manner that sounds like natural speech

Guided Practice
Select a short passage from an appropriate *Leveled Reader*. Work with the group, sentence-by-sentence. Read aloud the first sentence, starting very slowly, and have children echo-read it. Point out phrases or groups of words that you read a little more quickly. Increase your speed gradually. Then move on to the next sentence.

MONITOR PROGRESS

Fluency After small-group instruction, are children able to vary their reading rate as needed to read text fluently and accurately?

If not, provide additional small-group practice. See the *Strategic Intervention Resource Kit* for additional support.

Strategic ▶ Intervention Resource Kit

BELOW-LEVEL **RETEACH**

Echo-Reading

Routine Card 8 Remind children that to read aloud fluently, a good reader reads accurately and quickly, but not so fast that the words don't make sense. Review things children can do to increase their reading rate:

- Choose a short text that is easy to read, with no hard words.

- Read this text aloud to a partner three to five times, trying to read a little bit faster each time.

- Have your partner tell you how quick and accurate each reading is.

Distribute *Mountain Gorillas*, and read it aloud to children. Then select pages that have easy text, and have children echo-read with you to show them how to increase their reading rate. Then ask them to read the book with a partner, and then to pick a passage to practice reading at an increased rate. Circulate and provide feedback on the accuracy and rate of their readings.

Echo-Reading

Routine Card 10 Remind children that in order to become more fluent readers, they must work to increase their reading rate while still reading the words accurately. Note, however, that the point is not to read so fast that the listener can't follow what is being read. Distribute copies of *Orangutans*. Read each page aloud to children, and have them match your rate. Then revisit a passage, and show children how to practice. Start slowly and smoothly, having children echo-read. Increase your speed on three subsequent readings, with children echo-reading. Now have them read the book aloud with a partner, page by page. Then have partners pick a passage to practice 3–5 times, giving one another feedback.

Partner Reading

Routine Card 9 Have children discuss what it means to read fluently, making sure that they include appropriate reading rate and accuracy. Tell children that partners are going to read a book aloud to one another. Then each partner will pick a short passage from the book to practice reading at a more rapid rate. To do this, they will be doing timed readings. While one child reads aloud, the other uses a stopwatch, or the classroom clock, having the reader start when the second hand is on 12 and counting the seconds that pass. Explain that the goal is to increase reading rate, so they should do their first reading at a comfortable speed. Then they should do 3 or 4 more readings, trying to increase their speed a little bit each time. Distribute copies of *Watching Arctic Wolves*. Remind them that their goal is to read accurately, smoothly, and quickly, in a way that sounds like natural speech. They should not try to read so quickly that the words make no sense to the listener.

LEVELED READERS

● BELOW-LEVEL

▲ Mountain Gorillas

● ON-LEVEL

▲ Orangutans

● ADVANCED

▲ Watching Arctic Wolves

Comprehension

Use Graphic Aids

Objective
To use graphic aids to understand nonfiction selections

E L L

Clarify Meaning   Preview the subject of the diagram on *Student Edition* page 280. Display a picture of a plant or an actual plant as you identify its parts (stem, leaves, root). Work with children to identify and differentiate between the diagram's title and its labels. Then have children identify the title and labels in the diagram on page 281.

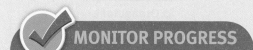
MONITOR PROGRESS

Comprehension   After small-group instruction, are children able to recognize various graphic aids, and to understand and use charts and diagrams?

If not, provide additional small-group practice with the skill. See the *Strategic Intervention Resource Kit* for additional support.

Strategic ▶
Intervention
Resource Kit

BELOW-LEVEL   RETEACH

Guided Review

Have children turn to pages 280–281 in the *Student Edition*. Read aloud the text on this page to review different kinds of graphic aids. Focus on a diagram. Have children tell you what part of the diagram tells what it shows. (the title) Have children read the title of the diagram on page 280 aloud. Then, as you read aloud each label, have a different child point to the part of the flower that the label names. Follow a similar procedure with the labels for the diagram on page 281, after you have read aloud and discussed the article that precedes it. Finally, have children respond to the prompts about this diagram at the bottom of page 281.

Move on to display a simple chart, one that includes an explanatory title, from children's science or social studies textbook. Have children tell you what the chart is about, referring them to the title if necessary. Help them read the information in the chart. Then ask them questions that they can answer by locating specific information in the chart.

Analyze Diagrams and Charts

Use *Student Edition* page 280 to review various kinds of graphic aids with children. Divide the class into two groups. Have one team look through their content-area textbooks for a diagram. Have the other team look through their textbooks for a chart. Direct both teams to decide on and record three questions on a piece of paper that can be answered by looking at their particular graphic aid, putting their answers on the back of the paper. Have teams take turns telling the others which page to open to and then posing their questions. Afterward, have the group work together to identify and discuss the parts of a diagram and of a chart.

Create Diagrams

Have children identify and discuss different kinds of graphic aids that can be found in nonfiction texts, making sure they include diagrams, charts, maps, timelines, and graphs. Use the diagram on *Student Edition* page 280 to review the parts of a diagram (title, illustration, labels) and the function of a diagram (to tell how something is put together or how it works). Have children brainstorm animals or things that they know the important parts of, such as a dog or a bike. Ask them to pick one to diagram as a group. Provide a picture of the subject or have them select a group member to draw its picture. Then have children discuss and decide on the labels they want to use in their diagram. Work together to spell and list the label names on the board. Then have group members take turns writing one of these labels in an appropriate area on the diagram and using a ruler to show what part of the diagram the label identifies. Finally, have children choose a title for their diagram.

Dog

Vocabulary
Synonyms

Objective
To identify and substitute synonyms

Guided Review

Remind children that synonyms are words that have similar meanings. Write this sentence on the board.

> **I was nervous because the dog looked big and scary.**

Read the sentence to children, and circle the words *big* and *scary*. Point out that you want to use better descriptive words that will help a reader picture a dog that looks like a monster about to attack. Model coming up with synonyms for *scary*. After considering *frightening, terrifying,* and *alarming*, settle on *terrifying* because it makes you think of a monster. Then work with children, consulting a thesaurus or synonym finder to think of a strong synonym for *big*, such as *large, huge, gigantic, enormous,* or *colossal*. Have children select the one they think sounds most like a monster. Then display pictures of different kinds of trees—for example, a giant oak, a delicate cherry tree, and a sugar maple in fall. Help children replace *pretty* in the sentence ***The tree is pretty***, finding a synonym that fits each tree. (Possible responses: *majestic, delicate, brilliant*)

MONITOR PROGRESS

Vocabulary   After small-group instruction, are children able to identify synonyms and decide which word is more descriptive or better suited?

If not, provide additional small-group practice with the skill. See the *Strategic Intervention Resource Kit* for additional support.

Strategic ▶ Intervention Resource Kit

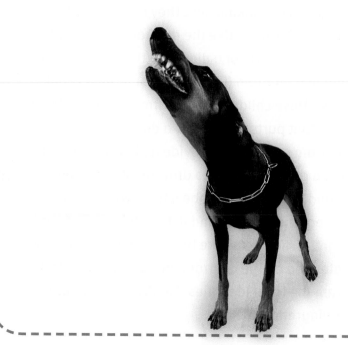

ON-LEVEL REINFORCE

Compare Synonyms

Display pairs of synonyms, and work with children to discuss and decide which word works better in the situation in parentheses. Look words up in a dictionary, if needed, to clarify meaning:

pale, sickly (a girl who has the flu)

slender, skinny (a snake hiding in a small hole)

look, stare (a boy who is being rude)

chuckle, giggle (a boy who thinks something is really, really funny)

march, trudge (a family that is walking through mud)

ADVANCED EXTEND

Play Mad Libs

Copy short passages from familiar stories that have some good descriptive adjectives and strong verbs. Leave blanks where these words occur, writing them in small print underneath. Tell children that they will be rewriting a story by using synonyms in the blanks. Then, read through one of the passages, stopping to elicit synonyms that you write in the blanks. Afterward, read the passage as it was originally written, as well as children's revised version. Then compare each sentence that has a replacement word with its original wording: Which version do children think works better? Why? You may want them to consult a dictionary from time to time, to explore the differences between two particular synonyms. Encourage children to begin to think more deeply about shades of meaning when choosing the descriptive word that works best in a particular context.

Toad will be __shocked__ .
surprised

Visual Shades of Meaning

Display a picture of a horse for *big*, an elephant for *huge*, and a whale for *enormous*. Then show children pictures of a large hill, a small mountain, and a snow capped mountain. Have children create oral sentences for each picture, using *big, huge,* or *enormous*. Point out that while each synonym describes something large, they should use the one with the clearest meaning for their sentence.

Robust Vocabulary

Objective
To review robust vocabulary

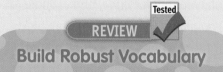

Build Robust Vocabulary

extinct	cradled
pledge	raggedy
patience	distance
tedious	personalities
blended	crumpled

Robust Vocabulary   After small-group instruction, are children able to use and understand the Vocabulary Words?

If not, provide additional small-group practice with the words. See the *Strategic Intervention Resource Kit* for additional support.

Strategic ▶ Intervention Resource Kit

BELOW-LEVEL RETEACH

Reintroduce the Words

Routine Card 3 Use *Routine Card 3* and **Transparencies R132 and R133** to reintroduce the words to children. Review the Student-Friendly Explanations until children are familiar with the words. Then use prompts such as the following to check understanding. Be sure children explain their answers.

extinct	Which of these animals is extinct—the tiger or the dinosaur?
pledge	Which person made a pledge? Dan promised he would save fifty cents every week. Nan recited a poem in class.
patience	Which person shows patience? Leo shows his little brother how to tie a shoe and then helps him practice several times. Cleo gets mad when her little brother doesn't learn right away and ties his shoe for him.
tedious	Which task is tedious: playing in the sand or counting grains of sand?
blended	If blue and yellow paint are blended, do you end up with blue or yellow paint? Why or why not?
cradled	Which one would you cradle in your lap—a rock or a baby?
raggedy	If a tablecloth looks raggedy, does it look old or new?
distance	Which one can you easily see from far away—a leaf or a tree?
personalities	Which ones have personalities—pets, plants, or colors?
crumpled	If a shirt is crumpled, has it been ironed or does it need ironing?

ON-LEVEL REINFORCE

Apply Word Knowledge

Review for children the Student-Friendly Explanations. Then display the Vocabulary Words, and write the following sentences on the board, with words or phrases underlined as shown.

The vase was <u>carefully held</u>. (cradled)

The dinosaur is <u>long dead</u>. (extinct)

The cake batter has to be <u>mixed</u>. (blended)

This chore is <u>boring</u>. (tedious)

I made a <u>promise</u>. (pledge)

Pets have different <u>ways of behaving</u>. (personalities)

The piece of paper was <u>crushed</u>. (crumpled)

I see a bird flying in the <u>sky far away</u>. (distance)

Have children replace the underlined words with a Vocabulary Word.

  ADVANCED EXTEND

Word Associations

Display all the Vocabulary Words. Ask questions such as the following, and have children explain their responses.

Which word goes with *Tyrannosaurus Rex*? (extinct)
Which word goes with *far away*? (distance)
Which word goes with *boredom*? (tedious)
Which word names something all of us have? (personalities)
Which word goes with *thrown-away paper*? (crumpled)
Which word goes with *old clothes*? (raggedy)
Which word goes with *allegiance*? (pledge)
Which word goes with *careful* and *breakable*? (cradled)
Which word goes with *calm* and *understanding*? (patience)
Which word goes with *stir*? (blended)

Clarify Meaning Have children use props, pictures, and pantomime to demonstrate each word's meaning. For example, they might cradle something breakable, display a picture of a extinct animal, and act out people with different personalities (happy, sad, silly).

Student-Friendly Explanations

extinct	If an animal is extinct, there are no more of that kind of animal alive.
pledge	When you make a pledge, you promise to do something.
patience	If you can wait for someone or something without complaining or getting restless, you have patience.
tedious	When something is boring and takes a long time to do, it is tedious.

Grade 2, Lesson 24   R132   Vocabulary

Transparencies R132, R133

Grammar and Writing
Language Arts Checkpoint

Objectives
- *To recognize forms of the verb* be: *am, is, are, was, were*
- *To write a paragraph that compares or contrasts*

Transparency LA49

Forms of *be*

1. Gary is a gorilla.
2. I am glad Gary lives in the wild.
3. Great apes are special creatures.
4. They are almost extinct.
5. We are pleased about the pledge to save the great apes.
6. I am ready to help Gary survive.

Grade 2, Lesson 24   LA49   Grammar

BELOW-LEVEL   RETEACH

Review Forms of the Verb *be*

Remind children that some verbs do not show action. They tell what something is or was like. Review these points:

- **The verbs** *am*, *is*, **and** *are* **tell about now.**

- **The verbs** *was* **and** *were* **tell about the past.**

Display these pairs of sentences: **Today I __ in school. Yesterday I __ in school.** Read aloud each sentence, have children identify the form of *be* that goes in the blank. Then change the subject of the sentence to *You, She,* and *They,* repeating the same process each time. Display **Transparency LA49,** reminding children that they have seen it before. Guide them in identifying a form of the verb *be* in each sentence.

REVIEW PARAGRAPHS THAT COMPARE AND CONTRAST   Remind children that a paragraph that compares or contrasts tells how two people, places, animals, or things are alike or different. Display the following paragraph:

> **A butterfly and a moth are different in many ways. A butterfly flies around during the day. Unlike a butterfly, a moth flies only at night. A butterfly has brightly-colored wings and a slim body. A moth has duller wings and a plump body.**

Read the paragraph to children, and use it to review features of a paragraph that compares or contrasts:

- The first sentence introduces the topic or one of the subjects that is being compared or contrasted.

- Other sentences tell how two things are alike or different.

- The writer often uses signal or clue words to help readers, such as *like, same, similar, different,* and *unlike.*

Have children find two signal words in the paragraph. (*different, unlike*) Work with children to compare or contrast two other similar animals.

ON-LEVEL REINFORCE

Connect Grammar and Writing

Point out that when writers create paragraphs that compare or contrast two things, they give information about both things. Display the following sets of opening sentences for a paragraph that contrasts:

The tyrannosaurus and the apatosaurus were two different dinosaurs. Unlike the apatosaurus, the tyrannosaurus was a meat eater.

The shark and the dolphin are two animals that live in the sea. The shark is a fish, but the dolphin is a mammal.

Read the first set of sentences to children, asking them to identify the two things being contrasted and to locate all the verbs that are forms of *be*. Do the same with the second set of sentences. Then have the group choose one set to work on, using their knowledge and classroom resources to add sentences to complete the paragraph.

ADVANCED EXTEND

Compare or Contrast Two Animals

Have the group suggest two animals that they would like to compare or contrast, animals that they know something about. Begin by brainstorming ways in which the two animals are alike, listing these similarities on the board in complete sentences. Then brainstorm ways in which they are different, listing the differences on the board in complete sentences. List some good signal words to include in the paragraph, such as *like, similar, same, unlike,* and *different.* Work together to craft a paragraph that compares or contrasts, beginning with a sentence that identifies what the paragraph is about. Afterward, revisit the paragraph to identify the forms of the verb be that were used in the paragraph. For each one, have children tell what verb they would use if the sentence were in the past tense. Reread the sentence together using the past-tense form of the verb.

ELL

Chart Verbs Help children learn the forms of the verb *be* by using and praticing with a chart:

	Now	Past
I	am	was
You	are	were
He, She, It	is	was
We	are	were
You	are	were

Teacher's Notes

Assessment

Assessment

Good assessments tell you what your students need to learn to meet grade-level standards.

It's not just about scoring the students—or the teacher, for that matter. It's about helping teachers **know what to teach and how much.**

Reading education is a **growing science.** We know more about how children learn to read than we did in the past. This **knowledge gives us the power** to use assessment to inform instruction. Assessment exposes the missing skills so that teachers can fill in the gaps.

Good assessment is part of instruction.

Think about it: if you are testing what you are teaching, then the test is another **practice and application** opportunity for children. In addition, when tests focus on the skills that are essential to better reading, testing informs teachers about which students need more instruction in those essential skills.

What is the best kind of assessment to use?

Using more than one kind of assessment will give you the clearest picture of your students' progress. **Multiple measures** are the key to a well-rounded view.

First, consider the assessments that are already **mandated** for you: your school, your district, and your state will, of course, tell you which tests you must use, and when. In addition to these, you should use **curriculum-based assessments** to monitor your students' progress in *StoryTown.*

"RESEARCH SAYS"

"Every teacher's primary concern is helping students learn. . . . Teachers are primarily interested in the kind of information that will support the daily instructional decisions they need to make."

—Roger Farr

The following curriculum-based assessments are built into *StoryTown.*

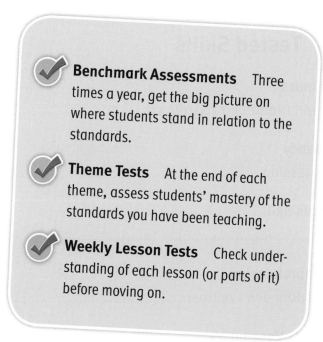

Benchmark Assessments Three times a year, get the big picture on where students stand in relation to the standards.

Theme Tests At the end of each theme, assess students' mastery of the standards you have been teaching.

Weekly Lesson Tests Check understanding of each lesson (or parts of it) before moving on.

On a daily basis, point-of-use **Monitor Progress** notes help you check understanding and reteach or extend instruction. Additional checklists and rubrics are provided to help you monitor students' comprehension, writing, listening, and speaking.

The *Benchmark Assessments,* the *Theme Tests,* and the *Weekly Lesson Tests* are all available online. Students can take the tests on the computer, or you can use pencil-and-paper and enter the scores into the database later. Either way, *StoryTown Online Assessment* will help you track students' progress and share their growth with administrators and families.

 StoryTown Online Assessment

Weekly Test

Using Assessment to Inform Instruction

Specific prescriptions based on Harcourt Reading Assessments.

✔ Tested Skills   Prescriptions

Phonics

Vowel Diphthong /ou/*ou, ow* ....Reteach, pp. S2–S3

Fluency

Expression ....Reteach, pp. S4–S5

Focus Skill

Plot..Reteach, pp. S6–S7

Comprehension

Compare and Contrast ....Reteach, pp. S8–S9

Robust Vocabulary

Lesson 21..Reteach, pp. S10–S11

Grammar/Writing

Present-Tense Action Verbs ....Reteach, pp. S12–S13

Lesson 22 Weekly Test

✔ Tested Skills

Prescriptions

Phonics
r-Controlled Vowel /ôr/*or, ore, our*................................. Reteach, pp. S14–S15

Fluency
Expression .... Reteach, pp. S16–S17

Focus Skill
Plot... Reteach, pp. S18–S19

Comprehension
Compare and Contrast .... Reteach, pp. S20–S21

Robust Vocabulary
Lesson 22 .... Reteach, pp. S22–S23

Grammar/Writing
Subject-Verb Agreement................................. Reteach, pp. S24–S25

Weekly Test

☑ Tested Skills

Prescriptions

Phonics

Vowel Variant /$\overline{oo}$/oo, ew, ue, ui, ou ....Reteach, pp. S26–S27

Fluency

Reading Rate ....Reteach, pp. S28–S29

Focus Skill

Use Graphic Aids..Reteach, pp. S30–S31

Vocabulary

Synonyms..Reteach, pp. S32–S33

Robust Vocabulary

Lesson 23 ....Reteach, pp. S34–S35

Grammar/Writing

Past-Tense Verbs ....Reteach, pp. S36–S37

Weekly Tests

✔ Lesson 24 Tested Skills   Prescriptions

Phonics
r-Controlled Vowel /âr/*air, are* .... Reteach, pp. S38–S39

Fluency
Reading Rate .... Reteach, pp. S40–S41

Focus Skill
Use Graphic Aids... Reteach, pp. S42–S43

Vocabulary
Synonyms... Reteach, pp. S44–S45

Robust Vocabulary
Lesson 24 .... Reteach, pp. S46–S47

Grammar/Writing
Forms of *Be* .... Reteach, pp. S48–S49

✔ Lesson 25 Tested Skills

Selection Comprehension
"Town Hall" .... Monitor Comprehension,
                                              pp. T401–T406

Robust Vocabulary
Lesson 25 .... Build Robust Vocabulary,
                                              pp. T407, T417, T427, T439

Theme 5 Test

✓ Tested Skills

Prescriptions

Phonics .... Reteach,
pp. S2–S3, S14–S15,
S26–S27, S38–S39

Focus Skill .... Reteach,
pp. S6–S7, S18–S19,
S30–S31, S42–S43

Comprehension .... Reteach,
pp. S8–S9, S20–S21

Robust Vocabulary... Reteach,
pp. S10–S11, S22–S23,
S32–S33, S34–S35, S44–S45,
S46–S47

Grammar/Writing .... Reteach,
pp. S12–S13, S24–S25,
S36–S37, S48–S49

Fluency.. Reteach,
pp. S4–S5, S16–S17,
S28–S29, S40–S41

 BELOW-LEVEL RETEACH

- Below-Level Leveled Readers
- Leveled Readers System
- Extra Support Copying Masters
- Strategic Intervention Resource Kit
- Intervention Station, Primary

 ON-LEVEL REINFORCE

- On-Level Leveled Readers
- Leveled Readers System
- Practice Book

 ADVANCED EXTEND

- Advanced Leveled Readers
- Leveled Readers System
- Challenge Copying Masters
- Challenge Resource Kit

To determine whether students need even more support, use your district-approved diagnostic and screening assessments.

Resources

ADDITIONAL RESOURCES

Rubrics

    Using Rubrics...R2

    Retell and Summarize Fiction.....................................R3

    Summarize Nonfiction...R4

    Presentations...R5

    Writing Rubric: Short and Extended Responses...........R6

    6-Point Rubric for Writing..R7

    4-Point Rubric for Writing..R8

Additional Reading...R9

Lesson Vocabulary..R10

Cumulative Vocabulary and High-Frequency Words..........R11

Handwriting Instruction and Models................................R12

**Student Edition Glossary
and Index of Titles and Authors**..R18

Professional Bibliography...R22

Program Reviewers & Advisors...R24

Scope and Sequence...R26

Index...R34

Acknowledgments..R86

Using Rubrics

A rubric is a tool a teacher can use to score a student's work.

A rubric lists the criteria for evaluating the work, and it describes different levels of success in meeting those criteria.

Rubrics are useful assessment tools for teachers, but they can be just as useful for students. They explain expectations, and can be powerful teaching tools.

RUBRIC Rubrics for Retelling and Summarizing

- There are separate rubrics for fiction and nonfiction. Before students begin their retellings or summaries, ask them which rubric should be used. Then point out the criteria and discuss each one.

- Have students focus on the criteria for excellence listed on the rubric so that they have specific goals to aim for.

RUBRIC Rubrics for Presentations

- Before students give a presentation, discuss the criteria listed on the rubric. Help them focus on the criteria for excellence listed on the rubric so that they have specific goals to aim for.

- Discuss the criteria for listening with students who will be in the audience. Point out the criteria for excellence listed on the rubric so that they have specific goals to aim for.

RUBRIC Rubrics for Short- and Extended-Responses

- Before students begin a short- or extended-response, discuss the criteria for excellence listed on the rubrics so that they have specific goals to aim for.

- Tell students that the short-response task should take about five to ten minutes to complete, and the extended-response should take much longer to complete.

RUBRIC Rubric for Writing

- When you introduce students to a new kind of writing through a writing model, discuss the criteria listed on the rubric, and ask students to decide how well the model meets each criterion.

- Before students attempt a new kind of writing, have them focus on the criteria for excellence listed on the rubric so that they have specific goals to aim for.

- During both the drafting and revising stages, remind students to check their writing against the rubric to keep their focus and to determine if there are any aspects of their writing they can improve.

- Students can use the rubrics to score their own writing. They can keep the marked rubric in their portfolios with the piece of writing it refers to. The marked rubrics will help students see their progress through the school year. In conferences with students and family members, you can refer to the rubrics to point out both strengths and weaknesses.

Score of 4

The student:

- names and describes the main and supporting characters and tells their actions
- tells about the setting, including both time and place
- retells the plot in detail
- describes the problems and solutions in the story
- uses phrases, language, vocabulary, or sentence structure from the story
- accurately defines the theme or meaning of the story
- provides extensions of the story such as making connections to other texts, relating experiences, making inferences and/or making generalizations
- discriminates between reality and fantasy, fact and fiction
- requires little or no prompting

Score of 3

The student:

- names and describes the main characters
- tells about the setting
- retells most of the plot accurately with some details
- describes some of the problems and solutions in the story
- uses some phrases, language, or vocabulary from the story
- relates some aspects of the theme or meaning of the story
- provides some extensions of the story such as making connections to other texts or relating relevant experiences
- discriminates between reality and fantasy, fact and fiction
- may require some prompting

Score of 2

The student:

- tells some details about the story elements, including characters, setting, and plot, with some omissions or errors
- cannot correctly identify problems or corresponding solutions in the story
- uses very little language and vocabulary from story
- shows minimal understanding of the theme or meaning
- provides minimal extensions of the story
- confuses reality and fantasy, and fact and fiction
- requires some prompting to retell the story

Score of 1

The student:

- tells few if any details about the story elements, possibly with errors
- has little or no awareness of the theme of the story
- provides no extensions of the story
- confuses reality and fantasy, and fact and fiction
- unable to retell the story without prompting

Score of 4

The student:
- provides a summarizing statement
- relates the main idea and important supporting details
- creates a focused, coherent, logical, and organized structure; stays on topic; and relates important points to the text
- understands relationships in the text such as recognizing cause and effect relationships, chronological order, or comparing and contrasting information
- uses phrases, language, or vocabulary from the text
- clearly identifies the conclusion
- identifies the author's purpose for creating the text
- provides extensions of the text such as making connections to other texts, relating relevant experiences, making inferences and/or making generalizations
- requires little or no prompting

Score of 3

The student:
- tells the topic of the text
- relates the main idea and relevant details
- creates a coherent structure and stays on topic
- mostly understands relationships in the text such as recognizing cause and effect relationships, chronological order, or comparing and contrasting information
- uses some language, or vocabulary from the text
- tells the conclusion or point of the text
- identifies the author's purpose
- provides some extensions of the text such as making connections to other texts or relating relevant experiences
- may require some prompting

Score of 2

The student:
- minimally relates the topic of the text
- shows minimal understanding of main idea and omits many important details
- provides some structure; might stray from topic
- understands few, if any, relationships in the text or recognizes chronological order
- uses little or no language and vocabulary from the text
- does not fully understand conclusion or point of the text
- shows some awareness of author's purpose
- provides few, if any, extensions of the text
- requires some prompting to retell the story

Score of 1

The student:
- shows little or no understanding of main idea and omits important details
- provides a poorly organized or unclear structure
- does not understand relationships in or of the text
- does not understand conclusion of the text
- provides no extensions of the text
- is unable to retell the story without prompting

	Score of 6	Score of 5	Score of 4	Score of 3	Score of 2	Score of 1
HANDWRITING	The slant of the letters is consistent throughout. The letters are clearly formed, spaced equally, and easy to read.	The slant of the letters is almost the same throughout. The letters are clearly formed. Spacing is nearly equal.	The slant and form of the letters is usually consistent. The spacing between words is usually equal.	The handwriting is readable. There are some inconsistencies in shape, form, slant, and spacing.	The handwriting is somewhat readable. There are many inconsistencies in shape, form, slant, and spacing.	The letters are not shaped, formed, slanted, or spaced correctly. The paper is very difficult to read.
WORD PROCESSING	Fonts and sizes are used very well, which helps the reader enjoy reading the text.	Fonts and sizes are used well.	Fonts and sizes are used fairly well, but could be improved upon.	Fonts and sizes are used well in some places, but make the paper look cluttered in others.	Fonts and sizes are not used well. The paper looks cluttered.	The writer has used too many different fonts and sizes. It is very distracting to the reader.
MARKERS	The title, side heads, page numbers, and bullets are used very well. They make it easy for the reader to find information in the text.	The title, side heads, page numbers, and bullets are used well. They help the reader find most information.	The title, side heads, page numbers, and bullets are used fairly well. They usually help the reader find information.	The writer uses a title, or page numbers, or bullets. Improvement is needed.	The writer uses very few markers. This makes it hard for the reader to find and understand the information in the text.	There are no markers such as title, page numbers, bullets, or side heads.
VISUALS	The writer uses visuals such as illustrations and props. The text and visuals clearly relate.	The writer uses visuals well. The text and visuals relate to each other.	The writer uses visuals fairly well.	The writer uses visuals with the text, but the reader may not understand how they are related.	The writer uses visuals with the text, but the reader is confused by them.	The visuals do not make sense with the text.
SPEAKING	The speaker uses very effective pacing, volume, intonation, and expression.	The speaker uses effective pacing, volume, intonation, and expression consistently.	The speaker uses effective pacing, volume, intonation, and expression fairly consistently.	The speaker uses effective pacing, volume, intonation, and expression, but not consistently.	The speaker needs to work on pacing, volume, intonation, and expression.	The speaker's techniques are unclear or distracting to the listener.

	Score of 4	Score of 3	Score of 2	Score of 1	Score of 0
SHORT-RESPONSE			The response indicates that the student has a complete understanding of the reading concept embodied in the task. The student has provided a response that is accurate, complete, and fulfills all the requirements of the task. Necessary support and/or examples are included, and the information given is clearly text-based.	The response indicates that the student has a partial understanding of the reading concept embodied in the task. The student has provided a response that includes information that is essentially correct and text-based, but the information is too general or too simplistic. Some of the support and/or examples may be incomplete or omitted.	The response indicates that the student does not demonstrate an understanding of the reading concept embodied in the task. The student has provided a response that is inaccurate; the response has an insufficient amount of information to determine the student's understanding of the task; or the student has failed to respond to the task.
EXTENDED-RESPONSE	The response indicates that the student has a thorough understanding of the reading concept embodied in the task. The student has provided a response that is accurate, complete, and fulfills all the requirements of the task. Necessary support and/or examples are included, and the information is clearly text-based.	The response indicates that the student has an understanding of the reading concept embodied in the task. The student has provided a response that is accurate and fulfills all the requirements of the task, but the required support and/or details are not complete or clearly text-based.	The response indicates that the student has a partial understanding of the reading concept embodied in the task. The student has provided a response that includes information that is essentially correct and text-based, but the information is too general or too simplistic. Some of the support and/or examples and requirements of the task may be incomplete or omitted.	The response indicates that the student has very limited understanding of the reading concept embodied in the task. The response is incomplete, may exhibit many flaws, and may not address all requirements of the task.	The response indicates that the student does not demonstrate an understanding of the reading concept embodied in the task. The student has provided a response that is inaccurate; the response has an insufficient amount of information to determine the student's understanding of the task; or the student has failed to respond to the task.

Scoring RUBRIC for Writing

	FOCUS	ORGANIZATION	SUPPORT	CONVENTIONS
Score of 6	The writing is narrowly focused on the main topic and subtopics, and has a clearly defined purpose.	The ideas in the paper are well-organized and presented in logical order. The paper seems complete to the reader.	The writing has strong, specific details. The word choices are clear and fresh.	The writer uses a variety of sentences. There are few or no errors in grammar, spelling, punctuation, and capitalization.
Score of 5	The writing is focused on the topic and purpose.	The organization of the paper is mostly clear. The paper seems complete.	The writing has strong, specific details and clear word choices.	The writer uses a variety of sentences. There are a few errors in grammar, spelling, punctuation, and capitalization.
Score of 4	The writing is generally focused on the topic and purpose with occasional drifts.	The organization is mostly clear, but the paper may seem unfinished.	The writing has supporting details and some variety in word choice.	The writer uses some variety in sentences. There are quite a few errors in grammar, spelling, punctuation, and capitalization.
Score of 3	The writing is somewhat focused on the topic and purpose with off-topic sentences common.	The paper is somewhat organized, but seems unfinished.	The writing has few supporting details. It needs more variety in word choice.	The writer uses simple sentences. There are often errors in grammar, spelling, punctuation, and capitalization.
Score of 2	The writing is related to the topic but does not have a clear focus.	There is little organization to the paper.	The writing uses few supporting details and very little variety in word choice.	The writer uses unclear sentences. There are many errors in grammar, spelling, punctuation, and capitalization.
Score of 1	The writing is not focused on the topic and/or purpose.	There is no organization to the paper.	There are few or no supporting details. The word choices are unclear, misused, or confusing.	The writer uses awkward sentences. There are numerous errors in grammar, spelling, punctuation, and capitalization.

Scoring RUBRIC for Writing

	IDEAS	ORGANIZATION	VOICE	WORD CHOICE	SENTENCE FLUENCY	CONVENTIONS
Score of 4	The paper is clear and focused. It is engaging and includes enriching details.	The ideas are well organized and in a logical order.	The writer consistently uses creative ideas and expressions.	The writing uses vivid verbs, specific nouns, and colorful adjectives well. The writing is very detailed.	The writing flows smoothly. The writer uses transitions, and a variety of sentences.	The writer uses standard writing conventions well, with few or no errors.
Score of 3	The paper is generally clear and includes supporting details, with minor focusing problems.	The paper is generally well organized and in a logical order.	The writer's ideas and expressions are generally creative.	The writing may use some vivid verbs, specific nouns, and colorful adjectives. The writing is detailed.	The writing flows generally well. The writer uses some variety in sentences.	The writer uses most standard writing conventions well, but makes some errors.
Score of 2	The paper is somewhat clear but the writer does not effectively use supporting details.	The ideas are somewhat organized.	The writer's ideas and expressions are somewhat creative.	The writing may use few interesting words. The writing is only somewhat detailed.	The writing flows somewhat. The writer does not use much variety in his or her sentence structure.	The writer uses some writing conventions well, but makes distracting errors.
Score of 1	The paper has no clear central theme. The details are either missing or sketchy.	The ideas are not well organized and there is no logical order.	The writer lacks creativity in ideas and expressions.	The writing lacks interesting word choice. The writing also lacks detail.	The writing does not flow. The writer uses little or no variety in sentences, and some sentences are unclear.	The writer makes continuous errors with most writing conventions, making text difficult to read.

Additional Reading

BLAST OFF! This list is a compilation of the additional theme- and topic-related books cited in the lesson plans. You may wish to use this list to provide students with opportunities **to read at least thirty minutes a day** outside of class.

Theme 5) BETTER TOGETHER

Barraclough, Sue.
Animals in the Wild (Animal Worlds). Raintree, 2005. An enriching and dynamic look at various wildlife creatures. Explores the differences between the animals, including habitats, sounds, and movements. **EASY**

Barraclough, Sue.
Bees (Creepy Creatures). Raintree, 2005. Readers learn how bees eat, grow, and reproduce in this colorful and un-bee-lievable book. **EASY**

Goodall, Jane.
Dr. White. North-South, 2003. Every day, a small white dog goes to the hospital to visit sick children and help them recover. *Teachers' Choice.* **CHALLENGE**

Granowsky, Alvin.
At the Park (My World). Copper Beech, 2001. A father and son enjoy spending a day at the park with their dog, where they can run, play, and see many interesting sights. **EASY**

Jackson, Abby.
Making Money. Yellow Umbrella, 2004. Simple text and photographs introduce the purpose of money, how old coins and paper money are disposed of, and how new money is made. **AVERAGE**

Nelson, Robin.
From Flower to Honey. Lerner, 2002. Describes the process of making honey, from a bee's collection of nectar to honey production on a beekeeper's farm. *Award-Winning Author.* **AVERAGE**

Pancella, Peggy.
Small Town (Neighborhood Walk). Heinemann, 2005. Readers tour a small town, and learn about workplaces, schools, transportation, and professions. **CHALLENGE**

Pedersen, Janet.
Millie Wants to Play! Candlewick, 2004. Millie the cow wakes early in the morning but waits until she hears the other animals making noise before she joins them in play. *Award-Winning Author.* **EASY**

Sayre, April Pulley.
Good Morning, Africa! (Our Amazing Continents). Millbrook, 2003. If you woke up in Africa, what might you see? Find out in this adventurous exploration of wildlife reserves, natural resources, and African cities. *Award-Winning Author.* **AVERAGE**

Sayre, April Pulley.
The Bumblebee Queen. Charlesbridge, 2006. The queen of the hive has a lot of work to do! Join her as she leads her colony through the seasons of the year. *Award-Winning Author.* **CHALLENGE**

Trumbauer, Lisa.
Living in a Small Town. Capstone, 2005. Simple text and photographs describe life in small towns. **EASY**

Wheeler, Lisa.
Farmer Dale's Red Pickup Truck. Harcourt, 2006. One by one, Farmer Dale picks up animals that want a ride to town in his rickety old pickup truck. *Award-Winning Author.* **CHALLENGE**

Williams, Vera B.
Something Special for Me. HarperTrophy, 1986. Rosa has difficulty choosing a special birthday present to buy with the coins her mother and grandmother have saved, until she hears a man playing beautiful music on an accordion. **CHALLENGE**

Wong, Janet S.
Apple Pie 4th of July. Harcourt, 2006. A Chinese American child fears that the food her parents are preparing to sell on the Fourth of July will not be eaten. Booklist *Editors' Choice.* **AVERAGE**

Ziefert, Harriet.
The Cow in the House. Puffin, 1997. Bothered by his noisy house, a man goes to a wise man for advice. *Award-Winning Author.* **AVERAGE**

Lesson Vocabulary

Theme 5

The following Robust Vocabulary Words are introduced in Lessons 21–25.

Lesson 21	Lesson 22	Lesson 23	Lesson 24	Lesson 25
allowance	absurd	attack	blended	accomplish
bargain	acquired	carefully	cradled	alternatives
boost	admit	crowd (v.)	crumpled	area
comfortable	assumed	diligent	distance	attend
delivered	attempt	disappear	extinct	feasible
exchanged	barely	pattern	patience	juggling
industrious	extremely	plentiful	personalities	preference
rosy	hilarious	role	pledge	race
spoiled	serious	sealed	raggedy	report
thrifty	witty	thickens	tedious	serve

Cumulative Vocabulary

The following words appear in the *Student Edition* selections in Grade 2.

absolutely*	beneath*	creative	except	housed*	nominate*	recreation*	spoiled
absurd*	bewildered*	crop	exchanged	identify*	noticed	refuse*	squatted*
accent*	beyond	crowd (v.)	excitable*	ignore*	official*	relieved	startle*
accolade*	bizarre*	crumpled	executive*	immense*	opinionated*	renowned*	statue
accomplish	blended	dangerous*	experiments	impatiently*	opponent*	replied	stomped
accurately	blockades*	dappled*	expression	impressive	original*	report	struggle*
ached*	boost	defeated*	extinct*	improve*	originated*	request*	strutted*
acquired*	brew*	delay	extinguish*	improvise*	paced*	responds	style*
admit	brisk*	delivered	extravaganza*	impulsive*	passion*	responsibility*	superior*
adorable*	budge	deny*	extremely	industrious*	patience*	review	supplies
adorn*	bulk*	depend*	fantastic	inexplicable*	pattern	rickety*	swirling*
affinity*	career*	described*	feasible	innovation*	peered	risk	technique*
agile*	carefree	diligent*	fellow*	instantly*	penalty*	role*	tedious*
allowance*	carefully	disability*	feud*	instead	performance	romp*	territory*
alternatives*	celebrate	disappear	filthy*	insult (v.)*	personalities	rosy*	thickens*
announcement*	challenge*	discovery	fleeing*	itinerary*	pleaded	route*	thrifty*
anonymous*	chilly*	distance	flitted*	journeyed*	pledge*	satisfied*	thrilled
area	circling*	distraught*	flutters*	jubilant*	plentiful*	scampering	traction*
archaic*	clambered*	distrust*	fragrant	juggling*	position*	screeching	trance*
aspire*	clumsy*	disturb*	frail*	kin*	positive*	sealed	trooped (v.)*
assistance*	clutched*	diversion*	frisky*	last (v.)	preference*	selected*	underestimate*
assortment*	collection	drench*	gently	leisurely*	previous*	semblance*	underneath*
assumed*	comfortable	durable*	gobbled*	literature	principles*	separated	universal*
attached*	committee	earn	grand	location*	priorities*	serious	unselfish*
attack	common	edge*	grunted	lock*	procrastinate*	serve	upbeat
attempt*	competitive*	edible*	habitat*	majestic	proficient*	settled	ventured*
attend	compromise*	efficient*	halfheartedly*	master (v.)*	provide	sipped	volume
attract*	concentrate	enchanting	hazard*	melodious*	prying*	sleuths	wilting*
audible*	consider*	encountered*	heed*	minor*	race*	smothered	witness*
award	correspond*	entertain	hesitate*	misplaced*	raggedy	snug*	witty
barely	cozy	enthusiast*	hilarious	mull*	ramble*	soaked*	worthwhile*
bargain	cradled	entire	historical	native*	rare	spare	zoom*
beautifying*	crave*	entranced*	horrendous*	negotiate*	rattling*	specially*	
belongings*	create	evasive*	host	neighborly*	recently*	spectator*	

High-Frequency Words

above	caught	ears	finally	lose	sign	tough
accept	cheer	eight	guess	million	sometimes	understand
ago	children	enjoy	half	minute	special	wash
already	clear	enough	hundred	picture	straight	wear
believe	coming	especially	idea	police	sugar	woman
bicycle	cook	everything	imagine	popular	sure	woods
board	covered	exercise	impossible	prove	sweat	world
bought	curve	expensive	interesting	question	though	worry
brother	different	fair	knee	quite	through	year
brought	draw	father	laughed	shoes	thumb	young
care	early	favorite	learn	short	touch	

Handwriting

Individual students have various levels of handwriting skills, but they all have the desire to communicate effectively. To write correctly, they must be familiar with concepts of

- **size (tall, short)**
- **open and closed**
- **capital and lowercase letters**
- **manuscript vs. cursive letters**
- **letter and word spacing**
- **punctuation**

To assess students' handwriting skills, review samples of their written work. Note whether they use correct letter formation and appropriate size and spacing. Note whether students follow the conventions of print, such as correct capitalization and punctuation. Encourage students to edit and proofread their work and to use editing marks. When writing messages, notes, and letters, or when publishing their writing, students should leave adequate margins and indent new paragraphs to help make their work more readable for their audience.

Stroke and Letter Formation

Most manuscript letters are formed with a continuous stroke, so students do not often pick up their pencils when writing a single letter. When students begin to use cursive handwriting, they will have to lift their pencils from the paper less frequently and will be able to write more fluently. Models for Harcourt and D'Nealian handwriting are provided on pages R14–R17.

Position for Writing

Establishing the correct posture, pen or pencil grip, and paper position for writing will help prevent handwriting problems.

Posture Students should sit with both feet on the floor and with hips to the back of the chair. They can lean forward slightly but should not slouch. The writing surface should be smooth and flat and at a height that allows the upper arms to be perpendicular to the surface and the elbows to be under the shoulders.

Writing Instrument An adult-sized number-two lead pencil is a satisfactory writing tool for most students. As students become proficient in the use of cursive handwriting, have them use pens for writing final drafts. Use your judgment in determining what type of instrument is most suitable.

Paper Position and Pencil Grip The paper is slanted along the line of the student's writing arm, and the student uses his or her nonwriting hand to hold the paper in place. The student holds the pencil or pen slightly above the paint line—about one inch from the lead tip.

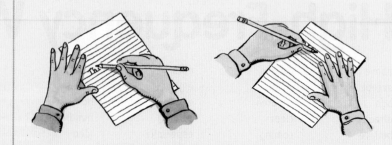

Meeting the Needs of All Learners

The best instruction builds on what students already know and can do. Given the wide range in students' handwriting abilities, a variety of approaches may be needed.

Extra Support For students who need more practice keeping their handwriting legible, one of the most important understandings is that legible writing is important for clear communication. Provide as many opportunities for classroom writing as possible. For example, students can

- Make a class directory listing the names of their classmates.
- Draw and label graphic organizers, pictures, and maps.
- Contribute entries weekly to their vocabulary journals.
- Write and post messages about class assignments or group activities.
- Record observations during activities.

ELL English-Language Learners can participate in meaningful print experiences. They can

- Write signs, labels for centers, and other messages.
- Label graphic organizers and drawings.
- Contribute in group writing activities.
- Write independently in journals.

You may also want to have students practice handwriting skills in their first language.

Challenge To ensure continued rapid advancement of students who come to second grade writing fluently, provide

- A wide range of writing assignments.
- Opportunities for independent writing on self-selected and assigned topics.

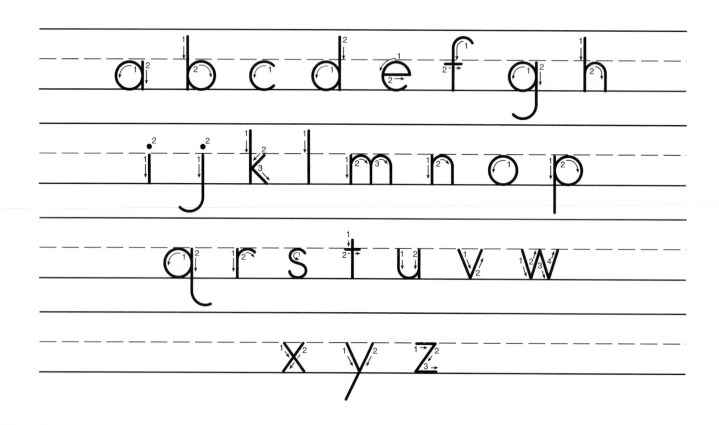

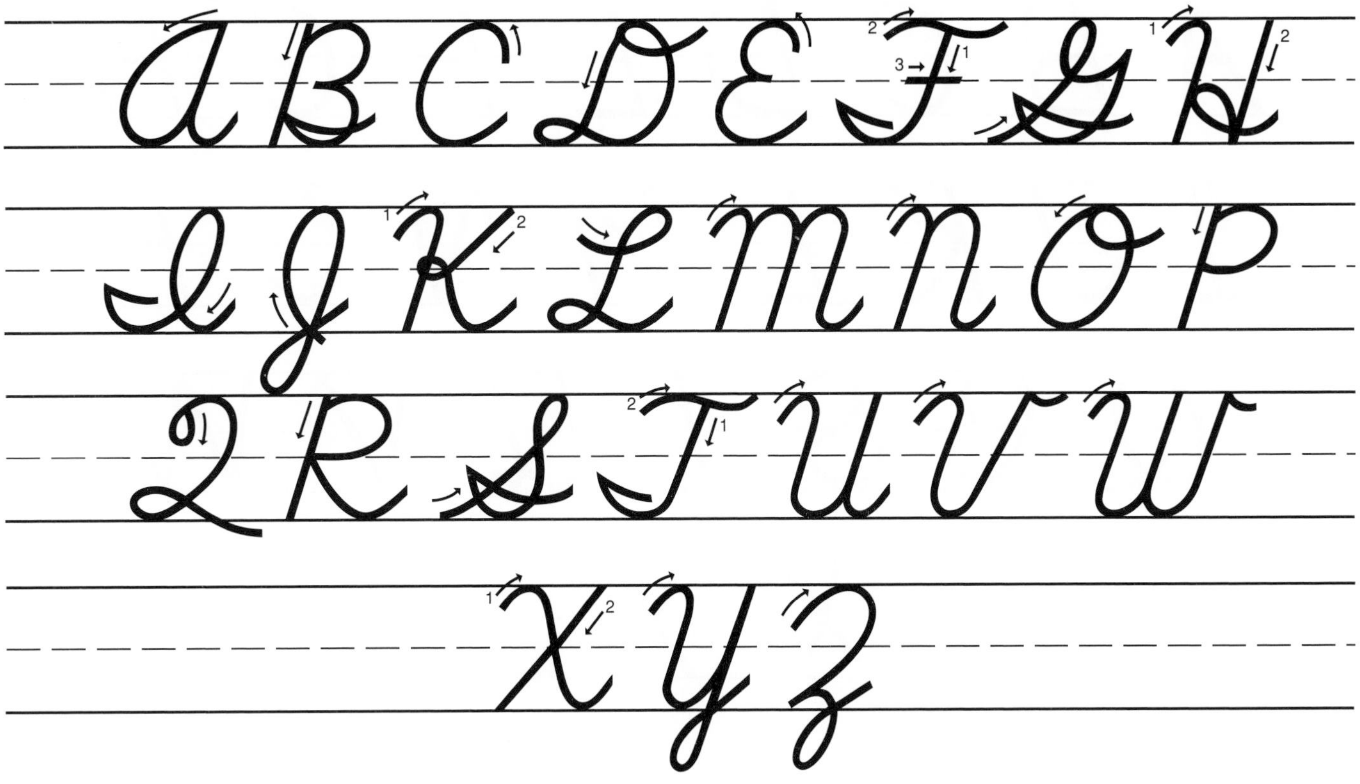

$\mathcal{A}$ $\mathcal{B}$ $\mathcal{C}$ $\mathcal{D}$ $\mathcal{E}$ $\mathcal{F}$ $\mathcal{G}$ $\mathcal{H}$

$\mathcal{I}$ $\mathcal{J}$ $\mathcal{K}$ $\mathcal{L}$ $\mathcal{M}$ $\mathcal{N}$ $\mathcal{O}$ $\mathcal{P}$

$\mathcal{Q}$ $\mathcal{R}$ $\mathcal{S}$ $\mathcal{T}$ $\mathcal{U}$ $\mathcal{V}$ $\mathcal{W}$

$\mathcal{X}$ $\mathcal{Y}$ $\mathcal{Z}$

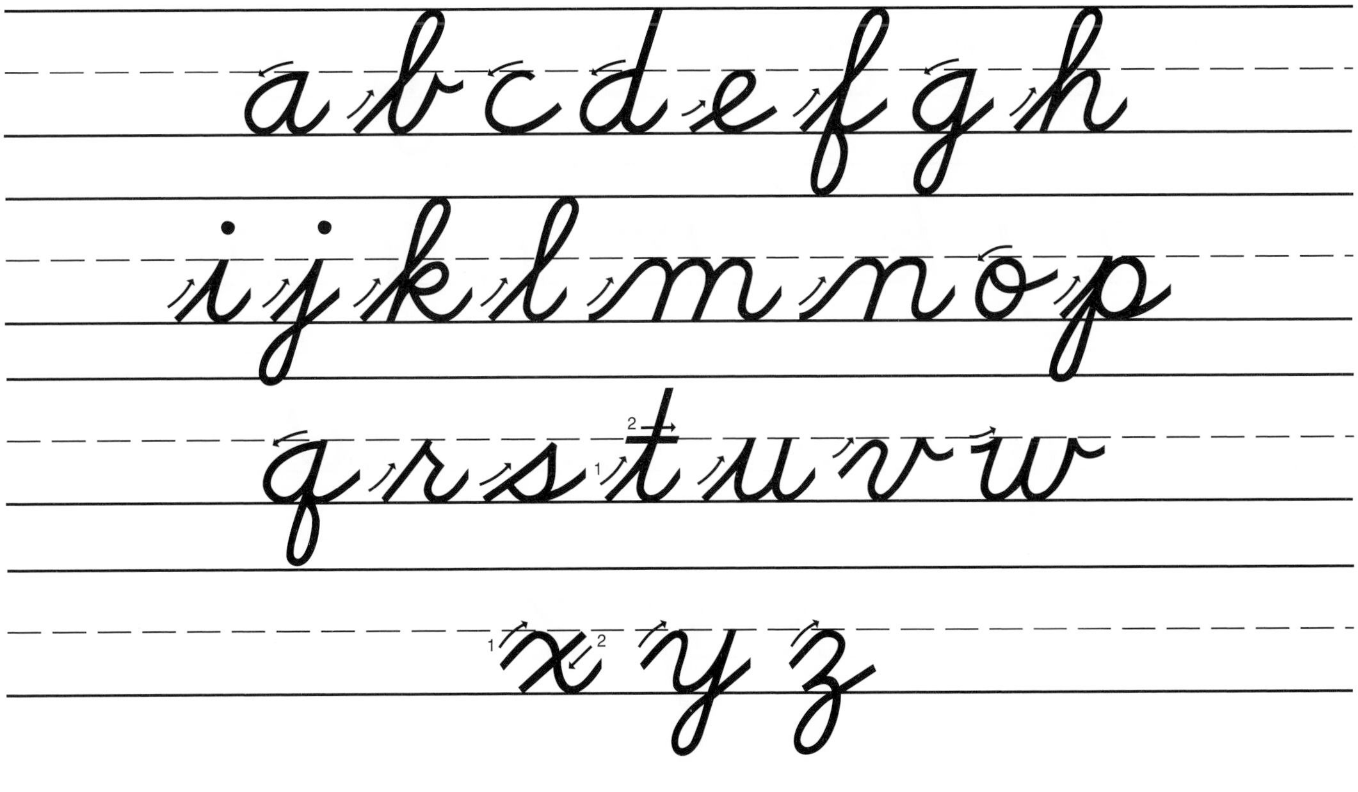

a b c d e f g h

i j k l m n o p

q r s t u v w

x y z

A B C D E F G H
I J K L M N O P
Q R S T U V W
X Y Z

a b c d e f g h
i j k l m n o p
q r s t u v w
x y z

D'Nealian Handwriting Cursive Alphabet

A B C D E F G H

I J K L M N O P

Q R S T U V W

X Y Z

a b c d e f g h

i j k l m n o p

q r s t u v w

x y z

Introducing the Glossary

MODEL USING THE GLOSSARY Explain to children that a glossary often is included in a book so that readers can find the meanings of words used in the book.

- Read aloud the introductory page.
- Model looking up one or more words.
- Point out how you rely on **alphabetical order** and the **guide words** at the top of the Glossary pages to locate the **entry word**.

As children look over the Glossary, point out that illustrations accompany some of the Student-Friendly Explanations.

Encourage children to look up several words in the Glossary, identifying the correct page and the guide words. Then have them explain how using alphabetical order and the guide words at the top of each page helped them locate the words.

Tell children to use the Glossary to confirm the pronunciation of Vocabulary Words during reading and to help them better understand the meanings of unfamiliar words.

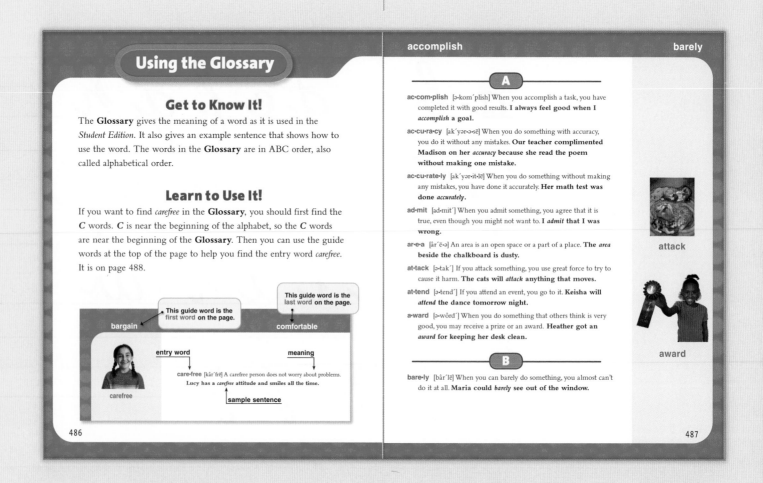

Using the Glossary

Get to Know It!

The **Glossary** gives the meaning of a word as it is used in the *Student Edition*. It also gives an example sentence that shows how to use the word. The words in the **Glossary** are in ABC order, also called alphabetical order.

Learn to Use It!

If you want to find *carefree* in the **Glossary**, you should first find the **C** words. **C** is near the beginning of the alphabet, so the **C** words are near the beginning of the **Glossary**. Then you can use the guide words at the top of the page to help you find the entry word *carefree*. It is on page 488.

This guide word is the first word on the page.

This guide word is the last word on the page.

bargain   comfortable

entry word   meaning

care·free [kâr′frē] A carefree person does not worry about problems. Lucy has a *carefree* attitude and smiles all the time.

carefree

sample sentence

486

---

accomplish   barely

A

ac·com·plish [ə·kom′plish] When you accomplish a task, you have completed it with good results. **I always feel good when I** *accomplish* **a goal.**

ac·cu·ra·cy [ak′yər·ə·sē] When you do something with accuracy, you do it without any mistakes. **Our teacher complimented Madison on her** *accuracy* **because she read the poem without making one mistake.**

ac·cu·rate·ly [ak′yər·it·lē] When you do something without making any mistakes, you have done it accurately. **Her math test was done** *accurately*.

ad·mit [ad·mit′] When you admit something, you agree that it is true, even though you might not want to. **I** *admit* **that I was wrong.**

ar·e·a [âr′ē·ə] An area is an open space or a part of a place. **The** *area* **beside the chalkboard is dusty.**

at·tack [ə·tak′] If you attack something, you use great force to try to cause it harm. **The cats will** *attack* **anything that moves.**

at·tend [ə·tend′] If you attend an event, you go to it. **Keisha will** *attend* **the dance tomorrow night.**

a·ward [ə·wôrd′] When you do something that others think is very good, you may receive a prize or an award. **Heather got an** *award* **for keeping her desk clean.**

attack

award

B

bare·ly [bâr′lē] When you can barely do something, you almost can't do it at all. **Maria could** *barely* **see out of the window.**

487

bar·gain [bär´gən] If you didn't have to pay much to buy something good, you got a bargain. **The pencil was a *bargain* at only five cents.**

be·yond [bi·yond´] Something that is beyond something else is farther away. *Beyond the fence was a field with cows.*

blend·ed [blend´əd] When things are blended, they are mixed together so that you can't tell there are separate parts. **Melissa *blended* yellow and blue to make green.**

boost [bōōst] If you give someone a boost, you help lift him or her up to reach something. **He will need a *boost* to reach the water fountain.**

budge [buj] If you budge something, you move it just a little. **I can't seem to *budge* this heavy box.**

<hr>
C

care·free [kâr´frē] A carefree person does not worry about problems. **Lucy has a *carefree* attitude and smiles all the time.**

care·ful·ly [kâr´fəl·lē] When you do something carefully, you pay close attention to what you are doing so that you don't make a mistake. **Grandma unwraps presents *carefully* so that she doesn't rip the paper.**

cel·e·brate [sel´ə·brāt] If you are happy about something, you may have a party to celebrate. **He likes to *celebrate* his birthday with friends.**

col·lec·tion [kə·lek´shən] When you have a collection, you have a group of things that are kept together. **Jane has a large doll *collection*.**

com·fort·a·ble [kum´fər·tə·bəl] When you are comfortable, you feel good just as you are. **I feel *comfortable* wearing this soft jacket.**

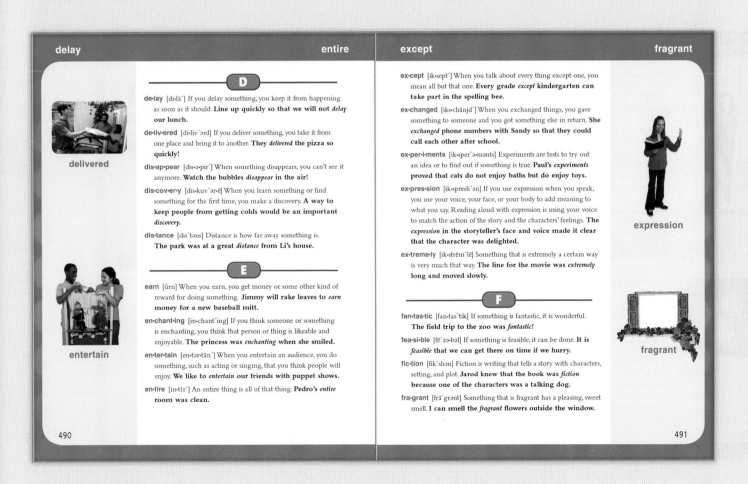

carefree

celebrate

488

com·mit·tee [kə·mit´ē] When you are on a committee, you work with a group of people on a project or for a special reason. **A *committee* will decide who wins the art contest.**

com·mon [kom´ən] If something is common, there is a lot of it or it happens often. **It is *common* to see crabs running on the beach.**

con·cen·trate [kon´sən·trāt] When you concentrate, you put all of your attention on one thing. **You must *concentrate* to solve the puzzle.**

co·zy [kō´zē] If a place is cozy, it makes you feel warm, happy, and comfortable. **The kitten curls up in its *cozy* little cat bed.**

cra·dled [krād´(ə)ld] If you cradle something, you hold it closely as if you were taking care of it. **Laura *cradled* her guinea pig.**

cre·ate [krē·āt´] When you create, you use your imagination to make something new. **He can *create* such funny stories.**

cre·a·tive [krē·ā´tiv] If you are creative, you use new or different ideas to make or do something. **Dawn is very *creative* in the way she uses colors in her art.**

crop [krop] A large planting of one kind of plant is a crop. **We grew a large *crop* of pumpkins this year.**

crowd [kroud] When people or animals gather in large numbers, they crowd together. **The children began to *crowd* around the artist as he painted a picture.**

crum·pled [krum´pəld] If you crumple something, you gently crush it or bunch it up. **The writer *crumpled* his story and threw it in the trash.**

cradled

creative

crop

489

<hr>
D

de·lay [di·lā´] If you delay something, you keep it from happening as soon as it should. **Line up quickly so that we will not *delay* our lunch.**

de·liv·ered [di·liv´ərd] If you deliver something, you take it from one place and bring it to another. **They *delivered* the pizza so quickly!**

dis·ap·pear [dis·ə·pir´] When something disappears, you can't see it anymore. **Watch the bubbles *disappear* in the air!**

dis·cov·er·y [dis·kuv´ər·ē] When you learn something or find something for the first time, you make a discovery. **A way to keep people from getting colds would be an important *discovery*.**

dis·tance [dis´təns] Distance is how far away something is. **The park was at a great *distance* from Li's house.**

<hr>
E

earn [ûrn] When you earn, you get money or some other kind of reward for doing something. **Jimmy will rake leaves to *earn* money for a new baseball mitt.**

en·chant·ing [in·chant´ing] If you think someone or something is enchanting, you think that person or thing is likeable and enjoyable. **The princess was *enchanting* when she smiled.**

en·ter·tain [en·tər·tān´] When you entertain an audience, you do something, such as acting or singing, that you think people will enjoy. **We like to *entertain* our friends with puppet shows.**

en·tire [in·tīr´] An entire thing is all of that thing. **Pedro's *entire* room was clean.**

delivered

entertain

490

ex·cept [ik·sept´] When you talk about every thing except one, you mean all but that one. **Every grade *except* kindergarten can take part in the spelling bee.**

ex·changed [iks·chānjd´] When you exchanged things, you gave something to someone and you got something else in return. **She *exchanged* phone numbers with Sandy so that they could call each other after school.**

ex·per·i·ments [ik·sper´ə·mənts] Experiments are tests to try out an idea or to find out if something is true. **Paul's *experiments* proved that cats do not enjoy baths but do enjoy toys.**

ex·pres·sion [ik·spresh´ən] If you use expression when you speak, you use your voice, your face, or your body to add meaning to what you say. Reading aloud with expression is using your voice to match the action of the story and the characters' feelings. **The *expression* in the storyteller's face and voice made it clear that the character was delighted.**

ex·treme·ly [ik·strēm´lē] Something that is extremely a certain way is very much that way. **The line for the movie was *extremely* long and moved slowly.**

<hr>
F

fan·tas·tic [fan·tas´tik] If something is fantastic, it is wonderful. **The field trip to the zoo was *fantastic*!**

fea·si·ble [fē´zə·bəl] If something is feasible, it can be done. **It is *feasible* that we can get there on time if we hurry.**

fic·tion [fik´shən] Fiction is writing that tells a story with characters, setting, and plot. **Jarod knew that the book was *fiction* because one of the characters was a talking dog.**

fra·grant [frā´grənt] Something that is fragrant has a pleasing, sweet smell. **I can smell the *fragrant* flowers outside the window.**

expression

fragrant

491

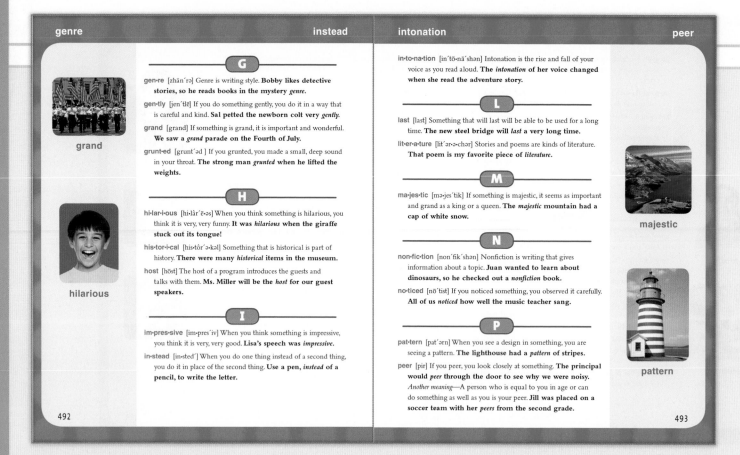

G

gen·re [zhän´rə] Genre is writing style. **Bobby likes detective stories, so he reads books in the mystery *genre*.**

gen·tly [jen´tlē] If you do something gently, you do it in a way that is careful and kind. **Sal petted the newborn colt very *gently*.**

grand [grand] If something is grand, it is important and wonderful. **We saw a *grand* parade on the Fourth of July.**

grunt·ed [grunt´əd] If you grunted, you made a small, deep sound in your throat. **The strong man *grunted* when he lifted the weights.**

grand

H

hi·lar·i·ous [hi·lâr´ē·əs] When you think something is hilarious, you think it is very, very funny. **It was *hilarious* when the giraffe stuck out its tongue!**

his·tor·i·cal [his·tôr´ə·kəl] Something that is historical is part of history. **There were many *historical* items in the museum.**

host [hōst] The host of a program introduces the guests and talks with them. **Ms. Miller will be the *host* for our guest speakers.**

hilarious

I

im·pres·sive [im·pres´iv] When you think something is impressive, you think it is very, very good. **Lisa's speech was *impressive*.**

in·stead [in·sted´] When you do one thing instead of a second thing, you do it in place of the second thing. **Use a pen, *instead* of a pencil, to write the letter.**

492

in·to·na·tion [in´tō·nā´shən] Intonation is the rise and fall of your voice as you read aloud. **The *intonation* of her voice changed when she read the adventure story.**

L

last [last] Something that will last will be able to be used for a long time. **The new steel bridge will *last* a very long time.**

lit·er·a·ture [lit´ər·ə·chər] Stories and poems are kinds of literature. **That poem is my favorite piece of *literature*.**

M

ma·jes·tic [mə·jes´tik] If something is majestic, it seems as important and grand as a king or a queen. **The *majestic* mountain had a cap of white snow.**

majestic

N

non·fic·tion [non·fik´shən] Nonfiction is writing that gives information about a topic. **Juan wanted to learn about dinosaurs, so he checked out a *nonfiction* book.**

no·ticed [nō´tist] If you noticed something, you observed it carefully. **All of us *noticed* how well the music teacher sang.**

P

pat·tern [pat´ərn] When you see a design in something, you are seeing a pattern. **The lighthouse had a *pattern* of stripes.**

peer [pir] If you peer, you look closely at something. **The principal would *peer* through the door to see why we were noisy.** *Another meaning*—A person who is equal to you in age or can do something as well as you is your peer. **Jill was placed on a soccer team with her *peers* from the second grade.**

pattern

493

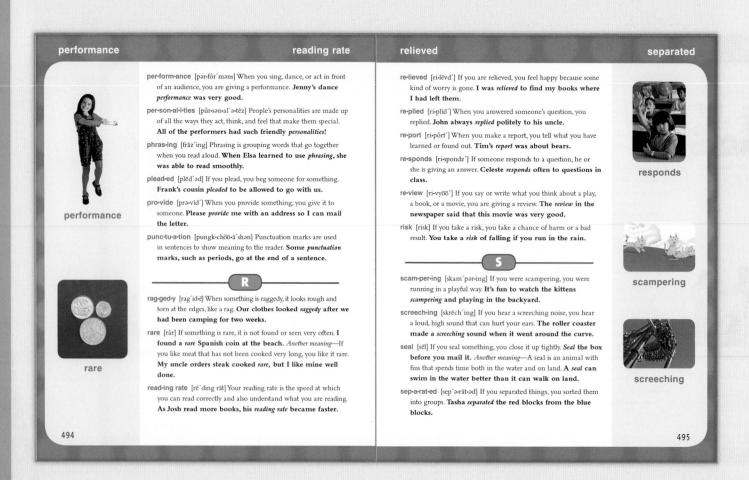

per·form·ance [pər·fôr´məns] When you sing, dance, or act in front of an audience, you are giving a performance. **Jenny's dance *performance* was very good.**

per·son·al·i·ties [pûr´sən·al´ə·tēz] People's personalities are made up of all the ways they act, think, and feel that make them special. **All of the performers had such friendly *personalities*!**

phras·ing [frāz´ing] Phrasing is grouping words that go together when you read aloud. **When Elsa learned to use *phrasing*, she was able to read smoothly.**

plead·ed [plēd´əd] If you plead, you beg someone for something. **Frank's cousin *pleaded* to be allowed to go with us.**

pro·vide [prə·vīd´] When you provide something, you give it to someone. **Please *provide* me with an address so I can mail the letter.**

punc·tu·a·tion [pungk·chōō·ā´shən] Punctuation marks are used in sentences to show meaning to the reader. **Some *punctuation* marks, such as periods, go at the end of a sentence.**

performance

R

rag·ged·y [rag´id·ē] When something is raggedy, it looks rough and torn at the edges, like a rag. **Our clothes looked *raggedy* after we had been camping for two weeks.**

rare [râr] If something is rare, it is not found or seen very often. **I found a *rare* Spanish coin at the beach.** *Another meaning*—If you like meat that has not been cooked very long, you like it rare. **My uncle orders steak cooked *rare*, but I like mine well done.**

read·ing rate [rē´ding rāt] Your reading rate is the speed at which you can read correctly and also understand what you are reading. **As Josh read more books, his *reading rate* became faster.**

rare

494

re·lieved [ri·lēvd´] If you are relieved, you feel happy because some kind of worry is gone. **I was *relieved* to find my books where I had left them.**

re·plied [ri·plīd´] When you answered someone's question, you replied. **John always *replied* politely to his uncle.**

re·port [ri·pôrt´] When you make a report, you tell what you have learned or found out. **Tim's *report* was about bears.**

re·sponds [ri·spondz´] If someone responds to a question, he or she is giving an answer. **Celeste *responds* often to questions in class.**

re·view [ri·vyōō´] If you say or write what you think about a play, a book, or a movie, you are giving a review. **The *review* in the newspaper said that this movie was very good.**

risk [risk] If you take a risk, you take a chance of harm or a bad result. **You take a *risk* of falling if you run in the rain.**

responds

S

scam·per·ing [skam´pər·ing] If you were scampering, you were running in a playful way. **It's fun to watch the kittens *scampering* and playing in the backyard.**

screech·ing [skrēch´ing] If you hear a screeching noise, you hear a loud, high sound that can hurt your ears. **The roller coaster made a *screeching* sound when it went around the curve.**

seal [sēl] If you seal something, you close it up tightly. **Seal the box before you mail it.** *Another meaning*—A seal is an animal with fins that spends time both in the water and on land. **A *seal* can swim in the water better than it can walk on land.**

sep·a·rat·ed [sep´ə·rāt·əd] If you separated things, you sorted them into groups. **Tasha *separated* the red blocks from the blue blocks.**

scampering

screeching

495

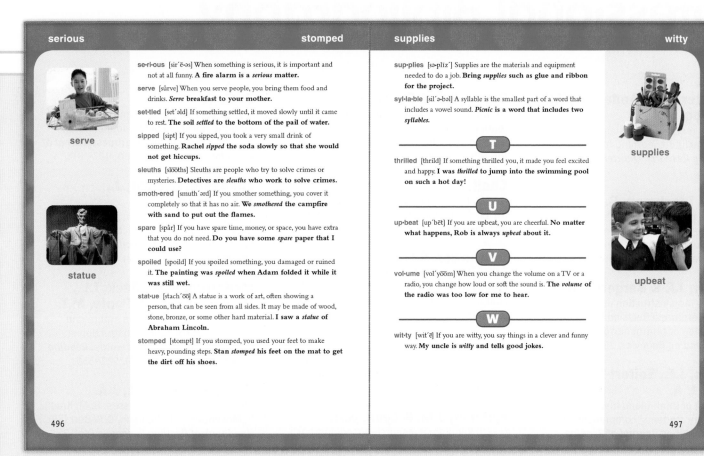

serve

statue

se·ri·ous [sîr´ē·əs] When something is serious, it is important and not at all funny. **A fire alarm is a *serious* matter.**

serve [sûrve] When you serve people, you bring them food and drinks. ***Serve* breakfast to your mother.**

set·tled [set´əld] If something settled, it moved slowly until it came to rest. **The soil *settled* to the bottom of the pail of water.**

sipped [sipt] If you sipped, you took a very small drink of something. **Rachel *sipped* the soda slowly so that she would not get hiccups.**

sleuths [slo͞oths] Sleuths are people who try to solve crimes or mysteries. **Detectives are *sleuths* who work to solve crimes.**

smoth·ered [smuth´ərd] If you smother something, you cover it completely so that it has no air. **We *smothered* the campfire with sand to put out the flames.**

spare [spâr] If you have spare time, money, or space, you have extra that you do not need. **Do you have some *spare* paper that I could use?**

spoiled [spoild] If you spoiled something, you damaged or ruined it. **The painting was *spoiled* when Adam folded it while it was still wet.**

stat·ue [stach´o͞o] A statue is a work of art, often showing a person, that can be seen from all sides. It may be made of wood, stone, bronze, or some other hard material. **I saw a *statue* of Abraham Lincoln.**

stomped [stompt] If you stomped, you used your feet to make heavy, pounding steps. **Stan *stomped* his feet on the mat to get the dirt off his shoes.**

496

---

sup·plies [sə·plīz´] Supplies are the materials and equipment needed to do a job. **Bring *supplies* such as glue and ribbon for the project.**

syl·la·ble [sil´ə·bəl] A syllable is the smallest part of a word that includes a vowel sound. ***Picnic* is a word that includes two *syllables*.**

T

thrilled [thrild] If something thrilled you, it made you feel excited and happy. **I was *thrilled* to jump into the swimming pool on such a hot day!**

U

up·beat [up´bēt] If you are upbeat, you are cheerful. **No matter what happens, Rob is always *upbeat* about it.**

V

vol·ume [vol´yo͞om] When you change the volume on a TV or a radio, you change how loud or soft the sound is. **The *volume* of the radio was too low for me to hear.**

W

wit·ty [wit´ē] If you are witty, you say things in a clever and funny way. **My uncle is *witty* and tells good jokes.**

supplies

upbeat

497

Index of Titles and Authors

Page numbers in green refer to biographical information.

Ada, Alma Flor, 386, 434, 462
"Ah, Music!," 98
Aliki, 98, 111
"Annie's Gifts," 58
"Be Sun Safe," 464
"Bee, The," 244
"Beyond Old MacDonald," 234
Brown, Monica, 368, 385
"California Bee Business," 274
Campoy, F. Isabel, 386
"Chair For My Mother, A," 166
"Chimp Computer Whiz," 298
"Come, My Little Children, Here Are Songs for You," 112
Crewe, Sabrina, 244, 273
"Cross-Country Vacation," 470
Egan, Tim, 208, 233
Firestone, Mary, 192
"Gabriela Mistral: A Poet's Life In Photos," 386
Gans, Roma, 398, 423
Haberle, Susan E., 354
Hennessey, Gail Skroback, 136
Hoce, Charley, 234
"Interview With Author Loreen Leedy," 44

Katz, Susan, 88
"Let's Go Rock Collecting," 398
"Life of George Washington Carver, The," 122
"Lizard and the Sun, The," 434
Lynch, Tom, 316
Medearis, Angela Shelf, 58, 87
"Mr. Putter and Tabby Write the Book," 22
"My Name Is Gabriela," 368
"North America," 154
"Nutty Facts About Peanuts," 136
Park, Frances and Ginger, 328, 352
"Pebbles," 424
Rylant, Cynthia, 22, 43
"Sarah Enters a Painting," 88
"Saving Money," 192
"Serious Farm," 208
Simon, Charnan, 284, 297
"South Korea," 354
Stevens, Joli K., 122
Stevenson, Robert Louis, 112
"Summer Safety," 482
"Time for Patience, A," 316
"Town Hall," 304
"Watching in the Wild," 284
"What's My Job?," 142
"Where on Earth Is My Bagel?," 328
Williams, Vera B., 166, 191
Worth, Valerie, 424

498   499

Professional Bibliography

Armbruster, B.B., Anderson, T.H., & Ostertag, J.
(1987). Does text structure/summarization instruction facilitate learning from expository text? *Reading Research Quarterly,* 22 (3), 331–346.

Ball, E. & Blachman, B.
(1991). Does phoneme awareness training in kindergarten make a difference in early word recognition and developmental spelling? *Reading Research Quarterly,* 26 (1), 49–66.

Baumann, J.F. & Bergeron, B.S.
(1993). Story map instruction using children's literature: effects on first graders' comprehension of central narrative elements. *Journal of Reading Behavior,* 25 (4), 407–437.

Baumann, J.F., Seifert-Kessell, N., & Jones, L.A.
(1992). Effect of think-aloud instruction on elementary students' comprehension monitoring abilities. *Journal of Reading Behavior,* 24 (2), 143–172.

Beck, I.L., Perfetti, C.A., & McKeown, M.G.
(1982). Effects of long-term vocabulary instruction on lexical access and reading comprehension. *Journal of Educational Psychology,* 74 (4), 506–521.

Bereiter, C. & Bird, M.
(1985). Use of thinking aloud in identification and teaching of reading comprehension strategies. *Cognition and Instruction,* 2, 131–156.

Blachman, B.
(2000). Phonological awareness. In M. Kamil, P. Mosenthal, P.D. Pearson, & R. Barr (Eds.), *Handbook of Reading Research,* (Vol. 3). Mahwah, NJ: Erlbaum.

Blachman, B., Ball, E.W., Black, R.S., & Tangel, D.M.
(1994). Kindergarten teachers develop phoneme awareness in low-income, inner-city classrooms: Does it make a difference? *Reading and Writing: An Interdisciplinary Journal,* 6 (1), 1–18.

Brown, I.S. & Felton, R.H.
(1990). Effects of instruction on beginning reading skills in children at risk for reading disability. *Reading and Writing: An Interdisciplinary Journal,* 2 (3), 223–241.

Chall, J.
(1996). *Learning to read: The great debate* (revised, with a new foreword). New York: McGraw-Hill.

Dowhower, S.L.
(1987). Effects of repeated reading on second-grade transitional readers' fluency and comprehension. *Reading Research Quarterly,* 22 (4), 389–406.

Ehri, L. & Wilce, L.
(1987). Does learning to spell help beginners learn to read words? *Reading Research Quarterly,* 22 (1), 48–65.

Fletcher, J.M. & Lyon, G.R.
(1998) Reading: A research-based approach. In Evers, W.M. (Ed.) *What's Gone Wrong in America's Classroom,* Palo Alto, CA: Hoover Institution Press, Stanford University.

Foorman, B., Francis, D., Fletcher, J., Schatschneider, C., & Mehta, P.
(1998). The role of instruction in learning to read: Preventing reading failure in at-risk children. *Journal of Educational Psychology,* 90 (1), 37–55.

Fukkink, R.G. & de Glopper, K.
(1998). Effects of instruction in deriving word meaning from context: A meta-analysis. *Review of Educational Research,* 68 (4), 450–469.

Gipe, J.P. & Arnold, R.D.
(1979). Teaching vocabulary through familiar associations and contexts. *Journal of Reading Behavior,* 11 (3), 281–285.

Griffith, P.L., Klesius, J.P., & Kromrey, J.D.
(1992). The effect of phonemic awareness on the literacy development of first grade children in a traditional or a whole language classroom. *Journal of Research in Childhood Education,* 6 (2), 85–92.

Juel, C.
(1988). Learning to read and write: A longitudinal study of fifty-four children from first through fourth grades. *Journal of Educational Psychology,* 80, 437–447.

Lundberg, I., Frost, J., & Petersen, O.
(1988). Effects of an extensive program for stimulating phonological awareness in preschool children. *Reading Research Quarterly,* 23 (3), 263–284.

McKeown, M.G., Beck, I.L., Omanson, R.C., & Pople, M.T.
(1985). Some effects of the nature and frequency of vocabulary instruction on the knowledge and use of words. *Reading Research Quarterly,* 20 (5), 522–535.

Nagy, W.E. & Scott, J.A.
(2000). Vocabulary processes. In M. Kamil, P. Mosenthal, P.D. Pearson, & R. Barr (Eds.), *Handbook of Reading Research,* (Vol. 3) Mahwah, NJ: Erlbaum.

National Reading Panel
(2000). *Teaching Children to Read.* National Institute of Child Health and Human Development, National Institutes of Health, Washington, D.C.

O'Connor, R., Jenkins, J.R., & Slocum, T.A.
(1995). Transfer among phonological tasks in kindergarten: Essential instructional content. *Journal of Educational Psychology,* 87 (2), 202–217.

O'Shea, L.J., Sindelar, P.T., & O'Shea, D.J.
(1985). The effects of repeated readings and attentional cues on reading fluency and comprehension. *Journal of Reading Behavior,* 17 (2), 129–142.

Paris, S.G., Cross, D.R., & Lipson, M.Y.
(1984). Informed strategies for learning: A program to improve children's reading awareness and comprehension. *Journal of Educational Psychology,* 76 (6), 1239–1252.

Payne, B.D. & Manning, B.H.
(1992). Basal reader instruction: Effects of comprehension monitoring training on reading comprehension, strategy use and attitude. *Reading Research and Instruction,* 32 (1), 29–38.

Rasinski, T.V., Padak, N., Linek, W., & Sturtevant, E.
(1994). Effects of fluency development on urban second-grade readers. *Journal of Educational Research,* 87 (3), 158–165.

Rinehart, S.D., Stahl, S.A., & Erickson, L.G.
(1986). Some effects of summarization training on reading and studying. *Reading Research Quarterly,* 21 (4), 422–438.

Robbins, C. & Ehri, L.C.
(1994). Reading storybooks to kindergartners helps them learn new vocabulary words. *Journal of Educational Psychology,* 86 (1), 54–64.

Rosenshine, B. & Meister, C.
(1994). Reciprocal teaching: A review of research. *Review of Educational Research,* 64 (4), 479–530.

Rosenshine, B., Meister, C., & Chapman, S.
(1996). Teaching students to generate questions: A review of the intervention studies. *Review of Educational Research,* 66 (2), 181–221.

Sénéchal, M.
(1997). The differential effect of storybook reading on preschoolers' acquisition of expressive and receptive vocabulary. *Journal of Child Language,* 24 (1), 123–138.

Shany, M.T. & Biemiller, A.
(1995) Assisted reading practice: Effects on performance for poor readers in grades 3 and 4. *Reading Research Quarterly,* 30 (3), 382–395.

Sindelar, P.T., Monda, L.E., & O'Shea, L.J.
(1990). Effects of repeated readings on instructional- and mastery-level readers. *Journal of Educational Research,* 83 (4), 220–226.

Snow, C.E., Burns, S.M., & Griffin, P.
(1998). *Preventing Reading Difficulties in Young Children.* Washington, D.C.: National Academy Press.

Stahl, S.A. & Fairbanks, M.M.
(1986). The effects of vocabulary instruction: A model-based meta-analysis. *Review of Educational Research,* 56 (1), 72–110.

Stanovich, K.E.
(1986) Matthew effects in reading: Some consequences of individual differences in the acquisition of literacy. *Reading Research Quarterly,* 21 (4), 360–406.

Torgesen, J., Morgan, S., & Davis, C.
(1992). Effects of two types of phonological awareness training on word learning in kindergarten children. *Journal of Educational Psychology,* 84 (3), 364–370.

Torgesen, J., Wagner, R., Rashotte, C., Rose, E., Lindamood, P., Conway, T., & Garvan, C.
(1999). Preventing reading failure in young children with phonological processing disabilities: Group and individual responses to instruction. *Journal of Educational Psychology,* 91(4), 579–593.

Vellutino, F.R. & Scanlon, D.M.
(1987). Phonological coding, phonological awareness, and reading ability: Evidence from a longitudinal and experimental study. *Merrill-Palmer Quarterly,* 33 (3), 321–363.

White, T.G., Graves, M.F., & Slater, W.H.
(1990). Growth of reading vocabulary in diverse elementary schools: Decoding and word meaning. *Journal of Educational Psychology,* 82 (2), 281–290.

Wixson, K.K.
(1986). Vocabulary instruction and children's comprehension of basal stories. *Reading Research Quarterly,* 21 (3), 317–329.

Program Reviewers & Advisors

Elizabeth A. Adkins,
Teacher
Ford Middle School
Brook Park, Ohio

Jean Bell,
Principal
Littleton Elementary School
Avondale, Arizona

Emily Brown,
Teacher
Orange Center Elementary School
Orlando, Florida

Stephen Bundy,
Teacher
Ventura Elementary School
Kissimmee, Florida

Helen Comba,
Language Arts Supervisor K-5
Southern Boulevard School
Chatham, New Jersey

Marsha Creese,
Reading/Language Arts Consultant
Marlborough Elementary School
Marlborough, Connecticut

Wyndy M. Crozier,
Teacher
Mary Bryant Elementary School
Tampa, Florida

Shirley Eyler,
Principal
Martin Luther King School
Piscataway, New Jersey

Sandy Hoffman,
Teacher
Heights Elementary School
Fort Myers, Florida

Amy Martin,
Reading Coach
Kingswood Elementary School
Wickenburg, Arizona

Rachel A. Musser,
Reading Coach
Chumuckla Elementary School
Jay, Florida

Dr. Carol Newton,
Director of Elementary Curriculum
Millard Public Schools
Omaha, Nebraska

Alda P. Pill,
Teacher
Mandarin Oaks Elementary School
Jacksonville, Florida

Dr. Elizabeth V. Primas,
Director
Office of Curriculum and Instruction
Washington, District of Columbia

Candice Ross,
Staff Development Teacher
A. Mario Loiderman Middle School
Silver Spring, Maryland

Sharon Sailor,
Teacher
Conrad Fischer Elementary School
Elmhurst, Illinois

Lucia Schneck,
Supervisor/Language Arts, Literacy
Irvington Board of Education
Irvington, New Jersey

RuthAnn Shauf,
District Resource Teacher
Hillsborough County Public Schools
Tampa, Florida

Jolene Topping,
Teacher
Palmetto Ridge High School
Bonita Springs, Florida

Betty Tubon,
Bilingual Teacher
New Field Primary School
Chicago, Illinois

Janet White,
Assistant Principal
MacFarlane Park Elementary School
Tampa, Florida

KINDERGARTEN REVIEWERS

Denise Bir,
Teacher
Destin Elementary School
Destin, Florida

Linda H. Butler,
Reading First State Director
Office of Academic Services
Washington, District of Columbia

Julie Elvers,
Teacher
Aldrich Elementary School
Omaha, Nebraska

Rosalyn Glavin,
Principal
Walter White Elementary School
River Rouge, Michigan

Jo Anne M. Kershaw,
Language Arts Program Leader, K-5
Longhill Administration Building
Trumbull, Connecticut

Beverly Kibbe,
Teacher
Cherry Brook Elementary School
Canton, Connecticut

Bonnie B. Macintosh,
Teacher
Glenallan Elementary School
Silver Spring, Maryland

Laurin MacLeish,
Teacher
Orange Center Elementary School
Orlando, Florida

Mindy Steighner,
Teacher
Randall Elementary School
Waukesha, Wisconsin

Paula Stutzman,
Teacher
Seven Springs Elementary School
New Port Richey, Florida

Martha Tully,
Teacher
Fleming Island Elementary School
Orange Park, Florida

EDITORIAL ADVISORS

Sharon J. Coburn,
National Reading Consultant

Hector J. Ramirez,
National Reading Consultant

Dr. Nancy I. Updegraff,
National Reading Consultant

Scope and Sequence

Reading	Gr K	Gr 1	Gr 2	Gr 3	Gr 4	Gr 5	Gr 6
Concepts About Print							
Understand that print provides information	░						
Understand how print is organized and read	░						
Know left-to-right and top-to-bottom directionality	░						
Distinguish letters from words	░						
Recognize name	░						
Name and match all uppercase and lowercase letter forms	░						
Understand the concept of word and construct meaning from shared text, illustrations, graphics, and charts	░						
Identify letters, words, and sentences	░						
Recognize that sentences in print are made up of words	░						
Identify the front cover, back cover, title page, title, and author of a book	░	░	░				
Match oral words to printed words	░	░	░				
Phonemic Awareness							
Understand that spoken words and syllables are made up of sequence of sounds	░						
Count and track sounds in a syllable, syllables in words, and words in sentences	•						
Know the sounds of letters	•	░					
Track and represent the number, sameness, difference, and order of two or more isolated phonemes	•						
Match, identify, distinguish, and segment sounds in initial, final, and medial position in single-syllable spoken words	•	░					
Blend sounds (onset-rimes/phonemes) to make words or syllables	•						
Track and represent changes in syllables and words as target sound is added, substituted, omitted, shifted, or repeated	•						
Distinguish long- and short-vowel sounds in orally stated words	░	░					
Identify and produce rhyming words	•						
Decoding: Phonic Analysis							
Understand and apply the alphabetic principle	░	░					
Consonants; single, blends, digraphs in initial, final, medial positions	•	•	•	•			
Vowels: short, long, digraphs, r-controlled, variant, schwa	•	•	•	•			
Match all consonant and short-vowel sounds to appropriate letters	•	•					
Understand that as letters in words change, so do the sounds	•	•					
Blend vowel-consonant sounds orally to make words or syllables	•	•					
Blend sounds from letters and letter patterns into recognizable words	•						
Decoding: Structural Analysis							
Inflectional endings, with and without spelling changes: plurals, verb tenses, possessives, comparatives-superlatives		•	•	•			
Contractions, abbreviations, and compound words		•	•	•			
Prefixes, suffixes, derivations, and root words				•	•	•	•
Greek and Latin roots					•	•	•
Letter, spelling, and syllable patterns		░	░	░	░	░	░
Phonograms/word families/onset-rimes	░	░	░	░	░	░	░
Syllable rules and patterns			░	░	░	░	░
Decoding: Strategies							
Visual cues: sound/symbol relationships, letter patterns, and spelling patterns	░	•					
Structural cues: compound words, contractions, inflectional endings, prefixes, suffixes, Greek and Latin roots, root words, spelling patterns, and word families	░	•					
Cross check visual and structural cues to confirm meaning							

Key:

Shaded area - Explicit Instruction/Modeling/Practice and Application

• *Tested—Assessment Resources: Weekly Lesson Tests, Theme Tests, Benchmark Assessments*

	Gr K	Gr 1	Gr 2	Gr 3	Gr 4	Gr 5	Gr 6
Word Recognition							
One-syllable and high-frequency words	•	•	•				
Common, irregular sight words	•	•	•				
Common abbreviations			•				
Lesson vocabulary		•	•	•	•	•	•
Fluency							
Read aloud in a manner that sounds like natural speech							
Read aloud accurately and with appropriate intonation and expression		•	•	•	•	•	•
Read aloud narrative and expository text with appropriate pacing, intonation, and expression			•	•	•	•	•
Read aloud prose and poetry with rhythm and pace, appropriate intonation, and vocal patterns			•	•	•	•	•
Vocabulary and Concept Development							
Academic language							
Classify-categorize		•					
Antonyms			•	•	•	•	
Synonyms			•	•	•	•	
Homographs				•			
Homophones				•			
Multiple-meaning words			•		•	•	•
Figurative and idiomatic language					•		•
Context/context clues			•	•	•	•	•
Content-area words							
Dictionary, glossary, thesaurus			•	•	•		
Foreign words							•
Connotation-denotation							
Word origins (acronyms, clipped and coined words, regional variations, etymologies, jargon, slang)							
Analogies							
Word structure clues to determine meaning			•	•	•		•
Inflected nouns and verbs, comparatives-superlatives, possessives, compound words, prefixes, suffixes, root words			•	•	•	•	•
Greek and Latin roots, prefixes, suffixes, derivations, and root words					•	•	•
Develop vocabulary							
Listen to and discuss text read aloud							
Read independently							
Use reference books							
Comprehension and Analysis of Text							
Ask/answer questions							
Author's purpose		•	•	•	•	•	
Author's perspective					•	•	
Propaganda/bias							
Background knowledge: prior knowledge and experiences							
Cause-effect		•	•	•	•		
Compare-contrast		•	•	•	•	•	•
Details		•	•	•	•	•	•
Directions: one-, two-, multi-step			•	•	•		
Draw conclusions	•	•			•	•	•
Fact-fiction				•	•	•	

Key:

Shaded area - Explicit Instruction/Modeling/Practice and Application

- *Tested—Assessment Resources: Weekly Lesson Tests, Theme Tests, Benchmark Assessments*

	Gr K	Gr 1	Gr 2	Gr 3	Gr 4	Gr 5	Gr 6
Fact-opinion					•	•	
Higher order thinking							
Analyze, critique and evaluate, synthesize, and visualize text and information							
Interpret information from graphic aids			•	•		•	
Locate information			•		•		
Book parts				•	•		
Text features				•	•		
Alphabetical order		•		•			
Main idea: stated/unstated		•			•	•	•
Main idea and supporting details	•	•	•	•	•	•	•
Make generalizations						•	
Make inferences		•	•	•		•	
Make judgments						•	•
Make predictions/predict outcomes	•	•	•	•	•		
Monitor comprehension							
Adjust reading rate, create mental images, reread, read ahead, set/adjust purpose, self-question, summarize/paraphrase, use graphic aids, text features, and text adjuncts					•		
Organize information							
Alphabetical order							
Numerical systems/outlines							
Graphic organizers							
Paraphrase/restate facts and details					•	•	
Preview							
Purpose for reading							
Referents							
Retell stories and ideas			•	•			
Sequence		•		•	•	•	•
Summarize			•	•	•	•	•
Text structure							
Narrative text			•	•	•	•	
Informational text (compare and contrast, cause and effect, sequence/chronological order, proposition and support, problem and solution)			•	•	•	•	•

Study Skills

	Gr K	Gr 1	Gr 2	Gr 3	Gr 4	Gr 5	Gr 6
Follow and give directions				•	•		•
Apply plans and strategies: KWL, question-answer relationships, skim and scan, note taking, outline, questioning the author, reciprocal teaching							•
Practice test-taking strategies							

Research and Information

	Gr K	Gr 1	Gr 2	Gr 3	Gr 4	Gr 5	Gr 6
Use resources and references			•		•	•	•
Understand the purpose, structure, and organization of various reference materials							
Title page, table of contents, chapter titles, chapter headings, index, glossary, guide words, citations, end notes, bibliography			•	•	•		
Picture dictionary, software, dictionary, thesaurus, atlas, globe, encyclopedia, telephone directory, on-line information, card catalog, electronic search engines and data bases, almanac, newspaper, journals, periodicals			•	•	•	•	•
Charts, maps, diagrams, time lines, schedules, calendar, graphs, photos			•		•	•	•
Choose reference materials appropriate to research purpose					•	•	•

Viewing/Media

	Gr K	Gr 1	Gr 2	Gr 3	Gr 4	Gr 5	Gr 6
Interpret information from visuals (graphics, media, including illustrations, tables, maps, charts, graphs, diagrams, time lines)			•	•			•

Key:

Shaded area - Explicit Instruction/Modeling/Practice and Application

- *Tested—Assessment Resources: Weekly Lesson Tests, Theme Tests, Benchmark Assessments*

	Gr K	Gr 1	Gr 2	Gr 3	Gr 4	Gr 5	Gr 6
Analyze the ways visuals, graphics, and media represent, contribute to, and support meaning of text							•
Select, organize, and produce visuals to complement and extend meaning							
Use technology or appropriate media to communicate information and ideas							
Use technology or appropriate media to compare ideas, information, and viewpoints							
Compare, contrast, and evaluate print and broadcast media							
Distinguish between fact and opinion							
Evaluate the role of media							
Analyze media as sources for information, entertainment, persuasion, interpretation of events, and transmission of culture							
Identify persuasive and propaganda techniques used in television and identify false and misleading information							
Summarize main concept and list supporting details and identify biases, stereotypes, and persuasive techniques in a nonprint message							
Support opinions with detailed evidence and with visual or media displays that use appropriate technology							

Literary Response and Analysis

Genre Characteristics

	Gr K	Gr 1	Gr 2	Gr 3	Gr 4	Gr 5	Gr 6
Know a variety of literary genres and their basic characteristics			•	•			
Distinguish between fantasy and realistic text							
Distinguish between informational and persuasive texts							
Understand the distinguishing features of literary and nonfiction texts: everyday print materials, poetry, drama, fantasies, fables, myths, legends, and fairy tales			•	•			
Explain the appropriateness of the literary forms chosen by an author for a specific purpose							

Literary Elements

Plot/Plot Development	Gr K	Gr 1	Gr 2	Gr 3	Gr 4	Gr 5	Gr 6
Important events		•	•	•			
Beginning, middle, ending of story	•	•	•	•			
Problem/solution		•	•	•			•
Conflict					•	•	•
Conflict and resolution/causes and effects					•	•	•
Compare and contrast			•	•	•	•	

Character	Gr K	Gr 1	Gr 2	Gr 3	Gr 4	Gr 5	Gr 6
Identify	•	•	•				
Identify, describe, compare and contrast				•	•	•	
Relate characters and events							•
Traits, actions, motives					•	•	•
Cause for character's actions					•	•	
Character's qualities and effect on plot					•	•	•

Setting	Gr K	Gr 1	Gr 2	Gr 3	Gr 4	Gr 5	Gr 6
Identify and describe	•	•	•	•			
Compare and contrast			•	•			•
Relate to problem/resolution							•

Theme	Gr K	Gr 1	Gr 2	Gr 3	Gr 4	Gr 5	Gr 6
Theme/essential message					•	•	•
Universal themes							•

Mood/Tone	Gr K	Gr 1	Gr 2	Gr 3	Gr 4	Gr 5	Gr 6
Identify							•
Compare and contrast							

Key:

Shaded area - Explicit Instruction/Modeling/Practice and Application

    • *Tested—Assessment Resources: Weekly Lesson Tests, Theme Tests, Benchmark Assessments*

	Gr K	Gr 1	Gr 2	Gr 3	Gr 4	Gr 5	Gr 6
Literary Devices/Author's Craft							
Rhythm, rhyme, pattern, and repetition							•
Alliteration, onomatopoeia, assonance, imagery						•	•
Figurative language (similes, metaphors, idioms, personification, hyperbole)				•	•	•	•
Characterization/character development				•	•	•	•
Dialogue							
Narrator/narration							
Point of view (first-person, third-person, omniscient)						•	•
Informal language (idioms, slang, jargon, dialect)							
Response to Text							
Relate characters and events to own life							
Read to perform a task or learn a new task							
Recollect, talk, and write about books read							
Describe the roles and contributions of authors and illustrators							
Generate alternative endings and identify the reason and impact of the alternatives							
Compare and contrast versions of the same stories that reflect different cultures							
Make connections between information in texts and stories and historical events							
Form ideas about what has been read and use specific information from the text to support these ideas							
Know that the attitudes and values that exist in a time period or culture affect stories and informational articles written during that time period							
Self-Selected Reading							
Select material to read for pleasure							
Read a variety of self-selected and assigned literary and informational texts							
Use knowledge of authors' styles, themes, and genres to choose own reading							
Read literature by authors from various cultural and historical backgrounds							
Cultural Awareness							
Connect information and events in texts to life and life to text experiences							
Compare language, oral traditions, and literature that reflect customs, regions, and cultures							
Identify how language reflects regions and cultures							
View concepts and issues from diverse perspectives							
Recognize the universality of literary themes across cultures and language							
Writing							
Writing Strategies							
Writing process: prewriting, drafting, revising, proofreading, publishing							
Collaborative, shared, timed writing, writing to prompts		•	•	•	•	•	•
Evaluate own and others' writing							
Proofread writing to correct convention errors in mechanics, usage, and punctuation, using handbooks and references as appropriate				•	•	•	•
Organization and Focus							
Use models and traditional structures for writing							
Select a focus, structure, and viewpoint							
Address purpose, audience, length, and format requirements							
Write single- and multiple-paragraph compositions			•	•	•	•	•
Revision Skills							
Correct sentence fragments and run-ons							
Vary sentence structure, word order, and sentence length							
Combine sentences							

Key:

Shaded area - Explicit Instruction/Modeling/Practice and Application

• *Tested—Assessment Resources: Weekly Lesson Tests, Theme Tests, Benchmark Assessments*

	Gr K	Gr 1	Gr 2	Gr 3	Gr 4	Gr 5	Gr 6
Improve coherence, unity, consistency, and progression of ideas	▨	▨	▨	▨	▨	▨	▨
Add, delete, consolidate, clarify, rearrange text	▨	▨	▨	▨	▨	▨	▨
Choose appropriate and effective words: exact/precise words, vivid words, trite/overused words	▨	▨	▨	▨	▨	▨	▨
Elaborate: details, examples, dialogue, quotations	▨	▨	▨	▨	▨	▨	▨
Revise using a rubric		▨	▨	▨	▨	▨	▨

Penmanship/Handwriting

	Gr K	Gr 1	Gr 2	Gr 3	Gr 4	Gr 5	Gr 6
Write uppercase and lowercase letters	▨	▨	▨	▨			
Write legibly, using appropriate word and letter spacing	▨	▨	▨	▨	▨	▨	▨
Write legibly, using spacing, margins, and indention		▨	▨	▨	▨	▨	▨

Writing Applications

	Gr K	Gr 1	Gr 2	Gr 3	Gr 4	Gr 5	Gr 6
Narrative writing (stories, paragraphs, personal narratives, journal, plays, poetry)	▨	•	•	•	•	•	•
Descriptive writing (titles, captions, ads, posters, paragraphs, stories, poems)	▨	•	•	▨	▨	▨	▨
Expository writing (comparison-contrast, explanation, directions, speech, how-to article, friendly/business letter, news story, essay, report, invitation)	▨	▨	▨	▨	•	•	•
Persuasive writing (paragraph, essay, letter, ad, poster)	▨				•	•	•
Cross-curricular writing (paragraph, report, poster, list, chart)	▨	▨	▨	▨	▨	▨	▨
Everyday writing (journal, message, forms, notes, summary, label, caption)	▨	▨	▨	▨	▨	▨	▨

Written and Oral English Language Conventions

Sentence Structure

	Gr K	Gr 1	Gr 2	Gr 3	Gr 4	Gr 5	Gr 6
Types (declarative, interrogative, exclamatory, imperative, interjection)	▨	•	•	•	•	•	•
Structure (simple, compound, complex, compound-complex)	▨	•	•	•	•	•	•
Parts (subjects/predicates: complete, simple, compound; clauses: independent, dependent, subordinate; phrase)	▨	•	•	•	•	•	•
Direct/indirect object						•	•
Word order	▨	•					

Grammar

	Gr K	Gr 1	Gr 2	Gr 3	Gr 4	Gr 5	Gr 6
Nouns (singular, plural, common, proper, possessive, collective, abstract, concrete, abbreviations, appositives)	▨	•	•	•	•	•	•
Verbs (action, helping, linking, transitive, intransitive, regular, irregular; subject-verb agreement)	▨	•	•	•	•	•	•
Verb tenses (present, past, future; present, past, and future perfect)	▨	•	•	•	•	•	•
Participles; infinitives						•	•
Adjectives (common, proper; articles; comparative, superlative)	▨	•	•	•	•	•	•
Adverbs (place, time, manner, degree)					•	•	•
Pronouns (subject, object, possessive, reflexive, demonstrative, antecedents)	▨	•	•	•	•	•	•
Prepositions; prepositional phrases					•	•	•
Conjunctions					•	•	•
Abbreviations, contractions	▨	▨	•	•	•	•	•

Punctuation

	Gr K	Gr 1	Gr 2	Gr 3	Gr 4	Gr 5	Gr 6
Period, exclamation point, or question mark at end of sentences	▨	•	•	•	•	•	•
Comma							
Greeting and closure of a letter		▨	▨	▨	▨	•	•
Dates, locations, and addresses			▨	▨	▨	•	•
For items in a series		▨	▨	▨	•	•	•
Direct quotations		▨	▨	▨	•	•	•
Link two clauses with a conjunction in compound sentences					•	•	•
Quotation Marks							
Dialogue, exact words of a speaker	▨	▨	▨	▨	•	•	•
Titles of books, stories, poems, magazines					•	•	•

Key:

Shaded area - Explicit Instruction/Modeling/Practice and Application

   • *Tested—Assessment Resources: Weekly Lesson Tests, Theme Tests, Benchmark Assessments*

	Gr K	Gr 1	Gr 2	Gr 3	Gr 4	Gr 5	Gr 6
Parentheses/dash/hyphen						•	•
Apostrophes in possessive case of nouns and in contractions		•	•	•	•	•	•
Underlining or italics to identify title of documents					•	•	•
Colon							
Separate hours and minutes						•	•
Introduce a list						•	•
After the salutation in business letters						•	•
Semicolons to connect dependent clauses							

Capitalization

	Gr K	Gr 1	Gr 2	Gr 3	Gr 4	Gr 5	Gr 6
First word of a sentence, names of people, and the pronoun *I*		•	•	•	•	•	•
Proper nouns, words at the beginning of sentences and greetings, months and days of the week, and titles and initials of people		•	•	•	•	•	•
Geographical names, holidays, historical periods, and special events			•	•			
Names of magazines, newspapers, works of art, musical compositions, organizations, and the first word in quotations when appropriate						•	•
Use conventions of punctuation and capitalization			•	•	•	•	•

Spelling

	Gr K	Gr 1	Gr 2	Gr 3	Gr 4	Gr 5	Gr 6
Spell independently by using pre-phonetic knowledge, sounds of the alphabet, and knowledge of letter names							
Use spelling approximations and some conventional spelling							
Common, phonetically regular words		•	•	•	•	•	•
Frequently used, irregular words		•	•	•	•	•	•
One-syllable words with consonant blends			•	•	•	•	•
Contractions, compounds, orthographic patterns, and common homophones				•	•	•	•
Greek and Latin roots, inflections, suffixes, prefixes, and syllable constructions				•	•	•	•
Use a variety of strategies and resources to spell words							

Listening and Speaking

Listening Skills and Strategies

	Gr K	Gr 1	Gr 2	Gr 3	Gr 4	Gr 5	Gr 6
Listen to a variety of oral presentations such as stories, poems, skits, songs, personal accounts, or informational speeches							
Listen attentively to the speaker (make eye contact and demonstrate appropriate body language)							
Listen for a purpose							
Follow oral directions (one-, two-, three-, and multi-step)							
For specific information							
For enjoyment							
To distinguish between the speaker's opinions and verifiable facts							
To actively participate in class discussions							
To expand and enhance personal interest and personal preferences							
To identify, analyze, and critique persuasive techniques							
To identify logical fallacies used in oral presentations and media messages							
To make inferences or draw conclusions							
To interpret a speaker's verbal and nonverbal messages, purposes, and perspectives							
To identify the tone, mood, and emotion							
To analyze the use of rhetorical devices for intent and effect							
To evaluate classroom presentations							
To respond to a variety of media and speakers							
To paraphrase/summarize directions and information							
For language reflecting regions and cultures							

Key:

Shaded area - Explicit Instruction/Modeling/Practice and Application

    • *Tested—Assessment Resources: Weekly Lesson Tests, Theme Tests, Benchmark Assessments*

	Gr K	Gr 1	Gr 2	Gr 3	Gr 4	Gr 5	Gr 6
To recognize emotional and logical arguments							
To identify the musical elements of language			▓	▓	▓	▓	
Listen critically to relate the speaker's verbal communication to the nonverbal message					▓		

Speaking Skills and Strategies

	Gr K	Gr 1	Gr 2	Gr 3	Gr 4	Gr 5	Gr 6
Speak clearly and audibly and use appropriate volume and pace in different settings	▓	▓	▓	▓	▓	▓	▓
Use formal and informal English appropriately	▓	▓	▓	▓	▓	▓	▓
Follow rules of conversation	▓	▓	▓	▓	▓	▓	▓
Stay on the topic when speaking		▓	▓	▓	▓	▓	▓
Use descriptive words		▓	▓	▓	▓	▓	▓
Recount experiences in a logical sequence		▓	▓	▓	▓	▓	▓
Clarify and support spoken ideas with evidence and examples		▓	▓	▓		▓	▓
Use eye contact, appropriate gestures, and props to enhance oral presentations and engage the audience		▓	▓	▓	▓	▓	▓
Give and follow two-, three-, and four-step directions		▓	▓	▓	▓	▓	▓
Recite poems, rhymes, songs, stories, soliloquies, or dramatic dialogues	▓	▓	▓	▓	▓	▓	▓
Plan and present dramatic interpretations with clear diction, pitch, tempo, and tone		▓	▓	▓	▓	▓	▓
Organize presentations to maintain a clear focus		▓	▓	▓	▓	▓	▓
Use language appropriate to situation, purpose, and audience		▓	▓	▓	▓	▓	▓
Make/deliver							
Oral narrative, descriptive, informational, and persuasive presentations			▓	▓	▓	▓	▓
Oral summaries of articles and books			▓	▓	▓	▓	▓
Oral responses to literature			▓	▓	▓	▓	▓
Presentations on problems and solutions			▓	▓	▓	▓	▓
Presentation or speech for specific occasions, audiences, and purposes			▓	▓	▓	▓	▓
Vary language according to situation, audience, and purpose			▓	▓	▓	▓	▓
Select a focus, organizational structure, and point of view for an oral presentation					▓	▓	▓
Participate in classroom activities and discussions	▓	▓	▓	▓	▓	▓	▓

Key:

Shaded area - Explicit Instruction/Modeling/Practice and Application

- *Tested— Assessment Resources: Weekly Lesson Tests, Theme Tests, Benchmark Assessments*

Index

Abbreviations
See **Decoding/Word Work,**
abbreviations; **Grammar,**
abbreviations
Academic Language
See **Vocabulary**
Academic Vocabulary
See **Student Edition,** Glossary;
Vocabulary
Accelerated Reader, 2-1: T18, T116,
T200, T280; **2-2:** T18, T116, T202,
T286; **2-3:** T18, T114, T282; **2-4:**
T18, T118, T208, T292; **2-5:** T18,
T120, T208, T300; **2-6:** T18, T120,
T204, T294
Accuracy
See **Fluency,** accuracy
Acknowledgments, 2-1: R86; **2-2:** R86;
2-3: R50; **2-4:** R86; **2-5:** R86; **2-6:**
R86
Activity Cards
See **Literacy Centers**
Adjectives
See **Grammar,** adjectives
Adjust Reading Rate
See **Fluency,** reading rate
Advanced Learners, Activities for
See **Differentiated Instruction,**
Advanced Learners, notes for
Advanced Readers
See **Leveled Readers,** Advanced
Readers
Affixes
See **Decoding/Word Work,** inflections,
prefixes, suffixes; **Vocabulary,**
prefixes, suffixes, roots
Alliteration
See **Comprehension Skills,** figurative/
poetic language, alliteration

Alphabetical Order
See **Comprehension Skills,**
alphabetical order
Answer Questions
See **Focus Strategies,** answer
questions
Antonyms
See **Vocabulary,** antonyms
Art
See **Content-Area Reading,** art;
Cross-Curricular Connections,
art; fine art
Articles
See **Genre,** magazine article
Ask Questions
See **Focus Strategies,** ask questions
Assessment, 2-1: A1–A6; **2-2:** A1–A6;
2-3: A1–A6; **2-4:** A1–A6; **2-5:**
A1–A6; **2-6:** A1–A6
See also **Monitor Progress; Rubrics**
Benchmark Assessments, **2-1:** T436;
2-2: T448; **2-3:** T436; **2-4:** T448;
2-5: T456; **2-6:** T458
decoding assessment, **2-1:** T43, T97,
T141, T193, T225, T273, T305,
T355; **2-2:** T43, T97, T141, T227,
T311; **2-3:** T43, T95, T139, T189,
T221, T275, T307, T357; **2-4:**
T43, T143, T233, T285, T317,
T367; **2-5:** T43, T145, T233,
T325; **2-6:** T43, T145, T229, T319
Oral Reading Fluency Assessment,
2-1: T60, T69, T83, T93, T154,
T163, T179, T189, T236, T245,
T259, T269, T318, T327, T341,
T351; **2-2:** T58, T83, T93, T156,
T181, T191, T242, T251, T265,
T275, T328, T353, T363; **2-3:**
T67, T81, T91, T152, T161, T175,
T185, T261, T271, T343, T353;
2-4: T82, T94, T162, T186, T196,
T244, T268, T280, T328, T352,
T362; **2-5:** T60, T84, T96, T162,
T186, T196, T252, T276, T288,

T336, T360, T370; **2-6:** T60, T84,
T96, T182, T192, T270, T282,
T362, T372
Portfolio Opportunity, **2-1:** T73, T111,
T113, T169, T249, T331; **2-2:** T73,
T111, T113, T171, T255, T343;
2-3: T71, T109, T111, T165, T251,
T333; **2-4:** T73, T113, T115, T177,
T259, T343; **2-5:** T115, T117,
T265, T349; **2-6:** T115, T117,
T171, T259, T351
prescriptions, **2-1:** T97, T193, T273,
T355, A2–A6; **2-2:** T97, T195,
T279, T367, A2–A6; **2-3:** T95,
T189, T275, T357, A2–A6; **2-4:**
T99, T201, T285, T367, A2–A6;
2-5: T101, T201, T293, T375,
A2–A6; **2-6:** T101, T197, T287,
T377, A2–A6
Self-Assessment, **2-1:** T110–T111,
T434; **2-2:** T110–T111; **2-3:**
T108–T109, T434; **2-4:** T112–
T113, T446; **2-5:** T114–T115,
T454; **2-6:** T114–T115, T456
Spelling Posttest, **2-1:** T91, T187,
T267, T349, T424; **2-2:** T91,
T189, T273, T361, T436; **2-3:**
T89, T183, T269, T351, T424;
2-4: T93, T195, T279, T361, T436;
2-5: T95, T195, T287, T369, T444;
2-6: T95, T191, T281, T371, T446
Spelling Pretest, **2-1:** T33, T131,
T215, T295, T376; **2-2:** T33,
T131, T217, T301, T388; **2-3:**
T33, T129, T211, T297, T378; **2-4:**
T33, T133, T223, T307, T388;
2-5: T33, T135, T223, T315, T396;
2-6: T33, T135, T219, T309, T398
StoryTown Online Assessment, **2-1:**
T7, T436; **2-2:** T7, T448;
2-3: T7, T436; **2-4:** T7, T448; **2-5:**
T7, T456; **2-6:** T7, T458

Theme Test, **2-1:** T436; **2-2:** T448;
2-3: T436; **2-4:** T448; **2-5:** T456;
2-6: T458

Weekly Lesson Test, **2-1:** T97, T193,
T273, T355, T429; **2-2:** T97,
T195, T279, T367, T441; **2-3:**
T95, T189, T275, T357, T429;
2-4: T99, T201, T285, T367,
T441; **2-5:** T101, T201, T293,
T375, T449; **2-6:** T101, T197,
T287, T377, T451

Assessment Prescriptions

See **Assessment,** prescriptions

Atlas

See **Research/Study Skills,** atlas,
reference sources

Audience

See **Speaking and Listening,**
audience; **Writing,** audience

Audiotext

See **Technology,** technology resources,
Audiotext

Author Features

See **Student Edition,** author features

Author's Craft

See **Comprehension Skills,** author's
craft/language use

Authors, Program, 2-1: iii; **2-2:** iii; **2-3:**
iii; **2-4:** iii; **2-5:** iii; **2-6:** iii

Author's Purpose

See **Comprehension Skills,** author's
purpose; **Focus Skills,** author's
purpose

Authors, Student Edition Literature

See **Student Edition,** author features

Author's Viewpoint

See **Comprehension Skills,** author's
viewpoint

Autobiography

See **Genre,** autobiography

Backdrops

See **Teacher Resource Book,** Readers'
Theater Backdrops

Background, Build, 2-1: T14, T47, T98,
T99, T100, T101, T145, T194,
T195, T196, T197, T229, T274,
T275, T276, T277, T309, T356,
T357, T358, T359, T380, T430,
T431, T432, T433; **2-2:** T14, T47,
T98, T99, T100, T101, T145, T196,
T197, T198, T199, T231, T280,
T281, T282, T283, T315, T368,
T369, T370, T371, T392, T442,
T443, T444, T445; **2-3:** T14, T47,
T96, T97, T98, T99, T143, T190,
T191, T192, T193, T225, T276,
T277, T278, T279, T311, T358,
T359, T360, T361, T382, T430,
T431, T432, T433; **2-4:** T14, T47,
T100, T101, T102, T103, T147,
T202, T203, T204, T205, T237,
T286, T287, T288, T289, T321,
T368, T369, T370, T371, T392,
T442, T443, T444, T445; **2-5:**
T14, T47, T97, T102, T103, T104,
T105, T149, T202, T203, T204,
T205, T237, T294, T295, T296,
T297, T329, T376, T377, T378,
T379, T400, T450, T451, T452,
T453; **2-6:** T14, T47, T102, T103,
T104, T105, T149, T198, T199,
T200, T201, T233, T288, T289,
T290, T291, T323, T378, T379,
T380, T381, T402, T452, T453,
T454, T455

Background Knowledge

See **Prior Knowledge**

Base Words

See **Decoding/Word Work,** base
words

Beginning, Middle, End

See **Focus Skills,** plot

Below-Level Learners, activities for

See **Differentiated Instruction,**
Below-Level Learners, notes for

Below-Level Readers

See **Leveled Readers,** Below-Level
Readers

Benchmark Assessments

See **Assessment,** Benchmark
Assessments

Bibliography, Professional, 2-1:
R22–R23; **2-2:** R22–R23; **2-3:**
R22–R23; **2-4:** R22–R23; **2-5:**
R22–R23; **2-6:** R22–R23

Big Book of Rhymes and Poems

"Aliona Says," **2-3:** T257, T267, T423

"Always Be Kind to Animals," **2-3:**
T339, T349, T411

"At the Bike Rack," **2-2:** T139, T161

"Bat Habits," **2-2:** T225, T247, T413

"Benita Beane," **2-4:** T265, T277

"Bookworm," **2-1:** T79, T89, T423

"Brush Dance," **2-3:** T77, T87

"Bumblebees," **2-5:** T231, T257, T421

"Chimpanzee," **2-5:** T323, T341

"Cowscape," **2-2:** T349, T359

"Did You Ever Think?" **2-3:** T219,
T243, T401

"Dogs," **2-1:** T303, T323, T411

"The Drum," **2-4:** T141, T167, T403

"Far Away," **2-6:** T41, T65

"First Snow," **2-4:** T79, T91

"The Gentle Cow," **2-2:** T309, T333,
T423

"Grown-Ups," **2-5:** T41, T65

"Here Comes the Band," **2-4:** T231,
T249, T263, T413

"Hide-and-Seek," **2-5:** T357, T367,
T431

"Home," **2-5:** T81, T93, T393

"I've Got a Dog," **2-1:** T337, T347

"Keepsakes," **2-6:** T267, T279, T423

"The Lizard," **2-6:** T317, T343

"Macaw," **2-3:** T305, T325

"Mix a Pancake," **2-6:** T81, T93, T395

"My Bike," **2-2:** T177, T187, T403

"My Cat and I," **2-4:** T41, T63, T385

"My Name," **2-3:** T41, T63, T375

"My Snake," **2-1:** T255, T265

"New Notebook," **2-4:** T183, T193, T435

"Night Creature," **2-2:** T261, T271

"Night Game," **2-2:** T79, T89, T435

"Nuts to You and Nuts to Me!" **2-4:** T315, T333

"People," **2-6:** T143, T163

"Play," **2-3:** T137, T157, T391

"The Poet Pencil," **2-6:** T179, T189, T413, T445

"The Purple Cow," **2-5:** T143, T167

"Quiet Morning," **2-1:** T223, T241, T401

"Rocks," **2-6:** T227, T251

"Sharing the Swing," **2-3:** T171, T181

"Soccer Feet," **2-2:** T41, T63, T385

"Sun," **2-6:** T359, T369, T433

"The Swarm of Bees," **2-5:** T273, T285, T443

"Tiny Seeds," **2-4:** T349, T359, T423

"The Tree Frog," **2-1:** T139, T159

"When You Can Read," **2-1:** T65, T373

"Who Has Seen the Wind?" **2-1:** T175, T185, T391

"A Young Farmer of Leeds," **2-5:** T183, T193, T411

Biography

See **Genre,** biography

Book Parts

See **Research/Study Skills,** book parts

Books on Tape

See **Technology,** technology resources, Audiotext

Brainstorming

See **Writing,** process writing, prewrite

Capitalization

See **Grammar,** abbreviations; sentences

Captions

See **Comprehension Skills,** text structure

Cause and Effect

See **Comprehension Skills,** cause and effect; **Focus Skills,** cause and effect; **Graphic Organizers,** cause-and-effect diagram

Center Activity Kit Cards

See **Literacy Centers,** Center Activity Kit Cards

Centers

See **Literacy Centers**

Challenge Copying Masters

See **Differentiated Instruction,** Challenge Copying Masters

Challenge Resource Kit

See **Differentiated Instruction,** Challenge Resource Kit

Challenge Teacher Guide

See **Differentiated Instruction,** Challenge Teacher Guide

Characters

See **Comprehension Skills,** characters, characters' emotions, characters' traits; **Focus Skills,** characters

Charts

See **Graphic Organizers,** charts

Choral-Read

See **Fluency,** choral-read

Classify/Categorize

See **Comprehension Skills,** classify/categorize

Classroom Library Collection

See also **Literacy Centers,** Reading Center

Ant Cities, **2-3:** T3, T25, T121, T203, T289, T371; **2-5:** T25, T127, T215, T307, T389

Billy's Bucket, **2-4:** T3, T25, T125, T215, T299, T381

Buster, **2-3:** T3, T25, T121, T203, T289, T371; **2-6:** T25, T127, T211, T301, T391

Clown Fish, **2-1:** T3, T25, T123, T207, T287, T369; **2-3:** T25, T121, T203, T289, T371

Cradles in the Trees, **2-2:** T3, T25, T123, T209, T293, T381

The Dot, **2-4:** T3, T25, T125, T215, T299, T381

Duck on a Bike, **2-1:** T25, T123, T207, T287, T369; **2-2:** T3, T25, T26, T123, T209, T293, T381

A Log's Life, **2-5:** T3, T25, T127, T215, T307, T389

Mae Jemison, **2-4:** T25, T125, T215, T299, T381; **2-6:** T3, T25, T127, T211, T301, T391

Puppy Mudge Finds a Friend, **2-1:** T3, T25, T123, T207, T287, T369

The Quetzal's Journey, **2-6:** T3, T25, T127, T211, T301, T391

Treasure Map, **2-2:** T25, T123, T209, T293, T381; **2-5:** T3, T25, T127, T215, T307, T389

Classroom Library Teacher Guide, 2-1: T3, T25, T123, T207, T287, T369; **2-2:** T3, T25, T123, T209, T293, T381; **2-3:** T3, T25, T121, T203, T289, T371; **2-4:** T3, T25, T125, T215, T299, T381; **2-5:** T3, T25, T127, T215, T307, T389; **2-6:** T3, T25, T127, T211, T301, T391

Classroom Management

See **Lesson Planner,** 5-Day Small-Group Planner; **Literacy Centers**

Commas

 See **Fluency,** punctuation; **Writing,**
  forms, friendly letter

Common Errors

 See **Grammar**

Communication Skills

 See **Speaking and Listening**

Compare and Contrast

 See **Comprehension Skills,** compare
  and contrast

Comparing Texts

 See **Student Edition,** comparing texts;

Comparisons, Make

 See **Comprehension Skills,**
  comparisons, make

Compound Words

 See **Decoding/Word Work,**
  compound words

Comprehension Skills

 See also **Focus Skills**

 alphabetical order, **2-5:** T185; **2-6:**
  T273

 author's craft/important details, **2-1:**
  T234

 author's craft/language use, **2-2:** T252,
  T316; **2-3:** T236, T313, T319; **2-4:**
  T57, T150, T152, T153, T154,
  T156, T157, T160, T161, T242;
  2-5: T153; **2-6:** T151, T328, T335

 author's purpose

  See **Focus Skills**

 author's viewpoint **2-3:** T146

 cause and effect

  See **Focus Skills**

 characters

  See **Focus Skills**

 characters' emotions, **2-1:** T57, T149,
  T195, T231, T274, T275; **2-2:**
  T146, T196, T235, T280, T281,
  T370; **2-3:** T52, T55, T277, T278;
  2-4: T54, T56, T150, T154, T156,
  T161, T203, T204; **2-5:** T52,
  T157; **2-6:** T50, T103, T379, T404

characters, identify with, **2-1:** T100;
 2-2: T99, T198, T282, T319,
 T369; **2-3:** T57, T96, T97; **2-4:**
 T101, T158, T370; **2-6:** T380

characters' motivations, **2-1:** T50,
 T148; **2-2:** T55, T282, T369; **2-3:**
 T50; **2-4:** T157; **2-5:** T332

characters' traits, **2-1:** T150, T232;
 2-2: T56, T100, T368; **2-3:** T48,
 T232, T430, T431; **2-4:** T53, T55,
 T394, T395; **2-6:** T102

classify/categorize, **2-1:** T313

compare and contrast, **2-1:** T51, T100,
 T317, T385; **2-2:** T71, T320; **2-3:**
 T98, T145, T150, T163, T192,
 T359, T384; **2-4:** T149, T202,
 T204, T205; **2-5:** T70–T71, T136,
 T152, T160, T172–T173, T197,
 T240, T244; **2-6:** T70, T154,
 T237, T245, T328

comparisons, make, **2-1:** T98, T277,
 T310; **2-2:** T52, T54, T282, T320,
 T370; **2-3:** T190, T226, T312,
 T313, T314, T315; **2-4:** T187; **2-5:**
 T334; **2-6:** T359, T368, T369, T379

conclusions, draw, **2-1:** T58, T98, T99,
 T151, T152, T197, T231, T234,
 T311, T313, T356, T357, T382,
 T383; **2-2:** T48, T147, T237,
 T240, T281, T322, T326, T371,
 T394; **2-3:** T49, T50, T56, T96,
 T97, T98, T99, T144, T226, T229,
 T235, T317, T386; **2-4:** T50, T57,
 T100, T101, T102, T149, T150,
 T151, T160, T161, T202, T203,
 T243, T287, T322, T324, T326,
 T327, T368, T397, T398; **2-5:**
 T51, T55, T59, T157, T161, T238,
 T243, T245, T246, T247, T248,
 T251, T331, T403; **2-6:** T48, T58,
 T104, T157, T200, T201, T243,
 T324, T336, T407

connections, make, **2-5:** T332

details, important, **2-1:** T58, T233,
 T317; **2-2:** T56, T146, T147,
 T149, T152, T154, T169, T323,
 T326; **2-3:** T57, T151, T319; **2-4:**
 T57, T287, T327; **2-5:** T59, T161,
 T251, T335; **2-6:** T58, T157,
 T243, T245, T336

details, note, **2-1:** T48, T49, T51, T52,
 T53, T54, T55, T56, T57, T71,
 T98, T146, T147, T152, T165,
 T166, T167, T194, T196, T230,
 T275, T276, T310, T311, T312,
 T314, T315, T356, T357, T358;
 2-2: T48, T49, T50, T51, T98,
 T99, T100, T196, T198, T238,
 T280, T281, T324, T370, T393,
 T442, T443, T444; **2-3:** T48, T49,
 T52, T53, T96, T97, T98, T144,
 T145, T147, T150, T190, T192,
 T228, T233, T276, T278, T312,
 T313, T314, T316, T317, T318,
 T358, T359, T360, T383, T385,
 T430, T431, T432; **2-4:** T49, T51,
 T53, T100, T148, T149, T151,
 T152, T202, T203, T204, T238,
 T286, T287, T288, T322, T323,
 T324, T325, T326, T368, T369,
 T370; **2-5:** T48, T50, T52, T54,
 T56, T58, T73, T238, T242, T245,
 T330, T333, T401; **2-6:** T48, T49,
 T53, T55, T56, T70, T102, T103,
 T150, T153, T155, T198, T199,
 T200, T237, T240, T241, T244,
 T289, T290, T324, T325, T326,
 T329, T331, T332, T333, T335,
 T378, T452

fact and opinion, **2-1:** T356, T358;
 2-6: T289, T290

fantasy/realistic text, **2-2:** T232, T239,
 T280

fiction and nonfiction

 See **Focus Skills**

figurative/poetic language, **2-2:** T317;
 2-4: T36, T50, T149, T153, T154,

T156, T193; **2-5:** T55, T174, T175; **2-6:** T138, T189

alliteration, **2-1:** T323; **2-4:** T174; **2-5:** T367; **2-6:** T53, T179

metaphor, **2-2:** T153, T261

onomatopoeia, **2-4:** T226, T229, T247, T249, T263

repetition, **2-2:** T333; **2-3:** T63, T137, T391; **2-4:** T256; **2-5:** T93; **2-6:** T65, T163, T179, T227, T267

rhyme, **2-1:** T304; **2-2:** T226, T247, T309, T310; **2-3:** T87, T181, T243, T249, T267, T349, T401; **2-4:** T63, T79, T157, T174, T229, T231, T256, T263, T277, T359; **2-5:** T65, T133, T138, T167, T193, T232, T257, T341; **2-6:** T65, T143, T144, T171, T181, T251, T259

rhythm, **2-1:** T347; **2-2:** T63; **2-3:** T243; **2-4:** T157, T167, T174, T256, T275, T333; **2-5:** T93, T167, T193, T273, T285; **2-6:** T93, T151, T256

follow directions, **2-4:** T68–T69, T172–T173; **2-6:** T81, T87, T89

generalize, **2-1:** T357; **2-5:** T158; **2-6:** T288

genre, **2-1:** T71, T247, T329; **2-2:** T169, T341; **2-3:** T69, T249; **2-4:** T70, T174, T256, T340; **2-5:** T73, T151, T154, T174, T262, T346; **2-6:** T70, T169, T348

graphic aids
   See **Focus Skills**

inferences, make
   See **Focus Skills**

judgments, make, **2-1:** T310; **2-2:** T321, T324; **2-3:** T228; **2-4:** T153; **2-5:** T159, T404; **2-6:** T153, T234

locate information
   See **Focus Skills**

main idea, **2-1:** T234; **2-2:** T283, T317; **2-3:** T51, T149; **2-4:** T270, T286, T289, T371; **2-5:** T249, T262; **2-6:** T63, T105, T238, T242, T289, T290, T291, T378, T381

main idea and details
   See **Focus Skills**

metacognitive, **2-6:** T453, T454

personal opinions, express, **2-1:** T99, T100, T234, T357, T358; **2-2:** T50, T51, T101, T154, T235, T237, T282, T321, T370, T396; **2-3:** T55, T146, T316, T358, T359, T384; **2-4:** T49, T51, T100, T101, T102, T160, T325; **2-5:** T50, T150, T155, T160, T246; **2-6:** T151, T153, T155, T156, T241, T244; T289

personal response, **2-1:** T71, T98, T167, T194, T195, T196, T247, T274, T275, T276, T329, T356; **2-2:** T71, T98, T99, T100, T196, T197, T198, T280, T281, T282, T341, T398; **2-3:** T69, T96, T98, T163, T249, T276, T277, T278, T331, T431; **2-4:** T70, T174, T202, T203, T204, T256, T287, T340, T368, T369, T370; **2-5:** T73, T174, T262, T346, T406; **2-6:** T70, T102, T103, T104, T169, T198, T199, T200, T256, T288, T290, T348, T378, T379, T380, T452, T453, T454

plot, **2-2:** T218–T219, T252, T266, T276, T280, T281, T282, T302–T303, T338–T339, T354, T364, T368, T369, T370, T371, T416, T428, T437, T442, T443, T444, T445; **2-4:** T85; **2-5:** T34–T35, T36, T49, T53, T57, T60, T69, T75, T85, T97, T102, T103, T104, T105, T136–T137, T138, T148, T151, T153, T156, T159, T161,

T162, T171, T187, T197, T202, T203, T204, T205, T436; **2-6:** T86

predictions, make and confirm
   See **Focus Skills**

prior knowledge, **2-1:** T36, T71, T99, T134, T165, T218, T247, T298, T315, T329; **2-2:** T29, T36, T46, T48, T50, T127, T134, T144, T146, T151, T169, T220, T304, T341; **2-3:** T36, T69, T132, T147, T163, T214, T300; **2-4:** T36, T70, T136, T226, T237, T240, T256, T310, T321, T340; **2-5:** T36, T56, T72, T86, T138, T152, T174, T226, T237, T262, T318, T329, T346; **2-6:** T36, T47, T70, T138, T168, T222, T233, T255, T256, T271, T283, T312, T348

problem/solution, **2-1:** T195, T356; **2-2:** T148, T198, T368; **2-3:** T98, T277; **2-4:** T100, T103, T158, T370; **2-5:** T136, T138, T148, T150, T151, T156, T158, T160, T162, T171, T187, T197; **2-6:** T56, T103, T104

reference sources, use, **2-1:** T12; **2-4:** T12, T254–T255, T338–T339; **2-6:** T12, T152, T273

sequence, **2-1:** T99, T149, T151, T165, T166, T194, T312; **2-2:** T153, T237; **2-3:** T96, T97, T359; **2-4:** T50, T52, T100, T101, T287, T324; **2-5:** T226, T241, T242, T245, T246; **2-6:** T56, T104, T242, T332, T334, T357, T379, T453

setting
   See **Focus Skills**

speculate, **2-1:** T196, T314, T316, T357; **2-2:** T152, T197, T235, T240, T325; **2-3:** T147, T148, T191, T192, T227; **2-4:** T241, T248, T368; **2-5:** T48, T54, T59;

2-6: T198, T240, T243, T288, T290, T330

story elements

  See **Comprehension,** characters; plot; setting; **Focus Skills,** characters; plot; setting

summarize, **2-1:** T50; **2-2:** T50, T154, T234, T394; **2-3:** T50, T54; **2-4:** T101, T156, T369, T370, T396; **2-5:** T155, T333; **2-6:** T103, T169

synthesize, **2-2:** T396; **2-4:** T238; **2-5:** T250, T402, T406

text structure, **2-2:** T98, T99, T100, T442, T444; **2-3:** T358, T414, T415, T432; **2-4:** T70, T239, T340; **2-5:** T262; **2-6:** T198, T200, T452

theme, **2-1:** T14–T15, T362; **2-2:** T14–T15, T55, T374; **2-3:** T14–T15, T53, T196, T364; **2-4:** T14–T15, T18, T118, T153, T208, T240, T292, T374; **2-5:** T14–T15, T382; **2-6:** T14–T15, T256, T279, T384

Comprehension Strategies

  See **Focus Strategies; Review Lessons**

Computer Skills

  See **Literacy Centers,** technology; **Technology**

Conclusions, Draw

  See **Comprehension Skills,** conclusions, draw

Conferences

  See **Writing,** conference

Connections

  See **Student Edition,** Connections

Consonant Digraphs

  See **Decoding/Word Work,** digraphs

Consonants

  See **Decoding/Word Work,** consonants

Consultants, Program, 2-1: R24–R25; **2-2:** R24–R25; **2-3:** R24–R25;

2-4: R24–R25; **2-5:** R24–R25; **2-6:** R24–R25

Content-Area Reading:

art

  "Jamaica Louise James," **2-3:** T47–T57

  "Sarah Enters a Painting," **2-4:** T174–T175

language arts

  "Arthur's Reading Race," **2-1:** T47–T59

  "The Bat," **2-2:** T253

  "Beyond Old MacDonald," **2-5:** T174–T175

  "The Book," **2-2:** T426–T428

  "Changing," **2-3:** T249

  "Dogs," **2-1:** T247

  "Friendliness," **2-1:** T414–T416

  "The Great Ball Game," **2-2:** T231–T241

  "Interview with Author Loreen Leedy," **2-4:** T70–T71

  "A Lazy Thought," **2-3:** T69

  "The Lizard and the Sun," **2-6:** T323–T337

  "Mr. Putter and Tabby Write the Book," **2-4:** T47–T57

  "A Time for Patience," **2-5:** T434–T436

  "Two Races," **2-2:** T70–T71

music

  "Ah, Music!" **2-4:** T237–T243

  "Come, My Little Children, Here Are Songs For You," **2-4:** T256–T257

science

  "Animals Have Special Jobs," **2-1:** T329

  "Baby Tapir Is Born!" **2-3:** T331

  "Be Sun Safe," **2-6:** T348–T349

  "The Bee," **2-5:** T237–T251

  "A Birthday Mystery," **2-3:** T383–T386

  "Chimp Computer Whiz," **2-5:** T346–T347

  "Dogs," **2-1:** T309–T317

  "Let's Go Rock Collecting," **2-6:** T233–T245

  "Life as a Frog," **2-1:** T165–T167

  "The Life Cycle of a Frog," **2-3:** T415–T416

  "Nutty Facts About Peanuts," **2-4:** T340–T341

  "Pebbles," **2-6:** T256–T257

  "Rain Forest Babies," **2-3:** T311–T319

  "Rock-a-Bye Cows," **2-2:** T340–T341

  "Watching in the Wild," **2-5:** T329–T335

social studies

  "Annie's Gifts," **2-4:** T147–T161

  "At Play: Long Ago and Today," **2-3:** T143–T151

  "Big Bushy Mustache," **2-3:** T225–T237

  "California Bee Business," **2-5:** T262–T263

  "A Chair for My Mother," **2-5:** T47–T59

  "Click, Clack, Moo: Cows That Type," **2-2:** T294, T315–T327

  "Cross-Country Vacation," **2-6:** T403–T408

  "Frog and Toad All Year," **2-1:** T145–T153

  "Gabriela Mistral: A Poet's Life in Photos," **2-6:** T168–T169

  "Gus and Grandpa and the Two-Wheeled Bike," **2-2:** T145–T155

  "Henry and Mudge," **2-1:** T229–T235

  "A History of Games and Toys in the United States," **2-3:** T163

  "The Life of George Washington Carver," **2-4:** T321–T327

"My Name Is Gabriela," **2-6:** T149–T157

"Neighborhood News," **2-1:** T381–T386

"No Helmet? Pay Up!" **2-2:** T168–T169

"North America," **2-4:** T427–T428

"Reading with Your Fingers," **2-1:** T71

"Saving Money," **2-5:** T72–T73

"Serious Farm," **2-5:** T149–T161

"South Korea," **2-6:** T70–T71

"Summer Safety," **2-6:** T436–T438

"Town Hall," **2-5:** T401–T406

"A Trip to the Fire Station," **2-2:** T382, T393–T398

"What's My Job?" **2-4:** T393–T398

"Where on Earth Is My Bagel?" **2-6:** T47–T59

"Winners Never Quit!" **2-2:** T47–T57

Content-Area Vocabulary

See **Vocabulary,** content-area vocabulary

Context Clues

See **Vocabulary,** context clues

Contract

See **Teacher Resource Book,** My Weekly Contract

Contractions

See **Decoding/Word Work,** contractions; **Grammar**

Conventions

See **Grammar; Writing,** traits, conventions

Critical Thinking

See **Comprehension Skills; Student Edition,** Connections; Think Critically

Cross-Curricular Connections

art, **2-3:** T46–T57; **2-4:** T398; **2-5:** T12, T240, T455; **2-6:** T237

fine art, **2-1:** xviii–T1, T15; **2-2:** xviii–T1, T15; **2-3:** T1, T15; **2-4:** xviii–T1, T15; **2-5:** xviii–T1, T15; **2-6:** xviii–T1, T15

music, **2-4:** T13, T218, T230, T264, T447

science, **2-1:** T150, T165, T166, T247, T316, T329, T381, T385; **2-2:** T55, T237; **2-3:** T69, T310–T319, T331, T415–T416; **2-4:** T55, T175, T239, T325; **2-5:** T247; **2-6:** T244, T257, T333, T349, T408

social studies, **2-1:** T55, T71, T231; **2-2:** T149, T323, T393; **2-3:** T52, T142–T151, T163 T228, T249, T312, T384; **2-4:** T71, T149, T341, T393; **2-5:** T48, T175, T263, T347, T401, T405; **2-6:** T51, T71, T156, T403

Cumulative Review

See **Vocabulary,** vocabulary review, cumulative

Daily Proofreading, 2-1: T38, T62, T76, T86, T96, T136, T156, T172, T182, T192, T220, T238, T252, T262, T272, T300, T320, T334, T344, T354, T388, T398, T408, T420, T428; **2-2:** T38, T76, T86, T96, T136, T158, T174, T184, T194, T222, T244, T258, T268, T278, T306, T330, T346, T356, T366, T400, T410, T420, T432, T440; **2-3:** T38, T60, T74, T84, T94, T134, T154, T168, T178, T188, T216, T240, T254, T264, T274, T302, T322, T336, T346, T356, T388, T398, T408, T420, T428; **2-4:** T38, T60, T76, T88, T98, T138, T164, T180, T190, T200, T228, T246, T262, T274, T284, T312, T330, T346, T356, T366, T400, T410, T420, T432, T440; **2-5:** T38, T62, T78, T90, T100, T140, T164, T180, T190, T200, T228, T254, T270, T282, T292, T320, T338, T354, T364, T374, T408, T418, T428, T440, T448; **2-6:** T38, T62, T78, T90, T100, T140, T160, T176, T186, T196, T224, T248, T264, T276, T286, T314, T340, T356, T366, T376, T410, T420, T430, T442, T450

Daily Routines

See **Question of the Day; Routine Cards; Speaking and Listening,** read aloud

Data-Driven Instruction, 2-1: viii–ix; **2-2:** viii–ix; **2-3:** viii–ix

Declarative Sentences

See **Grammar**

Decodable Books, 2-1: T60, T154, T236, T318; **2-2:** T156, T242, T328; **2-3:** T32, T58, T65, T67, T122, T152, T161, T238, T247, T320, T329, T372; **2-4:** T58, T66, T170, T244, T252, T328; **2-5:** T60, T68, T162, T170, T252, T260, T336, T344; **2-6:** T60, T68, T158, T166, T246, T254, T338, T346

See also **Literacy Centers,** Reading Center

Decodable Book 1

"Al at Bat," **2-1:** T32

"Ants," **2-1:** T67

"Big Pig," **2-1:** T32

"Will It Fit?" **2-1:** T67

Decodable Book 2

"A Hunt," **2-1:** T130

"The Lost Dog," **2-1:** T130

"My Pet Jess," **2-1:** T130

"Pug and Bug," **2-1:** T161

"A Vet Can Help," **2-1:** T161

"What Has Rod Got?" **2-1:** T161

Decodable Book 3

"A Big, Red Rose Grove," **2-1:** T243

"Bikes," **2-1:** T243

"Cole and Rose Make Fake Noses," **2-1:** T214

"Dale Lake," **2-1:** T243

"Fun in June," **2-1:** T243

"Mike and Spike," **2-1:** T214

"The Not-in-Tune Flute," **2-1:** T214

"The Trade," **2-1:** T214

Decodable Book 4

"Lee and Peep," **2-1:** T325

"Sled Dog Team," **2-1:** T294

Decodable Book 5

"Bats Take Flight," **2-2:** T65

"Bright Lights at Night," **2-2:** T32

Decodable Book 6

"A Gray Day in Maine," **2-2:** T130

"On the Trail by the Bay," **2-2:** T163

Decodable Book 7

"Mark the Star," **2-2:** T124, T216

"On Park Farm," **2-2:** T124, T249

Decodable Book 8

"Boats at Work, Boats at Play," **2-2:** T294, T335

"Off with His Coat," **2-2:** T294, T300

Decodable Book 9

"The Bad Itch," **2-3:** T32

"Beth, Seth, and the Pie Contest," **2-3:** T32

"Flash Gets a Shave," **2-3:** T32

"Hatch!" **2-3:** T65

"Shark Cove," **2-3:** T65

"These Are the Ways That We Travel," **2-3:** T65

Decodable Book 10

"Monkeys," **2-3:** T159

"Silly Donkey and His Missing Key," **2-3:** T128

Decodable Book 11

"City Bake Shop," **2-3:** T210

"A Nice Place for Mice," **2-3:** T245

"Sarge Sits," **2-3:** T210

"Strange Gadgets," **2-3:** T245

Decodable Book 12

"A Birthday Surprise for Bird," **2-3:** T296

"Earth Day" **2-3:** T327

"Bertha, the Sales Clerk," **2-3:** T296

"A Pet That Purrs," **2-3:** T327

Decodable Book 13

"Dolphins," **2-4:** T32

"A Fun Day with Phil," **2-4:** T65

"Fun with Tricky Knots," **2-4:** T65

"The Gentle Knight," **2-4:** T32

"The Twice-Wrapped Gifts," **2-4:** T65

"Wrap It Up!" **2-4:** T32

Decodable Book 14

"Get Ready, Get Fit, Go!" **2-4:** T132

"Monkey and the Wealthy Cat," **2-4:** T169

Decodable Book 15

"The Best Toy," **2-4:** T222

"Coins, Coins, Coins," **2-4:** T251

Decodable Book 16

"Cheers and Tears," **2-4:** T306

"A Year at the Leary Place," **2-4:** T335

Decodable Book 17

"Found in the Ground!" **2-5:** T67

"Meg and the Groundhog," **2-5:** T32

Decodable Book 18

"Courtney's Plans," **2-5:** T169

"Courtyards," **2-5:** T134

"Mort's Sports Store," **2-5:** T134

"Not Your Normal Fish!" **2-5:** T169

Decodable Book 19

"How to Groom Your Dog," **2-5:** T222

"Ouzels," **2-5:** T259

"Seafood Stew," **2-5:** T259

"Soup Tale," **2-5:** T222

"Sue Hunts for Clues," **2-5:** T222

"True Buddies," **2-5:** T259

Decodable Book 20

"Blair and His Lair," **2-5:** T314

"A Visit to the County Fair," **2-5:** T343

Decodable Book 21

"Booker's Cookies," **2-6:** T67

"Bookstores," **2-6:** T32

Decodable Book 22

"Paul and Maggie," **2-6:** T134

"Paw Prints," **2-6:** T165

Decodable Book 23

"At the Ballpark," **2-6:** T253

"Waldo Wins," **2-6:** T218

Decodable Book 24

"Eight Street," **2-6:** T345

"Greyhounds and More," **2-6:** T345

"Lucy, the Great Big Great Dane," **2-6:** T308

"Obey Miss Muffet," **2-6:** T308

Decoding Assessment

See **Assessment,** decoding assessment

Decoding/Word Work

See also **Monitor Progress,** phonics abbreviations

introduce, **2-4:** T82

See also **Grammar,** abbreviations

base words, **2-3:** T172, T182, T258, T268

See also **Decoding/Word Work,** root words

closed syllables, **2-1:** T31, T80, T90, T129; **2-3:** T78, T88, T205, T269, T291, T294, T295, T306, T307, T326, T327, T333, T340, T341, T350, T351, T358, T359, T360, T373, T402–T403, T412, T413; **2-4:** T305; **2-6:** T360

compound words, **2-2:** T125; **2-6:** T228

introduce, **2-2:** T178

review, **2-2:** T188, T350, T360

consonant plus -*le*

   See **Decoding/Word Work,**
     multisyllabic words, syllable
     pattern C-*le*

consonants

   /s/*c*; /j/*g, dge,* **2-3:** T205, T251,
     T276, T277, T278, T279

     reintroduce, **2-3:** T208–T211

     review, **2-3:** T220–221,
       T244–T245, T259, T269,
       T402–T403

contractions, **2-1:** T53

   reintroduce, **2-5:** T358

   review, **2-5:** T368

   See also **Grammar,** contractions

CVC, **2-1:** T31, T80, T90, T129; **2-4:**
   T305

CVCe, **2-1:** T209, T212–T215, T224–
   T225, T242–243, T249, T256,
   T257, T266, T267, T371, T402

digraphs

   /ch/*ch, tch;* /sh/*sh;* /th/*th,* **2-3:** T27,
     T71, T96, T97, T98, T373

     reintroduce, **2-3:** T30–T33

     review, **2-3:** T42–T43, T64–
       T65, T79, T89, T376

   /n/*kn;* /r/*wr;* /f/*gh, ph,* **2-4:** T27,
     T73, T100, T101, T102, T383

     reintroduce, **2-4:** T30–T33

     review, **2-4:** T42–T43, T64–
       T65, T81, T93, T386–T387

diphthongs

   See **Decoding/Word Work,** vowel
     diphthongs

inflections

   -*ed, -es* (*y* to *i*)

     introduce, **2-3:** T172

     review, **2-3:** T182

   -*ed, -ing* (double final consonant)

     introduce, **2-3:** T258

     review, **2-3:** T268

   -*ed, -ing* (drop final *e*)

     introduce, **2-2:** T80

review, **2-2:** T90; **2-4:** T323

   -*ed, -ing* (no spelling change)

     introduce, **2-1:** T338

     review, **2-1:** T348

   -*er, -est*

     introduce, **2-6:** T360

     review, **2-6:** T370

   -*es* (*f* to *v*)

     introduce, **2-6:** T180

     review, **2-6:** T190

   -*s, -es*

     introduce, **2-1:** 176

     review, **2-1:** T186

long vowels

   /ā/*a-e;* /ī/*i-e;* /ō/*o-e;* /(y) o͞o/*u-e,*
     2-1: T209, T249, T274, T275,
     T276, T277, T371

     reintroduce, **2-1:** T212–T215

     review, **2-1:** T224–T225,
       T242–243, T257, T267,
       T402

   /ā/*ai, ay,* **2-2:** T125, T171, T383

     reintroduce, **2-2:** T128–T131

     review, **2-2:** T140–T141,
       T162–T163, T179, T189,
       T404

   /ā/*ea, ei(gh), ey,* **2-6:** T303, T351

     reintroduce, **2-6:** T306–T309

     review, **2-6:** T318–T319,
       T344–T345, T361, T371,
       T434

   /ē/*ee, ea,* **2-1:** T289, T331, T356,
     T357, T358, T359, T371

     reintroduce, **2-1:** T292–T295

     review, **2-1:** T304–T305,
       T324–T325, T339, T349,
       T412

   /ē/*ey, y,* **2-3:** T123; **2-4:** T131

     reintroduce, **2-3:** T126–T129

     review, **2-3:** T138–T139,
       T158–T159, T165, T183,
       T392–T393

   /ī/*ie, igh,* **2-2:** T27, T73, T383

     reintroduce, **2-2:** T30–T33

review, **2-2:** T42–T43, T64–
   T65, T81, T91, T386–T387

   /ō/*oa, ow,* **2-2:** T295, T343, T383

     reintroduce, **2-2:** T298–T301

     review, **2-2:** T310–T311,
       T334–T335, T351, T361,
       T424

multisyllabic words

   CVC pattern in longer words, **2-6:**
     T360

     introduce, **2-1:** T80

     review, **2-1:** T90; **2-4:** T305

   CVCe pattern in longer words

     introduce, **2-1:** T256

     review, **2-1:** T266

   syllable pattern C-*le*

     introduce, **2-2:** T262

     review, **2-2:** T272

   syllable pattern VCCV

     introduce, **2-3:** T78

     review, **2-3:** T88, T340, T350

   syllable pattern V/CV

     introduce, **2-4:** T184

     review, **2-4:** T194; **2-5:** T184,
       T194

   syllable pattern VC/V

     introduce, **2-4:** T350

     review, **2-4:** T360; **2-5:** T184,
       T194

nonsense words, **2-1:** T80, T176,
   T256, T338; **2-2:** T178, T262,
   T350; **2-3:** T78, T340; **2-5:** T274;
   2-6: T82

open syllables, **2-3:** T123, T126–
   T129, T138–T139, T158–T159,
   T165, T183, T373, T392–T393;
   2-4: T184, T194; **2-5:** T184, T194

phonograms, **2-1:** T66, T73, T160,
   T224, T242, T249, T324; **2-2:**
   T64, T162, T248, T334; **2-3:** T64,
   T244, T326; **2-4:** T64, T168,
   T250, T334; **2-5:** T66, T168,
   T258, T342; **2-6:** T66, T164,
   T252, T344

prefixes
    dis-, over-, pre-
        reintroduce, **2-6:** T82
        review, **2-6:** T94
    mis-, re-, un-
        reintroduce, **2-5:** T274
        review, **2-5:** T286
r-controlled vowels
    /âr/*air, are,* **2-5:** T309, T349, T391
        reintroduce, **2-5:** T312–T315
        review, **2-5:** T324–T325,
            T342–T343, T359, T369,
            T432
    /är/*ar,* **2-2:** T211, T255
        reintroduce, **2-2:** T214–T217
        review, **2-2:** T226–T227,
            T248–T249, T263, T273,
            T414
    /ir/*ear, eer,* **2-4:** T301, T343, T368,
        T369, T370, T383
        reintroduce, **2-4:** T304–T307
        review, **2-4:** T316–T317, T334–
            T335, T351, T361, T424
    /ôr/*or, ore, our,* **2-5:** T129, T177,
        T391
        reintroduce, **2-5:** T132–T133
        review, **2-5:** T144–T145,
            T168–T169, T185, T195,
            T412
    /ûr/*ir, ur, er, ear,* **2-3:** T291, T333,
        T373
        introduce, **2-3:** T294–T295
        review, **2-3:** T306–T307,
            T326–T327, T341, T351,
            T412–T413
root words, **2-4:** T42, T80, T92
    See also **Decoding/Word Work,**
        base words
short vowels
    /a/*a;* /i/*i,* **2-1:** T27, T73, T98, T99,
        T100
        reintroduce, **2-1:** T30–T33
        review, **2-1:** T42–T43, T66–
            T67, T81, T90, T374–T375

    /e/*e;* /o/*o;* /u/*u,* **2-1:** T125, T169,
        T194, T195, T196
        reintroduce, **2-1:** T128–T131
        review, **2-1:** T140–T141,
            T160–T161, T177, T392
    /e/*ea,* **2-4:** T127, T177, T202,
        T203, T204, T383
        reintroduce, **2-4:** T130–T133
        review, **2-4:** T142–T143,
            T168–T169, T185, T195,
            T404
suffixes
    -ful, -less
        reintroduce, **2-4:** T266
        review, **2-4:** T278
    -ly, -ness
        reintroduce, **2-4:** T80
        review, **2-4:** T92
    -tion
        reintroduce, **2-6:** T268
        review, **2-6:** T280
vowel diphthongs
    /oi/*oi, oy,* **2-4:** T217, T259, T286,
        T287, T288, T383
        reintroduce, **2-4:** T220–T223
        review, **2-4:** T232–T233,
            T250–T251, T267, T279,
            T414
    /ou/*ou, ow,* **2-5:** T27, T75, T391
        reintroduce, **2-5:** T30–T33
        review, **2-5:** T42–T43, T66–
            T67, T83, T95, T394
vowel variants
    /ô/*a(l), ough,* **2-6:** T213, T259,
        T393
        reintroduce, **2-6:** T216–T219
        review, **2-6:** T228–T229,
            T252–T253, T269, T281,
            T424
    /ô/*aw, au(gh),* **2-6:** T129, T171,
        T393
        reintroduce, **2-6:** T132–T135

        review, **2-6:** T144–T145,
            T164–T165, T181, T191,
            T414
    /o͞o/*oo, ew, ue, ui, ou,* **2-5:** T217,
        T265, T391
        reintroduce, **2-5:** T220–T223
        review, **2-5:** T232–T233,
            T258–T259, T275, T287,
            T422
    /o͝o/*oo, ou,* **2-6:** T27, T73, T393
        reintroduce, **2-6:** T30–T33
        review, **2-6:** T42–T43, T66–
            T67, T83, T95, T396
word blending, **2-1:** T43, T80, T141,
    T176, T225, T256, T293, T305,
    T338; **2-2:** T43, T141, T178,
    T227, T262, T311; **2-3:** T78,
    T340; **2-4:** T80, T184, T194,
    T232, T233, T266, T350; **2-5:**
    T144, T145, T184, T194, T232,
    T233, T274, T286, T358; **2-6:**
    T42, T43, T82, T94, T145, T229,
    T268, T280, T318, T319, T360,
    T370
word building, **2-1:** T42, T66, T81,
    T140, T160, T177, T224, T242,
    T257, T289, T304, T324, T339;
    2-2: T27, T42, T64, T81, T125,
    T140, T162, T179, T211, T226,
    T248, T263, T295, T310, T334,
    T351; **2-3:** T27, T42, T64, T79,
    T123, T138, T158, T173, T205,
    T220, T244, T259, T306, T326,
    T341; **2-4:** T27, T42, T64, T81,
    T127, T142, T168, T185, T217,
    T232, T250, T267, T301, T316,
    T334, T351; **2-5:** T42, T66, T83,
    T144, T168, T185, T232, T258,
    T275, T309, T324, T342, T359;
    2-6: T27, T42, T66, T83, T129,
    T144, T164, T181, T213, T228,
    T252, T269, T303, T318, T344,
    T361

Description
   See **Writing,** forms, description
Details
   See **Comprehension Skills,** details,
    important; details, note
Diagnostic Check
   See **Monitor Progress**
Diagrams, Use and Interpret
   See **Graphic Aids; Research/Study**
    Skills
Dialogue
   See **Readers' Theater; Writing,**
    dialogue; forms, response to
    literature, story: dialogue
DIBELS, 2-1: T60, T69, T83, T93, T154,
   T163, T179, T189, T236, T245,
   T259, T269, T318, T327, T341,
   T351; **2-2:** T58, T67, T83, T93,
   T156, T165, T181, T191, T242,
   T251, T265, T275, T328, T337,
   T353, T363; **2-3:** T58, T67, T81,
   T91, T152, T161, T175, T185,
   T238, T247, T261, T271, T320,
   T329, T343, T353; **2-4:** T58, T66,
   T82, T94, T162, T170, T186,
   T196, T244, T252, T268, T280,
   T328, T336, T352, T362; **2-5:** T60,
   T68, T84, T96, T162, T170, T186,
   T196, T252, T260, T276, T288,
   T336, T344, T360, T370; **2-6:** T60,
   T68, T84, T96, T158, T166, T182,
   T192, T246, T254, T270, T282,
   T338, T346, T362, T372

Differentiated Instruction
   See also **English-Language**
    Learners; Intervention; Leveled
    Readers; Practice Book
   Advanced Learners, notes for, **2-1:**
    T42, T46, T77, T129, T140, T144,
    T224, T228, T253, T304, T308,
    T315, T335, T375, T392, T412,
    T417; **2-2:** T42, T46, T132, T140,
    T144, T153 T226, T230, T310,
    T314, T319, T404, T415, T424,

T429; **2-3:** T34, T42, T46, T53,
   T129, T130, T138, T142, T220,
   T224, T253, T306, T310, T337,
   T377, T392, T412, T417; **2-4:** T31,
   T42, T46, T131, T142, T146, T152,
   T181, T232, T236, T275, T305,
   T316, T320, T347, T387, T404,
   T424; **2-5:** T31, T42, T53, T79,
   T133, T144, T148, T232, T236,
   T271, T313, T324, T328, T355,
   T412, T432; **2-6:** T31, T42, T46,
   T53, T133, T144, T148, T177,
   T228, T232, T241, T265, T307,
   T318, T322, T328, T397, T414,
   T434
   Advanced-Leveled Readers, **2-1:**
    T100, T196, T276, T358, T432;
    2-2: T100, T198, T282, T370,
    T444; **2-3:** T98, T192, T278,
    T360, T432; **2-4:** T102, T204,
    T288, T370, T444; **2-5:** T104,
    T204, T296, T378, T452; **2-6:**
    T104, T200, T290, T380, T454
   Attention Deficit Hyperactivity
    disorder (ADHD), **2-4:** T52
   Below-Level Learners, notes for, **2-1:**
    T13, T31, T42, T46, T60, T69,
    T81, T83, T140, T144, T157, T163,
    T173, T177, T179, T183, T190,
    T217, T224, T228, T236, T245,
    T251, T257, T259, T263, T293,
    T304, T308, T318, T327, T339,
    T341, T392, T403, T412, T414,
    T417; **2-2:** T13, T31, T34, T42,
    T46, T58, T67, T75, T77, T81, T83,
    T129, T140, T144, T148, T159,
    T165, T169, T173, T175, T192,
    T226, T230, T242, T251, T263,
    T265, T269, T276, T299, T310,
    T314, T318, T337, T341, T345,
    T351, T353, T357, T364, T404,
    T424, T426, T429; **2-3:** T13, T31,
    T42, T46, T56, T58, T67, T75,
    T79, T81, T127, T138, T142, T152,

T155, T161, T169, T173, T175,
   T179, T220, T224, T232, T238,
   T247, T259, T261, T265, T295,
   T298, T306, T310, T320, T329,
   T341, T343, T392, T403, T412,
   T414, T417; **2-4:** T13, T42, T46,
   T52, T58, T61, T66, T77, T81, T82,
   T142, T146, T152, T170, T185,
   T186, T191, T232, T236, T247,
   T252, T267, T268, T305, T316,
   T320, T323, T328, T336, T351,
   T352, T357, T363, T404, T415,
   T424, T426; **2-5:** T13, T42, T46,
   T51, T56, T60, T68, T69, T83,
   T84, T91, T144, T148, T153, T162,
   T170, T185, T186, T197, T232,
   T236, T240, T242, T252, T255,
   T260, T275, T276, T324, T328,
   T334, T336, T359; **2-6:** T13, T42,
   T46, T55, T60, T68, T69, T71, T79,
   T83, T84, T91, T144, T148, T152,
   T166, T181, T182, T187, T228,
   T232, T238, T246, T254, T269,
   T270, T277, T318, T322, T327,
   T330, T338, T346, T347, T357,
   T361, T362, T414, T425, T434,
   T436
   Below-Level Readers, **2-1:** T98, T194,
    T274, T356, T430; **2-2:** T98,
    T196, T280, T368, T442; **2-3:**
    T96, T190, T276, T358, T430;
    2-4: T100, T202, T286, T368,
    T442; **2-5:** T102, T202, T294,
    T376, T450; **2-6:** T102, T198,
    T288, T378, T452
   Challenge Copying Masters, **2-1:** T32,
    T35, T43, T45, T90, T130, T133,
    T141, T143, T186, T214, T217,
    T225, T227, T266, T294, T297,
    T305, T307, T348, T375, T378,
    T393, T395, T403, T413, T425;
    2-2: T32, T35, T43, T45, T90,
    T130, T133, T141, T143, T188,
    T216, T219, T227, T229, T272,

T300, T303, T311, T313, T360;
2-3: T32, T35, T43, T45, T88,
T128, T131, T139, T141, T182,
T210, T213, T221, T223, T268,
T296, T299, T307, T309, T350,
T377, T380, T393, T394, T395,
T413, T425; **2-4:** T32, T35, T43,
T45, T69, T92, T132, T135, T143,
T145, T173, T194, T222, T225,
T233, T235, T255, T278, T306,
T309, T317, T319, T339, T360,
T387, T405, T406, T415, T417,
T419, T425, T437, T438; **2-5:**
T32, T35, T43, T45, T71, T94,
T134, T137, T145, T147, T173,
T194, T222, T225, T233, T235,
T269, T286, T314, T317, T325,
T327, T353, T368, T395, T413,
T414, T423, T425, T427, T433,
T445, T446; **2-6:** T32, T35, T43,
T45, T77, T94, T134, T137, T145,
T147, T175, T190, T218, T221,
T229, T231, T263, T280, T308,
T311, T319, T321, T355, T370,
T397, T415, T416, T425, T427,
T429, T435, T447, T448

Challenge Resource Kit, **2-1:** T5, T19,
T117, T201, T281, T363; **2-2:** T5,
T19, T117, T203, T287, T375; **2-3:**
T5, T19, T115, T197, T283, T365;
2-4: T5, T19, T119, T209, T293,
T375; **2-5:** T5, T19, T121, T209,
T301, T383; **2-6:** T5, T19, T121,
T205, T295, T385

Challenge Teacher Guide, **2-1:** T5;
2-2: T5; **2-3:** T5; **2-4:** T5; **2-5:** T5;
2-6: T5

ELL Copying Masters, **2-1:** T5, T19,
T117, T201, T281, T363; **2-2:** T5,
T19, T117, T203, T287, T375; **2-3:**
T5, T19, T115, T197, T283, T365;
2-4: T5, T19, T119, T209, T293,
T375; **2-5:** T5, T19, T121, T209,

T301, T383; **2-6:** T5, T19, T121,
T205, T295, T385

ELL Extra Support Kit, **2-1:** T5, T19,
T117, T201, T281, T363; **2-2:** T5,
T19, T117, T203, T287, T375; **2-3:**
T5, T19, T115, T197, T283, T365;
2-4: T5, T19, T119, T209, T293,
T375; **2-5:** T5, T19, T121, T209,
T301, T383; **2-6:** T5, T19, T121,
T205, T295, T385

ELL-Level Readers, **2-1:** T101, T197,
T277, T359, T433; **2-2:** T101,
T199, T283, T371, T445; **2-3:**
T99, T193, T279, T361, T433;
2-4: T103, T205, T289, T371,
T445; **2-5:** T105, T205, T297,
T379, T453; **2-6:** T105, T201,
T291, T381, T455

ELL Teacher Guide, **2-1:** T32, T35,
T43, T45, T90, T130, T133, T141,
T143, T186, T214, T217, T225,
T227, T266, T294, T297, T305,
T306, T307, T348, T375, T395,
T403, T413, T425; **2-2:** T32, T35,
T43, T45, T130, T133, T141,
T142, T143, T188, T216, T219,
T227, T228, T229, T272, T300,
T303, T311, T313, T360; **2-3:**
T32, T35, T43, T45, T88, T128,
T131, T139, T182, T210, T213,
T222, T223, T268, T296, T299,
T307, T309, T350, T380, T393,
T394, T395, T403, T413, T425;
2-4: T32, T35, T43, T45, T69,
T92, T132, T135, T143, T145,
T173, T194, T222, T225, T233,
T235, T255, T278, T306, T309,
T317, T319, T339, T360, T387,
T405, T406, T415, T419, T425,
T437, T438; **2-5:** T32, T35, T43,
T45, T71, T94, T134, T137, T145,
T147, T173, T194, T222, T225,
T233, T235, T269, T286, T314,
T317, T325, T327, T353, T368,

T395, T413, T414, T423, T425,
T427, T433, T445, T446; **2-6:**
T32, T35, T43, T45, T77, T94,
T134, T137, T145, T147, T175,
T190, T218, T221, T229, T231,
T263, T280, T308, T311, T319,
T321, T355, T370, T415, T416,
T425, T427, T429, T435, T447,
T448

English-Language Learners, notes
for, **2-1:** T13, T31, T32, T34,
T35, T36, T43, T44, T45, T49,
T52, T56, T62, T63, T68, T75,
T87, T90, T93, T94, T105, T109,
T129, T130, T132, T133, T134,
T141, T142, T143, T147, T154,
T156, T162, T171, T186, T189,
T214, T217, T218, T225, T226,
T227, T232, T239, T244, T266,
T269, T270, T293, T296, T298,
T306, T311, T320, T321, T326,
T333, T345, T351, T352, T375,
T380, T389, T394, T395, T403,
T406, T413, T425; **2-2:** T13, T32,
T35, T36, T43, T44, T45, T49,
T53, T61, T71, T105, T109, T129,
T130, T133, T134, T141, T142,
T143, T147, T150, T164, T181,
T185, T188, T191, T216, T219,
T220, T227, T228, T229, T234,
T235, T250, T257, T259, T272,
T275, T299, T300, T302, T303,
T304, T311, T312, T313, T320,
T328, T330, T331, T336, T339,
T347, T360, T363, T387, T390,
T401, T405, T406, T407, T415,
T418, T425, T437; **2-3:** T13, T31,
T32, T35, T36, T43, T44, T45,
T49, T51, T61, T66, T73, T85,
T88, T91, T92, T103, T107, T127,
T128, T131, T132, T139, T140,
T141, T146, T160, T167, T182,
T185, T186, T210, T212, T213,
T214, T221, T222, T223, T227,

T241, T246, T255, T268, T271, T272, T295, T296, T299, T300, T307, T308, T309, T314, T323, T328, T335, T347, T350, T353, T354, T377, T380, T382, T389, T393, T394, T395, T403, T406, T413, T425; **2-4:** T13, T31, T34, T36, T50, T60, T71, T89, T94, T95, T107, T111, T136, T150, T153, T156, T162, T164, T165, T175, T196, T197, T224, T226, T257, T263, T280, T281, T308, T310, T324, T331, T362, T392, T401, T418; **2-5:** T13, T36, T54, T55, T63, T73, T96, T97, T109, T113, T133, T136, T138, T151, T165, T175, T191, T196, T226, T245, T283, T288, T289, T313, T316, T318, T338, T339, T347, T370, T371, T395, T413, T414, T423, T425, T426, T427, T433, T445, T446; **2-6:** T13, T31, T34, T36, T48, T52, T56, T63, T96, T97, T109, T113, T133, T138, T160, T161, T167, T169, T192, T193, T222, T237, T248, T249, T257, T282, T283, T307, T310, T312, T325, T329, T332, T334, T341, T349, T353, T372, T373, T397, T402, T411, T428

Extra Support Copying Masters, **2-1:** T32, T35, T43, T45, T90, T130, T133, T141, T143, T186, T214, T217, T225, T227, T266, T294, T297, T305, T307, T348, T375, T378, T393, T395, T403, T413, T425; **2-2:** T32, T35, T43, T45, T130, T133, T141, T143, T188, T216, T219, T227, T229, T272, T300, T303, T311, T313, T360, T387, T390, T405, T406, T407, T415, T425, T437; **2-3:** T32, T35, T43, T45, T88, T128, T131, T139, T141, T182, T210, T213, T221,

T223, T268, T296, T299, T307, T309, T350, T377, T380, T393, T394, T395, T413, T425; **2-4:** T32, T35, T43, T45, T69, T92, T132, T135, T143, T145, T173, T194, T222, T225, T233, T235, T255, T278, T306, T309, T317, T319, T339, T360, T387, T405, T406, T415, T417, T419, T425, T437, T438; **2-5:** T32, T35, T43, T45, T71, T94, T134, T137, T145, T147, T173, T194, T222, T225, T233, T235, T269, T286, T314, T317, T325, T327, T353, T368, T395, T413, T414, T423, T425, T427, T433, T445, T446; **2-6:** T32, T35, T43, T45, T77, T94, T134, T137, T145, T147, T175, T190, T218, T221, T229, T231, T263, T280, T308, T311, T319, T321, T355, T370, T397, T415, T416, T425, T427, T429, T435, T447, T448

On-Level Learners, notes for, **2-1:** T46, T144, T228, T308; **2-2:** T46, T144, T230, T314; **2-3:** T46, T142, T224, T230, T310; **2-4:** T46, T146, T236, T320; **2-5:** T46, T148, T236, T328; **2-6:** T46, T148, T232, T322

On-Level Readers, **2-1:** T99, T195, T275, T357, T431; **2-2:** T99, T197, T281, T369, T443; **2-3:** T97, T191, T277, T359, T431; **2-4:** T101, T203, T287, T369, T443; **2-5:** T103, T203, T295, T377, T451; **2-6:** T103, T199, T289, T379, T453

Options for Reading, **2-1:** T46, T144, T228, T308; **2-2:** T46, T144, T230, T314; **2-3:** T46, T142, T224, T310; **2-4:** T46, T146, T236, T320; **2-5:** T46, T148,

T236, T328; **2-6:** T46, T148, T232, T322

Scaffold Instruction, **2-2:** T147, T148, T150, T153

Scaffolded Language Development, **2-1:** T101, T197, T277, T359, T433; **2-2:** T101, T199, T283, T371, T445; **2-3:** T99, T193, T279, T361, T433; **2-4:** T103, T205, T289, T371, T445; **2-5:** T105, T205, T297, T379, T453; **2-6:** T105, T201, T291, T381, T455

Small-Group Instruction, **2-1:** S1–S49; **2-2:** S1–S49; **2-3:** S1–S49; **2-4:** S1–S49; **2-5:** S1–S49; **2-6:** S1–S49

Special Needs, **2-4:** T155; **2-5:** T332

Total Physical Response, **2-1:** T52, T321; **2-2:** T245; **2-4:** T94; **2-6:** T56, T282, T332

Digital Classroom
  See **Technology,** technology resources

Digraphs
  See **Decoding/Word Work,** digraphs

Diphthongs
  See **Decoding/Word Work,** vowel diphthongs

Draft
  See **Reading-Writing Connection,** process writing, draft; **Writing,** process writing, draft

Drama
  See **Genre,** play; **Readers' Theater**

Draw Conclusions
  See **Comprehension Skills,** conclusions, draw

eBook
  See **Technology,** technology resources

Echo-Read
  See **Fluency,** echo-read

Edit

See **Writing,** process writing, edit

Editor's Marks, 2-1: T87, T110, T183, T262, T273, T345, T399; **2-2:** T97, T110, T185, T195, T269, T357; **2-3:** T85, T108, T178, T179, T264, T265, T347, T399; **2-4:** T88, T89, T99, T112, T191, T201, T275, T356, T357; **2-5:** T91, T114, T191, T283, T365; **2-6:** T91, T114, T186, T187, T197, T276, T277, T366, T367, T421

E-mail

See **Writing,** forms, e-mail

End-of-Selection Test

See **Assessment,** Weekly Lesson Test

English-Language Development

See **Differentiated Instruction,** English-Language Learners, notes for; **English-Language Learners,** ELL Notes

English-Language Learners

See also **Lesson Planner,** 5-Day Small-Group Planner

ELL Copying Masters, **2-1:** T5, T19, T117, T201, T281, T363; **2-2:** T5, T19, T117, T203, T287, T375; **2-3:** T5, T19, T115, T197, T283, T365; **2-4:** T5, T19, T119, T209, T293, T375; **2-5:** T5, T19, T121, T209, T301, T383; **2-6:** T5, T19, T121, T205, T295, T385

ELL Extra Support Kit, **2-1:** T5, T19, T117, T201, T281, T363; **2-2:** T5, T19, T117, T203, T287, T375; **2-3:** T5, T19, T115, T197, T283, T365; **2-4:** T5, T19, T119, T209, T293, T375; **2-5:** T5, T19, T121, T209, T301, T383; **2-6:** T5, T19, T121, T205, T295, T385

ELL-Level Readers, **2-1:** T101, T197, T277, T359, T433; **2-2:** T101, T199, T283, T371, T445; **2-3:** T99, T193, T279, T361, T433;

2-4: T103, T205, T289, T371, T445; **2-5:** T105, T205, T297, T379, T453; **2-6:** T105, T201, T291, T381, T455

ELL Notes, **2-1:** T13, T31, T32, T34, T35, T36, T43, T44, T45, T49, T52, T56, T62, T63, T68, T75, T87, T90, T93, T94, T105, T109, T129, T130, T132, T133, T134, T141, T142, T143, T147, T154, T156, T162, T171, T186, T189, T214, T217, T218, T225, T226, T227, T232, T239, T244, T266, T269, T270, T293, T296, T298, T306, T311, T320, T321, T326, T333, T345, T351, T352, T375, T380, T389, T394, T395, T403, T406, T413, T425; **2-2:** T13, T32, T35, T36, T43, T44, T45, T49, T53, T61, T71, T105, T109, T129, T130, T133, T134, T141, T142, T143, T147, T150, T164, T181, T185, T188, T191, T216, T219, T220, T227, T228, T229, T234, T235, T250, T257, T259, T272, T275, T299, T300, T302, T303, T304, T311, T312, T313, T320, T328, T330, T331, T336, T339, T347, T360, T363, T387, T390, T401, T405, T406, T407, T415, T418, T425, T437; **2-3:** T13, T31, T32, T35, T36, T43, T44, T45, T49, T51, T61, T66, T73, T85, T88, T91, T92, T103, T107, T127, T128, T131, T132, T139, T140, T141, T146, T160, T167, T182, T185, T186, T210, T212, T213, T214, T221, T222, T223, T227, T241, T246, T255, T268, T271, T272, T295, T296, T299, T300, T307, T308, T309, T314, T323, T328, T335, T347, T350, T353, T354, T377, T380, T382, T389, T393, T394, T395, T403, T406,

T413, T425; **2-4:** T31, T34, T36, T50, T60, T71, T89, T94, T95, T107, T111, T136, T150, T153, T156, T162, T164, T165, T175, T196, T197, T224, T226, T257, T263, T280, T281, T308, T310, T324, T331, T362, T392, T401, T418; **2-5:** T13, T36, T54, T55, T63, T73, T96, T97, T109, T113, T133, T136, T138, T151, T165, T175, T191, T196, T226, T245, T283, T288, T289, T313, T316, T318, T338, T339, T347, T370, T371, T395, T413, T414, T423, T425, T426, T427, T433, T445, T446; **2-6:** T13, T31, T34, T36, T48, T52, T56, T63, T96, T97, T109, T113, T133, T138, T160, T167, T169, T192, T193, T222, T237, T248, T249, T257, T282, T283, T307, T310, T312, T325, T329, T332, T334, T341, T349, T353, T372, T373, T397, T402, T411, T428

ELL Student Handbook, **2-1:** T22, T120, T204, T284, T366; **2-2:** T22, T120, T206, T290, T378; **2-3:** T22, T118, T200, T286, T368; **2-4:** T22, T122, T212, T296, T378; **2-5:** T22, T124, T212, T304, T386; **2-6:** T22, T124, T208, T298, T388

ELL Teacher Guide, **2-1:** T32, T35, T43, T45, T90, T130, T133, T141, T143, T186, T214, T217, T225, T227, T266, T294, T297, T305, T306, T307, T348, T375, T395, T403, T413, T425; **2-2:** T32, T35, T43, T45, T130, T133, T141, T142, T143, T188, T216, T219, T227, T228, T229, T272, T300, T303, T311, T313, T360; **2-3:** T32, T35, T43, T45, T88, T128, T131, T139, T182, T210, T213, T222, T223, T268, T296, T299,

T307, T309, T350, T380, T393,
T394, T395, T403, T413, T425;
2-4: T32, T35, T43, T45, T69,
T92, T132, T135, T143, T145,
T173, T194, T222, T225, T233,
T235, T255, T278, T306, T309,
T317, T319, T339, T360, T387,
T405, T406, T415, T419, T425,
T437, T438; **2-5:** T32, T35, T43,
T45, T71, T94, T134, T137, T145,
T147, T173, T194, T222, T225,
T233, T235, T269, T286, T314,
T317, T325, T327, T353, T368,
T395, T413, T414, T423, T425,
T427, T433, T445, T446; **2-6:**
T32, T35, T43, T45, T77, T94,
T134, T137, T145, T147, T175,
T190, T218, T221, T229, T231,
T263, T280, T308, T311, T319,
T321, T355, T370, T415, T416,
T425, T427, T429, T435, T447,
T448

Enrichment
  See **Differentiated Instruction,**
  Advanced Learners, notes for

ePlanner
  See **Technology,** technology resources,
  ePlanner

Etymologies
  See **Vocabulary**

Evaluate Writing
  See **Reading-Writing Connection,**
  writing, evaluate/publish; **Writing,**
  process writing, evaluate

Everyday Print Materials
  See **Genre,** functional text

Exclamatory Sentences
  See **Grammar,** commands and
  exclamations

Expository Texts
  See **Genre,** nonfiction

Expository Writing
  See **Writing,** forms, paragraph that
  explains

Expression
  See **Fluency,** expression

Extra Support Copying Masters
  See **Differentiated Instruction,** Extra
  Support Copying Masters

Fable
  See **Genre,** fable

Fact and Opinion
  See **Comprehension Skills,** fact and
  opinion

Family Involvement
  See **Teacher Resource Book,** School-
  Home Connections

Fantasy
  See **Genre,** fantasy

Fantasy/Realistic Text
  See **Comprehension Skills,** fantasy/
  realistic text

Fiction
  See **Focus Skills,** fiction and
  nonfiction; **Genre,** fiction

Fiction and Nonfiction
  See **Focus Skills,** fiction and
  nonfiction

Fine Art
  See **Cross-Curricular Connections,**
  art; fine art

Flexible Grouping
  See **Lesson Planner,** 5-Day Small-
  Group Planner

Fluency
  See also **Assessment,** Oral Reading
  Fluency Assessment; **Literacy**
  Centers, Listening and Speaking
  Center; **Monitor Progress,** fluency
  accuracy, **2-1:** T29, T36, T60, T69,
  T83, T93, T98, T99, T100,
  T101, T127, T134, T154, T163,
  T179, T189, T194, T195, T196,
  T197, T298, T379, T380, T383,

T386, T396, T406, T418, T427;
2-3: T381; **2-4:** T219, T226,
T244, T252, T259, T268, T280,
T286, T287, T288, T289, T303,
T310, T328, T336, T343, T352,
T362, T368, T369, T370, T371,
T394, T396, T408, T418, T430,
T439; **2-5:** T96, T186, T370

Additional Related Reading, **2-1:**
T69, T163, T327, R9; **2-2:**
T67, T165, T251, T337, R9;
2-3: T67, T161, T247, T329,
R9; **2-4:** T66, T170, T252,
T336, R9; **2-5:** T68, T170,
T260, T344, R9; **2-6:** T68,
T166, T254, T346, R9

choral-read, **2-1:** T98, T101,
T197, T274, T277, T294,
T340, T347, T359; **2-2:** T181,
T242, T392; **2-3:** T64, T158,
T261; **2-4:** T82, T162, T256;
2-5: T252, T276, T336; **2-6:**
T84, T169, T182, T362

echo-read, **2-1:** T60, T83, T236,
T341; **2-2:** T58, T83, T156,
T265, T328; **2-3:** T142, T152,
T261, T320; **2-4:** T58, T82,
T186, T244, T268, T280,
T328, T352; **2-5:** T60, T84,
T162, T360; **2-6:** T60, T84,
T158, T182, T232, T246,
T256, T270, T279, T338, T362

expression, **2-2:** T242, T251,
T255, T265, T275, T304,
T328, T337, T353, T363;
2-3: T71, T191, T277, T360,
T381, T396, T418, T430; **2-4:**
T73, T391, T392; **2-5:** T29,
T36, T60, T68, T75, T84,
T96, T131, T138, T162, T170,
T177, T186, T403, T406,
T416, T426, T438, T447

intonation, **2-2:** T36, T58, T67,
T83, T134, T156, T165, T181,

T191, T394, T397, T398, T408, T418, T430, T439; **2-3:** T71, T191, T204, T277, T360, T381; **2-4:** T29, T36, T58, T66, T82, T94, T100, T101, T102, T103, T129, T136, T162, T170, T177, T186, T196, T202, T203, T204, T205, T391, T392, T395, T397, T408, T418, T430, T439; **2-5:** T153

pace, **2-1:** T211, T218, T236, T245, T259, T269, T274, T275, T276, T277, T291, T318, T327, T331, T341, T351, T356, T357, T358, T359, T380, T382, T384, T396, T406, T418, T427; **2-3:** T381; **2-5:** T311, T318, T336, T344, T349, T360, T370, T402, T404, T416, T426, T438, T447

partner-read, **2-1:** T73, T100, T154, T169, T179, T196, T259, T275, T276, T318, T327, T331, T356, T357, T358; **2-2:** T73, T171, T343, T353; **2-3:** T238, T247, T251, T261, T333; **2-4:** T66, T73, T101, T102, T103, T170, T177, T202, T203, T204, T205, T252, T259, T286, T287, T289, T336, T343, T368, T369, T370, T371; **2-5:** T68, T75, T170, T260, T344, T349; **2-6:** T68, T102, T104, T105, T166, T171, T198, T199, T201, T254, T259, T288, T289, T290, T291, T346, T351, T381, T452, T453, T454, T455

phrasing, **2-3:** T207, T214, T238, T247, T251, T261, T271, T276, T279, T293, T300, T320, T329, T343, T353,

T358, T359, T361, T382, T386, T396, T406, T418, T427, T430, T432, T433; **2-5:** T288; **2-6:** T215, T246, T254, T259, T270, T282, T288, T290, T291, T312, T338, T346, T362, T372, T378, T379, T381, T402, T404, T406, T407, T418, T428, T440, T449, T452, T453, T454, T455

prosody, **2-2:** T36, T58, T67, T83, T134, T156, T165, T181, T191, T394, T397, T398, T408, T418, T430, T439; **2-3:** T204, T381; **2-4:** T29, T36, T58, T66, T82, T94, T100, T101, T102, T103, T129, T136, T162, T170, T177, T186, T196, T202, T203, T204, T205, T391, T392, T395, T397, T408, T418, T430, T439; **2-5:** T153

punctuation, **2-3:** T29, T36, T58, T81, T91, T97, T98, T99, T122, T125, T132, T152, T161, T175, T185, T190, T192, T193, T372, T383, T385, T396, T406, T418, T427, T430, T432, T433; **2-4:** T66, T82, T196; **2-5:** T84; **2-6:** T29, T36, T60, T68, T73, T84, T96, T102, T103, T104, T105, T131, T138, T158, T166, T171, T182, T192, T198, T199, T201, T222, T270, T282, T305, T312, T346, T351, T362, T402, T405, T418, T428, T440, T449, T452, T453, T454, T455

Readers' Theater, **2-1:** T93, T99, T189, T269, T351, T379–T386, T396, T406, T418, T427; **2-2:** T93, T191, T275, T363, T391–T398, T408, T418, T430,

T439; **2-3:** T91, T185, T271, T278, T353, T381–T386, T396, T406, T418, T427; **2-4:** T94, T196, T280, T288, T362, T391–T398, T408; **2-5:** T96, T177, T196, T288, T370, T399–T406, T416, T426, T438, T447; **2-6:** T73, T96, T103, T192, T282, T372, T378, T379, T380, T401–T408, T418, T428, T440, T449

reading rate, **2-1:** T211, T218, T236, T245, T259, T269, T274, T275, T276, T277, T291, T318, T327, T331, T341, T351, T356, T357, T358, T359, T380, T382, T384, T396, T406, T418, T427; **2-3:** T381; **2-5:** T260, T311, T318, T336, T344, T349, T360, T370, T402, T404, T416, T426, T438, T447

repeated reading, **2-1:** T98, T99, T100, T101, T194, T195, T196, T197, T274, T275, T276, T277, T356, T357, T358, T359, T418; **2-2:** T98, T99, T100, T101, T196, T197, T198, T199, T280, T281, T282, T283, T368, T369, T370, T371, T430, T442, T443, T444, T445; **2-3:** T96, T97, T98, T99, T190, T191, T192, T193, T276, T277, T278, T279, T358, T359, T360, T361; **2-4:** T100, T101, T102, T103, T162, T202, T203, T204, T205, T286, T287, T288, T289, T368, T369, T370, T371, T442, T443, T444, T445; **2-5:** T102, T103, T104, T105, T202, T203, T204, T205, T294, T295, T296, T297, T376,

T377, T378, T379, T450,
T451, T452, T453; **2-6:** T102,
T103, T104, T105, T198,
T199, T200, T201, T288,
T289, T290, T291, T378,
T379, T380, T381, T452,
T453, T454, T455
Support Materials, **2-1:** T93, T189,
T269, T351, T396, T406,
T418; **2-2:** T93, T191, T275,
T363, T408, T418, T430; **2-3:**
T91, T185, T271, T353; **2-4:**
T94, T196, T280, T362, T408,
T418, T430; **2-5:** T96, T196,
T288, T370, T416, T426,
T438; **2-6:** T96, T192, T282,
T372, T418, T428, T440
timed reading, **2-1:** T93, T189,
T249, T269, T351; **2-2:** T93,
T191, T275, T363; **2-3:** T91,
T165, T185, T271, T353; **2-4:**
T94, T196, T280, T362; **2-5:**
T96, T196, T265, T288; **2-6:**
T96, T192, T282, T372
Fluency Builders, 2-1: T93, T189, T269,
T351, T396, T406, T418; **2-2:** T93,
T191, T275, T363, T408, T418,
T430; **2-3:** T91, T185, T271, T353,
T427; **2-4:** T94, T196, T280, T362,
T408, T418, T430; **2-5:** T96, T196,
T288, T370, T416, T426, T438;
2-6: T96, T192, T282, T372, T418,
T428, T440
Focus
See **Writing,** traits, ideas/focus
Focus Skills
See also **Leveled Reader Teacher**
Guide, Comprehension; **Monitor**
Progress; Speaking and
Listening, comprehension/focus
skills
author's purpose, **2-1:** T53, T98,
T149, T312, T314, T317; **2-2:**
T54, T56, T154, T238; **2-3:**

T36, T48, T51, T54, T55, T56,
T57, T58, T96, T97, T98,
T99, T122, T125, T132, T145,
T149, T151, T152, T190,
T191, T192, T193, T234,
T360, T383, T385, T416,
T430, T431, T432, T433; **2-4:**
T56, T155, T159, T160, T241,
T286, T327; **2-5:** T58, T159,
T248, T278, T333, T334,
T335; **2-6:** T54, T155, T157,
T199, T235, T242, T244, T336
introduce, **2-3:** T34–T35
maintain, **2-5:** T278
review, **2-3:** T68, T82, T92,
T130–T131, T162, T176,
T186, T379, T394
cause and effect, **2-1:** T99, T100,
T150, T195, T275, T276, T314,
T316, T358, T384, T386;
2-2: T54, T149, T151, T233,
T238, T318, T321, T341,
T397; **2-3:** T57, T148, T149,
T190, T276, T277, T360; **2-4:**
T48, T54, T102, T148, T242,
T286, T288, T369; **2-5:** T50,
T55, T152, T239, T241, T243,
T244, T249, T335; **2-6:** T29,
T36, T46, T50, T51, T52, T55,
T57, T58, T60, T102, T103,
T104, T105, T138, T148,
T151, T154, T156, T157,
T158, T169, T198, T199,
T200, T201, T236, T239,
T242, T289, T325, T326,
T329, T330, T331, T335,
T380, T404, T406, T408,
T438, T452, T453, T454, T455
introduce, **2-6:** T34–T35
review, **2-6:** T69, T85, T97,
T136–T137, T167, T183,
T193
characters, **2-1:** T36, T49, T50,
T52, T54, T56, T58, T60, T98,

T99, T100, T101, T134, T146,
T147, T148, T149, T150, T152,
T194, T195, T196, T197, T232,
T381, T384; **2-2:** T55, T56,
T98, T99, T100, T146, T196,
T235, T280, T281, T282, T316,
T368, T369, T370; **2-4:** T204,
T368, T369; **2-5:** T49; **2-6:**
T199, T380, T404
introduce, **2-1:** T34–T35
maintain, **2-4:** T84
review, **2-1:** T70, T84, T94,
T132–T133, T164, T180,
T190, T377, T394
fiction and nonfiction, **2-2:** T326;
2-3: T214, T227, T236, T238,
T248, T276, T277, T278,
T279, T298, T300, T314,
T319, T320, T331, T358,
T359, T360, T361, T384,
T416, T430, T431, T432, T433
introduce, **2-3:** T212–T213
maintain, **2-4:** T271
review, **2-3:** T262, T272, T330,
T344, T354, T404, T425
graphic aids, **2-5:** T226, T236,
T239, T240, T250, T251,
T252, T294, T295, T296,
T297, T318, T330, T334,
T335, T336, T376, T377,
T378, T379, T401, T403,
T405, T436; **2-6:** T198, T235,
T236, T238, T239, T241, T245
chart, **2-5:** T224–T225, T226,
T261, T262, T277, T289,
T316, T345, T361, T371
diagram, **2-5:** T219, T224–
T225, T226, T239, T240,
T250, T252, T261, T262,
T265, T277, T289, T316,
T345, T361, T371; **2-6:**
T235, T236, T239, T241,
T242, T257, T272

graph, **2-5:** T224, T289, T316,
 T345, T361, T371

introduce, **2-5:** T224–T225

maintain, **2-6:** T272

map, **2-5:** T224–T225, T226,
 T261, T262, T263, T277,
 T289, T310, T316, T318,
 T345, T361, T371; **2-6:**
 T70

review, **2-5:** T261, T277, T289,
 T316–T317, T345, T361,
 T371

time line, **2-5:** T224–T225,
 T261, T277, T289, T334,
 T345, T370, T371

locate information, **2-1:** T12; **2-4:**
 T219, T226, T239, T241, T243,
 T244, T286, T287, T288, T289,
 T310, T324, T327, T328, T340,
 T368, T369, T370, T371, T394,
 T396, T428

introduce, **2-4:** T224–T225

maintain, **2-5:** T279

review, **2-4:** T253, T269, T281,
 T308–T309, T337, T353, T363

See also **Research/Study Skills**

main idea and details, **2-1:** T233,
 T234, T247, T274, T275, T276,
 T277, T316, T329, T356, T357,
 T358, T359, T382, T383, T385,
 T386, T416; **2-2:** T317; **2-3:** T190,
 T191, T192, T293, T358, T359,
 T360; **2-4:** T226, T236, T398; **2-5:**
 T229, T236, T239, T244, T249,
 T252, T255, T271, T283, T293,
 T331, T332, T402, T404; **2-6:**
 T403, T405, T408

introduce, **2-1:** T216–T217

maintain, **2-4:** T270

review, **2-1:** T246, T260, T270,
 T296–T297, T328, T342,
 T352, T404, T425

make inferences, **2-1:** T48, T51, T52,
 T53, T58, T146, T152, T230, T232,

T233, T274, T311, T315, T381,
 T383, T386; **2-2:** T53, T147, T148,
 T150, T153, T316, T317, T323,
 T369; **2-3:** T49, T193, T226, T228,
 T230, T232, T233, T234, T235,
 T279, T312, T316, T317, T361,
 T383; **2-4:** T48, T151, T157, T323,
 T326, T327, T397; **2-5:** T49, T51,
 T52, T57, T58, T158, T161, T242,
 T247, T251, T330, T331, T333,
 T405; **2-6:** T49, T52, T53, T54,
 T57, T58, T155, T222, T236, T237,
 T238, T241, T245, T246, T288,
 T289, T290, T291, T312, T325,
 T326, T327, T331, T336, T338,
 T348, T378, T379, T380, T381,
 T403, T405, T406, T407, T438,
 T452, T453, T454, T455

introduce, **2-6:** T220–T221

review, **2-6:** T255, T271, T283,
 T310–T311, T347, T363, T373

make predictions, **2-1:** T50, T54, T57,
 T100, T101, T148, T194, T195,
 T196, T229, T232, T274, T275,
 T276, T309; **2-2:** T49, T51, T52,
 T53, T56, T98, T99, T100, T101,
 T146, T148, T150, T151, T152,
 T154, T169, T196, T197, T198,
 T199, T234, T281, T318, T319,
 T323, T368, T369, T393, T395,
 T397, T398, T428, T442, T443,
 T444, T445; **2-3:** T143, T225,
 T229, T230, T233, T276, T277,
 T278, T385; **2-4:** T47, T48, T52,
 T147, T152, T155, T159, T237,
 T321, T322, T393; **2-5:** T47, T53,
 T55, T56, T58, T149, T154, T155,
 T156, T237, T241, T329; **2-6:**
 T47, T48, T51, T54, T55, T57,
 T149, T152, T154, T199, T200,
 T233, T240, T323, T329, T330,
 T333, T334, T335

introduce, **2-2:** T34–T35

maintain, **2-5:** T86

review, **2-2:** T68–T69, T84, T94,
 T132–T133, T166–T167,
 T182, T192

plot, **2-2:** T280, T281, T282, T368,
 T369, T370, T371, T428, T442,
 T443, T444, T445; **2-5:** T36, T49,
 T53, T57, T59, T60, T75, T102,
 T103, T104, T105, T138, T148,
 T151, T153, T156, T159, T161,
 T162, T202, T203, T204, T205,
 T436

introduce, **2-2:** T218–T219

maintain, **2-4:** T85; **2-6:** T86

review, **2-2:** T252, T266, T276,
 T302–T303, T338–T339,
 T354, T364,T416, T437; **2-5:**
 T34–T35, T69, T85, T97,
 T136–T137, T171, T187, T197

setting, **2-4:** T29, T36, T49, T51, T55,
 T56, T57, T58, T73, T100, T101,
 T102, T103, T129, T136, T146,
 T148, T154, T159, T161, T174,
 T177, T202, T203, T204, T205,
 T393, T395; **2-5:** T51; **2-6:** T102,
 T104, T150

introduce, **2-4:** T34–T35

maintain, **2-5:** T87

review, **2-4:** T67, T83, T95, T134–
 T135, T171, T187, T197

Focus Strategies

answer questions, **2-1:** T228, T230,
 T233, T308, T310, T312, T416;
 2-4: T236, T238, T242, T320, T322

ask questions, **2-3:** T46, T48, T54,
 T142, T145, T150, T229, T414,
 T416; **2-4:** T326; **2-6:** T49, T326

monitor comprehension: reread, **2-3:**
 T224, T226, T233, T235, T310,
 T313, T315; **2-5:** T52; **2-6:** T232,
 T235, T240, T243

overview, **2-1:** xvii; **2-2:** xvii; **2-3:**
 xvii; **2-4:** xvii; **2-5:** xvii; **2-6:** xvii

read ahead, **2-4:** T46, T49, T54, T146,
 T148, T154, T428; **2-5:** T154

reread, **2-3:** T416; **2-5:** T52; **2-6:** T232, T235, T240, T243, T322, T324, T331, T438

summarize, **2-5:** T236, T239, T244, T328, T330; **2-6:** T153

use graphic organizers, **2-1:** T46, T50, T54, T57, T144, T146, T151; **2-3:** T50; **2-4:** T51, T158; **2-5:** T241; **2-6:** T46, T50, T57, T148, T151, T154, T236, T238

use multiple strategies, **2-1:** T51; **2-2:** T51, T152, T233, T321; **2-3:** T147, T229, T316; **2-4:** T158, T240, T326; **2-5:** T52, T152, T154, T241; **2-6:** T49, T153, T236, T326

use prior knowledge, **2-2:** T46, T48, T50, T144, T146, T151; **2-4:** T240; **2-5:** T152

use story structure, **2-4:** T158; **2-5:** T46, T49, T50, T57, T148, T150, T156, T160, T436

Folktales
   See **Genre,** folktale
Following Directions
   See **Comprehension Skills,** follow directions; **Writing,** forms, directions
Formal Assessment
   See **Assessment**
Forms of Text
   See **Genre**
Friendly Letter
   See **Writing,** forms
Functional Text
   See **Genre,** functional text

Generalize
   See **Comprehension Skills,** generalize
Generating Ideas
   See **Writing,** traits, ideas

Generating Questions
   See **Focus Strategies,** ask questions
Genre
   See also **Comprehension Skills,** genre; **Writing,** forms
autobiography, **2-2:** T46
biography, **2-4:** T320; **2-6:** T148, T149, T157
expository nonfiction, **2-4:** T310
fable, **2-2:** T70; **2-5:** T334–T436
fantasy, **2-2:** T220; **2-4:** T28; **2-5:** T138, T148, T151, T154
fiction, **2-1:** T46, T70, T134, T144, T218; **2-2:** T314, T426–T428; **2-3:** T300, T430, T431, T432, T433; **2-4:** T36, T46, T47, T136, T146; **2-6:** T36, T46, T138, T222
folktale, **2-2:** T70, T304; **2-6:** T322, T323
   See also **Writing,** forms
functional text
   recipe, **2-6:** T87
interview, **2-4:** T70–T71
magazine article, **2-1:** T329; **2-4:** T340; **2-5:** T346; **2-6:** T348
mystery, **2-3:** T382, T396; **2-6:** T312
mystery play, **2-3:** T382–T386, T392
narrative
   See **Writing,** forms, personal narrative
news script, **2-1:** T380, T396
nonfiction, **2-1:** T298, T308; **2-3:** T99, T132, T142, T163, T190, T191, T192, T310, T358, T359, T360, T361, T414–T415; **2-4:** T226, T236, T310; **2-5:** T72, T226, T236, T262, T278, T318, T328; **2-6:** T70, T215, T232
nonfiction script, **2-2:** T392–T398, T408; **2-6:** T402–T406, T418
personal narrative, **2-2:** T36
photo essay, **2-6:** T168–T169

play, **2-1:** T379–T386; **2-2:** T391–T398; **2-3:** T381–T386; **2-4:** T393–T398; **2-5:** T401–T406; **2-6:** T403–T408
poetry, **2-1:** T14, T41, T65, T79, T89, T139, T159, T175, T185, T223, T241, T255, T265, T303, T323; **2-2:** T14, T41, T63, T79, T89, T139, T161, T177, T187, T225, T247, T253, T261, T271, T309, T333, T349, T359; **2-3:** T14, T69, T249; **2-4:** T14, T41, T63, T79, T91, T174, T231, T249, T256, T265, T277; **2-5:** T14, T143, T167, T174, T183, T193, T231, T257, T273, T285; **2-6:** T14, T41, T65, T81, T93, T227, T256, T317, T343, T359, T369
pourquoi tale, **2-2:** 230
realistic fiction, **2-1:** T228; **2-2:** T134, T144; **2-3:** T36, T46, T96, T97, T98, T193, T224, T276, T277, T278, T279; **2-4:** T36, T46, T47, T146; **2-5:** T36, T46; **2-6:** T222, T312
textbook, social studies, **2-4:** T426–T428
time line, **2-3:** T163; **2-5:** T334
Web sites, **2-3:** T331
Genre Study
   See **Genre**
Gifted and Talented Students
   See **Differentiated Instruction,** Advanced Learners, notes for; **Small-Group Instruction**
Glossary
   See **Student Edition,** Glossary
Grammar
   See also **Writing,** Grammar-Writing Connection
abbreviations, **2-3:** T11; **2-5:** T101
   introduce, **2-3:** T38
   review, **2-3:** T60, T74, T84, T94, T388, T428
   See also **Decoding/Word Work,** abbreviations

action words, **2-3:** T51; **2-4:** T282; **2-5:** T198, T200, T229, T245, T271, T283, T290, T293; **2-6:** T81

adjectives, **2-4:** T86, T89, T99, T282; **2-5:** T198, T290

  introduce, **2-4:** T38

  review, **2-4:** T60, T76, T88, T98, T400, T440

adjectives for senses, **2-4:** T139, T165, T174, T181, T191, T259

  introduce, **2-4:** T138

  review, **2-4:** T164, T180, T190, T200, T410, T440

commands and exclamations, **2-4:** T77, T89

  introduce, **2-1:** T220

  review, **2-1:** T238, T252, T262, T272, T408

contractions, **2-1:** T53

  introduce, **2-6:** T314

  review, **2-6:** T340, T356, T366, T376, T442, T450

  See also **Decoding/Word Work,** contractions

daily proofreading, **2-1:** T38, T62, T76, T86, T96, T136, T156, T172, T182, T192, T220, T238, T252, T262, T272, T300, T320, T334, T344, T354, T388, T398, T408, T420, T428; **2-2:** T38, T60, T76, T86, T96, T136, T158, T174, T184, T194, T222, T244, T258, T268, T278, T306, T330, T346, T356, T366, T400, T410, T420, T432, T440; **2-3:** T38, T60, T74, T84, T94, T134, T154, T168, T178, T188, T216, T240, T254, T264, T274, T302, T322, T336, T346, T356, T388, T398, T408, T420, T428; **2-4:** T38, T60, T76, T88, T98, T138, T164, T180, T190, T200, T228, T246, T262, T274, T284, T312, T330, T346, T356, T366, T400, T410, T420,

T432, T440; **2-5:** T38, T62, T78, T90, T100, T140, T164, T180, T190, T200, T228, T254, T270, T282, T292, T320, T338, T354, T364, T374, T408, T418, T428, T440, T448; **2-6:** T38, T62, T78, T90, T100, T140, T160, T176, T186, T196, T224, T248, T264, T276, T286, T314, T340, T356, T366, T376, T410, T420, T430, T442, T450

forms of *be*

  introduce, **2-5:** T320

  review, **2-5:** T338, T354, T364, T374, T440, T448

helping verbs, **2-6:** T265, T277, T287

  introduce, **2-6:** T224

  review, **2-6:** T248, T264, T276, T286, T430, T450

irregular verbs, **2-6:** T91, T187, T197

  introduce, **2-6:** T38

  review, **2-6:** T62, T78, T90, T100, T140, T160, T176, T186, T196, T410, T420, T450

nouns

  introduce, **2-2:** T38

  review, **2-2:** T60, T76, T86, T96, T400, T440

number words

  introduce, **2-4:** T228

  review, **2-4:** T246, T262, T274, T284, T420, T440

parts of a sentence

  introduce, **2-1:** T300

  review, **2-1:** T320, T334, T344, T354, T420, T428

past-tense verbs, **2-5:** T229, T271

  introduce, **2-5:** T228

  review, **2-5:** T254, T270, T282, T292, T428, T448

plural possessive nouns

  introduce, **2-3:** T216

  review, **2-3:** T240, T254, T264, T274, T408, T428

present-tense action verbs, **2-5:** T91, T101, T198

  introduce, **2-5:** T38

  review, **2-5:** T62, T78, T90, T100, T408, T448

pronouns

  introduce, **2-3:** T302

  review, **2-3:** T322, T336, T346, T356, T420, T428

proper nouns, **2-5:** T101

  introduce, **2-2:** T222

  review, **2-2:** T244, T258, T268, T278, T306, T330, T346, T356, T366, T420, T432, T440

sentences

  introduce, **2-1:** T38

  review, **2-1:** T62, T76, T86, T96, T388, T428

singular and plural nouns, **2-5:** T242

  introduce, **2-2:** T136

  review, **2-2:** T158, T174, T184, T194, T410, T440

singular possessive nouns, **2-3:** T254

  introduce, **2-3:** T134

  review, **2-3:** T154, T168, T178, T188, T398, T428

statements and questions

  introduce, **2-1:** T136

  review, **2-1:** T156, T172, T182, T192, T398, T428

subject-verb agreement, **2-5:** T191

  introduce, **2-5:** T140

  review, **2-5:** T164, T180, T190, T200, T418, T448

words that compare

  introduce, **2-4:** T312

  review, **2-4:** T330, T346, T356, T366, T432, T440

Grammar Glossary

  See **Technology,** technology resources, Grammar Glossary

Grammar Practice Book, 2-1: T62, T76, T86, T156, T172, T182, T238, T252, T262, T320, T334, T344,

T398, T420; **2-2:** T60, T76, T86,
T158, T174, T184, T244, T258,
T268, T330, T346, T356; **2-3:**
T60, T74, T84, T154, T168, T178,
T188, T240, T254, T264, T322,
T336, T346, T356, T398, T420;
2-4: T60, T76, T88, T164, T180,
T190, T246, T262, T274, T330,
T346, T356; **2-5:** T62, T78, T90,
T164, T180, T190, T254, T270,
T282, T338, T354, T364; **2-6:**
T62, T78, T90, T160, T176, T186,
T248, T264, T276, T340, T356,
T366, T420

Grammar-Writing Connection
See **Writing,** Grammar-Writing
Connection

Graphic Organizers
See also **Focus Strategies,** use graphic
organizers; **Teacher Resource
Book,** graphic organizers;
Transparencies, graphic
organizers

cause-and-effect diagram, **2-6:** T35,
T46, T50, T57, T60, T69, T73,
T97, T136, T148, T151, T154,
T158, T167, T171, T193

charts, **2-1:** T46, T50, T54, T57, T60,
T90, T92, T94, T134, T144, T154,
T157, T188, T190, T208, T216,
T217, T228, T239, T246, T249,
T266, T268, T270, T298, T321,
T331, T348, T350, T352, T353,
T377, T426; **2-2:** T34, T35, T46,
T68, T70, T132, T133, T144,
T146, T151, T159, T162, T166,
T190, T192, T193, T248, T272,
T274, T276, T277, T320, T334,
T343, T360, T362, T364; **2-3:**
T36, T46, T61, T88, T90, T92,
T142, T155, T182, T184, T212,
T213, T268, T270, T272, T273,
T310, T316, T320, T323, T350,
T352, T354, T373, T379, T394,

T404, T425, T426; **2-4:** T34, T46,
T64, T67, T73, T84, T92, T95,
T96, T110, T134, T142, T165,
T168, T171, T184, T197, T236,
T244, T247, T250, T270, T271,
T278, T281, T282, T308, T331,
T334, T335, T350, T360, T363,
T364, T420, T438; **2-5:** T66, T70,
T71, T87, T94, T168, T173, T177,
T194, T198, T236, T252, T255,
T258, T265, T274, T278, T286,
T289, T290, T324, T345, T349,
T368, T371; **2-6:** T50, T66, T73,
T94, T109, T136, T148, T151,
T154, T164, T167, T171, T176,
T185, T190, T193, T194, T195,
T221, T222, T232, T233, T236,
T249, T252, T255, T259, T273,
T275, T283, T310, T344, T347,
T351, T370, T373, T399, T416,
T426, T447

diagram, **2-6:** T241

graph, **2-2:** T12

sequence chart, **2-2:** T105; **2-4:** T61,
T320, T328; **2-5:** T138, T241,
T328, T336, T349; **2-6:** T161

story map, **2-1:** T105; **2-2:** T61, T218,
T220, T230, T232, T236, T239,
T242, T245, T255, T276, T302,
T303, T304, T314, T316, T325,
T328, T416, T426; **2-3:** T50,
T224, T241; **2-4:** T46, T51, T85,
T107, T111, T146, T158; **2-5:** T34,
T46, T49, T50, T57, T60, T69,
T97, T148, T150, T156, T162,
T165, T197, T397; **2-6:** T322,
T324, T331, T338, T341, T351

Venn diagram, **2-4:** T149; **2-5:** T339,
T415; **2-6:** T226,

word web, **2-1:** T95, T191; **2-2:** T75;
2-3: T93, T187, T355; **2-4:** T198,
T226, T310; **2-5:** T109, T372; **2-6:**
T98, T284, T374

Graphs
See **Focus Skills,** graphic aids;
Graphic Organizers

Handwriting, 2-1: T67, T161, T243,
T325, T349, T403, T421, R12–
R17; **2-2:** T65, T163, T249, T335,
T415, T421, T433, R12–R17; **2-3:**
T65, T245, T327, T403, T409,
T421, R12–R17; **2-4:** T65, T169,
T251, T335, T415, T433, R12–
R17; **2-5:** T67, T101, T169, T259,
T343, T423, T441, R12–R17; **2-6:**
T67, T165, T253, T287, T345,
T425, T443, R12–R17

High-Frequency Words, 2-1: T27, T29,
T41, T44–T45, T65, T68, T79,
T82, T89, T92, T98, T99, T100,
T101, T125, T127, T139, T142–
T143, T159, T162, T175, T178,
T185, T188, T194, T195, T196,
T197, T209, T211, T223, T226–
T227, T241, T244, T255, T258,
T265, T268, T274, T275, T276,
T277, T289, T291, T303, T306–
T307, T323, T326, T337, T340,
T347, T350, T356, T357, T358,
T359, T371, T373, T378, T380,
T391, T395, T401, T405, T411,
T417, T423, T426, T430, T431,
T432, T433; **2-2:** T27, T29, T41,
T44–T45, T63, T66, T79, T82,
T89, T92, T98, T99, T100, T101,
T125, T127, T139, T142–T143,
T161, T164, T177, T180, T187,
T190, T196, T197, T198, T199,
T211, T213, T225, T228–T229,
T247, T250, T261, T264, T271,
T274, T280, T281, T282, T283,
T295, T297, T309, T312–T313,
T333, T336, T349, T352, T359,

T362, T368, T369, T370, T371, T383, T385, T390, T392, T403, T407, T413, T417, T423, T429, T435, T438, T442, T443, T444, T445; **2-3:** T27, T29, T41, T44–T45, T63, T66, T77, T80, T87, T90, T96, T97, T98, T99, T123, T125, T137, T140–T141, T157, T160, T174, T181, T190, T191, T192, T193, T207, T219, T222–T223, T243, T257, T260, T267, T270, T276, T277, T278, T293, T305, T308–309, T325, T339, T342, T349, T352, T358, T359, T360, T373, T375, T380, T391, T395, T401, T405, T411, T417, T423, T426, T430, T431, T432, R11; **2-4:** T29, T41, T63, T65, T79, T91, T129, T141, T167, T169, T183, T193, T219, T231, T249, T251, T265, T277, T303, T315, T333, T335, T349, T359, T385, T403, T413, T423, T435; **2-5:** T29, T41, T65, T81, T93, T131, T143, T167, T183, T193, T219, T231, T257, T273, T285, T311, T323, T341, T357, T367, T393, T411, T421, T431, T443; **2-6:** T29, T41, T65, T81, T93, T131, T143, T163, T179, T189, T215, T227, T251, T267, T279, T305, T317, T343, T359, T369, T395, T413, T423, T433, T445

See also **Leveled Readers Teacher Guide,** high-frequency words; **Literacy Centers,** Word Work Center; **Monitor Progress,** high-frequency words; **Vocabulary,** vocabulary review, cumulative

History/Social Science
See **Cross-Curricular Connections,** social studies

Homework, 2-4: T44, T144, T234, T318; **2-5:** T44, T146, T234, T326; **2-6:** T44, T146, T230, T320
See also **Literacy Centers,** Homework Copying Master; **Teacher Resource Book,** School-Home Connections

Homophones
See **Vocabulary,** homophones

How-to Writing
See **Writing,** forms, how-to paragraph

Ideas
See **Writing,** traits, ideas/focus

Illustrators, Student Edition Literature
See **Student Edition,** illustrator features

Index of Titles and Authors
See **Student Edition,** Index of Titles and Authors

Inferences, Make
See **Comprehension Skills,** inferences, make; **Focus Skills,** make inferences

Inflected Forms
See **Decoding/Word Work,** inflections

Inflections
See **Decoding/Word Work,** inflections

Informal Assessment
See **Assessment; Monitor Progress**

Information Books
See **Genre,** nonfiction

Informational Text
See **Genre,** nonfiction

Inquiry
See **Theme Project**

Intensive Intervention Program
See **Intervention,** Intensive Intervention Program

Internet
See **Technology,** Web site

Interrogative Sentences
See **Grammar**

Intervention
See also **Lesson Planner,** 5-Day Small-Group Planner
Intensive Intervention Program, **2-1:** T5; **2-2:** T5; **2-3:** T5; **2-4:** T5; **2-5:** T5; **2-6:** T5
Strategic Intervention Interactive Reader, **2-1:** T69, T163, T245, T318, T327; **2-2:** T165, T251, T337; **2-3:** T58, T67, T152, T161, T238, T247, T329; **2-4:** T58, T66, T170, T252, T328, T336; **2-5:** T60, T68, T170, T252, T260, T336, T344; **2-6:** T60, T68, T158, T166, T254, T338, T346
Strategic Intervention Resource Kit, **2-1:** T5, T19, T117, T201, T281, T363; **2-2:** T5, T19, T117, T203, T287, T375; **2-3:** T5, T19, T115, T197, T283, T365; **2-4:** T5, T19, T119, T209, T293, T375; **2-5:** T5, T19, T121, T209, T301, T383; **2-6:** T5, T19, T121, T205, T295, T385
Strategic Intervention Teacher Guide, **2-1:** T5, T93, T189, T269, T351; **2-2:** T5, T93, T191, T275, T363; **2-3:** T5, T91, T185, T271, T353; **2-4:** T94, T280, T362; **2-5:** T96, T196, T288, T370; **2-6:** T96, T192, T282, T372

Intervention Reader
See **Intervention,** Strategic Intervention Interactive Reader

Intonation
See **Fluency,** intonation

Introduce the Theme, 2-1: T14–T15; **2-2:** T14–T15; **2-3:** T14–T15; **2-4:** T14–T15; **2-5:** T14–T15; **2-6:** T14–T15

Introducing the Book, 2-1: xvi; **2-2:** xvi; **2-3:** xvi; **2-4:** xvi; **2-5:** xvi; **2-6:** xvi

Journal
  See **Spelling,** notebook; **Writing,**
    notebook
Judgments, Make
  See **Comprehension Skills,**
    judgments, make

KWL Charts, 2-3: T316; **2-6:** T232, T233,
  T235, T236
  See also **Graphic Organizers,** charts

Labels, 2-3: T415–T416
Language Arts
  See **Content-Area Reading,** language
    arts; **Grammar; Spelling;**
    Transparencies, language arts;
    Writing
Language Arts Checkpoint, 2-1: T96,
  T192, T272, T354; **2-2:** T96, T194,
  T278, T366; **2-3:** T94, T188, T274,
  T356; **2-4:** T98, T200, T284, T366;
  2-5: T100, T200, T292, T374; **2-6:**
  T100, T196, T286, T376
Language Development
  See **English-Language Learners;**
    Lesson Planner, 5-Day Small-
    Group Planner; **Literacy Centers**
Language Structures
  See **Grammar**
Learning Centers
  See **Literacy Centers**
Learning Stations
  See **Literacy Centers**

Lesson Opener, 2-1: T16–T17,
  T114–T115, T198–T199,
  T278–T279, T360–T361; **2-2:**
  T16–T17, T114–T115, T200–T201,
  T284–T285, T372–T373; **2-3:**
  T16–T17, T112–T113, T194–T195,
  T280–T281, T362–T363; **2-4:**
  T16–T17, T116–T117, T206–T207,
  T290–T291, T372–T373; **2-5:**
  T16–T17, T118–T119, T206–T207,
  T298–T299, T380–T381; **2-6:**
  T16–T17, T118–T119, T202–T203,
  T292–T293, T382–T383
Lesson Overview, 2-1: xii–xv; **2-2:** xii–
  xv; **2-3:** xii–xv; **2-4:** xii–xv; **2-5:**
  xii–xv; **2-6:** xii–xv
Lesson Planner
  5-Day Small-Group Planner, **2-1:**
    T22–T23, T120–T121, T204–
    T205, T284–T285, T366–T367;
    2-2: T22–T23, T120–T121, T206–
    T207, T290–T291, T378–T379;
    2-3: T22–T23, T118–T119, T200–
    T201, T286–T287, T368–T369;
    2-4: T22–T23, T122–T123, T212–
    T213, T296–T297, T378–T379;
    2-5: T22–T23, T124–T125, T212–
    T213, T304–T305, T386–T387;
    2-6: T22–T23, T124–T125, T208–
    T209, T298–T299, T388–T389
  5-Day Whole-Group Planner, **2-1:**
    T20–T21, T118–T119, T202–
    T203, T282–T283, T364–T365;
    2-2: T20–T21, T118–T119, T204–
    T205, T288–T289, T376–T377;
    2-3: T20–T21, T116–T117, T198–
    T199, T284–T285, T366–T367;
    2-4: T20–T21, T120–T121, T210–
    T211, T294–T295, T376–T377;
    2-5: T20–T21, T122–T123, T210–
    T211, T302–T303, T384–T385;
    2-6: T20–T21, T122–T123, T206–
    T207, T296–T297, T386–T387

Lesson Resources, 2-1: T18–T19,
  T116–T117, T200–T201, T280–
  T281, T362–T363; **2-2:** T18–T19,
  T116–T117, T202–T203, T286–
  T287, T374–T375; **2-3:** T18–T19,
  T114–T115, T196–T197, T282–
  T283, T364–T365; **2-4:** T18–T19,
  T118–T119, T208–T209, T292–
  T293, T374–T375; **2-5:** T18–T19,
  T120–T121, T208–T209, T300–
  T301, T382–T383; **2-6:** T18–T19,
  T120–T121, T204–T205, T294–
  T295, T384–T385
Letters
  See **Writing**
Leveled Activities
  See **Differentiated Instruction**
Leveled Practice
  See **Differentiated Instruction**
Leveled Readers
  See also **Leveled Readers and**
    Practice; Leveled Readers
    Lesson Plans; Literacy Centers,
    Reading Center; **Technology**
  Advanced Readers
    "An Artist Named Tomie," **2-6:**
      T200
    "At the Museum," **2-5:** T452
    "Board Riding: Long Ago and
      Today," **2-3:** T192
    "Book Week News," **2-1:** T432
    "Clues for Grandma," **2-3:** T432
    "Cyrus McCormick: Friend to
      Farmers," **2-4:** T370
    "The Dinosaur Drawing Delivery,"
      2-3: T278
    "First Prize," **2-4:** T102
    "Hamsters," **2-1:** T358
    "Happy Again," **2-5:** T104
    "Have You Seen Grandma's
      Panpipe?" **2-6:** T104
    "Hunter's Secret," **2-4:** T204
    "Let's Look for Fossils," **2-6:**
      T290

"Music for Everyone," **2-4:** T288

"On Stage!" **2-3:** T98

"Peacock and Crane," **2-2:** T209, T210, T282

"Pelé—Soccer Legend," **2-2:** T25, T100

"A Pet that Fits," **2-1:** T276

"Prairie Babies," **2-3:** T360

"The Prairie Dog," **2-5:** T296

"A Present for Charlie," **2-2:** T198

"Puppy Tricks," **2-5:** T204

"Rescue Helicopter," **2-2:** T381, T444

"Rooster's Sore Throat," **2-2:** T293, T370

"The Surprise by the Stream," **2-1:** T196

"Watching Arctic Wolves," **2-5:** T378

"Wendy's Great Catch," **2-1:** T100

"What a Trip!" **2-6:** T454

"What's My Hobby?" **2-4:** T444

"Why Tree Frogs Sing at Night," **2-6:** T380

Below-Level Readers

"Abalone and the Sea," **2-6:** T378

"Apples for Sheep and Goat," **2-2:** T292, T368

"At the Library," **2-5:** T450

"At the Police Station," **2-2:** T382, T442

"Ben and Sooty," **2-1:** T274

"Better than AJ," **2-1:** T98

"The Book Sale," **2-5:** T102

"Cats," **2-1:** T356

"Family Trip," **2-6:** T452

"A Going-Away Present," **2-3:** T430

"Grandma's Rain Song," **2-2:** T196

"The Hamster Escape," **2-3:** T276

"Hannah's Dance," **2-4:** T202

"Having Fun: Long Ago and Today," **2-3:** T190

"Just Like the Moon," **2-6:** T102

"Let's Look at Gems," **2-6:** T288

"Lucia's Gift," **2-3:** T96

"Mountain Babies," **2-3:** T358

"Mountain Gorillas," **2-5:** T376

"Music Is About Sounds," **2-4:** T286

"Nancy Lopez—Super Golfer," **2-2:** T24, T98

"A New Painting," **2-4:** T100

"News from the Market," **2-1:** T430

"No More Fish!" **2-5:** T202

"The Penguin," **2-5:** T294

"A Surprise for Squirrel and Rabbit," **2-1:** T194

"Thomas Alva Edison: A Great Inventor," **2-4:** T368

"What's My Pet?" **2-4:** T442

"Why Raven Is Black," **2-2:** T208, T280

"A Writer Named Jean," **2-6:** T198

ELL-Leveled Readers

"All About Bikes," **2-2:** T123, T199

"Art in the Subway," **2-3:** T99

"The Art of Sculpture," **2-4:** T445

"A Birthday Surprise," **2-3:** T433

"Collecting Seashells," **2-6:** T291

"Down on the Farm," **2-2:** T371

"The Fall," **2-1:** T197

"Farmer Bert," **2-5:** T205

"The Firefighter," **2-2:** T381, T445

"Food Around the World," **2-6:** T105

"Guitar Lessons," **2-4:** T205

"I Love to Write," **2-6:** T201

"I Read the TV News," **2-1:** T433

"In Our Neighborhood," **2-5:** T105

"Insects," **2-5:** T297

"It's Fun to Dance," **2-4:** T289

"Just Like Olivia," **2-3:** T279

"Katie's Book," **2-4:** T103

"Let's Play Sports," **2-2:** T25, T101

"Lots of Dogs," **2-1:** T277

"Many Kinds of Birds," **2-2:** T209, T283

"My Community," **2-5:** T453

"My Travel Journal," **2-6:** T455

"Peanuts," **2-4:** T371

"Puppy School," **2-1:** T359

"Rainforest Homes," **2-3:** T361

"Reptiles," **2-6:** T381

"Signs All Around Us," **2-1:** T101

"Toys: Long Ago and Today," **2-3:** T193

"A Wild Animal Tour," **2-5:** T379

On-Level Readers

"The Ant," **2-5:** T295

"The Best Birthday," **2-4:** T101

"Bump!" **2-1:** T195

"A Chat with the Principal," **2-5:** T451

"The Country Show," **2-2:** T292, T369

"Desert Babies," **2-3:** T359

"How the Tortoise Got Its Shell," **2-6:** T379

"Hummingbird and Heron," **2-2:** T208, T281

"An Interesting Trip," **2-6:** T453

"Jackson's Tree," **2-5:** T103

"Joshua and the Tigers," **2-4:** T203

"Let's Discover Gold," **2-6:** T289

"Lucy and Billy," **2-1:** T275

"Madam C.J. Walker: Making Dreams Happen," **2-4:** T369

"Measuring Max," **2-3:** T97

"Michael Jordan—No Quitter," **2-2:** T24, T99

"Monkey Business," **2-5:** T203

"Morning News from the Fair," **2-1:** T431

"Orangutans," **2-5:** T377

"Playing in an Orchestra," **2-4:** T287

"Ponies," **2-1:** T357

"The Rabbit Suit Rescue," **2-3:** T277

"Riding Bicycles: Long Ago and Today," **2-3:** T191

"Ski Patrol," **2-2:** T382, T443

"A Surprise for Mom," T431

"Swimming with Pops," **2-2:** T197

"The Vegetable Garden," **2-1:** T99

"What's My Sport?" **2-4:** T443

"Who Is Dr. Seuss?" **2-6:** T199

"Wishing for Star Fruit," **2-6:** T103

Think Critically, **2-1:** T98, T99, T100, T194, T195, T196, T274, T275, T276, T356, T357, T358, T430, T431, T432; **2-2:** T98, T99, T100, T196, T197, T198, T280, T281, T282, T368, T369, T370, T442, T443, T444; **2-3:** T96, T97, T98, T190, T191, T192, T276, T277, T278, T358, T359, T360, T430, T431, T432; **2-4:** T100, T101, T102, T202, T203, T204, T286, T287, T288, T368, T369, T370, T442, T443, T444; **2-5:** T102, T103, T104, T202, T203, T204, T294, T295, T296, T376, T377, T378, T450, T451, T452; **2-6:** T102, T103, T104, T198, T199, T200, T288, T289, T290, T378, T379, T380, T452, T453, T454

Leveled Readers and Practice, 2-1: T24–T25, T122–T123, T206–T207, T286–T287, T368–T369; **2-2:** T24–T25, T122–T123, T208–T209, T292–T293, T380–T381; **2-3:** T24–T25, T120–T121, T202–T203, T288–T289, T370–T371; **2-4:** T24–T25, T124–T125, T214–T215, T298–T299, T380–T381; **2-5:** T24–T25, T126–T127, T214–T215, T306–T307, T388–T389;

2-6: T24–T25, T126–T127, T210–T211, T300–T301, T390–T391

Leveled Readers Lesson Plans, 2-1: T98–T101, T194–T197, T274–T277, T356–T359, T430–T433; **2-2:** T98–T101, T196–T199, T280–T283, T368–T371, T442–T445; **2-3:** T96–T99, T190–T193, T276–T279, T358–T361, T430–T433; **2-4:** T100–T103, T202–T205, T286–T289, T368–T371, T442–T445; **2-5:** T102–T105, T202–T205, T294–T297, T376–T379, T450–T453; **2-6:** T102–T105, T198–T201, T288–T291, T378–T381, T452–T455

Leveled Readers System, 2-1: T4, T24, T122, T206, T286, T368; **2-2:** T4, T24, T122, T208, T292, T380; **2-3:** T4, T24, T120, T202, T288, T370; **2-4:** T4, T24, T124, T214, T298, T380; **2-5:** T4, T24, T126, T214, T306, T388; **2-6:** T4, T24, T126, T210, T300, T390

Leveled Readers Teacher Guide

build background, **2-1:** T101, T197, T277, T359, T433; **2-2:** T101, T199, T283, T371, T445; **2-3:** T99, T193, T279, T361, T433; **2-4:** T103, T205, T289, T371, T445; **2-5:** T105, T205, T297, T379, T453; **2-6:** T105, T201, T291, T381, T455

comprehension, **2-1:** T98, T99, T100, T194, T195, T196, T274, T275, T276, T356, T357, T358, T430, T431, T432; **2-2:** T98, T99, T100, T101, T196, T197, T198, T199, T280, T281, T282, T283, T368, T369, T370, T371, T442, T443, T444, T445; **2-3:** T96, T97, T98, T99, T190, T191, T192, T193, T276, T277, T278, T279, T358, T359, T360, T361, T430, T431,

T432, T433; **2-4:** T100, T101, T102, T103, T202, T203, T204, T286, T287, T288, T368, T369, T370, T371, T442, T443, T444; **2-5:** T102, T103, T104, T105, T202, T203, T204, T205, T294, T295, T296, T297, T376, T377, T378, T379, T450, T451, T452, T453; **2-6:** T102, T103, T104, T198, T199, T200, T288, T289, T290, T378, T379, T380, T452, T453, T454

high-frequency words, **2-1:** T98, T99, T100, T194, T195, T196, T274, T275, T276, T356, T357, T358, T430, T431, T432; **2-2:** T98, T99, T100, T101, T196, T197, T198, T199, T280, T281, T282, T283, T368, T369, T370, T371, T442, T443, T444, T445; **2-3:** T96, T97, T98, T190, T191, T192, T276, T277, T278, T358, T359, T360, T430, T431, T432

scaffolded language development, **2-1:** T101, T197, T277, T359, T433; **2-2:** T101, T199, T283, T371, T445; **2-3:** T99, T193, T279, T361, T433; **2-4:** T103, T205, T289, T371, T445; **2-5:** T105, T205, T297, T379, T453; **2-6:** T105, T201, T291, T381, T455

vocabulary, **2-4:** T100, T101, T102, T103, T202, T203, T204, T205, T286, T287, T288, T289, T368, T369, T370, T371, T442, T443, T444, T445; **2-5:** T102, T103, T104, T105, T202, T203, T204, T205, T294, T295, T296, T297, T376, T377, T378, T379, T450, T451, T452, T453; **2-6:** T102, T103, T104, T105, T198, T199, T200, T201, T288, T289, T290, T291, T378, T379, T380, T381, T452, T453, T454, T455

Leveled Resources, 2-1: T4–T5; **2-2:** T4–T5; **2-3:** T4–T5; **2-4:** T4–T5; **2-5:** T4–T5; **2-6:** T4–T5

Library Books

See **Classroom Library Collection**

Library/Media Center

See **Research/Study Skills; Technology**

Listening and Speaking

See **Speaking and Listening**

Listening and Speaking Center

See **Literacy Centers,** Listening and Speaking Center

Listening and Speaking Vocabulary

See **Vocabulary,** robust vocabulary

Listening Comprehension, 2-1: T13, T14–T15, T28, T36, T40, T64, T78, T88, T126, T134, T138, T158, T174, T184, T210, T218, T222, T240, T254, T264, T290, T298, T322, T336, T346, T372, T390, T400, T410, T422; **2-2:** T13, T14–T15, T28, T36, T40, T62, T78, T88, T126, T134, T138, T160, T176, T186, T212, T220, T224, T246, T260, T270, T296, T304, T308, T332, T348, T358, T384, T402, T412, T422, T434; **2-3:** T13, T14–T15, T28, T36, T40, T62, T76, T206, T214, T218, T242, T256, T266, T292, T300, T304, T324, T338, T348, T374, T390, T400, T410, T422, T434, T435; **2-4:** T13, T14–T15, T28, T36, T40, T62, T78, T90, T128, T136, T140, T166, T182, T192, T218, T226, T230, T248, T264, T276, T302, T310, T314, T332, T348, T358, T384, T402, T412, T422, T434; **2-5:** T13, T14–T15, T28, T36, T40, T64, T80, T92, T130, T138, T142, T166, T182, T192, T218, T226, T230, T256, T272, T284, T310, T318, T322, T340, T356, T366,

T392, T410, T420, T430, T442; **2-6:** T13, T14–T15, T28, T36, T40, T64, T80, T92, T130, T138, T142, T162, T178, T188, T214, T222, T226, T250, T266, T278, T304, T312, T316, T342, T358, T368, T394, T412, T422, T432, T444

See also **Speaking and Listening,** read aloud

Listening to Literature Selections

See **Technology,** Audiotext

Literacy Center Cards

See **Literacy Center,** Center Activity Kit Cards

Literacy Centers

See also **Technology,** Resources for Parents and Teachers: Homework Help

Center Activity Kit Cards, **2-1:** T26–T27, T124–T125, T208–T209, T288–T289, T370–T371; **2-2:** T26–T27, T124–T125, T210–T211, T294–T295, T382–T383; **2-3:** T26–T27, T122–T123, T204–T205, T290–T291, T372–T373; **2-4:** T26–T27, T126–T127, T216–T217, T300–T301, T382–T383; **2-5:** T26–T27, T128–T129, T216–T217, T308–T309, T390–T391; **2-6:** T26–T27, T128–T129, T212–T213, T302–T303, T392–T393

fluency, **2-1:** T26, T124, T208, T288, T370; **2-2:** T26, T124, T210, T294, T382; **2-3:** T26, T122, T204, T290, T372; **2-4:** T26, T126, T216, T300, T382; **2-5:** T26, T128, T216, T308, T390; **2-6:** T26, T128, T212, T302, T392

Homework Copying Master, **2-1:** T26, T124, T208, T288, T370; **2-2:** T26, T124, T210, T294, T382; **2-3:** T26, T122, T204, T290, T372; **2-4:** T26, T126, T216, T300, T382;

2-5: T26, T128, T216, T308, T390; **2-6:** T26, T128, T212, T302, T392

Letters and Sounds Center, **2-1:** T27, T125, T209, T289, T371; **2-2:** T27, T125, T211, T295, T383; **2-3:** T27, T123, T205, T291, T373; **2-4:** T27, T127, T217, T301, T383; **2-5:** T27, T129, T217, T309, T391; **2-6:** T27, T129, T213, T303, T393

Listening and Speaking Center, **2-1:** T26, T124, T208, T288, T370; **2-2:** T26, T124, T210, T294, T382; **2-3:** T26, T122, T204, T290, T372; **2-4:** T26, T126, T216, T300, T382; **2-5:** T26, T128, T216, T308, T390; **2-6:** T26, T128, T212, T302, T392

Phonics Center, **2-1:** T27, T125, T209, T289, T371; **2-2:** T27, T125, T211, T295, T383; **2-3:** T27, T123, T205, T291, T373; **2-4:** T27, T127, T217, T301, T383; **2-5:** T27, T129, T217, T309, T391; **2-6:** T27, T129, T213, T303, T393

Reading Center, **2-1:** T26, T124, T208, T288, T370; **2-2:** T26, T124, T210, T294, T382; **2-3:** T26, T122, T204, T290, T372; **2-4:** T26, T126, T216, T300, T382; **2-5:** T26, T128, T216, T308, T390; **2-6:** T26, T128, T212, T302, T392

technology, **2-1:** T26, T27, T124, T125, T208, T209, T288, T289, T370, T371; **2-2:** T26, T27, T124, T210, T294, T295, T382; **2-3:** T26, T27, T122, T123, T204, T290, T372; **2-4:** T26, T126, T127, T216, T300, T382; **2-5:** T26, T128, T216, T308, T309, T390; **2-6:** T26, T128, T212, T302, T392

vocabulary, **2-1:** T27, T125, T209, T289, T371; **2-2:** T27, T125, T211, T295, T383; **2-3:** T27, T123,

T205, T291, T373; **2-4:** T27,
T127, T217, T301, T383; **2-5:**
T27, T129, T217, T309, T391;
2-6: T27, T129, T213, T303, T393
web site, Harcourt School Publishers
Online
Additional Literacy Center
Activities, **2-1:** T27, T125,
T209, T289, T371; **2-2:** T27,
T125, T211, T295, T383; **2-3:**
T27, T123, T205, T291, T373;
2-4: T27, T127, T217, T301,
T383; **2-5:** T27, T129, T217,
T309, T391; **2-6:** T27, T129,
T213, T303, T393
Resources for Parents and
Teachers, **2-1:** T27, T125,
T209, T289, T371; **2-2:** T27,
T125, T211, T295, T383; **2-3:**
T27, T123, T205, T291, T373;
2-4: T27, T127, T217, T301,
T383; **2-5:** T27, T129, T217,
T309, T391; **2-6:** T27, T129,
T213, T303, T393
Word Work Center, **2-1:** T27, T125,
T209, T289, T371; **2-2:** T27,
T125, T211, T295, T383; **2-3:** T27,
T123, T205, T291, T373; **2-4:**
T27, T127, T217, T301, T383;
2-5: T27, T129, T217, T309, T391;
2-6: T27, T129, T213, T303, T393
Writing Center, **2-1:** T27, T125, T209,
T289, T371; **2-2:** T27, T125, T211,
T295, T383; **2-3:** T27, T123,
T205, T291, T373; **2-4:** T27,
T127, T217, T301, T383; **2-5:**
T27, T129, T217, T309, T391;
2-6: T27, T129, T213, T303, T393
Literacy Centers Kit, 2-1: T3, T26–
T27, T124–T125, T208–T209,
T288–T289, T370–T371; **2-2:** T3,
T26–T27, T124–T125, T210–T211,
T294–T295, T382–T383; **2-3:** T3,
T26–T27, T122–T123, T204–T205,

T290–T291, T372–T373; **2-4:** T3,
T26–T27, T126–T127, T216–T217,
T300–T301, T382–T383; **2-5:** T3,
T26–T27, T128–T129, T216–T217,
T308–T309, T390–T391; **2-6:** T3,
T26–T27, T128–T129, T212–T213,
T302–T303, T392–T393
Literacy Centers Pocket Chart, 2-1: T26,
T124, T208, T288, T370; **2-2:** T26,
T124, T210, T294, T382; **2-3:** T26,
T122, T204, T290, T372; **2-4:** T26,
T126, T216, T300, T382; **2-5:** T26,
T128, T216, T308, T390; **2-6:** T26,
T128, T212, T302, T392
Literary Forms
See **Genre**
Literary Response
See **Writing,** forms, response to
literature
Literature
See **Classroom Library Collection;**
Read-Aloud Anthology; Reading,
Additional Related; **Student**
Edition, literature selections
Long Vowels
See **Decoding/Word Work,** long vowels

Magazine Articles
See **Genre,** magazine articles
Main Idea
See **Comprehension Skills,** main
idea; main idea and details; **Focus**
Skills, main idea and details
Main Selections
See **Student Edition,** literature
selections
Mass Media
See **Technology**
Meeting Individual Needs
See **Differentiated Instruction;**
Leveled Readers

Mentor Text
See **Writing,** mentor text
Metaphor
See **Comprehension Skills,** figurative/
poetic language, metaphor
Modeling
See **Think Aloud**
Models of Writing
See **Writing,** mentor text; Student-
Writing Models
Monitor Comprehension: Reread
See **Focus Strategies,** monitor
comprehension: reread
Monitor Progress, 2-1: T7, T436; **2-2:**
T7, T448; **2-3:** T7, T436; **2-4:**
T7, T448; **2-5:** T7, T456; **2-6:** T7,
T458

See also **Tested Skills**
comprehension, **2-1:** T34, T132, T216,
T296; **2-2:** T34, T132, T219, T302;
2-3: T34, T130, T212, T298; **2-4:**
T34, T69, T134, T172, T224, T254,
T308, T338; **2-5:** T34, T70, T136,
T172, T224, T316; **2-6:** T34, T76,
T136, T175, T220, T262, T310
fluency, **2-1:** T83, T93, T179, T189,
T259, T269, T341, T351; **2-2:** T83,
T93, T181, T191, T265, T275,
T353, T363; **2-3:** T81, T91, T175,
T185, T261, T271, T343, T353;
2-4: T82, T94, T186, T196, T268,
T280, T352, T362; **2-5:** T84, T96,
T186, T196, T276, T288, T360,
T370; **2-6:** T84, T96, T182, T192,
T270, T282, T362, T372
Focus Skill, **2-1:** T34, T132, T216,
T296; **2-2:** T34, T132, T219,
T302; **2-3:** T34, T130, T212,
T298; **2-4:** T34, T134, T224,
T308; **2-5:** T34, T136, T224,
T316; **2-6:** T34, T136, T220, T310
high-frequency words, **2-1:** T68, T162,
T244, T326; **2-2:** T66, T164,

T250, T336; **2-3:** T66, T160,
T246, T328

phonics, **2-1:** T43, T141, T225, T305;
2-2: T43, T141, T227, T311; **2-3:**
T43, T139, T221, T307; **2-4:**
T43, T143, T233, T317; **2-5:** T43,
T145, T233, T325; **2-6:** T43,
T145, T229, T319

robust vocabulary, **2-1:** T95, T191,
T271, T353; **2-2:** T95, T193, T277,
T365; **2-3:** T93, T187, T273, T355;
2-4: T97, T199, T283, T365; **2-5:**
T99, T199, T291, T373; **2-6:** T99,
T195, T285, T375

vocabulary, **2-1:** T68, T95, T162,
T191, T244, T271, T326, T353;
2-2: T66, T95, T164, T193, T250,
T277, T336, T365; **2-3:** T66, T93,
T160, T187, T246, T273, T328,
T355; **2-4:** T97, T199, T283, T365;
2-5: T99, T199, T268, T291, T352,
T373; **2-6:** T76, T99, T175, T195,
T262, T285, T355, T375

Multiple-Meaning Words
See **Vocabulary**

Multiple Strategies
See **Focus Strategies,** use multiple
strategies

Multisyllabic Words
See **Decoding/Word Work,**
multisyllabic words

Music
See **Cross-Curricular Connections,**
music

Musical Elements of Language
See **Comprehension Skills,** figurative/
poetic language, rhyme

My Reading Log
See **Teacher Resource Book,** My
Reading Log

Mystery
See **Genre,** mystery

My Weekly Contract, 2-1: T26, T124,
T208, T288, T370; **2-2:** T26, T124,

T210, T294, T382; **2-3:** T26, T122,
T204, T290, T372; **2-4:** T26, T126,
T216, T300, T382; **2-5:** T26, T128,
T216, T308, T390; **2-6:** T26, T128,
T212, T302, T392
See **Teacher Resource Book,** My
Weekly Contract

Narrative
See **Writing,** forms, personal
narrative; story
See **Genre,** nonfiction

Narrative Writing
See **Writing,** forms, personal
narrative; story
See **Genre,** nonfiction

Nonfiction
See **Genre,** nonfiction

Nonsense Words
See **Decoding/Word Work,** nonsense
words

Nonverbal Cues
See **Speaking and Listening**

Notebook
See **Spelling,** notebook; **Vocabulary,**
notebook; **Writing,** notebook

Ongoing Assessment
See **Monitor Progress**

On-Level Notes
See **Differentiated Instruction,** On-
Level Learners, notes for

On-Level Readers
See **Leveled Readers,** On-Level
Readers

Onset-Rime Blending
See **Phonemic Awareness**

Onset-Rime Segmentation

See **Phonemic Awareness**

Options for Reading
See **Differentiated Instruction,**
Options for Reading

Oral Language
See **Listening Comprehension;**
Question of the Day; Speaking
and Listening

Oral Language Conventions
See **Grammar; Speaking and Listening**

Oral Reading Fluency
See **Fluency**

Oral Reading Fluency Assessment
See **Assessment,** Oral Reading
Fluency Assessment

Organization
See **Writing,** traits, organization

Outlining
See **Reading-Writing Connection;**
Research/Study Skills

Pace
See **Fluency,** pace

Paragraphs
See **Writing,** forms, paragraph that
explains; forms, paragraph that
gives information; paragraph

Paraphrase, 2-5: T271

Parent Involvement
See **Teacher Resource Book,** School-
Home Connections

Partner-Read
See **Fluency,** partner-read

Parts of Speech
See **Grammar**

Patterns and Cutouts
See **Teacher Resource Book,** Patterns
and Cutouts

Penmanship
See **Handwriting**

Periods
See **Grammar,** abbreviations; sentences

Personal Narrative
See **Writing,** forms, personal narrative

Personal Opinions, Express
See **Comprehension Skills,** personal opinions, express

Personal Response
See **Comprehension Skills,** personal response

Persuasive Writing
See **Writing,** forms, persuasive writing

Phonemic Awareness, 2-1: T30–T31, T128–T129, T214–T215, T292–T293, T374–T375, **2-2:** T30–T31, T128–T129, T214–T215, T298–T299, T386–T387; **2-3:** T30–T32, T42–T43, T126–T127, T208–T209, T294–T295, T376–T377; **2-4:** T30–T31, T130–T131, T220–T221, T304–T305, T386–T387; **2-5:** T30–T31, T132–T133, T220–T221, T312–T313, T394–T395; **2-6:** T30–T31, T132–T133, T216–T217, T306–T307, T396–T397

Phonics
See **Decoding/Word Work; Monitor Progress,** phonics

Phonics CD-ROM
See **Technology,** technology resources, *Splash into Phonics* CD-ROM

Phonics Practice Book, 2-1: T43, T141, T225, T305; **2-2:** T43, T141, T227, T311; **2-3:** T43, T139, T221, T307; **2-4:** T43, T143, T233, T317; **2-5:** T43, T145, T233, T325; **2-6:** T43, T145, T229, T319

Phonograms
See **Decoding/Word Work,** phonograms

Phrasing
See **Fluency,** phrasing

Picture Books
See **Classroom Library Collection**

Picture Cards, 2-1: T31, T34, T36, T44, T129, T142, T226, T293, T306; **2-2:** T36, T44, T129, T185, T228, T299, T312; **2-3:** T31, T44, T127, T140, T222, T300, T308; **2-4:** T95, T136, T156, T175; **2-5:** T31, T34, T177, T283, T339, T347; **2-6:** T34, T310

Planning
See **Lesson Planner; Technology; Theme Planner**

Planning for Reading Success, 2-1: T10–T11; **2-2:** T10–T11; **2-3:** T10–T11; **2-4:** T10–T11; **2-5:** T10–T11; **2-6:** T10–T11

Play
See **Genre,** play; **Readers' Theater**

Plot
See **Focus Skills,** plot

Plural Nouns
See **Grammar,** nouns

Plural Possessive Nouns
See **Grammar,** plural possessive nouns

Poetry, 2-1: T14, T41, T65, T79, T89, T139, T159, T175, T185, T223, T241, T255, T265, T303, T323; **2-2:** T14, T41, T63, T79, T89, T139, T161, T177, T187, T225, T247, T253, T261, T271, T309, T333, T349, T359; **2-3:** T14, T41, T63, T69, T77, T87, T137, T157, T171, T181, T219, T243, T257, T267, T305, T325, T339, T349, T375, T391, T401, T411, T423; **2-4:** T14, T41, T63, T79, T91, T141, T157, T167, T174, T175, T183; **2-5:** T14, T41, T65, T81, T93, T138, T143, T167, T174, T183, T192, T193, T231, T257, T273, T285, T323, T341, T357, T367; **2-6:** T14, T41, T65, T81, T93, T143, T163, T179, T189, T317, T343, T359, T369
See **Genre,** poetry; **Writing,** poem

Point of View
See **Comprehension Skills,** author's viewpoint

Portfolio Opportunity
See **Assessment,** Portfolio Opportunity

Practice Book, 2-1: T32, T33, T35, T43, T90, T96, T130, T131, T133, T141, T143, T186, T192, T214, T215, T217, T225, T227, T266, T272, T294, T295, T297, T305, T307, T348, T354, T375, T376, T378, T393, T395, T403, T413, T425; **2-2:** T32, T33, T35, T43, T45, T90, T96, T130, T131, T133, T141, T143, T188, T194, T216, T217, T219, T227, T229, T272, T278, T300, T301, T303, T311, T313, T360, T366, T387, T388, T390, T405, T406, T407, T410, T415, T425, T432, T437; **2-3:** T32, T33, T35, T43, T45, T94, T128, T129, T131, T139, T141, T182, T188, T210, T211, T213, T223, T268, T274, T296, T297, T299, T307, T309, T350, T356, T377, T380, T393, T394, T395, T403, T413, T425; **2-4:** T32, T33, T35, T43, T45, T69, T92, T98, T132, T133, T135, T143, T145, T173, T194, T200, T222, T223, T225, T233, T235, T278, T306, T309, T317, T319, T339, T360, T387, T388, T405, T406, T410, T415, T417, T419, T425, T432, T437, T438; **2-5:** T32, T33, T35, T43, T45, T71, T94, T100, T134, T135, T137, T145, T147, T194, T200, T222, T223, T225, T233, T235, T286, T292, T314, T315, T317, T325, T327, T353, T368, T374, T395, T413, T414, T418, T423, T425, T427, T433, T440,

T445, T446; **2-6:** T32, T33, T35,
T43, T94, T100, T134, T135, T137,
T145, T147, T190, T196, T218,
T219, T221, T229, T231, T263,
T280, T286, T308, T309, T311,
T319, T321, T355, T370, T376,
T397, T398, T415, T416, T425,
T427, T429, T435, T442, T447,
T448

Predictions, Make

See **Comprehension Skills,**
predictions, make and confirm;
Focus Skills, make predictions

Predict Outcomes

See **Comprehension Skills,**
predictions, make and confirm;
Focus Skills, make predictions

Prefixes

See **Decoding/Word Work,** prefixes;
Spelling

Prescriptions

See **Assessment,** prescriptions

Presentation

See **Reading-Writing Connection;**
Writing, traits, presentation

Prewrite Strategies

See **Reading-Writing Connection,**
process writing, prewrite; **Writing,**
process writing, prewrite

Prior Knowledge, 2-1: T36, T71, T134,
T165, T218, T247, T298, T315,
T329; **2-2:** T29, T36, T46, T48,
T50, T71, T127, T134, T144,
T146, T151, T169, T220, T253,
T304, T341; **2-3:** T36, T69, T132,
T147, T163, T214, T300; **2-4:** T36,
T70, T136, T226, T237, T240,
T256, T310, T321, T340; **2-5:** T36,
T56, T72, T86, T138, T152, T174,
T226, T237, T262, T318, T329,
T346; **2-6:** T36, T47, T70, T138,
T168, T222, T233, T255, T256,
T271, T283, T312, T348

See also **Purpose Setting**

Problem/Solution

See **Comprehension Skills,** problem/
solution; **Focus Skills,** plot

Process Writing

See **Writing,** process writing

Professional Development

See also **Bibliography, Professional**
Professional Development for Reading
Courses, **2-1:** T3; **2-2:** T3; **2-3:**
T3; **2-4:** T3; **2-5:** T3; **2-6:** T3
Research Citations, **2-1:** T74, T171,
T217, T298, T418; **2-2:** T30,
T167, T257, T337, T430; **2-3:**
T30, T167; **2-4:** T30, T136, T252,
T304; **2-5:** T61, T171, T260,
T312; **2-6:** T74, T172, T221,
T307, T440

Program Reviewers, 2-1: R24–R25; **2-2:**
R24–R25; **2-3:** R24–R25; **2-4:**
R24–R25; **2-5:** R24–R25; **2-6:**
R24–R25

Progress-Monitoring

See **Assessment; Monitor Progress**

Prompts for Writing

See **Writing,** writing prompts

Pronouns

See **Grammar,** pronouns

Proofread

See **Daily Proofreading; Grammar;**
Reading-Writing Connection,
proofread; **Writing,** process
writing, proofread

Proper Nouns

See **Grammar**

Prosody

See **Fluency,** prosody

Publish

See **Reading-Writing Connection,**
process writing, publish; **Writing,**
process writing, publish

Punctuation

See **Fluency,** punctuation; **Grammar,**
abbreviations; commands

and exclamations; sentences;
statements and questions,

Purpose Setting

purpose for listening, **2-1:** T29, T36,
T41, T65, T79, T84, T94, T127,
T134, T139, T159, T175, T185,
T190, T211, T218, T223, T241,
T255, T265, T270, T291, T298,
T303, T323, T337, T347, T352,
T380; **2-2:** T29, T36, T94, T192,
T213, T297, T392; **2-3:** T29, T41,
T92, T125, T137, T186, T207,
T214, T219, T257, T272, T293,
T305, T325, T339, T354, T375,
T381, T391, T411, T423; **2-4:**
T29, T36, T41, T63, T79, T91,
T95, T129, T136, T141, T167,
T183, T193, T197, T219, T226,
T231, T249, T256, T303, T310,
T315, T333, T349, T359, T363,
T392; **2-5:** T29, T36, T41, T65,
T72, T81, T93, T97, T131, T138,
T143, T167, T183, T193, T197,
T219, T226, T231, T257, T273,
T285, T289, T311, T318, T323,
T341, T346, T357, T367, T371,
T400; **2-6:** T29, T36, T41, T65,
T81, T93, T97, T131, T138, T143,
T163, T179, T215, T222, T227,
T251, T283, T305, T312, T317,
T343, T359, T369, T373

purpose for reading, **2-1:** T48, T49,
T50, T51, T52, T53, T54, T55,
T56, T57, T71, T98, T99, T100,
T101, T145, T146, T147, T148,
T149, T150, T151, T165, T166,
T167, T194, T195, T196, T197,
T229, T230, T231, T233, T247,
T274, T275, T276, T277, T309,
T310, T311, T312, T313, T314,
T315, T316, T329, T356, T357,
T358, T359, T381, T382, T383,
T384, T385, T386, T414, T430,
T431, T432, T433; **2-2:** T47, T48,

T49, T50, T51, T52, T53, T54, T55, T70, T98, T99, T100, T101, T145, T146, T147, T148, T149, T150, T151, T152, T153, T169, T196, T197, T198, T199, T231, T232, T233, T234, T235, T236, T237, T238, T239, T252, T280, T281, T282, T283, T315, T316, T317, T318, T319, T320, T321, T322, T323, T324, T325, T368, T369, T370, T371, T393, T394, T395, T396, T397, T398, T426, T442, T443, T444, T445; **2-3:** T15, T47, T48, T49, T50, T51, T52, T53, T54, T55, T56, T69, T96, T97, T98, T99, T143, T144, T145, T146, T147, T148, T149, T150, T163, T190, T191, T192, T193, T225, T226, T227, T228, T229, T230, T231, T232, T233, T234, T235, T249, T276, T277, T278, T279, T311, T312, T313, T314, T315, T316, T317, T318, T331, T358, T359, T360, T361, T382, T383, T384, T385, T386, T414, T416, T430, T431, T432, T433; **2-4:** T47, T48, T49, T50, T51, T52, T53, T54, T55, T56, T100, T101, T102, T103, T147, T148, T149, T150, T151, T152, T153, T154, T155, T156, T157, T158, T159, T160, T202, T203, T204, T205, T237, T238, T239, T240, T241, T242, T286, T287, T288, T289, T321, T322, T323, T324, T325, T326, T368, T369, T370, T371, T393, T394, T395, T396, T397, T398, T426, T427, T442, T443, T444, T445; **2-5:** T47, T48, T49, T50, T51, T52, T53, T54, T55, T56, T57, T58, T102, T103, T104, T105, T149, T150, T151, T152, T153, T154, T155, T156, T157, T158, T159,

T160, T202, T203, T204, T205, T237, T238, T239, T240, T241, T242, T243, T244, T245, T246, T247, T248, T249, T250, T294, T295, T296, T297, T329, T330, T331, T332, T333, T334, T376, T377, T378, T379, T401, T402, T403, T404, T405, T406, T434, T450, T451, T452, T453; **2-6:** T47, T48, T49, T50, T51, T52, T53, T54, T55, T56, T57, T102, T103, T104, T105, T149, T150, T151, T152, T153, T154, T155, T156, T198, T199, T200, T201, T233, T234, T235, T236, T237, T238, T239, T240, T241, T242, T243, T244, T288, T289, T290, T291, T323, T324, T325, T326, T327, T328, T329, T330, T331, T332, T333, T334, T335, T378, T379, T380, T381, T402, T403, T404, T405, T406, T407, T408, T437, T438, T452, T453, T454, T455

purpose for writing, **2-1:** T104, T105, T106–T107, T108, T112; **2-2:** T104, T105, T106–T107, T108, T112; **2-3:** T102, T103, T104–105, T106, T110; **2-4:** T106, T107, T108–T109, T110, T114; **2-5:** T108, T109, T110–T111, T112, T116; **2-6:** T39, T63, T79, T91, T106, T107, T108–T109, T110, T114

Question of the Day, 2-1: T28, T40, T64, T78, T88, T126, T138, T158, T174, T184, T210, T222, T240, T254, T264, T290, T302, T322, T336, T346, T372, T390, T400, T410, T422; **2-2:** T28, T40, T62,

T78, T88, T126, T138, T160, T176, T186, T212, T224, T246, T260, T270, T296, T308, T332, T348, T358, T384, T402, T412, T422, T434; **2-3:** T28, T40, T62, T76, T86, T124, T136, T156, T170, T180, T206, T218, T256, T266, T292, T304, T324, T338, T348, T374, T390, T400, T410, T422; **2-4:** T28, T40, T62, T78, T90, T128, T140, T166, T182, T192, T218, T230, T248, T264, T276, T302, T314, T332, T348, T358, T384, T402, T412, T422, T434; **2-5:** T28, T40, T64, T80, T92, T130, T142, T166, T182, T192, T218, T230, T256, T272, T284, T310, T322, T340, T356, T366, T392, T410, T420, T430, T442; **2-6:** T28, T40, T64, T80, T92, T130, T142, T162, T178, T188, T214, T226, T250, T266, T278, T304, T316, T342, T358, T368, T394, T412, T422, T432, T444

Questions
  See **Focus Strategies,** answer questions; ask questions; **Grammar**

Quotation Marks
  See **Grammar,** punctuation; **Writing,** forms, story: dialogue; traits, conventions

***r*-Controlled Vowels**
  See **Decoding/Word Work,** *r*-Controlled vowels

Reaching All Learners
  See **Differentiated Instruction**

Read Ahead
  See **Focus Strategies,** read ahead

Read Aloud

See **Speaking and Listening**

Read-Aloud Anthology

"The Best Story Ever," **2-4:** T36, T38, T95

"Brilliant Bees," **2-5:** T226, T228, T289

"Butterfly Boy," **2-3:** T214, T216, T272

"Cardboard Box Joins Toy Hall of Fame," **2-3:** T132, T134, T186

"The Cat Who Walked Across France," **2-6:** T36, T38, T97

"Clarence, the Copy Cat," **2-1:** T218, T220, T270

"Climb Your Mountain," **2-2:** T36, T38, T94

"Dig This," **2-6:** T222, T224, T283

"Driving Back in Time," **2-6:** T419

"Friend Frog," **2-1:** T134, T136, T190

"From Study Hall to City Hall," **2-5:** T417

"Go Fetch!" **2-1:** T298, T300, T352

"Hanging On," **2-5:** T318, T320, T371

"How to Make an Apple Pie and See the World," **2-6:** T138, T140, T193

"The Just Right Gift," **2-5:** T36, T38, T97

"Laurel's Rainforest," **2-3:** T300, T302, T354

"Lights! Camera! Action!" **2-1:** T397

"The Missing Baseball Mystery," **2-3:** T397

"Mount Rushmore," **2-4:** T409

"My Father's Grandfather and the Time Machine," **2-2:** T134, T136, T192

"The Mystery in Grandma's Garden," **2-6:** T312, T314, T373

"On the Job at Fire Station 16," **2-2:** T409

"The Rooster That Crowed at Nightfall," **2-5:** T138, T140, T197

"The Rooster Who Went to His Uncle's Wedding," **2-2:** T304, T306, T364

"Sophie's Masterpiece," **2-4:** T136, T138, T197

"Sounds All Around," **2-4:** T226, T228

"Stellaluna," **2-2:** T220, T222, T276

"Tanya's City Garden," **2-3:** T36, T38, T92

"Wolf!" **2-1:** T36, T38, T94

"Young Inventors," **2-4:** T310, T363

Readers' Theater, 2-1: T93, T99, T189, T269, T351, T379–T386, T396, T406, T418, T427; **2-2:** T93, T191, T275, T363, T391–T398, T408, T418, T430, T439; **2-3:** T91, T185, T271, T353, T381–T386, T396, T406, T418, T427; **2-4:** T94, T196, T280, T288, T362, T391–T398, T408; **2-5:** T96, T177, T196, T288, T370, T399–T406, T416, T426, T438, T447; **2-6:** T73, T96, T103, T192, T282, T372, T378, T379, T380, T401–T408, T418, T428, T440, T449

See also **Student Edition,** Readers' Theater

Readers' Theater Backdrops

See **Teacher Resource Book,** Readers' Theater Backdrops

Readers' Theater Scripts

See **Teacher Resource Book,** Readers' Theater Scripts

Reading, Additional Related, 2-1: T69, T163, T327, R9; **2-2:** T67, T165, T251, T337, R9; **2-3:** T67, T161, T247, T329, R9; **2-4:** T66, T170, T252, T336, R9; **2-5:** T68, T170, T260, T344, R9; **2-6:** T68, T166, T254, T346, R9

Reading Across Texts

See **Student Edition,** Connections

Reading Center

See **Literacy Centers,** Reading Center

Reading for Information

See **Purpose Setting,** purposes for reading

Reading Intervention Kit

See **Intervention,** Strategic Intervention Resource Kit

Reading Rate

See **Fluency,** reading rate

Reading Transparencies

See **Transparencies,** reading

Reading-Writing Connection

opener, **2-1:** T102–T103; **2-2:** T102–T103; **2-3:** T100–T101; **2-4:** T104–T105; **2-5:** T106–T107; **2-6:** T106–T107

process writing

draft, **2-1:** T109; **2-2:** T109; **2-3:** T107; **2-4:** T111; **2-5:** T113; **2-6:** T113

evaluate/publish, **2-1:** T111; **2-2:** T111; **2-3:** T109; **2-4:** T113; **2-5:** T115; **2-6:** T115

prewrite, **2-1:** T108; **2-2:** T108; **2-3:** T106; **2-4:** T110; **2-5:** T112; **2-6:** T112

revise/proofread, **2-1:** T110; **2-2:** T110; **2-3:** T108; **2-4:** T112; **2-5:** T114; **2-6:** T114

Set the Stage, **2-1:** T104–T105; **2-2:** T104–T105; **2-3:** T102–T103; **2-4:** T106–T107; **2-5:** T108–T109; **2-6:** T108–T109

Student-Writing Model, **2-1:** T106–T107; **2-2:** T106–T107; **2-3:** T104–T105; **2-4:** T108–T109; **2-5:** T110–T111; **2-6:** T110–T111

Writing on Demand, **2-1:** T112–T113; **2-2:** T112–T113; **2-3:** T110–T111; **2-4:** T114–T115; **2-5:** T116–T117; **2-6:** T116–T117

Realistic Fiction

See **Genre,** realistic fiction

Recipes

See **Genre,** functional text, recipe

Recognize Story Structure

See **Focus Strategies,** use story structure

Reference Materials, 2-1: vi–vii; **2-2:** vi–vii; **2-3:** vi–vii; **2-4:** vi–vii; **2-5:** vi–vii; **2-6:** vi–vii

Repeated Reading
See **Fluency,** repeated reading

Rereading
See **Fluency,** repeated reading; **Focus Strategies,** monitor comprehension: reread

Research
See **Research/Study Skills**

Research Base, Scientific
See **Bibliography, Professional**

Research Citations
See **Professional Development,** Research Citations

Research Report
See **Reading-Writing Connection; Writing,** forms, research report

Research/Study Skills
atlas, **2-4:** T254–T255; **2-6:** T273
book parts
glossary, **2-4:** T224, T253, T269, T281; **2-5:** T279
index, **2-4:** T224, T226, T253, T269, T281; **2-5:** T279
table of contents, **2-4:** T224, T226, T253, T269, T281; **2-5:** T279
dictionary, **2-4:** T254–T255; **2-5:** T144, T268, T352; **2-6:** T152, T262, T263, T284, T354
encyclopedia, **2-4:** T254–T255; **2-5:** T271; **2-6:** T12, T273
guide words, **2-4:** T224, T253, T281
headings, **2-4:** T224, T236, T239, T241, T242, T253, T269, T281; **2-5:** T279
locate information, **2-1:** T12; **2-4:** T224–T225, T226, T239, T241, T243, T244, T253, T269, T281, T286, T287, T288, T289, T308–T309, T310, T324, T327, T328, T337, T340, T353, T363, T368, T369, T370, T371, T394, T396, T428; **2-5:** T279
maps, **2-5:** T224–T225, T226, T261, T262, T263, T277, T289, T310, T316, T318, T345, T361, T371; **2-6:** T70, T71, T156
reference sources, use, **2-1:** T12; **2-4:** T12, T254–T255, T338–T339; **2-6:** T12, T273
thesaurus, **2-4:** T254–T255; **2-5:** T268, T352; **2-6:** T174, T265, T284
Web site, **2-1:** T12; **2-4:** T12; **2-6:** T12, T115, T273

Resources, 2-1: R2–R86; **2-2:** R2–R86; **2-3:** R2–R86; **2-4:** R2–R86; **2-5:** R2–R86; **2-6:** R2–R86

Response to Literature
See **Comprehension Skills; Speaking and Listening,** comprehension/focus skills; **Student Edition,** Connections; Think Critically; **Writing,** forms, response to literature

Reteaching
See **Differentiated Instruction,** Small-Group Instruction

Retelling, 2-1: T60, T154, T196, T236, T359; **2-2:** T98, T156, T242, T328; **2-3:** T58, T238; **2-4:** T58, T162; **2-5:** T60, T152, T162; **2-6:** T60, T338, T378, T379

Retelling Rubrics
See **Rubrics,** retell and summarize fiction

Review Lessons
comprehension strategies, **2-1:** T414–T416; **2-2:** T426–T428; **2-3:** T414–T416; **2-4:** T426–T428; **2-5:** T434–T436; **2-6:** T436–T438
decoding/word work
consonants /s/c; /j/g, dge, **2-3:** T220–T221, T244–T245, T259, T269, T402–T403
digraphs /ch/ch, tch; /sh/sh; /th/th, **2-3:** T42–T43, T64–T65, T79, T89, T376
digraphs /n/kn; /r/wr; /f/gh, ph, **2-4:** T42–T43, T64–T65, T93, T386–T387
diphthong /oi/oi, oy, **2-4:** T232–T233, T250–T251, T267, T279, T414
diphthong /o͞o/oo, ew, ue, ui, ou, **2-5:** T232–T233, T258–T259, T275, T287, T422
diphthong /ou/ou, ow, **2-5:** T42–T43, T66–T67, T83, T95, T394
long vowels /ā/a-e, /ī/i-e, /ō/o-e, /(y)o͞o/u-e, **2-1:** T224–T225, T242–T243, T257, T267, T402
long vowel /ā/ai, ay, **2-2:** T140–T141, T162–T163, T179, T189, T404
long vowel /ē/ea, ei(gh), ey, **2-6:** T318–T319, T344–T345, T361, T370, T434
long vowel /ē/ee, ea, **2-1:** T304–T305, T324–T325, T339, T349, T412
long vowel /ē/ey, y, **2-3:** T138–T139, T158–T159, T165, T183, T392–T393
long vowel /ī/ie, igh, **2-2:** T42–T43, T64–T65, T81, T91, T386–T387
long vowel /ō/oa, ow, **2-2:** T310–T311, T334–T335, T351, T361, T424
r-Controlled Vowel, /âr/air, are, **2-5:** T324–T325, T342–T343, T359, T369, T432
r-Controlled Vowel, /är/ar, **2-2:** T226–T227, T248–T249, T263, T273, T414
r-Controlled Vowel, /ir/ear, eer, **2-4:** T316–T317, T334–T335, T351, T361, T424

r-Controlled Vowel, /ôr/*or, ore, our,* **2-5:** T144–T145, T168–T169, T185, T195, T412

r-Controlled Vowel, /ûr/*ir, ur, er, ear,* **2-3:** T306–T307, T326–T327, T341, T351, T412–T413

short vowels /a/*a, /i/i,* **2-1:** T42–T43, T66–T67, T81, T91, T374–T375

short vowels /e/*e, /o/o, /u/u,* **2-1:** T140–T141, T160–T161, T177, T187, T392

short vowel /e/*ea,* **2-4:** T142–T143, T168–T169, T185, T195, T404–T405

vowel variant /ô/*a(l), ough,* **2-6:** T228–T229, T252–T253, T269, T281, T424

vowel variant /ô/*aw, au(gh),* **2-6:** T144–T145, T164–T165, T181, T191, T414

vowel variant /o͞o/*oo, ou,* **2-6:** T42–T43, T66–T67, T83, T95, T396

focus skills

  author's purpose, **2-3:** T68, T82, T92, T130–T131, T162, T176, T186, T379, T394

  cause and effect, **2-6:** T69, T85, T97, T136–T137, T167, T183, T193, T399, T416

  characters, **2-1:** T70, T84, T94, T132–T133, T164, T180, T377, T394

  fiction and nonfiction, **2-3:** T262, T272, T330, T344, T354, T404, T425

  graphic aids, use, **2-5:** T261, T277, T289, T316–T317, T345, T361, T371, T424

  locate information, **2-4:** T253, T269, T281, T308–T309, T337, T353, T363, T416

main idea and details, **2-1:** T246, T260, T270, T296–T297, T328, T342, T352, T404, T425

make inferences, **2-6:** T255, T271, T283, T310–T311, T347, T363, T373, T426

make predictions, **2-2:** T68–T69, T84, T94, T132–T133, T166–T167, T182, T192, T389, T406

plot, **2-2:** T252, T266, T276, T302–T303, T338–T339, T354, T364, T416, T437; **2-5:** T34–T35, T69, T85, T97, T136–T137, T171, T187, T197, T397, T414

setting, **2-4:** T67, T83, T95, T134–T135, T174, T187, T197, T389, T406

grammar

  abbreviations, **2-3:** T60, T74, T84, T94, T388, T428

  adjectives, **2-4:** T60, T76, T88, T98, T400, T440

  adjectives for senses, **2-4:** T164, T180, T190, T200, T410, T440

  commands and exclamations, **2-1:** T252, T262, T272, T408, T428

  contractions, **2-6:** T340, T356, T366, T376, T442, T450

  forms of *be,* **2-5:** T338, T354, T364, T374, T440, T448

  helping verbs, **2-6:** T248, T264, T276, T286, T430, T450

  irregular verbs, **2-6:** T62, T78, T90, T100, T140, T160, T176, T186, T196, T410, T420, T450

  nouns, **2-2:** T60, T76, T86, T96, T400, T440

  number words, **2-4:** T246, T262, T274, T284, T420, T440

  past-tense verbs, **2-5:** T254, T270, T282, T292, T428, T448

plural possessive nouns, **2-3:** T240, T254, T264, T274, T408, T428

present-tense action verbs, **2-5:** T62, T78, T90, T100, T408, T448

pronouns, **2-3:** T322, T336, T346, T356, T420, T428

proper nouns, **2-2:** T244, T258, T268, T278, T306, T330, T346, T356, T366, T420, T432, T440

sentence, parts of a, **2-1:** T320, T334, T344, T354, T420, T428

sentences, **2-1:** T62, T76, T86, T96, T388, T428

singular and plural nouns, **2-2:** T158, T174, T184, T194, T410, T440

singular possessive nouns, **2-3:** T154, T168, T178, T188, T398, T428

statements and questions, **2-1:** T156, T172, T182, T192, T398, T428

subject-verb agreement, **2-5:** T164, T180, T190, T200, T418, T448

words that compare, **2-4:** T330, T346, T356, T366, T432, T440

high-frequency words, **2-1:** T378, T395, T405, T417, T426; **2-2:** T390, T407, T417, T429, T438; **2-3:** T380, T395, T405, T417, T426

robust vocabulary, **2-1:** T407, T419; **2-2:** T419, T431; **2-3:** T407, T419; **2-4:** T419, T431; **2-5:** T427, T439; **2-6:** T429, T441

spelling

  consonants /s/*c; /j/g, dge,* words with; **2-3:** T403

  digraphs /ch/*ch, tch; /sh/sh; /th/th,* words with, **2-3:** T378

digraphs /n/*kn;* /r/*wr;* /f/*gh, ph,*
    words with, **2-4:** T388

diphthong /oi/*oi, oy,* words with,
    2-4: T415

diphthong /ou/*ou, ow,* words with,
    2-5: T396

long vowels /ā/*a-e,* /ī/*i-e,* /ō/*o-e,*
    /(y)o͞o/*u-e,* words with, **2-1:**
    T403

long vowel /ā/*ai, ay,* words with,
    2-2: T405

long vowel /ē/*ea, ei(gh), ey,* words
    with, **2-6:** T435

long vowel /ē/*ee, ea,* words with,
    2-1: T412–T413

long vowel /ē/*ey, y,* words with,
    2-3: T392–T393

long vowel /ī/*ie, igh,* words with,
    2-2: T388

long vowel /ō/*oa, ow,* words with,
    2-2: T425

r-Controlled Vowel, /âr/*air, are,*
    words with, **2-5:** T432

r-Controlled Vowel, /är/*ar,* words
    with, **2-2:** T415

r-Controlled Vowel, /ir/*ear, eer,*
    words with, **2-4:** T424

r-Controlled Vowel, /ôr/*or, ore,*
    our, words with, **2-5:** T413

r-Controlled Vowel, /ûr/*ir, ur, er,*
    ear, words with, **2-3:** T412–
    T413

short vowels /a/*a,* /i/*i,* words with,
    2-1: T376

short vowels /e/*e,* /o/*o,* /u/*u,* words
    with, **2-1:** T392

short vowel /e/*ea,* words with, **2-4:**
    T405

Spelling Test, **2-1:** T424; **2-2:**
    T436; **2-3:** T424; **2-4:** T436;
    2-5: T444; **2-6:** T446

vowel variant /ô/*a(l), ough,* words
    with, **2-6:** T424, T425

vowel variant /ô/*aw, au(gh),* words
    with, **2-6:** T424, T415

vowel variant /o͞o/*oo, ew, ue, ui,*
    ou, words with, **2-5:** T423

vowel variant /o͝o/*oo, ou,* words
    with, **2-6:** T398

Revise

    See **Reading-Writing Connection,**
    process writing, revise/proofread;
    Writing, process writing, revise

Rhyme

    See **Comprehension Skills,** figurative/
    poetic language, rhyme

Robust Vocabulary

    See **Monitor Progress,** robust
    vocabulary; **Vocabulary,** robust
    vocabulary

Root Words

    See **Decoding/Word Work,** root words

Routine Cards, 2-1: T30, T36, T37, T44,
    T47, T60, T69, T80, T83, T128,
    T134, T135, T142, T155, T176,
    T179, T212, T218, T219, T226,
    T229, T236, T237, T245, T256,
    T259, T292, T298, T299, T306,
    T309, T319, T327, T338, T341,
    T349, T374, T387, T397, T402;
    2-2: T30, T36, T37, T44, T47, T58,
    T67, T83, T128, T135, T142, T145,
    T156, T157, T165, T214, T220,
    T221, T228, T231, T242, T243,
    T251, T262, T265, T298, T304,
    T305, T312, T315, T328, T329,
    T337, T350, T353, T386, T399,
    T409, T414; **2-3:** T30, T37, T44,
    T59, T126, T133, T140, T143, T153,
    T208, T215, T222, T225, T239,
    T294, T301, T308, T321, T376,
    T387, T397, T402; **2-4:** T30, T37,
    T44, T47, T59, T66, T82, T130,
    T136, T137, T144, T147, T162,
    T163, T184, T220, T226, T227,
    T237, T304, T310, T311, T318,
    T321, T329, T336, T352, T386,
    T392, T399, T409, T414; **2-5:** T37,
    T44, T47, T60, T61, T132, T139,
    T146, T149, T163, T220, T227,
    T234, T237, T253, T312, T318,
    T319, T326, T329, T336, T337,
    T344, T360, T394, T398, T407,
    T417, T422; **2-6:** T138, T139, T146,
    T149, T158, T159, T166, T182,
    T216, T223, T230, T233, T246,
    T247, T306, T313, T323, T396,
    T400, T409, T419, T424

Routines

    See **Question of the Day; Phonemic**
    Awareness; Routine Cards;
    Word Wall

Rubrics, 2-1: R2–R8; **2-2:** R2–R8; **2-3:**
    R2–R8; **2-4:** R2–R8; **2-5:** R2–R8;
    2-6: R2–R8

presentation: speaking and listening,
    2-1: T435, R5; **2-2:** T447, R5;
    2-3: T427, T435, R5; **2-4:** T447,
    R5; **2-5:** T455, R5; **2-6:** T457, R5

retell and summarize fiction, **2-1:** T60,
    T154, T236; **2-2:** T156, T242, T328;
    2-3: T58, T238; **2-4:** T58, T162;
    2-5: T60, T162; **2-6:** T60, T338

retelling, **2-1:** T60, T154, T236, T318;
    2-2: T58, T156, T242, T328; **2-3:**
    T58, T152, T238, T320; **2-4:** T58,
    T162, T244, T328; **2-5:** T60,
    T162, T252, T336; **2-6:** T60,
    T158, T246, T338

summarize nonfiction, **2-1:** T318; **2-2:**
    T58; **2-3:** T152, T320; **2-4:** T244,
    T328; **2-5:** T252, T336; **2-6:** T158,
    T246

using, **2-1:** R2; **2-2:** R2; **2-3:** R2; **2-4:**
    R2; **2-5:** R2; **2-6:** R2

writing

    extended response, **2-1:** R6; **2-2:**
    R6; **2-3:** R6; **2-4:** R6; **2-5:** R6;
    2-6: R6

    4-point rubric, **2-1:** T97, T111, T113,
    T193, T273, T355, T429, R8;

2-2: T97, T111, T113, T195, T279, T367, T441, R8; **2-3:** T95, T189, T275, T357, T429, R8; **2-4:** T99, T113, T115, T201, T285, T367, T441, R8; **2-5:** T101, T115, T117, T201, T293, T375, T449, R8; **2-6:** T101, T115, T117, T197, T287, T377, T451, R8

short response, **2-1:** R6; **2-2:** R6; **2-3:** R6; **2-4:** R6; **2-5:** R6; **2-6:** R6

6-point rubric, **2-1:** T97, T111, T113, T193, T273, T355, T429, R7; **2-2:** T97, T111, T113, T195, T279, T367, T441, R7; **2-3:** T189, T275, T357, T429, R7; **2-4:** T99, T113, T115, T201, T285, T367, T441, R7; **2-5:** T101, T115, T117, T201, T293, T375, T449, R7; **2-6:** T101, T115, T117, T197, T287, T377, T451, R7

Scaffolded Language Development
See **Differentiated Instruction,** Scaffolded Language Development

School-Home Connection, 2-1: T13, T435; **2-2:** T13, T447; **2-3:** T13, T435; **2-4:** T13, T447; **2-5:** T13, T455; **2-6:** T13, T457
See also **Teacher Resource Book,** School-Home Connections

Science
See **Content-Area Reading,** science; **Cross-Curricular Connections,** science

Scope and Sequence, 2-1: R26–R33; **2-2:** R26–R33; **2-3:** R26–R33; **2-4:** R26–R33; **2-5:** R26–R33; **2-6:** R26–R33

Second-Language Support
See **English-Language Learners**

Selecting Topics
See **Writing,** process writing, prewrite

Self-Assessment
See **Assessment,** Self-Assessment

Self-Selected Reading
See **Classroom Library Collection**

Sentence Fluency
See **Writing,** traits, sentence fluency

Sentence Structure
See **Grammar,** sentences; **Writing,** forms, sentences

Sentence Variety
See **Writing,** traits, sentence fluency

Sentences
See **Grammar,** sentences

Sequence
See **Comprehension Skills,** sequence

Setting
See **Comprehension Skills,** setting; **Focus Skills,** setting

Short Response
See **Rubrics,** writing, short response

Short Vowels
See **Decoding/Word Work,** short vowels

Sight Words
See **High-Frequency Words**

Singular Possessive Nouns
See **Grammar,** singular possessive nouns

Six Traits of Writing
See **Writing,** traits

Small-Group Instruction
See **Differentiated Instruction,** Small-Group Instruction

Small-Group Planner
See **Lesson Planner,** 5-Day Small-Group Planner

Social Studies
See **Content-Area Reading,** social studies; **Cross-Curricular Connections,** social studies

Software
See **Technology,** technology resources

Sound/Spelling Cards, 2-1: T30, T128, T212, T292, T374, T402; **2-2:** T30, T128, T214, T298, T386, T414; **2-3:** T30, T126, T208, T294, T376, T402; **2-4:** T30, T130, T220, T304, T386, T414; **2-5:** T30, T132, T220, T312, T394, T422; **2-6:** T30, T132, T216, T306, T396, T424

Speaking and Listening
See also **Vocabulary,** robust vocabulary
audience, **2-1:** T418, T427; **2-2:** T430, T439; **2-3:** T418, T427; **2-4:** T430, T439; **2-5:** T438, T447; **2-6:** T440, T449
comprehension/focus skills, **2-1:** T94, T190, T270, T352; **2-2:** T94, T192, T276, T364; **2-3:** T92, T186, T272, T354; **2-4:** T95, T197, T281, T363; **2-5:** T97, T197, T289, T371; **2-6:** T97, T193, T283, T373
oral language, **2-1:** T13, T14–T15, T28, T40, T64, T78, T88, T126, T138, T158, T174, T184, T210, T222, T240, T254, T264, T290, T302, T322, T336, T346, T372, T390, T400, T410, T422, T435; **2-2:** T13, T14–T15, T28, T40, T62, T78, T88, T126, T138, T160, T176, T186, T212, T224, T246, T260, T270, T296, T308, T332, T348, T358, T384, T402, T412, T422, T434, T447; **2-3:** T13, T14–T15, T28, T40, T62, T76, T86, T124, T136, T156, T170, T180, T206, T218, T256, T266, T292, T304, T324, T338, T348, T374, T390, T400, T410, T422, T435; **2-4:** T13, T14–T15, T28, T40, T62, T78, T90, T128, T140, T166, T182, T192, T218, T230, T248, T264, T276, T302, T314, T332, T348, T358, T384, T402, T412, T422, T434,

T447; **2-5:** T13, T14–T15, T28, T40, T64, T80, T92, T130, T142, T166, T182, T192, T218, T230, T256, T272, T284, T310, T322, T340, T356, T366, T392, T410, T420, T430, T442, T455; **2-6:** T13, T14–T15, T28, T40, T64, T80, T92, T130, T142, T162, T178, T188, T214, T226, T250, T266, T278, T304, T316, T342, T358, T368, T394, T412, T422, T432, T444, T457

read aloud, **2-1:** T29, T36, T41, T65, T69, T79, T83, T89, T93, T127, T134, T139, T159, T163, T175, T179, T185, T189, T211, T218, T223, T241, T245, T255, T259, T265, T291, T298, T303, T323, T327, T337, T341, T347, T373, T379, T380–T386, T391, T396, T401, T406, T411, T418, T423, T427; **2-2:** T29, T36, T41, T83, T127, T134, T139, T161, T165, T177, T181, T187, T191, T213, T220, T225, T247, T251, T261, T265, T271, T275, T297, T304, T309, T333, T337, T349, T353, T359, T363, T385, T391, T392– T398, T403, T408, T413, T418, T423, T430, T435, T439; **2-3:** T26, T29, T36, T41, T63, T77, T81, T87, T122, T125, T132, T137, T157, T171, T175, T181, T207, T214, T219, T243, T257, T261, T267, T293, T300, T305, T325, T339, T343, T349, T375, T381, T382– T386, T391, T396, T401, T406, T411, T418, T423, T427; **2-4:** T29, T36, T41, T63, T66, T79, T82, T91, T94, T129, T136, T141, T167, T170, T183, T186, T193, T196, T219, T226, T231, T249, T252, T265, T268, T277, T280, T303, T310, T315, T333, T336, T349,

T352, T359, T362, T385, T391, T392–T398, T403, T408, T413, T418, T423, T430, T435, T439; **2-5:** T29, T36, T41, T65, T68, T81, T84, T93, T96, T131, T138, T143, T167, T170, T183, T186, T193, T196, T219, T226, T231, T257, T260, T273, T276, T285, T288, T311, T318, T323, T341, T344, T357, T360, T367, T370, T393, T399, T400–T406, T411, T416, T421, T426, T431, T438, T443, T447; **2-6:** T29, T36, T41, T65, T81, T84, T93, T96, T131, T138, T143, T163, T166, T179, T182, T189, T192, T215, T222, T227, T251, T254, T267, T270, T279, T282, T305, T312, T317, T343, T346, T359, T362, T369, T372, T395, T401, T402–T408, T413, T418, T423, T428, T433, T440, T445, T449

Speculate

See **Comprehension Skills,** speculate

Spelling

See also **Assessment,** Spelling Posttest; Spelling Pretest

consonants /s/*c* or /j/*g, dge,* words with, **2-3:** T211, T220–T221, T245, T259, T269, T378, T402– T403, T424

digraphs /ch/*ch, tch;* /sh/*sh;* /th/*th,* words with, **2-3:** T33, T42–T43, T65, T79, T89, T378, T424

digraphs /n/*kn;* /r/*wr;* /f/*gh, ph,* words with, **2-4:** T33, T42–T43, T65, T81, T93, T388, T436

diphthong /oi/*oi, oy,* words with, **2-4:** T223, T232–T233, T251, T267, T279, T414, T436

diphthong /ou/*ou, ow,* words with, **2-5:** T33, T42–T43, T67, T83, T95, T396

long vowels /ā/*a-e,* /ī/*i-e,* /ō/*o-e,* /(y)o͞o/*u-e,* words with, **2-1:** T215, T224–T225, T243, T257, T267, T403, T424

long vowel /ā/*ai, ay,* words with, **2-2:** T131, T140–T141, T163, T179, T189, T405, T436

long vowel /ē/*ea, ei(gh), ey,* words with, **2-6:** T309, T318–T319, T345, T361, T371, T435, T446

long vowels /ē/*ee, ea,* words with, **2-1:** T295, T304–T305, T325, T339, T348, T412, T413, T424

long vowel /ē/*ey, y,* words with, **2-3:** T129, T138–139, T159, T173, T183, T378, T392–T393, T424

long vowel /ī/*ie, igh,* words with, **2-2:** T33, T42–T43, T65, T81, T91, T388, T436

long vowel /ō/*oa, ow,* words with, **2-2:** T301, T310–T311, T335, T351, T361, T425, T436

notebook, **2-1:** T43, T67, T141, T161, T225, T243, T305, T325, T393, T403; **2-2:** T43, T65, T141, T163, T227, T249, T311, T335, T415; **2-3:** T43, T65, T139, T159, T221, T245, T307, T327, T393, T403; **2-4:** T43, T65, T143, T169, T233, T251, T317, T335, T415; **2-5:** T43, T67, T145, T169, T233, T259, T325, T343, T423; **2-6:** T43, T67, T145, T165, T181, T229, T253, T319, T345, T425

palindromes, **2-1:** T42

r-Controlled Vowel, /âr/*air, are,* words with, **2-5:** T315, T324–T325, T343, T359, T369, T433

r-Controlled Vowel, /är/*ar,* words with, **2-2:** T217, T226–T227, T249, T263, T273, T415, T436

r-Controlled Vowel, /ir/*ear, eer,* words with, **2-4:** T307, T316–T317, T335, T351, T361, T424, T436

r-Controlled Vowel, /ôr/*or, ore, our,*
words with, **2-5:** T135, T144–
T145, T169, T185, T195, T413

r-Controlled Vowel, /ûr/*ir, ur, er,* or
ear, words with, **2-3:** T297, T306–
T307, T327, T341, T351, T378,

short vowels /a/*a, /*i/*i,* words with, **2-1:**
T33, T42–T43, T67, T81, T91,
T376, T424

short vowels /e/*e, /*o/*o, /*u/*u,* words
with, **2-1:** T131, T140–T141,
T161, T177, T187, T393, T424

short vowel /e/*ea,* words with, **2-4:**
T133, T142–T143, T169, T185,
T195, T405, T436

Spelling Test, **2-1:** T33, T91, T131,
T187, T215, T267, T295, T349,
T376, T424; **2-2:** T33, T91, T131,
T189, T217, T273, T301, T361,
T388, T436; **2-3:** T33, T89, T129,
T183, T211, T269, T297, T351,
T378, T424; **2-4:** T33, T93, T133,
T195, T223, T279, T307, T361,
T388, T436; **2-5:** T33, T95, T135,
T195, T223, T287, T315, T369,
T396, T444; **2-6:** T33, T95, T135,
T191, T219, T281, T309, T371,
T398, T446

vowel variant /ô/*a(l), ough,* words
with, **2-6:** T219, T228–T229,
T253, T269, T281, T425, T446

vowel variant /ô/*aw, au(gh),* words
with, **2-6:** T135, T144–T145,
T165, T181, T191, T415, T446

vowel variant /o͞o/*oo, ew, ue, ui, ou,*
words with, **2-5:** T223, T232–
T233, T259, T275, T287, T423

vowel variant /o͝o/*oo, ou,* words with,
2-6: T33, T42–T43, T67, T83,
T95, T398, T446

Writing Application, **2-1:** T91, T187,
T267, T349; **2-2:** T91, T189,
T273, T361; **2-3:** T89, T183,
T269, T351; **2-4:** T93, T195,

T279, T361; **2-5:** T95, T195,
T287, T369; **2-6:** T95, T191,
T281, T311

Spelling Practice Book, 2-1: T67, T81,
T161, T177, T243, T257, T325,
T339, T392, T402, T412, T424;
2-2: T65, T81, T163, T179, T249,
T263, T335, T351, T414, T424,
T436; **2-3:** T33, T65, T79, T129,
T159, T173, T211, T245, T259,
T297, T327, T341, T424; **2-4:** T65,
T81, T169, T185, T251, T267,
T335, T351, T414, T424, T436;
2-5: T67, T83, T169, T185, T259,
T275, T343, T359, T412, T422,
T432, T444; **2-6:** T67, T83, T165,
T181, T253, T269, T345, T361,
T414, T424, T434, T446

Staff Development
See **Professional Development**

Stations
See **Literacy Centers**

Story
See **Student Edition,** Literature
Selections; **Writing,** forms,
personal narrative

Story Elements
See **Focus Skills,** characters; plot;
setting

Story Events
See **Focus Skills,** plot

Story Grammar
See **Focus Skills,** characters; plot;
setting

Story Map
See **Graphic Organizers,** story map

Story Retelling Cards, 2-1: T60, T154,
T236, T318; **2-2:** T58, T156, T242,
T328; **2-3:** T58, T152, T238, T320;
2-4: T58, T162, T244, T328; **2-5:**
T60, T162, T252, T336; **2-6:** T60,
T158, T246, T338

Story Structure
See **Focus Strategies,** use story
structure

Strategic Intervention Resource Kit
See **Intervention,** Strategic
Intervention Resource Kit

Strategic Intervention Teacher Guide
See **Intervention,** Strategic
Intervention Teacher Guide

Structural Analysis
See **Decoding/Word Work**

Structural Cues
See **Decoding/Word Work**

Structural Features
See **Decoding/Word Work**

Student Edition
author features, **2-1:** T59, T153, T235,
T317; **2-2:** T57, T155, T241,
T327; **2-3:** T57, T237, T319;
2-4: T57, T161, T243, T257; **2-5:**
T59, T161, T251, T335; **2-6:** T59,
T157, T245, T337

comparing texts, **2-1:** T72–T73, T168–
T169, T248–T249, T330–T331;
2-2: T72–T73, T170–T171, T254–
T255, T342–T343; **2-3:** T70–T71,
T164–T165, T250–T251, T332–
T333; **2-4:** T72–T73, T176–T177,
T258–T259, T342–T343; **2-5:**
T74–T75, T176–T177, T264–
T265, T348–T349; **2-6:** T72–T73,
T170–T171, T258–T259, T350–
T351

comprehension strategies, **2-1:** T46–
T47, T144–T145, T228–T229,
T308–T309; **2-2:** T46–T47,
T144–T145, T230–T231, T314–
T315; **2-3:** T46–T47, T142–T143,
T224–T225, T310–T311; **2-4:**
T46–T47, T146–T147, T236–
T237, T320–T321; **2-5:** T46–T47,
T148–T149, T236–T237, T328–
T329; **2-6:** T46–T47, T148–T149,
T232–T233, T322–T323

Connections, **2-1:** T72–T73, T168–
T169, T248–T249, T330–T331;
2-2: T72–T73, T170–T171, T254–
T255, T342–T343; **2-3:** T70–T71,
T164–T165, T250–T251, T332–
T333; **2-4:** T72–T73, T176–T177,
T258–T259, T342–T343; **2-5:**
T74–T75, T176–T177, T264–
T265, T348–T349; **2-6:** T72–T73,
T170–T171, T258–T259, T350–
T351
decoding/word work, **2-1:** T73, T169,
T212–T213, T249, T331; **2-2:**
T73, T171, T255, T343; **2-3:** T71,
T165, T208–T209, T251, T333;
2-4: T73, T177, T220–T221, T259,
T343; **2-5:** T75, T177, T220–
T221, T265, T349; **2-6:** T73,
T171, T216–T217, T259, T351
Glossary, **2-1:** R18–R21; **2-2:**
R18–R21; **2-3:** R18–R21; **2-4:**
R18–R21; **2-5:** R18–R21; **2-6:**
R18–R21
illustrator features, **2-1:** T59, T153,
T235; **2-2:** T155, T241, T327; **2-3:**
T57, T237; **2-4:** T57, T161, T243;
2-5: T59, T161; **2-6:** T59, T157,
T245, T337
Index, **2-1:** R21; **2-2:** R21; **2-3:** R21;
2-4: R21; **2-5:** R21; **2-6:** R21
Index of Titles and Authors, **2-1:** R21;
2-2: R21; T-3: R21; **2-4:** R21; **2-5:**
R21; **2-6:** R21
Literature Selections
"Ah, Music!" **2-4:** T236–T243
"Animals Have Special Jobs," **2-1:**
T329
"Annie's Gifts," **2-4:** T146–T161
"Arthur's Reading Race," **2-1:**
T46–T59
"At Play: Long Ago and Today,"
2-3: T142–T151
"Baby Tapir Is Born," **2-3:** T331
"The Bat," **2-2:** T253

"Be Sun Safe," **2-6:** T348–T349
"The Bee," **2-5:** T236–T251
"Beyond Old MacDonald," **2-5:**
T174–T175
"Big Bushy Mustache," **2-3:**
T224–T237
"California Bee Business," **2-5:**
T262–T263
"A Chair for My Mother," **2-5:**
T46–T59
"Changing," **2-3:** T249
"Chimp Computer Whiz," **2-5:**
T346–T347
"Click, Clack, Moo: Cows That
Type," **2-2:** T314–T327
"Come, My Little Children, Here
Are Songs for You," **2-4:**
T256–T257
"Dogs," **2-1:** T247
"Dogs," **2-1:** T308–T317
"Frog and Toad All Year," **2-1:**
T144–T153
"Gabriela Mistral: A Poet's Life In
Photos," **2-6:** T168–T169
"The Great Ball Game," **2-2:**
T230–T241
"Gus and Grandpa and the Two-
Wheeled Bike," **2-2:** T144–
T155
"Henry and Mudge," **2-1:** T228–
T235
"A History of Games and Toys in
the United States," **2-3:** T163
"Interview with Author Loreen
Leedy," **2-4:** T70–T71
"Jamaica Louise James," **2-3:**
T46–T57
"A Lazy Thought," **2-3:** T69
"Let's Go Rock Collecting," **2-6:**
T233–T245
"Life as a Frog," **2-1:** T165–T167
"Life Cycle of a Frog," **2-3:**
T414–T416

"The Life of George Washington
Carver," **2-4:** T320–T327
"The Lizard and the Sun," **2-6:**
T322–T337
"Mr. Putter and Tabby Write the
Book," **2-4:** T46–T57
"My Name Is Gabriela," **2-6:**
T148–T157
"No Helmet? Pay Up!" **2-2:**
T168–T169
"Nutty Facts About Peanuts," **2-4:**
T340–T341
"Pebbles," **2-6:** T256–T257
"Rain Forest Babies," **2-3:** T310–
T319
"Reading with Your Fingers," **2-1:**
T71
"Rock-a-Bye Cows," **2-2:** T340–
T341
"Sarah Enters a Painting," **2-4:**
T174–T175
"Saving Money," **2-5:** T72–T73
"Serious Farm," **2-5:** T148–T161
"South Korea," **2-6:** T70–T71
"Two Races," **2-2:** T70–T71
"Watching in the Wild," **2-5:**
T328–T335
"Where on Earth Is My Bagel?"
2-6: T46–T59
"Winners Never Quit," **2-2:**
T46–T57
Readers' Theater, **2-1:** "Neighborhood
News," T379–T386; **2-2:** "A Trip
to the Fire Station," T391–T398;
2-3: "A Birthday Mystery," T381–
T386; **2-4:** "What's My Job?"
T393–T398; **2-5:** "Town Hall,"
T401–T406; **2-6:** "Cross-Country
Vacation," T403–T408
Student-Writing Models, **2-1:** T107;
2-2: T107; **2-3:** T105; **2-4:** T109;
2-5: T111; **2-6:** T111
Theme Opener, **2-1:** T14–T15; **2-2:**
T14–T15; **2-3:** T14–T15; **2-4:**

T14–T15; **2-5:** T14–T15; **2-6:** T14–T15

Think Critically, **2-1:** T58, T152, T234, T317; **2-2:** T56, T154, T240, T326; **2-3:** T57, T151, T236, T319; **2-4:** T57, T161, T243, T327; **2-5:** T59, T161, T251, T335; **2-6:** T58, T157, T245, T336

Vocabulary, **2-1:** T44–T45, T142–T143, T226–T227, T306–T307; **2-2:** T44–T45, T142–T143, T228–T229, T312–T313; **2-3:** T44–T45, T140–T141, T222–T223, T308–T309; **2-4:** T44–T45, T144–T145, T234–T235, T318–T319; **2-5:** T44–T45, T146–T147, T234–T235, T326–T327; **2-6:** T44–T45, T146–T147, T230–T231, T320–T321

Student-Friendly Explanations

See **Vocabulary,** Student-Friendly Explanations

Student-Writing Models

See **Reader-Writing Connection,** Student-Writing Model; **Student Edition,** Student-Writing Models

Suffixes

See **Decoding/Word Work**

Summarize, 2-1: T318; **2-2:** T58; **2-3:** T152, T320; **2-4:** T36, T244, T328; **2-5:** T252, T336; **2-6:** T60, T158, T169, T246, T330, T338

See also **Comprehension Skills,** summarize; **Focus Strategies,** summarize

Summative Assessment

See **Assessment,** Benchmark Assessments

Summary

See **Writing,** forms

Supporting Standards

See **Cross-Curricular Connections**

Syllabication

See **Decoding/Word Work,** syllables

Syllables

See **Decoding/Word Work,** multisyllabic words

Synonyms

See **Vocabulary,** synonyms

Table of Contents

See **Research/Study Skills,** book parts

Teacher Read-Aloud

See **Big Book of Rhymes and Poems; Read-Aloud Anthology**

Teacher Resource Book, 2-1: T26, T124, T208, T288, T370, T379, T396, T418, T427; **2-2:** T26, T124, T178, T210, T262, T294, T350, T382, T391, T408, T430, T439; **2-3:** T26, T122, T204, T290, T372, T381, T396, T418, T427; **2-4:** T26, T126, T216, T300, T382, T391, T408, T430, T439; **2-5:** T26, T128, T216, T308, T390, T399, T416, T438, T447; **2-6:** T26, T128, T212, T302, T392, T401, T418, T440, T449

Homework Copying Master, **2-1:** T26, T124, T208, T288, T370; **2-2:** T26, T124, T210, T294, T382; **2-3:** T26, T122, T204, T290, T372; **2-4:** T26, T126, T216, T300, T382; **2-5:** T26, T128, T216, T308, T390; **2-6:** T26, T128, T212, T302, T392

My Reading Log, **2-1:** T434; **2-2:** T446; **2-3:** T434; **2-4:** T446; **2-5:** T454; **2-6:** T456

My Weekly Contract, **2-1:** T26, T124, T208, T288, T370; **2-2:** T26, T124, T210, T294, T382; **2-3:** T26, T122, T204, T290, T372; **2-4:** T26, T126, T216, T300, T382; **2-5:** T26, T128,

T216, T308, T390; **2-6:** T26, T128, T212, T302, T392

Readers' Theater Backdrops, **2-1:** T379, T427; **2-2:** T391, T439; **2-3:** T381, T427; **2-4:** T391, T430, T439; **2-5:** T399, T416, T438, T447

Readers' Theater Scripts, **2-1:** T379, T396, T418, T427; **2-2:** T391, T408, T430, T439; **2-3:** T381, T396; **2-4:** T391, T408, T430, T439; **2-5:** T399, T416, T438, T447; **2-6:** T401, T402, T418, T440, T449

School-Home Connections, **2-1:** T26, T124, T208, T288, T370; **2-2:** T26, T124, T210, T294, T382; **2-3:** T26, T122, T204, T290, T372; **2-4:** T26, T126, T216, T300, T382; **2-5:** T26, T128, T216, T308, T390; **2-6:** T26, T128, T212, T302, T392

syllabication cards, **2-1:** T80; **2-2:** T262, T350; **2-3:** T78, T340; **2-4:** T80, T266, T350; **2-5:** T184, T274; **2-6:** T82

word cards, **2-1:** T89, T127, T291, T303, T323, T326, T337, T347; **2-2:** T29, T41, T63, T79, T127, T139, T161, T177, T187, T213, T225, T247, T261, T271, T297, T309, T333, T349, T359; **2-3:** T66, T160, T246, T328, T405, T417; **2-4:** T29, T41, T63, T79, T91, T129, T141, T167, T183, T193, T219, T231, T249, T265, T277, T303, T315, T333, T349, T359; **2-5:** T29, T41, T65, T81, T93, T131, T143, T167, T183, T193, T219, T231, T257, T273, T285, T311, T323, T341, T357, T367; **2-6:** T29, T41,

T65, T81, T93, T131, T143, T163, T179, T189, T215, T227, T251, T267, T279, T305, T317, T343, T359, T369

Teacher Training

See **Professional Development**

Technology

search engine, use, **2-5:** T319

technology resources, **2-1:** T6; **2-2:** T6; **2-3:** T6; **2-4:** T6; **2-5:** T6; **2-6:** T6

Audiotext, **2-1:** T18, T47, T93, T116, T145, T189, T200, T229, T280, T309, T351, T362, T380, T406, T418; **2-2:** T18, T47, T116, T145, T202, T231, T286, T315, T363, T374, T392, T408, T418, T430; **2-3:** T18, T47, T91, T114, T122, T143, T185, T196, T225, T271, T282, T290, T311, T353, T364, T372, T382, T396, T406, T418; **2-4:** T18, T47, T94, T118, T147, T196, T208, T237, T280, T292, T321, T362, T374, T392, T408, T418, T430; **2-5:** T18, T47, T96, T120, T149, T208, T237, T300, T329, T382, T400, T416, T426; **2-6:** T18, T47, T96, T120, T149, T192, T204, T233, T282, T294, T323, T372, T384, T402

Decodable Books, online

Take-Home Version, **2-1:** T32, T67, T130, T161, T214, T243, T294, T325; **2-2:** T32, T65, T130, T163, T216, T249, T300, T335; **2-3:** T32, T65, T128, T159, T210, T245, T296, T327; **2-4:** T32, T65, T132, T169, T222, T251, T306, T335; **2-5:** T32, T67, T134, T169, T222, T259, T314, T343;

2-6: T32, T67, T134, T165, T218, T253, T308, T345

Digital Classroom, **2-1:** T6, T17, T115, T199, T279, T361; **2-2:** T6, T17, T115, T201, T285, T373; **2-3:** T6, T17, T113, T195, T281, T363; **2-4:** T6, T17, T117, T207, T291, T373; **2-5:** T6, T17, T119, T207, T299, T381; **2-6:** T6, T17, T119, T203, T293, T383

eBook, **2-1:** T2, T47, T145, T229, T309, T380; **2-2:** T2, T47, T145, T231, T315, T392; **2-3:** T2, T47, T143, T225, T311, T382; **2-4:** T2, T47, T147, T237, T321, T392; **2-5:** T2, T47, T149, T237, T329, T400; **2-6:** T2, T47, T149, T233, T256, T323, T402

ePlanner, **2-1:** T6; **2-2:** T6; **2-3:** T6; **2-4:** T6; **2-5:** T6; **2-6:** T6

Grammar Glossary, **2-1:** T38, T136, T220, T300; **2-2:** T38, T136, T222, T306; **2-3:** T38, T134, T216, T302; **2-4:** T38, T138, T228, T312; **2-5:** T38, T140, T228, T320; **2-6:** T38, T140, T224, T314

podcasting, **2-1:** T60, T97, T154, T193, T236, T273, T308, T318, T429; **2-2:** T97, T195, T230, T242, T314, T328, T367, T391, T441; **2-3:** T429; **2-4:** T58, T244, T285, T441; **2-5:** T162, T201, T252, T449; **2-6:** T60, T101, T158, T338, T377, T451

Resources for Parents and Teachers: Homework Help, **2-1:** T27, T125, T209, T289, T371; **2-2:** T27, T125, T211, T295, T383; **2-3:** T27, T123, T205, T291, T373; **2-4:** T27,

T127, T217, T301, T383; **2-5:** T27, T129, T217, T309, T391; **2-6:** T27, T129, T213, T303, T393

Splash into Phonics CD-ROM, **2-1:** T6; **2-2:** T6; **2-3:** T6; **2-4:** T6; **2-5:** T6; **2-6:** T6

web site, Harcourt School Publishers Online

Assessment and ExamView, **2-1:** T97, T193, T273, T355; **2-2:** T97, T195, T279, T367; **2-3:** T95, T189, T275, T357; **2-4:** T99, T201, T285, T367, T441; **2-5:** T101, T201, T293, T375, T449; **2-6:** T101, T197, T287, T377, T451

Leveled Readers online, **2-1:** T4, T99, T101, T195, T197, T275, T277, T357, T359; **2-2:** T4, T99, T101, T197, T199, T281, T283, T369, T371; **2-3:** T4, T97, T99, T191, T193, T277, T279, T359, T361, T431; **2-4:** T101, T103, T203, T205, T287, T289, T369, T371, T443, T445; **2-5:** T103, T105, T203, T205, T295, T297, T377, T379, T451, T453; **2-6:** T103, T105, T199, T201, T289, T379, T381, T453, T455

technology skills

word-processing skills, **2-1:** T421; **2-2:** T111, T433; **2-3:** T109, T421; **2-4:** T113; **2-5:** T115, T441; **2-6:** T443

Technology Center

See **Literacy Centers**

Technology Resources

See **Technology,** technology resources

Technology Skills

See **Technology,** technology skills

Test Preparation, 2-1: T11; **2-2:** T11; **2-3:** T11; **2-4:** T11; **2-5:** T11; **2-6:** T11

Tested or Timed Writing

See **Writing,** Writing on Demand

Tested Skills, 2-1: T7; **2-2:** T7; **2-3:** T7; **2-4:** T7; **2-5:** T7; **2-6:** T7

Theme

See **Comprehension Skills,** theme

Theme Introduction

See **Introduce the Theme**

Theme Opener, 2-1: T1; **2-2:** T1; **2-3:** T1; **2-4:** T1; **2-5:** T1; **2-6:** T1

See also **Student Edition,** Theme Opener

Theme Overview, 2-1: x–xi; **2-2:** x–xi; **2-3:** x–xi; **2-4:** x–xi; **2-5:** x–xi; **2-6:** x–xi

Theme Planner, 2-1: T8–T9; **2-2:** T8–T9; **2-3:** T8–T9; **2-4:** T8–T9; **2-5:** T8–T9; **2-6:** T8–T9

Theme Project, 2-1: T12–T13, T435; **2-2:** T12–T13, T447; **2-3:** T12–T13, T435; **2-4:** T12–T13, T447; **2-5:** T12–T13, T455; **2-6:** T12–T13, T457

Journey Board Games, **2-6:** T12–T13, T457

Musical Creations, **2-4:** T12–T13, T447

Pet Handbook, **2-1:** T12–T13, T435

School Community Mural, **2-5:** T12–T13, T455

Sports Poll, **2-2:** T12–T13, T447

Then-and-Now Display, **2-3:** T12–T13, T435

Theme Resources, 2-1: T2–T3; **2-2:** T2–T3; **2-3:** T2–T3; **2-4:** T2–T3; **2-5:** T2–T3; **2-6:** T2–T3

Theme Table of Contents, 2-1: iv–v; **2-2:** iv–v; **2-3:** iv–v; **2-4:** iv–v; **2-5:** iv–v; **2-6:** iv–v

Theme Test

See **Assessment,** Theme Test

Theme Wrap-Up and Review, 2-1: T434–T435; **2-2:** T446–T447; **2-3:** T434–T435; **2-4:** T446–T447; **2-5:** T454–T455; **2-6:** T456–T457

Thesaurus

See **Research/Study Skills,** thesaurus

Think Aloud, 2-1: T34, T36, T46, T50, T54, T57, T69, T83, T132, T134, T144, T146, T151, T163, T179, T216, T218, T230, T233, T245, T259, T296, T298, T308, T310, T312, T377, T380, T382, T383, T399, T416, T418, T421; **2-2:** T34, T36, T48, T50, T67, T68, T132, T146, T151, T165, T166, T181, T218, T220, T232, T236, T251, T265, T302, T304, T316, T337, T353, T389, T392, T394, T395, T398, T406, T408, T411, T428, T430, T433; **2-3:** T34, T36, T46, T48, T50, T54, T67, T81, T102, T106, T132, T145, T150, T161, T175, T212, T214, T226, T233, T235, T247, T261, T298, T300, T313, T315, T329, T343, T379, T382, T383, T385, T394, T396, T416, T418, T421; **2-4:** T34, T36, T49, T54, T66, T67, T68, T82, T84, T85, T134, T136, T148, T154, T158, T170, T171, T172, T186, T226, T238, T242, T252, T268, T270, T308, T310, T322, T336, T337, T338, T352, T389, T392, T394, T395, T406, T407, T408, T411, T428, T430, T433; **2-5:** T34, T36, T49, T50, T57, T68, T70, T84, T86, T87, T136, T138, T150, T156, T160, T170, T186, T224, T226, T236, T239, T244, T260, T261, T268, T276, T278, T279, T316, T318, T328, T330, T344, T352, T360, T397, T400, T402, T403, T414, T415, T416, T419, T436, T438, T441, T446; **2-6:** T34, T36, T50, T57, T68, T76, T84, T87, T136, T138, T151, T153, T166, T174, T182, T220, T222, T225, T235, T236, T240, T243, T248, T254, T270, T272, T273, T310, T312, T324, T331, T346, T362, T399, T402, T404, T405, T416, T418, T421, T426, T438, T440, T443, T448

Think Critically

See **Leveled Readers,** Think Critically; **Student Edition,** Think Critically

Tier Two Words

See **Vocabulary,** robust vocabulary

Timed Reading, 2-1: T93, T189, T269, T351; **2-2:** T93, T191, T275, T363; **2-3:** T91, T165, T185, T271, T353; **2-4:** T94, T196, T280, T362; **2-5:** T96, T196, T265, T288; **2-6:** T96, T192, T282, T372

Timed Writing, 2-1: T112–T113; **2-2:** T112–T113; **2-3:** T110–T111; **2-4:** T114–T115; **2-5:** T116–T117; **2-6:** T116–T117

Trade Books

See **Classroom Library Collection**

Traits of Good Writing

See **Writing,** traits

Transparencies

graphic organizers, **2-1:** T46, T60, T95, T105, T108, T109, T144, T154, T191, T228, T236, T271, T308, T318; **2-2:** T46, T58, T68, T95, T105, T108, T144, T156, T166, T193, T230, T242, T277, T314, T328, T365; **2-3:** T46, T58, T93, T142, T152, T187, T224, T238, T273, T310, T355; **2-4:** T46, T58, T96, T107, T146, T162, T198, T236, T244, T320, T328; **2-5:** T46, T60, T98, T109, T112, T148, T162, T198, T236, T252, T328, T336,

T372; **2-6:** T46, T60, T98, T136,
T148, T158, T194, T232, T246,
T322, T338, T374
language arts, **2-1:** T38, T39, T110,
T112, T136, T137, T220, T221,
T300, T301; **2-2:** T38, T39, T109,
T112, T136, T137, T222, T223,
T306, T307; **2-3:** T38, T39, T134,
T135, T216, T217, T302, T303;
2-4: T38, T39, T112, T114, T138,
T139, T228, T229, T312, T313;
2-5: T38, T39, T114, T116, T140,
T141, T228, T229, T320, T321;
2-6: T38, T39, T109, T112, T116,
T140, T141, T224, T225, T314,
T315
reading, **2-1:** T29, T32, T37, T61, T66,
T75, T80, T82, T84, T85, T127,
T130, T135, T155, T160, T170,
T176, T178, T180, T181, T211,
T214, T219, T237, T242, T250,
T256, T258, T260, T261, T291,
T294, T299, T319, T324, T332,
T338, T340, T342, T343, T387,
T397, T407; **2-2:** T29, T32, T37,
T59, T64, T74, T80, T82, T84,
T85, T127, T130, T135, T157,
T162, T172, T178, T180, T182,
T183, T213, T216, T221, T243,
T248, T256, T262, T264, T266,
T267, T297, T300, T305, T329,
T334, T344, T350, T352, T354,
T355, T399, T409, T419, T431;
2-3: T29, T32, T37, T59, T64,
T72, T78, T80, T82, T83, T125,
T128, T133, T153, T158, T166,
T172, T174, T176, T177, T207,
T210, T215, T239, T244, T252,
T258, T260, T262, T263, T293,
T296, T301, T321, T326, T334,
T340, T342, T344, T345, T387,
T397, T407, T419; **2-4:** T29, T32,
T37, T44, T59, T64, T68, T80,
T83, T87, T129, T132, T137,

T144, T163, T168, T173, T179,
T184, T187, T189, T219, T222,
T227, T234, T245, T250, T255,
T261, T266, T269, T273, T303,
T306, T311, T318, T329, T334,
T339, T345, T350, T353, T355,
T399, T409; **2-5:** T29, T32, T37,
T44, T61, T66, T71, T77, T82,
T85, T89, T98, T131, T134, T139,
T146, T163, T168, T173, T179,
T184, T187, T189, T219, T222,
T224, T227, T234, T253, T258,
T267, T269, T274, T277, T281,
T311, T314, T319, T326, T337,
T342, T351, T353, T358, T361,
T363, T398, T407, T417; **2-6:**
T29, T32, T37, T44, T61, T66,
T75, T82, T85, T89, T131, T134,
T139, T146, T159, T164, T173,
T174, T180, T183, T215, T218,
T223, T230, T247, T252, T261,
T263, T268, T271, T275, T305,
T308, T313, T320, T339, T344,
T353, T354, T360, T363, T365,
T409, T419

Variant Vowels
  See **Decoding/Word Work,** variant
    vowels
Venn diagram
  See **Graphic Organizers,** Venn diagram
Verbs
  See **Grammar,** verbs
Vocabulary
  See also **High-Frequency Words;**
    Literacy Centers, Word Work
    Center; **Monitor Progress,**
    vocabulary; **Student Edition,**
    Vocabulary; **Word Wall**
antonyms, **2-1:** T333, T353; **2-4:**
  T87, T189; **2-5:** T281, T363; **2-6:**
  T76–T77, T174–T175
base words, **2-3:** T172, T182, T258,
  T268; **2-4:** T273
categories of words, **2-4:** T96; **2-5:**
  T185; **2-6:** T284
compound words, **2-2:** T125, T178,
  T188, T350, T360; **2-6:** T228
connotations, **2-4:** T96
content-area vocabulary, **2-1:** T55,
  T150, T247; **2-2:** T55, T149,
  T237, T253, T323; **2-3:** T59,
  T153, T321; **2-4:** T71, T239,
  T325, T341; **2-5:** T48, T73, T242;
  2-6: T51, T235, T257, T333
context clues, **2-1:** T37, T61, T74–
  T75, T85, T135, T155, T170–
  T171, T181, T194, T219, T237,
  T250–T251, T261, T299, T319,
  T332–T333, T343, T387, T393,
  T397, T402, T413, T419; **2-2:** T37,
  T59, T74–T75, T85, T135, T157,
  T172–T173, T183, T198, T221,
  T243, T256–T257, T282, T305,
  T318, T320, T329, T344–T345,
  T355, T399, T405, T409, T414,
  T419, T425, T431; **2-3:** T37, T59,

Universal Access
  See **Differentiated Instruction**
Usage
  See **Grammar**
Use Graphic Organizers
  See **Focus Strategies,** use graphic
    organizers
Use Multiple Strategies
  See **Focus Strategies,** use multiple
    strategies
Use Story Structure
  See **Focus Strategies,** use story structure

T72, T73, T83, T133, T153, T166–T167, T177, T191, T215, T239, T252–T253, T263, T301, T321, T334–T335, T345, T387, T393, T397, T407, T413, T419; **2-4:** T37, T43, T44, T59, T74–T75, T86, T96, T97, T102, T137, T144, T163, T178–T179, T188–T189, T202, T227, T233, T234, T240, T245, T257, T260–T261, T272–T273, T283, T288, T311, T318, T324, T344–T345, T354, T365, T399, T405, T409, T414, T419, T425, T431; **2-5:** T37, T44, T61, T76–T77, T88, T96, T99, T139, T146, T151, T163, T178–T179, T188, T196, T227, T234, T253, T266, T280, T319, T326, T337, T350–T351, T362, T372, T373, T407, T413, T417, T422, T427, T433, T439; **2-6:** T37, T43, T44, T48, T52, T55, T61, T66, T74–T75, T88, T99, T139, T146, T152, T159, T172–T173, T184, T192, T194, T223, T234, T247, T260, T262–T263, T274, T285, T313, T319, T320, T325, T327, T329, T334, T339, T352–T353, T354, T364, T375, T378, T409, T415, T419, T424, T429, T435, T441

homophones, **2-4:** T31, T316; **2-5:** T133; **2-6:** T133, T318

idioms, **2-1:** T56; **2-2:** T235; **2-4:** T50; **2-5:** T55; **2-6:** T138

multiple-meaning words, **2-1:** T147; **2-2:** T424; **2-4:** T257; **2-5:** T174, T175; **2-6:** T192, T262–T263, T354–T355

prefixes, suffixes, roots, **2-4:** T42, T80, T92, T266, T278; **2-5:** T274, T286; **2-6:** T82, T94, T268, T275, T280

robust vocabulary, **2-1:** T11, T37, T61, T74–T75, T85, T95, T135, T155,

T170–T171, T181, T191, T219, T237, T250–T251, T261, T271, T299, T319, T332–T333, T343, T353, T387, T397, T407, T419; **2-2:** T11, T37, T59, T74–T75, T85, T95, T135, T157, T172–T173, T183, T193, T221, T243, T256–T257, T267, T277, T305, T329, T344–T345, T355, T365, T399, T409, T419, T431; **2-3:** T11, T37, T59, T72–T73, T83, T93, T133, T153, T166–T167, T177, T187, T215, T239, T252–T253, T263, T273, T301, T321, T334–T335, T345, T355, T387, T397, T407, T419; **2-4:** T11, T37, T44–T45, T59, T74–T75, T86–T87, T96–T97, T137, T144–T145, T163, T178–T179, T188–T189, T198–T199, T227, T234–T235, T245, T260–T261, T272–T273, T282–T283, T311, T318–T319, T329, T344–T345, T354–T355, T364–T365, T390, T399, T409, T419, T431; **2-5:** T11, T37, T44–T45, T61, T76–T77, T88–T89, T98–T99, T139, T146–T147, T163, T178–T179, T188–T189, T198–T199, T227, T234–T235, T253, T266–T267, T280–T281, T290–T291, T319, T326–T327, T337, T350–T351, T362–T363, T372–T373, T398, T407, T417, T427, T439; **2-6:** T11, T37, T44–T45, T61, T74–T75, T88–T89, T98–T99, T139, T146–T147, T159, T172–T173, T184–T185, T194–T195, T223, T230–T231, T247, T260–T261, T274–T275, T284–T285, T313, T320–T321, T339, T352–T353, T364–T365, T374–T375, T400, T409, T419, T429, T441

Student-Friendly Explanations, **2-1:** T37, T61, T75, T85, T95, T135, T155, T170, T181, T191, T219, T237, T250, T261, T271, T299, T319, T332, T343, T353, T387, T397, T407, T419; **2-2:** T37, T59, T74, T85, T95, T135, T157, T172, T183, T193, T221, T243, T256, T267, T277, T305, T329, T344, T355, T365, T399, T409, T419, T431; **2-3:** T37, T59, T72, T83, T133, T153, T166, T177, T215, T239, T252, T263, T301, T321, T334, T345, T387, T397, T407, T419; **2-4:** T37, T44, T59, T75, T87, T137, T144, T163, T179, T189, T198, T227, T234, T245, T261, T273, T282, T311, T318, T329, T345, T355, T364, T390, T399, T409, T419, T431; **2-5:** T11, T37, T44, T61, T77, T89, T139, T146, T163, T179, T189, T227, T234, T253, T267, T281, T319, T326, T337, T351, T363, T398, T407, T417, T427, T439; **2-6:** T11, T37, T44, T61, T75, T89, T139, T146, T159, T173, T185, T223, T230, T247, T261, T275, T313, T320, T339, T353, T365, T400, T409, T419, T429, T441

synonyms, **2-1:** T333, T353; **2-4:** T189, T273, T355; **2-5:** T89, T189, T268–T269, T352–T353, T363, T365, T375; **2-6:** T89, T195, T257, T265, T365

vocabulary and concept development, **2-1:** T11, T37, T61, T74–T75, T85, T95, T135, T155, T170–T171, T181, T191, T219, T237, T250–T251, T261, T271, T299, T315, T319, T332–T333, T343, T353, T387, T397, T407, T419; **2-2:** T11, T37, T59, T74–T75, T85, T95, T135, T157, T172–

T173, T183, T193, T221, T243,
T256–T257, T267, T277, T305,
T329, T344–T345, T355, T365,
T399, T409, T419, T431; **2-3:**
T11, T37, T59, T72–T73, T83,
T93, T133, T153, T166–T167,
T177, T187, T215, T239, T252–
T253, T263, T273, T301, T321,
T334–T335, T345, T355, T387,
T397, T407, T419; **2-4:** T11, T37,
T44–T45, T59, T74–T75, T86–
T87, T96–T97, T137, T144–T145,
T163, T178–T179, T188–T189,
T198–T199, T227, T234–T235,
T245, T260–T261, T272–T273,
T282–T283, T311, T318–T319,
T329, T344–T345, T354–T355,
T364–T365, T390, T399, T409,
T419, T431; **2-5:** T11, T37, T44–
T45, T61, T76–T77, T88–T89,
T98–T99, T139, T146–T147,
T163, T178–T179, T188–T189,
T198–T199, T227, T234–T235,
T253, T266–T267, T280–T281,
T290–T291, T319, T326–T327,
T337, T350–T351, T362–T363,
T372–T373, T398, T407, T417,
T427, T439; **2-6:** T11, T37, T44–
T45, T61, T74–T75, T88–T89,
T98–T99, T139, T146–T147,
T159, T172–T173, T184–T185,
T194–T195, T223, T230–T231,
T247, T260–T261, T274–T275,
T284–T285, T313, T320–T321,
T339, T352–T353, T364–T365,
T374–T375, T400, T409, T419,
T429, T441

vocabulary review, cumulative, **2-1:**
T92, T95, T188, T191, T268,
T271, T350, T353, R11; **2-2:** T92,
T95, T190, T193, T274, T277,
T362, T365, R11; **2-3:** T90, T93,
T184, T187, T270, T273, T352,
T355, R11; **2-4:** T96–T97, T198–

T199, T282–T283, T364–T365,
R11; **2-5:** T98–T99, T198–T199,
T290–T291, T372–T373; **2-6:**
T98–T99, T194–T195, T284–
T285, T374–T375

word meaning, **2-1:** T11, T37, T61,
T74–T75, T85, T95, T135, T155,
T170–T171, T181, T191, T219,
T237, T250–T251, T261, T271,
T299, T315, T319, T332–T333,
T343, T353, T387, T397, T407,
T419; **2-2:** T11, T37, T59, T74–
T75, T85, T95, T135, T157, T172–
T173, T183, T193, T221, T243,
T256–T257, T267, T277, T305,
T329, T344–T345, T355, T365,
T399, T409, T419, T431; **2-3:**
T11, T37, T59, T72–T73, T83,
T93, T133, T153, T166–T167,
T177, T187, T215, T239, T252–
T253, T263, T273, T301, T321,
T334–T335, T345, T355, T387,
T397, T407, T419; **2-4:** T11, T37,
T44–T45, T59, T74–T75, T86–
T87, T96–T97, T137, T144–T145,
T163, T178–T179, T188–T189,
T198–T199, T227, T234–T235,
T245, T260–T261, T272–T273,
T282–T283, T311, T318–T319,
T329, T344–T345, T354–T355,
T364–T365, T390, T399, T409,
T419, T431; **2-5:** T11, T37, T44–
T45, T61, T76–T77, T88–T89,
T98–T99, T139, T146–T147,
T163, T178–T179, T188–T189,
T198–T199, T227, T234–T235,
T253, T266–T267, T280–T281,
T290–T291, T319, T326–T327,
T337, T350–T351, T362–T363,
T372–T373, T398, T407, T417,
T427, T439; **2-6:** T11, T37, T44–
T45, T61, T74–T75, T88–T89,
T98–T99, T139, T146–T147,
T159, T172–T173, T184–T185,

T194–T195, T223, T230–T231,
T247, T260–T261, T274–T275,
T284–T285, T313, T320–T321,
T339, T352–T353, T364–T365,
T374–T375, T400, T409, T419,
T429, T441

word sort, **2-1:** T92, T188, T268,
T350; **2-4:** T64, T73, T92, T232,
T250, T278, T282, T316, T364;
2-5: T42, T94, T144, T185, T194,
T198, T290; **2-6:** T66, T94, T185,
T190, T194, T195, T252, T259,
T275, T280, T344, T370

word wall, **2-1:** T29, T41, T65, T79,
T89, T127, T139, T159, T175, T185,
T211, T223, T241, T255, T265,
T291, T303, T323, T337, T347,
T373, T391, T401, T411, T423; **2-2:**
T29, T41, T63, T79, T89, T127,
T139, T161, T177, T187, T213,
T225, T247, T261, T271, T297,
T309, T333, T349, T359, T385,
T403, T413, T423, T435; **2-3:** T29,
T41, T63, T77, T87, T125, T137,
T157, T171, T181, T207, T219,
T243, T257, T267, T293, T305,
T325, T339, T349, T375, T391,
T401, T411, T423; **2-4:** T29, T41,
T63, T79, T91, T129, T141, T167,
T183, T193, T219, T231, T249,
T265, T277, T303, T315, T333,
T349, T359, T385, T403, T413,
T423, T435; **2-5:** T29, T41, T65,
T81, T93, T131, T143, T167, T183,
T193, T219, T231, T257, T273,
T285, T311, T323, T341, T357,
T367, T393, T411, T421, T431,
T443; **2-6:** T29, T41, T65, T81, T93,
T131, T143, T163, T179, T189,
T215, T227, T251, T267, T279,
T305, T317, T343, T359, T369,
T395, T413, T423, T433, T445

word web, **2-1:** T95, T191; **2-2:** T75;
2-3: T93, T187, T355; **2-4:** T198,

T226, T310; **2-5:** T63, T372; **2-6:** T98, T284, T374

Vocabulary and Concept Development

See **Vocabulary,** vocabulary and concept development

Voice

See **Writing,** traits, voice

Vowel Diphthongs

See **Decoding/Word Work,** diphthongs, vowel diphthongs

Web Site

See **Technology,** technology resources

Weekly Lesson Tests

See **Assessment,** Weekly Lesson Test

Whole-Group Planner

See **Lesson Planners,** 5-Day Whole-Group Planner

Word Analysis

See **Decoding/Word Work**

Word Attack

See **Decoding/Word Work**

Word Blending

See **Decoding/Word Work,** word blending

Word Building

See **Decoding/Word Work,** word building

Word Cards

See **Teacher Resource Book,** word cards

Word Choice

See **Writing,** traits

Word Families, 2-1: T66–T67, T160–T161, T242–T243, T324–T325; **2-2:** T64–T65, T162–T163, T248–T249, T334–T335; **2-3:** T64–T65, T158–T159, T244–T245, T326–T327; **2-4:** T42, T64–T65, T168–T169, T250–T251, T334–T335; **2-5:** T66–T67, T168–T169, T258–

T259, T342–T343; **2-6:** T66–T67, T164–T165, T252–T253, T344–T345

Word-Learning Strategies, 2-1: T11, T37, T61, T74–T75, T85, T95, T135, T155, T170–T171, T181, T191, T219, T237, T250–T251, T261, T271, T299, T319, T332–T333, T343, T353, T387, T397, T407, T419; **2-2:** T11, T37, T59, T74–T75, T85, T95, T135, T157, T172–T173, T183, T193, T221, T243, T256–T257, T267, T277, T305, T329, T344–T345, T355, T365, T399, T409, T419, T431; **2-3:** T11, T37, T59, T72–T73, T83, T93, T133, T153, T166–T167, T177, T187, T215, T239, T252–T253, T263, T273, T301, T321, T334–T335, T345, T355, T387, T397, T407, T419; **2-4:** T11, T37, T44–T45, T59, T74–T75, T86–T87, T96–T97, T137, T144–T145, T163, T178–T179, T188–T189, T198–T199, T227, T234–T235, T245, T260–T261, T272–T273, T282–T283, T311, T318–T319, T329, T344–T345, T354–T355, T364–T365, T390, T399, T409, T419, T431; **2-5:** T11, T37, T44–T45, T61, T76–T77, T88–T89, T98–T99, T139, T146–T147, T163, T178–T179, T188–T189, T198–T199, T227, T234–T235, T253, T266–T267, T280–T281, T290–T291, T319, T326–T327, T337, T350–T351, T362–T363, T372–T373, T398, T407, T417, T427, T439; **2-6:** T11, T37, T44–T45, T61, T74–T75, T88–T89, T98–T99, T139, T146–T147, T159, T172–T173, T184–T185, T194–T195, T223, T230–T231, T247, T260–T261, T274–T275,

T284–T285, T313, T320–T321, T339, T352–T353, T364–T365, T374–T375, T400, T409, T419, T429, T441

Word Lists, 2-1: T29, T33, T37, T41, T42, T44, T61, T65, T67, T68, T74, T79, T81, T82, T85, T89, T91, T92, T95, T127, T131, T135, T139, T140, T142, T155, T159, T161, T162, T170, T175, T177, T178, T181, T185, T187, T188, T191, T211, T215, T219, T223, T226, T237, T241, T243, T244, T250, T255, T257, T261, T265, T267, T268, T271, T291, T293, T295, T299, T303, T304, T306, T319, T323, T325, T326, T332, T338, T339, T340, T343, T347, T349, T350, T353, T373, T376, T378, T387, T391, T392, T395, T397, T401, T403, T405, T407, T411, T419, T423, T424, T426; **2-2:** T29, T33, T37, T41, T44, T59, T63, T65, T66, T74, T79, T81, T82, T85, T127, T131, T135, T139, T142, T157, T161, T163, T164, T172, T179, T180, T183, T189, T190, T193, T213, T217, T221, T225, T228, T243, T247, T249, T250, T256, T261, T263, T264, T267, T271, T273, T274, T277, T297, T301, T305, T312, T329, T333, T335, T336, T344, T349, T351, T352, T355, T359, T361, T362, T365, T385, T388, T390, T399, T403, T404, T407, T409, T413, T415, T417, T419, T423, T424, T429, T431, T435, T436, T438; **2-3:** T33, T44, T65, T66, T79, T80, T140, T159, T160, T222, T245, T246, T308, T327, T328, T375, T378, T380, T387, T391, T392, T395, T397, T401, T403, T405, T407, T411,

T412, T417, T419, T423, T424, T426; **2-4:** T29, T33, T37, T41, T42, T44, T59, T63, T65, T74, T79, T81, T86, T93, T129, T133, T137, T141, T142, T144, T163, T167, T169, T178, T179, T183, T185, T188, T189, T193, T195, T198, T219, T223, T227, T231, T232, T234, T245, T249, T251, T260, T265, T267, T272, T277, T279, T282, T303, T307, T311, T315, T316, T318, T329, T333, T335, T344, T345, T349, T351, T354, T355, T359, T361, T364, T385, T388, T399, T403, T404, T409, T413, T415, T419, T423, T424, T431, T435, T436; **2-5:** T29, T33, T37, T41, T42, T44, T61, T65, T67, T76, T81, T83, T88, T93, T95, T98, T131, T135, T139, T143, T144, T146, T163, T167, T179, T183, T185, T188, T193, T195, T198, T219, T223, T227, T231, T232, T234, T253, T257, T259, T266, T273, T275, T280, T285, T287, T290, T311, T315, T319, T323, T324, T326, T337, T341, T343, T350, T357, T359, T362, T367, T369, T372, T393, T396, T398, T407, T411, T412, T417, T421, T423, T427, T431, T432, T439, T443, T444; **2-6:** T29, T33, T37, T41, T42, T44, T61, T65, T67, T74, T81, T83, T88, T93, T95, T98, T131, T135, T139, T143, T144, T146, T159, T163, T165, T172, T179, T181, T184, T189, T191, T194, T215, T219, T223, T227, T228, T230, T247, T251, T253, T260, T267, T269, T274, T279, T281, T284, T305, T309, T313, T317, T318, T320, T339, T343, T345, T352, T359, T361, T364, T369, T371, T374,

T395, T398, T400, T409, T413, T414, T419, T423, T425, T429, T433, T434, T441, T445, T446

Word Order, 2-1: T62, T86, T96; **2-4:** T60

Word-Processing Skills

  See **Technology,** technology skills, word-processing skills

Word Recognition

  See **Decoding/Word Work; High-Frequency Words; Word Wall**

Word Sort, 2-1: T92, T188, T268, T348, T350, T426; **2-2:** T92, T190, T274, T362, T438; **2-3:** T88, T90, T184, T270, T326, T327, T350, T352, T426; **2-4:** T64, T73, T92, T232, T250, T278, T282, T316, T364; **2-5:** T42, T94, T144, T185, T194, T198, T290; **2-6:** T66, T94, T185, T190, T194, T195, T252, T259, T275, T280, T344, T370

Words to Know

  See **High-Frequency Words**

Word Wall, 2-1: T29, T41, T65, T79, T89, T127, T139, T159, T175, T185, T211, T223, T241, T255, T265, T291, T303, T323, T337, T347, T373, T391, T401, T411, T423; **2-2:** T29, T41, T63, T79, T89, T127, T139, T161, T177, T187, T213, T225, T247, T261, T271, T297, T309, T333, T349, T359, T385, T403, T413, T423, T435; **2-3:** T29, T41, T63, T77, T87, T125, T137, T157, T171, T181, T207, T219, T243, T257, T267, T293, T305, T325, T339, T349, T375, T391, T401, T411, T423; **2-4:** T29, T41, T63, T79, T91, T129, T141, T167, T183, T193, T219, T231, T249, T265, T277, T303, T315, T333, T349, T359, T385, T403, T413, T423, T435; **2-5:** T29, T41, T65, T81, T93, T131, T143, T167, T183,

T193, T219, T231, T257, T273, T285, T311, T323, T341, T357, T367, T393, T411, T421, T431, T443; **2-6:** T29, T41, T65, T81, T93, T131, T143, T163, T179, T189, T215, T227, T251, T267, T279, T305, T317, T343, T359, T369, T395, T413, T423, T433, T445

  See also **High-Frequency Words**

Word Web

  See **Graphic Organizers,** word web; **Vocabulary,** word web

Word Work, 2-1: T27, T30–T33, T42–T45, T66–T68, T80–T82, T90–T92, T125, T128–T131, T140–T143, T160–T162, T176–T178, T186–T188, T209, T212–T215, T224–T227, T242–T244, T256–T258, T266–T268, T289, T292–T295, T304–T307, T324–T326, T338–T340, T348–T350, T371, T374–T376, T378, T392–T393, T395, T402–T403, T405, T412–T413, T417, T424, T426; **2-2:** T27, T30–T33, T42–T45, T64–T66, T80–T82, T90–T92, T125, T128–T131, T140–T143, T162–T164, T178–T180, T188–T190, T211, T214–T217, T226–T227, T248–T250, T262, T272–T274, T295, T298–T301, T310–T312, T334–T336, T350–T352, T360–T362, T383, T386–T388, T390, T404–T405, T407, T414–415, T417, T424–T425, T429, T436, T438; **2-3:** T27, T30–T33, T42–T45, T64–T66, T78–T80, T88–T90, T123, T126–T129, T138–T141, T158–T160, T172–T174, T182–T184, T205, T208–T211, T220–T221, T268–T270, T291, T294–T296, T306, T326–T328, T340–T341, T350–T352, T373, T376–T378, T380, T392–T393, T395, T402–T403, T405, T412–

T413, T417, T424, T426; **2-4:** T27,
T30–T33, T42–T43, T64–T65,
T80–T81, T92–T93, T127, T130–
T133, T142–T143, T168–T169,
T184–T185, T194–T195, T217,
T220–T223, T232–T233, T250–
T251, T266–T267, T278–T279,
T301, T304–T307, T316–T317,
T334–T335, T350–T351,
T360–T361, T383, T386–T389,
T404–T405, T414–T415, T424–
T425, T436; **2-5:** T27, T30–T33,
T42–T43, T66–T67, T82–T83,
T94–T95, T129, T132–T133, T144–
T145, T168–T169, T184–T185,
T194–T195, T217, T223, T232–
T233, T258–T259, T274–T275,
T286–T287, T309, T312–T315,
T324–T325, T342–T343, T358–
T359, T368–T369, T394–T395,
T412–T413, T422–T423, T432–
T433, T444; **2-6:** T27, T30–T33,
T42–T43, T66–T67, T82–T83,
T94–T95, T129, T132–T135, T144–
T145, T164–T165, T180–T181,
T190–T191, T213, T216–T219,
T228–T229, T252–T253, T268–
T269, T280–T281, T303, T306–
T309, T318–T319, T344–T345,
T360–T361, T370–T371, T393,
T396–T398, T414–T415, T424–
T425, T434–T435, T446–T447

Word Work Center
See **Literacy Centers,** Word Work
Center

Writer's Companion, 2-1: T77, T105,
T173, T253, T335, T399; **2-2:** T77,
T175, T259, T347, T411; **2-3:** T75,
T169, T255, T337, T399; **2-4:** T77,
T181, T263, T347, T411; **2-5:** T79,
T181, T271, T355, T419; **2-6:** T79,
T177, T265, T357, T421

Writer's Craft
See **Writing,** traits

Writing
See also **Reading-Writing
Connection**
audience, **2-1:** T108, T110, T111; **2-3:**
T105-T106, T429; **2-4:** T39, T89,
T99, T111, T112, T229, T247,
T263, T275, T285, T313; **2-5:**
T109, T112, T113, T165; **2-6:** T79,
T91, T141, T161, T177, T187
conference, **2-1:** T77, T173, T253,
T335, T389, T399; **2-2:** T77,
T175, T259, T347, T401, T411;
2-3: T75, T169, T255, T337, T399;
2-4: T77, T181, T263, T347, T411;
2-5: T79, T181, T271, T355, T419;
2-6: T79, T177, T265, T357, T421
dialogue, **2-3:** T205, T217, T241,
T255, T265, T275, T373; **2-4:**
T112
forms
book report, **2-6:** T213
introduce, **2-6:** T225
review, **2-6:** T249, T265, T277,
T287
description, **2-1:** T208; **2-4:** T127;
2-5: T106–T115
introduce, **2-1:** T221
review, **2-1:** T239, T253, T263,
T273; **2-4:** T139, T165,
T181, T191, T201
directions, **2-2:** T125, T171
introduce, **2-2:** T137
review, **2-2:** T159, T175, T185,
T195
fantasy, **2-5:** T129; **2-6:** T245,
introduce, **2-5:** T141
review, **2-5:** T165, T181, T191,
T201
folktale, **2-6:** T302
introduce, **2-6:** T315
review, **2-6:** T341, T357, T367,
T377
friendly letter, **2-2:** T295; **2-3:**
T102–T109

how-to paragraph, **2-4:** T27
introduce, **2-4:** T39
review, **2-4:** T61, T77, T89,
T99
letter of invitation/request, **2-2:**
T295
introduce, **2-2:** T307
review, **2-2:** T331, T347, T357,
T367
narrative: biography, **2-4:** T301
introduce, **2-4:** T313
review, **2-4:** T331, T347, T357,
T367
paragraph, **2-1:** T125; **2-2:** T73;
T383; **2-4:** T259; **2-6:** T73,
T367
introduce, **2-1:** T137
review, **2-1:** T157, T173, T183,
T193
paragraph of information, **2-1:**
T289; **2-5:** T217
introduce, **2-1:** T301
review, **2-1:** T321, T335, T345,
T355; **2-5:** T229, T255,
T271, T283, T293
paragraph that compares (or
contrasts), **2-5:** T308
introduce, **2-5:** T321
review, **2-5:** T339, T355, T365,
T375
paragraph that explains, **2-3:** T291
introduce, **2-3:** T303
review, **2-3:** T323, T337, T347,
T357
paragraph that gives information,
2-3: T123
introduce, **2-3:** T135
review, **2-3:** T155, T169, T179,
T189
personal narrative, **2-1:** T102–
T113; **2-3:** T27; **2-4:** T343;
2-5: T26
introduce, **2-3:** T39

review, **2-3:** T61, T75, T85,
T95; **2-5:** T39, T63, T79,
T91, T101
poem, **2-4:** T217, T256, T361;
2-6: T256
introduce, **2-4:** T229
review, **2-4:** T247, T263, T275,
T285
report about a person, **2-6:** T129
introduce, **2-6:** T141
review, **2-6:** T161, T177, T187,
T197
research report, **2-6:** T106–T115
respond to a story, **2-2:** T102–T111
response to literature
extended response **2-1:** T112–
T113; **2-2:** T112–T113;
2-3: T110–T111; **2-4:**
T161; **2-5:** T335
personal response, **2-3:** T69,
T163, T249, T331
short response, **2-1:** T58, T152,
T234, T317; **2-2:** T56,
T154, T240, T326; **2-3:**
T57, T151, T236, T319;
2-4: T57, T243, T327; **2-5:**
T59, T161; **2-6:** T58, T157,
T336
riddle, **2-5:** T42, T95
sentences about a picture, **2-1:** T27
introduce, **2-1:** T39
review, **2-1:** T63, T77, T87,
T97
story, **2-2:** T211, T255; **2-4:**
T104–T115; **2-5:** T75, T177;
2-6: T351
introduce, **2-2:** T223
review, **2-2:** T245, T259, T269,
T279
story: dialogue, **2-3:** T205
introduce, **2-3:** T217
review, **2-3:** T241, T255,
T265, T275
summary, **2-2:** T27; **2-4:** T36

introduce, **2-2:** T39
review, **2-2:** T61, T77, T87,
T97
thank-you note, **2-2:** T343
Grammar-Writing Connection, **2-1:**
T389, T399; **2-2:** T401, T411; **2-3:**
T389, T399; **2-4:** T401, T411; **2-5:**
T409, T419; **2-6:** T411, T421
mentor text, **2-1:** T106–T107; **2-2:**
T106–T107; **2-3:** T104–T105; **2-4:**
T108–T109; **2-5:** T110–T111; **2-6:**
T110–T111
notebook, **2-1:** T43, T67, T141, T161,
T225, T243, T305, T325, T339,
T389, T399; **2-2:** T43, T65, T141,
T163, T227, T249, T311, T335,
T401; **2-3:** T43, T65, T139, T159,
T221, T245, T307, T327, T389;
2-4: T43, T65, T143, T169, T233,
T251, T317, T335, T401; **2-5:**
T43, T67, T145, T169, T233,
T259, T325, T343; **2-6:** T43, T67,
T145, T165, T229, T253, T319,
T345, T411
paragraph, **2-1:** T125, T137, T157,
T173, T183, T193; **2-2:** T73;
T383; **2-4:** T259; **2-6:** T73, T367
poem, **2-3:** T333; **2-4:** T217, T229,
T247, T256, T263, T275, T285;
2-6: T256
process writing
prewrite, **2-1:** T39, T63, T108,
T137, T157, T221, T239,
T301, T321; **2-2:** T61, T108,
T159, T245, T307, T331; **2-3:**
T39, T61, T106, T135, T155,
T217, T241, T303, T323; **2-4:**
T39, T61, T110, T139, T165,
T229, T247, T313, T331; **2-5:**
T39, T63, T112, T141, T165,
T229, T255, T321, T339; **2-6:**
T39, T63, T112, T141, T161,
T225, T249, T315, T341

draft, **2-1:** T39, T77, T109, T137,
T173, T253, T335; **2-2:** T77,
T109, T175, T259, T347; **2-3:**
T75, T107, T169, T255, T337;
2-4: T77, T111, T181, T263,
T347; **2-5:** T79, T113, T181,
T271, T355; **2-6:** T79, T113,
T177, T265, T357
revise, **2-1:** T87, T97, T110, T183,
T193, T263, T273, T345,
T355, T389, T399; **2-2:** T87,
T97, T110, T185, T195, T269,
T279, T357, T367, T401,
T411; **2-3:** T85, T95, T108,
T179, T189, T265, T275,
T347, T357, T389, T399; **2-4:**
T89, T99, T112, T191, T201,
T275, T285, T357, T367,
T401, T411; **2-5:** T91, T101,
T114, T191, T283, T293, T365,
T375, T409, T419; **2-6:** T91,
T101, T114, T187, T197, T277,
T287, T367, T377, T411, T421
edit, **2-1:** T87, T110, T183, T193,
T263, T273, T345, T355, T389,
T399; **2-2:** T87, T97, T110,
T185, T195, T269, T279, T357,
T367, T401, T411; **2-3:** T85,
T95, T108, T179, T189, T265,
T275, T347, T357, T389, T399;
2-4: T89, T99, T112, T191,
T201, T275, T285, T357, T367,
T401, T411; **2-5:** T91, T101,
T114, T191, T283, T293, T365,
T375, T409, T419; **2-6:** T91,
T101, T114, T187, T197, T277,
T287, T367, T377, T411, T421
proofread, **2-1:** T97, T110; **2-2:**
T110; **2-3:** T108; **2-4:** T112;
2-5: T114; **2-6:** T114
evaluate, **2-1:** T111; **2-2:** T111;
2-3: T109; **2-4:** T89, T113;
2-5: T91, T115; **2-6:** T115,
T187, T265

publish, **2-1:** T97, T111, T409; **2-2:** T111, T421, T433; **2-3:** T109, T409, T429; **2-4:** T113, T421, T433; **2-5:** T115, T429; **2-6:** T115, T431, T443

purposes for writing, **2-1:** T104, T112; **2-2:** T104, T112; **2-3:** T102, T103, T104–105, T106, T110; **2-4:** T106, T114; **2-5:** T108, T116; **2-6:** T39, T63, T79, T91, T108, T116

rubrics, **2-1:** T97, T111, T193, T273, T355, T429, R6–R8; **2-2:** T97, T111, T195, T279, T441, R6–R8; **2-3:** T95, T109, T189, T275, T357, T429, R6–R8; **2-4:** T99, T113, T201, T285, T367, T441, R6–R8; **2-5:** T101, T115, T201, T293, T375, T449, R6–R8; **2-6:** T101, T115, T197, T287, T377, T451, R6–R8

self-selected writing, **2-1:** T97, T389; **2-2:** T367, T401; **2-3:** T389; **2-4:** T401; **2-5:** T409; **2-6:** T411

short response
   See **Writing,** forms, response to literature

Student-Writing Models, **2-1:** T106–T107; **2-2:** T106–T107; **2-3:** T104–T105; **2-4:** T108–T109; **2-5:** T110–T111; **2-6:** T110–T111

timed writing, **2-1:** T112–T113; **2-2:** T112–T113; **2-3:** T110–T111; **2-4:** T114–T115; **2-5:** T116–T117; **2-6:** T116–T117

traits
  conventions, **2-1:** T110, T421, T429; **2-2:** T110, T433, T441; **2-3:** T107, T108, T217, T241, T255, T265, T275, T303, T323, T337, T347, T357, T421, T429; **2-4:** T112, T433; **2-5:** T114, T201, T441; **2-6:** T114, T225, T249, T265, T277, T287, T315, T341, T357, T367, T377, T443, T451

ideas/focus, **2-1:** T39, T63, T77, T87, T108, T137, T157, T173, T183, T193, T389, T399; **2-2:** T108; **2-3:** T106, T389, T399; **2-4:** T110; **2-5:** T112; **2-6:** T39, T63, T79, T91, T101, T112, T113, T141, T161, T177, T187, T197, T411, T421

organization, **2-1:** T108, T109, T221, T239, T253, T263, T273, T301, T321, T335, T355; **2-3:** T107; **2-4:** T39, T61, T77, T89, T99, T110, T111, T139, T165, T181, T191, T201, T411; **2-5:** T113; **2-6:** T112, T113

presentation, **2-1:** T111, T409, T435; **2-2:** T111, T421, T447; **2-3:** T109, T435; **2-4:** T113, T447; **2-5:** T115, T429, T455; **2-6:** T115, T431

sentence fluency, **2-2:** T109, T110, T223, T245, T259, T269, T279, T307, T331, T347, T357, T367; **2-5:** T39, T63, T79, T91, T101, T113, T165, T181, T191, T201, T419, T449
   See also **Writing,** forms, friendly letter

voice, **2-2:** T39; **2-3:** T106, T108

word choice, **2-2:** T61, T77, T97, T108, T109, T137, T159, T175, T185, T195; **2-4:** T111, T112, T229, T247, T263, T275, T285, T313, T331, T347, T357, T367, T411; **2-5:** T112, T114, T229, T255, T271, T283, T293, T321, T339, T355, T365, T375, T409
   See also **Writing,** dialogue

Writing on Demand, **2-1:** T112–T113; **2-2:** T112–T113; **2-3:** T110–T111;

2-4: T114–T115; **2-5:** T116–T117; **2-6:** T116–T117

writing prompts, **2-1:** T39, T63, T77, T87, T97, T137, T157, T173, T183, T193, T221, T239, T253, T263, T273, T301, T321, T335, T345, T355, T389, T399, T409, T421; **2-2:** T39, T61, T77, T87, T97, T137, T159, T175, T185, T195, T223, T245, T259, T269, T279, T307, T331, T347, T357, T367, T401, T411, T421, T433; **2-3:** T39, T61, T75, T85, T95, T135, T155, T169, T179, T189, T217, T241, T255, T265, T275, T303, T323, T337, T347, T357, T389, T399, T421; **2-4:** T39, T61, T77, T89, T99, T139, T165, T174, T181, T191, T201, T229, T247, T263, T275, T285, T313, T331, T340, T347, T357, T367, T401, T411, T421, T433; **2-5:** T39, T63, T79, T91, T101, T141, T165, T181, T191, T201, T229, T255, T262, T271, T283, T293, T321, T339, T346, T365, T409, T419, T429, T441; **2-6:** T39, T63, T70, T79, T91, T101, T141, T161, T177, T187, T197, T225, T249, T256, T265, T277, T287, T315, T341, T348, T357, T367, T377, T421, T443

writing strategies, **2-1:** T39, T63, T108, T137, T157, T221, T239, T301, T321; **2-2:** T39, T61, T108, T137, T159, T223, T245, T307, T331; **2-3:** T39, T61, T106, T135, T155, T217, T241, T303, T323; **2-4:** T39, T61, T110, T139, T165, T229, T247, T313, T331; **2-5:** T39, T63, T112, T141, T165, T229, T255, T321, T339; **2-6:** T39, T63, T112, T141, T161, T225, T249, T315, T341

Writing Center
    See **Literacy Centers,** Writing Center
Writing Prompts
    See **Writing,** writing prompts
Writing Strategies
    See **Writing,** writing strategies
Writing Traits
    See **Writing,** traits
Written Language Conventions
    See **Grammar; Writing,** traits,
    conventions

Teacher's Notes

Acknowledgments

For permission to reprint copyrighted material, grateful acknowledgment is made to the following sources:

Robin Bernard: "Brush Dance" by Robin Bernard. Text copyright © 2004 by Robin Bernard.

Georges Borchardt, Inc., on behalf of the Estate of John Gardner: "Always Be Kind to Animals" and "The Lizard" from *A Child's Bestiary* by John Gardner. Text copyright © 1977 by Boskydell Artists, Ltd.

Boyds Mills Press, Inc.: "Bumblebees" from *Lemonade Sun and Other Summer Poems* by Rebecca Kai Dotlich. Text copyright © 1998 by Rebecca Kai Dotlich. Published by Wordsong, an imprint of Boyds Mills Press.

Curtis Brown, Ltd.: "My Name" from *Kim's Place and Other Poems* by Lee Bennett Hopkins. Text copyright © 1974 by Lee Bennett Hopkins. Published by Henry Holt and Company. "Night Game" from *Sports! Sports! Sports!* by Lee Bennett Hopkins. Text copyright © 1999 by Lee Bennett Hopkins. Published by HarperCollins Publishers. "Quiet Morning" by Karen Winnick from *Climb Into My Lap,* selected by Lee Bennett Hopkins. Text copyright © 1998 by Karen Winnick. Published by Simon & Schuster, Inc.

Sandra Gilbert Brüg: "Soccer Feet" by Sandra Gilbert Brüg.

Estate of William Rossa Cole: "Here Comes the Band" by William Cole.

Trustees of Mrs. F. C. Cornford Will Trust: "Dogs" from *Collected Poems* by Frances Cornford. Published by Cresset Press, 1954.

The Cricket Magazine Group, a division of Carus Publishing Company: "Bat Habits" by Mary Ann Coleman and Oliver M. Coleman, Jr. from *Click* Magazine, April 2004. Text © 2004 by Mary Ann Coleman.

Farrar, Straus and Giroux, LLC: "the drum" from *Spin a Soft Black Song, Revised Edition* by Nikki Giovanni. Text copyright © 1971, 1985 by Nikki Giovanni. "sun" from *All the Small Poems and Fourteen More* by Valerie Worth. Text copyright © 1987, 1994 by Valerie Worth.

Betsy Franco: "At the Bike Rack" by Betsy Franco. Text copyright © 2004 by Betsy Franco.

Emily George: "Aliona Says" by Emily George from *Pocket Poems,* selected by Bobbi Katz. Text copyright © 2004 by Emily George.

Harcourt, Inc.: "Nuts to You and Nuts to Me" from *The Llama Who Had No Pajama: 100 Favorite Poems* by Mary Ann Hoberman. Text copyright © 1974 by Mary Ann Hoberman.

HarperCollins Publishers: "Play" from *Country Pie* by Frank Asch. Text copyright © 1979 by Frank Asch. "Benita Beane" from *Something BIG Has Been Here* by Jack Prelutsky. Text copyright © 1990 by Jack Prelutsky.

Florence Parry Heide: "Rocks" by Florence Parry Heide. Text copyright © 1969 by Florence Parry Heide.

Henry Holt and Company, LLC: "Keepsakes" from *Is Somewhere Always Far Away?* by Leland B. Jacobs. Text © 1967 by Leland B. Jacobs; text © 1995 by Allen D. Jacobs.

Judith Infante: "The Poet Pencil" by Jesús Carlos Soto Morfín, translated by Judith Infante from *The Tree Is Older Than You Are,* selected by Naomi Shihab Nye. Text copyright © by Jesús Carlos Soto Morfín; English translation copyright © by Judith Infante.

Bobbi Katz: From "Did You Ever Think?" by Bobbi Katz. Text copyright © 1981, renewed 1996 by Bobbi Katz. "When You Can Read" from *Could We Be Friends? Poems for Pals* by Bobbi Katz. Text copyright © 1994 by Bobbi Katz. Published by Mondo Publishing, 1997.

Little, Brown and Co. Inc.: "Far Away" from *One at a Time* by David McCord. Text copyright © 1965, 1966 by David McCord.

Gina Maccoby Literary Agency: "Bookworm" by Mary Ann Hoberman. Text copyright © 1975 by Mary Ann Hoberman.

Marian Reiner: "Macaw" from *I Never Told and Other Poems* by Myra Cohn Livingston. Text copyright © 1992 by Myra Cohn Livingston. "Night Creature" from *Little Raccoon and Poems from the Woods* by Lilian Moore. Text copyright © 1975 by Lilian Moore.

Marian Reiner, on behalf of the Boulder Public Library Foundation, Inc.: "My Cat and I" from *Out in the Dark and Daylight* by Aileen Fisher. Text copyright © 1980 by Aileen Fisher.

Marian Reiner, on behalf of Constance Levy: "Cowscape" from *A Crack in the Clouds and Other Poems* by Constance Levy. Text copyright © 1998 by Constance Kling Levy. "Hide-and-Seek" from *A Tree Place and Other Poems* by Constance Levy. Text copyright © 1994 by Constance Kling Levy.

Marian Reiner, on behalf of Judith Thurman: "New Notebook" from *Flashlight and Other Poems* by Judith Thurman. Text copyright © 1976 by Judith Thurman.

Joanne M. Roberts: "My Snake" by Jo Roberts. Text copyright © 2004 by Jo Roberts.

Scholastic Inc.: "The Swarm of Bees" by Elsa Gorham Baker, "Sharing the Swing" by Alice Crowell Hoffman, "My Bike" by Bobbe Indgin, and "Tiny Seeds" by Vera L. Stafford from *Poetry Place Anthology.* Text copyright © 1983 by Edgell Communications, Inc. Published by Scholastic Teaching Resources.

Tiger Tales, an imprint of ME Media LLC, Wilton, CT: "Chimpanzee" from *Rumble in the Jungle* by Giles Andreae. Text © 1996 by Giles Andreae.

S©ott Treimel NY: "First Snow" and "Grown-ups" from *Seasons: A Book of Poems* by Charlotte Zolotow. Text copyright © 2002 by Charlotte Zolotow. "People" from *All That Sunlight* by Charlotte Zolotow. Text copyright © 1967, text copyright renewed © 1995 by Charlotte Zolotow. Published by HarperCollins Publishers.

Photo Credits

Placement key: (r) right, (l) left, (c) center, (b) bottom

S32 (b) Geral Nowak/Westend61/Getty Images; S44 (b) Digital Vision/Getty Images; T27 (bl) Blue Line Pictures/Iconia/Getty Images; T28 (br) Jamye Thorton/The Image bank/Getty Images; T29 (r) @Imagebroker/Alamy; T40 (b) Digital Vision/Getty Images; T64 (b) Digital Vision/Tom LeGoff/Getty Images; T80 (b) Asia Images/Wang Leng/ Getty Images; T92 (b) Photolibrary/Getty Images; T130 (b) Myrleen Ferguson Cate/PhotoEdit; T131 (r) Stone/Freudenthal Verhagen/Getty Images; T157 (br) Owaki-kulla/Corbis; T182 (br) Adrian Burke/Corbis; T199 (b) Alex Mares-Manton/Asia Images/Getty Images; T218 (b) It stockfree; T219 (r) James Robinson/Animals Animals; T230 (b) Tony Freeman/PhotoEdit; T247 (br) Lena Untidt/ Bonnier Publications/Photo Researchers Inc; T256 (b) Dennis Macdonald/PhotoEdit; T263 (bl) D Hurst/Alamy; T284 (b) Phillip Bailey/Corbis; T310 (b) Corbis; T311 (r) Daryl Balfour/Getty Images; T322 (b) P Kumar/Taxi/Getty Images; T347 (bl) Bettmann/Corbis; T356 (b) O'Brien Productions/ Corbis; T366 (b) Tim Hall/Stone/Getty Images; T410 (b) Altrendo/Getty Images; T420 (b) Digital Visions/ Getty Images; T424 (b) National Geographic/Getty Images; T430 (b) Photodisc Green/Getty Images.

All other photos property of Harcourt School Publishers

Teacher's Notes

Teacher's Notes

Teacher's Notes

Teacher's Notes

Teacher's Notes

Teacher's Notes

Teacher's Notes

Teacher's Notes